hamlyn

COMPLETE
COOK

Executive Editor Polly Manguel
Project Manager Joanna Smith
Copy Editors Linda Doeser, Barbara Horn, Shirley Patton
Proofreaders Sharon Ashman, Sharyn Conlan, Anne Crane,
Sarah Ford, Cara Frost, Cathy Lowne, Joanna Smith
Creative Director Keith Martin
Designer Peter Gerrish
Jacket Designer Martin Topping
Senior Production Controller Katherine Hockley
Picture Researchers Sally Claxton, Christine Junemann
Indexer Hilary Bird
Typists Kim Griffiths, Gillian Towner

First published in 2000 by Hamlyn
an imprint of Octopus Publishing Group Limited

This edition published 2005 by Bounty Books
a division of Octopus Publishing Group Limited
2–4 Heron Quays, London E14 4JP

Reprinted 2005, 2006

Design and illustrations copyright © 2000 Octopus Publishing
Group Limited
Text copyright © 2000 Octopus Publishing Group Limited
Photography: copyright © 2000 Octopus Publishing Group Limited
Jacket Photography: copyright © 2000 Octopus Publishing Group
Ltd; David Loftus, Ian Wallace

British Library Cataloguing-in-Publication Data
A catalogue record for this book is available from the British Library

ISBN-13: 978-0753711-25-5
ISBN-10: 0-753711-25-7

Produced by Toppan
Printed in China

Notes

Standard level spoon measurements are used in all recipes.
1 tablespoon = one 15 ml spoon
1 teaspoon = one 5 ml spoon

Both imperial and metric measurements have been given in
all recipes. Use one set of measurements only and not a mixture
of both.

Measurements for canned food have been given as a standard
metric equivalent.

Do not re-freeze a dish that has been frozen previously.

Pepper should be freshly ground black pepper unless otherwise
stated.

Fresh herbs should be used, unless otherwise stated. If unavailable,
use dried herbs as an alternative but halve the quantities stated.

Eggs should be medium (size 3) unless otherwise stated.

Ovens should be preheated to the specified temperature – if using a
fan assisted oven, follow the manufacturer's instructions for
adjusting the time and temperature.

This book includes dishes made with nuts and nut derivatives. It is
advisable for customers with known allergic reactions to nuts and
nut derivatives and those who may be potentially vulnerable to these
allergies, such as pregnant and nursing mothers, invalids, the
elderly, babies and children, to avoid dishes made with nuts and nut
oils. It is also prudent to check the labels of pre-prepared
ingredients for the possible inclusion of nut derivatives.

hamlyn
COMPLETE
COOK

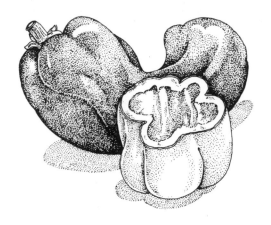

ℬℬ Bounty
Books

basic recipes & techniques 84

recipes 154

contents

This comprehensive book is aimed at those who, through a love of food or just simple necessity, want to learn about food and cooking so they can produce family meals or entertain with confidence. This practical, accessible volume contains everything the beginner or experienced cook needs to know about selecting, preparing and cooking all the basic foodstuffs, plus many more exotic dishes from the great cuisines of the world.

It starts, in Section 1, by describing a wide range of everyday and more unusual ingredients, divided into a number of easy-reference categories, offering hints on buying, storing and preparing the foods, plus tips on the best cooking methods.

It then goes on, in Section 2, to explain the tools of the trade – a wide selection of the knives, utensils, pots and pans and kitchen appliances that are available. Many cooks won't need them all, but using the right tools for the job does give a much better result.

Section 3 gives a good grounding in the basics, starting with a glossary explaining the culinary terms which may otherwise mystify the novice. It then describes, with the aid of clear illustrations, all those useful, basic cooking techniques that people are afraid to try, such as making bread, how to carve a leg of lamb, making simple homemade pasta, how to fillet a fish or clean a crab, making delicious stocks, the best ways to cook rice, and how to skin tomatoes and peppers. The aim throughout is to explain the basic skills simply and easily, with illustrations to clarify any difficult points. It takes the mystery out of the basic skills and builds up confidence to tackle the recipes later in the book.

Section 4, the recipes section, contains over 1000 tried-and-tested recipes for mouth-watering dishes suitable for every possible occasion, including after-work meals, dinner parties and special occasions, snacks and light lunches, and afternoon tea; there is even a section on drinks and finger foods for those party occasions. The dishes range from good, traditional home cooking to recipes hailing from all corners of the world, including places as far apart as India, Thailand, China, Mexico, Morocco, Italy, Spain, Ireland and North America.

There are many dishes suitable for vegetarians, plus lots that are quick and easy to prepare, making perfect meals for simple midweek suppers. Such recipes are easy to find because preparation and cooking times, along with the number of servings, are included for every recipe.

introduction

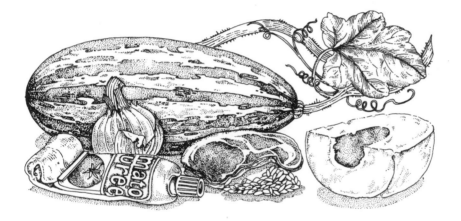

buying and storing

Ageing (the hanging of carcasses) tenderizes beef and lamb and gives it a good flavour. Flesh that has a dark red colour indicates that the carcass has been well hung. When you buy beef, the lean of the meat should be bright to dark red with the fat a creamy white. Small flecks of fat should be visible throughout the lean meat. A bright red colour often indicates that the meat is very fresh and unhung or not hung long enough for the flavour to develop properly. Pork and veal are not aged and have a much paler appearance.

Store pre-packed meat in its film-covered plastic tray on a plate in the refrigerator. Any meat that is not pre-packed should be wrapped in foil or greaseproof paper and then refrigerated. Chops deteriorate faster than joints of meat.

cuts of beef

brisket

This has an excellent flavour, but tends to be fatty so always look for a lean piece. It is best boned and rolled, when some of the excess fat can be discarded. Cook by a long slow method such as braising or pot-roasting.

silverside

This is a popular joint, always boneless, which can also be bought salted to serve as the traditional boiled beef and carrots. It needs the long slow cooking achieved by boiling or braising, or if preferred, pot-roasting.

cuts of beef

1 Neck
2 Chuck and blade
3 Fore, top and back ribs
4 Sirloin
5 Fillet
6 Rump

7 Topside
8 Silverside
9 Leg
10 Flank
11 Brisket
12 Shin

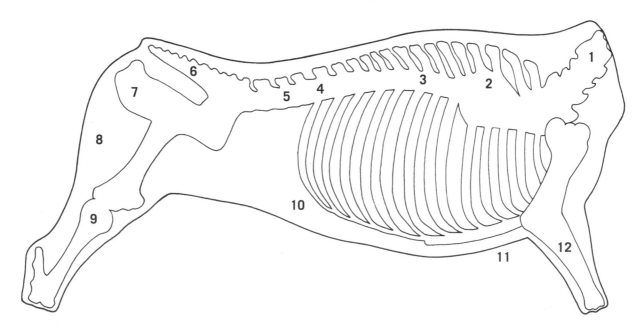

beef

sirloin

A boned and rolled joint with a good layer of fat to protect it, coming from the back of the animal. It is very suitable for roasting. It can be bought with the 'undercut' (fillet) on it. The rolled joints are usually about 18 cm/ 7 inches across. Steaks can also be cut from the sirloin.

ribs

Ribs come as wing rib, top rib and fore rib joints and they too can be bought on the bone or as boned and rolled joints. The flavour is particularly good when cooked on the bone, and this joint makes a most impressive centrepiece. Roast for preference, but these joints can also be pot-roasted or braised.

stewing meats

These include leg and shin which are the cheapest cuts and need the longest and slowest of cooking to really tenderize them, though the flavour is excellent. Chuck and blade steak are the best cuts of stewing steak and they require less cooking. These cuts should not have too much thick fat on the outside, but the flesh of the meat should be well marbled or streaked with flecks of fat. For all stewing steak, either stew, braise or casserole. It can also be used in meat pies, and boiled for stock.

topside

This joint is usually boned and rolled. As it is a very lean cut with little or no fat of its own, a strip of extra fat (barding fat) is often tied on by the butcher to prevent it from becoming over-dry when cooked. It can be roasted, although pot-roasting or braising often gives a better result, as the liquid involved keeps it more moist.

minced or ground beef

Various qualities of mince are available, some of which, such as minced steak at the top end of the price market, are almost fat free. At the other end of the market is the cheapest quality which does contain a lot of fat. Mince tends to make use of the cheaper cuts of beef, like the flank. Mince may be sold finely minced, medium minced and coarsely minced; each to be used for different purposes.

steaks

Steaks come in several different cuts, and are all suitable to grill or fry. *Rump* is the joint next to the sirloin and one of the most usual cuts made into steaks and used for grilling and frying. There is a layer of fat all along the top edge of this steak. *Fillet* is cut from the centre of the sirloin. It is probably one of the best known and most expensive cuts of beef, and steaks cut from it have no fat at all. It is very tender, but the flavour is probably not as good as that of rump. *Sirloin* is cut into two parts to give the porterhouse steak and the T-bone steak. The upper part of the sirloin is cut into thin steaks which are called 'minute steaks'. *Entrecôte* is really the part of the meat between the ribs of beef, but a slice from the sirloin or rump, which is thin rather than thick, can also be termed an entrecôte. *Châteaubriand* is a thick slice taken from the end of the fillet, weighing from 375 g/12 oz upwards, which can be grilled or roasted. It is an excellent cut and well worth trying for a special occasion. It is often offered in restaurants as a 2-portion serving, so that it can be cooked in the piece to keep it succulent.

bacon and ham

Bacon and *ham* are the flesh of the pig which has been salted or cured in brine and then smoked. Green or unsmoked bacon is cured, but not smoked and is consequently less strong in flavour and will not keep for the same length of time as its smoked counterpart. As the name suggests, back bacon comes from the back of the pig; streaky bacon comes from the belly part of the pig.
Gammon is the hind leg of the pig which is cured on the side of bacon; if the leg is then cut off and cooked and served cold, it is known as ham. A true ham, however, is the hind leg of the pig, detached before curing, and which is then cured, salted, matured, hung or smoked, depending on the manufacturer's process.

cuts of pork

leg
A large lean joint often boned and rolled, although excellent when cooked on the bone. It can be cut into various sizes of joints which are usually roasted.

shoulder
Often sub-divided into spare rib and blade. This is a tender cut, available on the bone or boneless. It can be roasted, stuffed, grilled or casseroled.

spare rib
Not to be confused with spare ribs, this is a fairly lean joint, from the shoulder, which sometimes has more fat than other joints. It should be moderately priced and has an excellent flavour. Good for roasting, it can also be cut up to braise, casserole or stew.

spare ribs
Taken from the belly, they are removed in one piece and then cut up into ribs with the meat left all around the bones. These are very popular and are usually barbecued, grilled or casseroled.

loin
This is a prime roasting joint which can be bought on or off the bone. It sometimes includes the kidney and can be excellent if stuffed and rolled. The loin is also cut into chops and also boneless chops (or steaks as they are often called) which can be grilled or fried.

fillet or tenderloin
A prime piece of meat with very little fat. Very versatile, and excellent for kebabs, escalopes, pan-frying and for grilling or frying. It can also be sliced lengthways and stuffed. Quite expensive but it goes a long way.

belly
Cheap and fatty but full of flavour, it can be used on and off the bone, either as a joint or cut into slices. Bone and roll it with a stuffing to roast or pot-roast; or use the slices to grill, fry or casserole, or cook on a barbecue.

hand and spring
This is the foreleg of the pig, suitable for roasting, boiling, stewing and casseroling. It is relatively inexpensive and is often minced and used for stuffings, meatballs and pork pâtés.

pork & veal

cuts of veal

fillet

This is the prime cut of the calf, from the hindquarters, and is usually sliced into escalopes to fry or grill. However, it can be used as a very expensive roasting joint or cut into cubes for kebabs.

veal escalopes

These are probably the most popular cut of veal and are the most expensive. The escalopes should be cut from the best part or fillet end of the leg, and they should be cut between about 5 mm/¼ inch and 1 cm/½ inch thick. They should always be cut across the grain of the meat, not along it. Once cut, escalopes are usually beaten so they are very much thinner.

chops

These come from the loin. Those from the bottom end, with a small round bone, are known as chump chops; those from the other end are called cutlets although one cutlet is quite large. All chops are suitable for frying, grilling (if basted well) and pan-frying, but need good flavourings or a good sauce as an accompaniment.

knuckle

This is a cheaper, bony cut from the end of the leg. It is good for stewing and casseroling and is used in the classic Italian dish, Osso Buco.

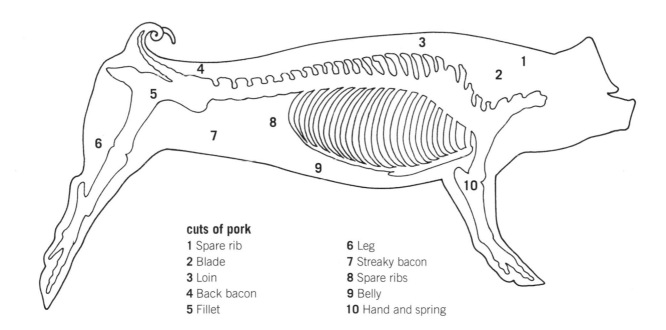

cuts of pork

1 Spare rib
2 Blade
3 Loin
4 Back bacon
5 Fillet
6 Leg
7 Streaky bacon
8 Spare ribs
9 Belly
10 Hand and spring

cuts of lamb

chops and cutlets

Loin chops contain part of the backbone, and are cut from the loin as single or double loin chops (also known as butterfly chops).

Chump chops come from between the loin and the leg and are the largest and leanest.

Leg chops are slices taken straight across the leg joint and have an 'eye' of bone in the centre.

Cutlets are taken from the best end of neck. They have a small eye of meat and a long bone which can be left with meat on it or be trimmed both in length and free of meat.

Boneless chops include noisettes, which are taken from a boned-out best end of neck (or sometimes a small loin): the meat is rolled up tightly and secured with cocktail sticks or string and then cut into slices.

Lamb steaks are slices taken from a boned leg of lamb. They can be beaten out between two layers of clingfilm to make them thinner, if required.

loin

This is a prime cut which is usually roasted on the bone or boned and rolled with or without a stuffing. It can also be pot-roasted. This part of the animal can be cut up and made into an assortment of chops.

best end of neck

This is also a prime roasting joint either on the bone or boned and rolled. It is from this joint that the spectacular crown roast of lamb and guard of honour roasts are made. It can be cut into cutlets which are left as they are or can be trimmed.

breast

This is a versatile and cheap cut of lamb which is very tasty but also very fatty. It is ideal for casseroling, but should be cooked the day before required, so it can be cooled and the resulting layer of fat on the surface removed before the dish is reheated. It can be boned, stuffed, rolled and slow roasted or pot-roasted with great success.

leg

This is a prime joint which is quite large and always rather expensive. It is often cut in half and sold as half legs, as the fillet end (or top half) and the shank end (or lower half). The fillet end is sometimes boned out and it is good for kebabs and casseroling.

Leg of lamb, whether whole or in halves, is usually roasted although it can also be pot-roasted with great success.

shoulder

One of the sweetest and most tender parts of the animal but it does have a fair amount of fat on it and is one of the most difficult of all joints to carve. It is always succulent and most often roasted either on the bone, or boned and rolled when some of the fat can be discarded. Shoulder meat can also be boned to use for kebabs, casseroles and mince, when excess fat can be trimmed off before cooking.

middle and scrag end of neck

These are the cheap cuts with a rather high percentage of bone and some fat, but again with a good flavour. Well worth using for casseroles. Chops can be cut from the middle neck.

lamb & offal

liver & kidney

liver

There are several types of liver available and all are good value. They vary in flavour and texture, however, and therefore require different types of cooking to serve at their best.

Ox liver is the cheapest of the livers, has a strong flavour, and can be tough because the texture is rather coarse. It is best used for slow braising or casseroling.

Calves' liver is the finest and most expensive of all the livers. It is very tender with a delicate flavour and is best simply and lightly fried in butter, grilled, or pan-fried.

Pigs' liver is fairly cheap, and has a very distinct and rather strong flavour. It is best braised or casseroled and is the most popular liver (along with chicken livers) for making pâtés and terrines.

Lambs' liver is probably the most popular of the livers, with a good flavour which is not as strong or pronounced as pigs' or ox liver. Although not as tender as calves' liver, it is much cheaper.

Chicken or *turkey livers* are very tender and easily obtained. They make excellent pâté and are good fried.

kidney

All kidneys are covered in a thin transparent skin which must be removed before cooking, as must the fatty core. It is best to snip out the core with a pair of scissors.

Kidneys can be grilled or fried, pan-fried or sautéed and may also be put into casseroles along with other meats, and added to stuffings, risottos and many other dishes. They should not be overcooked, though, as they are virtually fatless and therefore shrivel and dry out easily.

Ox kidney is the largest and cheapest. It has a fairly strong flavour and needs a little more cooking than the smaller kidneys. Good for steak and kidney pie.

Calves' kidneys are much smaller and paler in colour than ox kidney. They are more tender and more delicate in flavour, but can be cooked in the same ways.

Lambs' kidneys are small and well flavoured but do not have a harsh or overpowering taste. They can be cooked whole or halved or cut into pieces, simply by frying in butter or grilling, but do not overcook or they will become tough and dry.

Pigs' kidney is larger than lambs' kidney, more elongated in shape and slightly lighter and more orangey in colour. They are also stronger in flavour, but can still be fried or grilled, as well as being diced to add to casseroles for flavour.

cuts of lamb

1 Scrag end of neck
2 Middle end of neck
3 Best end of neck
4 Loin

5 Chump
6 Leg, fillet end
7 Leg, shank end
8 Breast
9 Shoulder

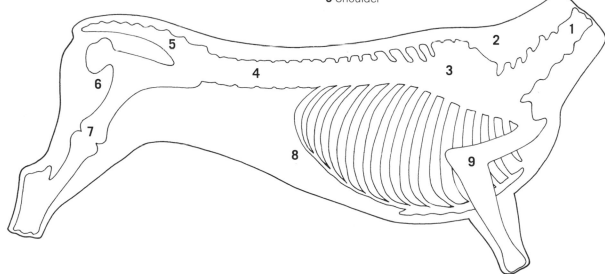

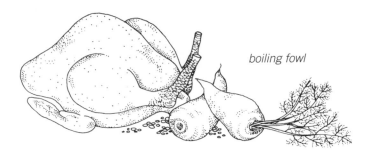

boiling fowl

buying and storing

If buying a fresh chicken – one that has not been frozen in any way – the way to tell its age is to feel the breastbone with your thumb and finger: a young bird should feel soft and flexible.

Fresh poultry is always more expensive than frozen but has a better flavour, and free-range chicken has the best flavour of all. A fresh bird will keep for up to 2 days in the refrigerator before cooking, but remove any tight wrappings, and cover loosely to allow air to circulate. For longer storage, freeze on the day of purchase. Remove the giblets too, and store them separately.

types of chicken

Chickens are sold under different names according to their age, ranging from the poussin of a few weeks old to the boiling fowl, which is usually at least a year and a half old. Any chicken younger than 6 months is best grilled, sautéed or roasted, to develop the best flavour.

poulet
This is an immature spring chicken. Allow one bird for two people.

poussin
Baby chicken. Allow one per person. It is a bit fiddly and bony, so eat with your fingers.

roasting chicken
Use for most chicken recipes. Allow a 2 kg/4 lb bird to feed 4–6 people.

boiling fowl
An old bird, tough and cheap with a good flavour. Use for dishes requiring a long gentle simmer. Perfect for stocks and stews.

other poultry and game

duck
'Duckling' describes birds aged up to 6 months. If too young, the bird will not have enough meat to be worth eating. Look for a breast that, when pinched, feels meaty. Duck freezes well because of its high fat content. It is also available as portions and as boneless breasts.

goose
Choose a young bird with pliable breastbone and a plump, well-filled breast. A gosling weighs up to 2 kg/4 lb. When it reaches 8–9 months old it becomes a goose and weighs 3–6 kg/6–12 lb. Thereafter it becomes much fatter and tougher, and needs much longer cooking.

grouse
As with most other game, grouse is much better if well hung, for about 4–5 days, sometimes even as long as 2 weeks for those who prefer a really gamey flavour. They are usually only available fresh. The breastbone of young birds should feel soft and pliable. They are best roasted. One grouse will usually serve only one person, although sometimes the really large ones will serve two.

guinea fowl
A close relative of the chicken, this fairly dry, dark meat has a mild, gamey flavour. Cook as for chicken, but bear in mind the dryness of the meat. Moist cooking methods such as casseroling are recommended. Also suitable for roasting, when the breast should be covered with bacon to keep it moist.

hare
Hare is akin to rabbit in flavour, though it is much darker and more gamey. It is often marinated before cooking as it tends to be dry, and is then roasted or casseroled.

poultry & game

ostrich

A relatively new product to appear in this country, ostrich meat is now being farmed quite extensively. It is very dark red and is not dissimilar to beef, but with a much lower fat content. Because it has so little fat, however, care must be taken not to allow it to dry out during cooking.

partridge

These are small game birds which will serve only one portion each. Young plucked birds weigh up to 425 g/14 oz. They are best roasted, but are also good to cook under the grill or on a barbecue. Older birds will weigh 500 g/1 lb or more.

pheasant

This is probably the best known and most popular of all the game birds. It is available fresh and frozen and can often be found in larger supermarkets. Pheasant should be hung for at least 3 days for a good flavour to develop.

Young birds are best roasted but more mature birds – which have a better flavour – will be tougher, so need the longer cooking of casseroling, braising or pot-roasting to ensure they are tender. One pheasant will serve two or three people when roasted, and larger mature birds may serve up to four when casseroled with other ingredients.

pigeon

Pigeons do not need to be hung. If plump and young, one bird will serve a portion. They have a rich, dark meat.

quail

These are the smallest European game birds, like tiny partridges. As they are so small, two birds can be served for a good portion, but one is usually enough, and eating them with fingers is almost obligatory. Quails must be eaten really fresh – within 24 hours of being killed – and they are most usually simply roasted.

rabbit

Rabbit has lean meat and small, thin bones. The flesh of the wild rabbit is dark with a gamey flavour, while the flesh of farmed rabbits is pale with a delicate texture and flavour. Soak in cold, salted water for several hours before cooking. Stew, roast or sauté.

turkey

For best flavour, choose a hen bird, hung for 3 days, with moist skin tinted pearly white. A whole frozen turkey takes at least 48 hours to defrost; let it thaw gradually in the refrigerator and finally at room temperature for a few hours. Once thawed, cook as soon as possible. It must be cooked through to the centre. Allow 500 g/1 lb per person. Turkey is also often available boneless and diced, and as leg and breast portions.

venison

The deep red meat of the farmed deer is lean, tender and delicately flavoured but lacks the gamey flavour of wild deer. The meat is suitable for pan-frying, grilling, barbecuing, roasting and casseroling. Marinating improves the flavour and slight dryness.

wild boar

Wild boar is now available in some supermarkets and butchers' shops. It is similar to pork, but with a more intense, gamey flavour. It is often used in sausages, but it is also suitable for roasting or casseroling, depending on the cut.

hare

buying and storing

Seafood perishes more quickly than meat and poultry, so take great care, when you come to buy it, that it is fresh. Look for all the following signs: the smell should be slightly sweet, certainly not unpleasant. Whole fish should be stiff and firm, not limp. Eyes should be full, shiny and bright, and never sunken or opaque. The skin should be shiny, not dry and gritty and the gills should be a rosy pink, not brownish or dry. Fish fillets should be translucent (not milky-white), firm and springy to the touch with no sign of discoloration. The flesh should be intact. Fish should be eaten as fresh as possible, at most within 24 hours of purchase. Otherwise it should be cleaned, gutted and frozen. Fish fillets and steaks can be prepared up to 12 hours in advance, loosely covered in foil and refrigerated. To keep fish overnight, wrap in several layers of newspaper and put in the coldest part of the refrigerator.

fish

bass
A round fish, silver in colour. The flesh is white and delicate in flavour and texture. Sold whole. To cook: bake, steam, poach or grill.

bream, sea
A round fish with very coarse big scales, it is identifiable by a black spot behind the eyes. The flesh is pink and delicate. Sold whole or in fillets. To cook: steam, bake or fry. Particularly good steamed with herbs.

brill
A salt-water flat fish, similar to turbot in appearance but smaller, with a brownish-yellow skin with small scales. The flesh is a creamy-white, and delicate, breaking up easily. Sold whole or filleted. To cook: bake, steam, poach, fry or grill.

carp
A freshwater fish whose habitat is generally muddy ponds, lakes and rivers. It is a round fish with coarse scales, a small mouth and no teeth. Available whole, or in steaks and fillets. To cook: soak in salt water for 4–6 hours before cooking to remove the muddy flavour and aroma. Best stuffed and baked whole.

cod
A very large round salt-water fish with a silver-grey skin with small yellow and brown spots. The flesh should be pure white and firm with a coarse texture. Available fresh, as steaks or fillets, and salted, smoked and dried. To cook: use in pies, grill, fry, poach or steam.

coley
A round salt-water fish with a very dark charcoal-grey skin and a greyish-pink flesh, which turns white when cooked. Always sold in fillets. To cook: fry, bake, use in soups and pies.

dogfish (huss, rock salmon, rock eel)
Always sold skinned and split through. This salt-water fish is related to the shark family. It has a white flesh which is soft and a little oily in texture. To cook: use for soups and pies, poached in a sauce or deep-fried.

fish & seafood

eel, common

A freshwater fish with a long thin body. The skin is a shiny grey-black colour, and the flesh white, firm and rich. Also available jellied from stalls and specialist shops, and smoked. Sold whole or in fillets. To cook: steam, deep-fry or braise.

eel, conger

The most common salt-water eel. The flesh is very firm and white, stronger in flavour than the fresh-water eel and the skin is pale silvery-grey to black. Can be smoked. Sold whole or in chunks. To cook: steam or boil; use for soups and stews.

flounder

Related to the plaice and brill. A flat salt-water fish with a rounded body. The underside is cream coloured, the top pale brown. Sold whole. To cook: best grilled or fried.

haddock

A round salt-water fish, related to the cod family. It has a greyish-silver skin with a dark line which runs along both flanks. Its white flesh is firm and tasty but coarse in texture. Available whole, in fillets and cutlets. To cook: grill, fry, poach or bake.

hake

A round salt-water fish with a thin, sleek body and pointed nose, and large fins. The skin is a silver-grey and the flesh is firm, white, flaky and easy to digest. Sold as fillets, steaks and cutlets. To cook: bake, poach, stew or casserole.

halibut

This is the largest flat salt-water fish. The flesh is firm, coarse and white; that of smaller fish – known as chicken halibut – is finer. Available in steaks, fillets and whole for small ones. To cook: grill, poach, fry, bake or steam.

herring

A smallish silvery-blue skinned salt-water fish, with a brownish-white flesh. The skin should be shiny. Very bony, but delicately flavoured. Sold whole or filleted. To cook: grill, fry or bake. Rollmops are salted herring fillets, rolled up with onion and pickled in jars of vinegar and spices.

John Dory

Grey body, large ugly head. The firm white flesh is moist and sweet. Best cooked by steaming, baking or frying. Use small ones in soup.

mackerel

A silver-skinned salt-water fish with blue and black stripes from the head to the tail along its back. The flesh is pinkish brown and firm, the flavour is fairly rich. Sold whole. To cook: grill, fry, barbecue or bake. Best served with a sour or mustard sauce.

monkfish (angler fish)

A deep-sea fish with a large ugly head; usually only the tail is sold. The skin is blackish; the flesh is white, firm and succulent. To cook: poach, steam, fry, grill, stew or bake.

mullet, grey

A salt-water fish with large scales, and a grey skin. The flesh is greyish-white, firm and rather fatty. Sold whole. To cook: steam, bake, poach or grill.

mullet, red

A small salt-water fish with pinky-red skin and large scales. The flesh is white and firm. Difficult to buy fresh – usually frozen. Sold whole. To cook: grill or fry, with the liver left inside for flavour.

pike

A freshwater fish with a long lean body, a large pointed mouth and numerous teeth. The flesh is white and coarse and may require soaking in water before cooking if the fish is from muddy waters. Sold whole or in fillets. To cook: boil, bake, poach, fry or grill.

plaice

A flat salt-water fish with a brownish-grey upperside with bright orange spots; the underside is a creamy colour. The flesh is white and easily digested. Sold whole or in fillets. To cook: fry, poach, steam, bake or grill.

salmon

A fish which matures in the sea, but which spawns in fresh water. The skin is silvery with small scales, the flesh pink to dark red and close textured, with a delicate flavour. Scotch salmon is the best. Sold whole or in steaks or cutlets. Also frozen and smoked. To cook: poach, steam or grill.

sardine

A silver-skinned small salt-water fish, which is a young and immature pilchard. Sardines are sold fresh or canned. To cook: when fresh they are best grilled.

skate

A flat salt-water fish, shaped like a ray. Only the wings are sold. The flesh is a pinkish-cream colour and meaty. To cook: fry, poach or grill.

snapper

A very large family of fish, some of which are now imported. A very versatile fish with well-flavoured juicy flesh. To cook: best grilled, barbecued, baked or poached.

sole, Dover

A flat salt-water fish with an oval body and fairly small fins. The skin on one side is brownish-grey, the underside is creamy-white. The flesh is fine textured with a delicate flavour: it is considered the finest of the flat fish. Sold whole or in fillets. To cook: poach, fry, steam or grill.

sole, lemon

Considered inferior in flavour and texture to Dover sole, but still with a delicate, fresh flavour. It is wider and has a more pointed nose than Dover sole. Sold whole or in fillets. To cook: poach, fry, steam or grill.

sprat

A member of the herring family. A small silvery-skinned salt-water fish. To cook: deep-fry, shallow-fry or grill.

trout, rainbow

A silver-skinned fresh-water fish with rainbow colours flecked over the body. The skin should be slimy, the flesh is firm and either pink or creamy white. Sold whole. To cook: grill, fry, poach or bake.

trout, river or brown

A brown-skinned fresh-water fish with dark brown spots. The flesh is finer than that of the rainbow trout. To cook: grill, fry, poach or bake.

trout, sea or salmon

Fresh-water river trout which has spent a season or more at sea has a silver skin with silvery scales and a pale pink flesh – because of a diet of crustaceans – and a flavour similar to salmon. To cook: steam, poach or bake. Fry or grill fillets.

tuna

A large fish, found only in warm seas, it is sold as steaks with firm pink flesh. To cook: grill or griddle, bake or braise.

tuna

turbot

A large flat salt-water fish with a dark brown-black skin; the underside is white. The flesh is firm and white with a delicate flavour. Sold whole or in cutlets, steaks or fillets. To cook: bake, steam, poach, fry or grill.

whitebait

These are the fry of young sprats or herring. These tiny salt-water fish are silver in colour with a fine white flesh. Eaten whole. Available fresh and frozen. To cook: deep-fry whole, ungutted, in seasoned flour.

whiting

A member of the cod family. This round salt-water fish has a greyish-green upper skin, which is silvery-cream underneath. It has rather a bland flavour and a flaky texture. To cook: steam, poach, bake or fry. Good served with sauces.

seafood

buying and storing

Shellfish are best bought live and killed and cooked at home to ensure freshness and flavour. Lobsters, crabs, oysters, cockles, clams and mussels can all generally be bought alive. Live mussel, clam and oyster shells should close tightly when tapped; any which do not are dead and should be discarded.

Crustaceans such as crabs and lobsters are often sold cooked. They should have dry bright shells, and should feel heavy for their size. Cooked shrimps and prawns should be bright pink, and smell fresh and pleasant.

As with all seafood, it is essential to buy shellfish and cook or use it on the same day. It deteriorates quickly, and if not absolutely fresh can be toxic.

clam

Clams have a greyish thick, very tightly-fitting shell, and are usually sold live. As they are sandy, they must be washed several times in cold water, then soaked in cold water with a little oatmeal. Scrub before cooking. To cook whole, simmer in lightly salted water or wine for 5–10 minutes (depending on size) until the shells open. Use in soups, such as chowders, fish stews, or as a starter.

cockle

Tiny shellfish enclosed in a whitish fluted shell. Usually sold cooked. If fresh, soak in a bucket of salt water for at least an hour before cooking to remove the sand. Scrub the shells before cooking. To cook, simmer in lightly salted water for 4–5 minutes until the shells open. Use in fish soups, pies or as a starter.

crab

A raw crab is pinkish-brown when alive, the shell turning to an orange-red when cooked. Usually sold cooked, but they are available alive. The body contains soft brown meat; the white meat comes from the legs and claws. Allow one large crab for two people or a small to medium crab per person for a main-course dish. Best served freshly cooked, and dressed, or cold with mayonnaise.

salmon

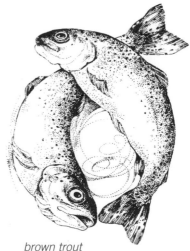

brown trout

octopus
Bluish-grey, 8-legged creature like a squid. The tentacles are covered with suckers. The flesh is pinkish-white and can be tough, so pre-cook in boiling water to tenderize the flesh and remove the skin, or cook long and slow. It can also be tenderized by beating the flesh with a meat mallet. To cook: boil, stew or fry.

oyster
The most prized of molluscs. The shells should be tightly closed when bought. Usually served raw, although sometimes cooked very lightly. The shell should be opened just before the oyster is eaten. Serve raw in the half shell on a bed of crushed ice. Allow 6 per person as a starter.

prawn
Prawns have a greyish shell which turns pink when cooked. Only the body and tail are edible. Most are cooked and frozen on the boats which catch them, but some are available raw. If uncooked, simmer in lightly salted water for about 5 minutes, until they turn pink.

prawn, Dublin Bay
Also called langoustine, these are shaped like a lobster with a slender orange body and long, thin claws. Mainly eaten as scampi (their tails). If raw, cook in their shells in gently boiling water for no more than 10 minutes and eat with melted butter. If pre-boiled, reheat gently but do not recook as they easily toughen.

lobster
These are a dark blue-black colour when live, which cooks to a bright red. The flesh of the female is finer than that of the male, and the body contains the coral, or roe (bright orange when cooked), which is highly prized; it is used to make sauces with a lovely pink colour, or for garnish. Lobsters are sold both live and cooked. Avoid ones with white blemishes on the shell, which is a sign of age. Use in salads, soups or starters. Lobster can be grilled and is especially good cold, served with mayonnaise.

mussel
Deep blue-purple to black shells. Usually sold live in the shell. They should be put into a bucket of cold water, with a sprinkling of flour or oatmeal to plump them, and left for a few hours to remove any sand or grit. Most mussels are farmed these days, so the shells should be clean and require little preparation. Mussels vary in size greatly. The larger ones require less cleaning for their weight. Large green-lipped mussels are available frozen in the half shell.

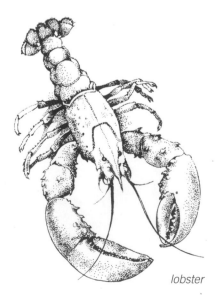

lobster

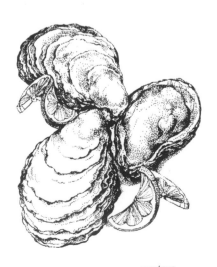

oysters

prawn, Pacific

The largest of the prawn family, measuring up to 15 cm/6 inches long. The pinkish-orange shell encloses the fine pink flesh. These are usually imported frozen, and are available throughout the year either cooked or uncooked. If bought uncooked, cook in boiling water for 5–10 minutes.

scallop

The scallop is a creamish-white nugget of firm flesh with a bright orange coral (roe). King and queen scallops are available, king scallops being much larger. Queen scallops are small and sweet. They should look plump and firm. Also available in closed shells and frozen off the shell. Suitable for poaching, baking and grilling, as well as for use in soups and stews.

shrimp, brown or common

Tiny transparent crustaceans, much smaller than prawns. The shell turns brown when cooked. Available either fresh or frozen. Usually served with brown bread and butter, in salads, or potted with butter and mace.

shrimp, pink

Usually sold cooked, these grey-shelled shrimps are slightly larger than the brown or common variety. The flesh turns bright pink when cooked. Serve as for brown shrimps.

squid

Squid are soft-bodied sea creatures covered with a fine purplish membrane which must be removed to reveal the tender white flesh. The tentacles and body are edible. Fry in oil or stew. Large ones can be stuffed. The ink sac can be used to colour the cooking liquid and in pasta or risotto dishes.

whelk

Snail-shaped brown or grey shells which are quite large. The flesh is brownish in colour. Usually sold cooked but they can be found uncooked. To cook, boil in salted water for 5–7 minutes, and remove from the shell before serving. Usually served with vinegar and brown bread and butter.

winkle

Similar to whelks, but much smaller. The shell is greyish-brown. Usually sold cooked, but can also be found uncooked. Cook in lightly salted boiling water for about 4 minutes. A pin is required to remove the flesh from the shell. Serve with vinegar and brown bread and butter.

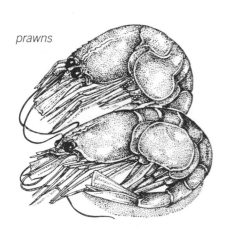

prawns

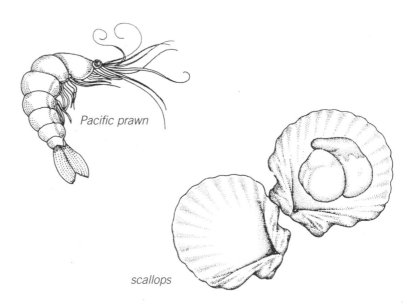

Pacific prawn

scallops

milk

Most of the milk we buy is pasteurized cows' milk. *Fresh milk* is available as whole milk, which has a full flavour and usually a layer of cream at the top if left to stand.
Skimmed milk is where the cream has been removed from the milk to give a virtually fat-free product; *semi-skimmed* milk is where about half of the cream has been removed; and *homogenized milk* is where the milk has been treated so that the cream is evenly distributed throughout the milk.
Goats' and sheep's milk are now increasingly available; goats' milk offers the advantage of being easily digestible and is therefore ideal for toddlers and some individuals on special diets. In cooking, milk should be heated gently and cooked at a low temperature.

yogurt

Full-fat yogurt is nutritionally similar to full-fat cows' milk; low-fat yogurts are also widely available. Fruit yogurts sometimes have sugar, edible gum and gelatine added to them. Natural yogurt can be used as a marinade for meat and a substitute for cream in sauces and soups but it must be heated gently to avoid separation. Greek yogurt is full-fat natural yogurt that has been strained to make it thicker and creamier.

double cream

Double cream has a high fat content (48%) and is thick and rich. It can be whipped to fill or decorate cakes and puddings but care must be taken not to overwhip: aim to stop whipping when soft peaks form otherwise it may turn granular. Double cream can be used to spoon over fruit.

whipping cream

Whipping cream has a fat content of 35% and is not as rich as double cream. It should be whipped with a balloon whisk until it doubles in volume. Used in ice creams, soufflés and mousses where a light, aerated mixture is required.

single cream

The fat content of single cream is 18% and it cannot be whipped because of its lower fat content. This cream is thinner than double and whipping cream and is ideal for soups and sauces and for pouring over desserts.

soured cream

This is cream that has had a culture added to it to give it a sour flavour. It should never be boiled and instead should be added to hot dishes towards the end of cooking. Used mainly in savoury dishes, especially soups and sauces.

crème fraîche

Although it too has had a culture added, the flavour of crème fraîche is not as sour as that of soured cream. Crème fraîche has a creamy flavour and a silky texture. Use in soups and sauces and with fresh fruit and desserts.

butter

Butter is available salted or unsalted. Unsalted butter has a delicate, sweet taste and is more suitable than salted butter for making cakes and biscuits. Salted butter burns at a lower temperature than unsalted butter therefore unsalted butter makes a better choice for frying. Salted butter keeps better than unsalted because the salt improves the keeping qualities.

cheese

buying and storing

When selecting cheeses, avoid anything that looks dry, sweaty or has blue mould on the surface. When choosing soft cheeses such as Brie and Camembert, press the top surface lightly with the fingertips. The cheese should yield slightly. It should be creamy in texture throughout, without any chalkiness in the centre. This chalkiness means that the cheese has not been ripened sufficiently and will remain in this condition.

Ideally, cheese should be stored in a cool, draught-free larder – a refrigerator is the next best thing. Cheese should be removed from the refrigerator and unwrapped at least an hour before it is required so that it has time to come to room temperature, which is best for appreciating the full flavour and the texture of the cheese. Fresh goats' cheeses should be consumed on the day they are purchased, as the flavour soon becomes soapy.

Brie

A soft, whitish cheese, made from cows' milk, with a white crust. It is smooth and creamy inside and has a mild flavour. It should be soft throughout, without any chalky solid centre. Generally, Brie is eaten uncooked but it may be cooked, usually with the crust removed, in tarts and flans. Smoked Brie is also available, as well as a variety with a thickly-peppered crust.

blue Brie

This is generally a thicker cheese than plain Brie, with blue veining throughout. Use as for plain Brie.

Caerphilly

A hard, crumbly Cheddar-like cheese with a sharp taste and pale, almost white colour. Caerphilly is made in Wales and Somerset. It is delicious served with crusty bread and pickles, but also makes a flavoursome addition to an after dinner cheese board. It can be used in place of a basic Cheddar in sauces, gratins or other cooked dishes. It melts well and gives a tangier flavour than Cheddar.

Camembert

A similar, but stronger-flavoured cheese than Brie, Camembert should bulge but not run when the top surface is lightly pressed. It is usually about 2.5 cm/1 inch thicker than Brie, coming in large or small, flat disks, packed in wooden boxes. Perfect with bread, biscuits or salad. It may be cooked and is commonly deep-fried with a crisp coating and served with redcurrant jelly or other tangy sauce.

Cheddar

Probably the most popular of British cheeses. Its flavour ranges from very mild to a fully matured strong nutty flavour. Ideal for grating and cooking, and for eating with bread or biscuits and pickle or chutney, or with fruit.

cottage cheese

A mild-flavoured cheese, very low in calories, as it is made from skimmed milk curds and is therefore low in fat. It is often flavoured with herbs or fruit. Usually used uncooked but it may be used for flans, cheesecakes and some sweet or savoury dishes. It is sieved when used in cheesecakes to give a smoother texture without the lumps.

dairy products

cream cheese

Usually a full-fat cheese, though it is available in low-fat varieties. It has a rich creamy flavour which is rather bland. Use cooked or uncooked. Ideal for savoury and sweet dishes including cheesecakes, desserts and icings, sauces, pâtés and bakes.

curd cheese

A soft unripened, slightly grainy cheese, with a clean acidic, bland taste. Used generally for cooking, in both sweet and savoury dishes, and it is often added to cheesecakes.

Dolcelatte

A creamy white Italian cheese with bluish green veins, a robust yet creamy flavour and a creamy moist texture. Usually used uncooked, but may be used for cheese sauces, especially with pasta.

Edam

Made from partly skimmed milk, this yellow cheese has a bright red rind and a rubbery texture. It has a mild creamy flavour and is relatively low in calories. Suitable for cooking or for eating uncooked in sandwiches and salads. It slices well.

Emmenthal

A buttery-yellow Swiss cheese with large holes. It is slightly rubbery in texture and has a mild to strong sweet nutty flavour. Ideal uncooked or cooked. It melts well and is often used in fondues.

feta

A semi-soft curd cheese made from sheep's milk. Brilliant white in colour, with a crumbly texture. It has a salty bland flavour. Use uncooked in salads or in cooked dishes. It is best known for its use in Greek salads.

Fontina

An Italian, soft full-fat cheese, straw coloured, with a few holes. It has an orange rind and the flavour is nutty and delicate. Use uncooked or for cooking. It melts easily and is perfect for grating and for making sauces.

fromage frais

Fromage frais is a smooth, creamy-textured cheese made from either skimmed or whole cows' milk that has had a culture added to it. You can buy either virtually fat-free fromage frais or one that has about 8% fat. Fromage frais is extremely versatile and can be used instead of cream or yogurt in cooking, as it is less liable to curdle, or can be served simply with fruit as a dessert. Fromage blanc is similar but smoother in texture.

goats' cheese

Cheeses made from goats' milk come in a wide range of flavours, textures and types. There are some hard varieties available but most continental goats' cheeses are soft. Mature continental goats' cheeses have a blue mould rind, a thick, white rind or are sometimes coated in ash. Some of the most popular goats' cheeses are the French log-shaped ones that have a thick, fluted white rind and are often sold in slices. Fresh goats' cheeses are soft and chalky and should be eaten soon after they are made.

Gorgonzola

A strongly-flavoured pale yellow Italian cheese with bluish-green marbling and a coarse brown rind. Although it is a semi-soft cheese, it should be firm and fairly dry. Mild and creamy varieties are available. It can be used uncooked, but is also delicious if lightly melted into sauces and risotto.

Gruyère

A pale yellow cheese with small holes, similar in texture to Emmenthal. It has a rich, full flavour with a little sweetness. It is an excellent cooking cheese as it melts well and is often served grated on top of fish soup in France. Equally good used uncooked.

haloumi

Haloumi is a goats' cheese from the Middle East and parts of Europe. It is quite salty and stringy, with a rubbery texture and mild flavour. It can be eaten as it is, or marinated, grilled, barbecued or fried. The surface becomes crisp and the inside melts. It is quite delicious grilled and served with salad.

mascarpone

A rich, creamy cheese made from cows' milk, mascarpone has the consistency of soft butter. It may replace cream in many recipes, such as pasta sauces and desserts, or may be served as an accompaniment to desserts. It is used to make tiramisu.

mozzarella

A soft compact curd cheese, usually moulded into a ball or egg shape. It is also sold in oblong blocks, sealed with plastic. This type is not to be recommended as the texture and flavour can be rubbery. It forms long strands during cooking, and becomes rather hard if overcooked. Serve raw in salads where it has an affinity with tomatoes and basil, or in pasta dishes. Perhaps best known as a topping for pizza.

panir

An Indian curd cheese with a rubbery texture and bland, salty flavour, used in many dishes, particularly vegetarian curries. It is now available in larger supermarkets and Asian shops. It is most flavoursome when cut into cubes and browned in oil before adding to a moist dish.

Parmesan

A very hard Italian cheese, yellowish in colour and fairly grainy. It is strong flavoured and should be grated just before it is required. When fresh, it has a fairly soft texture, similar to Cheddar. If very fresh, it is a good dessert cheese. The mature cheese (3–4 years old) is usually used for cooking or serving grated and sprinkled over pasta and soups.

Pecorino

A whole family of sheep's milk cheeses come under this name, the best known being Pecorino Romano. They have a pronounced piquant flavour and are available in fresher or more mature varieties. Fresher Pecorino goes particularly well with fresh country bread. The mature variety is used in the same way as Parmesan, grated in many regional Italian dishes. It is one of the main ingredients of traditional pesto.

Pont l'Evêque

A French, semi-soft pale yellow cheese with a yellow crust. It has a rich creamy flavour, stronger than Camembert. Serve with soft, crusty bread as part of a cheeseboard.

Port Salut

A French cheese with a thin orange rind. It is semi-hard with a rubbery texture and has a creamy bland flavour which gets stronger when it is fully ripe. Suitable for a cheeseboard and for cooking.

quark

Quark is a type of skimmed milk curd cheese made in Germany. Slightly acidic in flavour, it has a low fat content. Rarely served by itself, quark may be made into savoury dips or spreads, mixed with fruit purées or made into desserts. It is a good substitute for whipped cream as an accompaniment to sweet pies and flans or stewed fruit dishes.

ricotta

Made from sheep's milk, this cheese has a soft bland flavour and texture. It has a low fat content. Used a great deal in Italian cooking, it can be mixed with spinach and cooked potato and made into gnocchi or used as a filling for ravioli and cannelloni. It also makes a delicious base for a cheesecake.

Roquefort

A French cheese made from sheep's milk curds. It has bluish-green veins. A crumbly, semi-soft cheese with a strong, salty flavour. May be used cooked or uncooked. Perfect for salad dressings or crumbled over salads with nuts and croûtons.

Stilton

A creamy, salty English blue cheese, perfect for serving after dinner with a glass of port. It should be very creamy and not dry in texture. The blue veining should be evenly distributed throughout the pale cream cheese. If the cheese is white in colour, it is a sign of immaturity.
Stilton is best served uncooked, but it may be used in some flans or sauces to add a rich, creamy blue cheese flavour.

hard white fat

Made from vegetable oil, white fat is used for frying and pastry-making. It gives a similar result to lard, but is preferable for health reasons.

lard

Lard is made from rendered pork fat. It used to be used widely in baking and for shallow and deep-frying but for health reasons it is no longer popular. Some cooks use a mixture of lard and butter in pastry-making where it produces a light, crumbly texture.

margarine

All margarines are made from solidified vegetable oil. Margarine can perform the same functions in the kitchen as butter with the exception of frying. Soft margarine is not ideal for making pastry and low-fat spreads should not be used for cooking as they contain a high percentage of water.

ghee

Ghee is unsalted butter from which all the water and milk solids have been removed. The result is a clarified butter that can be heated to very high temperatures without burning. This means it can be used for frying at temperatures at which normal butter would burn. It is used extensively in Indian cooking to give a rich, buttery flavour to both sweet and savoury dishes.

groundnut oil

Also known as peanut oil, groundnut oil is valuable to the cook because it can be heated to a very high temperature. It is for this reason that it is the ideal oil for stir-frying. It is relatively flavourless, making it suitable for many different dishes.

flavoured oils

These are oils which have had flavourings, such as herbs, spices, sun-dried tomatoes or lemon peel, added. Most are used in salads and dressings for pasta. Chilli oil, made by adding fresh or dried chillies to vegetable oil and leaving them to infuse, is used in Oriental cooking. Truffle oil is another flavoured oil, made by scenting good quality olive oil with fresh truffles. It has the earthy, pungent aroma of truffles and is used in Italian cooking to flavour pasta, risotto, salads and mushroom dishes. It is extremely expensive, but is used very sparingly so a bottle lasts a long time.

corn oil

Corn oil, also called maize oil, has a distinctive golden yellow colour and is crushed from the germ of corn kernels. It can be heated to a very high temperature and is very economical. It is commonly used for deep-frying and is high in polyunsaturates, making it a good choice for low-cholesterol diets.

cooking fats & oils

olive oil

Olive oil is notable because of the sheer variety of types that are available, ranging from sweet and mellow to sharp-tasting, and from golden to green in colour. The best and most expensive olive oils are extra virgin and virgin oils which have a delicious fruity flavour and often a greenish colour. They are extracted from the first cold pressing of the olives. Ordinary olive oil is usually a blend of oils and is blander and paler than the virgin variety as it has been refined. Use extra virgin and virgin oils to dress salads, pasta and grilled meats and fish, and choose a less expensive olive oil for frying and cooking, when the flavour of the oil is less important.

pumpkin seed oil

A rich, nutty oil extracted from toasted pumpkin seeds and used in Italian cookery. It has a deep golden colour and sweet, smoky aroma. It is used sparingly to flavour pasta, risotto and meat dishes.

rapeseed oil

Also known as canola, rapeseed oil has a pale colour and can be used for frying and in salad dressings. It is particularly high in monounsaturated fats and low in saturated fats.

safflower oil

Another light oil that can be used interchangeably with sunflower oil. It is made from the safflower plant which is a type of thistle. Safflower oil is particularly low in unsaturated fats and is recommended for use in low-cholesterol diets.

sesame oil

With a strong, nutty flavour and golden brown colour, this oil is used widely in Chinese cooking. It should be used for flavouring rather than cooking as it burns readily when heated. It is extracted from toasted sesame seeds.

suet

Suet is the hard fat from around the kidneys of beef or mutton. Fresh suet used to be an important ingredient in dishes such as Roly Poly Pudding but nowadays suet is usually bought ready-shredded in packets. Vegetarian suet is now produced for those who do not eat meat.

sunflower oil

Sunflower oil is pale in colour with a rather bland flavour. It is excellent as an all-purpose cooking oil, perfect for deep-frying, and can be used in salad dressings combined with a stronger, more expensive olive oil to give flavour. It can also be used to make a mild mayonnaise.

vegetable oil

This is usually a mixture of the blander oils such as safflower, sunflower, corn and groundnut oil. Vegetable oil is a good all-purpose oil, particularly suited to cooking as it can be heated to a high temperature.

walnut oil

With a strong nutty flavour, this oil is used as a flavouring and is especially good in salads. It should be used sparingly and should not be used for frying as it cannot withstand high temperatures. Buy in small quantities and store in the refrigerator as it does not keep well.

rice

The type of rice chosen for a dish should be matched carefully to the result desired: pudding rice will not produce the separate grains vital for a pilau; and a long-grain basmati will not produce the moist, clinging texture characteristic of the best risotto, which needs arborio or carnaroli rice to succeed.

arborio and carnaroli rice

These are examples of Italian short-grain rice and are both used in risotto dishes. A key feature of these two types of rice is their ability to absorb a large amount of liquid without turning soft and slushy.

basmati rice

A long-grain, thin rice that stays firm and separate when cooked. Basmati has an aromatic, delicate flavour and is traditionally used in Indian cooking.

brown rice

This is the rice grain with nothing but the inedible outer husk removed. Because it retains the bran, brown rice is greatly superior in food value, and has a nutty texture and flavour when cooked. White, polished or pearled rice is produced when the bran is removed by milling.

glutinous or sticky rice

Widely used in Chinese cookery, these grains stick together and thus are easy to pick up with the fingers or chopsticks. It is also used, because of its sweetness, in baking and confectionery.

ground rice or rice flour

This is rice that has been ground to a fine powder. Use for thickening and in cakes, puddings and biscuits.

long-grain rice

The grains are up to five times as long as they are wide, and are fluffy and separate when cooked. They are ideal, therefore, for use in salads, and with curries, stews, chicken and meat dishes.

short-grain rice

Also called pudding rice, this rice is almost as wide as it is long. A glutinous rice that contains a lot of starch, its grains tend to cling together when cooked, making it suitable for puddings.

Thai fragrant rice

A long-grain rice with a fragrant aroma, that is slightly sticky when cooked. In Thai cooking, it is usually cooked and served without the addition of spices or salt.

wild rice

This is not actually a rice, but the seeds of a grass grown in the United States and the Far East. It is used for savoury dishes, particularly poultry and game stuffings, and is blackish-brown in colour.

grains

barley

Used to make beer, whisky and barley water, it is also good in soups, stews and casseroles.

buckwheat

Buckwheat can be used in pilafs or stuffings. Buckwheat flour is used to make blinis, crêpes and noodles.

bulgar wheat

Wheat grains which are hulled and steamed and then cracked and dried. Popular in Middle Eastern cooking, especially vegetarian dishes such as tabbouleh.

cornflour

Used to thicken sauces, cornflour is usually added at the end of cooking. To avoid lumps forming, cornflour should be blended with a small amount of cold water and then added gradually to the boiling mixture.

rice & grains

couscous
Made from semolina coated in flour, these tiny pellets are available in an instant variety, which takes about 5 minutes to prepare. Traditional couscous takes at least 1 hour to cook.

millet
This has a nutty, polenta-like flavour and, when toasted, the aroma of roasted corn. Used in combination with other grains in bread-making.

oatmeal
Small pieces of the whole grain, ground into coarse particles. Used in baking.

plain flour
This flour contains no raising agents and is particularly suitable for pastry and biscuits. It may also be used as a thickening agent when making sauces such as white sauce and cheese sauce.

polenta
Polenta is a flour with a granular texture and is usually made from yellow corn. Bring to a simmer in water and cook to a porridge-like consistency. Butter, herbs and/or olive oil may be added for additional flavour. Eat when soft and hot or allow to cool and cut into slices, which can be grilled or fried. Instant polenta can be used in the same way but requires much less cooking time.

rolled oats
Popularly known as porridge oats, these are oats that have been steamed and flattened. Also used in muesli and baking.

rye flakes
Similar to rolled oats, these are steamed and rolled rye grains. They may be eaten as porridge for breakfast and sprinkled on loaves before baking.

self-raising flour
Generally, self-raising flour is used for scones and cakes. It contains a raising agent, commonly a mixture of cream of tartar and bicarbonate of soda.

semolina
This is the ground endosperm of hard durum wheat, the wheat of choice in pasta making. Also used to make Indian dosas and couscous. Good for making bread and in desserts.

strong bread flour
Strong bread flour has a high gluten content and is used in bread-making.

wheat germ
This is removed from the grain during the milling process and is sold separately. It has a nutty flavour and can be added to breakfast cereals, fruit or yogurt, or bread and scones. It is a rich source of vitamins and should be kept in the refrigerator once opened.

white flour
To produce white flour, the bran and germ of the grain are discarded during the milling process. White self-raising, plain and strong bread flours are all available.

wholemeal flour
Wholemeal flour contains the outer layers of the grain (the bran) and the germ. Not only do these parts of the grain contribute a nutty flavour to wholemeal flour, they also provide valuable nutrients, particularly the B vitamins. Wholemeal self-raising, plain and strong bread flours are all available.

storing, soaking and cooking

Store dried pulses in an airtight container in a cool, dark place. Most dried pulses need to be soaked in about 3 times their volume of cold water before cooking; leave to soak overnight in a cool place, then drain and rinse well under cold running water. Kidney beans, black beans, adzuki beans and black-eyed beans must be brought to the boil and boiled fast for 15–20 minutes to destroy the toxins. Salt should be added at the end of cooking when the pulses are soft.

adzuki beans

Also known as aduki beans, these small red, shiny beans are popular in China and Japan. They have a sweetish flavour and are often made into red bean paste as a filling for pancakes and dumplings. Use in soups, salads, or with other vegetables, or grow as bean sprouts.

black beans

A member of the kidney bean family. These shiny black beans may be substituted for red kidney beans in any recipe. They have a strong and meaty taste, and are particularly effective when cooked with rice. They may be mixed into salads, casseroles, soups and main dishes.

black-eyed beans

Also known as black-eyed peas or cowpeas, these cream-coloured beans with a black spot are similar in shape to kidney beans, but smaller. Widely used in spicy African, Caribbean and Indian cooking.

borlotti beans

Kidney shaped, speckled and ranging in colour from creamy-pink to deep brownish-pink, these are the beans traditionally used in Italian cooking. Use in rustic salads, soups and pasta dishes, or substitute them in recipes using kidney beans. Pinto beans look rather like borlotti beans.

butter beans

Large, flattish, creamy white beans with a mild flavour and floury texture, which tend to turn mushy if overcooked. They are good added to mixed bean salads or used in rich stews, where they absorb other flavours.

cannellini beans

A member of the kidney bean family. These beans are small and creamy white. They are very similar to haricots and are interchangeable with them. They may be used in soups, stews and casseroles. They are particularly good in flavoursome salads.

chickpeas

Also known as garbanzo beans, these look rather like small hazelnuts, and have a nutty flavour. They are popular in the Mediterranean region, the Middle East, India and many other countries. They are added whole to salads, chunky soups, curries and stews, puréed in dips, toasted with spices as an appetizer, or ground and made into chickpea flour.

soaking and rinsing pulses

flageolet beans

Pale green or white, these are very tender young haricot beans with a delicate flavour. Add them to other beans for a salad, or serve in a creamy, garlicky sauce as an accompaniment to roast lamb.

haricot beans

Creamy white and oval shaped, the familiar 'baked beans' are ideal for dishes which need long slow cooking – with sausages, meat, tomatoes or herbs – such as the cassoulet of France, because they readily absorb other flavours. They can be used in salads, soups or as bean purées.

lentils

Lentils need no soaking, just rinsing. Red and yellow lentils, often sold split, cook quickly to a purée. They are used in Indian cooking for soups, rissoles, and to thicken curries. Brown and green (or continental) lentils keep their disc shape when cooked and have a distinctive earthy flavour, which goes well with sausages, ham and bacon. Puy lentils are smaller and fatter than brown or green lentils. They are slate grey-green in colour with a superb texture and mild peppery flavour.

mung beans

Small, oval-shaped, olive green beans, which are sweet tasting and have a soft texture. They may be cooked without soaking. Best known in their sprouted form as bean sprouts, which are used in salads and Oriental stir-fry dishes.

peas, dried

Available as yellow or green split peas or as whole peas, these need only 1–2 hours soaking, and cook in less than an hour. Split peas become a purée as they cook, and do not need to be mashed or blended.

pinto beans

A member of the kidney bean family. These oval beans are slightly rounded and pinkish-peach in colour with darker speckles. They are related to borlotti beans, are pink when cooked, and have a distinctive flavour. They are a key ingredient in Mexican cooking and can be used for salads, stews and hearty casseroles.

red kidney beans

The meaty flavour and texture of these beans makes them a popular choice for salads, soups, casseroles and hot, spicy dishes such as chilli con carne. They hold their shape well and should always be boiled fast for at least 15 minutes at the beginning of their cooking time.

soya beans

Small, round and yellowish-brown, these have the highest protein content of all pulses and are used to make tofu (bean curd), soya milk and soy sauce. They are bland in flavour, so always use them in combination with strongly flavoured herbs and spices. Soya beans should be boiled fast for the first hour of cooking to destroy a substance that prevents the body absorbing protein.

pulses

pasta & noodles

types of pasta

Made from durum (hard wheat) flour, pasta is the familiar pale straw colour, but it is brown if made from buckwheat or wholewheat flour. Colouring is added by spinach (green), tomato purée (red), beetroot juice (red or pink), saffron or turmeric (yellow), and squid or octopus ink (black). Durum wheat can be difficult to work with and, to make it easier, it is sometimes mixed with soft wheat flour which reduces the protein content and makes the product more starchy. Look for pasta that is made from 100% durum wheat for best results.

Egg pasta (pasta all'uovo) is the pasta of flour and eggs which originated from the Emilia-Romagna region of Italy and is available fresh or dried. This is often used for stuffed pasta.

common pasta shapes

cannelloni
These are available shaped as large, smooth or ridged, hollow tubes. Suitable for filling and then baking with sauces.

conchiglie
These are shell-shaped pasta – their name translates as little shells or conches. They come in various sizes and may have a smooth surface or a ribbed texture.

farfalle
The name of this small shape translates as bows or butterflies, and it is available in a variety of sizes. Farfalline is the name given to the very tiny ones.

fettuccine
This is a ribbon-shaped pasta, slightly wider than tagliatelle. It is especially good with creamy and butter-based sauces.

fusilli
Resembling a spring, these pasta shapes are also known as twists. Fusilli lunghi is a hollow pasta shape in the form of a long corkscrew.

fiorelli
The name of this pretty little pasta shape means flower. It is sold in packets of mixed colours – white, green and red – the colours of the Italian national flag.

gnocchi
Gnocchi is usually included when describing types of pasta, although it is really a small dumpling. It may be made of flour and water; potato flour and water, or even polenta. Gnocchi is usually added to soups or cooked in a simmering liquid and then tossed in butter or a sauce.

lasagne
Lasagne is made in broad flat sheets. The sheets are usually cooked layered with meat, cheese, vegetables and a sauce, or sauces, and baked in the oven. Cannelloni are sometimes made with rolled sheets of lasagne.

pappardelle
This is a wide ribbon noodle, sometimes made even more distinctive by a crinkly edge. Like tagliatelle, it can be found coiled into nests.

ravioli

penne
The name of this short tubular-shaped pasta means quills, recalling the quill pens of the past. Penne may be smooth or with a ridged surface, in which case they are called penne rigate.

ravioli
This is a filled square or round pasta shape that comes with a variety of fillings, ricotta and spinach being a favourite. They are available in small, medium or large sizes.

spaghetti
The classic pasta, and possibly the universal favourite. Other long strings of pasta include spaghettini (a very thin type of spaghetti); vermicelli (a size in between spaghetti and spaghettini); capellini (a very fine pasta); and fedelini (slightly thicker than capellini).

tagliatelle
Tagliatelle is flat ribbon pasta and so technically a noodle. It is usually sold coiled into nests. The combination of green and yellow tagliatelle is known as paglia e fieno or straw and hay noodles.

tortellini
Tortellini are a small version of tortelli, a stuffed pasta shape. Spinach and ricotta is a favourite filling for tortellini; they are sold ready-filled or you can make your own. Like ravioli, they are served with a sauce or with melted butter and grated Parmesan cheese.

noodles

bean thread noodles
These are commonly made from soya or mung bean starch. Also known as cellophane noodles, as they are transparent, they are good in stir-fries and salads. Although bean thread noodles can be cooked like pasta, it is usual to soak them first to soften them.

dried egg noodles
These are Chinese-style noodles made from wheat flour and eggs and sold in layers in packets. They cook very quickly and two types are widely available: thin or medium thick. They hold flavours well; after cooking they can be tossed in sesame oil or soy sauce.

rice noodles
Made from rice flour, these noodles are available as rice sticks or vermicelli. They can be confused with bean thread noodles as rice sticks also require soaking before cooking them. Good in stir-fries with rich sauces.

wheat noodles
Japanese wheat noodles, called udon and somen, are now increasingly available. Somen noodles are particularly fine in appearance and are sold wrapped in bundles. Both somen and udon noodles may be used in hot noodle soups or in stir-fries.

tagliatelle

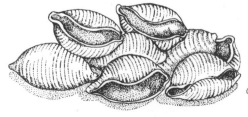

conchiglie

artichoke, globe

This edible flower bud belongs to the thistle family. To check for freshness, look for heads with leaves that are tightly packed. Artichokes should be used as soon as possible after purchasing and must be stored in a refrigerator. Before cooking, cut off the stalk and outer leaves. They can be boiled, steamed or braised.

artichoke, Jerusalem

These knobbly, tuberous vegetables are not true artichokes, despite their name. They have a delicate flavour that resembles that of the globe artichoke. Choose firm tubers with as few knobbles as possible for ease of preparation. Scrub and peel (or leave unpeeled), then cut into pieces or slices. Place in iced water as you work to prevent discoloration. Serve as a vegetable accompaniment, make into soups or add to stews and casseroles.

asparagus

Asparagus is the edible member of the lily family and is considered to be a luxury vegetable. Stalks range from slender and green to thick, white and fleshy. It is delicious served hot, warm or cold. It can be served as an accompaniment, a first course, or combined with other ingredients. If served on its own, it is best eaten with fingers. Asparagus should have firm, straight stalks.

aubergine

There are many varieties of aubergine from white to almost black. They should be smooth, firm and shiny with no blemishes. The large aubergines have little taste and are spongy. They should be used as soon as possible after buying as they deteriorate quickly. If not, they can be stored, covered, in the refrigerator.

avocado

Avocados are native to Central and South America. They are easy to digest and are rich in fat, protein and vitamins. They can be round or pear shaped and green, purple or a blackish colour. Avocados have a pale, creamy, green flesh. They are ripe when they yield slightly if pressed gently in the hand.

bean, broad

These are the seeds of bean plants. They are bought in a pod which is then split open to reveal the oval, pale green beans. They can be eaten fresh as a boiled vegetable or they can be dried and used as a pulse.

bean, green or French

Green or French beans are beans that are picked before they reach maturity and so the pods are thin in appearance. They should be cooked as runner beans, topped and tailed and then boiled, steamed or braised.

bean, runner

The runner bean is native to South America. It is a long green pod that holds seeds. Before cooking, beans should be topped and tailed and may be sliced or eaten whole. They can be boiled or steamed. If possible they should be eaten whilst young as they can become tough and stringy as they mature.

aubergine

asparagus

globe artichokes

bean sprouts

Bean sprouts have been used for hundreds of years in Oriental cooking and have gradually become more popular in Western dishes. The most commonly used bean for sprouting is the mung bean. Other types are also used such as soya, lentils and alfalfa. The sprouts can be eaten raw in salads or cooked in savoury dishes.

beetroot

Beetroot is a root vegetable with a sweet, red flesh. They should not be peeled or cut before cooking, as this loses some of the rich colour. Cooked beetroot is delicious sliced and heated through, or heated in the juice and grated rind of an orange for a tangy flavour. Grated cooked beetroot is often used as a salad garnish.

broccoli

Broccoli is a member of the cabbage family. Choose broccoli with tight heads, which are fresh and a dark green colour, with no trace of yellow. Most of the stalks should be cut off before cooking. Broccoli can be boiled in lightly salted water or steamed.

Brussels sprout

For the best flavour, choose small sprouts that have tight heads and show no traces of yellow. They should be stored for a few days in a refrigerator before being used. They can be boiled in salted water, braised or steamed.

cabbage

Cabbage comes in many varieties and is available all year round – from spring cabbages and greens to the harder red and white cabbages later in the year. Savoy cabbages, with their dark green, crinkled leaves, are among the most popular. Select firm heads with no trace of yellow. Before cooking, the outer leaves should be removed. Cabbage can be boiled, steamed or pickled, or eaten raw in salads.

cabbage, Chinese

Chinese cabbage is a lesser known member of the cabbage family. It is pale green in colour and more slender in shape. It also has a milder taste than other cabbages. It can be prepared and cooked just like other cabbages although it is excellent stir-fried.

carrot

The young carrots that are available in late spring with their characteristic feathery green tops are sweet in flavour. Older carrots may lack colour and flavour in the winter months. They have a distinctive orange colour and are conical in shape. They can be used in many ways and often appear in salads and casseroles. They should be topped and tailed before cooking; young carrots need only be scrubbed whereas older carrots should be scraped. They can be steamed or boiled.

cauliflower

Cauliflower, native to the eastern Mediterranean countries, is a member of the cabbage family. A fresh cauliflower should have white florets that are packed close together, and fresh green leaves. Prepare for cooking by cutting off the outer leaves and separating into florets or cooking whole. They may be steamed or boiled.

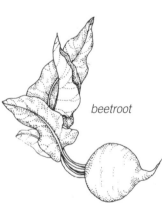

beetroot

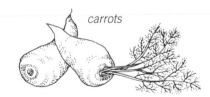

carrots

runner beans

vegetables

celeriac

This root vegetable is a type of celery. Only the large round root may be eaten as the stalks are not edible. Choose firm, small roots – really large heads of celeriac may be hollow or woody inside. Celeriac can be eaten raw in salads, boiled or steamed as a vegetable accompaniment, or in savoury dishes such as casseroles. It should be peeled before cooking.

celery

Celery is pale green to creamy white in colour and can be used in a variety of ways. It has a sweet to bitter-sweet taste and may be eaten raw in salads or used cooked in savoury dishes such as soups and casseroles.

chicory

Chicory has tightly-packed white leaves with green tips and tastes slightly bitter. It can be served cooked as a vegetable accompaniment or raw in salads.

courgette

Also called zucchini, this vegetable is a member of the marrow family. It has a dark green or bright yellow skin and a slightly sweeter flavour than other types of marrow. It is used in savoury dishes and may be cooked whole or in slices by boiling, steaming, baking, frying or stir-frying.

cucumber

The cucumber belongs to the marrow family. It is usually only eaten raw in salads or sandwiches but makes a good addition to the flavour of soups and hot vegetable dishes. The insides may also be scooped out and stuffed with savoury vegetables or fish mousse.

endive

This is a member of the chicory family and is so called in America. It has a bitter taste that goes well with other vegetables in a salad. To prepare, tear off the outer leaves and use the inner leaves. Wash thoroughly and dry before using.

fennel

Fennel is prized for its delicate aniseed flavour and is delicious both raw in salads and cooked. It should be prepared by trimming the top of the bulb and scrubbing the outside leaves, then cut into slices or quarters. When cooked the aniseed flavour becomes much milder. Fennel can be sautéed, steamed, stir-fried or used in pasta sauces, soups, stews and casseroles.

kohlrabi

This is a member of the cabbage family and is not a root vegetable, but the swollen stem of the plant. It should be prepared and used in the same way as turnips and has a similar, if milder, flavour. It can also be used grated in salads.

leek

The leek is a member of the onion family. Its white stem is the part that is eaten and it has a sweeter taste than onions. Fresh leeks should be firm with fresh green tops and no blemishes. In preparation for cooking, the roots and the topmost green leaves should be trimmed off. Clean very carefully by making several cuts lengthways down through the outer leaves and wash thoroughly under cold running water to remove any soil. Leeks can be cooked whole or sliced and can be boiled or steamed.

fennel

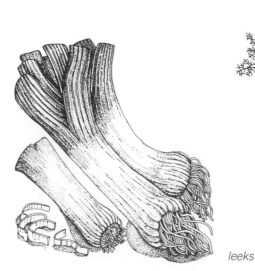

leeks

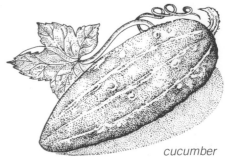

cucumber

lettuce

There are many varieties of this leafy green or red vegetable, from the crisp iceberg to the crunchy long-leaved Cos and the soft round lettuce. They are traditionally served in salads but can be used in other ways, such as in soups, or they can be braised. The main thing to look for in a fresh lettuce is unwilted leaves that retain a fresh colour. Do not buy lettuces with yellow or discoloured leaves. Prepare by removing the coarse outer leaves and washing thoroughly.

mangetout

This vegetable is also called the snow pea, sugar pea or Chinese pea. It is a pea pod, but the seeds don't really develop, so the whole pod is eaten as a crisp vegetable. They are prepared in just the same way as runner beans, being topped and tailed before steaming, boiling or stir-frying.

marrow

The marrow has a smooth skin with light and dark green stripes that run along its length. Marrow tastes best when eaten young and can be served with sauces and stuffings or cooked in chutneys. Choose unblemished marrows that are relatively small. To prepare for cooking, peel, take out the seeds and cut the flesh into cubes or stuff whole.

mushroom

Cultivated mushrooms are edible fungi that come in many shapes and sizes. There are also wild varieties that are edible. Mushrooms should be stored in a paper bag or box in the refrigerator. They should not be peeled unless they are very dirty; instead, merely wipe them with a damp cloth. They can then be sliced, chopped or cooked whole, in soups, casseroles and sauces or served as a vegetable accompaniment.

okra

Okra, also called lady's fingers, is a fleshy green seed pod with a flavour resembling aubergines. It is used in curries and Middle Eastern dishes, as well as being a vital part of Creole cooking. Fresh okra should be green in colour and snap easily. Choose small undamaged pods with no brown patches. The seeds should be firm but not hard. Okra is prepared by washing and trimming the stems. Take care not to expose the seeds or juices inside the pods during cooking.

onion

Onions are members of the same family as chives, leeks and garlic. They are used to flavour stocks, soups, sauces and meat and vegetable dishes. Onions should be firm with no bruising and should be stored in a cool dry place. There are several different types of onions including brown, Spanish, red and white varieties. To prepare for use, they should be topped, tailed and peeled, then sliced or chopped.

okra

mushrooms

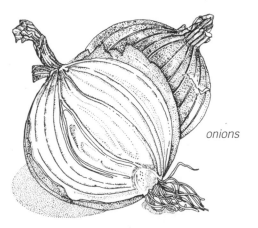

onions

parsnip

Parsnips have a slightly sweet flavour which goes well with roast meats. They can also be used in soups and stews or puréed. Choose firm parsnips that have no brown blemishes. The roots and tops should be cut off and the outer skin peeled thinly in preparation for cooking. If the vegetable is mature the hard core will need to be removed.

pea

Peas are one of the most popular vegetables. They grow in a flat pod which is green in colour like the resulting seeds themselves. It is these seeds that are the edible part. There are many varieties of pea, but all taste best when eaten young. Young peas may be eaten raw in salads; boiled or steamed as a vegetable accompaniment, or added to soups and savoury dishes.

pepper

These are related to hot chillies. They come in many colours with red being the fully ripe ones and green and yellow being stronger in flavour. When choosing fresh peppers look for ones with no soft spots or wrinkled flesh. They should be stored in a refrigerator and used within a week. They can be used raw in salads, stuffed and baked whole, roasted, or combined in savoury dishes such as soups, casseroles and pasta dishes.

potato

Potatoes are the tubers of a plant that is native to South America. There are many varieties of potato and the appearance of the vegetable varies according to the type. New potatoes, which are usually small, are generally used in salads. There are certain varieties of potato that are best suited to boiling, roasting and baking. They are nutritious and are extremely versatile.

pumpkin

The pumpkin is a member of the squash family and is usually only available in the autumn and winter. The flavour is slightly sweet and nutty. Pumpkin is prepared by peeling it and then removing the seeds. It is used in many dishes, both sweet and savoury, such as soups, pies and salads. Pumpkin may also be stuffed and baked.

radicchio

This is a member of the endive family and is the Italian name for chicory. It looks like a small red cabbage and has a distinctive, slightly bitter taste. Radicchio can be used raw in salads and should be prepared like a lettuce; the outer leaves should be removed and the remaining leaves washed thoroughly. It may also be grilled or roasted until slightly wilted and used in cheese and pasta dishes.

radish

Radishes are root vegetables that are members of the mustard family and are native to southern Asia. There are many varieties of radish ranging from white to red to black; the shape can vary from round to cone-shaped. Radishes are normally eaten raw in salads although they can be eaten cooked especially in some Oriental dishes. To prepare radishes for eating, they should be topped and tailed and washed thoroughly.

salsify

This is a white-skinned root vegetable whose young leaves are sometimes used in salads. Salsify has a distinctive flavour that is said to resemble that of oysters and so it is sometimes called the oyster plant. It can be eaten raw or in savoury dishes, but to obtain the best results boil it on its own as a vegetable and serve tossed in butter and plenty of black pepper.

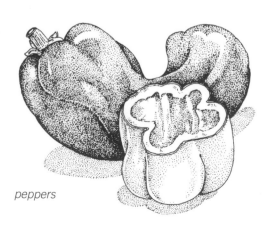

peppers

shallot

The shallot is a member of the onion family. The flavour is said to be a combination of onion and garlic. It is, however, sweeter and less pungent than both onion and garlic; shallots can be used in the same way as onions but can also be used whole in soups, stews and casseroles.

sorrel

Sorrel is a leafy vegetable that is native to Europe and the Middle East. It is green and has small leaves with a bitter lemon flavour. It can be used in the same way as spinach or it can be puréed and used in omelettes. Sorrel can also be used raw in salads or cooked in sauces. It is excellent with fish and combines well with the flavours of duck, pork and veal.

spinach

Spinach is a leafy green vegetable that is high in vitamins and minerals. When preparing spinach for cooking, the leaves must be washed thoroughly. If it is very young it may be eaten raw in salads. Spinach should be cooked with only the water clinging to its leaves after washing, for the shortest possible time. Use as a vegetable accompaniment, or puréed or chopped in quiches, soups and savoury dishes.

swede

Swede is a bulbous root vegetable with orange flesh that is related to the turnip. Traditionally it is cooked and mashed and served as an accompaniment to meat dishes. It can however be used in many other ways, such as roasted or added to stews. Choose small swedes, as large roots can be woody. To prepare them for use, they should be peeled thinly until the flesh is showing, then topped, tailed and chopped.

sweetcorn (corn-on-the-cob)

Sweetcorn is native to North and South America. To check if it is fresh you should make sure the kernels are plump and that the husk is green and fresh. Before cooking, the leaves and threads should be removed. It can be boiled, grilled or barbecued whole, or the kernels can be cut off the cob and boiled by themselves. Whole cobs can be eaten as a snack, starter or accompaniment to a meal, or the kernels can be used in soups, salads or casseroles.

tomato

There are many varieties of tomato and they come in all shapes and sizes, from the small sweet cherry tomato to the oval-shaped plum tomato and the larger beefsteak tomato. They can be used raw in salads, or cooked in sauces, soups and other savoury dishes; they can also be puréed or made into a drink.

turnip

The turnip is a root vegetable that is bulbous in shape. The skin varies in colour from white to green to purple. Turnips are best eaten when small and young as the larger ones can be woody. They can be grated and used in salads or used in savoury dishes such as soups and stews, and as a vegetable accompaniment to meat dishes.

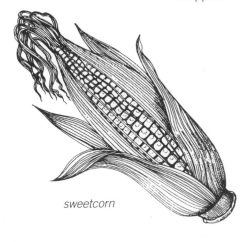

sweetcorn

tomatoes

apple

There are numerous varieties of apples, but they can generally be divided into cooking apples and eating apples. Apples are extremely versatile and can be baked, stewed, puréed, used in puddings, pickles and chutneys, or used raw in salads and with savoury meals. Apples can be stored in the refrigerator or in a cool, dark place.

apricot

The apricot is a member of the peach family and is a small, golden-coloured fruit. Apricots should be stored in the refrigerator in a covered container or in a plastic bag with holes for air to circulate. Apricots can be poached, simmered or boiled and are used in puddings, jams and savoury dishes.

banana

Bananas should be bought with smooth, unblemished skins and in a bunch rather than separated, as they keep better. Green bananas can be used for cooking, but for eating raw, allow bananas to ripen at room temperature. When slicing bananas to be used in fruit salads or as cake decorations, mix them with a small amount of lemon juice to prevent them from turning brown.

blackberry

Fresh blackberries are only available for a short season from late summer to early autumn, but they can also be found canned or frozen. They are round or oval-shaped and generally about 2.5 cm/1 inch long. They can be eaten on their own, in fruit salads or in cooked dishes and preserves. Before eating them, however, wash them carefully to remove any dirt or bugs.

blackcurrant

The blackcurrant is a small, round, seeded berry that is black in colour. Choose firm, plump, perfectly ripe fruits – avoid green or wrinkled fruits. Blackcurrants may be eaten fresh or removed from their stalks and stewed and puréed. Use in desserts such as fools, crumbles and summer pudding, or serve in sauces and casseroles with fatty meats and poultry.

cherry

Cherries can be eaten fresh or can be stewed for 5–10 minutes in a sugar syrup which may be flavoured with a cinnamon stick, lemon peel and brandy. Cherries have a very short season, but can be preserved and enjoyed all year round.

coconut

This is the fruit of a tropical palm which is native to much of Africa and Asia. Fresh coconuts are worth buying for use in cooking because the flavour of fresh coconut flesh is far superior to that of dried or desiccated coconut. When choosing coconuts, hold the fruits in your hand – they should feel heavy. When you shake one, you should hear the sound of the coconut water inside. Coconuts are used in both sweet and savoury dishes.

crab apple

These members of the apple family are the wild fruits of the crab apple tree. They are small green apples that are very sour. For this reason they are not eaten raw but can be used in preserves because they contain a lot of the gelling agent pectin.

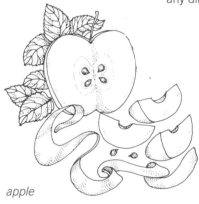

apple

apricot

blackberries

cranberry

This is the fruit of an evergreen shrub which belongs to the heather family. There are various different species so the size and colour depends on the variety. They have a very sharp taste which means they are not eaten raw, but they have many uses in sauces, both sweet and savoury, jams, desserts and baking. Cranberries may also be served as a juice.

date

Dates grow in large hanging bunches on the date palm and can either be eaten fresh or dried. Fresh dates should be purchased only if plump and moist with skins that are smooth and shiny brown – do not buy if they are dry and shrivelled. Eat as a snack or use chopped in sweet and savoury salads; stuff them with cream cheese or use in baking.

fig

Figs are best eaten at room temperature as the flavour is lost if they are too cold. Choose plump fruits that are soft and ripe with skin that is not split or bruised. Fresh figs are sweet and juicy when eaten raw, whereas dried figs are a lot sweeter and are best used in cakes and puddings or stewed.

gooseberry

Gooseberries are summer fruits and are categorised by their colour – red, yellow or green. Some varieties, mostly yellow, are suitable as dessert fruit whereas others, usually the green varieties, are suitable only for cookery. Gooseberries are used in desserts, jams and sauces, or they can be poached in syrup that may be flavoured with elderflower.

grape

Grapes are the fruit of a climbing vine. They come in many varieties and colours from pale green to deep red or black, both with and without seeds, and in a range of sizes. They are small and oval in shape with thin skins and sweet flesh. Grapes may be used raw in fruit salads, jellies and other desserts, or used in savoury cooked dishes. They also make a delicious non-alcoholic drink. Certain varieties of grape are used for wine-making.

grapefruit

Grapefruit is the fruit of an evergreen tree. It is larger than other citrus fruits and has yellow or slightly pinkish skin. It is mainly used raw as a breakfast dish, in marmalade or as a juice.

kiwifruit

Kiwifruit is also known as the Chinese gooseberry as it is an oval, hairy fruit which is native to China. It has green flesh with black seeds. When choosing kiwifruits, look for fruits that are firm but which give when squeezed gently. To prepare, carefully peel off the skin with a small sharp knife. They are most commonly used sliced in fruit salads and as garnishes but can be used in other desserts, such as pies, and in preserves.

figs

blackcurrants

fruits

kumquat

The tiniest of all the citrus fruits, the kumquat is about the size of an olive. It can be eaten whole, including the skin. It is an extremely versatile fruit, with a bitter-sweet, piquant flavour which is both refreshing and thirst-quenching. Ideal for fruit salads and preserves, and excellent cooked and served with duck as a substitute for orange.

lemon

Lemons are widely used in many cuisines and their versatility and number of uses makes them an indispensable ingredient in the kitchen. Both the juice and the rind of the lemon can be used to flavour and season dishes. The maximum amount of juice can be extracted from a lemon by first placing it in a preheated moderate oven for two minutes, before halving and squeezing it. The rind can be removed using a fine grater, rubbed off with sugar lumps or pared thinly with a vegetable peeler.

lime

Limes can be pale or dark green and are often used instead of lemon as a flavouring for sweet and savoury dishes. They are delicious when made into marmalade and are used in Indian cuisine to make pickles and as an accompaniment to many curry dishes. Limes are also popular in Mexican and Creole cooking, as well as in making refreshing drinks such as Margaritas and Daiquiris.

loganberry

These are the fruits of a plant which is related to the rose family. It is a cross between a raspberry and either a blackberry or the closely-related dewberry. They are dark red oval berries, slightly larger than the raspberry. The flavour is more sour than the blackberry but milder than the raspberry. They can be eaten raw and used in any dish that is suitable for blackberries or raspberries.

lychee

Fresh lychees are encased in a brittle, knobbly-looking outer covering. The flesh inside is juicy and translucent with a large stone. The flavour of lychees is often likened to that of the muscat grape, with a slightly acid after-taste. Eat as a dessert fruit or with duck, pork and chicken dishes.

mango

Mangoes are cultivated in many tropical countries and offer a profusion of tastes. Mangoes do not travel well and the best flavour is achieved when the fruit is allowed to ripen to an orange-yellow colour. Choose fruits that have a firm flesh and a smooth texture. Prepare by peeling away the skin and cutting the flesh away from the large flat stone. Mango slices may be added to fruit salads or curries, made into pickles and chutneys or they can be dried.

mango

kumquat

melon

melon

The melon comes from the same family as the cucumber and the marrow. There are many different varieties of melon including the small, green-skinned Charentais, the cantaloupe with its sectioned skin and yellow flesh, and the oval honeydew melons with their bright yellow skin and green flesh. The flesh can be used in many sweet and savoury dishes including fruit salads. The seeds are edible and may be eaten roasted.

nectarine

The nectarine is a member of the peach family and has a smooth skin with a pinky red colour. The flesh is firm and ranges from a creamy white to a deep orange. There are many varieties, and nectarines can be used in most recipes requiring peaches.

orange

The orange is a very popular citrus fruit which is available all year round. It is widely used in savoury and sweet cooking as well as being eaten as a fresh fruit. Orange juice contains a high level of vitamin C and should be freshly squeezed. Oranges should have bright shiny skins with no bruising and they should feel firm and heavy for their size.

papaya

Papaya or paw paw is a large tropical fruit with a thin, smooth skin that turns yellow when ripe. The juicy flesh varies from yellow to orange; in the centre of the flesh is a large cavity containing black seeds which should be scooped out and discarded. Ripe papaya may be eaten raw on its own or in fruit salads. Papaya also contains an enzyme that gives the fruit tenderizing properties: in the tropics it is widely used to tenderize meat.

passionfruit

Passionfruit has a thick purple skin that is not edible. When the skin becomes crinkled and soft, the fruit is ripe. The simplest way to enjoy passionfruit is to cut it in half, scoop out the pulp with a teaspoon and eat it straight away. The pulp may also be added to desserts such as pavlova, gâteaux, fruit salads and ice creams.

peach

Peaches can have white or yellow flesh and are best eaten when they are perfectly ripe and slightly chilled. Peaches go well with other summer fruits in fruit salads and make a simple dessert on their own. They also add flavour to meat and poultry dishes.

passionfruit

nectarine

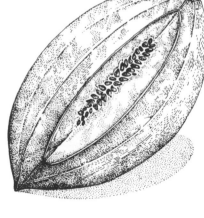

papaya

pear

Pears can be divided into dessert and cooking varieties. Dessert pears have the best flavour when eaten raw on their own or in fruit salads. Cooking pears are best stewed or used in dishes such as crumbles, tarts and pies. Some pears are also used exclusively for making pear brandy.

pineapple

Pineapples are available all year round. They are grown in tropical and sub-tropical climates. Fresh pineapple is best served simply when it is fully ripe. It also combines well with pork and chicken. Ripe pineapples should be golden with firm, yet tender flesh. Pineapples can be prepared by cutting off the crown, then removing a 1 cm/$^1/_2$ inch slice from each end. Stand the fruit upright and cut off the skin in strips using a sharp knife. Then slice the fruit into rings and remove the tough central core on larger fruits.

pomegranate

Pomegranates are the fruits of a tree that is native to Iran. They are now grown in tropical and sub-tropical areas. They are spherical in shape with a hard skin that is a yellow-reddish brown colour. Inside there are tiny seeds encased in sweet pink flesh and this is the part that is eaten. They are embedded in pith that is bitter tasting and should be discarded. The flesh is used in fruit salads or sorbets and in some savoury dishes.

quince

These are pear-shaped fruits with a thin yellow skin. The white flesh is too sour to eat raw and for this reason they are used in preserves and sauces. They are not widely available.

raspberry

Raspberries have a very short season, but frozen raspberries can be bought all year round. Fresh raspberries can be served simply with cream or a soft fresh cheese. They combine well with other fruits, either fresh or cooked. Raspberries can be made into jam or jelly, or they can be frozen whole or as a purée, when they can be kept for 6 months.

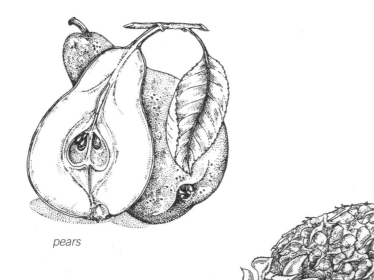

pears

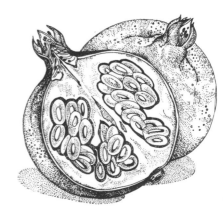

pomegranates

pineapple

redcurrant

The redcurrant is a small, round red berry, related to the blackcurrant. It is not eaten raw, but is mainly used in jams, drinks and cooked sweet and savoury dishes.

rhubarb

Rhubarb is available all year round and must be eaten cooked. Forced rhubarb is the pale pink type with thin, tender, sweet stalks. The other 'outdoor' type is stronger in flavour and coarser in texture. It works particularly well with citrus flavourings and also with spices, such as ginger. It is used to make desserts such as pies, fools, mousses, ice creams and sorbets; in jams and preserves; and in some savoury dishes.

satsuma

This is a cultivated version of the tangerine. It is a small citrus fruit with a sweet taste. Satsumas are eaten on their own as a snack or are used in fruit salads.

strawberry

There are many varieties of strawberry – from tiny wild strawberries to larger modern cultivated ones. They have a sweet taste and are at their best when fully ripe. They may be eaten in a variety of ways, such as by themselves with cream, or in desserts such as fruit salads, flans, tarts, mousses or ice creams. They may also be made into sauces or preserves.

tangerine

Also called mandarins because they originated in China, these are the fruits of an evergreen tree which is a member of the orange family. The skin peels away easily and is darker than other members of the orange family. The flesh is sweet tasting and may be eaten on its own or used in any dish that calls for oranges.

watermelon

This is a member of the melon family but should be considered in a class of its own. It is larger than any of the other varieties and has a dark green skin. Inside, the flesh is a pinky red colour and it is here the seeds are contained. It has a slightly milder flavour than other melons and a higher water content. The flesh is refreshing if eaten on its own or it may be used in fruit salads.

raspberries

strawberries

almond

This is the seed of a tree that is native to western Asia, a member of the peach family. Almonds come in two varieties, bitter and sweet. They are oval in shape and off-white in colour. They are available whole, blanched (with the brown skins removed), slivered (fairly thickly sliced lengthways), flaked (shaved into paper-thin slices), or ground. Almonds may be used in both sweet and savoury dishes in baking, confectionery, salads, stuffings and rice dishes. Ground almonds may be made into marzipan, added to pastry or used as a thickening agent.

brazil

These are the seeds of a tropical South American tree. They have brown shells and a creamy white kernel. They can be purchased whole in their shells or shelled, in chopped or ground form. They are mostly used in cakes and desserts.

cashew

Cashew nuts are the seeds of a native South American tree. They are kidney shaped and have a sweet flavour and soft texture. They may be eaten as a snack or used in a variety of sweet dishes, and savoury dishes like nut roasts and curries.

chestnut

The edible chestnut is sweet tasting, starchy and has a low fat content. Chestnuts can be used in both sweet and savoury dishes. Use in soups, stuffings or with vegetables. Sweetened chestnut purée may be used in desserts where it combines well with chocolate. Whole chestnuts are available canned, while sweetened or unsweetened purée can be bought in cans or metal tubes.

hazelnut

These are also called cobnuts. They are the small, round nut of the hazel tree found in Europe and North America. To prepare, they should be shelled and then they can be eaten whole, chopped or ground. The flavour improves if the nuts are roasted in a medium oven for 10 minutes. They can be puréed with other ingredients to make a spread. Hazelnuts are used in both sweet and savoury dishes.

peanut

Also known as a groundnut, the peanut is the seed of a pulse found in the tropics. As well as being a very popular snack, peanuts can be used to make peanut butter and can be found in Thai and West African cooking. They can be roasted in a moderate oven for 10 minutes to concentrate the flavour.

pecan

Closely related to the walnut, the pecan nut is native to the United States. Pecans can be eaten as a snack or used in pecan pie, ice cream and cakes. They can also be used in savoury stuffings for poultry.

pine nut

These are also called pine kernels and are the kernels from the cones of certain types of pine trees, some of which are common around the Mediterranean. They are long, with an off-white colour. They may be chopped or ground, toasted or eaten raw. They are a vital ingredient in pesto, but can also be used in salads, risotto and pilaf.

pistachio

Pistachio nuts are native to Syria but are also grown in other areas with warm climates. They have a creamy-coloured shell that splits at one end. The nut inside is a green colour. They are often available salted and roasted, but have other uses. Pistachios may be made into ice cream, added to cakes and fruit salads, or used to make praline. They are also used as colouring agents for milk puddings.

walnut

Walnuts are enclosed in a hard shell that has a wrinkled appearance. Walnuts can be eaten whole on their own, or in sweet or savoury dishes, halved or in chopped or ground form. They make an excellent addition to salads, cakes, pasta sauces and stuffings.

chestnuts

candied peel

Candying is a slow process that involves saturating fruit or peel with a sugar solution. Candied citrus peel – mostly oranges and lemons – is commonly sold chopped. Long strips of candied orange, lemon, citron and grapefruit peel have a superior flavour and attractive appearance and are usually available at Christmas. Use in mincemeat or in baking, such as Christmas cakes.

currant

Currants come from a smaller, bushier vine than that of raisins or sultanas. They are seedless and very small and sweet. Currants may be eaten as a snack or used in cakes, puddings and savoury dishes.

dried apple

These are ripe apples which have been peeled, cored and cut into rings or pieces, and dried in hot-air tunnels. Dried apples are a healthy snack or may be used in desserts, baking, muesli and stuffings. To reconstitute, soak them in boiling water for 30 minutes.

dried apricot

Dried apricots have a sweet flavour with a hint of sharpness. They may be reconstituted by soaking in cold water overnight or for 30 minutes in boiling water. Purée and serve as a sweet or savoury sauce; or add to fruit salads, muesli, cakes and sweet breads, or savoury rice dishes.

dried date

The date is the fruit of the date palm. They are either sun-dried or dried in hot-air tunnels. Top quality dessert dates have a golden, amber colour and are soft and fleshy in texture. Cheaper dates, used mainly for cooking, are dark and short and have a coarser texture. Dates can be eaten as a snack or used in cakes, puddings, breads, preserves or savoury dishes.

dried fig

Dried figs are an excellent source of dietary fibre and contain minerals and vitamins. They make a nutritious snack food or they can be chopped up and used in cakes, puddings, breads and savoury dishes, including stuffings. Dried figs can be soaked and poached and eaten by themselves with yogurt or cream, or combined with other fresh and dried fruits in a compote.

glacé fruits

This is candied fruit that is given a glacé finish by dipping the fruit into a sugar syrup solution. Candied fruit that is dipped first in water and then caster sugar is known as crystallized fruit. A wide range of glacé and crystallized fruit is now available. Most can be used in cakes, added to muesli or eaten as snacks.

prune

This is a dried purple-skinned plum. Prunes are usually available whole, stoned or unstoned, and have a naturally sweet flavour and soft, juicy texture. Prunes are graded according to size, with the larger or 'jumbo' prunes the best and most succulent. Whole prunes may be eaten as a snack or added to fruit salads; they may also be stewed and added to compotes. Chopped prunes may be used in breads, cakes and savoury dishes.

raisin

Raisins are dried white or black grapes. They come in a variety of colours, flavours and sizes, depending on the variety of grape. Muscat raisins are very sweet and succulent with a pronounced flavour. Raisins may be eaten raw or used in cakes and puddings, salads, savoury dishes or pickles and chutneys.

sultana

Sultanas are dried seedless white grapes that are golden brown in appearance. They are very sweet and succulent and can be used in the same way as currants and raisins.

pecans

nuts & dried fruits

basil

Basil is a popular ingredient in Italian cooking, its peppery flavour particularly complementing tomatoes. It is available fresh, either cut or growing in a pot and can be preserved well in oil. It can also be bought dried, but unlike many other herbs, the flavour is completely altered during drying.

bay

Bay leaves come from the sweet bay tree. Ideally the leaves should be used 3–4 days after they have been picked. They can also be dried by hanging them in a cool place for a week and then storing them in an airtight jar. Bay leaves are particularly good for flavouring sauces, soups, pickles, kebabs and meat. Avoid old or dried leaves which will not have much flavour.

borage

Borage has grey-green leaves that are pointed and long. It has edible flowers of an intense blue, which may be added to salads. The leaves have a mild flavour resembling cucumber and are often added to fruit drinks such as Pimms and other punches.

chervil

This herb is related to the carrot family. The leaves, which are small and green in colour, resemble parsley in taste and may be used to add flavour to soups, salads, sauces, egg, chicken and fish.

chilli

Chillies are available in all shapes and sizes and are important ingredients in Mexican, Indian and Asian dishes, especially in Thai cooking. On the whole, the smaller the chilli, the more intense will be its heat. Birdseye chillies are small and thin-skinned with a deep, fiery heat and are used in salsas and stir-fries. Jalapeño and poblano chillies are used in Mexican cooking and are both medium hot.

chive

The chive is a member of the onion family and has a vivid green colour and a delicate flavour. Chives are used to give a mild onion flavour and go especially well with cheese, potatoes and eggs and as a flavouring for soured cream. They also make a colourful and attractive garnish for many dishes. They are best cut using scissors, to avoid bruising, and should be added to food just before it is served.

coriander

Coriander is a widely used herb with a distinctive smell and taste. The plant has delicate, feathery leaves and it is often sold planted or with the roots still attached. It is used extensively in Mediterranean, Mexican and Asian cooking. It is an essential ingredient in Thai green curry.

chervil

basil

bay leaves

dill

The flavour of dill bears similarities to both fennel and parsley. It is dark green with feathery leaves and is often used as a garnish. It is used widely in Scandinavian and Russian cooking and is often combined with yogurt and soured cream to accompany savoury dishes. It is an extremely versatile flavouring and chopped dill combines well with new potatoes, salmon, cucumber and mayonnaise.

fennel

Fennel is available as a herb and a vegetable. The herb is a tall plant with willowy leaves and green stalks. The flavour of fennel can vary, depending on the variety, from sweet to bitter, but has a distinctive aniseed taste. The leaves provide a delicate flavouring to fish and meat and can also be chopped and used in pasta dishes and salads.

garlic

Garlic is probably one of the most well-known and widely used herbs. It is a member of the onion family and consists of a bulb which is made up of a number of cloves. It is a basic ingredient in the cuisines of France, Italy and Spain as well as the Middle and Far East. Garlic cloves can be added whole to dishes when cooking and then removed before serving for a subtle flavour, or chopped and combined with the other ingredients. Garlic is used in curries and to add flavour to otherwise bland dishes.

ginger

Fresh ginger is available as a knobbly root that should have a firm and shiny appearance. It is used extensively in Asian cooking and is usually peeled and finely chopped, grated or cut into matchstick strips.

lemon grass

These are stalks with an intense lemon flavour, that are usually sold trimmed in supermarkets. Lemon grass will keep in the refrigerator for 2–3 weeks. Prepare by removing any damaged outer leaves and finely slice or chop. It may also be available dried, either sliced or powdered.

lime leaf

Shiny Kaffir lime leaves add a delicious fragrant citrus flavour to Thai food. They keep well if chilled and should be finely shredded before being added to curries and spicy soups.

lovage

Lovage is an old English potherb. The leaves have a strong flavour that is a mixture of citrus fruits and celery. It can be used in a variety of dishes from meat and vegetable dishes to salads and cottage cheese.

marjoram

There are three types of marjoram available; sweet, pot and wild. The sweet variety is the most common and is grown in many gardens. Marjoram combines particularly well with thyme and can be added to almost any dish that is flavoured with thyme. It is mainly used to flavour poultry, pork or beef and some fish dishes. It can also be used in salads and soups.

herbs

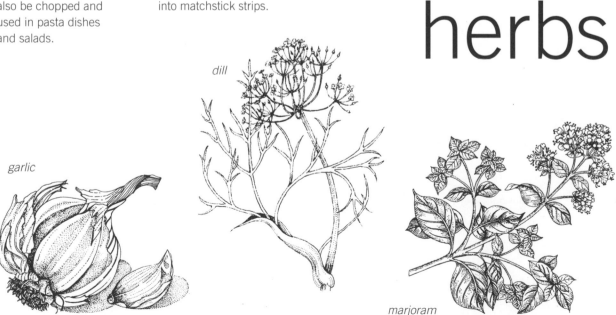

garlic

dill

marjoram

mint

There are more than 40 varieties of mint, but the variety found in most gardens is the round-leaf variety. Mint has a very fresh, clean flavour, but as a rule, it should not be used with other herbs or with garlic. It is good with new potatoes, peas, lamb and duck, but does not work well with other meats. However, it goes well with vegetables and is one of the few herbs that can be used in sweet dishes. Use sprigs as a garnish or in drinks.

oregano

Oregano is related to marjoram, but has a much more pungent flavour. It grows well in warmer climates, particularly in Mediterranean countries. It is widely used in southern Italian dishes, including pasta sauces, pizzas, vegetables and seafood dishes.

parsley

Parsley is one of the most essential herbs to have in the kitchen. There are two main varieties, curly leaf and flat leaf. Parsley has a high vitamin C and mineral content and is considered to be one of the best natural tonics. Chopped parsley adds flavour to potatoes, steamed vegetables, scrambled eggs, sauces, salads and stuffings.

rocket

Also known as arugula, the leaves have a peppery flavour and look like dandelion leaves. May be used as a salad leaf or added to hot food such as pasta, risotto, soups and stews. Pesto may be made using rocket as a base.

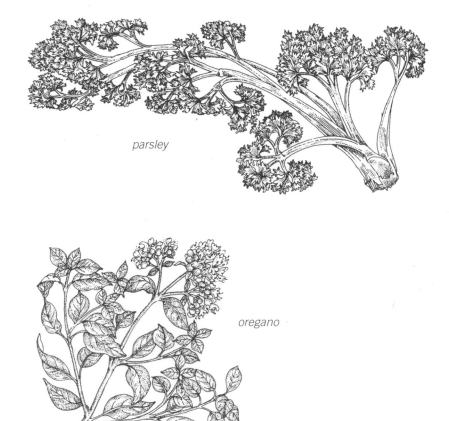

parsley

mint

oregano

rosemary

Rosemary grows wild in many countries, and can easily be grown in a warm dry place in the garden. Rosemary has a unique fragrance and flavour which works particularly well with veal, pork and lamb. Butter or olive oil can be scented with rosemary and is used to sauté potatoes and tomatoes. It is best used fresh, but dried rosemary can also be used as a flavouring for puddings and creamy dishes.

sage

Sage has a strong, bitter flavour. It is best to use young, fresh sage leaves. It is a common herb in English and European cuisines, with one of its most popular uses being to flavour stuffings for meats. It is also used to flavour breads and cheese. Use sparingly as too much sage can be rather overpowering.

tarragon

This herb is native to Siberia. The flavour of the small leaves is said to resemble a cross between aniseed and mint. It is the main flavouring in Béarnaise sauce. It combines well with poultry and shellfish dishes and also with many vegetables.

thyme

Thyme is one of the herbs used in a bouquet garni and is an indispensable ingredient in stews and stocks. Thyme sprigs can be dried but the fresh herb is available all year round, and easy to find. Thyme is also used to flavour marinades for meat and poultry and goes very well with rabbit.

rosemary

tarragon

sage

thyme

allspice

Allspice is the round pea-like fruit of an evergreen tree that is native to the West Indies and South America. It also goes by the name of pimento. The berries are picked whilst unripe and still green and are left to dry in the sun for about a week so that they turn red. It can be used whole in chutneys, pickles and stews, and in marinades for meat and game. It can also be ground and added to apples and tomato sauce as well as cakes and desserts, including milk puddings.

aniseed

Aniseed is a tall plant with a distinctive liquorice flavour. The full flavour of the seeds can be released if they are crushed, but use them sparingly as the flavour can dominate a dish. Aniseed is good in fish dishes, especially fish and seafood curries. It is also added to breads, cakes and cheeses as well as alcoholic drinks.

asafoetida

This is the dried sap of a perennial plant which is native to Iran, Afghanistan and India. When in liquid form the sap smells vile but once dried it is used to give an onion flavour to Indian vegetarian dishes. It can be bought in this dried powder form and is a pale yellow colour.

caraway

Caraway is a biennial plant that is native to Europe. The seeds are brown in colour and have a sweet, sharp flavour. They are the main flavour in rye bread and are also used to flavour cheeses and kummel liqueur.

cardamom

The dried seed pods and the small aromatic seeds of cardamom are widely used in pickles, curries and sweet dishes. There are a number of varieties of cardamom, but whichever you use, it is best to buy the seed pods and grind the seeds as and when required for the freshest flavour.

cayenne

This hot spice is a member of the pepper family. It is sold as a powder that is produced by grinding dried red chilli peppers. It is used in small amounts to flavour curries and spicy dishes and as a seasoning for sauces, marinades and fish dishes. Only a pinch of cayenne is needed to add sufficient flavour and heat to a dish.

spices

chilli powder

Chillies are small, hot members of the pepper family, important in Latin American, Indian and South-east Asian cuisine. They are dried and ground to make chilli powder. Fresh chillies vary in their heat and the resulting chilli powders do, too. Chilli powder is available in hot, medium and mild varieties. It is used to add heat and flavour to curries, chilli con carne and other spicy dishes.

cinnamon

Cinnamon is the dried bark of the cinnamon tree. It has a spicy, sweet smell and adds a delicious flavour to many foods. The finest quality cinnamon is a pale yellow colour. Cinnamon sticks can be used whole when cooking beef or pork and in curry and rice dishes. It is also used in pickling and poaching. Ground cinnamon is widely used in baking, fruit dishes and other desserts.

clove

Cloves are a popular and widely used spice. The small clove buds vary in size depending on their age and origin. They should be bought whole rather than ground for a better flavour, and if only a little is needed, the central core of the clove can easily be crushed. Use in meat and fish dishes, pastries and mulled wine.

cumin

Cumin seeds are very aromatic and can be used whole or ground. They are used to spice chicken, rice, lamb and vegetables in Middle Eastern, Latin American and Indian cooking. Cumin looks similar to aniseed and caraway seeds, but its aroma is very different.

dill seed

Used in Scandinavian food, in particular for preparing fish and seafood dishes. Also used for pickling. It is said to have a soothing and calming effect.

fennel seed

These seeds, which have a slight aniseed flavour, are used in pickling, in Indian food and as a flavouring for bread.

fenugreek

Fenugreek is used extensively in Indian cooking. The seeds are small, flat and beige-coloured and are ground and used in curries. The seeds should be roasted lightly before they are ground, but if they are roasted for too long, a bitter flavour will develop.

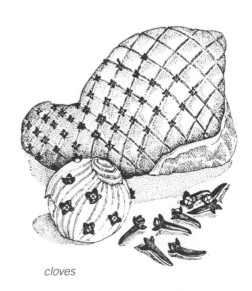

cloves

mace

Mace is the outer yellow, lacy covering of the nutmeg and has a similar flavour. It is available in strips or ground and is used in curries and pickles and as a flavouring in some sausages.

nutmeg

mace

ginger, ground

Ground ginger is mostly used in baking cakes, biscuits and pies, in jams – especially rhubarb – and for flavouring drinks. It is also used in some savoury dishes.

juniper berry

Used whole or crushed, these berries combine extremely well with game. Sauerkraut is greatly improved with the addition of a few crushed berries. They are also used to flavour gin and schnapps.

mustard seed

White and black mustard seeds are available. White mustard seeds are used in Asian cooking, in most ready-made mustards and in marinades. Black seeds are used to flavour spicy dishes.

nutmeg

When ripe, the nutmeg fruit dries and splits open. The seeds are dried either in the sun or over charcoal fires. They can be kept in airtight containers for long periods of time. Nutmeg has its best flavour when it is freshly grated into the dish, as after it has been grated it loses its flavour rapidly. Nutmeg works equally well in sweet and savoury dishes, but is used more extensively in cakes and sweet dishes.

paprika

Paprika is made from a sweet variety of red pepper which is grown widely in Europe. It should be a deep, rich, red colour and have a mild, sweet aroma. Paprika is often used in dishes to provide a vibrant colour. It should always be bought in small quantities as even the best paprika will lose its spicy qualities when it is stored for a long time.

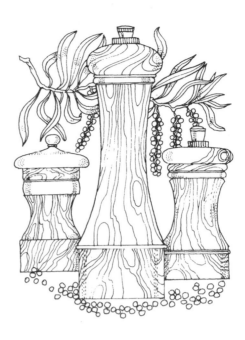

pepper

Pepper is the world's most important spice and is grown in tropical countries such as Indonesia and India. It is very aromatic and has a pungent flavour and is used to season all kinds of savoury dishes. The most common varieties of pepper are black and white, both of which can be found as peppercorns or as ground pepper. Like most other spices, the flavour deteriorates after grinding and it is therefore best when freshly ground.

poppy seed

These are the seeds of the poppy plant which are used a lot in Asian and European cooking. The poppy has medicinal properties including the relief of toothache. Poppy seeds are sprinkled on bread and savoury biscuits before baking and add a nutty flavour. They are also used in cakes, either whole or ground.

saffron

Saffron is an expensive spice, but only a small amount is required to add a distinctive flavour to a dish. It is the dried stigmas from a variety of crocus and is used in rice dishes and with seafood in particular. Saffron can be bought either as stigmas or as a powder. The stigmas can be ground or used whole, soaked in liquid or stock which is then used to flavour the dish.

sesame seed

Sesame seeds have a variety of uses, but are most often sprinkled on vegetables or salads or scattered over breads and biscuits. Sesame seeds contain minerals and protein and also have a high oil content. They can be crushed to make the thick paste, tahini. which is used widely in the Middle East.

star anise

This pretty star-shaped spice has an aniseed flavour. Available whole or ground, it is used to flavour Chinese and Indian dishes such as stir-fries and biryanis.

tamarind

This spice adds a sour flavour to many Indian dishes. It is available as a pulp or paste and when unavailable, lemon juice is usually suggested as a substitute. Tamarind water is made by soaking the pulp in warm water, then draining off and using the liquid.

turmeric

Turmeric is used widely in Indian cookery and is one of the ingredients in curry powder. It is obtained from the dried root of a plant of the ginger family. Turmeric has a bright yellow colour and gives both flavour and colour to food. It is often used instead of saffron for its colour, although the flavour is quite different.

anchovy paste
Made from mashed anchovy fillets, this paste imparts a salty flavour to fish dishes and tomato sauces. Excellent spread very thinly on hot buttered toast.

balsamic vinegar
From the Modena region in northern Italy, this sweet, rich, dark brown vinegar is aged for many years in wooden barrels. Use sparingly in dressings or sprinkled over fish, meat, chicken or vegetables.

caper
This is the pickled, unopened green flower bud of a Mediterranean plant. The smaller capers are prized for their subtle flavour. They are indispensable in tartare sauce and puttanesca sauce for pasta, and also go very well with shellfish salads.

chilli sauce
The heat of these sauces may vary greatly so add sparingly. Thick and bright red, these sauces do not generally need refrigeration. Use in Chinese and South-east Asian food.

cider vinegar
Made from crushed apples, this vinegar has a distinctive taste of cider. Sharper than wine vinegar, it may be used in dressings and chutneys.

coarse grain mustard
This is a mild mustard with a grainy texture. Use in dressings, sauces, casseroles and soups or serve as a condiment.

Dijon mustard
This popular, smooth mustard has a slightly sweet flavour and is medium hot. It is the ideal mustard for making mayonnaise.

fish sauce
Made from fermented fish or prawns, this sauce is indispensable in Thai cooking. Used to offset the richness of coconut curries and soups, and also in fish stocks and fish dishes.

hoisin sauce
This is a pungent, sweet and spicy, reddish-brown sauce that should be used sparingly. Made from soya beans with various spices, garlic and chillies, it is an essential ingredient eaten with Peking duck.

horseradish
Freshly grated, this root may be used in sauces to add piquancy to meat, fish and chicken. Horseradish sauce is available ready-made in jars and is the classic accompaniment to roast beef and is excellent with smoked fish.

malt vinegar
Brewed from malted barley, the brown colour of this vinegar is achieved by adding caramel. Excellent for pickling and with fish and chips.

mirin
A Japanese sweetened rice wine used in extensively in many Japanese dishes.

savoury flavourings

mustard powder
Made from mustard flour, wheat flour and spices, mustard powder is usually prepared by mixing with an equal amount of cold water. Make up as required, otherwise it will lose its robust flavour. Use as a condiment with meat, especially ham, or use in powder form in cooking.

oyster sauce
A thick, brown sauce used in Chinese cooking. Made from oysters, it imparts a rich, salty flavour to Chinese dishes. Once opened, keep refrigerated.

raspberry vinegar
This is a wine vinegar that has the natural flavour of raspberries added to it. Excellent in warm salads and in salad dressings.

rice vinegar
This vinegar has a sweet, delicate flavour and is used in many Japanese and South-east Asian dishes. An important ingredient in sushi.

salt
The flavour of ordinary table salt is inferior to sea salt and rock salt, but it is good for baking and useful when you require a fine sprinkling of salt. Sea salt is comprised of large crystals of pure salt and is made by evaporating sea water. It contains natural iodine and has the best flavour. Rock salt is hard and coarse and needs to be used in a salt mill or pounded with a pestle in a mortar.

sherry vinegar
Made from sweet sherry, this vinegar can be used instead of balsamic vinegar but the result will be slightly drier. Used in meat cookery, it combines particularly well with kidneys and chicken livers.

soy sauce
Used extensively in Chinese and Japanese cooking, soy sauce has a rich aroma and a strong, salty flavour. May also be used in marinades and barbecue sauces.

tomato purée
Made from highly concentrated tomatoes, a tablespoon or two can be added to pasta sauces, soups, stews and casseroles to give an intense tomato flavour.

wasabi
Bright green in colour, and also known as Japanese horseradish, wasabi is usually served as an accompaniment to Japanese dishes such as sushi. Wasabi can be bought in powder form or as a paste in tubes.

wine vinegar
Red and white wine vinegars are available. White wine vinegar is the best choice for making mayonnaise and Hollandaise sauce. Red wine vinegar can be used in meat cookery. Use in salad dressings, marinades and pickles.

Worcestershire sauce
Made from a long list of ingredients including mushrooms, vinegar, caramel and anchovies, this is a dark brown liquid sauce with a pungent flavour. Use in cooking and in the classic cocktail, Bloody Mary.

caster sugar

Finer than granulated sugar, this is a fine sugar which dissolves easily. Use to make cakes, pastries, biscuits, puddings, custards and sweet mousses.

chocolate

Plain (or dark) chocolate is widely available and is the best type to use for cooking. For the best flavour, choose one with at least 50% cocoa solids. Milk chocolate is very rarely used in cooking as it contains a high proportion of sugar and low proportion of cocoa solids. When melting chocolate, melt it slowly as it scorches very easily if overheated.

cocoa

Cocoa is produced by pulverizing the residue of the cocoa bean after most of the cocoa butter has been extracted. Cocoa powder may be used in baking or made into a hot drink with milk and sugar. To stop lumps forming in the drink, mix the cocoa to a paste with a little water or milk.

coffee

The flavour of coffee depends on the type of bean and how it is roasted. To use coffee as a flavouring ingredient, mix together small and equal amounts of instant coffee and boiling water. Alternatively brew some fresh coffee and then boil it until thick and reduced.

demerara sugar

This sugar has a coarse texture with large golden crystals. It is made from partly refined sugar syrup and contains a small amount of treacle. Use in coffee or sweet yeast breads, or sprinkle on top of cakes before baking for a crunchy topping.

golden syrup

A rich gold in colour, this syrup can add flavour and moistness to cakes, puddings and biscuits. Also popular on its own as a topping for pancakes or porridge.

granulated sugar

This is a refined white sugar, coarser than caster sugar. Use to sweeten beverages, such as tea and coffee; for sweetening stewed fruit and for making boiled icings and frostings, fudges and toffees.

honey

Honey can range enormously in texture, colour and flavour. The finest honeys are named after their flower source such as orange blossom, heather and lavender. Blended honey tends to be cheaper and usually comes from various countries. Clear clover honey is ideal for baking.

sweet flavourings

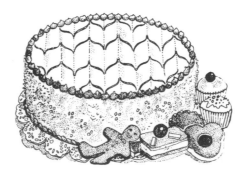

maple syrup

Made from the sap of North American and Canadian maple trees, this syrup has a sweet distinctive flavour. It has a thin consistency and can be used to drizzle over pancakes. It can be used in baking and ice-cream-making instead of honey or treacle.

orange flower water

Distilled from the blossom of oranges, this water is popular in the Mediterranean countries and the Middle East. Used to flavour pastries, cream and preserves.

palm sugar

Also known as jaggery, this sugar is made from palm sap. It has a flavour reminiscent of black treacle, and is used widely in Thai cooking – in stews, curries and sweet puddings.

rosewater

Distilled from rose petals, this perfumed water is used in sorbets, spicy chicken dishes and sweets such as Turkish Delight. Store away from heat and light.

soft brown sugar

This is simply white sugar that has been mixed with black treacle to provide colour, moistness and limited flavour. Dark soft brown sugar has had a higher percentage of black treacle added to it than has light soft brown sugar.

treacle

Treacle is an extremely thick and dark syrup with a strong, slightly bitter flavour. Use in rich fruit cakes, gingerbread, and bread and scones to add flavour and colour.

vanilla

Vanilla is available as whole pods, extract or essence. The pod has the best flavour and can be used, split in half, to flavour hot liquid such as milk. For an even stronger vanilla flavour some of the small black seeds may be scraped out of the pod and added to the liquid. The vanilla pod may be reused if rinsed and dried.

For long-term wear, buy the best saucepans you can afford. Stainless steel with a copper base or a thick layer of aluminium is a combination that is hard to beat and will ensure even cooking; it will cut down on energy consumption and give you a lifetime's service. Buying cheap pans is a false economy – they quickly burn and soon reach the throwing-away stage. Good pans should be well balanced, easy to hold, have welded handles and lids that fit tightly. You will need three or four saucepans in the range of about 1–7 litres/2–12 pints.

deep-fryer
Although electric models are available, a traditional deep-fryer is best if made of steel with a well-fitting basket that is used to lower and raise the food in and out of the fat. It is important that the pan is deep enough for the oil to bubble without spilling over.

casserole pan
A lidded casserole pan should be deep with a thick base. Used for stewing, braising and pot-roasting, evaporation is prevented by a heavy, well-fitting lid. Casseroles are available in stainless steel and heavy earthenware.

milk pan
A small saucepan with sloping sides, a thick base to heat milk evenly and prevent burning, and a spout in the rim for pouring.

paella pan
A wide, shallow pan with sloping sides used for making the famous Spanish rice dish. A paella pan should have a heavy base to prevent burning; most are made from cast iron. They usually have two heatproof handles for ease of lifting.

preserving pan
An enormous wide pan with sloping sides and a spout in the rim. Used for making jams and pickles, allowing fast evaporation.

sauté pan
Often made of lined copper or stainless steel, a sauté pan has a wide base and low sides to allow steam to escape. The base should be heavy to spread heat evenly. Many have heatproof handles to allow them to be put in the oven, like a casserole.

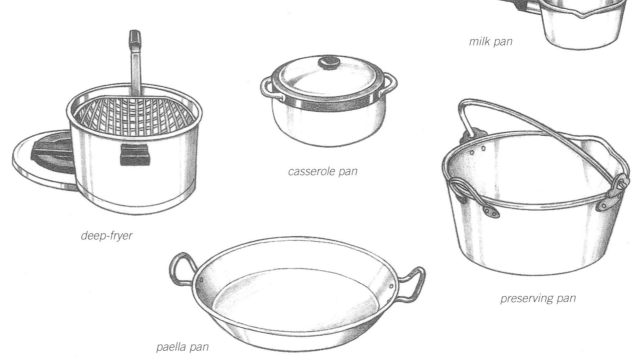

milk pan

casserole pan

deep-fryer

preserving pan

paella pan

pots & pans

omelette pan

Plain steel pans are best for making omelettes and pancakes although aluminium or cast iron are also acceptable. An omelette pan should have a thick base for even heat distribution, and gently sloping sides. If you want to use slightly less oil or butter, heat the pan for 2–3 minutes over a moderate heat before adding the oil or butter. Do not heat an empty pan over a high heat because this simply makes the pan too hot too quickly and will mean your ingredients dry out and burn. To season steel pans, heat slightly and wash to remove the protective coating. Dry and reheat with cooking oil to a fairly high temperature. Run oil over the base and up the sides to cover the whole area. Cool and wipe out the surplus.

frying pan

A shallow pan used for frying. The base should be thick to allow heat to spread evenly. Copper and cast iron are the best materials. Nonstick frying pans are available, allowing foods to be cooked in a minimum of fat, but the nonstick surface can be scratched quite easily.

wok

A large, round-bottomed pan used in Oriental cooking, mainly for stir-frying. A new steel wok has a protective film of grease. Remove by filling the wok with water and boiling for 30 minutes. Scrub the wok with an abrasive cloth, rinse and dry over heat for about 5 minutes. When cool, wipe the sides thoroughly with vegetable oil. Clean after each use; wash with water, using a mild detergent if necessary. Dry and rub with oil. Nonstick woks are easier to clean but they have a shorter life as the coating soon wears off.

pressure cooker

A heavy pan with a very tight-fitting lid in which steam pressure builds up so that foods cook quickly at temperatures above boiling point. A safety valve releases any excess steam. This cooking method is suited to moist dishes which take a long time to cook.

pressure cooker

sauté pan

frying pan

omelette pan

wok

double boiler

This comprises a large pan for heating water, and a smaller pan which sits in the top suspended over the heat but not in direct contact with it. It is used for making delicate sauces and melting chocolate at low temperatures.

griddle

A heavy, flat metal plate, usually made from cast iron, used for cooking pancakes, scones and other dry foods. It usually has a handle which folds down flat.

griddle pan

A type of frying pan, usually square, with a nonstick surface and ridged base, designed for cooking foods without any extra oil or fat. The pan is heated before the food is added. The food is sealed on both sides at high temperatures to retain moisture. It is then cooked through at a slightly lower heat.

pasta pan

If you love pasta then you will need a pot that is large enough so that it can cook in plenty of boiling salted water with enough room for it to move without sticking. A 7 litre/12 pint pot is large enough for 7–8 portions and is fitted with a stainless steel draining basket. Its thick base means this saucepan can also be used for making stock, soups and stews.

fish kettle

A long, narrow pan, about as deep as it is wide, for poaching fish in the minimum amount of liquid. Once cooked, the fish is lifted out with the rack that fits in the base of the poacher. Usually made from stainless steel or copper.

steamer

Usually made of stainless steel, this is a perforated container that sits snugly over a pan of boiling water. It can be bought as a steamer set with a number of stacking compartments. Ideal for cooking vegetables and fish to perfection.

asparagus pan

griddle

double boiler (illustration)

double boiler

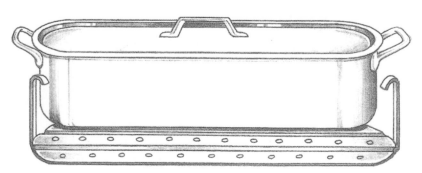

fish kettle

steamer

bamboo steamer

A bamboo steamer is a slatted steaming basket. Stand the steamer in a wok or over a deep saucepan, containing about 5 cm/2 inches of boiling water, then place the food in the basket, wrapped in leaves or on a plate, and cover with the lid. Turn up the heat; fish should cook very quickly, but also try vegetables and Oriental dumplings.

couscoussière

A large double pot, much like a steamer, used for cooking the north African dish of couscous. A stew is cooked in the bottom pan, while the couscous, which is served with it, steams in the pan above. This is a very efficient use of energy.

asparagus pan

A tall, thin pan used for cooking asparagus. The asparagus stands upright. The stems are immersed in boiling water and the tips, which need less cooking, cook in the steam above.

expanding steamer

A stainless steel folding steaming platform which adjusts to fit most pan sizes. It is a very useful cookware item if you don't have a steamer unit in your saucepan range. Steaming allows you to cook food quickly and retain a high proportion of flavour and nutrients.

cast-iron cooking pot

Vitreous enamelled cast iron cooking pots last a lifetime. If used on top of the stove, heat the pan very slowly over low-to-medium heat. Casseroles can be started off on the hob, then moved into the oven to finish cooking.

marmite

A traditional French cooking pot, made from cast iron or earthenware, which is used for stews, cassoulet and pot-au-feu. It sometimes has feet, from the days when it would have stood on an open fire.

cast-iron cooking pot

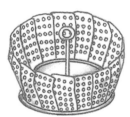

expanding steamer

couscoussière

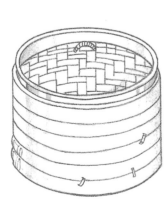

bamboo steamer

marmite

baking tins & dishes

ramekin

This is a miniature version of a soufflé dish. Ramekins are used to make individual sweet and savoury, hot and cold dishes such as soufflés and mousses. They can also be used as moulds for individual summer puddings or rice.

loaf tin

A rectangular-shaped tin with high, slightly sloping sides. Used to make bread, teabreads and fruit cakes.

soufflé dish

These are available in a variety of sizes and are usually measured by volume, not diameter. A soufflé dish is always round with straight sides and is traditionally made of white porcelain with a fluted design on the outside.

Swiss roll tin

A large rectangular tin with sides about 2 cm/³/₄ inch high. Choose tins that are sturdy to avoid them warping once heated. Use for making roulades and Swiss rolls and to make sheets of cake for shaping and cutting into novelty shapes.

roasting tin

Roasting tins should be smooth and have no seams or crevices in which fat can collect or germs breed. Those with a rolled top edge or a generous rim are easy to lift. A roasting rack sits in the tin and keeps meat or poultry from frying in fat.

pizza tray

Made of ceramic or terracotta, these are used in place of baking trays, to give pizza its characteristic crisp base.

ramekin

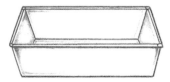

roasting tin

pizza tray

soufflé dish

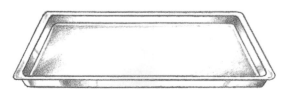

Swiss roll tin

flan tin

Some flan tins have fluted edges and a choice of removable or fixed bases. Some are deep, others are shallow. Fluted rings can be difficult to clean because food sticks to them, so always soak them in hot water after use. Metal flan tins are preferable to porcelain flan dishes as they conduct heat very well, making the pastry crisp.

cake tin

Cake tins can have loose bases or spring clips to allow for easy removal of the cake. When using the latter, make sure the base fits into the groove at the side and won't move or allow the mixture to escape. Place the base, rim side up, on the worktop, place the round above it and then close the clips. Tins can then be greased and floured or base-lined.

gratin dish

These are made in a range of materials such as earthenware, glass, china, or enamelled cast iron. A shallow oval or round dish, usually with two small handles, a gratin dish is used for baked pasta or other savoury or sweet dishes that require browning, often with a cheese or a breadcrumb topping.

pie dish

An oval dish with a wide flat rim to secure the pastry. Used to make traditional fruit and savoury pies.

baking sheet

A baking sheet has raised sides which prevent anything sliding off when the tin is removed from the oven. Tinned steel or aluminium are the most versatile but make sure they are not too thin otherwise they will warp once heated.

gratin dishes

pie dishes

flan tin

cake tin

baking sheet

utensils

cleaver

general kitchen knife

filleting knife

small cook's knife

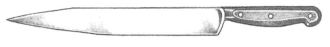
carving knife

bread knife

Good, sharp knives are essential tools in the kitchen. They should be comfortable to hold and take the hard work out of food preparation. Six or seven knives will provide a good selection that will enable you to deal easily with various tasks. They should all be stored in a knife box or a wall rack, inaccessible to children. Keeping knives in drawers will damage their blades and you are more likely to cut your hands when taking them out. Choose a knife that feels comfortable in the hand, heavy and well balanced.

The part of the blade that extends into the handle should run the whole length and be securely rivetted in place. Although expensive, high-carbon stainless steel knives are good buys: they last a long time, hold a fine edge and are easy to clean. Carbon steel is easy to sharpen but soon rusts and discolours. Knives should always be kept razor-sharp. A blunt knife is frustrating and dangerous to use – it performs badly, needing a great deal of force, and can easily slip out of control.

bread knife
Choose one with a fairly long blade with deep serrations as this will be most effective.

carving knife
Used together with a carving fork for cutting thin slices from roast and cooked meats. Carving knives should be kept very sharp.

filleting knife
This has a flexible, pointed blade to follow the contours of a fish, lifting the flesh from the bones.

general kitchen knife
A strong, general-purpose knife, usually about 15–25 cm/6–10 inches long, used for chopping, slicing, paring and cutting.

small cook's knife
A small, pointed knife, invaluable for many different tasks in the kitchen, including peeling vegetables and fruit, testing to see if food is cooked through and for chopping and slicing small quantities of ingredients.

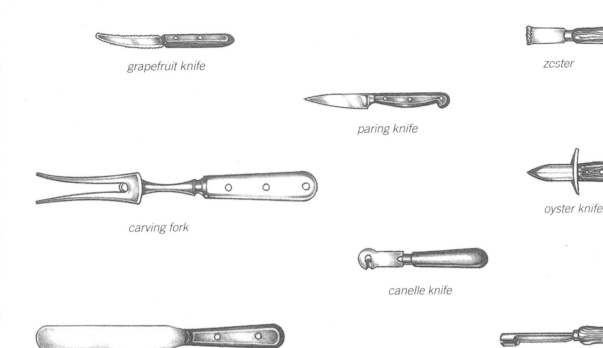

grapefruit knife

zester

paring knife

carving fork

oyster knife

canelle knife

palette knife

corer

cleaver
This is the heaviest knife, which comes in various different sizes. It is used for chopping through bone. It has a broad, rectangular blade which can also be used for crushing garlic – place the garlic under the blade on a board and hit the blade with your fist.

palette knife
A knife with a flexible blade with a rounded end used for spreading jam, butter cream and icing over cakes and pastries.

paring knife
Designed to peel fruit and vegetables, a paring knife usually has a plain or serrated stainless steel blade, 7.5 cm/3 inches in length.

grapefruit knife
This is a small knife with a double serrated curved edge for loosening grapefruit flesh.

oyster knife
This has a very short, broad blade with a point at the end. It is used for prising open the shells of oysters and other types of shellfish.

zester
A useful tool for removing fine strips of rind from citrus fruits such as oranges, lemons and limes. A zester consists of a flat metal plate perforated with five angled holes which are drawn across the skin of the fruit and remove fine slivers of zest for use in sweet and savoury dishes.

corer
A sharp-edged cylinder used to remove the cores from fruits such as apples and pears.

canelle knife
A knife with a short flat blade with a U-shaped indentation, used to cut strips of lemon or orange rind or to create patterns in the skin of cucumbers and other vegetables.

carving fork
This is used to lift roast meat and keep it steady while carving. It should have a guard to prevent the knife slipping. The long, usually straight tines are essential for bigger cuts of meat.

vegetable peeler

As well as removing the peel from root vegetables, vegetable peelers are also invaluable for paring the rind from citrus fruits, to use as an ingredient or a garnish, and for making Parmesan cheese shavings.

steel

The traditional way of sharpening knives is to use a sharpening steel. The blade of the knife is drawn across the steel, one side at a time.

mezzaluna

A half-moon shaped blade, with two handles, used for finely chopping mushrooms, herbs and other ingredients, using a rocking motion. They sometimes come with their own wooden chopping bowl.

knife sharpener

A knife sharpener has two small steels inside a plastic casing. The knife is drawn through a groove in the casing, sharpening both sides of the blade at the same time.

poultry shears

These make light work of cutting through gristle and bone, either during the preparation of raw food or when serving cooked food. The pointed tips enable the shears to reach and operate effectively in small, awkward places.

cheese slicer

A compact slice, usually made of stainless steel, used for paring thin, even slices from hard cheeses such as Cheddar, Edam and Parmesan.

melon baller

A small, rounded spoon used to scoop balls from a melon. This is one of the most attractive ways to serve melon.

kitchen scissors

These should be very sharp, strong and made of stainless steel. The lower handle should be large enough to take the last three fingers of the cutting hand. A serrated edge will give an extra bite to the first cut and the blades should cut evenly right down to the tips.

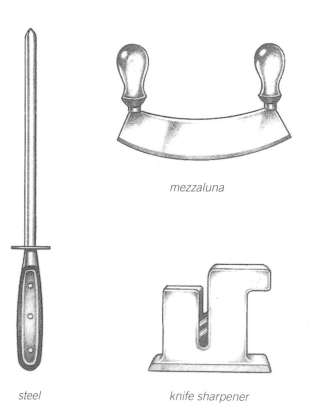

mezzaluna

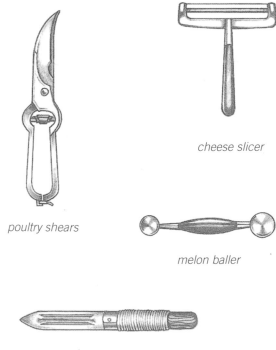

cheese slicer

poultry shears

melon baller

steel

knife sharpener

vegetable peeler

kebab skewer

A metal or wooden skewer used for threading pieces of meat, fish or vegetables during cooking. Wooden skewers should be soaked in water for 20 minutes before use to prevent them burning during cooking. Kebabs are generally grilled or barbecued.

lobster pick

A fine metal shaft, forked at one end and flattened at the other, used to remove meat from lobster and crab shells.

can opener

It is worthwhile investing in the best can opener that you can afford as cheap ones are difficult to use and soon need to be replaced. Make sure you choose one with a comfortable handle and grip.

pizza wheel

A multi-purpose implement used for cutting cooked pizza and raw pastry and pasta dough. When choosing a pizza wheel, make sure that the wheel turns freely.

egg slicer

A small device with a number of fine, parallel wires which pass through a shelled, boiled egg, slicing it into neat, even slices for salads and sandwiches.

butcher's skewer

A large metal skewer used for many tasks during the cooking of meat, but particularly to secure the stuffed opening of a chicken or hold a spatchcocked bird flat during cooking.

bulb baster

A hollow plastic shaft with a flexible bulb on one end and a hole in the other. It is used to baste roasting meat by drawing the cooking juices into the shaft, allowing them to be distributed back over the meat to keep it moist during cooking.

butter curler

A utensil with a metal blade that is curled over at the end, used to draw across a pat of butter and remove neat curls.

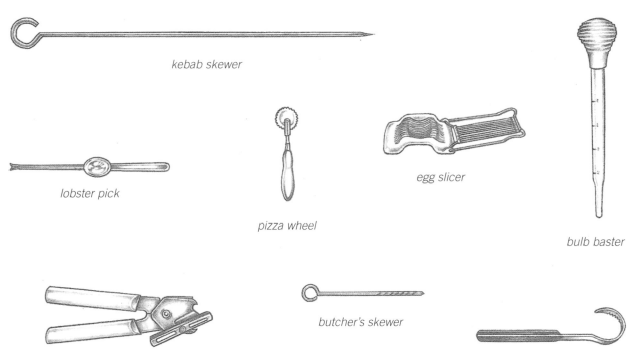

kebab skewer

lobster pick

pizza wheel

egg slicer

bulb baster

can opener

butcher's skewer

butter curler

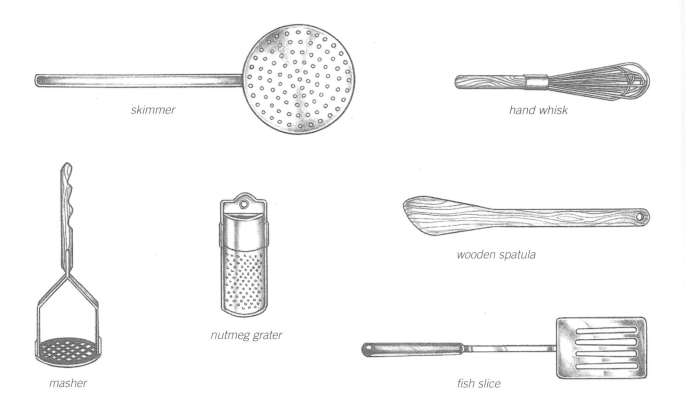

skimmer

hand whisk

wooden spatula

masher

nutmeg grater

fish slice

masher
Many vegetables can be mashed, not just potatoes. Try mashed carrot, swede, celeriac or other root vegetables as an accompaniment to roast meat, fish or vegetable courses.

nutmeg grater
A tiny flat metal grater or box grater designed specifically for grating nutmeg.

skimmer
A long-handled, shallow metal spoon usually circular in shape. The bowl is perforated so when it is used to lift food, any liquid will simply drain away. It is also used for removing fat or scum from the surface of liquids.

hand whisk
Perfect for whipping cream, beating eggs and making batters, as well as stirring sauces as they thicken to remove any lumps that form.

wooden spatula
Wooden spatulas are the perfect tools for use in nonstick pans as they will not damage the coating. The slanted straight end will fit snugly against the sides of pans and bowls, making it easy to remove all the food.

metal spoon
A metal spoon can be used to transfer food from pan to dish, to fold gently together delicate mixtures and to make last minute checks on soups and sauces. Wooden spoons cannot be used for tasting as they retain flavours and smells.

fish slice
Also known as a turner, a fish slice must be able to slide under food without damaging it and be broad and firm enough to turn over or lift food from a pan. Perforations in the fish slice allow excess fat or oil to drain from the food. They are usually made from stainless steel or plastic.

spatula
Usually made from plastic, a spatula has a wide, blunt blade. It is used for moving food around a bowl and for scraping ingredients out from round the edge of a mixing bowl.

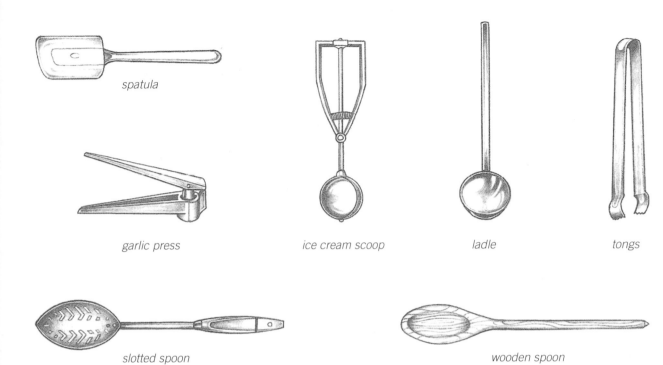

spatula

garlic press

ice cream scoop

ladle

tongs

slotted spoon

wooden spoon

slotted spoon

A large plastic or metal spoon with a slotted (perforated) bowl used to remove foods from liquids such as stock or oil. Metal spoons are better suited for use when cooking with boiling oil.

pasta spoon

A long-handled spoon, made from stainless steel or plastic, used for transferring pasta from the saucepan to the serving dish. This useful gadget has teeth which grip and support the long strands of pasta, while any water drains away through the hole in the middle of the bowl.

ice cream scoop

A rounded spoon, used to make neat ice cream balls. Stand it in warm water before use to make scooping easier.

ladle

A type of spoon with a very deep bowl used to transfer liquids such as stock or soup from one receptacle to another. Ladles come in many different sizes. Metal ladles can be used for warming spirits over a flame, ready for flambéing.

tongs

Usually made of wood or stainless steel, tongs are invaluable for moving hot foods around during cooking, either in a frying pan, under a grill or on a barbecue. They grip well, are easy to handle and prevent fingers being burned.

garlic press

Garlic presses are used to crush garlic cloves to speed up cooking and to release the full flavour into the food.

wooden spoon

The wooden spoon is one of the most useful tools in the kitchen, invaluable for beating, mixing and stirring. It will not burn your hand because wood is a bad conductor of heat and will not scratch or wear saucepans. The best are those made of close-grained wood which is less likely to split.

meat thermometer

A thermometer inserted into roasting meat to measure the temperature in the centre of the joint and thus determine whether it is cooked inside. These are most often used by professional cooks as a measure against bacterial food poisoning, as certain bacteria are killed at certain temperatures.

roasting rack

A wire or metal grid which is placed in a roasting tin to hold a joint of meat or poultry above the base of the tin. This allows the meat to be roasted evenly on all sides and prevents it sitting in the cooking juices or fat which have collected in the tin beneath.

mortar and pestle

A cup-shaped bowl and grinder used to grind spices to a fine powder or fresh herbs to a pulp for use in dressings or sauces.

salt and pepper mills

Made from plastic or wood, mills are used to grind whole peppercorns or rock salt down to a size that can be used for seasoning. They tend to grind quite coarsely, giving the dish a better texture and appearance. Freshly ground black pepper is far superior to pepper that is bought ready ground.

colander

Literally a stainless steel or plastic bowl with holes in it, a colander is used for separating liquids and solids and for draining and rinsing food.

chopping board

It is best to have at least two chopping boards, one made from a hard wood, such as maple, which you can use for most tasks, and another non-porous board to be kept for the preparation of raw meat. Choose wooden boards at least 4 cm/1¼ inches thick, ideally with the grain on the main board running in the opposite direction to that on the reinforced ends. Melamine boards may look attractive when new but their hard surfaces soon blunt knife blades and may cause knives to slip.

meat thermometer

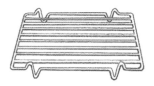

roasting rack

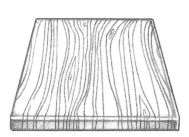

chopping board

salt and pepper mills

colander

mortar and pestle

measuring jug
These are available in glass, stainless steel and plastic. All types have a handle and a pouring lip. Heatproof jugs, such as those made of Pyrex, will withstand boiling liquids. Some plastic jugs are marked for solids and liquids and are useful for measuring small quantities.

sugar thermometer
A vital piece of equipment for cooks who make confectionery, a sugar thermometer measures the temperature of sugar syrup as it boils. The temperature that the syrup has reached determines the consistency it will be when it cools down.

pudding basin
An earthenware, glass or plastic basin with a wider rim around the top, designed for cooking steamed puddings. The mixture is poured into the basin, the top is covered with greased paper which is tied in place under the wide rim, and the basin is placed in a saucepan of gently simmering water.

wire sieve
Round, fine mesh sieves can be used for sifting flour, sugar and cocoa as well as straining and puréeing moist foods. For sifting, never fill too full and knock the side of the frame gently against the palm of your hand.

egg timer
A very basic timer used to time an egg boiling. It consists of a glass tube with a narrow central section, filled with sand. The sand collects in the lower section of the tube, but when the tube is turned the other way up, the sand seeps through the narrow section into the other end of the tube. This is designed to take exactly 3 minutes, the time it takes to soft-boil an egg to perfection.

salad spinner
A large receptacle, usually made from plastic, with a basket that fits inside and a lid with a handle. It is used to dry salad leaves and spinach prior to use. The basket is filled with the recently-washed leaves. When the handle is turned, the basket spins round quickly, causing the water to fall into the receptacle beneath the basket.

sugar thermometer

pudding basin

measuring jug

egg timer

wire sieve

salad spinner

other equipment

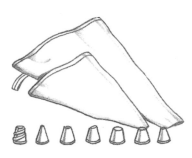

icing bag and nozzles

ravioli cutter

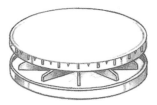

icing turntable

pastry brush

citrus juicer

box grater

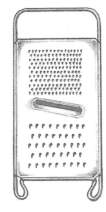

flat grater

icing bag and nozzles

Icing bags can be made from folded greaseproof paper, but more permanent nylon bags are available in many different sizes. They are used in conjunction with stainless steel or plastic nozzles. Nozzles come in a variety of sizes and designs, star and plain nozzles being the most common. Use to pipe whipped cream, butter cream or royal icing on cakes and desserts. Very small bags and delicate nozzles are used for piping intricate designs in royal icing on wedding and Christmas cakes.

citrus juicer

Many recipes require lemon, lime or orange juice and freshly-squeezed juice is far superior to the juice you can buy in bottles. Juice squeezers are a quick, clean and easy way to remove the juice. Some have a reservoir to catch the juice while others are more simple in design.

ravioli cutter

A fluted-edged metal cutter with a wooden handle used for stamping out individual ravioli and other pasta shapes. Ravioli cutters are made in a variety of shapes and sizes.

icing turntable

Perfect for keen cake decorators, an icing turntable allows a cake to be gently and easily turned during icing, making all sides equally accessible. This is particularly important for icing borders and other designs which follow right around the edge of a cake.

grater

Available as a flat sheet or in a box shape, graters have a selection of different-sized perforations for grating a variety of ingredients, including spices and citrus rind, vegetables and cheese.

pastry brush

A small brush, usually with nylon bristles, used for a variety of tasks, particularly glazing pastry dishes with a glaze such as beaten egg or milk. Also useful for basting vegetables and meats during grilling or barbecuing with flavoured oils or marinades. Pastry brushes can also be used for greasing baking sheets and cake tins with melted butter or oil.

mixing bowl

A mixing bowl should be wide enough to allow mixtures to be beaten or folded. The bowl should be rested on a grip stand or a cloth during use to prevent it slipping.

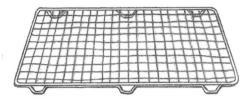

wire rack

pie funnel

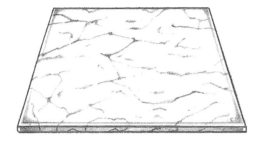

marble pastry slab

biscuit cutters

pastry wheel

dredger

rolling pin

wire rack

Cooling racks are either circular, specifically for cakes, or rectangular for all types of baked food, and are meshed to allow good circulation of air. They are used for cooling cakes and biscuits without allowing them to sweat. It is better to buy one that is larger than you think you need, and it should stand fairly high. If leaving food – especially cakes – overnight, cover with a tea towel to prevent them becoming crusty and dry.

pastry wheel

Similar to a pizza wheel, a pastry wheel is used to cut pastry or pasta dough into strips or shapes. Available with either a straight or fluted edge.

biscuit cutter

Usually made of stainless steel or rigid plastic, biscuit cutters are used to cut shapes from biscuit and pastry doughs prior to cooking. They are available in many different sizes and shapes. The most common shape is circular, but many novelty shapes are available, such as animals and shapes for gingerbread men.

funnel

Made from stainless steel or plastic, a funnel is used to transfer liquids or fine, dry ingredients from a wide-necked receptacle to one with a narrow neck without spillage.

dredger

A stainless steel, glass or plastic receptacle with a perforated lid, a dredger is used to sift flour on to a work surface for rolling and kneading pastry and bread doughs. It can also be used for sifting sugar and cocoa powder over cakes and desserts.

pie funnel

A small ceramic funnel which is placed, narrow end uppermost, in a pie. The point of the funnel sticks out through a hole in the pastry lid, allowing steam to escape from the middle of the pie. This allows the pastry to crisp.

marble pastry slab

With most pastries, the outcome is more successful if the dough has been kept as cold as possible during preparation and rolling. Marble slabs are much cooler than normal work surfaces, making them excellent for pastry.

rolling pin

Used for rolling out pasta, bread dough and pastry, rolling pins are usually made from wood or marble. Choose a heavy rolling pin to make rolling easier and always dust it with flour before use to stop the foods from sticking to it.

Electrical equipment is expensive and can take up lots of space in a kitchen, so it is worth making quite certain before buying that its use will repay its cost.

blender/liquidizer

This machine is used to purée wet foods such as soups, stews, milkshakes and fruit desserts. It will only be successful if the food contains a high percentage of water. Also available as an attachment which sits on top of a food processor.

food processor

These are perfect for the busy cook or for someone who cooks a lot for many people. They work fast, chopping, slicing, grinding and puréeing, and come with other attachments which allow more specialised work, such as making fruit juice or pasta.

coffee grinder

Freshly-ground coffee is far more flavoursome than commercially available ground coffee, and whole roasted beans are readily available for grinding at home. This machine will also allow you to make your own blends, by grinding a mixture of different beans together.

juicer

Perfect for large families, juicers extract the juice from fresh fruits to make freshly-squeezed orange juice or mixed fruit drinks. Some models squeeze only citrus fruits, others can cope with all sorts of fruits and vegetables. Freshly-squeezed juice is a world apart from shop-bought alternatives and allows you to experiment with your own cocktails.

hand-held beater

Probably the most generally useful of all electrical appliances, a hand-held beater and whisk takes the hard work out of all the most difficult of kitchen tasks, such as whisking egg whites and cream, beating cake mixtures and making mayonnaise.

knife sharpener

Blunt knives are a hazard in the kitchen so some kind of knife sharpener is vital for every cook. Many manual models are available, but electric knife sharpeners give a better finish, without any effort. Like any electrical appliances, however, they are not cheap, so make sure you will really find it useful before you buy.

knife sharpener

blender

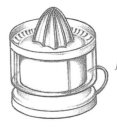

juicer

coffee grinder

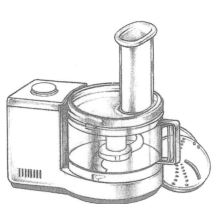

food processor

hand-held beater

coffee machine

coffee machine

Electric coffee machines allow you to make the perfect jug of filter coffee and have it hot and ready to hand whenever you want it throughout the day. They are simple to use and to clean. If you are really serious about your coffee, consider an electric espresso and cappuccino maker. It is the only way of getting sufficient pressure to make authentic espresso and cappuccino at home.

food slicer

Mainly used for slicing meats, this is perfect for large families or those who eat a lot of sandwiches. It does, however, take up a lot of counter space in the kitchen.

carving knife

Perfect for neat and accurate slicing of boneless meat joints, and for joints with bones after a bit of practice. Allows meat and bread to be sliced thinly and evenly. Some models can cut through bone or through frozen foods.

deep-fryer

This machine offers a clean and easy way of deep-frying foods, and leaves less of the smell of frying in the house than a traditional chip pan because the lid is in place during frying. Most models have a temperature control and a timer for safe and accurate frying.

slow cooker

Ideal for making soups, stocks and casseroles. The machine keeps the food cooking at an even temperature so you do not have to keep an eye on a pan on the stove to check it doesn't boil over or come off the boil. The timer allows the food to start cooking while you are out at work.

toaster

Probably the most used of all electrical appliances, toasters are perfect for toasting bread, buns, waffles, muffins and crumpets, allowing both sides to be toasted at the same time. Some models take four pieces of bread at one time, others just two. Some take only bread, others have much wider slots that can be used for buns and muffins.

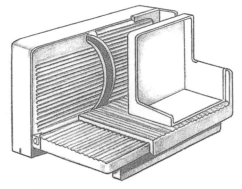

food slicer

slow cooker

toaster

deep-fryer

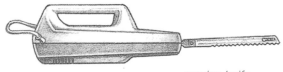

carving knife

electrical machines

food mill

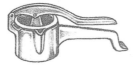

potato ricer

puréeing machine

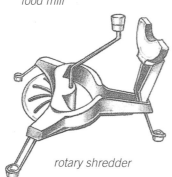

rotary shredder

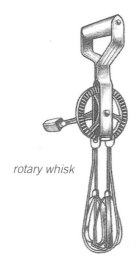

rotary whisk

barbecue

food mill
A type of manual food processor. Foods are pushed into the funnel at the top and come out of the spout ground down into much smaller pieces. They are collected in the tray underneath. Great for making stuffings, burgers, meatballs and breadcrumbs.

rotary shredder
Also called a mouli-légumes, this appliance stands on a table top and is used for shredding raw vegetables. The vegetables are pressed against the blade which is rotated by turning the handle on top.

potato ricer
A handy little appliance for making perfect mashed potatoes or other vegetable purées. The peeled, cooked potatoes are placed in the drum and the two halves are pressed together to push the potato through the holes in the base of the drum, much in the manner of a garlic crusher. It gives a good, smooth consistency, much better than an electric food processor which will over-mash potatoes. The potato ricer can also be used for making purées from cooked carrots, parsnips, swede and squash. Simply add butter and season to taste.

puréeing machine
This is also sometimes referred to as a mouli and is used to purée small amounts of cooked foods such as vegetables, casseroles and fruits. The food is placed in the machine, then the blade is rotated by turning the handle on top. This is useful for making baby foods.

rotary whisk
Because of the clever design, the two whisk heads rotate extremely quickly when the handle is turned. This allows you to whisk egg whites and cream in a fraction of the time it takes using a balloon whisk. It is, however, only really suitable for whisking small quantities of ingredients at one time.

barbecue
Nothing can beat the taste of food grilled over charcoal and nothing can create that taste apart from a barbecue. Models vary hugely, but the feature that is most important is the ability to adjust the cooking height. This allows you to cook in a controlled manner when the coals are very hot, and move the griddle down as the coals cool down. It also allows you to cook different foods at different temperatures. Cast-iron barbecues are particularly good as they hold the heat, keeping the coals hot for longer.

other appliances

mincer

kitchen scales

corkscrew

pasta machine

kitchen timers

mincer

A strong, metal machine that is clamped to the edge of a work surface and is used for mincing foods, such as raw or cooked meats, breadcrumbs and vegetables. Food is placed into the funnel at the top and is drawn down between the spiral blades as they are turned with the handle, and spat out of the far end. Good for making burgers, sausages and mincing baby foods.

pasta machine

This takes all the hard work out of rolling pasta. The rested dough is fed between the rotating rollers which draw it through and flatten it, much in the manner of a mangle. The rolled dough is fed through repeatedly until it is smooth and elastic. The rollers are adjusted so they are increasingly closer together to make the dough thinner and thinner. Cutting blades then cut the sheets of pasta into noodles, if required. Ravioli-making attachments are also available.

kitchen scales

Used for measuring out ingredients to be used in a recipe or for weighing joints of meat or fish to calculate the cooking time needed. Both digital and old-fashioned balancing scales are available. Digital scales are more accurate, especially when weighing small quantities of ingredients, but many people prefer balancing scales which come with a selection of weights of different sizes. These are accurate enough for most purposes in the kitchen.

kitchen timer

Useful for the busy cook, these can be either mechanical or digital and are designed to remind the cook when the food is done. They are set to a certain number of minutes and when that time has passed, an alarm sounds. Many ovens come with a timer built in to them.

corkscrew

No kitchen should be without one as it is extremely difficult to remove a cork from a bottle with anything else.

acidulated water Water with added acid, such as lemon juice or vinegar, which prevents discoloration in fruit and vegetables such as artichokes and apples.

al dente The Italians say that pasta is ready to eat when it is *al dente* which, when literally translated, means 'firm to the bite'.

antipasti Italian *hors d'oeuvres*. The literal Italian translation is 'before the meal' and it usually denotes an assortment of cold meats, vegetables and cheeses which are often marinated.

arborio The Italian rice used in making risotto. It is similar in shape to pudding rice, but never quite softens in the middle.

au gratin A cheese and breadcrumb topping, browned under the grill.

bain-marie A large, water-filled pan in which smaller dishes are set for cooking when an indirect, gentle heat is required.

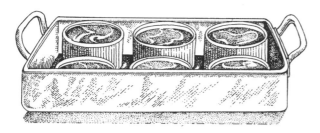

bain-marie

barbecue To cook over glowing coals, often charcoal.

baste To spoon pan juices (usually fat-based) over meat or vegetables to moisten during cooking.

beignets Fritters.

beurre manié Flour and butter worked into a paste, then used to thicken soups, stew juices and casseroles.

beurre noir Butter heated to a light brown colour, usually served with fish.

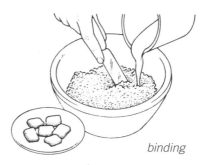

binding

bind To hold dry ingredients together with egg or liquid.

bisque Smooth and thickened shellfish soup.

blanch To immerse food briefly in boiling water to soften, remove skin, par-cook, set a colour, or remove a strong flavour.

boiling Cooking in liquid at a temperature of 100°C/212°F.

bouillon Broth or unclarified stock obtained from boiling meat or vegetables.

boiling

bouquet garni
Classically made up of a bay leaf, a sprig of thyme and two or three sprigs of parsley, which are either bound together with string or tied into a small muslin bag. It is used to flavour almost any savoury dish that needs long cooking, and is removed before the dish is served.

braise To cook food very slowly in a small amount of liquid in a pan or pot with a tight-fitting lid, after initial browning.

glossary of basic cooking terms

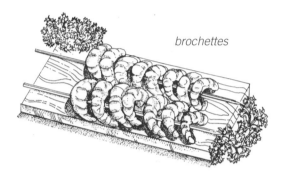

brochettes

brochette Food grilled and served on a skewer.
butterfly To slit a piece of food in half horizontally, almost cutting through so that when opened it resembles butterfly wings. Often used for king prawns, chops and thick fillets of fish.
canapé Small appetizer of pastry, biscuits and so on, with a savoury topping.
caramelize To cook sugar or sugar syrup to the caramel stage. The term is also used when grilling a sugar topping until browned.
cassis A fruit liqueur or syrup made from blackcurrants.
cassoulet A French dish which consists of haricot beans cooked in a stewpot with pork, other meat and poultry, seasoning and a gratin topping. Sausages and duck or goose portions are often added.

bouquet garni

ceps (dried) Dried wild mushrooms with a rich flavour that need reconstituting in boiling water before using. Also known as *porcini*, which is their Italian name.
clarify To melt and strain butter of its milk particles and impurities; to clear stocks by filtering.
compôte Fresh or dried fruit served cold in a syrup.
consommé Concentrated clear meat or poultry stock.
coulis A thick liquid purée, usually of fresh or cooked fruit or vegetables, which can be poured.
court-bouillon Aromatic liquid generally used for poaching fish or shellfish.
crackling The crisp cooked rind of a joint of pork.
cream To beat fat and sugar together to a pale, light consistency.

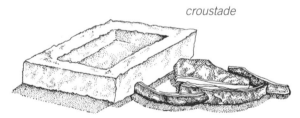

croustade

croustade Small bread cases, brushed with melted butter and baked or deep-fried until crisp.
croûte A slice of fried or toasted bread on which food is served.
croûton Small shapes (usually dice) of fried or occasionally toasted bread used as a garnish.

dredger

fines herbes

crudités Raw vegetables such as carrot, cucumber and celery, usually cut into sticks or slices and served with a dipping sauce.

curdle To cause milk or sauce to separate into solid and liquid parts. Often used to describe any mixture that separates.

dariole A small castle-shaped mould, used for cakes and mousses.

deglaze To free congealed cooking juices and sediments from the bottom of a roasting tin or pan by adding water, stock or wine and stirring over heat. The juices may be used to make gravy or added to a sauce.

degorge To sprinkle with salt or to soak to remove indigestible or strong-tasting juices from meat, fish or vegetables.

degrease To skim grease from the surface of a liquid.

devilled A food seasoned with a hot-tasting sauce and grilled or fried.

dredge To sprinkle the surface of food with flour, sugar or icing sugar.

dress To pluck, draw and truss poultry or game birds; or to put dressing on salad or pasta and toss.

dropping consistency The stage reached when a spoonful of a mixture held upside down will drop off a spoon reluctantly.

emulsion A milky liquid prepared by mixing liquids that are not soluble, such as oil and water, or other substances. A good example is mayonnaise.

en croûte To cook food in a pastry case.

en papillote To cook food enclosed in paper.

escalope A thin slice of meat from the fillet or leg.

fines herbes A mixture of finely chopped fresh herbs. Traditionally these are chervil, chives, parsley and tarragon.

flake To separate cooked meat or fish into very small pieces.

flamber To pour warmed spirit, often brandy, over food and set it alight.

florentine A dish that is made with spinach.

flute To make decorative indentations in the edges of pastry pies.

fold in To combine two mixtures gently with a metal spoon to retain their lightness.

folding in

garnishes

frying There are two main methods of frying. Shallow-frying is carried out over a medium heat using equal amounts of sizzling oil and butter, or just oil. Deep-frying uses hot oil that should come no more than halfway up a deep pan. The food is immersed in the hot oil which seals the outside of the food, preventing moisture escaping and fat soaking in.

galette Any sweet or savoury mixture that is shaped in a flat round.

garam masala A ready-made spice powder made up of several different Indian spices.

garnish To decorate a savoury dish.

glaze A mixture that is brushed on the surface of food to give colour and shine.

glazing

goujons Small strips of meat or fish, coated and deep-fried.

grilling A method of cooking where the food is placed on a grill pan below the heat. The grill should be preheated at its highest setting for at least 10 minutes.

hard ball A stage of sugar boiling used in making sweets.

hors d'oeuvres The first course or savoury morsels served with drinks.

hull To remove the green calyx from fruit.

infuse To extract flavour by steeping food in hot liquid.

julienne Matchstick strips of vegetables, citrus rind or meat, used as a garnish.

kibbled Coarsely chopped, used particularly for wheat.

knead To work dough by stretching and folding it to distribute the yeast and give a springy consistency.

knock back To punch or knead air from yeast dough after rising.

knocking back

knock up To slightly separate the layers of raw puff pastry with the blade of a knife, to help rising during cooking.

lard To thread strips of fat (usually pork) into lean meat to moisten it during cooking.

lardons Small cooked strips or cubes of pork or bacon fat, used to flavour or garnish a dish.

liaison Ingredients used to bind or thicken.

macerate To steep raw food, usually fruit, in sugar syrup or alcohol.

magret A boned breast of duck, presented with the skin and underlying layer of fat attached.

marinade The liquid in which food is marinated.

marinate To soak raw food (usually meat, poultry or game) in liquid, often wine or oil, to tenderize it and give flavour.

medallions Small rounds of meat, evenly cut.

paring

Niçoise

mesclun This is a French salad using a mixture of wild salad leaves and grasses.

Niçoise Food cooked or served with tomato, garlic, French beans, anchovies and olives.

noisette A boneless rack of lamb, rolled and cut into rounds; surrounded by a thin band of fat.

pan-frying A cooking method in which food cooks in its own juices in a preheated heavy-based pan.

parboil To boil until partially cooked.

pare To peel or trim.

passata Sieved tomatoes.

pâte The French for a pastry dough.

pâté A savoury paste of liver, pork or game.

pâtisserie A French cake shop or a term for sweet cakes and pastries.

praline Caramelized sugar and browned almonds mixed together.

proving

prove To put yeast dough to rise before baking.

pulses The dried seeds of members of the bean and pea families.

purée Cooked food, mashed or sieved until smooth.

reduce To concentrate – or thicken – a liquid, by boiling it rapidly to decrease its volume.

refresh To rinse freshly cooked food under cold running water or by plunging into iced water to stop the cooking process and to set the colour, used particularly for vegetables.

relax or **rest** In pastry, to allow the gluten in the flour to contract after rolling out; to allow the starch cells in the flour of a batter to expand.

render To melt and strain animal fat.

roasting Cooking food in an oven with currents of hot, dry air, often with the addition of fat or liquid.

roux A basic liaison of melted fat (usually butter) and flour, cooked as a thickening for sauces and soups.

rub in To mix fat into flour, using the fingertips, to give a mixture resembling fine breadcrumbs.

salsa In Mexico this term usually applies to uncooked sauces served as a dip or accompaniment. Mexican salsas are usually made from chillies and tomatoes; in Italy the term is often used for pasta sauces.

sauté To fry food in very little fat over a high heat. The food is moved constantly throughout the process to prevent it sticking to the pan and burning.

scald To heat liquid, usually milk, to just below boiling point. Also to rinse with boiling water.

score To make shallow or deep cuts over the surface of meat or fish before cooking to allow the heat to penetrate evenly.

stewing

sealing or **searing** Sealing the surface of food, to retain the juices, goodness and flavour.

seasoned flour Flour with salt and pepper added.

simmering To cook food gently in liquid at just below boiling point.

skim To remove any scum or fat from the surface of a liquid with a metal spoon or small ladle.

spatchcock A chicken or poussin split open with poultry shears and spread out flat before cooking.

steam To cook food in the steam above boiling water, in a perforated dish or a special steamer.

steep To soak in warm or cold liquid in order to soften food and draw out strong flavours.

stewing To cook food slowly in a small quantity of liquid in a closed dish or pan in the oven or on the hob.

stir-fry an Oriental cooking method in which food is lightly cooked in a little oil over a high heat with constant stirring.

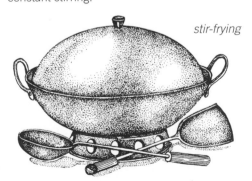

stir-frying

suprême A choice piece of meat, usually a breast of poultry, and also a rich, creamy white sauce.

sweat To soften food, usually vegetables, in a little fat over a very low heat until the juices run.

tempura A Japanese style of deep-frying pieces of meat, fish, poultry and vegetables in a light batter. These are then served with a dipping sauce of soy sauce.

terrine A pâté or minced mixture cooked in a loaf-shaped dish.

timbale A dish cooked in a drum-shaped mould.

tortillas These are a flat type of bread unique to Mexico and are made from dried cornflour or from wheat flour. They are the basis for many Mexican dishes such as tacos and enchiladas.

vanilla sugar Caster sugar flavoured with pure vanilla extract or essence. This can be made by adding a vanilla pod to a jar of caster sugar.

vinaigrette A French salad dressing made with olive oil and vinegar or lemon juice.

well The hollow made in a heap or bowl of flour into which eggs, liquid or fats are put prior to mixing in.

zest The thin outer layer of citrus fruit containing the citrus oil.

well

poultry

preparing poultry for cooking

Remove the giblet bag as soon as possible after buying a bird to allow air to get into the cavity. If taking the bird straight from the refrigerator to the oven, increase the cooking time by 10–15 minutes to compensate. Weigh poultry and game after stuffing and then calculate the cooking time to ensure that the bird and stuffing will be cooked right through. Game birds are lean and need to be barded. This involves placing a thin layer of fatty bacon on top of the bird which should be removed for the last 10 minutes of cooking. Before roasting chicken, turkey or poussin, spread a thin layer of butter over the skin and lay a few rashers of streaky bacon on top if wished; baste the meat from time to time during cooking to keep it moist. Duck and goose need to be pricked all over before roasting, so that their fat can both escape and baste them at the same time. As they have so much fat, they should be roasted on a rack over a roasting tin.

jointing a chicken or duck

If you want to cook poultry in portions it is much more economical to cut it up yourself.

All you need is a chopping board and a heavy knife. Poultry shears are also useful. The secret is to first find the joints and so cut through the tendons and cartilage, rather than hacking through bones.

- Place the bird with the legs facing you and pull one leg away from the body. Cut through the skin down to where the thigh joins the body. Bend the leg outwards to expose the ball and socket joint and cut down between the ball and socket to free the whole leg. Repeat with the other leg. A large leg can then be cut into drumstick and thigh portions, if required.
- Press down through the shoulder joint attaching the wing to the body, then cut down through the skin at the base of the wing. Repeat with the other wing.
- Place the knife inside the carcass and carefully slit along the ribs on both sides to separate the breast from the lower carcass. Pull the breast away from the back to expose the shoulder bones and cut down to detach the breast.
- Place the breast, skin side up, on the board and cut down on one side or other of the breastbone to give two breasts. With larger birds the breast portions can then be cut widthways to give 2 or 3 portions each.

roasting

Refer to the chart on page 95 for roasting information. Put the stuffing, if using, in the neck end only and fold the neck flap over to completely enclose the stuffing. Secure with a small skewer, or wooden cocktail sticks. Stuffing can be placed in the body cavity, but great care should be taken to ensure that the bird gets ample cooking time and that the meat and stuffing are cooked through thoroughly before serving. In any case, always allow about 15 minutes extra time when calculating the cooking time, just in case the bird is not quite done when you plan to serve it. Some birds are fleshier than others and require longer cooking time, despite being the same weight.

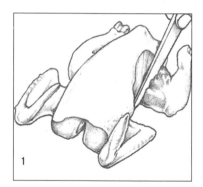

jointing a chicken

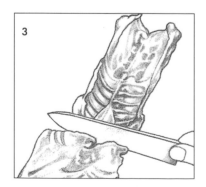

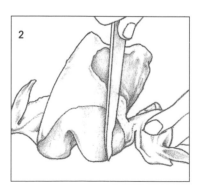

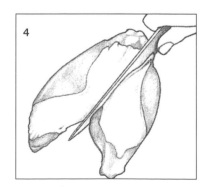

meat & poultry

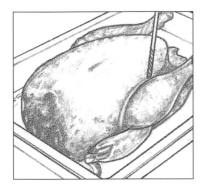

testing if cooked

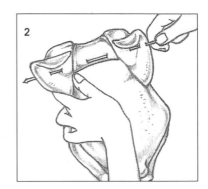

stuffing poultry

to test if cooked

To test if the chicken or other bird is cooked, take a fine skewer and pierce the thickest part of the thigh. If the juices run clear the bird is cooked; but if they are tinged pink, return to the oven for 10 minutes and test again.

resting a roast

A roast must be allowed to rest in a warm place for 10–15 minutes once it is cooked. Resting settles the meat so that it is easier to carve and loses less juice. Don't worry about it getting cold: a cooked bird has a lot of heat stored in it and would take hours to get cold.

apricot stuffing

1 onion, finely chopped
25 g/1 oz butter
125 g/4 oz ready-to-eat dried apricots, chopped
grated rind of $^1/_2$ lemon
2 tablespoons chopped parsley
pinch of mixed spice
75 g/3 oz fresh breadcrumbs
1 egg, beaten
salt and pepper

Fry the onion gently in the butter until soft but not coloured. Mix the onion and butter with the apricots, lemon rind, parsley and mixed spice and season to taste with salt and pepper. Stir in the breadcrumbs and enough beaten egg to bind the mixture, without making it too wet.

pecan stuffing

1 onion, finely chopped
25 g/1 oz butter
40 g/1$^1/_2$ oz boiled rice
1 tablespoon chopped parsley
$^1/_2$ teaspoon dried thyme
40 g/1$^1/_2$ oz pecan nuts, chopped
$^1/_2$ teaspoon ground coriander
1 egg, beaten
salt and pepper

Fry the onion gently in the butter until soft but not coloured. Mix the onion and butter with the rice, parsley, thyme, pecan nuts and coriander and season to taste with salt and pepper. Stir in enough beaten egg to bind the mixture, without making it too wet.

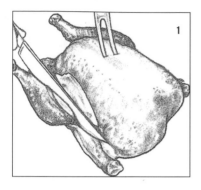 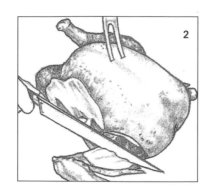 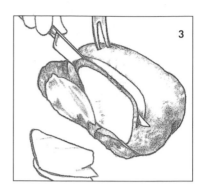

carving a turkey

carving poultry and game

Use a sharp knife for carving, which is much safer than a blunt one. If you are unsure about your carving skills, carve in the kitchen out of sight, keep the meat warm and serve it all at once. Always use a carving fork fitted with a safety guard.

carving a chicken
• Place the bird breast side up, remove the legs and wings on each side. If the chicken is large, separate the drumsticks from the thighs.
• Carve thin slices diagonally from each side of the breast and serve some white and some dark meat to each person.

carving a duck or game bird
Duck is difficult to carve, so use poultry shears to joint the bird once cooked. Insert the shears into the cavity and cut through the breast along the breastbone. Open up the duck and cut along each side of the backbone and remove it. Place each duck half, skin side up, on a board and cut between the wing and leg to give two portions, four in total. Serve a portion to each person.

carving a turkey
Stand the bird on a board or a large plate with the breast facing upwards. Allow the bird to rest for about 10 minutes before starting to carve.
• First remove one of the drumsticks, leaving the thigh on the bird. Slice the meat from the removed drumstick and place on a warmed serving plate.
• Carve slices from the thigh on the same side, then remove the wings and cut the meat off neatly.
• Carve thin slices lengthways from the breast of the bird, taking in slices from the stuffing as you reach it.
• Serve a mixture of white and dark meat for each portion, plus some stuffing. Finish carving one side of the bird completely before turning it round to carve the other side.
• Cover the carcass with foil after carving to keep any leftover meat warm, ready for second helpings.

carving a goose
Geese are large birds with very little flesh in relation to their size. They are quite different in shape to other poultry, so follow the steps below for carving.
Stand the bird on a board with the breast upwards. Remove any skewers or string which have been used to truss the bird. Allow it to rest for about 10 minutes prior to carving.
• First remove the legs and wings from the bird and place on a warmed serving plate.
• Carve thick slices from either side of the breastbone, taking the slices the whole length of the body. Arrange on the serving plate.
• If the bird is stuffed, carve off slices of the stuffing with the breast meat and remove the rest with a spoon if it is inaccessible. Serve each person with some white and dark meat and some stuffing.

a guide to roasting meat and poultry

	Slow roasting	Quick roasting
Chicken	160°C (325°F), Gas Mark 3 1–1.5 kg/2–3 lb bird: **45–60 minutes** 1.5–2.5 kg/3–5 lb bird: **1–1½ hours**	Cook for **30 minutes** at 220°C (425°F), Gas Mark 7, then reduce the temperature to 160°C (325°F), Gas Mark 3, and cook as follows: 1–1.5 kg/2–3 lb bird: **15–30 minutes** extra 1.5–2.5 kg/3–5 lb bird: **30–60 minutes** extra
Turkey	160°C (325°F), Gas Mark 3 3.5–5.5 kg/7–11 lb bird: **3½–4 hours** 6–7 kg/12–14 lb bird: **4–4½ hours** 7.5–10 kg/15–20 lb bird: **4½–5 hours**	Cook for **50 minutes** at 220°C (425°F), Gas Mark 7, then reduce the temperature to 160°C (325°F), Gas Mark 3, and cook as follows: 3.5–5.5 kg/7–11 lb bird: **1½–2 hours** extra 6–7 kg/12–14 lb bird: **2–2½ hours** extra 7.5–10 kg/15–20 lb bird: **2½–3 hours** extra
Duck	Not suitable	Cook for **30 minutes** at 220°C (425°F), Gas Mark 7, then reduce the temperature to 160°C (325°F), Gas Mark 3, and cook as follows: 1.5–3 kg/3–6 lb bird: **50 minutes–1½ hours** extra
Goose	180°C (350°F), Gas Mark 4 **30–35 minutes** per 500 g/1 lb, depending on how well cooked you want it, plus **35 minutes** extra	Cook for **45 minutes** at 220°C (425°F), Gas Mark 7, then reduce the temperature to 160°C (325°F), Gas Mark 3, and cook as follows: 3.5–4.5 kg/7–9 lb bird: **1½–2 hours** extra 5–6 kg/10–12 lb bird: **2–2½ hours** extra
Lamb*	180°C (350°F), Gas Mark 4 **40 minutes** per 500 g/1 lb, plus **40 minutes** extra	220°C (425°F), Gas Mark 7 Cook for just over **15 minutes** per 500 g/1 lb, plus a good **15 minutes** extra for very pink lamb; **18 minutes** per 500 g/1 lb, plus **18 minutes** extra for fairly pink lamb; **20 minutes** per 500 g/1 lb, plus **20 minutes** extra for well-cooked lamb
Pork and veal*	Not suitable	220°C (425°F), Gas Mark 7 **25–30 minutes** per 500 g/1 lb, plus **25–30 minutes** extra
Beef*	180°C (350°F), Gas Mark 4 **25 minutes** per 500 g/1 lb, plus **25 minutes** extra for rare beef; **30 minutes** per 500 g/1 lb, plus **30 minutes** extra for medium beef; **35 minutes** per 500 g/1 lb, plus **35 minutes** extra for well-cooked beef	220°C (425°F), Gas Mark 7 **15 minutes** per 500 g/1 lb, plus **15 minutes** extra for rare beef; **20 minutes** per 500 g/1 lb, plus **20 minutes** extra for medium beef; **25 minutes** per 500 g/1 lb, plus **25 minutes** extra for well-cooked beef

* For stuffed joints, weigh after stuffing and allow **5–10 minutes** per 500 g/1 lb extra cooking time.

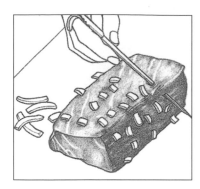

larding a fillet of beef

barding a lean joint

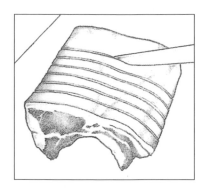

making pork crackling

meat

preparing meat for cooking

Tough meat can be prepared so that it arrives at the table full of flavour and juice, by marinating with acidic ingredients such as wine, lemon juice, vinegar, yogurt or pulped tomatoes. These acids help to break down the connective tissue that is mostly responsible for toughness. Pounding or cutting up and lengthy cooking also help to tenderize tough cuts.

Before grilling reasonably thick, good quality meat, brush on both sides with oil to prevent it drying out. To stop a joint drying out, tie large sheets of pork fat or fatty bacon rashers round it, a technique known as barding. This keeps the meat moist during cooking, preventing it becoming tough.

A lean piece of meat such as a fillet can also be larded to prevent it drying out during roasting. Cut some pork fat into short narrow strips. These are then threaded on to a larding needle, one by one, and threaded through the meat to make 'stitches' about 1 cm/½ inch deep. The fat keeps the outer layer of meat moist.

Before roasting lean beef, dripping or fat may be spread over the joint. This can then be collected from the roasting tin and used for basting during cooking. As lamb is already quite fatty, it does not require extra fat for roasting.

To make pork crackling, score the skin of the joint, marking thin strips with a sharp knife at frequent intervals then rub in oil and a generous amount of salt.

boning a leg of lamb

Lamb is a deliciously tender meat, perfect for roasting, and leg of lamb is one of the most popular cuts. Leg joints can be boned and stuffed before roasting, resulting in a flavoursome stuffing encased in thick, succulent meat. A stuffed leg of lamb is easy to carve and serve and makes an impressive centrepiece to a meal.

● To bone a leg of lamb, use a sharp, pointed knife to clear the meat away from the hip bone which protrudes from the thickest end of the leg. Scrape the meat away from the hip bone along its whole length, reaching inside the meat to do so. When it is free, remove the hip bone.

● Cut away the meat from the shank bone in the same way, this time working from the narrower end of the leg. Remove the shank bone.

● Working from the wider end of the leg again, clear the meat away from the middle bone, then remove it through the hip cavity.

● You should now be left with a boneless piece of meat, with a cavity running down the centre. Fill the cavity with stuffing and use butcher's string to tie the joint into a neat shape, tucking the narrow end of the lamb into the cavity to hold the stuffing in place.

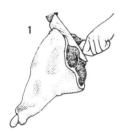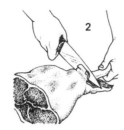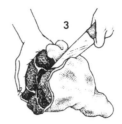

boning a leg of lamb

roasting

Refer to the chart on page 95 for information about roasting times and oven temperatures.

carving

Let the carved joint rest for at least 5 and up to 15 minutes before carving, to allow the juices to settle. This will make carving much easier. Make sure you have a well-sharpened knife so the blade will slide through the meat rather than sawing and tearing at the fibres. Stand the joint on a flat non-slip surface such as a wooden board or a metal carving plate with spikes on it. A carving fork with a guard will help hold the meat steady. Always start by removing any outer bones. As a general principle, most meat is carved across the grain because this shortens the meat fibres, making the individual slices more tender.

carving a wing rib of beef

● Start by removing the chine bone at the thickest end of the joint.
● Lay the meat on a flat surface, fat uppermost, and carve downwards into narrow slices, loosening the meat from the rib bones as you go.

carving a rib roast

● First remove any string from the joint, and stand it on its wide end, holding it securely with a carving fork. If necessary, remove the chine bone with a sharp knife to make it easier to carve.
● Cut across the joint in even, fairly thick slices, until the blade of the knife reaches the rib bone. Cut down close to the bone to loosen each slice.

carving a boned and rolled joint of beef

● Remove any skewers and any string which runs along the length of the joint as opposed to around it, and take off the first string around the joint.
● Carve downwards in neat, fairly thin slices, removing more string as it becomes necessary.
If carving a cold joint, all the string may be removed before you begin. An electric carving knife is ideal for boned and rolled joints.

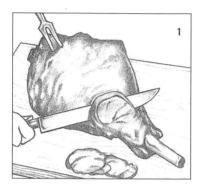
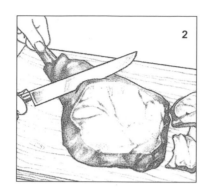

carving a leg of lamb

carving a leg of lamb

Lamb should not be carved too thinly; aim for slices about 5 mm/¼ inch thick.

• Holding the knuckle end firmly with the carving fork, carve a wedge-shaped slice from the centre of the meatiest side. Carve slices from each side of the cut, gradually turning the knife to get larger slices and ending parallel to the bone.

• Turn the joint over and carve in long horizontal slices.

carving a shoulder of lamb

The shoulder is probably the most difficult joint to carve. To simplify carving, you can loosen around the blade bone with a small sharp knife before cooking, but do not remove it entirely. When cooked, this loosened bone can then be pulled out to make carving easier.

• Lay the joint skin side uppermost and make a series of parallel cuts downwards, starting at the elbow and ending at the shoulder blade.

• Run the knife horizontally along the length of the bone underneath the slices to free them.

• Turn the joint over, remove any surface fat, then carve the meat on the other side of the joint into long horizontal slices.

carving loin of lamb or best end of neck

With loin or best end of neck joints on the bone, ask the butcher to chine the joint first. This simply means that he chops partly through the backbone lengthways so the bone can easily be removed after cooking to make it easier to carve between the rib bones. If the bone were removed before cooking, the meat would shrink from the bones and look rather unattractive.

Alternatively, the joint can be chopped, which means each or every other chop is partly chopped through so when it is cooked, the cut just has to be completed. This does not, however, give such a good-looking or well-cooked joint.

• Stand the chined joint squarely on a plate or board and remove the backbone with a sharp knife.

• Carve between the ribs to divide the joint neatly into cutlets. Sometimes the slices will have no bone if the joint is from a large animal.

You could, alternatively, cut the joints quite thick, allowing two bones per portion which gives a mini-joint for each serving.

carving a loin of pork

• Remove the crackling first to make carving easier. Cut the crackling into thin strips, following the scored lines, and place on the serving dish.

• Sever the chined bone from the chop bones and discard it.

• Divide the joint into chops, cutting between the rib bones, and arrange on the serving dish with the crackling. Alternatively, loosen the meat from the rib bones and then cut off in neat slices, without dividing it into chops.

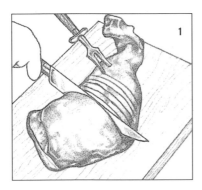 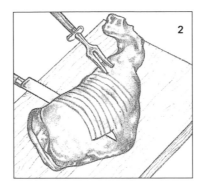 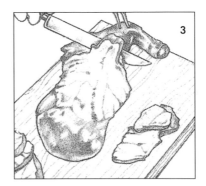

carving a shoulder of lamb

carving a leg of pork

● As with pork loin, use the knife to cut through the crackling and remove it before carving the meat. This makes carving much easier. Do not, however, take off and serve the crackling from meat which you will not be carving. Carve the leg of pork in a similar way to a shoulder of lamb.
● Make a series of vertical parallel cuts down to the bone, keeping the slices fairly thin.
● Slice horizontally along the bone, freeing all the vertical slices.
● Then turn the joint over and cut horizontal slices from the other side of the joint.

carving a loin of pork

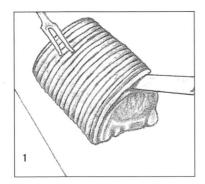 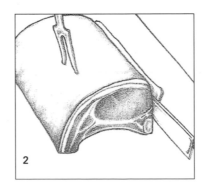 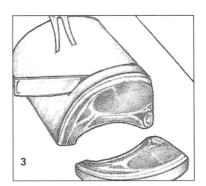

accompaniments for roast meats

chicken

To accompany roast chicken, serve bacon rolls, bread sauce and thin gravy. Sage and onion stuffing is also a popular accompaniment, which can either be made into stuffing balls, or can be stuffed into the neck end of the bird to cook.

turkey

Roast turkey should be served with chipolata sausages, bacon rolls, cranberry sauce, Brussels sprouts and roast potatoes. You can also stuff the bird with sausagemeat.

goose

The traditional accompaniments for roast goose are apple or gooseberry sauce, fried onion rings, sage and onion stuffing and thin gravy. Take care to remove all the fat from the pan juices before making the gravy as goose is very fatty.

beef

Serve horseradish sauce, horseradish cream or a horseradish mustard with roast beef. It is also traditional to serve Yorkshire pudding, either one large pudding or individual ones made in small patty tins, and a good thin gravy made from the meat juices. Many people also like a plain mustard with beef.

pork

To accompany roast pork, it is traditional to serve apple sauce, sage and onion stuffing and gravy.

lamb

With lamb, serve mint sauce, mint jelly or redcurrant jelly. If the joint has been spiked with garlic and herbs, you may simply prefer to serve a good gravy, made from the pan juices and slightly thickened.

yorkshire puddings

a little dripping or vegetable oil, for greasing
¹/₂ quantity Basic Batter (see page 126)

1 Put some of the dripping from the joint, or a little oil, into 4 Yorkshire pudding tins or 12 patty tins and place in the oven until the fat is really hot.

2 Pour the batter into the tins so that they are no more than two-thirds full and bake in a preheated oven, 220°C (425°F), Gas Mark 7, until puffed up and golden brown.

Serves 4
Preparation time: 5 minutes, plus standing
Cooking time: about 25 minutes

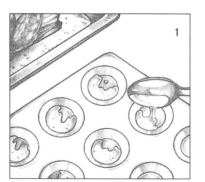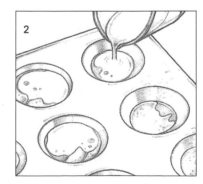

making Yorkshire puddings

sage and onion stuffing

2 large onions, chopped
25 g/1 oz butter
125 g/4 oz fresh breadcrumbs
2 teaspoons dried sage
salt and pepper

1 Put the onions into a pan of water, bring to the boil and simmer for 5 minutes; drain well.

2 Melt the butter in a pan, add the onions and fry for a minute or so.

3 Put the breadcrumbs into a bowl and mix in the sage and seasonings. Add the onions and the butter and mix well together.

4 Press lightly into a greased ovenproof shallow dish and cook in the oven below the meat for 30–40 minutes or until lightly browned on top and crisp. Cut into wedges to serve. Alternatively, use to stuff the neck end of a chicken or goose and carve with the meat.

Serves 4
Preparation time: about 2 minutes
Cooking time: 35–45 minutes

making meat gravy

gravy

There is no need to use gravy mix, gravy browning or stock cubes to make a delicious gravy. All that is required is the roasting tin with its fat and juices from the roast meat. The liquid used can be stock made from the giblets, if you are roasting poultry, or vegetable water from boiling your accompanying vegetables. This thick gravy uses a little flour for thickening.

meat gravy

To make a thin gravy, omit the fat and flour and cook for only 30 seconds at step 2.

2 tablespoons fat (from roasting the meat)
1 tablespoon flour
300 ml/½ pint hot vegetable water or stock
salt and pepper
1 tablespoon sherry or wine (optional)

1 Pour off the excess fat from the roasting pan, leaving the sediment and approximately 2 tablespoons of fat behind.

2 Sprinkle the flour into the pan, and stir very well, scraping up and mixing in all the sediment and meat juices. Cook over gentle heat on the hob for about 2 minutes, stirring constantly, to brown the flour, taking care not to burn it.

3 Gradually stir the hot vegetable water or stock into the pan, stirring well. Bring to the boil, stirring constantly. Cook for 2 minutes, season and add the sherry or wine.

4 Strain through a fine sieve and serve very hot.

Makes 300 ml/½ pint
Preparation time: about 2 minutes
Cooking time: 5 minutes

preparing rabbit

Rabbit is a wonderfully versatile meat, blending equally well with red or white wine sauces, with herbs and spices, with mushrooms and prunes, yet it is little used or appreciated today. It is therefore great value for money and since it is very lean, it is healthy and invaluable in diets where fatty foods and cholesterol should be kept to a minimum.

A whole rabbit usually weighs about 1 kg/2 lb and will serve 4–5 people. Very small young rabbits are sometimes available in spring; these have a mild flavour and are very tender. Some butchers sell rabbit pieces so you can buy the choicest part of the rabbit, the loin, and avoid the bonier rib section.

As it contains little fat, rabbit flesh does tend to be a bit dry, so it is best cooked with liquid, such as wine or stock. Cooking times will depend on the age of the rabbit: older rabbits may need up to 1½ hours, while young rabbits will be cooked in 30 minutes.

Many recipes call for a rabbit to be jointed. This is actually quite a similar process to cutting up a chicken and is relatively straightforward.
● Start by removing the two back legs, separating the pieces at the hip joints to give two meaty thighs. It will be easier if you find the hip joints exactly, then cut through the cartilage of the joint, rather than trying to cut through the bone.
● Next cut the meaty loin of the rabbit into one or two sections, cutting through the backbone, across the animal.
● Finally cut the rib cage section into two pieces, this time cutting along the backbone. This will result in four or five serving portions.

preparing liver

Liver has outstanding nutritional properties, and when it is properly prepared it is delicious. Liver, kidneys and many other types of offal are becoming popular again and deservedly so.

Ox, calf, lamb, pig and poultry livers are used in the cuisines of many nations. Liver and bacon is a natural combination enjoyed in many countries, using lamb, ox or calves' liver. Goose and ducks' livers are made into the famous pâtés and terrines of France and Hungary. Chicken livers are used in risotto in Italy, and in pâtés and pan-fried in salads in much of Europe.

Most of these livers are widely available in supermarkets and butchers' shops in this country. Lamb and calves' livers are best enjoyed thinly sliced and pan-fried in a little butter until crisp on the outside and still pink in the middle. They can be served with a simple accompaniment of onions or bacon, or are equally delicious dressed with herbs and balsamic vinegar or a simple creamy sauce. Ox and pigs' liver are less tender and stronger in flavour and are best braised in pies or casseroles. Pigs' liver also makes good pâté. Chicken livers are tender and sweet and are excellent for pâtés as well as salads and barbecues.
● To prepare liver, first pull the thin veil of membrane away from the outside and discard it. Also cut away any fat or gristle from the outside.
● Cut out any large veins which run through the flesh, by gently scraping the flesh away from them, holding them taut in one hand. Use a small, sharp, pointed knife for this.
● Now slice the liver or leave whole, depending on its size and the recipe.

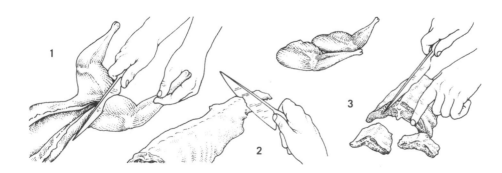

preparing rabbit

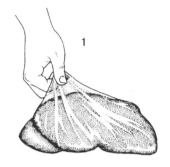

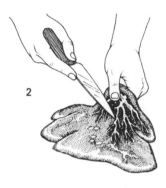

preparing liver

preparing kidneys

Kidneys are another type of offal with a rich and delicious flavour. The different types of kidneys vary greatly in strength of flavour, but the following are used in cookery: ox, lamb, veal and, less frequently, pigs'.

Lambs' kidneys are one of the most delectable morsels; calves' kidneys even more so, especially for those who find other kidneys, especially ox, too strong. Ox kidneys are mainly used in steak and kidney pies and puddings, though they can be quite tasty used in a casserole.

Unless directed to cook them whole with some of their skin and fat still around them, kidneys should be prepared in the following way.

● Remove the outer layer of white suet which encloses the kidney. If you have bought the kidneys in a supermarket, this may already have been done.

● Next remove the outer membrane, using a sharp pair of kitchen scissors to pierce it. Peel it away from the kidney flesh.

● Cut the kidneys open and remove the central white core with kitchen scissors or a small, sharp knife. This will be too tough to eat. If the kidneys are large, cut into smaller pieces to cook.

● Eat all types of kidneys as fresh as possible and store them in the refrigerator for no more than about 24 hours before use.

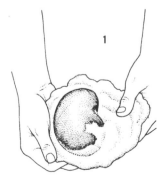

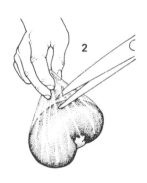

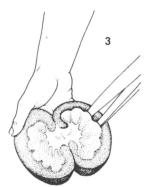

preparing kidneys

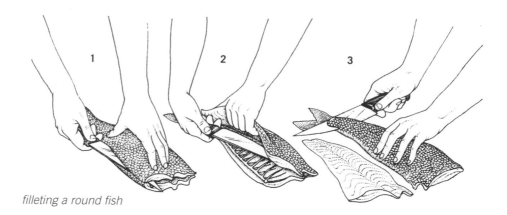

filleting a round fish

cooking fish

As fish has such a small amount of connective tissue, it requires very little cooking. If it is overcooked, the flakes fall apart and the fibres become tough, dry and tasteless.

There are several ways of cooking fish, but the cooking process should, in general, be short and gentle. Although fillets are more popular, most cooks agree that fish on the bone – as with meat – has more flavour.

frying

This is a popular method, and fish can be both shallow- or deep-fried. For both processes the flesh of the fish must be coated with egg and breadcrumbs, batter, flour or oatmeal – to protect the delicate flesh. Usually fillets of fish are cooked in this way. A vegetable oil should be used (if deep-frying, the oil should only be used for fish), but a combination of butter and oil is best and tastiest for shallow-frying.

grilling

This method is used for whole fish, steaks, fillets and cutlets, particularly oily fish such as mackerel, salmon and trout. The flesh is usually scored with a knife (if the fish is on the bone) to ensure even and thorough cooking. The fish should be dotted with butter to prevent it drying out. The grill should be set at a moderate heat, rather than on high, so that the fish does not dry out. The smaller the fish, the higher the grill. Line the grill with foil so that the pan and the rack don't have lingering fish flavours.

baking

Fish can be baked whole, brushed with butter or oil, and stuffed; they may be open or lightly covered with buttered foil for protection. They can also be baked in a liquid (milk, sauce, wine or stock).

poaching

This method ensures that the fish remains moist throughout cooking. The fish is cooked in a liquid, such as fish stock, wine, water or milk, which can be flavoured with herbs, a little onion or lemon juice. The fish may be cooked on top of the stove in a pan or fish kettle, or in the oven. If the pan is not covered the fish should be basted frequently. The cooking liquid is usually used as a basis for the accompanying sauce.

steaming

The fish is cooked in the steam above a pan of simmering water. It should be placed between two buttered plates, or on a plate covered in foil to prevent the natural juices escaping into the water beneath.

en papillote

Fish, whole or in fillets or steaks, can be wrapped up in foil, greaseproof or cellophane with various flavourings (butter, lemon juice, wine, onion, garlic, herbs) and poached, steamed, baked or deep-fried. All the essential flavours and juices are retained making it one of the best ways to cook fish.

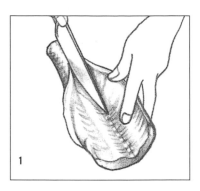 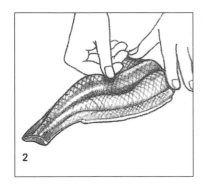 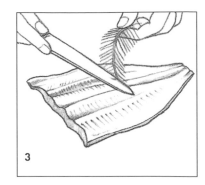

boning a round fish

preparing fish

filleting a round fish (such as trout, herring or mackerel)

- Using a sharp, flexible knife, remove the head of the fish, then remove the guts and rinse the fish. Cut the fish along the backbone.
- Holding the knife at a slight angle and starting along the backbone, work the upper fillet away from the ribs using a stroking action with the blade of the knife. Pull the flesh away with the other hand as you work.
- Turn the fish over and repeat the process. This will leave you with two single fillets.

boning a round fish (such as a sardine or small herring)

- First cut off the head and the tail and cut down the belly of the fish to open it up completely.
- Lay the fish down, skin side up, and press firmly along the backbone with your thumb, to flatten the fish and loosen the bone.
- Turn the fish over and use a sharp knife to lift out the backbone, easing it gently away from the flesh, taking care not to break up the flesh. This method will result in one large double fish fillet, suitable for stuffing and reshaping or simply frying flat.

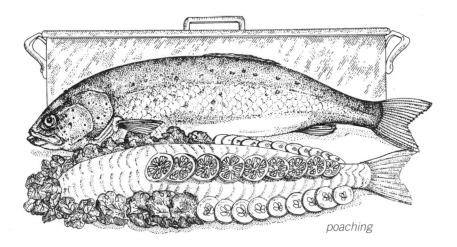

poaching

fish & seafood

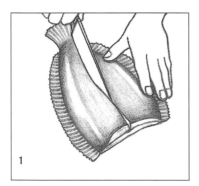

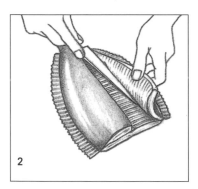

filleting a flat fish

filleting a flat fish (such as plaice or sole)

This method will give you four small fillets.

● Place the fish on a board with the head away from you. Using a sharp flexible knife, gut the fish and remove the head, then cut down the backbone from the head to the tail of the fish.

● To remove one fillet, hold your knife at a slight angle and insert along the backbone. Then work the flesh away from the bones towards one edge of the fish, using long strokes of the knife. Keep the knife flat against the bones and pull the flesh back with your other hand as you work.

● Turn the fish around with the head end facing you and remove the second fillet in the same way.

● Turn the fish over and remove the other two fillets using the same technique.

skinning a fish fillet

● Place the fish fillet, skin side down, on a flat board with the tail end toward you. Using a large sharp knife, cut through the flesh at the tail end, leaving the skin intact.

● Dip your fingers in salt to give a good grip and hold the tail firmly. Slip the knife between the flesh and skin, keeping it almost horizontal against the skin and the board.

● Separate the flesh from the skin using a sawing action with the knife and pull the skin towards you with the other hand.

skinning a flat fish (such as plaice or sole)

● Lay the fish, dark skin up, on a board. Make a cut across the skin at the tail end.

● Grip the tail firmly with one hand and pull the skin off the fish with the other hand in one movement towards the head. You will get a firmer grip on the skin if you dip your fingers in salt first.

● Turn the fish over and repeat with the white side.

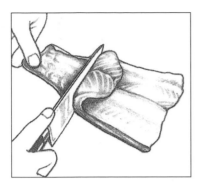

skinning a fish fillet

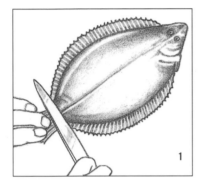

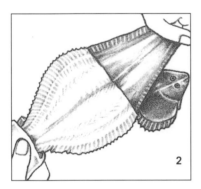

skinning a flat fish

preparing squid

Squid is a delicious but relatively cheap seafood, available fresh (usually whole), or prepared and frozen. It is worth buying it fresh as the flavour and texture are much better. You will, however, need to prepare it yourself.

If the recipe requires the ink from the squid to be used, prepare the squid over a dish to catch the ink.

The edible parts of a squid are the tentacles and body. The head and inner parts of the body must be removed and discarded.

● Start by pulling the head and tentacles from the body. The intestines will come away with the head.

● Remove the squid's wings, the flat pieces of flesh which are attached on either side of the body.

● Next, remove the speckled skin from the squid's body. It should come away easily, leaving white flesh underneath. Remove the skin from the wings, too, if you want to use them in the dish.

● Next cut the tentacles from the head, leaving them in one piece, and discard the head and intestines (apart from the ink sac if you want to save the ink). You will also need to cut or push out and discard the beak which is the hard mouthpart between the tentacles.

● Next remove the transparent 'backbone' from the body of the squid and discard. Wash the body, wings and tentacles thoroughly, paying most attention to the body cavity; you can turn the body inside out if it makes it easier to clean.

● Dry the squid flesh on absorbent kitchen paper and cut up or leave whole, according to the recipe and the size of the squid.

preparing squid

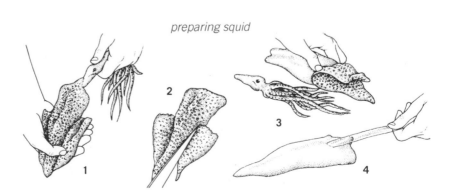

preparing crab

Fresh crab meat is so much more flavoursome than the canned variety, so it is well worth buying a fresh crab and preparing it yourself.

Crabs are available cooked or live. When choosing a cooked crab, make sure it has been cooked recently so it is still very fresh, as the flavour will be better. It should have a salty sweet smell. If the smell is at all unpleasant, do not buy it. Choose a crab that feels heavy for its size and is a fresh orange colour. Make sure none of the legs are missing or the crab may have filled up with water during cooking. Shake the crab to make sure it does not sound slushy inside: it may be full of water.

• To cook a live crab, plunge it into a large pan of salted boiling water, cover and bring back to the boil. Boil a small crab for 10–15 minutes, and a larger one for 20–25 minutes. Remove from the water and allow to cool.

• When cool, remove all the small legs and the two large claws and set aside. Also remove the 'tail' which curls under the shell and lies flat against it. Discard the tail.

• Next, lay the crab on its back and press down on the back of the shell with the heel of your hand. This should crack the undershell and release the central section from the main shell. Pull the body of the crab out of the shell. Pull away and discard the greyish-white stomach sac (just behind the mouth) and the long white pointed 'dead men's fingers'. These are quite obvious, and should be removed and discarded as they have an unpleasant texture.

• Remove the brown meat from the shell and set aside.

• Cut the main body of the crab in half down the centre. Using a skewer or crab pick, pick all the white meat from the cavities in the body halves. You should end up with an empty skeleton. Next remove the meat from the legs and claws using the same pick and add to the white meat. You will be left with a pile of brown meat and a pile of white meat. Either serve with brown bread, lemon wedges and mayonnaise, or use in a recipe, according to instructions.

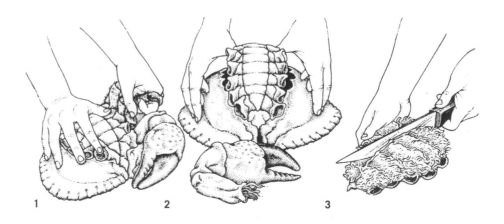

preparing a crab   1   2   3

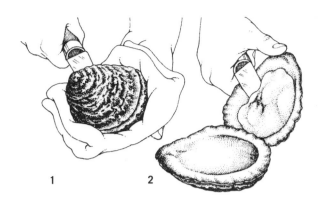

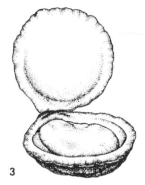

1   2   3

opening oysters

preparing fresh oysters

A much-prized mollusc, the oyster appears on menus throughout the world, its unique flavour and texture being unlike any other type of seafood. Many varieties are extensively cultivated around the world; the best European oysters include the English Whitstable oyster and the Belon and green Marenne from France. Most are sold raw, though a few are bottled or tinned in fresh water, or frozen.

Live rock oysters can survive unopened in the shell for up to two weeks if they are kept in a cool, damp place, preferably in a hessian bag, or wrapped in seaweed. If stored in a plastic bag or a refrigerator, they will soon die. Always discard oysters with partially open shells or those with an offensive odour as they are probably already dead and could be dangerous to eat.

Oysters should be plump and creamy and smell of the sea. Opened oysters should be eaten on the day of purchase.

Oyster opening is an acquired skill, but if you follow the instructions below, you should soon master it.
● You will need a short, strong, flat-bladed knife to open oysters, plus a cloth with which to protect the hand that is holding the shell. Insert the knife under the smooth lip of the joined shells, close to the hinge, where there is a gap in the corrugated shell edge. Lever the shells apart by twisting the knife quickly.
● As you pull the shells apart, take care to retain the liquid in the deeper bottom shell. Oyster liquid is much prized. Detach the oyster from the flatter top shell and place it in the deeper bottom shell, in its liquid.

Serve oysters with lemon wedges, for squeezing, and brown bread and butter, accompanied by a glass of crisp white wine. Alternatively, grill the oysters in their shells with a variety of other flavourings, such as spinach, cheese, cream, cayenne pepper or bacon. Oysters are also delicious in pies and soups.

preparing mussels and clams

Live mussels are now readily available in supermarkets and fishmongers; they are cheap to buy and can be used in many delicious dishes. Much mystery surrounds these tasty shellfish, but now that most are farmed, they need little cleaning and you are very unlikely to get a 'bad' mussel.
● Start by tipping the mussels into a bowl of cold water and picking over each one in turn, scraping off any barnacles with a sharp knife and removing the stringy beards by pulling them off.
● Discard any mussels that are gaping open, unless they close when you tap them on a hard surface.
● Rinse the shells well, scrubbing them with a brush if they are particularly dirty. They are now ready for cooking. Follow the recipe instructions for cooking and discard any mussels that do not open during the cooking process.

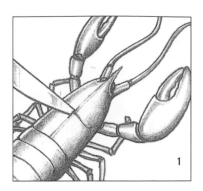 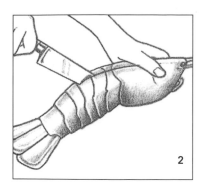 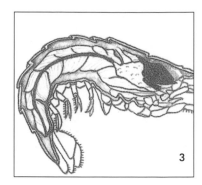

preparing lobster

preparing lobster

There are two ways of killing a lobster. One is to pierce its head, at the well-defined cross mark, with a strong sharp knife. This goes straight into the brain, and kills it instantly. The other method is given below.

● Tie the claws together with string or with a rubber band. If the lobster is alive you may prefer to place it in the freezer for 5–10 minutes prior to cooking, where it will quietly fall asleep.

● Place the lobster, dead or alive, in a large pan of salted water with flavouring vegetables, if liked, and slowly bring to the boil. Cover with a lid and simmer for 15–20 minutes until the dark shell turns bright red.

● Leave the lobster to cool in the cooking liquid.

● Twist off the claws and remove the legs. Using shellfish crackers, or a hammer, crack the claws and pull out the meat.

● Cut away the thin undershell of the tail section using sharp scissors, and carefully pull out the flesh.

● Place the lobster tail on a board and cut in half along its length with a sharp knife. Remove the thin grey vein of intestine running along its length.

● Scrape out the red coral (if present) and reserve.

● If liked, add the liver to the flesh. This is the green-grey flesh near the head, and is delicious.

● Carefully lift out the bony part of the head and break it into pieces. Using a lobster pick or skewer, pick out the flesh and any remaining liver and roe.

● Pull away the grey spongy gills and stomach sac from the top of the head and discard.

● Wash the shell and dry well. This method of preparation means that both the head and tail sections of the lobster may be used to hold and serve the meat.

scallops

Scallops have two shells like mussels: a large, flat fan-shaped shell on which the scallop sits, and a rounded shell in which the scallop is usually served. The flesh consists of a creamish white nugget of firm flesh with a bright orange coral or roe to one side.

Choose large scallops as the smaller ones are underdeveloped. They should look plump and firm and smell very sweet.

● To remove scallops from their shells, insert a strong, short knife between the two shells and twist firmly to prise the shells apart.

● Remove the flat greyish fringe around the scallop, reserving the nugget of white flesh and the orange coral. If it is visible, remove the black digestive cord from the side of the flesh.

● Scallops require very little cooking as the flesh is very tender and becomes tough if it is overcooked. They are best suited to poaching, grilling and stir-frying and lend themselves well to creamy sauces.

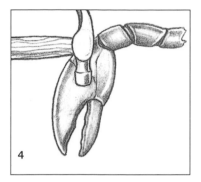

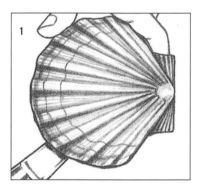

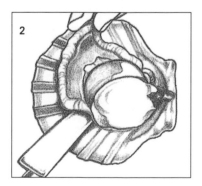

preparing scallops

preparing prawns

Prawns have a grey, hinged shell which turns pink when cooked. Small prawns are usually sold already cooked. Only the body and tail are edible.

● To prepare, pull off the head and legs and carefully peel away the shell on the body and tail.

● If uncooked, simmer the prawns in lightly salted water for 3–5 minutes until pink, then serve in a salad. Alternatively, use raw prawns in sauces or stir-fries, adding them raw to the pan. They will be cooked through in 3–5 minutes.

scampi, langoustines or Dublin Bay prawns

These are about 10 cm/4 inches in length, often with claws, and are a pale pink when raw, turning a deeper pink when cooked.

● Prepare in the same way as small prawns (above), with only the tail section being eaten.

● If uncooked, simmer the prawns in lightly salted water for 8–10 minutes until pink, then serve in a salad. Vegetables such as carrots, celery and fennel can be added to the cooking water to flavour the prawns, if liked. Alternatively, use the raw prawns in sauces or stir-fries, adding them raw to the pan. They will be cooked through in about 10 minutes.

Pacific prawns

The largest of the prawn family, measuring up to 15 cm/6 inches long. The shell is pinkish orange, enclosing fine pink flesh. They are imported frozen, both cooked and uncooked.

● Prepare in the same way as small prawns (above).

● If uncooked, simmer the prawns in lightly salted water for about 15 minutes until bright pink, then serve in a salad with Hollandaise Sauce (see page 144). Vegetables such as carrots, celery and fennel can be added to the cooking water to flavour the prawns, if liked.

● Alternatively, fry the prawns gently in garlic butter for about 10 minutes until cooked through. When cooked, the flesh will be opaque right through. Season with salt and pepper and add a dash of sherry, then serve with crusty bread.

degorging aubergines

preparing and cooking vegetables

Vegetables should really be 'prepared' as little as possible. They are good sources of vitamins and other nutrients, but these tend to concentrate in the outer darker leaves, or just under the skin. Trim vegetables as little as possible and scrub, rather than peel them, where you can.

Many of the nutrients in vegetables, especially Vitamin C, are water-soluble and can be lost in soaking water as well as during cooking. Always wash vegetables, if you have to, as briefly and speedily as possible before cooking. To retain the nutrients, prepare the vegetables as soon as possible before cooking or eating: once exposed to the air, the nutrients start to disappear. Indeed, as soon as it is picked, a vegetable starts to lose its nutrients, the best reason of all for growing your own vegetables.

Steaming is the healthiest way to cook vegetables, but if you boil them, use the minimum amount of water possible and use the cooking water to make gravy or stock.

To boil vegetables perfectly, the rule is to cook root vegetables in cold water to start, with a lid; and to cook green vegetables in hot water to start, with no lid, and refresh in cold water when tender.

degorging aubergines

Modern aubergine varieties are not as bitter as they used to be, but it is still a good idea to degorge them before cooking to draw out any bitter juices.
- Trim the stalk off the aubergine and slice or dice the flesh, as required.
- Place the pieces in a colander, then sprinkle them with salt and turn to make sure they are all coated. Leave for 30 minutes, with the colander standing in the sink, or on a plate to drain. Rinse the salt off the aubergine pieces, then drain thoroughly.

how to skin tomatoes

Tomato skins can be a bit tough, so remove them when making delicate sauces and soups, or special salads and salsas.
- Cut a shallow cross through the skin in the top end of each tomato furthest from the stalk.
- Place the tomatoes in a bowl of boiling water and leave for about 1 minute. The skin should start to come away from the flesh around the cuts.
- Remove one tomato and start to peel away the loosened skin. If it comes away easily, drain the remaining tomatoes and refresh in cold water. If it is not easy to peel the tomato, place it back in the bowl of boiling water and leave for another 15 seconds and try again. Slide the skins off all the tomatoes when they are ready.

vegetables

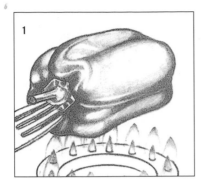

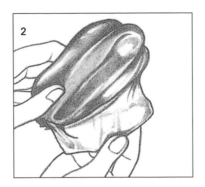

skinning peppers

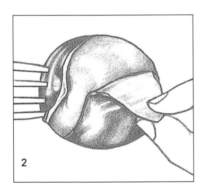

skinning tomatoes

skinning peppers

Pepper skins can be a little tough, so it is desirable to remove them when making smooth sauces or soups, or fresh salads.

- Spear the pepper on a fork and hold it over a gas flame, rotating it occasionally until the skin is blistered and charred on all sides.
- Alternatively, place the pepper on a grill pan under a preheated hot grill and turn occasionally until charred on all sides.
- Place the charred pepper in a plastic bag and leave until cool enough to handle.
- Remove the loosened skin and use the pepper flesh as required.

preparing Brussels sprouts

- Peel off any bruised or damaged outer leaves, removing them at the base with a small sharp knife.
- Trim down the stem if it is very long.
- Make a cross cut in the base of the stem to speed up the cooking process.

preparing Brussels sprouts

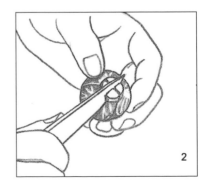

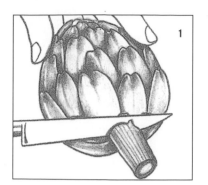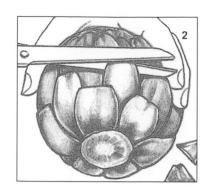

preparing globe artichokes

chopping onions
- Peel away the papery skin and any damaged inner leaves, leaving the root end intact to keep the leaves held together.
- Cut the onion in half lengthways from the top, through the root.
- Place the cut side of one half of the onion on a board. Holding it firmly, cut it into narrow strips from near the root end to the stalk end, leaving the root end uncut so the slices are still held together.
- Turn the onion round and, still holding it firmly, cut slices in the other direction, across the strips, working from the stalk end, so that the onion falls into tiny squares.
- Discard the root end and repeat with the other half of the onion.

preparing globe artichokes
- Cut off the stalk close to the base of the artichoke.
- Trim the points off the lower leaves using sharp kitchen scissors. If you are preparing the artichokes in advance of cooking, rub the cut edges with lemon juice to prevent discoloration.
- Using a sharp knife, cut the top third off the artichoke, to remove the upper leaves.
- Cook the artichokes in lightly salted boiling water for about 10–15 minutes, removing them when they are tender right through.

- Spoon the hairy choke out of the centre of each artichoke and serve them on individual serving plates. Fill the cavity with French Dressing (see page 146) or Hollandaise Sauce (see page 144). Suck the tender flesh from the plump leaves, removing them one at a time from the outside and dipping them in the sauce. Then eat the fleshy heart that remains.
- Alternatively, if you are going to stuff the artichokes, refresh them in cold water after removing from the pan, then remove the hairy chokes from the centres. Stuff the cavities with a stuffing mixture and bake. Serve with a tomato or cream-based sauce.

how to crush garlic with salt
You don't need any special equipment to crush a garlic clove with salt, apart from a heavy knife, and the process results in a very fine paste, suitable for salad dressings, pizza toppings, sauces and salsas.
- Peel the papery skin off the garlic clove and discard it. If this is difficult, merely crush the clove under the flat side of a heavy knife blade; this helps to release the skin from the garlic.
- Place the peeled garlic clove on a chopping board and sprinkle with salt.
- Lay the flat side of a knife blade on the clove and press down heavily with the flat of the hand against the blade, to crush the clove flat.
- Use the side of the tip of the blade to work the garlic and salt to a fine purée.

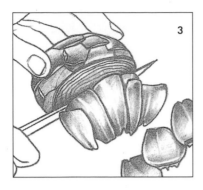

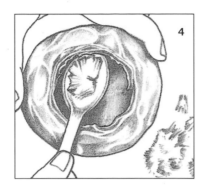

how to cut julienne strips

Julienne strips are vegetables cut into long, thin matchsticks. They are used, either raw or cooked, to garnish dishes. Many vegetables can be prepared in this way including carrots, leeks, celery, spring onions and potatoes. They look very attractive and aren't difficult to achieve.

• Peel and trim the vegetable. If using a rounded vegetable, such as a carrot, cut off the rounded edges to square it up.

• Cut it into even slices, then trim the slices to 5 cm/2 inches. Stack several slices on top of each other and ensure they are all aligned.

• Slice the block of slices vertically and lengthways into 3 mm/$\frac{1}{8}$ inch strips.

• Prepare leeks and spring onions by trimming into 5 cm/2 inch lengths, then slicing the lengths vertically and lengthways into 3 mm/$\frac{1}{8}$ inch slices, keeping the slices together. Rotate the piece of vegetable by a quarter turn and slice in the same way again.

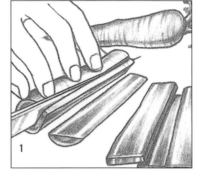

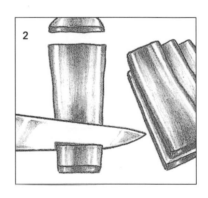

crushing garlic with salt

cutting julienne strips

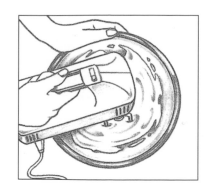

whisking egg whites by hand   *whisking egg whites with an electric whisk*

how to test for freshness

The fresher the egg, the higher its nutritional value. It is best to buy from a reliable source with a quick turnover, and if possible, choose free-range eggs where the birds have been fed on high-quality feed.

Each egg has an air space at the blunt end which increases as the egg ages, therefore the fresher the egg, the smaller the air space. If an egg is placed in a bowl of water, it should lie completely flat at the bottom if it is very fresh. If it tilts up slightly at one end, it is slightly stale, and if it floats to the surface, it should be cracked before use to check it is fresh enough to eat. If it smells bad inside, it should be discarded.

When an egg is broken, the white should be translucent and thickly clinging to the yolk. If the white runs away from the yolk, it is not as fresh as it might be.

storing eggs

Always store eggs in a cool place, preferably not the refrigerator, with the blunt end up and pointed end down. Store away from strong-smelling foods as the porous shell will absorb smells and flavours. Try not to keep eggs for more than two weeks; instead, buy them in smaller quantities to use them up more quickly.

Leftover whites or yolks can be stored in small covered containers in the refrigerator. Yolks, if whole, should be covered with a little water to keep them moist; they should be used within about 24 hours.

the uses of eggs

Eggs have many culinary uses. An egg yolk acts as a binding agent in stuffings, fish cakes and burgers, holding the surrounding ingredients together. They can also be used to aerate a mixture, egg whites having the ability to hold air and increase their volume by many times. This is put to good use in mousses and meringues which rely on air to make them light.

Eggs also act as thickening agents for soups and sauces, as well as in custards where the egg yolk thickens as it is heated, to hold the liquid in suspension. Egg yolks can be used as emulsifiers, holding oil or butter in suspension, keeping the two from separating. This is demonstrated in mayonnaise.

Lastly, whole eggs or egg yolks can be used for coating foods, or glazing them, giving a shiny finish.

how to separate an egg

Always break an egg into a cup or saucer before adding it to the dish, rather than breaking it directly into the food, in case it is bad.

To separate an egg, give the egg a firm, sharp knock against the rim of a basin or cup to break the shell cleanly in half. Carefully pass the yolk from one half of the shell to the other, so that the egg white drops into the basin. Then place the yolk into a separate cup or basin. If the egg yolk breaks, use a very clean teaspoon (or the shell half, as long as it has no egg yolk on it) to remove all specks of yellow from the whites as this will spoil the whisking ability of the whites.

eggs

whisking egg whites

Always have egg whites at room temperature before whisking as this gives better results. Check the recipe before starting to see whether you want the whites to form soft or firm peaks when whisked as this dictates the length of time you have to whisk. Generally, soft peaks are required for soufflés; the whites are whisked until they are slightly translucent and hold soft peaks. For meringues, however, the whites are whisked until they are opaque and hold firm peaks.

It is essential that all the utensils used – the mixing bowl, whisk and spoon – are completely free of grease and very clean. This is because the smallest amount of grease, including traces of egg yolk, can spoil the end result and stop the white from bulking up.

Egg whites can be beaten by hand with a balloon whisk, or with an electric whisk. The former leads to slightly better results, but this is greatly offset by the time and effort involved. A metal spoon or spatula should be used to fold the whisked egg white into whatever it is being added to. This is because it has a sharp, thin edge which cuts through the mixture, rather than squashing the air out of it.

The more egg white is whisked, the more air is incorporated. However, care must be taken not to overwhisk as this can cause the mixture to collapse during cooking. The amount of whisking should be gauged according to the recipe for which it is required. The general rule is that the texture of the egg white should be similar to the consistency of the mixture it is being added to.

Use whisked egg white immediately as it collapses if left for even a short time. If you are interrupted and the whites begin to collapse, simply whisk again until they reach the required texture.

folding in egg whites

When making a soufflé or mousse, it is vital to get the right technique for folding in the egg whites. The aim is to incorporate the whisked egg whites with the soufflé or mousse mixture without losing too much air from them, making the mixture as light as possible.

● First stir a big spoonful of the whites into the mixture to loosen it a little. Then scoop the rest of the whisked egg white on top.

● Using a metal spoon or spatula, cut down into the centre of the bowl.

● With a scooping action, bring the spoon up towards you, turning the mixture from bottom to top. Continue, turning the bowl and working clockwise until the whites are completely folded in.

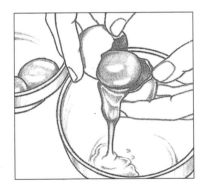

separating an egg

cooking eggs

boiled eggs

Eggs may be soft-, medium- or hard-boiled. Soft-boiled eggs have a softly set white and runny yolk. Medium-boiled eggs have a firmly set white with a just soft yolk, while hard-boiled eggs are firm throughout, the white being dry and the yolk solid.

It is essential when boiling eggs, that the egg is not cold to start with or the shell will crack in hot water. If the eggs are to be peeled, they should be at least a couple of days old, otherwise the white sticks to the shell, making peeling very difficult.

The fresher the eggs are, the longer they need to be cooked to achieve the same results.

To boil, lower eggs at room temperature into boiling water and reduce the heat to simmer. Cook the eggs for 3 minutes for light set and 4½ minutes for a firmer set. Eggs that are to be hard-boiled should be lowered into cold water and slowly brought to the boil. Simmer and time from this point for 10–12 minutes. As soon as the eggs are cooked, place them in a bowl under cold running water. As soon as they are cool, peel and use at once. This method helps prevent the eggs becoming tough and reduces the chance of a dark line forming around the yolk.

poached eggs

There are two methods for poaching eggs: in a deep frying pan filled with simmering water, or in a specially designed poacher, where the eggs are placed in individual cups and steamed over simmering water.

To poach eggs by the frying pan method, pour water into the pan to a depth of about 4 cm/1½ inches and bring to simmering point. Break each egg on to a saucer and gently lower the egg into the water. Cook for about 3 minutes, or until done to your liking. A lid can be used to cover the eggs, or they can be basted with the hot water during cooking. Use a fish slice or slotted spoon to lift the eggs carefully from the pan and drain them well before serving immediately.

To poach eggs in a poacher, place a knob of butter in each cup, half-fill the lower part of the pan with water and place the cups in position. Bring the water to the boil, lower the heat and break the eggs into the cups. Season to taste with salt and pepper. Simmer, covered, for about 4–5 minutes. Loosen each egg with a blunt-ended knife and tip the eggs out of the cups.

scrambled eggs

The art of scrambling eggs is not to overcook or overstir the mixture. The eggs should form large, creamy flakes when done.

For two people, break three or four eggs into a bowl and whisk lightly with a fork. Season with salt and pepper and stir in 2 tablespoons of milk or single cream. Melt about 25 g/1 oz of butter in a small pan over a low heat. Pour in the eggs and leave for about 30 seconds before gently stirring with a wooden spoon. Cook for a further 30 seconds–1 minute, stirring, until the eggs are just set. Serve immediately.

 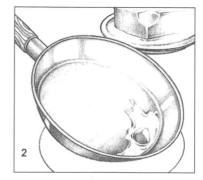

making an omelette

baked eggs

Eggs cooked in this way are cooked in individual ramekin or cocotte dishes. Lightly grease the dishes with a little butter. Place them in a roasting tin with 2.5 cm/1 inch of warm water in it. Break an egg into each dish and season well. Dot the surface with a little butter or a tablespoon or two of cream.

Cook in a preheated oven, 180°C (350°F), Gas Mark 4, for 8–10 minutes until the eggs are just set. Remove from the water at once, as they will continue cooking, and serve immediately. These eggs are even nicer if you place a small amount of flaked fish, fried onion or cooked bacon in the bottom of each ramekin before breaking the eggs on top.

omelettes

A good omelette should be lightly cooked, with a golden-brown outside and a creamy soft inside.

For best results, an omelette pan or round-sided frying pan should be used. The pan should be reserved for making omelettes and should not be washed after use, just wiped clean with kitchen paper.

To make the perfect omelette, make sure the butter is foaming before the egg is added so that it cooks the egg as soon as it reaches the pan. However, it is essential that the heat is not too high or the egg will toughen and the omelette will be ruined.

basic omelette

2 eggs
1 tablespoon cold water
15 g/½ oz butter
salt and pepper

1 Break the eggs into a basin and whisk lightly with a balloon whisk.

2 Whisk in the water and season well with salt and pepper. Do not overbeat as this will ruin the texture of the finished omelette.

3 Place the pan over a gentle heat and, when it is hot, add the butter. Tip the pan so that the entire inner surface is coated with the butter. When the butter is foaming, but not coloured, tip in the eggs.

4 Leave for about 2 seconds, then using a palette knife, draw the setting mixture away from the edge of the pan into the centre, allowing the egg to run into the sides. Repeat the process twice more, by which time the egg should have set. Cook for a further 30 seconds until the underside is golden brown and the top still slightly runny and creamy.

5 Tilt the pan, and with the help of the palette knife, carefully turn the omelette on to a plate, folding it in half in the process.

Serves 1
Preparation time: about 2 minutes
Cooking time: 2 minutes

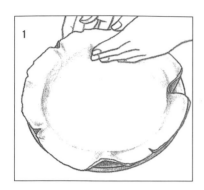
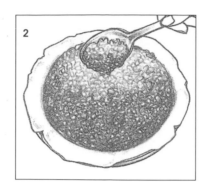

filling a pie

Pastry-making is one of the skills which every cook should master. There are no secrets to guarantee instant success, but with a little care, and plenty of practice, it can be a quick and simple process.

basic rules

Plain flour is used for all pastries, except suet crust. Wholemeal flour can be used for most pastries but extra water will be needed to bind it, and the pastry will be heavier. Self-raising flour can be used, but the pastry will be sponge-like in texture when baked. The fats used should be butter, for flavour, or hard margarine. Lard can be used in some pastries to give a short, crisp texture when baking. If using lard, use a quarter or a third of the total fat content. Choose hard fats as they are easier to rub in – avoid soft spreading margarines and vegetable fats.

One of the best tips for successful results is to keep everything cool. Pastry should be made as quickly as possible, handled with speed and agility. The fats should be cold when used and chilled water will help to keep the pastry cold while working with it.

When rubbing the fat into the flour, always use only the fingertips, as these are the coolest parts of the hand. A food processor or food mixer will give the same results in seconds.

The amount of water added to the pastry will vary each time as some flours will absorb more water than others. But make sure that the right amount of water is added, as too dry a mixture will make the pastry crumbly and impossible to handle, and too wet a mixture will make a tough, hard result to eat. Add the water a little at a time, stirring it quickly into the flour with a round-bladed knife. Turn the dough out of the bowl on to a lightly floured work surface and knead quickly until smooth, handling the pastry as little as possible. Wrap in clingfilm and chill for 10–15 minutes before using – this allows the pastry to firm up and relax before being used, and makes rolling easier.

rolling out

Roll out carefully using light even pressure with both hands on the rolling pin – light flowing movements are better than heavy abrupt actions. Always roll away from yourself. Keep the pastry in a round shape and lift and turn it often to make sure that it does not stick to the work surface and that it keeps its shape. Sprinkle with a little flour to prevent it sticking to the table or rolling pin, but do not turn the pastry over, as this will incorporate too much flour into the pastry. Before baking, the pastry should be lightly chilled in its finished shape to prevent excessive shrinkage in the oven.

filling a pie

Filling a pie is the same whatever pastry you use. Flaky, suet crust or shortcrust pastries are the best. Generally, the filling should be cooked before it is put into the pie, so that when you put the pie in the oven, you can choose the oven temperature and cooking time most suited to just cooking the pastry to perfection, without having to worry whether the filling is cooked.
- Cut the pastry in half and roll out one half to a circle

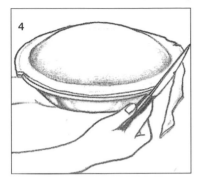

about 8 cm/3 inches wider than the pie dish. Use the circle to line the greased pie dish, placing it gently in position without stretching the pastry in the process. Use the rolling pin to help support the pastry as you manoeuvre it.

● Spoon the filling into the pie, doming it in the middle. Make sure the filling is not too wet or it will bubble up and leak out of the pie during cooking.

● Brush the edges of the pastry around the filling with beaten egg.

● Roll out the remaining pastry to a circle just slightly bigger than the pie dish and lay it on top of the pie, again taking care not to stretch the pastry. Press the edges together all around the pie to seal, then trim off the excess with a sharp knife.

● Roll out the pastry trimmings and cut shapes to decorate the top of the pie. Stick them in place with beaten egg, then brush the pie all over with more beaten egg. Make a small hole in the pie lid to allow the steam to escape, before baking the pie according to the recipe instructions.

lining a flan tin

● Choose a flan tin with a loose bottom, or a flan ring used on a baking sheet. China flan dishes do not conduct the heat quickly enough.

● Roll the pastry out thinly, about 3 mm/$\frac{1}{8}$ inch thick, to a circle 4 cm/1½ inches larger than the diameter of the flan tin.

● Lift the pastry on the rolling pin and lower it into the flan tin or ring. Press it carefully into the base and sides, taking care not to stretch it at any time.

● Trim the edges, using a rolling pin to roll the pastry level with the rim.

● Prick the base with a fork to allow any steam to escape while cooking.

● Chill the lined flan tin for at least 10 minutes.

making pastry

baking blind

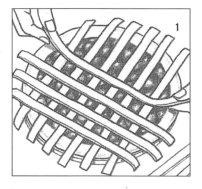

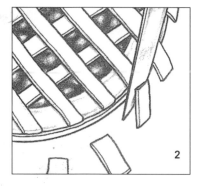

making a pastry lattice

baking blind
● The flan case is baked blind when the filling is to be cooked for only a short time or not at all, so the case has to be cooked separately and the base prevented from rising.
● Line the pastry case with greaseproof paper, foil, or a double layer of absorbent kitchen paper.
● Weight it down with dried beans (kept specially for this purpose, they can be used indefinitely). You can also buy special ceramic or aluminium beans. Take care to put in enough beans to compensate for the filling. Push them well to the edges to support and hold up the sides.
● Bake the pastry case in the centre of a preheated oven, 200°C (400°F), Gas Mark 6, for about 10–15 minutes.
● Remove the beans and paper and bake for a further 10 minutes or until the pastry is dry and golden-brown.
● Allow to cool on a wire rack before carefully removing from the flan tin.

pastry decorations

making a lattice top for open flans
● Line the pie dish or flan tin with pastry, and add the filling in the usual way. Roll out the pastry trimmings and cut them into 0.5–1 cm/^{1}/$_4$–^{1}/$_2$ inch wide strips, long enough to cover the flan.
● Moisten the edges of the flan case with water or beaten egg, then lay half the pastry strips across the filling, about 2.5 cm/1 inch apart. Press the ends on to the edges of the flan case to secure.
● Rotate the flan by a quarter turn, then repeat the process, laying the remaining pastry strips over the flan at right angles to the first set. Press the ends of the strips firmly in place.
● Trim off the excess pastry from around the flan with a sharp knife.
● For a more decorative effect, cut the strips a little longer and twist them before laying on top of the flan. Seal and trim as before.

decorative pastry leaves
● Cut some rolled pastry into strips about 2.5 cm/1 inch across, or larger if you prefer.
● Cut the strips diagonally across into diamond-shaped pieces.
● Mark the diamonds with the back of a knife to indicate the veins of a leaf.

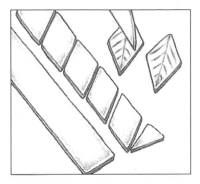

pastry leaves

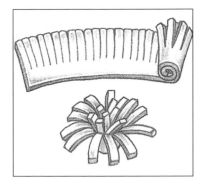

making a tassel for a pie

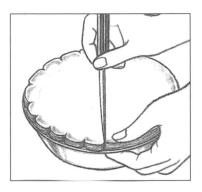

making a scalloped edge to a pie

making a tassel for a pie

● Cut some rolled pastry into a strip about 5 cm/2 inches across. Make a series of cuts across the strip at intervals of 5 mm/¼ inch, cutting just three-quarters of the way across.

● Roll up the strip neatly, then open out like a flower. Stick the tassel on top of a pie to decorate it.

to make a scalloped edge

● To make a scalloped edge to a pie or flan, press a thumb around the edges of the pie at 1 cm/½ inch intervals, drawing a knife between each thumb print back towards the centre of the pie to form a scalloped edge. Alternatively, use thumb and index finger to crimp the edges of the pie.

choux pastry

Choux pastry, used in profiteroles and chocolate eclairs, is softer than other pastries and is shaped with a spoon or a piping bag rather than rolled out. When cooked, it swells into crisp, golden shells that are hollow inside. The secret of making shells that will hold their shape is to make sure the pastry is cooked and dry right through.

50 g/2 oz butter or margarine
150 ml/¼ pint water
65 g/2½ oz plain flour, sifted
2 eggs, beaten

Melt the fat in a large pan, add the water and bring to the boil. When boiling well, remove from the heat and immediately add the flour all at once, beating hard until the mixture leaves the sides of the pan. Cool slightly, then add the eggs a little at a time, beating vigorously between each addition until all the egg is incorporated and the paste is smooth.

Preparation time: 10 minutes

making choux pastry

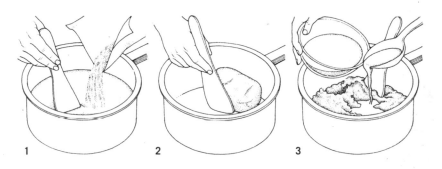

1   2   3

making shortcrust pastry

shortcrust pastry

This is the easiest of all pastry doughs and a favourite for both savoury and sweet pies.

175 g/6 oz plain flour
pinch of salt
75 g/3 oz butter, cut into 1 cm/½ inch cubes
2–3 tablespoons cold water

1 Mix together the flour, salt and butter with your fingertips or in a food processor until the mixture resembles fine breadcrumbs.

2 Add the water, a tablespoon at a time, until the dough binds together and knead it carefully. Wrap the dough in clingfilm and chill for 30 minutes.

Preparation time: 10 minutes, plus chilling

suet crust pastry

This is made by the same method as shortcrust, with twice as much flour as fat. Suet crust should be used immediately, once it is made.

350 g/12 oz self-raising flour
pinch of salt
175 g/6 oz shredded suet
175 ml/6 fl oz cold water

1 Sift the flour and salt into a bowl. Stir in the suet until coated evenly in the flour.

2 Stir in the water with a knife to form a soft pliable dough. Knead on a floured surface until smooth, then roll out and use at once. (This pastry does not need to rest.)

Preparation time: 10 minutes

making suet crust pastry

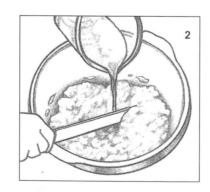
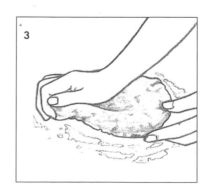

flaky pastry

This pastry has a light, flaky texture because of the way the fat is incorporated.

250 g/8 oz plain flour
pinch of salt
175 g/6 oz butter
about 125 ml/4 fl oz cold water

1 Sift the flour and salt together in a mixing bowl. Cut a quarter of the butter into small cubes and rub into the flour until the mixture resembles fine breadcrumbs.

2 Mix to a soft pliable dough with the water. Turn on to a lightly floured surface and knead until smooth.

3 Roll out the pastry to an oblong 10 x 30 cm/4 x 12 inches and mark into 3 sections. Cut the remaining butter into small cubes and cover the top two-thirds of the pastry with one-third of the butter. Fold the bottom third over the centre and the top third over the middle section and press the open ends together to seal.

4 Give the pastry a quarter turn and roll out again. Repeat twice more, using half of the remaining butter each time in the same way. Roll again and fold as before, but without any fat. Chill for 10–15 minutes. Roll out and fold again if still streaky. Use as required.

Preparation time: 25 minutes, plus chilling

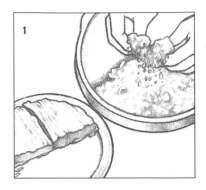

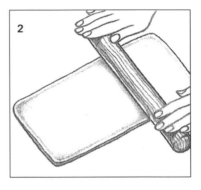

making flaky pastry

batters

The literal translation of batter is 'to beat'. This name is given to mixtures of flour with sufficient liquid to give a cream-like consistency. Batters are used to make Yorkshire pudding, pancakes, fritters, drop scones and sometimes cakes.

basic batter

This is the batter to use for Yorkshire pudding (see page 100); the same recipe can be used for toad in the hole.

125 g/4 oz plain flour
pinch of salt
1 egg
just under 300 ml/½ pint milk
2 tablespoons water

1 Sift the flour and salt into a mixing bowl, make a well in the centre and break the egg into it.

2 Mix the milk and water together, add a quarter of the milk to the well and, using a wooden spoon, draw the flour into the centre, beating well to incorporate the flour completely into the egg and liquid.

3 Gradually beat in the remaining milk, beating well between additions, to form a smooth batter. Leave to stand for 15 minutes.

Preparation time: 10 minutes, plus standing

toad in the hole
For toad in the hole, pour a little oil into an 18 cm/7 inch roasting tin. Place in a preheated oven, 220°C (425°F), Gas Mark 7, for 5–7 minutes until the oil is smoking.
   Place 6 cooked sausages in the tin. Pour the batter into the tin around the sausages, and cook for about 25 minutes until well risen and golden brown.

making pancakes

basic pancakes

The Basic Batter recipe can also be used to make pancakes. This amount of batter will make 12 pancakes, using an 18 cm/7 inch pancake or crêpe pan.

a little oil, for frying
1 quantity Basic Batter (see opposite)

1 Heat a little oil in a frying pan until really hot, running it around to coat the pan. Pour off any excess.

2 Pour or spoon just enough batter into the pan to cover the base, to give a thin even layer.

3 Cook quickly until tiny bubbles form on the upper surface of the pancake, and the underside is golden-brown.

4 Toss or turn the pancake over and cook the other side for about 1 minute until golden-brown.

5 Slip the pancake out of the pan, and keep warm inside a tea towel on a plate. Use as required. Repeat the process with the remaining batter, adding more oil as necessary.

6 If the pancakes are to be used at a later date, they may be stacked on top of each other, interleaved with greaseproof paper or foil, and frozen.

Makes 12 pancakes
Preparation time: 10 minutes, plus standing
Cooking time: about 25 minutes

crêpes

The batter for crêpes is richer than a normal pancake mixture. It is enriched with butter and is lighter in texture. This recipe is particularly light, making crêpes that are so thin they are transparent. They are very similar to the delicious crêpes sold on the streets of Normandy and Brittany.

3 eggs
125 g/4 oz plain flour
300 ml/½ pint milk
2 tablespoons melted butter
pinch of salt
a little oil, for frying

1 Place the eggs in the goblet of an electric blender.

2 Sprinkle the flour over the eggs, then add the milk, melted butter and salt.

3 Blend for 2 minutes on high. Leave to stand for 30 minutes.

4 To cook, follow the instructions for Basic Pancakes (left).

Makes 12–14 crêpes
Preparation time: 5 minutes, plus standing
Cooking time: about 25 minutes

Bread-making is one of the most satisfying of activities, yet most people are frightened of ever trying it. Follow the guidelines for using yeast, be patient and you will find it surprisingly easy.

Bread is basically a mixture of flour and water, leavened with yeast and baked in the oven. Bread can be made with wheat, rye or barley flour; you can also use buckwheat flour or cornmeal. It can even be cooked without yeast (unleavened) or risen with baking soda instead of yeast.

The most important lesson in bread-making is to learn about yeast. For successful results, you must wait for the yeast to be activated, allow the dough time to rise properly, and wait for the dough to prove after shaping. In fact, you could say that patience is the secret of bread-making. See pages 538–543 in the Baking section for bread dough recipes.

yeast

In general, there are two types of yeast suitable for bread-making.

fresh yeast
Fresh yeast is the yeast most often used by bakers. It is putty-coloured, smooth-textured and moist, and will cut easily with a knife, or will crumble readily when broken. It should smell fresh and slightly fruity, rather like wine. If it is already crumbly, dark or spotty, it is stale and not suitable for use. Fresh yeast is available in health-food shops, some baker's shops and supermarkets with an in-store bakery section.

It stays fresh for 4–5 days if stored in a loosely tied polythene bag in the refrigerator.

dried yeast
Dried yeast comes as small granules of compacted yeast and is sold in tins or packets which will keep for up to 6 months after opening if kept in an airtight container. There are always activating instructions on the packet or tin, and it is essential that the yeast is properly activated before adding to the dry ingredients or the dough will not rise.

It can be reconstituted in warm liquid with a little sugar added. It is then left in a warm place until the granules have dissolved and the liquid froths up – this usually takes 10–20 minutes. If the yeast does not froth up it is a sign the yeast is stale and should be discarded. Dried yeast is widely available. If substituting dried for fresh yeast, halve the quantity specified in the recipe.

fast-action dried yeast
'Fast-action' or 'easy-blend' dried yeast is a kind of granular dried yeast which is quick-acting and does not need to be reconstituted with liquid. It is simply mixed into the flour before the liquid is poured in. There are several varieties on the market, so simply follow the manufacturer's instructions.

activating fresh yeast

using dried yeast

bread

to activate the yeast
The liquid for bread-making is usually water, milk or a mixture of the two. The liquid, or part of it, is used to dissolve the yeast, and it must be warm – 37–43°C (98–110°F) – to make the yeast work. If it is too cool, the yeast will not be activated, and if too hot will simply kill the yeast. When the yeast looks frothy or 'sponges' you know it is working.

flour

A strong white, gluten-rich flour called a bread flour or strong flour should be used for bread-making. The higher gluten content of strong flour allows more absorption of liquid thus giving a greater volume and lighter bread.

Quite apart from the plain strong white flours, numerous other types of strong flour are available: wholewheat, wholemeal, granary and so on. These will produce a heavier, nuttier-tasting loaf.

making bread

kneading
All doughs must be kneaded after mixing to strengthen and develop the gluten in order to give a good rise and even texture to the baked loaf.

To knead dough, you form the dough into a ball and punch it down and away from you using the palm of your hand, then fold it over towards you and give it a quarter turn. Repeat until smooth and even and the dough feels elastic and is no longer sticky. This should take about 10 minutes (or as the recipe directs), and as you knead, it is possible to develop a rhythmic, rocking movement. Knead on a lightly floured surface, using as little extra flour as possible. You can also use an electric mixer with a dough hook.

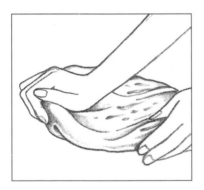

kneading bread dough by hand

kneading bread dough in an electric mixer

rising

All yeast doughs must rise at least once before baking. After kneading, the dough should be shaped into a ball and placed in a large, lightly oiled polythene bag loosely tied at the neck. It could also be put into a lightly greased bowl or plastic storage container. This must be large enough for the dough to double in size at least, and the dough must be kept covered to prevent a skin forming; either use a damp cloth, polythene, which has been lightly oiled, or clingfilm.

Rising times vary with room temperature. Allow 45–60 minutes in a warm place, 2 hours at room temperature, up to 12 hours in a cold room or larder, or up to 24 hours in the refrigerator. Remember that chilled dough must be allowed to return to room temperature before shaping. Surplus dough can be stored in a closed polythene bag or container in the refrigerator for up to 24 hours before use.

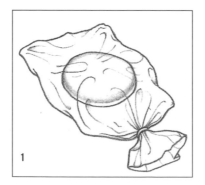

first rising of the dough

knocking back

This is simply a short second kneading of the dough which takes place after the first rising to knock out any large air bubbles and make it smooth and even, ready for shaping. It should only take 1–2 minutes: push down into the risen dough with your closed fist, then push the sides into the centre.

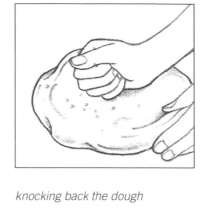

knocking back the dough

shaping and proving

The dough is now ready for shaping. Follow the recipe instructions for whatever type of dough you are making. This often takes place in a loaf tin, ready for baking. The shaped dough then requires a second rising (or proving). Proving usually takes 10–15 minutes in a warm kitchen. Put the loaf tins, cake tins or baking sheets into large oiled polythene bags or lay a sheet of oiled polythene loosely over them to prevent a skin forming; put in a warm place until the dough has doubled in size again and springs back when lightly pressed with a floured finger. Don't forget to remove the polythene before baking the bread.

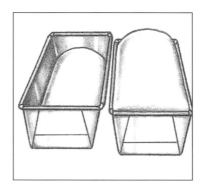

shaping and proving

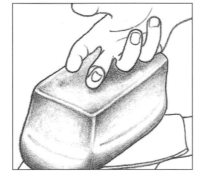

testing if the loaf is cooked

glazing

A glaze can be added to loaves or rolls before baking. Beaten egg, milk, salted water or a dredging of flour each give different finishes, and the loaves can also be sprinkled before baking with poppy seeds, sesame seeds, cracked wheat, oatmeal and so on.

baking

Most bread doughs are baked in a hot to very hot oven.

A cooked loaf should shrink slightly away from the sides of the tin. When it is turned out, the base should sound hollow when tapped with the knuckles. If the loaf is cooked, cool on a wire rack. If it is not cooked, replace it in the tin and continue cooking for a few minutes. (Some loaves benefit from a few minutes baking out of the tin: this gives a good crust.)

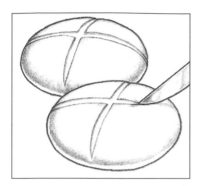

coburg loaves

making a cottage loaf

loaf shapes

There are many shapes of loaf which can be made simply from basic white or brown bread dough.

coburg

Shape half the recipe quantity of risen bread dough into a round ball. This is done by rolling the dough in a circular movement with the palm of your hand and gradually easing the pressure to give a smooth round ball – it takes practice to perfect. Place on a greased baking sheet and, if liked, brush all over with milk or beaten egg. With a sharp knife, cut a cross on top of the loaf. Set aside to prove as usual.

cob

This is a plain round loaf, again using half the basic recipe of risen bread dough. It is usually glazed and sprinkled with seeds, and used to be mainly made of brown dough. Sometimes the top of the loaf is slashed once across the top before proving.

cottage

The famous round loaf with a top-knot. Use a recipe quantity for a large loaf or divide it in two for smaller loaves. Remove one-third of the dough for the top-knot. Shape both pieces into round balls and place the larger piece on a greased baking sheet and flatten it slightly. Dampen the base of the top-knot and position it centrally on top of the large ball of dough; secure it by pushing two fingers right through the centre of the loaf to the base, taking care to keep the top-knot quite central. Brush with beaten egg or salted water and put to prove.

For a fancy notched cottage loaf, after shaping, make slashes all round the lower part of the loaf at an angle; and then around the top-knot.

plait

For whatever sized loaf you require, divide the dough into 3 equal portions and with the palms of the hands roll them into fairly thin, even sausage shapes of equal length. For thicker plaits simply roll the sausages thicker. Place the 3 pieces of dough next to each other on a greased baking sheet straight in front of you. Beginning in the centre, plait the pieces evenly towards you and pinch the ends together firmly. Carefully turn the baking sheet round so that the unplaited strands face you. Complete the plaiting, secure the ends by pinching together, and tuck the ends underneath the loaf. Plaits can be baked plain or glazed with milk, beaten egg or salted water, and then sprinkled, before baking, with poppy or sesame seeds for variety.

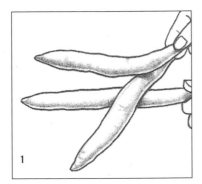

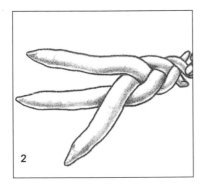

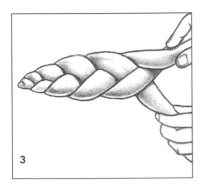

making a plait

bloomer

This is a long, fat, torpedo-shaped loaf with diagonal slashes along the top. It is usually crusty and can be sprinkled with poppy or sesame seeds. Use 1 recipe quantity of risen dough, or half the dough for smaller loaves. Shape each piece into an even thickness loaf by rolling the dough backwards and forwards with the palms of the hands. Tuck the ends underneath and place on a greased baking sheet. If liked, brush with milk, beaten egg or salted water, then cover with oiled polythene and put to prove until doubled in size. Remove the polythene, cut diagonal slashes all along the top of the loaf with a very sharp knife and bake for 30–40 minutes depending on size.

basic pizza dough

250 g/8 oz strong plain flour, plus extra for dusting
½ teaspoon salt
½ teaspoon fast-action dried yeast
125 ml/4 fl oz warm water
1 tablespoon olive oil, plus extra for oiling

1 Sift the flour and salt into a large bowl and stir in the dried yeast. Make a well in the centre and gradually stir in the measured water and oil to form a soft dough.

2 Turn out on to a lightly floured surface and knead for 8–10 minutes until smooth and elastic. Place in an oiled bowl; turn once to coat the dough with oil and cover with oiled clingfilm. Leave to rise in a warm, draught-free place for 45 minutes or until doubled in size.

3 Lightly knead the risen dough and divide and roll out as the recipe requires.

Makes two 23 cm/9 inch pizza bases
Preparation time: 15–20 minutes, plus rising

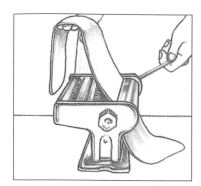

*rolling out the dough in a
pasta machine*

The word *pasta* means 'dough' in Italian, and is the
generic name for all forms of spaghetti, macaroni, ravioli
and so on. Choose from an amazing variety of dried
pasta shapes or make your own fresh pasta as described
here – it's much easier than you might think.

pasta shapes

Although pasta comes in what appears to be a
bewildering assortment of shapes and sizes, all these
may be classified as long and narrow, short and broad,
flat or tubular, solid or hollow, smooth or ridged. These
various shapes are not merely decorative, they are
specifically designed to affect the texture, character and
taste of the pasta, and determine how it will be served,
as each pasta shape has a certain form of sauce it will
particularly suit, or a filling that has been specifically
designed for it.

basic egg pasta dough

*Homemade pasta is very simple to make and has a
completely different texture and taste to dried pasta.*

**500 g/1 lb plain flour
large pinch of fine salt
2 large or 3 medium eggs
1 teaspoon olive oil
3–4 tablespoons water**

1 Sift the flour and salt into a large bowl (using
one attached to a large electric mixer will save you
kneading).

2 Make a well in the centre and drop in the eggs. Add
the oil, and draw the flour into the centre using your
hand. Gradually add the water, a tablespoon at a time. It
may not be necessary to add all the water, as this
depends on how absorbent the flour is. Knead to a firm
smooth dough (firmer than a pastry or bread dough).

3 Continue kneading until the dough is very elastic,
smooth and shiny – about 15–20 minutes by hand. (A
dough hook is ideal for this.) It is essential to knead the
dough very thoroughly so that it rolls out evenly without
breaking up.

4 Wrap the dough in clingfilm and leave to rest for a
minimum of 15 minutes and a maximum of 2 hours,
before using.

**Makes 500 g/1 lb
Preparation time:** about 25 minutes

rolling out pasta dough

Either roll out the dough on a lightly floured board or marble slab, or with a pasta machine. If using a machine, follow the manufacturer's instructions. The more the pasta is rolled, the better the end result. Rolling not only ensures that the dough is even in thickness but also helps to make it more elastic, essential when making pasta. It is often easier to do this in two batches.

● Place the kneaded dough on a floured board and flatten it with a very long floured rolling pin. Roll out, giving the dough a quarter turn between each rolling, always rolling away from yourself, until the dough measures 20–30 cm/8–12 inches in diameter. It should be about 3 mm/⅛ inch thick.

● This next stage takes a little practice. The objective is to stretch the pasta with a sideways pressure of the hands as you wrap it around the rolling pin. Curl the far end of the sheet of pasta around the centre of the rolling pin, and roll it towards you, with both of the palms of the hands cupped over the centre of the rolling pin. When about a quarter of the dough has been rolled on to the rolling pin, do not roll any more.

● Quickly roll the rolling pin backwards and forwards and at the same time slide the palms of your hands away from each other, towards the end of the rolling pin. Do not roll the dough but stretch it all the time.

● Continue rolling up until all the dough has been stretched and wrapped around the rolling pin. Give the rolling pin a quarter turn, so that it points towards you, and unfurl the sheet of dough, to open it out flat.

● Repeat the rolling and stretching until the dough is again wrapped around the rolling pin. Give the dough a quarter turn and unwrap as before.

● Continue the process until the sheet of dough measures 40–45 cm/16–18 inches square.

● This process must be done with great speed to prevent the dough drying out as it will be ruined. Roll out the dough paper-thin and use as required.

rolling the dough by hand

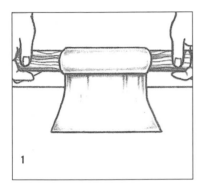

First curl the dough round the rolling pin and stretch

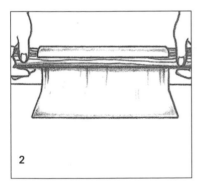

Next turn the dough sideways and roll and stretch again

pasta

 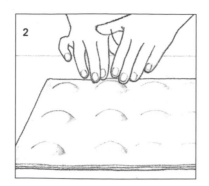 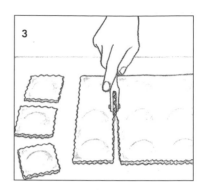

making ravioli

making ravioli

Ravioli are little pockets of fresh pasta dough, either round or square, stuffed with a filling and boiled. The choice of fillings is endless, though many are based on ricotta cheese. See pages 382–384 for some filling suggestions.

Ravioli can be cut out individually using special ravioli stamps which are available in many sizes and shapes. Special ravioli trays are also available, which are metal trays with square indentations. A sheet of pasta is laid on the tray, then the filling is spread on top. The second sheet of pasta is used to cover the filling, then a rolling pin is passed over the tray, sealing the edges between the pockets of filling and dividing the ravioli up in one go.

However, they can also be cut out simply with a knife, or a pasta wheel, with a fluted or straight edge.

- Make the pasta dough according to the recipe on page 134 and leave to rest.
- Divide the dough in half, wrap one piece in clingfilm and set aside. Roll out the remaining piece thinly on a lightly floured board to form a neat rectangle.
- Place teaspoonfuls of the filling mixture in lines about 5 cm/2 inches apart on the rolled dough. Brush the pasta with beaten egg between the mounds of filling.
- Roll out the second piece of pasta dough slightly larger than the first and carefully lay it over the top, pressing it down between the filling to seal.
- Using a pastry wheel or knife, cut around the mounds of filling to give ravioli squares.
- Check that each one is thoroughly sealed on all sides, then place on a floured board to dry for 15 minutes before cooking.
- Cook in lightly salted boiling water for 5–7 minutes, or until al dente (see below), or according to recipe instructions.

making tagliatelle

Tagliatelle strips are easily cut from fresh pasta dough. In fact, they are the easiest of pastas to shape.

- Make the pasta dough according to the recipe on page 134 and leave to rest.
- Roll out the pasta thinly on a lightly floured board and form into a rectangle shape. If it is easier, divide the dough in half first and roll out one piece at a time.
- Flour the top of the rectangle lightly, then roll up loosely.
- Cut the roll into even slices, about 1 cm/½ inch thick, or to the thickness you prefer.
- Open out the rolls to form long strips. Drape the strips on a pasta dryer or over the back of a chair for about 30 minutes to dry before cooking.

cooking spaghetti

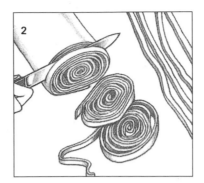
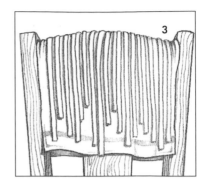

making tagliatelle

cooking pasta

Pasta should always be cooked in plenty of boiling salted water. Allow at least 4 litres/7 pints of water for every 500 g/1 lb of pasta.

The water should be boiling rapidly when the pasta is added, and returned to the boil as quickly as possible.

When adding long pasta, such as spaghetti, hold it in a bunch at one end and coil the strands around the sides of the pan as they soften until all the pasta is in the pan.

Do not cover the pan, as there is more chance of the water boiling over if the lid is on.

Always test the pasta throughout cooking and as soon as it is 'al dente', or tender with a slight bite in the centre, drain it immediately into a large colander. The pasta will continue cooking after draining, so always allow for this. There should be no need to wash it in either boiling or cold water, which will spoil it, just toss the cooked pasta in butter or oil.

suggested cooking times

Check with manufacturer's instructions for bought pasta, if available; the following times are a rough guide for dried pasta.

Spaghetti: 9 minutes
Long macaroni: 10 minutes
Lasagne: 10 minutes (add a sheet at a time)
Cannelloni: 10–12 minutes
Ravioli: 15 minutes
Tagliatelle: 10 minutes
Vermicelli: 5 minutes

Fresh pasta needs much less time – from a few minutes for unfilled types to 8–10 minutes for the stuffed varieties.

Some manufacturers produce a dried lasagne which requires no pre-cooking like fresh lasagne (the dried usually needs to be boiled before baking). Always allow a little extra sauce to moisten it, and help it to cook.

storing pasta

Fresh or homemade pasta should be eaten preferably on the day it is purchased or made but it can be stored in the refrigerator for up to 24 hours. The dough, or shaped dough, stores well in the freezer for up to three months.

Dried pasta keeps well in sealed jars or containers for up to 9 months. Ensure that the storage container is dry and airtight. It is best to store pasta in a dark, dry cupboard.

Most varieties of white rice should be washed before cooking. This ensures that the loose starch, which is a white powder, is removed. If the rice is not washed it is more likely that the grains will stick together. Put the rice in a large sieve and rinse under cold running water, until the water running through the sieve is clear.

There are several methods of cooking rice. It is a matter of choice which one you use, and will depend also on the type of rice used. If possible, follow the manufacturer's instructions.

absorption method

This is an easy way of cooking rice, and it ensures that the grains stay separate and fluffy. Both white and brown rices can be cooked in this way, but the brown rice will take longer.

• Measure the amount of rice required in a cup, and for each cup of rice use two cups of water or stock plus ½ teaspoon of salt.

• Bring the water to the boil in a large saucepan, add the salt and then the rice, which has been washed under cold running water, and stir well to separate the grains.

• As soon as the water boils, reduce the heat, cover with a very tight-fitting lid, and cook for 15 minutes (45 for brown). Do not be tempted to lift the lid at all during the time, or the steam will escape, and alter the cooking time required.

• When the 15 or 45 minutes have elapsed the rice will be perfectly cooked, the liquid completely absorbed and the rice tender and fluffy. Stir in a small knob of butter and use immediately.

the absorption method

preparing & cooking rice

 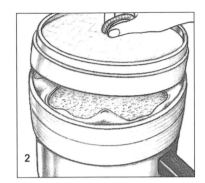

steaming rice

steaming

Steaming is a popular Chinese method of cooking rice so that the grains stay separate and fluffy.

● First soak the rice in cold water for at least 1 hour, then drain it.

● Fill the bottom half of a steamer, or a large saucepan, with water.

● Line the steamer, or a Chinese steamer basket, with muslin. Spoon in the rice and fold the muslin ends over the top of the rice.

● Cover and steam for 25–30 minutes, or until the rice is just tender.

boiling rice

Per 50 g/2 oz rice, use 600 ml/1 pint of water and ½ teaspoon of salt.

● Bring the water to the boil, add the salt, sprinkle in the rice, return to the boil and simmer for 12–13 minutes (25 for brown) until 'al dente' (see page 137).

● A tablespoon of oil in the water helps to prevent it boiling over and the rice grains from sticking together.

● Drain the rice in a sieve, return it to the saucepan, stir in a knob of butter and serve immediately.

To simplify draining, the rice can also be cooked in a rice boiler which is suspended by a chain which hooks over the side of the pan. Cook as for boiling rice, above. When the rice is cooked simply lift the boiler out of the pan and drain.

a rice boiler

making stock

A good stock is the foundation of all good soups, gravies and sauces. It is simple to make and, when stored in the refrigerator or freezer, it is as handy as any stock cube and much more flavoursome.

The basic ingredients are usually the raw bones of meat, fish, poultry or game, with added vegetables, herbs and seasonings, with perhaps a splash of wine or sherry to give additional flavour.

Stock cubes or powder are no substitute for a richly-flavoured homemade stock. They taint the finished dish with a distinctive artificial flavour which ruins the taste of the recipe.

basic rules

There are a few basic rules to remember when making stock. First, all the ingredients should be very fresh and of good quality. The stock should be simmered for several hours to give a well-flavoured, full-bodied consistency.

Secondly, never allow a stock to boil rapidly as this will spoil the clarity of it. A long, slow simmer produces a much better result. The longer the stock is cooked, the better the flavour, as the liquid reduces during cooking which concentrates the taste and makes it more likely that the stock will gel.

Never add salt until you are actually using the stock, as cooking and reducing the stock will concentrate the flavour and you could end up with very salty stock.

Always use a pan with a tight-fitting lid to ensure that the liquid does not evaporate too much, but allow the stock to cool with the lid half on.

It is important to remove any excess fat from meat and bones before cooking to prevent the stock becoming greasy. Once the stock is cooked, leave it to cool, then refrigerate for a couple of hours, when any fat will settle on the surface. It may then be removed by skimming it off with a flat spoon. Alternatively, use absorbent kitchen paper to soak up the fat from the surface of the stock.

The finished stock should not be kept for more than two or three days in the refrigerator without reboiling for 10–15 minutes. The best thing to do is to make a large quantity of stock at one time and freeze it in ice cube trays or small containers so it is ready to hand when needed. When it has been made and strained, boil the stock hard to reduce and concentrate it before freezing so that it takes up less space in the freezer.

vegetable stock

This is a well-flavoured stock which can also be varied to your own taste. You might wish to experiment with other flavourings. Try adding some bulb fennel for a mild aniseed flavour, or a sliver of orange rind for an added lift. The addition of tomatoes will give it richness of flavour and colour. Avoid any floury root vegetables, however, as these will make the stock cloudy.

500 g/1 lb mixed vegetables (carrots, leeks, celery, onions, mushrooms), chopped
1 garlic clove
6 black peppercorns
1 bouquet garni
1.2 litres/2 pints water

Place the vegetables, garlic, peppercorns and bouquet garni in a saucepan and cover with the water. Bring to the boil and simmer gently for 30 minutes, skimming when necessary. Strain the stock and cool it completely before refrigerating.

Makes 1 litre/1¾ pints
Preparation time: 5–10 minutes
Cooking time: about 45 minutes

beef stock

750 g/1½ lb shin of beef, cubed
2 onions, chopped
2–3 carrots, chopped
2 celery sticks, roughly chopped
1 bay leaf
1 bouquet garni
4–6 peppercorns
1.8 litres/3 pints water

Place all the ingredients in a large saucepan. Slowly bring to the boil, and immediately reduce the heat to a slow simmer. Cover with a well-fitting lid and simmer for 4 hours, removing any scum from the surface. Strain the stock through a muslin-lined sieve and leave to cool before refrigerating.

Makes about 1.5 litres/2½ pints
Preparation time: 15 minutes
Cooking time: about 4½ hours

chicken stock

Chicken stock is used extensively throughout the book, and a good recipe is essential to success. The following gives a light, delicate stock which has a good flavour, but will not overpower the ingredients in the final dish.

1 cooked chicken carcass
raw giblets and trimmings from the chicken
1 onion, roughly chopped
2 large carrots, roughly chopped
1 large celery stick, roughly chopped
1 bay leaf
a few parsley stalks, lightly crushed
1 thyme sprig
1.8 litres/3 pints water

1 Chop the chicken carcass into 3 or 4 pieces and place it in a large saucepan with the remaining ingredients.

2 Bring to the boil, removing any scum from the surface. Lower the heat and simmer for 2–2½ hours.

3 Strain the stock through a muslin-lined sieve and leave to cool completely before refrigerating.

4 When chilled remove the fat that has risen to the surface, to leave the clear stock underneath.

Makes 1 litre/1¾ pints
Preparation time: 5–10 minutes
Cooking time: about 2½ hours

making chicken stock

fish stock

When purchasing the trimmings for this stock, avoid buying the skin and bones of oily fish. It is very important that the stock does not boil as it will become very cloudy.

1.5 kg/3 lb fish trimmings
1 onion, sliced
1 small leek, white part only
1 celery stick
1 bay leaf
6 parsley stalks
10 black peppercorns
475 ml/16 fl oz dry white wine
1.8 litres/3 pints water

1 Place all the ingredients in a large saucepan and bring slowly to just below boiling point.

2 Simmer for 20 minutes, removing any scum from the surface. Strain the stock through a muslin-lined sieve and leave to cool before refrigerating.

Makes 1.8 litres/3 pints
Preparation time: 10 minutes
Cooking time: 20 minutes

ham stock

Use this as a basis for soups made with pulses or in pork or bacon dishes.

1 ham bone
1.8 litres/3 pints water
1 large onion, stuck with a clove
2 celery sticks, chopped
2 carrots, chopped
1 bay leaf

Cover the ham bone with the water, bring to the boil, add the vegetables and bay leaf and simmer for 3 hours. Strain and cool.

Makes 1 litre/1³/₄ pints
Preparation time: 10 minutes
Cooking time: 3 hours

thai stocks

For an authentic flavour, it is worth spending some time making up these stocks called for in Thai and other Oriental dishes. Thai soups, which are an important feature of Thai cooking, are incomparable when the proper stock is used. To save time, make up more stock than you need and freeze the leftovers.

thai vegetable stock

2 large onions, quartered
4 large fresh red chillies
250 g/8 oz carrots, halved
¹/₂ small white cabbage, halved
1 small celery head (including leaves), chopped
50 g/2 oz fresh coriander leaves, stalks and roots
25 g/1 oz basil leaves and stalks
¹/₂ head Chinese leaves, chopped
¹/₂ mooli radish, peeled
25 black peppercorns
¹/₂ teaspoon salt
1 teaspoon palm sugar or light muscovado sugar
2 litres/3¹/₂ pints water

1 Put all the ingredients, including the water, into a large, heavy-bottomed saucepan or casserole. Bring to the boil, cover and simmer for 1 hour.

2 Remove the lid and boil hard for 10 minutes. Allow to cool, then strain. Freeze any stock you are not using immediately.

Makes 1.8 litres/3 pints
Preparation time: 5–10 minutes
Cooking time: about 1¹/₂ hours

*remove the surface fat from
cooled stock using absorbent
kitchen paper*

thai fish stock

*500 g/1 lb heads and bones of raw white fish and heads
   and shells of prawns, if available*
2.4 litres/4 pints water
3 shallots
1 celery stick, including leaves, roughly chopped
1 lime leaf
½ lemon grass stalk
2 garlic cloves
25 g/1 oz fresh coriander stalks and roots

1 Put the fish heads and bones and water into a
saucepan and bring to the boil. Skim off any scum that
rises to the top.

2 Add the shallots, celery, lime leaf, lemon grass, garlic
and coriander and simmer for 50 minutes.

3 Strain the stock and freeze what you do not need to
use immediately.

Makes 2 litres/3½ pints
Preparation time: 3 minutes
Cooking time: 1 hour

thai chicken stock

1.75 kg/3½ lb boiling chicken
500 g/1 lb chicken giblets
1 onion, halved
1 carrot, roughly chopped
2 celery sticks, including leaves, roughly chopped
2 garlic cloves
1 lemon grass stalk, roughly chopped
10 black peppercorns
1.8 litres/3 pints water
1 lime leaf
3 large red chillies

1 Put the chicken into a large heavy-bottomed saucepan
or casserole with the giblets, onion, carrot and celery
and just cover them with cold water. Place over a very
low heat and bring to the boil as slowly as possible,
about 50 minutes. When it begins to simmer, remove the
scum from the top until only white foam rises.

2 Add the remaining ingredients and cook slowly for
2 hours, covered. Use a heat diffuser if you need to.

3 Remove the chicken and set aside for another use.
Strain the stock without pressing the juices from the
vegetables – this helps to keep it clear. You can use as
much as you need immediately and freeze the rest for
future use.

Makes 1.5 litres/2½ pints
Preparation time: 3 minutes
Cooking time: about 3 hours

Sauces and dressings should be chosen to complement or enhance whatever you are serving. Consider carefully the types of oil and vinegar used in mayonnaise and French dressing as this will influence the flavour of the end result.

classic white sauce

600 ml/1 pint milk
1 small onion, roughly chopped
1 bay leaf
50 g/2 oz butter
50 g/2 oz plain flour
salt and pepper

1 Put the milk, onion and bay leaf in a pan and heat until just boiling. Remove from the heat and set aside for 20 minutes. Strain and set aside again.

2 Melt the butter in a pan, stir in the flour and cook over a low heat for 1 minute. Remove from the heat and beat in the milk a little at a time until blended. Return to a low heat and stir constantly until thickened. Bring to a gentle boil, stirring all the time. Simmer for 2 minutes. Season with salt and pepper.

Makes about 600 ml/1 pint
Preparation time: 10 minutes, plus standing
Cooking time: 8–10 minutes

cheese sauce

Follow the recipe for Classic White Sauce (see above), adding 125 g/4 oz grated Cheddar or Gruyère cheese to the cooked sauce off the heat.

making white sauce

hollandaise sauce

2 egg yolks
pinch of sugar
½ teaspoon salt
1 tablespoon white wine vinegar
1 tablespoon water
1 teaspoon Dijon mustard
125 g/4 oz unsalted butter, diced
white pepper

1 Place all the ingredients, except the butter and pepper, in a bowl and whisk until frothy.

2 Set the bowl over a pan of gently simmering water and continue to whisk until the whisk leaves a trail.

3 Remove from the heat and whisk in the butter a little at a time, beating after each addition, until thickened. The sauce should be frothy and of a pouring consistency. Taste and adjust the seasoning and serve at once.

Makes about 200 ml/7 fl oz
Preparation time: 5 minutes
Cooking time: 5 minutes

basic sauces & dressings

mayonnaise

Homemade mayonnaise is much nicer than the shop-bought equivalent and, if you make your own, you can vary the type of oil and vinegar you use to achieve different flavours and textures.

Mayonnaise can be made either by hand or in an electric blender; both give good results. Whichever method you use, it is essential that all the ingredients are at room temperature before you start.

The oil should be added to the egg yolk extremely slowly. If it is added too quickly, the sauce will curdle. If this happens, place another egg yolk in a clean bowl and gradually add the curdled mixture to the yolk, whisking constantly as you do it, then add the remaining oil, drop by drop.

For perfect mayonnaise, the eggs you use should be very fresh (but not straight from the hen or the mayonnaise will not thicken).

The type of oil you use determines the flavour of the mayonnaise. A corn or vegetable oil gives a lighter flavour than a richer olive oil. Tailor the oil to the food you will be serving the mayonnaise with.

The type of vinegar used also affects the flavour. Choose white wine vinegar in most instances, but use a flavoured herb or fruit vinegar if it will complement the finished dish.

Add flavourings to the finished mayonnaise if you like. Finely grated lemon rind and juice, chopped herbs and spices all work well.

making mayonnaise in a blender

blender mayonnaise

1 egg
½ teaspoon mustard powder
1 tablespoon wine vinegar
300 ml/½ pint olive oil or vegetable oil
salt

1 Crack the egg into a blender or food processor and add the mustard and salt, to taste. Process for 30 seconds, then add the wine vinegar and blend again.

2 With the motor still running, pour in the oil in a thin steady stream. The sauce will thicken after half of the oil has been added. Continue to add the oil until it has all been absorbed.

3 Scrape the mayonnaise into a bowl with a rubber spatula and store, covered, in the refrigerator.

Makes 450 ml/¾ pint
Preparation time: 10 minutes

See overleaf for making mayonnaise by hand.

mayonnaise by hand

1 egg yolk
¼ teaspoon salt
½ teaspoon mustard powder
150 ml/¼ pint olive oil or vegetable oil
1 tablespoon white wine vinegar
white pepper

1 Place the egg yolk in a bowl and gradually beat in the salt, mustard and pepper to taste, using a balloon whisk.

2 Add the oil, drop by drop, whisking vigorously after each addition so that is absorbed completely before the next addition.

3 After about half the oil has been added, the mayonnaise will start to look shiny and thick. If so, the oil can now be added more rapidly, about a tablespoon at a time. (If the mixture is still runny, it has curdled. See page 145 for how to rectify this.)

4 As the mixture becomes very thick, add a little vinegar to soften it, then add the remaining oil.

5 Blend in the rest of the vinegar. Adjust the seasoning to taste. The consistency should be like whipped cream. Use straight away, or store in the refrigerator in a covered container for up to 2 weeks.

Makes about 150 ml/¼ pint
Preparation time: 10 minutes

making mayonnaise by hand

french dressing

1 tablespoon white or red wine vinegar
1 teaspoon Dijon mustard
pinch of sugar
6 tablespoons extra virgin olive oil
salt and pepper

Put the vinegar, mustard, sugar and salt and pepper into a small bowl and whisk well. Gradually whisk in the oil until well blended.

Makes about 100 ml/3½ fl oz
Preparation time: 2 minutes

pesto

50 g/2 oz pine nuts
2 garlic cloves, crushed
50 g/2 oz basil leaves
150 g/5 oz Parmesan cheese, freshly grated
2 tablespoons lemon juice
150 ml/¼ pint olive oil
salt and pepper

1 Put the pine nuts and the garlic into a mortar and pound the mixture to a thick paste. Alternatively, use a food processor or blender.

2 Tear the basil leaves into shreds and add to the pine nut mixture. Continue pounding or processing until you have a thick green paste. Transfer to a bowl.

3 Stir in the Parmesan and the lemon juice. Add the olive oil, a little at a time, beating well. Season to taste.

Makes 150 ml/¼ pint
Preparation time: 10 minutes

fresh tomato sauce

1 kg/2 lb ripe tomatoes, skinned and roughly chopped
2 tablespoons extra virgin olive oil
2 garlic cloves, chopped
2 tablespoons chopped basil
1 teaspoon grated lemon rind
pinch of sugar
salt and pepper

1 Place all the ingredients in a saucepan and bring to the boil. Cover and simmer gently for 30 minutes.

2 Remove the lid and simmer for 20 minutes until the sauce is thick. Taste and adjust the seasoning.

Makes about 600 ml/1 pint
Preparation time: 10 minutes
Cooking time: 50 minutes

quick tomato sauce

Use two 400 g/13 oz cans of chopped tomatoes in place of the fresh ones. Cook as above, but simmer for 10 minutes only.

mushroom gravy

15 g/½ oz dried ceps
25 g/1 oz butter
4 shallots, chopped
500 g/1 lb field mushrooms, sliced
2 tablespoons plain flour
150 ml/¼ pint dry sherry or white wine
4 thyme sprigs
4 rosemary sprigs
600 ml/1 pint Vegetable Stock (see page 140)
salt and pepper

1 Soak the ceps in 300 ml/½ pint boiling water for 30 minutes. Drain, reserving the liquid, and slice.

2 Melt the butter in a saucepan and fry the shallots for 5 minutes. Add the mushrooms and ceps and fry for a further 5 minutes until tender.

3 Stir in the flour and cook for 1 minute. Gradually whisk in the sherry or wine and cep liquid and boil for 5 minutes. Strain through a sieve into a clean saucepan.

4 Add the herbs and stock, and boil for 10–15 minutes until reduced by half. Season with salt and pepper, strain and serve immediately.

Makes about 400 ml/14 fl oz
Preparation time: 10 minutes, plus making stock and soaking
Cooking time: 30 minutes

bread sauce

600 ml/1 pint milk
1 small onion, grated
pinch of ground cloves
pinch of ground bay leaves
75 g/3 oz fresh white breadcrumbs
25 g/1 oz butter
ground nutmeg
salt

1 Pour the milk into a saucepan and add the onion, cloves and bay leaves.

2 Heat until the milk has almost reached boiling point. Stir in the breadcrumbs and butter. Remove the pan from the heat and leave for 5 minutes. Add nutmeg and salt to taste.

Serves 6
Preparation time: 10 minutes
Cooking time: 5 minutes

apple sauce

500 g/1 lb cooking apples, peeled and cored
2–3 tablespoons water
25 g/1 oz butter or margarine
a little sugar (optional)

1 Slice the apples into a small saucepan and add the water. Cover the pan and cook gently until very soft and pulpy – about 7–10 minutes – stirring occasionally.

2 Beat the apple with a wooden spoon until quite smooth, or rub through a sieve or purée in a blender.

3 Return to a clean pan and beat in the butter or margarine and a little sugar, to taste.

Serves 6
Preparation time: about 5 minutes
Cooking time: about 10 minutes

cranberry sauce

For an orange cranberry sauce, use orange juice in place of all or part of the water and add the grated rind of ½ orange with the cranberries.

175 g/6 oz sugar
150 ml/¼ pint water
250 g/8 oz cranberries, fresh or frozen
1–2 tablespoons port (optional)

1 Dissolve the sugar in the water in a saucepan, and bring to the boil. Stir occasionally and boil for about 5 minutes.

2 Add the cranberries, cover the pan and simmer gently until they have all popped. Remove the lid from the pan and continue simmering for about 5 minutes, until they are quite tender.

3 If liked, add 1–2 tablespoons port, and leave to cool. Serve with roast turkey, lamb or game.

Serves 6
Preparation time: about 5 minutes
Cooking time: about 15 minutes

thai red curry paste

10 large fresh red chillies
2 teaspoons coriander seeds
5 cm/2 inch piece of fresh root ginger, peeled
   and finely chopped
1 lemon grass stalk, finely chopped
4 garlic cloves, halved
1 shallot, roughly chopped
1 teaspoon lime juice
2 tablespoons groundnut oil

1 Put all the ingredients into a food processor or blender and blend to a thick paste. Alternatively, you can pound all the ingredients together using a pestle and mortar.

2 Transfer the paste to an airtight container; it can be stored in the refrigerator for up to 3 weeks.

Makes 1 jar
Preparation time: 15 minutes

thai green curry paste

15 small fresh green chillies
4 garlic cloves, halved
2 lemon grass stalks, finely chopped
2 lime leaves, torn
2 shallots, chopped
50 g/2 oz coriander leaves, stalks and roots
2.5 cm/1 inch piece of fresh root ginger, peeled
   and finely chopped
2 teaspoons black peppercorns
1 teaspoon pared lime rind
½ teaspoon salt
1 tablespoon groundnut oil

1 Put all the ingredients into a food processor or blender and blend to a thick paste. Alternatively, put the chillies in a mortar and crush with a pestle, then add the garlic and crush with the chillies, and so on with all the other ingredients, finally mixing in the oil with a spoon.

2 Transfer the paste to an airtight container; it can be stored in the refrigerator for up to 3 weeks.

Makes 1 jar
Preparation time: 15 minutes

A microwave oven can be a boon in the kitchen for the busy cook. As well as being used for cooking, it can be used for defrosting frozen dishes and reheating cooked foods. To get the best from a microwave, it is important to know how it works and how to use it to its best advantage.

how microwaves work

In the microwave oven, a magnetron converts electricity into electromagnetic waves or 'microwaves'. Microwaves pass through most objects without affecting them at all, but they are reflected by metals and absorbed by foods. The microwaves penetrate the food to a depth of about 5 cm/2 inches and cause the molecules of water in the food to vibrate, generating heat within it.

power output

The power output of microwave ovens varies between 450 and 700 watts. Some ovens, suitable for defrosting, reheating and simple cooking, have only two power settings: full power (100%) and low power (usually 30%). Others have completely variable power, permitting much more versatile cooking.

additional features

Extra features include the following:

removable shelf
This allows several dishes to be cooked at the same time, stacked one on top of the other.

temperature probe
This helps to control the internal temperature that you want the food to reach. This is especially useful when cooking meat.

programmable memory
This allows you to control the oven's starting time and temperature, and to change temperatures during cooking, all in advance. For example, you can set it to start cooking on high power to heat food quickly, then reduce power to cook gently or simmer.

food browners
These include small grills or integral convection ovens. Basic microwaves do not brown food because the food cooks too quickly to have time to brown.

cooking containers

These must be microwave transparent, that is, the microwaves must be able to pass through them. To check if a dish is suitable for microwaving, place a glass jug half full of water in the dish and microwave on full power for 1 minute. The dish should be cool when it comes out of the oven. If it is hot, it should not be used.

Some plastics melt when the food gets very hot. This is a problem when cooking foods with a high fat or sugar content, and these should only be cooked in pottery.

do use:
Heat-resistant glass, china, firm plastics and polythene, roasting and boiling bags, paper, wood, wicker. Use the last three for warming foods only.

don't use:
Crystal or cut glass, unglazed earthenware and pottery, soft polythene, metal, foil, dishes with silver or gold trim.

special microwave ware
Specially designed microwave cookware dishes are obviously good to use, and some ranges have some useful items. These include browning dishes, which are used to brown and crisp foods, and cooking racks, good for cooking meat, bacon and poultry, keeping it from sitting in its own fat during cooking.

cooking by microwave

Because microwaves penetrate the food from the outer edge first, foods arranged in a circle cook most evenly. Foods also cook more evenly if stirred or rearranged during microwaving. Foods which can't be stirred should be rotated, and most ovens have a turntable which does this for you. Uneven-shaped foods should be arranged so that the thinnest parts are in the centre where they will receive less energy.

Almost all foods are covered before cooking in a microwave. A solid lid or microwave-safe clingfilm will hold the steam in to keep foods moist, speed up cooking and stop splattering. Use for vegetables, fruits, fish, casseroles, pasta and rice. Absorbent paper is used to cover foods such as bacon, sausages and chops to stop them spattering and to wrap breads and cakes to absorb excess moisture.

Some vegetables and fruits, such as potatoes, tomatoes and apples, can be cooked uncovered, though the skins must be pricked before microwaving to prevent them bursting. Soups and sauces are sometimes microwaved without a lid, either to reduce the quantity or because they need stirring during cooking.

cooking times

The more food you put in the microwave at one time, the longer it takes to cook. If you double the quantities in a recipe, you will need to add between a third and a half to the cooking time. Conversely, if you reduce the quantity, you will also need to reduce the time.

The shapes of foods and dishes also affect the cooking time, with shallow dishes and thin foods cooking more quickly than thicker foods of the same weight.

The starting temperature of food makes a noticeable difference when microwaving because cooking times are so much shorter. Most microwave recipes give times for food at room temperature, so if you are taking food straight from the refrigerator, cook it for longer.

All food continues to cook for a short time after the microwave has been switched off. During this time, the heat on the outside of the food is conducted to the centre of the food so, ideally, food should be removed before it is completely cooked. It can then finish cooking during the 'standing time'.

what not to do

- Don't try to deep-fry in a microwave – you can't control the fat temperature.
- Do not cook eggs in their shells – they will explode.
- Do not switch on the microwave when empty – you may damage the magnetron.
- Do not use ordinary thermometers – use a special microwave thermometer.

microwave cooking

choosing a freezer

When deciding which freezer to buy, consider the space you have available to put it, the size of your household and the purpose for which you require the freezer. As a general guide, allow a minimum of 56 litres/2 cubic feet of freezer space for each member of the family, remembering that 28 litres/1 cubic foot should hold about 10 kg/20 lb of food.

chest freezers

These have top-opening hinged lids and are less expensive to buy than upright models. They are also less expensive to run because they use less electricity. They are, however, not so convenient as the food tends to be stacked up, making it difficult to gain access to the things at the bottom of the freezer. Chest freezers are, however, good for large families who need a lot of freezing space and have the room to accommodate one.

upright freezers

These tend to be more expensive to buy and run than chest freezers, but are much more convenient to use. When you open the door, all the food is easily visible and you can store different types of foods in the different drawers to allow you to find them quickly. They also tend to take up less floor space than chest freezers, so are perfect for fitting into small kitchens. Some are even small enough to stand on top of units or other appliances. Look for a model with drawers or shelves on runners for really easy access.

combination refrigerator/freezers

If your kitchen is small, this is an ideal model to buy because the two units together will only take up the floor space of one. Different models have different amounts of space dedicated to the refrigerator and freezer compartments, so make up your mind as to which you will use more and which you require to be bigger than the other.

defrosting

Regular defrosting is essential if the freezer is to run efficiently. It is impossible to say exactly how often this is necessary but, on average, it should be two or three times a year for an upright freezer, once or twice for a chest freezer. As a general guide, when the ice has built up to a thickness of more than 5 mm/$\frac{1}{4}$ inch inside the cabinet, it is time to defrost. Defrost when stocks in the freezer are low and the weather is cold.

thawing

Frozen foods should be thawed slowly at room temperature, or in the refrigerator. Unless using commercially-prepared frozen foods that indicate otherwise on the packet, foods should be thawed before cooking to ensure they cook through thoroughly. This is especially important with frozen poultry products. If you put a frozen chicken straight into the oven, the outside will be cooked and golden long before the inside has had a chance to thaw out and cook. The temperature in the cavity of the chicken would not get high enough to destroy harmful bacteria, thus making the chicken unsafe to eat.

All raw meat is best thawed slowly in the refrigerator so it absorbs as much of its juices as possible. It is, however, a slow process; you should allow 5 hours per 500 g/1 lb to thaw completely. Thawing at room temperature is much faster – allow 2 hours per 500 g/1 lb – but it is not advisable for pork.

Once food has been fully thawed, it should be used as soon as possible. Do not leave it lying around at room temperature and never refreeze thawed food.

freezing techniques

batch cooking

It is a good idea to cook a batch or a large quantity of the same dish, then to divide it into smaller portions to freeze for future use. This cuts down on cooking time in the long run and is perfect for busy cooks.

blanching

This procedure is essential for many vegetables, to preserve their quality during freezing. It consists of dropping the prepared vegetables into boiling water for up to 1–2 minutes, then refreshing them in cold water to stop the cooking process. The vegetables are then drained thoroughly and frozen.

cooling

This is one of the most vital stages in the preparation of cooked foods for the freezer. Food that is placed in the freezer must be as cold as possible to prevent moisture being trapped inside packages, and to avoid warming up other items in the freezer.

open freezing

Some foods, such as piped cream desserts and cakes, casseroles, bakes and mousses can be frozen without wrappings for a short time until solid, then wrapped and sealed in the freezer. This prevents them being squashed and misshapen by their wrappings.

overwrapping

Strong-smelling foods should be packed for freezing in the normal way, then wrapped again in foil or plastic to prevent them cross-flavouring other foods.

preforming

Pour liquid foods such as soups, casseroles, stocks and stews into a rigid container lined with a polythene bag and open freeze. When solid, remove the food, seal the bag and store in the freezer. This will take up less space than a rigid container.

storage times

Storage times recommended in recipes and by manufacturers of commercial foods err on the safe side. Food will not normally be harmful if eaten soon after the recommended storage time, but its quality, in terms of colour, flavour and texture, will not be as good.

what not to freeze

The following foods do not freeze successfully:
- eggs
- cream less than 40% butterfat, including soured cream
- all fruits high in water content
- raw bananas
- avocado
- raw celery
- boiled potatoes (mashed potatoes freeze well)
- salad vegetables
- raw tomatoes
- custards
- jellies
- yogurt
- soft meringue
- icings
- mayonnaise
- carbonated drinks (the bottle may split and leak)

freezing

soups & starters

spinach and broccoli soup

2 tablespoons olive oil
50 g/2 oz butter
1 onion, diced
1 garlic clove, crushed and chopped
2 potatoes, chopped
250 g/8 oz broccoli, chopped
300 g/10 oz spinach, washed and chopped
900 ml/1½ pints Chicken or Vegetable Stock
  (see pages 141 and 140)
125 g/4 oz Gorgonzola cheese, crumbled into small
  pieces
4–8 tablespoons lemon juice
½ teaspoon grated nutmeg
salt and pepper
75 g/3 oz toasted pine nuts, to garnish
warm crusty bread, to serve

1 Heat the oil and butter in a saucepan. Add the onion and garlic and fry over a low heat for 3 minutes.

2 Add the potatoes, broccoli, spinach and stock, bring to the boil and simmer for 15 minutes.

3 Transfer the soup to a food processor or blender and process to a purée, if liked. Return to the pan and warm through. Add the Gorgonzola, together with the lemon juice, nutmeg and salt and pepper to taste.

4 Transfer to a warm tureen, garnish with the toasted pine nuts and serve with warm crusty bread.

Serves 4
Preparation time: 10 minutes
Cooking time: 20 minutes

butternut squash and rosemary soup

1 butternut squash
few rosemary sprigs, plus extra to garnish
150 g/5 oz red lentils, washed
1 onion, finely chopped
900 ml/1½ pints Vegetable Stock (see page 140)
salt and pepper

1 Halve the squash and, using a spoon, scoop out the seeds and fibrous flesh. Cut the squash into smaller chunks and place in a roasting tin. Sprinkle over the rosemary and season with salt and pepper. Roast in a preheated oven, 200°C (400°F), Gas Mark 6, for 45 minutes.

2 Meanwhile, place the lentils in a saucepan. Cover with water, bring to the boil and boil rapidly for 10 minutes. Strain, then return the lentils to a clean saucepan with the onion and stock and simmer for 5 minutes. Season to taste with salt and pepper.

3 Remove the squash from the oven, mash with a fork and add to the soup. Simmer for 25 minutes and then ladle into warm bowls. Garnish with more rosemary before serving.

Serves 4
Preparation time: 15 minutes
Cooking time: 1 hour 10 minutes
Oven temperature: 200°C (400°F), Gas Mark 6

minestrone

Minestrone improves when it is made in advance and reheated. Cover and store in the refrigerator so that the flavours can blend.

2 tablespoons olive oil
1 onion, diced
1 garlic clove, crushed
2 celery sticks, chopped
1 leek, thinly sliced
1 carrot, chopped
400 g/13 oz can chopped tomatoes
600 ml/1 pint Chicken or Vegetable Stock
(see pages 141 and 140)
1 courgette, diced
½ small cabbage, shredded
1 bay leaf
75 g/3 oz canned haricot beans
75 g/3 oz spaghetti, broken into small pieces
1 tablespoon chopped flat leaf parsley
salt and pepper
50 g/2 oz Parmesan cheese, freshly grated, to serve

1 Heat the oil in a saucepan. Add the onion, garlic, celery, leek and carrot and fry over a low heat for 3 minutes.

2 Add the tomatoes, stock, courgette, cabbage, bay leaf and haricot beans. Bring to the boil and simmer for 10 minutes.

3 Add the spaghetti and season to taste with salt and pepper. Stir well and cook for a further 8 minutes. Keep stirring as the soup may stick to the bottom of the pan.

4 Just before serving, add the chopped parsley and stir well. Serve immediately with grated Parmesan.

Serves 4
Preparation time: 5 minutes
Cooking time: 25 minutes

broad bean and artichoke soup

250 g/8 oz broad beans
3 artichokes
3 tablespoons olive oil
½ onion, finely chopped
1.5 litres/2½ pints Vegetable Stock (see page 140)
2 large potatoes, thickly sliced
1 chicory head, thinly sliced
2 egg yolks
2 tablespoons single cream
2 tablespoons grated Parmesan cheese
15 g/½ oz parsley, chopped
salt and pepper
125 g/4 oz croûtons, to serve

1 Remove the skins from the broad beans. Remove any coarse outer leaves from the artichokes and chop them into bite-sized pieces, discarding the hairy choke.

2 Heat the oil in a deep saucepan over a low heat. Add the onion and cook for about 4 minutes until golden. Add 125 ml/4 fl oz of the stock and simmer for 4 minutes.

3 Add the broad beans and artichokes, mix well and cook for 5 minutes. Add the potatoes and chicory to the pan, then cover with the remaining stock and bring to the boil. Simmer for 45 minutes.

4 Remove the potato slices with a slotted spoon, mash and return to the soup.

5 Beat the egg yolks in a soup tureen, together with the cream, Parmesan and parsley. Season to taste with salt and pepper. Gently add the soup, then quickly stir to mix. Serve hot, with croûtons.

Serves 4
Preparation time: 10 minutes
Cooking time: 1 hour

mushroom soup

7 tablespoons olive oil
2 garlic cloves, crushed
500 g/1 lb field mushrooms, sliced
250 g/8 oz tomatoes, skinned and chopped
750 ml/1¼ pints Vegetable Stock (see page 140)
6 large slices hot toasted bread, cut into quarters
65 g/2½ oz Parmesan cheese, grated
2 eggs, beaten
salt and pepper

1 Heat the oil in a heavy pan. Add the garlic and fry gently until it begins to brown. Add the mushrooms and cook, stirring frequently, for 5 minutes.

2 Add the tomatoes and stock and season to taste with salt and pepper. Bring to the boil, then lower the heat, cover and simmer for 15 minutes.

3 Divide the toast slices between 6 individual soup bowls, then sprinkle them with about half of the Parmesan. Mix the eggs with the remaining Parmesan and add to the soup mixture in the pan. Remove from the heat immediately and stir vigorously. Pour the soup over the toast and serve immediately.

Serves 6
Preparation time: 5 minutes
Cooking time: 25 minutes

sweet red pepper soup

4 tablespoons olive oil
1 red onion, finely chopped
2 celery sticks, thinly sliced
2 red peppers, cored, deseeded and cut into very thin strips
2 plum tomatoes, roughly chopped

1 garlic clove, crushed
1 tablespoon plain flour
1 litre/1¾ pints Chicken or Vegetable Stock (see pages 141 and 140) or water
1 teaspoon sugar
2 eggs
4 thick slices rustic bread
salt and pepper
chopped flat leaf parsley, to garnish (optional)

1 Heat the oil in a large heavy-based saucepan. Add the onion, celery and red peppers and cook over a low heat, stirring frequently, for about 10 minutes until softened.

2 Add the tomatoes, garlic and flour and stir well to mix. Cook, stirring, for 1–2 minutes, then pour in the stock and bring to the boil. Add the sugar and season to taste with salt and pepper. Half cover the pan and simmer gently for 30 minutes.

3 Whisk the eggs in a bowl with salt and pepper to taste, then whisk in a ladleful or two of the hot soup. Pour this mixture into the pan of soup and heat very gently, without boiling, stirring constantly. Taste for seasoning.

4 Put a slice of bread in the base of 4 soup plates, ladle the soup over and garnish with parsley, if using. Serve hot.

Serves 4
Preparation time: 15 minutes
Cooking time: 40–45 minutes

spicy chinese chicken soup

Beanthread noodles, also called cellophane noodles, are made from mung bean flour. They must be soaked before using, to make them soft.

3 tablespoons sunflower oil
½ large onion, thinly sliced
2 garlic cloves, crushed
1 teaspoon chopped fresh root ginger
½ teaspoon pepper
pinch of turmeric
175 g/6 oz cooked chicken, coarsely chopped
1 tablespoon light soy sauce
1 litre/1¾ pints Chicken Stock (see page 141)
a handful of beanthread noodles, soaked until soft
75 g/3 oz beansprouts
chopped spring onions, to garnish

1 Heat the oil in a medium saucepan. Add the onion, garlic and ginger and fry until the onion is soft. Add the pepper, turmeric and chicken and stir for 30 seconds.

2 Add the soy sauce and stock and bring to the boil. Adjust the seasoning if necessary. Reduce the heat slightly and cook for 5 minutes.

3 Drain the noodles. Divide them equally between 4 warmed soup bowls. Divide the beansprouts between the bowls and pour the soup on top. Serve hot, garnished with chopped spring onions.

Serves 4
Preparation time: 15–20 minutes
Cooking time: 15 minutes

fish and coconut soup

500 g/1 lb monkfish or halibut fillet, skinned and cubed
25 g/1 oz desiccated coconut
6 shallots
6 almonds, blanched
2 garlic cloves, peeled
2.5 cm/1 inch piece of fresh root ginger, sliced
2 blades of lemon grass, trimmed
2–3 teaspoons turmeric
3 tablespoons oil
1 fresh red chilli, deseeded and sliced
salt
coriander leaves, to garnish

Coconut milk:
300 g/10 oz desiccated coconut
750 ml/1¼ pints boiling water

Coconut cream:
300 g/10 oz desiccated coconut
750 ml/1¼ pints boiling water

1 Make the coconut milk by placing the desiccated coconut and boiling water in a food processor or blender, and processing for 20 seconds. Pour into a bowl and leave to cool. Strain the cooled coconut milk into a clean bowl or jug.

2 Repeat the process to make the coconut cream, leaving the strained liquid to stand. When the cream rises to the top of the milk, skim it off – this is the coconut cream.

3 Sprinkle the fish with salt. Place the coconut in a wok or heavy-based frying pan and heat gently until it is golden and crisp. Remove from the pan and pound until oily. Set aside.

4 Put the shallots, almonds, garlic, ginger and 6 cm/2½ inches from the root end of the lemon grass (reserving the remainder) in a food processor or blender and process to a purée. Add the turmeric.

5 Heat the oil in a preheated wok or saucepan. Add the puréed mixture and fry for a few minutes. Add the coconut milk and bring to the boil, stirring constantly. Stir in the fish, chilli and the remaining lemon grass. Cook over a low heat for about 5 minutes.

6 Stir in the pounded coconut and cook for a further 5 minutes. Remove the blades of lemon grass and stir in the coconut cream. Serve hot, garnished with coriander.

Serves 4
Preparation time: 25 minutes
Cooking time: 15–20 minutes

indian split pea soup

250 g/8 oz yellow split peas
1.3 litres/2¼ pints water
½ teaspoon turmeric
2 tablespoons lemon juice
1 fresh green chilli, deseeded and finely chopped
1 teaspoon ground cumin
1 teaspoon ground coriander
½ small cucumber
3 spring onions
75 ml/3 fl oz natural yogurt
salt and pepper
mint leaves, to garnish

1 Pick over the yellow split peas to remove any grit, then wash under running cold water and drain them in a colander. Place the drained split peas in a large saucepan with the water and turmeric and bring to the boil. Reduce the heat, cover and simmer very gently for 1¼–1½ hours until cooked and tender. Remove from the heat.

2 Tip the split peas and their liquid into a food processor or blender. Add the lemon juice, chilli, cumin and coriander seeds and season to taste with salt and pepper. Process until smooth. If the soup is a little too thick, thin it down with water or more lemon juice. Transfer to a serving bowl and refrigerate until required.

3 Dice the cucumber and slice the spring onions just before serving. Swirl the yogurt into the chilled soup and serve garnished with the cucumber, spring onions and mint.

Serves 4
Preparation time: 20 minutes
Cooking time: 1¼–1½ hours

smoked ham and bean soup with garlic

375 g/12 oz dried borlotti or cannellini beans
2 litres/3½ pints water
1 carrot, chopped
1 onion, quartered
1 bouquet garni
125 g/4 oz cooked smoked ham, diced
40 g/1½ oz butter
2 shallots, finely chopped
1 garlic clove, crushed
1 tablespoon chopped parsley
salt and pepper
1½ teaspoons chopped parsley, to garnish
125 g/4 oz croûtons, to serve

1 Soak the beans overnight in cold water, then drain. Put the beans in a large saucepan with the water and a pinch of salt. Bring to the boil over a medium heat. Add the carrot, onion, bouquet garni and ham and simmer for 2 hours, or until the beans are tender.

2 Remove the bouquet garni and transfer the soup to a food processor or blender. Process to a purée, return it to the pan and reheat over a medium heat.

3 Melt the butter in a heavy-based frying pan. Add the shallots and garlic and fry until golden. Add the chopped parsley and mix quickly. Turn off the heat and add this mixture to the bean purée.

4 Mix well with a wooden spoon and season with pepper. Pour the soup into warmed individual bowls and garnish with parsley. Serve the croûtons separately.

Serves 4
Preparation time: 30 minutes, plus soaking
Cooking time: 2 hours

bacon and turnip soup

25 g/1 oz butter or margarine
125 g/4 oz smoked bacon, rinded and coarsely chopped
1 onion, chopped
375 g/12 oz potatoes, chopped
750 g/1½ lb turnips, chopped
1.2 litres/2 pints Chicken Stock (see page 141)
1 bay leaf
1 small thyme sprig or ¼ teaspoon dried thyme
150 ml/¼ pint milk
salt and pepper
1 tablespoon finely chopped parsley, to garnish (optional)

1 Melt the butter or margarine in a heavy-based saucepan. Add the bacon and cook over a moderate heat until crisp and golden. Remove the bacon with a slotted spoon and set aside.

2 Add the onion, potatoes and turnips to the pan and fry over a low heat for about 5 minutes. Add the stock, bay leaf and thyme. Bring to the boil, lower the heat and cook for 30–35 minutes, or until all the vegetables are soft. Remove and discard the bay leaf and sprig of thyme, if used.

3 Transfer the mixture to a blender or food processor in batches and process until smooth. Transfer each successive batch to a clean saucepan. Add the reserved bacon and the milk and season with salt and pepper if necessary.

4 Cook over a moderate heat, stirring frequently, for 3–5 minutes, or until the soup is hot but not boiling.

5 Ladle the soup into warmed soup plates or bowls, garnish with parsley, if liked, and serve immediately.

Serves 6
Preparation time: 20 minutes
Cooking time: 40–45 minutes

thai banana soup   p168

butternut squash and rosemary soup   p156

carrot and coriander pâté p178

moroccan fish soup p167

griddled tiger prawns with mint and lemon p188

marinated herring with horseradish cream p188

mussel chowder p161

roasted vine tomatoes with goats' cheese p197

prawn gumbo

50 g/2 oz white long grain rice
50 g/2 oz butter
2 garlic cloves, crushed
1 onion, chopped
1 red pepper, cored, deseeded and finely chopped
4 ripe tomatoes, skinned and chopped
¼–½ teaspoon cayenne pepper
1.2 litres/2 pints Fish Stock (see page 142)
375 g/12 oz okra, trimmed and sliced
375 g/12 oz cooked, peeled prawns, thawed if frozen and
    dried on kitchen paper
1 tablespoon lime juice
salt and pepper

1 Bring a large saucepan of lightly salted water to the boil. Add the rice and cook for 8–10 minutes, or until tender. Drain the rice and set aside.

2 Melt the butter in a large heavy-based saucepan. Add the garlic and onion and cook over a low heat for about 5 minutes until soft and slightly golden. Add the red pepper and cook over a moderate heat, stirring constantly, for a further 5 minutes.

3 Stir in the tomatoes and cayenne and mix well. Pour in the fish stock and bring the mixture to the boil. Add the okra, lower the heat, cover the pan and cook, stirring occasionally, for 20 minutes.

4 Add the prawns, rice and lime juice to the soup. Stir well, cover and simmer for a further 5–8 minutes. Season with salt and pepper and add a little more cayenne, if liked. Serve immediately.

Serves 4–6
Preparation time: 20 minutes
Cooking time: 50 minutes

mussel chowder

2 tablespoons olive oil
250 g/8 oz streaky bacon, rinded and chopped
2 onions, finely chopped
1 celery stick, finely sliced
1 green pepper, cored, deseeded and finely chopped
450 ml/¾ pint Fish Stock (see page 142)
250 g/8 oz potatoes, diced
1 bay leaf
½ teaspoon chopped marjoram leaves, or
    ¼ teaspoon dried marjoram
3 tablespoons plain white flour
300 ml/½ pint milk
500 g/1 lb mussels, cooked and shelled (see page 109)
150 ml/¼ pint single cream
salt and white pepper
1 tablespoon finely chopped parsley, to garnish
crusty French bread, to serve

1 Heat the olive oil in a heavy-based saucepan. Add the bacon and fry over a moderate heat until browned. Add the onions, celery and pepper and cook, stirring frequently, for 5 minutes, or until the vegetables soften.

2 Add the fish stock, potatoes, bay leaf and marjoram. Bring to the boil, then lower the heat, cover the pan and simmer for 15–20 minutes until the potatoes are tender.

3 Blend the flour with 150 ml/¼ pint of the milk in a small bowl. Whisk the mixture into the chowder, stir until it begins to boil, then slowly add the remaining milk. Season to taste with salt and pepper.

4 Lower the heat, add the mussels and simmer gently, stirring occasionally, for 5 minutes. Do not allow the chowder to boil. Stir in the cream and pour the chowder into a heated soup tureen. Sprinkle the parsley over the top to garnish and serve with crusty French bread.

Serves 4–6
Preparation time: 10–15 minutes
Cooking time: about 30 minutes

gazpacho

1 garlic clove, peeled
1 litre/1¾ pints tomato juice
3 tablespoons olive oil
2 tablespoons lemon juice
1 tablespoon lime juice
2 teaspoons sugar
150 g/5 oz cucumber, peeled and diced
75 g/3 oz mild red onion or spring onions, chopped
150 g/5 oz red pepper, deseeded and diced
75 g/3 oz avocado, diced
2 tablespoons chopped mixed herbs
salt and pepper

To serve:
ice cubes
tortilla chips, coarsely crushed
lime wedges

1 Cut the garlic clove in half and rub the cut surfaces over the base and around the sides of a large mixing bowl. Discard the garlic.

2 Pour the tomato juice into the bowl, add the olive oil, lemon and lime juices and sugar and season to taste with salt and pepper. Beat the mixture lightly until well combined.

3 Cover the bowl with clingfilm and chill in the refrigerator for at least 1 hour.

4 Beat the soup again and stir in all the remaining ingredients. Place some ice cubes in individual serving bowls and pour the soup over the top. Sprinkle with coarsely crushed tortilla chips and serve with lime wedges.

Serves 6–8
Preparation time: 20 minutes, plus chilling

tasty bean soup

375 g/12 oz dried haricot beans
1 carrot, finely chopped
1 onion, sliced
2 celery sticks, sliced
125 g/4 oz smoked sausage, diced
400 g/13 oz can chopped tomatoes
1 tablespoon tomato purée
2 teaspoons sugar
3 tablespoons olive oil
2 shallots, finely chopped
1 garlic clove, crushed
1 tablespoon chopped sage
salt and pepper

1 Soak the beans overnight in cold water and drain.

2 Place the beans in a large pan with 1¹/₂ litres/2¹/₂ pints water and bring to the boil over a medium heat. Boil for 1¹/₂ hours, or until the beans are just tender.

3 Add the carrot, onion, celery, sausage, tomatoes, tomato purée and sugar and simmer for 20–30 minutes.

4 Heat the oil in a heavy-based pan. Add the shallots and garlic and fry over a low heat until golden, but not brown. Add the sage and mix together. Add the shallot mixture to the bean soup.

5 Mix well with a wooden spoon, season to taste with salt and plenty of pepper, then pour into warmed individual serving bowls.

Serves 4
Preparation time: 30 minutes, plus soaking
Cooking time: 2 hours

lentil soup

2 tablespoons olive oil
1 tablespoon butter
1 large onion, finely chopped
1 large carrot, finely chopped
175 g/6 oz brown continental lentils
1–2 garlic cloves, crushed
2.4 litres/4 pints Chicken Stock (see page 141)
2 tablespoons tomato purée
1 teaspoon dried marjoram
salt and pepper

To serve:
marjoram leaves
freshly grated Parmesan cheese

1 Heat the oil and butter in a large heavy-based saucepan until foaming. Add the onion and carrot and cook over a low heat, stirring frequently, for about 5 minutes until softened.

2 Add the lentils and garlic and stir well to mix, then pour in the stock and bring to the boil. Add the tomato purée, stir until it is thoroughly mixed into the liquid, then add the marjoram and season with salt and pepper to taste. Half cover and simmer gently for 30 minutes.

3 Pour half of the soup into a food processor or blender and process until smooth, then return to the pan of soup and stir to mix. Add water to thin down the consistency, if necessary, then taste for seasoning. Serve hot, sprinkled with marjoram leaves and grated Parmesan.

Serves 4–6
Preparation time: 15 minutes
Cooking time: 40 minutes

french onion soup

50 g/2 oz butter
750 g/1½ lb onions, thinly sliced
2 teaspoons sugar
2 teaspoons plain flour
1 litre/1¾ pints Beef Stock (see page 141)
½ French bread stick, sliced
50 g/2 oz Gruyère cheese, grated
salt and pepper

1 Melt the butter in a large saucepan. Add the onions and sugar, reduce the heat to very low and cook the onions, stirring occasionally, for 20–30 minutes until they are soft and a really deep golden brown.

2 Stir the flour into the onion mixture and cook over a very low heat, stirring constantly, for about 5 minutes.

3 Add the beef stock and season to taste with salt and pepper. Increase the heat and bring to the boil, stirring constantly. Reduce the heat and simmer for 15–20 minutes. Taste the soup and adjust the seasoning, if necessary.

4 Meanwhile, toast the slices of French bread lightly on both sides. Sprinkle with the grated Gruyère. Pour the soup into a hot tureen. Place a piece of toast in each serving bowl and ladle the hot soup over the top.

Serves 4–5
Preparation time: 15 minutes
Cooking time: 1 hour

green bean and vegetable soup with pesto

Any unused pesto can be stored in a screw-top jar in the refrigerator for up to a week.

2 tablespoons extra virgin olive oil
1 leek, sliced
2 garlic cloves, crushed
1 potato, diced
1 celery stick, sliced
1 tablespoon chopped thyme
425 g/14 oz canned flageolet beans
600 ml/1 pint Vegetable Stock (see page 140)

1 courgette, diced
50 g/2 oz French beans, halved
125 g/4 oz frozen broad beans, thawed
salt and pepper

Pesto:
125 g/4 oz basil leaves
25 g/1 oz pine nuts
2 garlic cloves
¼ teaspoon coarse salt
50 g/2 oz freshly grated Parmesan cheese
125 ml/4 fl oz extra virgin olive oil

To serve:
French bread
freshly grated Parmesan cheese (optional)

1 First make the pesto. Put the basil, pine nuts, garlic and salt in a mortar and pound to a paste with a pestle. Mix in the Parmesan. Gradually add the olive oil, working it in well with a wooden spoon, until thick and creamy. Set aside.

2 Heat the oil in a large saucepan. Add the leek and garlic and fry for 5 minutes. Add the potato, celery and thyme and fry for a further 10 minutes until light golden.

3 Stir in the flageolet beans, together with their liquid and the vegetable stock, return to the boil, cover and simmer gently for 20 minutes. Add the courgette, French beans and broad beans and cook for a further 10 minutes. Season to taste with salt and pepper.

4 Ladle the soup into large bowls. Stir in a spoonful of pesto and serve immediately with crusty French bread and grated cheese, if wished.

Serves 4
Preparation time: 25 minutes
Cooking time: 35–40 minutes

smoky sweetcorn soup with lime butter

4 sweetcorn cobs, about 250 g/8 oz each
4 tablespoons extra virgin olive oil
1 onion, chopped
2 garlic cloves, chopped
250 g/8 oz potato, chopped
900 ml/1½ pints Vegetable Stock (see page 140)

300 ml/½ pint milk, warmed
pinch of cayenne pepper
salt and pepper

lime butter:
125 g/4 oz butter
grated rind and juice of 1 lime
2 tablespoons chopped coriander

1 First make the lime butter. In a small bowl beat together the butter, lime rind and juice and the coriander until evenly combined. Add a little salt and pepper to taste and roll into a log shape. Wrap in foil and refrigerate until required.

2 Strip away the outer leaves of the corn, brush each cob with oil and sprinkle with salt and pepper. Cook under a preheated grill for 15 minutes, turning frequently until charred on all sides. Remove from the heat and leave to cool slightly.

3 Heat the remaining oil in a saucepan. Add the onion and garlic and fry for 5 minutes until softened. Add the potato and fry for a further 5 minutes.

4 Hold the corn cobs vertically and cut downwards to remove the kernels. Add the kernels to the saucepan, together with the stock and milk. Bring to the boil, cover and simmer gently for 30 minutes. Transfer the soup to a food processor or blender and process until smooth.

5 Return the soup to the pan, add the cayenne and season to taste with salt and pepper. Heat through gently and serve hot, garnished with thin slices of lime butter.

Serves 6–8
Preparation time: 15 minutes
Cooking time: 45 minutes

cream of chicken soup

500 g/1 lb chicken pieces, skinned
1 onion, chopped
1 garlic clove, chopped
1 leek, sliced
2 carrots, thinly sliced
1 celery stick, sliced
600 ml/1 pint water
600 ml/1 pint Chicken Stock (see page 141)
150 ml/¼ pint single cream
salt and pepper

To garnish:
chopped parsley
paprika

1 Place the chicken pieces in a large saucepan. Add the onion, garlic and remaining vegetables. Season to taste with salt and pepper. Add the water and bring to the boil over a low heat, skimming off any scum that rises to the surface.

2 Cover and simmer over a low heat for 30 minutes. Stir in the stock and bring to the boil. Lower the heat, cover and simmer for a further 30 minutes. Adjust the seasoning, if necessary.

3 Lift out the chicken pieces with a slotted spoon. Remove and discard the bones. Place the meat in a food processor or blender. Add the soup and process until smooth (this may be done in batches).

4 Return the soup to the pan. If it is too thick, thin it down with a little more stock or water. Stir in the cream and heat through, but do not let the soup boil. Serve sprinkled with chopped parsley and paprika.

Serves 6
Preparation time: about 15 minutes
Cooking time: about 1¼ hours

mulligatawny soup

50 g/2 oz dried tamarind
1.2 litres/2 pints Beef Stock (see page 141)
50 g/2 oz butter
1 large onion, sliced
2 garlic cloves, sliced
1 teaspoon ground ginger
2 teaspoons pepper
2 teaspoons ground coriander
½ teaspoon ground fenugreek
½ teaspoon chilli powder
1½ teaspoons turmeric
1½ teaspoons salt
thinly sliced red and green peppers, to garnish

1 Put the dried tamarind into a saucepan, add just enough of the beef stock to cover, then bring to the boil. Remove the pan from the heat, cover and leave the tamarind to soak for 4 hours.

2 Melt the butter in a heavy-based saucepan. Add the onion and garlic and fry gently for about 4–5 minutes until soft.

3 Add the ginger, pepper, ground coriander, fenugreek, chilli powder, turmeric and salt and fry, stirring constantly, for 3 minutes. Stir in the remaining beef stock.

4 Strain the tamarind liquid through a wire sieve over a small bowl, pressing to extract as much liquid as possible. Add the tamarind juice to the pan and simmer for 15 minutes. Taste and adjust the seasoning before serving, garnished with the sliced peppers. Serve hot.

Serves 4
Preparation time: 10 minutes, plus soaking
Cooking time: 25 minutes

mexican chilled avocado soup

50 g/2 oz butter
4 tablespoons olive oil
1 onion, finely chopped
1 leek, finely chopped
1 carrot, finely chopped
2 garlic cloves, crushed
1.8 litres/3 pints Chicken Stock (see page 141)
4 ripe avocados, peeled and stoned
250 ml/8 fl oz natural yogurt
2 tablespoons lime juice
salt and pepper

To garnish:
125 ml/4 fl oz crème fraîche
2 tablespoons chopped coriander

1 Melt the butter and oil in a large saucepan. Add the onion, leek, carrot and garlic and fry over a low heat until tender. Add about 750 ml/1¼ pints of the stock and simmer gently for about 30 minutes.

2 Process the avocados in batches with the remaining stock in a food processor or blender until smooth. Add the vegetable mixture and continue to process to a smooth green purée.

3 Stir in the yogurt and season to taste with salt and pepper. Add the lime juice and chill for 1 hour. Serve with a swirl of crème fraîche, sprinkled with chopped coriander.

Serves 6–8
Preparation time: 10 minutes, plus chilling
Cooking time: 35–40 minutes

leek and potato soup

25 g/1 oz butter
2 large leeks, finely sliced
250 g/8 oz potatoes, roughly diced
1 onion, roughly chopped
750 ml/1¼ pints Chicken Stock (see page 141) or water
300 ml/½ pint milk
salt and pepper
1 tablespoon snipped chives, to garnish

1 Melt the butter in a large saucepan. Add the leeks, potatoes and onion and stir well to coat with the butter. Cover tightly with a piece of greaseproof paper and cook over a very low heat, stirring frequently, for about 15 minutes, or until softening, but not coloured.

2 Add the stock or water and milk and season to taste with salt and pepper. Bring to the boil, reduce the heat and simmer gently for about 20 minutes until the vegetables are tender.

3 Transfer the soup to a food processor or blender and process until smooth. Return the soup to the saucepan, adjust the seasoning if necessary and heat through. Pour into individual bowls, garnish with chives and serve immediately.

Serves 4–6
Preparation time: 15 minutes
Cooking time: 35 minutes

lentil and bacon broth

1 ham shank, weighing 500 g–1 kg/1–2 lb
175 g/6 oz split red lentils, rinsed
2 large onions, finely diced
2 large carrots, finely diced
175 g/6 oz turnip, finely diced
500 g/1 lb potatoes, finely diced
3 tablespoons finely chopped parsley
salt and pepper

1 Rinse the ham shank in cold water, then put it into a large saucepan and cover with water. Bring to the boil. Pour off this water and rinse the pan. Add 2.5 litres/ 4 pints fresh cold water to the pan. Add the lentils, onions, carrots and turnip, bring to the boil, then reduce the heat and simmer for 1½ hours.

2 Add the potatoes and cook for a further 30 minutes until the meat is tender and the broth rich and thick.

3 Remove the ham from the broth, peel off the skin and cut the meat into small cubes. Return to the broth, season to taste with salt and pepper and stir in the parsley. Serve hot.

Serves 8–10
Preparation time: 15 minutes
Cooking time: 2¼ hours

courgette soup

2 tablespoons olive oil
4 shallots, diced
1 garlic clove, chopped
6 courgettes, diced
2 potatoes, chopped
1.2 litres/2 pints Chicken Stock (see page 141)
75 g/3 oz farfallini or other small dried pasta
grated rind and juice of 1 lemon
large handful of chives, chopped
salt and pepper

1 Heat the oil in a saucepan. Add the shallots and garlic and fry over a low heat for 3 minutes.

2 Add the courgettes, potatoes and stock, bring to the boil and simmer for 15 minutes. Rub the mixture through a sieve or process in a food processor or blender until smooth.

3 Add the pasta and cook for about 7 minutes until soft.

4 Stir in the lemon rind, juice and chives. Season to taste with salt and pepper and serve immediately.

Serves 4
Preparation time: 5 minutes
Cooking time: 25 minutes

chicory soup

75 g/3 oz butter
1 onion, diced
2 chicory heads, finely chopped
50 ml/2 fl oz dry white wine
1 litre/1¾ pints milk
250 ml/8 fl oz Chicken Stock (see page 141)
2 tablespoons cornflour
2 tablespoons grated Parmesan cheese
8 slices of stale bread, buttered
salt and pepper

1 Heat 50 g/2 oz of the butter in a pan over a low heat. Add the onion and fry until golden. Add the chicory and cook gently in the butter for 10 minutes, then season with salt and pepper to taste.

2 Pour in the wine and when this has evaporated, stir in most of the milk and the stock. Bring to the boil. Mix the cornflour with the remaining milk and add to the pan, stirring constantly.

3 Cook for 25 minutes over a medium heat, then whisk in the grated Parmesan cheese and the remaining butter, cut into pieces.

4 Toast the stale bread in a preheated oven, 200°C (400°F), Gas Mark 6, for about 10 minutes until golden brown. Place the toast in warmed soup bowls and pour the soup over. Serve hot.

Serves 4
Preparation time: 5 minutes
Cooking time: 55 minutes
Oven temperature: 200°C (400°F), Gas Mark 6

carrot and herb soup

25 g/1 oz butter
1 large onion, finely sliced
500 g/1 lb carrots, sliced
1 small potato, sliced
1 garlic clove, chopped
1 litre/1¾ pints Chicken Stock (see page 141)
1 bouquet garni
pinch of ground mace
150 ml/¼ pint cream
2 tablespoons finely chopped coriander
1 tablespoon finely chopped parsley
1 tablespoon finely chopped chervil
salt and pepper
croûtons, to garnish

1 Melt the butter in a large saucepan, add the vegetables and garlic and cook over a low heat until soft but not brown. Add the stock, bouquet garni and mace and season to taste with salt and pepper. Bring to the boil, then reduce the heat and simmer gently for 45 minutes–1 hour until the vegetables are tender.

2 Remove and discard the bouquet garni. Transfer the soup to a food processor or blender and process until smooth. Return to the saucepan, add the cream and bring to the boil. Mix the herbs together and stir three-quarters of them into the soup.

3 Serve immediately in individual soup bowls garnished with the croûtons and remaining herbs.

Serves 6
Preparation time: 10 minutes
Cooking time: 1 hour

mussel soup with saffron and garlic

75 g/3 oz butter
1 onion, finely sliced
175 g/6 oz leeks, white part only, finely sliced
30–40 live mussels, about 1.5 kg/3 lb in total, scrubbed and beards removed (see page 109)
2 bouquet garni
125 ml/4 fl oz dry white wine
2 garlic cloves, crushed
175 g/6 oz carrot, thinly sliced
1 celery stick, thinly sliced
750 ml/1¼ pints Fish Stock (see page 142)
pinch of saffron
150 ml/¼ pint double cream
salt and pepper
chervil fronds, to garnish

1 Melt 25 g/1 oz of the butter in a very large saucepan. Add one-third of the onion and leeks and cook until soft. Add the mussels, bouquet garni and wine. Cover and cook over a high heat, stirring occasionally, for 4–5 minutes. When all the mussel shells have opened, strain through a muslin-lined strainer set over a bowl to catch the cooking juices. Remove the mussels from their shells, discarding any which remain closed. Refrigerate until required.

2 Melt the remaining butter in a saucepan. Add the remaining onion and leeks, the garlic, carrots and celery and fry over a low heat until soft. Add the stock and the reserved mussel juices. Reserve 12 mussels to garnish the soup, chop the remainder and add to the pan. Bring to the boil and cook gently for 20 minutes.

3 Add the saffron and stir in the cream. Transfer the soup to a food processor or blender and process until smooth.

4 Return to the pan, taste and adjust the seasoning, if necessary. Stir in the reserved whole mussels and bring back to the boil. Serve immediately in individual soup bowls garnished with chervil fronds.

Serves 4–6
Preparation time: 30 minutes
Cooking time: 35 minutes

moroccan fish soup

3 tablespoons olive oil
2 onions, chopped
2 celery sticks, sliced
4 garlic cloves, crushed
1 fresh red chilli, deseeded and chopped
½ teaspoon ground cumin
1 cinnamon stick
½ teaspoon ground coriander
2 large potatoes, chopped
1.5 litres/2½ pints Fish Stock (see page 142) or water

3 tablespoons lemon juice
2 kg/4 lb mixed white fish fillets and prepared shellfish
4 tomatoes, skinned, deseeded if liked, and chopped
1 large bunch mixed dill, parsley and coriander, chopped
salt and pepper

1 Heat the oil in a large saucepan. Add the onion and celery and fry over a low heat until soft and translucent. Add the garlic and chilli and fry for 1 minute. Add the cumin, cinnamon and coriander and fry, stirring, for 1 minute, then add the potatoes and cook, stirring, for a further 2 minutes.

2 Add the stock or water and the lemon juice. Heat to simmering point, then simmer gently for about 20 minutes until the potatoes are tender.

3 Add the fish and shellfish, tomatoes and herbs and season to taste with salt and pepper. Cook over a low heat until the fish and shellfish are tender. Serve immediately.

Serves 6–8
Preparation time: 10 minutes
Cooking time: 35–45 minutes

soupe au pistou

250 g/8 oz dried haricot beans
2 tablespoons olive oil
250 g/8 oz carrots, diced
2 leeks, diced
2 celery sticks, diced
375 g/12 oz tomatoes, skinned and roughly chopped
1.2 litres/2 pints water
250 g/8 oz potatoes, diced
250 g/8 oz thin French beans, cut into 1 cm/½ inch lengths
375 g/12 oz courgettes, diced
50 g/2 oz vermicelli
salt and pepper

Pistou:
3–4 garlic cloves, peeled
pinch of salt
20 large basil leaves
125 g/4 oz grated Parmesan cheese
125 ml/4 fl oz olive oil

1 Put the haricot beans in a large bowl and cover with cold water. Leave overnight or for at least 5 hours to soak. Drain the beans and transfer to a saucepan. Cover with fresh water and bring to the boil. Skim off any scum on the surface and boil for 10 minutes. Reduce the heat and simmer for 1 hour, or until tender. Drain and set aside.

2 Heat the olive oil in a large saucepan. Add the carrots, leeks, celery and tomatoes and fry over a low heat for 2 minutes, then add the water. Bring to the boil, reduce the heat immediately and simmer for 15 minutes.

3 Add the potatoes, French beans, courgettes, vermicelli and the reserved haricot beans and simmer for 15–20 minutes, until the pasta and all the vegetables are tender. Season to taste with salt and pepper.

4 Meanwhile, make the pistou. Put the garlic, salt and basil in a food processor or blender and process to a paste. Add the Parmesan and, with the motor running, pour in the olive oil in a thin trickle through the feed tube until you have a thick green paste. Stir into the soup just before serving, or hand the pistou separately.

Serves 6
Preparation time: 30 minutes, plus soaking
Cooking time: 1½ hours

thai banana soup

1 tablespoon groundnut oil
50 g/2 oz spring onions (including green shoots), sliced
25 g/1 oz garlic, sliced
200 ml/7 fl oz coconut milk
400 ml/1¼ pints Thai Vegetable Stock (see page 142)
¼ teaspoon ground white pepper
3 tablespoons Thai fish sauce or soy sauce
¼ teaspoon salt
½ teaspoon sugar
1 large banana, peeled and cut diagonally into thin slices
1 large fresh red chilli, sliced diagonally

To garnish:
coriander leaves
2 limes, quartered
spring onion strips

1 Heat the oil in a pan. Add the spring onion and garlic and fry over a medium heat, stirring constantly until soft. Add the remaining ingredients and cook for 5 minutes.

2 If you like, this soup can be puréed. Set aside about one-quarter of the banana and chilli slices, then process the rest, together with the soup, in a food processor or blender until smooth. Return the mixture to the pan, add the reserved banana and chilli slices and warm through for 3 minutes.

3 Serve hot, garnished with coriander leaves, lime quarters and spring onion strips.

Serves 4
Preparation time: 15 minutes
Cooking time: 8 minutes

tofu soup

750 ml/1¼ pints groundnut oil
250 g/8 oz block ready-fried tofu, diced
750 ml/1¼ pints water
1 lemon grass stalk
3 lime leaves
2.5 cm/1 inch piece of galangal, peeled and sliced
1½ teaspoons salt
1 teaspoon sugar
10 small fresh green chillies, chopped
3 tablespoons lime juice
1 teaspoon Thai fish sauce or soy sauce
2 spring onions, sliced lengthways
1 carrot, cut into matchsticks
1 fresh shiitake mushroom, finely sliced
50 g/2 oz coriander leaves, to garnish

1 Heat the oil in a wok to 180–190°C (350–375°F), or until a cube of bread browns in 30 seconds. Add the tofu and deep-fry for about 3 minutes until golden. Remove from the wok, drain and set aside.

2 Put the water, lemon grass, lime leaves, galangal, salt and sugar in a saucepan, bring to the boil and simmer for about 10 minutes. Remove the pan from the heat.

3 Add the chillies to the stock, together with the lime juice, fish sauce, spring onions, carrot and mushroom. Cook over a moderate heat for about 6 minutes, then stir in the tofu.

4 Serve hot, garnished with coriander leaves.

Serves 4
Preparation time: 15 minutes
Cooking time: 20 minutes

pork and bamboo shoot soup

450 ml/¾ pint Thai Chicken Stock (see page 143)
10 black peppercorns, crushed
2 garlic cloves, crushed
5 garlic cloves, roughly chopped
125 g/4 oz minced pork
4½ teaspoons light soy sauce
100 g/3½ oz bamboo shoots
3 tablespoons Thai fish sauce
pepper

To garnish:
1 spring onion, diagonally sliced
coriander leaves

1 Put the stock in a large saucepan and bring to the boil. Lower the heat, add the peppercorns and crushed and chopped garlic.

2 Meanwhile, mix together the pork and soy sauce and season with pepper. Form the mixture into small meatballs. Add them to the simmering stock and cook for 4 minutes.

3 Add the bamboo shoots and simmer gently for 5 minutes. Stir in the fish sauce and serve, garnished with the spring onion and coriander leaves.

Serves 2
Preparation time: 6–8 minutes
Cooking time: 11 minutes

thai mussel soup

500 g/1 lb mussels, scrubbed and debearded (see page 109)
300 ml/½ pint coconut milk
600 ml/1 pint Thai Fish Stock (see page 143)
75 g/3 oz rice vermicelli, soaked for 15–20 minutes
1 tablespoon finely chopped fresh root ginger
50 g/2 oz coriander stems and roots
½ lemon grass stalk, chopped
2 small red chillies, finely sliced
1 tablespoon Thai fish sauce
1 tablespoon lime juice
25 g/1 oz coriander leaves, to garnish

1 Put the mussels into a saucepan, cover and cook over a moderate heat for 3–4 minutes. Remove the mussels with a slotted spoon and reserve. Discard any that remain closed.

2 Add the remaining ingredients to the pan, bring to the boil and simmer over a low heat for 15 minutes.

3 Return the mussels to the pan and simmer for 1 minute. Serve, garnished with coriander leaves.

Serves 4
Preparation time: 20 minutes
Cooking time: 20 minutes

hot and sour prawn soup

1.2 litres/2 pints Thai Fish Stock (see page 143)
4 lime leaves, torn
1 lemon grass stalk, finely sliced diagonally
2.5 cm/1 inch piece of galangal or fresh root ginger, sliced
1 tablespoon palm sugar or light muscovado sugar
5 tablespoons lime juice
2 tablespoons chilli oil or 12 small green chillies, chopped
12–16 raw prawns
salt and pepper
coriander sprigs, to garnish

1 Put the stock, lime leaves, lemon grass, galangal or ginger, sugar, lime juice and chilli oil or chopped chillies in a large wok or saucepan and bring to the boil. Lower the heat and simmer gently for 15 minutes.

2 Add the prawns and cook for 1 minute until they have turned pink and are cooked through.

3 Season to taste with salt and pepper and serve immediately, garnished with sprigs of coriander.

Serves 4
Preparation time: 5 minutes
Cooking time: 20 minutes

potato, carrot and barley soup

50 g/2 oz butter or margarine
375 g/12 oz potatoes, peeled and cut into 2.5 cm/1 inch cubes
275 g/9 oz carrots, thinly sliced
1 large onion, chopped
1 tablespoon plain flour
1.2 litres/2 pints Chicken Stock (see page 141)
½ teaspoon dried mixed herbs
50 g/2 oz pearl barley, soaked overnight in cold water, drained
300 ml/½ pint milk
salt and pepper

To garnish:
croûtons
chopped parsley

1 Melt the butter or margarine in a large saucepan. Add the potatoes, carrots and onion and fry gently, stirring occasionally, for 5 minutes. Sprinkle in the flour and cook for 1 minute more, then add 900 ml/1½ pints of the stock and bring to the boil, stirring.

2 Lower the heat, add the herbs and season with salt and pepper to taste. Cover and simmer gently for 30 minutes, or until the vegetables are tender. Allow to cool slightly, then transfer to a food processor or blender and process for 30 seconds or until smooth. Alternatively, rub the mixture through a sieve.

3 Return the soup to the rinsed pan, stir in the remaining stock and the barley and bring to the boil. Lower the heat, cover and cook, stirring occasionally, for a further 30 minutes until the barley is tender.

4 Stir in the milk and taste and adjust the seasoning. Heat through gently. Serve the soup piping hot in warmed bowls, garnished with croûtons and parsley.

Serves 6
Preparation time: 10–15 minutes, plus soaking
Cooking time: 1¼ hours

creamy corn and chicken chowder

25 g/1 oz butter or margarine
1 large onion, chopped
1 small red pepper, cored, deseeded and diced
625 g/1¼ lb potatoes, peeled and diced
25 g/1 oz plain flour
750 ml/1¼ pints Chicken Stock (see page 141)
175 g/6 oz frozen sweetcorn, thawed
250 g/8 oz cooked chicken, diced
450 ml/¾ pint milk
½ teaspoon salt
freshly ground white pepper
3 tablespoons chopped parsley
crusty bread, to serve

1 Melt the butter or margarine in a large saucepan. Add the onions, red pepper and potatoes and fry over a moderate heat for 5 minutes, stirring from time to time.

2 Sprinkle in the flour and cook over a low heat for 1 minute. Gradually stir in the stock and bring to the boil, stirring, then lower the heat, cover and cook for 10 minutes.

3 Stir in the sweetcorn, chicken, milk, salt, pepper to taste, and parsley, then cover and simmer gently for a further 10 minutes until the potatoes are just tender. Taste and adjust the seasoning.

4 Serve the chowder hot in warmed soup bowls, with crusty bread.

Serves 4–6
Preparation time: 20 minutes
Cooking time: 30 minutes

curried cauliflower soup

1 tablespoon sunflower oil
1 onion, sliced
2 teaspoons curry powder (or to taste)
1 small cauliflower, roughly chopped
900 ml/1½ pints Chicken Stock (see page 141)
salt and pepper
4 tablespoons sunflower seeds, to garnish

1 Heat the oil in a large saucepan. Add the onion and fry over a moderate heat for 2 minutes. Stir in the curry powder and cook for 1 minute.

2 Add the cauliflower and stock, season with salt and pepper and bring to the boil. Cover the pan, lower the heat and simmer for 20 minutes.

3 Cool slightly, then transfer the vegetables and stock to a food processor or blender and process to a smooth purée. Alternatively, rub them through a sieve.

4 Return the purée to the rinsed pan. Taste and adjust the seasoning if necessary and reheat.

5 Serve the soup in warmed bowls, garnished with the sunflower seeds.

Serves 4–6
Preparation time: 10 minutes
Cooking time: 30 minutes

celeriac and orange soup

1 celeriac, about 375 g/12 oz, peeled and roughly
  chopped
1 potato, peeled and roughly chopped
2 carrots, sliced
1 litre/1¾ pints Chicken Stock (see page 141)
thinly pared rind of ½ orange
1 teaspoon grated orange rind
1 tablespoon orange juice
salt and pepper
single cream or crème fraîche, to garnish

1 Put the celeriac, potato and carrots into a saucepan with the stock and bring to the boil. Cover the pan, lower the heat and simmer for 30 minutes, or until all the vegetables are soft.

2 Cut the orange rind into very thin matchstick strips. Place them in a saucepan with a little boiling water and boil for 10 minutes, then drain. Reserve for the garnish.

3 Cool the vegetables and stock slightly, then transfer to a food processor or blender and process to a smooth purée. Alternatively, rub them through a sieve.

4 Return the purée to the rinsed pan, add the grated orange rind and juice and season with salt and pepper to taste. Bring back to the boil, then simmer for 5 minutes.

5 Serve the soup in heated dishes or bowls, adding a swirl of cream or crème fraîche to each portion and garnishing with the reserved strips of orange rind.

Serves 6
Preparation time: 15 minutes
Cooking time: 50 minutes

red lentil soup

4 streaky bacon rashers, rinded and diced
1 onion, sliced
125 g/4 oz celeriac, peeled and chopped
125 g/4 oz red lentils, washed and drained
1.2 litres/2 pints Chicken Stock (see page 141)
½ teaspoon dried mixed herbs
salt and pepper
croûtons or crusty bread, to serve

1 Place the bacon in a large nonstick saucepan and heat gently until the fat runs. Add the onion and fry gently for 5 minutes until softened.

2 Add the celeriac and stir well to mix. Stir in the lentils, stock and herbs and season with salt and pepper to taste. Bring to the boil, lower the heat and simmer for 45 minutes–1 hour, or until the lentils are tender.

3 Transfer the soup to a food processor or blender and process to a smooth purée. Alternatively, rub it through a sieve. Return the soup to the rinsed pan, reheat gently and adjust the seasoning to taste.

4 Serve in warmed soup bowls with croûtons or crusty bread broken into large chunks.

Serves 4–6
Preparation time: 10–15 minutes
Cooking time: 1–1¼ hours

courgette and yogurt soup

50 g/2 oz butter or margarine
1 onion, chopped
500 g/1 lb courgettes, cut into 5 mm/¼ inch slices
900 ml/1½ pints Chicken Stock (see page 141)
1 mint sprig
salt and pepper
150 ml/¼ pint natural yogurt, plus extra to garnish
brown bread and butter, to serve (optional)

1 Melt the butter or margarine in a large saucepan. Add the onion and courgettes and fry gently for 5 minutes.

2 Add the stock and mint and season to taste with salt and pepper. Bring to the boil, lower the heat, cover the pan and simmer for 20–30 minutes, or until the courgettes are soft.

3 Reserve a few courgette slices to garnish and transfer the soup to a food processor or blender and process to a smooth purée. Alternatively, rub it through a sieve. Transfer the soup to a bowl, stir in the yogurt and chill for 3 hours.

4 Serve in chilled individual soup bowls, garnished with the reserved courgette slices and the extra yogurt. Accompany with thin slices of brown bread and butter, if liked.

Serves 4–6
Preparation time: 10 minutes, plus chilling
Cooking time: 30–40 minutes

asparagus cheese soup

25 g/1 oz butter
1 small onion, chopped
750 g/1½ lb fresh asparagus, cut into 2.5 cm/1 inch pieces
1.2 litres/2 pints Chicken Stock (see page 141)
125 g/4 oz brie cheese, diced
few drops of green food colouring (optional)
salt and pepper

To garnish:
150 ml/¼ pint single cream
a few cooked asparagus spears

1 Melt the butter in a large saucepan. Add the onion and fry gently for 5 minutes until soft and lightly browned. Add the asparagus and cook for 1–2 minutes more.

2 Pour in the stock, season to taste with salt and pepper, then bring to the boil. Cover, lower the heat and simmer for about 25 minutes, or until the asparagus is tender.

3 Remove the pan from the heat. Transfer the soup to a food processor or blender and process to a smooth purée. Alternatively, rub it through a sieve. Add the diced cheese and mix thoroughly until smooth.

4 Return the soup to the rinsed pan and reheat. Adjust the seasoning to taste and add the green food colouring, if using.

5 Serve in warmed bowls, garnished with swirls of cream and asparagus spears.

Serves 6
Preparation time: 10 minutes
Cooking time: 35–40 minutes

cream of artichoke soup with parmesan croûtons

50 g/2 oz butter
500 g/1 lb Jerusalem artichokes, peeled and sliced
500 g/1 lb potatoes, peeled and sliced
2 onions, sliced
600 ml/1 pint milk
300 ml/½ pint Chicken Stock (see page 141)
150 ml/¼ pint single cream, to garnish
salt and pepper

Parmesan croûtons:
3 thick slices of white bread, crusts removed, cut into
*   1 cm/½ inch squares*
oil, for shallow frying
1 tablespoon grated Parmesan cheese

1 Melt the butter in a large heavy saucepan. Add the artichokes, potatoes and onions, stir well to coat all the vegetables, then cover. Cook for 20–25 minutes over a low heat, so that the vegetables sweat in the butter, but do not brown. Shake the pan from time to time to ensure even cooking.

2 Add the milk and chicken stock to the pan and season to taste with salt and pepper. Simmer the soup, stirring from time to time, for 45 minutes.

3 Cool the soup a little, then transfer to a food processor or blender and process to a smooth purée. Alternatively, rub it through a sieve. Return the soup to the rinsed pan and reheat gently.

4 Meanwhile, make the croûtons. Fry the cubes of bread in hot oil, turning constantly, for about 5 minutes. Drain on kitchen paper and toss in the grated Parmesan while still hot.

5 Serve the soup in warmed individual bowls with a swirl of cream to garnish, and add the Parmesan croûtons.

Serves 6
Preparation time: 20 minutes
Cooking time: about 1 hour 20 minutes

pumpkin and lemon soup

50 g/2 oz butter
1 large onion, sliced
500 g/1 lb pumpkin, peeled, deseeded and cut into
*   chunks*
250 g/8 oz potatoes, peeled and sliced
1 small garlic clove, crushed
1 thyme sprig
1.2 litres/2 pints Chicken Stock (see page 141)
4 tablespoons lemon juice
150 ml/¼ pint double cream
salt and pepper

1 Melt the butter in a large heavy saucepan. Add the onion and fry over a low heat for 3 minutes until soft and translucent.

2 Add the pumpkin, potatoes, garlic and thyme. Cover the pan and cook over a low heat for 20 minutes, or until the vegetables are soft.

3 Add the stock and season with salt and pepper to taste. Bring to the boil, lower the heat and simmer for 10 minutes. Remove the thyme sprig.

4 Transfer the soup to a food processor or blender and process to a smooth purée. Alternatively, rub it through a sieve. Return the soup to the rinsed pan. Add the lemon juice, stir in the cream and reheat without boiling.

5 Serve in warmed individual soup bowls.

Serves 6
Preparation time: 15 minutes
Cooking time: 40 minutes

pâté de campagne

50 g/2 oz butter, plus extra for greasing
2 onions, finely chopped
4 garlic cloves, crushed
500 g/1 lb pig's liver, diced
275 g/9 oz streaky bacon rashers, rinded
500 g/1 lb lean pork, minced or chopped
2 tablespoons chopped parsley
½ teaspoon dried sage
¼ teaspoon ground mace
¼ teaspoon ground nutmeg
2 egg whites
2 tablespoons brandy
2 bay leaves
salt and pepper
crusty bread or toast, to serve

1 Lightly grease a 500 g/1 lb terrine or loaf tin.

2 Melt the butter in a frying pan. Add the onions and garlic and fry over a low heat for a few minutes until tender and golden. Transfer to a large bowl. Add the liver to the pan and fry until lightly browned. Remove and mince or chop.

3 Chop 200 g/7 oz of the bacon and add to the bowl, together with the liver, pork, parsley, sage, mace, nutmeg, egg whites and brandy and season to taste with salt and pepper. Mix together until thoroughly combined.

4 Line the terrine or loaf tin with the remaining bacon rashers so that they hang over the sides. Fill with the pâté mixture and fold the bacon over the top. Put the bay leaves on top and place in a roasting tin. Add sufficient hot water to come halfway up the sides.

5 Cook in a preheated oven, 190°C (375°F), Gas Mark 5, for 1½ hours, or until the juices run clear and the pâté has shrunk from the sides of the tin.

6 Leave the pâté to cool for 30 minutes, then cover with a piece of greaseproof paper or foil and weigh it down with some light weights. Leave until completely cold and set. If you like, you can replace the bay leaves with fresh ones. Cover and refrigerate for about 36 hours. Serve sliced with toast or crusty bread.

Serves 8
Preparation time: 30 minutes, plus chilling
Cooking time: 1½ hours
Oven temperature: 190°C (375°F), Gas Mark 5

chicken liver pâté with sweet and sour onion salsa

250 g/8 oz chicken livers
50 g/2 oz butter
1 shallot, finely chopped
3 tablespoons Madeira
3 tablespoons double cream
1 teaspoon pink peppercorns, crushed
salt and pepper
crisp bread or toast, to serve

Sweet and sour onion salsa:
2 red onions, sliced
1 tablespoon olive oil
3 tablespoons balsamic vinegar
2 tablespoons soft brown sugar
1 rosemary sprig, bruised
4 tablespoons water

1 Trim the chicken livers discarding any discoloured parts, wash and dry well.

2 Melt the butter in a frying pan. Add the shallot and fry over a medium heat for 5 minutes.

3 Increase the heat and add the chicken livers. Fry for 3–4 minutes until browned on all sides, but still slightly pink in the centre.

4 Remove the livers using a slotted spoon and place in a food processor or blender. Add the Madeira to the frying pan and reduce by half, scraping the sediment from the base of the pan.

5 Scrape into the blender and add the cream and a little salt. Process to form a smooth paste and pass through a fine sieve. Stir in the peppercorns and spoon into a small dish. Leave to cool and then chill overnight.

6 To make the salsa, place all the ingredients in a saucepan and season with salt and pepper. Simmer over a low heat for 20 minutes until soft and caramelized. Leave to cool. Serve the pâté and salsa together with crisp bread or toast.

Serves: 4
Preparation time: 20 minutes, plus chilling
Cooking time: 30 minutes

smoked salmon mousse

175 g/6 oz smoked salmon pieces
50 g/2 oz cream cheese
150 ml/¼ pint soured cream
1 tablespoon fresh lemon juice
1 teaspoon grated lemon rind
cayenne pepper

To serve:
crudités
pumpernickel, thinly sliced

1 Put the smoked salmon into a food processor or blender and process for a few seconds. Add the cream cheese, soured cream, lemon juice and rind, and process until smooth.

2 Season the salmon mousse to taste with cayenne pepper. Serve with crudités and thinly sliced pumpernickel.

Serves: 8
Preparation time: 5 minutes

rillettes de porc

1.5 kg/3 lb belly pork on the bone
750 g/1½ lb pork bones
2 sage leaves
1 bouquet garni
salt and pepper

To serve:
crusty bread
salad

1 Place the pork, pork bones, sage leaves and bouquet garni in a large saucepan. Add just enough water to cover and season with a little salt and pepper. Cook over a low heat until the water has almost evaporated and the meat is falling off the bone.

2 Strain off the remaining juices, much of which will be pork fat, and set aside. Remove all the meat from the bones and place in a mixing bowl, discarding the sage and bouquet garni.

3 Using 2 forks, shred the meat finely. Check the seasoning. Place the meat in a terrine or 6 small ramekin dishes. The dishes should be only three-quarters full.

4 Strain the reserved juices over the meat and chill the rillettes in the refrigerator for at least 3 hours until set. Serve with crusty bread and a salad.

Serves 6–8
Preparation time: 10 minutes, plus chilling
Cooking time: 2–3 hours

creamed smoked mackerel pots

1 smoked mackerel, about 250 g/8 oz, skinned, boned and flaked
65 g/2½ oz butter, melted
50 g/2 oz full-fat soft cheese
1 teaspoon lemon juice
1 tablespoon chopped parsley
½–1 teaspoon creamed horseradish (optional)
pepper

To garnish:
lemon slices
parsley sprigs

1 Place the mackerel in a bowl. Add 25 g/1 oz of the melted butter and the cheese and stir well to mix.

2 Stir in the lemon juice, parsley, creamed horseradish, if using, and pepper to taste. Mix thoroughly until well combined.

3 Divide the mixture evenly between 4 small individual ramekins or serving pots and smooth the surface.

4 Pour the remaining melted butter over each ramekin and chill in the refrigerator for at least 2 hours before serving, garnished with lemon slices and parsley sprigs.

Serves 4
Preparation time: 15 minutes, plus chilling

ardennes pâté

500 g/1 lb pork fillet, diced
500 g/1 lb belly pork, diced
500 g/1 lb minced veal
750 g/1½ lb chicken livers, chopped
8 tablespoons brandy
4 teaspoons chopped thyme
2 tablespoons green peppercorns
butter, for greasing
8–12 streaky bacon rashers, rinded
salt and pepper
toast, to serve

To garnish:
thyme sprigs
lemon slices

1 Combine the pork, veal and chicken livers in a large bowl. Stir in the brandy, thyme and peppercorns and season to taste with salt and pepper. Cover and chill for 2 hours.

2 Lightly grease a 1 kg/2 lb loaf tin and spoon in the meat mixture. Stretch the bacon with the flat side of a knife and use to cover the pâté. Cover with foil and place in a roasting pan. Pour in enough boiling water to come halfway up the sides of the pan. Cook in a preheated moderate oven, 180°C (350°F), Gas Mark 4, for about 1½ hours.

3 Leave to cool in the tin and turn out when cold. Garnish with thyme and lemon slices, and serve with toast.

Serves 16
Preparation time: 30 minutes, plus chilling
Cooking time: 1½ hours
Oven temperature: 180°C (350°F), Gas Mark 4

liver and mushroom pâté

65 g/2½ oz butter
1 garlic clove, chopped
1 onion, thinly sliced
4 streaky bacon rashers, rinded and diced
125 g/4 oz button mushrooms, sliced
250 g/8 oz chicken livers, trimmed
150 ml/¼ pint Chicken Stock (see page 141)
2 hard-boiled eggs, chopped
3 tablespoons single cream
salt and pepper

To garnish:
4 bay leaves
black peppercorns

1 Melt 40 g/1½ oz of the butter in a frying pan. Add the garlic, onion and bacon and fry over a moderate heat for 5 minutes.

2 Add the mushrooms and chicken livers and fry, stirring, for 5 minutes more.

3 Add the stock and bring to the boil. Cover, lower the heat and simmer for 10 minutes.

4 Strain the mixture and process in a food processor or blender for about 30 seconds until smooth. Add the hard-boiled eggs and cream and season to taste with salt and pepper, then process again until smooth and combined. Add a little stock if necessary.

5 Turn the mixture into a 300 ml/½ pint serving dish and smooth the surface. Melt the remaining butter and pour it over the top. Garnish with the bay leaves and peppercorns, then chill in the refrigerator for at least 4 hours.

Serves 4–5
Preparation time: 15 minutes, plus chilling
Cooking time: 25 minutes

farmhouse terrine

10 streaky bacon rashers, rinded
500 g/1 lb pig's liver, coarsely minced
500 g/1 lb lean pork, coarsely minced
1 onion, finely chopped
2 garlic cloves, crushed
½ teaspoon dried thyme or mixed herbs
1 tablespoon dry sherry
50 g/2 oz fresh wholemeal breadcrumbs
½ teaspoon salt
pepper

1 Place the bacon rashers on a board and stretch them with the flat side of a knife, until double their original length. Line a 1 kg/2 lb loaf tin with the bacon rashers, arranging them crossways and slightly overlapping along the length of the tin, allowing the ends to overlap the rim of the tin on each of the longer sides.

2 Place the liver, pork, onion, garlic, herbs, sherry, breadcrumbs and salt and pepper in a bowl and stir well to mix.

3 Turn the mixture into the bacon-lined tin and smooth the surface. Fold the overlapping ends of the bacon rashers over the mixture.

4 Cover the loaf tin tightly with foil and place in a roasting tin. Pour in sufficient cold water to come halfway up the sides of the tin. Cook in a preheated oven, 160°C (325°F), Gas Mark 3, for 2½ hours.

5 Remove the foil and cover with fresh foil. Place a weight on the wrapped terrine to compress it. (A clean house brick, tightly wrapped, is ideal for this.) Leave the terrine to cool for 3 hours, then chill overnight, in the refrigerator, still weighted.

6 Run a knife around the edge of the terrine and turn on to a serving plate. Serve cut into chunky slices.

Serves 8–10
Preparation time: 25 minutes, plus chilling
Cooking time: 2½ hours
Oven temperature: 160°C (325°F), Gas Mark 3

pork and port pâté

1 large onion
1 garlic clove
500 g/1 lb belly pork
3 tablespoons port
1 teaspoon mint, chopped
250 g/8 oz lambs' liver, finely chopped
3 streaky bacon rashers, rinded and finely chopped
50 g/2 oz mushrooms, finely chopped
1 egg, beaten
salt and pepper
rosemary sprigs, to garnish

1 Put the onion, garlic and pork into a food processor and process until smooth. Turn into a bowl, stir in the port and mint and season to taste with salt and pepper. Cover closely and leave to marinate in the refrigerator overnight.

2 Mix the lambs' liver, bacon and mushrooms into the pork mixture. Stir in the egg. Spoon into a foil-lined 500 g/1lb loaf tin and bake in a preheated oven, 180°C (350°F), Gas Mark 4, for 1½ hours. Carefully pour off the fat and leave to cool.

3 To serve, remove the pâté from the tin, place on a serving dish and garnish with sprigs of rosemary.

Serves 8
Preparation time: 10–15 minutes, plus marinating
Cooking time: 1½ hours
Oven temperature: 180°C (350°F), Gas Mark 4

spinach and courgette pâté

2 tablespoons olive oil
1 onion, thinly sliced
375 g/12 oz cougettes, sliced
375 g/12 oz spinach, washed
½ teaspoon grated nutmeg
250 g/8 oz curd cheese
50 g/2 oz fresh white breadcrumbs
2 teaspoons chopped basil, or 1 teaspoon dried basil
2 teaspoons chopped marjoram, or 1 teaspoon dried marjoram
1 egg, beaten
2 tablespoons melted butter
salt and pepper

1 Heat the oil in a frying pan, add the onion and courgettes and fry gently for 5 minutes until softened and lightly browned. Remove from the pan with a slotted spoon and drain on kitchen paper. Purée in a food processor or blender or rub through a sieve.

2 Place the spinach in a saucepan with just the water that clings to the leaves after washing. Cook gently, stirring occasionally, for about 10 minutes or until tender. Drain and chop finely. Tip into a bowl, add the nutmeg and season to taste with salt and pepper.

3 Place the courgette purée in a heavy saucepan and set over a gentle heat for 2–3 minutes to dry out. Transfer to a bowl, then beat in the curd cheese, breadcrumbs, basil and marjoram and season to taste with salt and pepper. Stir in the beaten egg to bind.

4 Brush the inside of a 500 g/1 lb loaf tin liberally with melted butter. Line the base with greaseproof paper, then brush with more melted butter. Spoon half of the courgette mixture into the base of the tin, press down firmly and level the surface.

5 Spread the spinach in an even layer over the top, then cover with the remaining courgette mixture and press it down evenly.

6 Cover the tin with buttered foil, then place in a roasting tin. Pour boiling water into the roasting tin to come half way up the sides of the loaf tin. Place in a preheated oven, 160°C (325°F), Gas Mark 3, for 1¼ hours or until the mixture feels firm and set when a knife is inserted into the centre. Remove from the roasting tin and leave to cool completely. Chill in the refrigerator overnight.

7 Loosen the sides of the pâté from the tin with a knife, then turn out on to a serving plate; peel off the paper. Serve chilled, cut into slices.

Serves 6
Preparation time: 30 minutes
Cooking time: 1 hour 35 minutes
Oven temperature: 160°C (325°F), Gas Mark 3

aubergine pâté

2 large aubergines
1 garlic clove, crushed
2 teaspoons lemon juice
2 tablespoons olive oil
2 tablespoons chopped parsley
salt and pepper
wholemeal toast, to serve

To garnish:
chopped parsley
lemon wedges

1 Prick the aubergines all over with a fork, cut them in half and place, cut side down, on a greased baking sheet. Place in a preheated oven, 190°C (375°F), Gas Mark 5, for 30–40 minutes until softened.

2 Peel the aubergines and place in a food processor or blender with the garlic and lemon juice. Process, adding the oil a teaspoon at a time. Alternatively, chop the flesh finely and rub it through a sieve, then add the garlic, lemon juice and oil in a steady stream, beating until smooth.

3 Stir in the parsley, season to taste with salt and pepper and spoon into ramekin dishes. Chill in the refrigerator for at least 1 hour.

4 Garnish with parsley and lemon wedges. Serve with wholemeal toast.

Serves 4
Preparation time: 15 minutes, plus chilling
Cooking time: 30–40 minutes
Oven temperature: 190°C (375°F), Gas Mark 5

carrot and coriander pâté

500 g/1 lb carrots, grated
1 tablespoon ground coriander
175 ml/6 fl oz freshly squeezed orange juice
300 ml/½ pint water
50 g/2 oz medium-fat soft cheese
30 g/1¼ oz coriander leaves
salt and pepper
rustic bread, to serve

1 Place the grated carrot in a saucepan, together with the ground coriander, orange juice and water. Cover and simmer for 40 minutes until the carrots are cooked. Cool and transfer to a food processor or blender with a little of the cooking liquid.

2 Add the soft cheese and coriander leaves and process until smooth. Season to taste with salt and pepper and blend again. Spoon into small dishes and chill before serving with rustic bread.

Serves 4
Preparation time: 5 minutes, plus chilling
Cooking time: 40 minutes

smoked oyster tarts

250 g/8 oz Shortcrust Pastry dough (see page 124)
50 g/2 oz smoked oysters, drained and chopped
1 teaspoon chopped parsley
1 egg
150 ml/¼ pint single cream
cayenne pepper
pepper

1 Roll out the dough thinly on a lightly floured surface and cut into rounds using a 6 cm/2½ inch cutter. Line 12 greased mini tartlet tins with the dough rounds and prick all over with a fork.

2 Bake the pastry cases 'blind' (see page 122) in a preheated oven, 220°C (425°F), Gas Mark 7, for 10 minutes. Remove from the oven and reduce the temperature to 190°C (375°F), Gas Mark 5.

3 Divide the oysters and parsley between the pastry cases.

4 Mix together the egg and cream and season to taste with cayenne and pepper. Pour the mixture into the pastry cases.

5 Bake the tarts for a further 15–20 minutes, or until the filling is set and golden brown.

Makes 12
Preparation time: 20 minutes
Cooking time: 30 minutes
Oven temperature: 220°C (425°F), Gas Mark 7

tomato and anchovy tartlets

Pastry:
250 g/8 oz wholemeal flour
½ teaspoon salt
50 g/2 oz hard white fat, diced
50 g/2 oz butter or margarine, diced

Filling:
3 tablespoons olive oil
3 large onions, thinly sliced
6 tomatoes, skinned and roughly chopped
1 garlic clove, crushed
1 teaspoon dried mixed herbs
50 g/2 oz can anchovy fillets, drained and soaked in
*   2 tablespoons milk for 15 minutes, rinsed and drained*
10 black olives, pitted
salt and pepper
basil sprigs, to garnish

1 To make the pastry, sift the flour with the salt into a mixing bowl. Add the fat and butter or margarine and rub them in with the fingertips until the mixture resembles fine breadcrumbs. Add just enough water to bind to a stiff dough. Knead lightly until smooth.

2 Turn the dough on to a lightly floured surface, roll out to 5 mm/¼ inch thickness and use to line ten 7 cm/3 inch tartlet tins. Prick the pastry with a fork and chill in the refrigerator for 20 minutes.

3 Meanwhile, prepare the filling. Heat the oil in a saucepan. Add the onions and fry over a low heat for about 5 minutes, until soft and lightly browned. Stir in the tomatoes, garlic and herbs. Cook, uncovered, for 15 minutes, until the sauce is thick. Season to taste with salt and pepper.

4 Bake the tartlet cases 'blind' (see page 122) in a preheated oven, 180°C (350°F), Gas Mark 4, for 7 minutes. Remove the foil and beans. Spoon the tomato filling into the tartlet cases. Arrange the anchovy fillets and olives over the top.

5 Bake for 10 minutes, then remove from the oven. Cool in the tins for 10 minutes, then transfer to a wire rack. Serve cold, garnished with the basil.

Serves 5
Preparation time: 30 minutes, plus chilling
Cooking time: 40 minutes
Oven temperature: 180°C (350°F), Gas Mark 4

onion tart

50 g/2 oz butter
125 g/4 oz smoked bacon, rinded and diced
500 g/1 lb onions, finely sliced
25 g/1 oz plain flour
200 ml/7 fl oz milk
6 tablespoons single cream
2 egg yolks
pinch of grated nutmeg
salt and pepper

French flan pastry:
250 g/8 oz plain flour
½ teaspoon salt
140 g/4½ oz butter, chilled, plus extra for greasing
1 egg yolk
¼ teaspoon lemon juice
3–4 tablespoons iced water

1 First make the pastry. Sift the flour and salt together into a mixing bowl. Add the butter and rub it into the flour with the fingertips until the mixture resembles fine breadcrumbs.

2 Mix together the egg yolk, lemon juice and 3 tablespoons of the water. Add to the mixing bowl and mix lightly with a fork. Gather the dough together with your hand. If it is too dry and crumbly, add a little more water.

3 Turn the dough on to a work surface. Knead by pushing small pieces of it away from you with the heel of the hand, smearing them on the work surface. Continue kneading in this way until the dough is smooth and elastic and can be easily peeled away from the work surface. Shape into a ball, cover and chill in the refrigerator for 30 minutes–1 hour.

4 Melt the butter in a large frying pan. Add the bacon and onions and fry over a low heat until soft and golden. Add the flour and cook for 1 minute. Stir in the milk and cream and cook, stirring occasionally, for 5 minutes.

5 Remove the pan from the heat and add the egg yolks and grated nutmeg and season to taste with salt and pepper. Stir well and set aside to cool.

6 Grease a 25 cm/10 inch loose-based flan tin. Roll out the pastry dough on a lightly floured surface and use to line the flan tin. Prick the base of the pastry with a fork.

7 Pour the prepared onion mixture into the pastry case. Slide on to a baking tray and cook in a preheated oven, 180°C (350°F), Gas Mark 4, for 40 minutes until set and golden. Serve hot.

Serves 6
Preparation time: 45 minutes, plus chilling
Cooking time: 50 minutes
Oven temperature: 180°C (350°F), Gas Mark 4

spinach and ricotta tartlets

1 quantity Shortcrust Pastry dough (see page 124)
125 g/4 oz frozen leaf spinach, thawed and squeezed dry
200 g/7 oz ricotta cheese
2 tablespoons freshly grated Parmesan cheese
pinch of grated nutmeg
2 eggs, beaten
4 tablespoons single cream
salt and pepper

1 Divide the shortcrust dough into 6 and roll each piece out to line a 8.5 cm/3½ inch tartlet tin. Prick the base with a fork and chill for 20 minutes.

2 Meanwhile, prepare the filling. Place all the remaining ingredients in a bowl and mix until well blended. Season well with salt and pepper.

3 Bake the pastry cases 'blind' (see page 122) in a preheated oven, 200°C (400°F), Gas Mark 6, for 10 minutes. Remove the foil and beans and bake for a further 10 minutes until the pastry is crisp and golden.

4 Divide the filling between the cases, return to the oven and cook for 20 minutes more until risen and firm to the touch. Cool slightly and serve warm.

Serves 6
Preparation time: 30 minutes, plus chilling
Cooking time: 40 minutes
Oven temperature: 200°C (400°F), Gas Mark 6

leek and filo parcels

40 g/1½ oz butter
500 g/1 lb leeks, thinly sliced
1 garlic clove, crushed
4 tablespoons crème fraîche or fromage frais, plus extra
  to serve
1 tablespoon chopped chervil
freshly grated nutmeg
25 g/1 oz fresh white breadcrumbs
25 g/1 oz Parmesan cheese, grated
8 large sheets filo pastry, thawed if frozen
extra virgin olive oil, for brushing
salt and pepper
chervil sprigs, to garnish

1 Melt half the butter in a frying pan. Add the leeks and garlic and fry over a low heat for 4–5 minutes until the leeks are tender. Leave to cool slightly and then stir in the crème fraîche or fromage frais and chervil. Season to taste with nutmeg, salt and pepper.

2 Melt the remaining butter in another pan. Add the breadcrumbs and stir-fry for 4–5 minutes until golden. Stir into the leek mixture, together with the Parmesan.

3 Cut each sheet of pastry lengthways into 3 strips. Brush one strip with oil, place a second on top and brush again (keep the remaining sheets covered with a damp tea towel as you work, to prevent the pastry from drying out).

4 Place a heaped tablespoon of the leek mixture at one end of the filo pastry. Fold over on the diagonal and continue folding along the length of the pastry to enclose the filling. Brush with oil and transfer to an oiled baking sheet. Repeat to make 12 triangles.

5 Bake in a preheated oven, 200°C (400°F), Gas Mark 6, for 20–25 minutes until golden. Serve with extra crème fraîche. Garnish with chervil.

Serves 4–6
Preparation time: 15 minutes
Cooking time: 30–35 minutes
Oven temperature: 200°C (400°F), Gas Mark 6

pancakes with spinach and ricotta

1 quantity Basic Pancake Batter (see page 127)
vegetable oil, for frying

Tomato sauce:
2 tablespoons olive oil
1 shallot, finely chopped
1 carrot, finely chopped
1 celery stick, finely chopped
1 garlic clove, crushed
750 g/1½ lb bottle passata
250 ml/8 fl oz Vegetable Stock (see page 140) or water
1 teaspoon dried basil
2 tablespoons chopped flat leaf parsley
salt and pepper

Filling:
250 g/8 oz ricotta cheese
125 g/4 oz frozen leaf spinach, thawed and squeezed dry
2 eggs, beaten
1 tablespoon grated Parmesan cheese
pinch of grated nutmeg

Béchamel sauce:
50 g/2 oz butter
2 tablespoons plain flour
500 ml/17 fl oz milk
50 g/2 oz Parmesan cheese, grated

1 First, make the tomato sauce. Heat the oil in a saucepan. Add the shallot, carrot, celery and garlic and fry over a low heat, stirring frequently, for 2–3 minutes. Stir in the passata and stock or water, add the basil and season to taste with salt and pepper. Bring to the boil, then simmer, stirring occasionally, for 20–30 minutes until thickened.

2 Meanwhile, cook 12 pancakes in a lightly oiled 18 cm/7 inch frying pan, stacking the pancakes up, interleaved with greaseproof paper, as they are cooked.

3 Stir the parsley into the tomato sauce and spread half the sauce evenly over the base of a large ovenproof dish.

4 Mix together the ingredients for the filling and season to taste with salt and pepper. Put a spoon of the filling on one of the pancakes, spreading it down one side, then roll the pancake up around it. Place the pancake in the dish and then repeat with the remaining pancakes. Pour over the remaining tomato sauce.

5 To make the béchamel sauce, melt the butter in a saucepan. Add the flour and cook over a low heat, stirring constantly, for 1–2 minutes until golden. Gradually whisk in the milk and bring to the boil. Simmer, whisking constantly, for 2–3 minutes until thickened. Remove from the heat, stir in half the Parmesan and season to taste with salt and pepper.

6 Pour the béchamel over the pancakes, sprinkle with the remaining Parmesan and bake in a preheated oven, 180°C (350°F), Gas Mark 4, for 30–35 minutes. Serve hot, straight from the dish.

Serves 6
Preparation time: 20 minutes
Cooking time: 1 hour 25 minutes
Oven temperature: 180°C (350°F), Gas Mark 4

cheese soufflé

50 g/2 oz butter, plus extra for greasing
50 g/2 oz plain flour
250 ml/8 fl oz milk
2 tablespoons single cream
4 egg yolks
150 g/5 oz Gruyère cheese, grated
¼ teaspoon freshly grated nutmeg
5 egg whites
salt and white pepper

1 Grease a 1.2 litre/2 pint soufflé dish or two 600 ml/1 pint dishes with butter.

2 Melt the butter in a saucepan. Stir in the flour and cook, stirring constantly, over a low heat for 1–2 minutes. Gradually add the milk, stirring well between each addition until the sauce is thick and smooth. Cook very gently, stirring constantly with a wooden spoon, for 15 minutes.

3 Remove the pan from the heat and stir in the cream. Stir the egg yolks into the mixture, a little at a time. Add the Gruyère and nutmeg and season to taste with salt and pepper. Beat well until the cheese has melted and the mixture is really smooth.

4 Whisk the egg whites in a grease-free bowl until they are really stiff, but not dry. Fold them gently into the cheese mixture with a metal spoon using a figure-of-eight motion.

5 Transfer the mixture to the soufflé dish or dishes. Bake in a preheated oven, 180°C (350°F), Gas Mark 4, for 15 minutes. Increase the temperature to 200°C (400°F), Gas Mark 6 and cook for a further 15 minutes until the soufflé is well risen and golden. Serve immediately.

Serves 4
Preparation time: 20 minutes
Cooking time: 50 minutes
Oven temperature: 180°C (350°F), Gas Mark 4

kidneys cooked with sherry

8 veal or lambs' kidneys
4 tablespoons lemon juice
2 tablespoons olive oil
1 garlic clove, crushed
125 g/4 oz pancetta, chopped
50 ml/2 fl oz dry sherry
2 tablespoons chopped parsley
salt and pepper

1 Halve the kidneys and cut out the white cores. Place the kidneys in a bowl, add the lemon juice and set aside for 10 minutes.

2 Heat the oil in a frying pan. Add the kidneys, garlic and pancetta and fry over a high heat, stirring constantly, for 3–4 minutes until browned.

3 Add the sherry and simmer for a further 3–4 minutes until the sherry is reduced and the kidneys cooked through. Sprinkle over the parsley, season to taste with salt and pepper and serve at once.

Serves 4
Preparation time: 15 minutes, plus standing
Cooking time: 10 minutes

moroccan lamb kebabs

1 kg /2 lb boned shoulder of lamb, cut into 5 cm/2 inch
  cubes
salad and lemon wedges, to serve

Marinade:
3 tablespoons olive oil
2 tablespoons lemon juice
1 garlic clove, crushed
1½ tablespoons paprika
1 teaspoon ground cumin
1 teaspoon ground coriander
1 teaspoon harissa

1 Put the lamb into a bowl. Mix together all the marinade ingredients, add to the lamb and stir to mix thoroughly. Cover and leave at room temperature for 2 hours, or overnight in the refrigerator. If you put the lamb in the refrigerator, return it to room temperature 1 hour before cooking it.

2 Remove the lamb from the marinade and pat dry. Thread the lamb on to 6 long skewers. Cook on a heated barbecue or under a preheated grill, turning occasionally and brushing with any of the remaining marinade, for 10–15 minutes until browned on the outside but still pink on the inside.

3 Serve on a bed of salad with lemon wedges.

Serves 6
Preparation time: 10 minutes, plus marinating
Cooking time: 10–15 minutes

warm salad of red peppers and scallops

2 tablespoons lemon juice
3 tablespoons olive oil
2 red peppers, cored, deseeded and cut into thin strips
mixed salad leaves
375 g/12 oz scallops
50 g/2 oz black olives, pitted and quartered
2 tablespoons snipped chives
salt and pepper

1 In a small bowl, combine the lemon juice and 2 tablespoons of the oil. Season to taste with salt and pepper. Set aside.

2 Heat the remaining oil in a frying pan over a moderate heat. Add the red peppers with a pinch of salt and fry over a low heat for about 5 minutes until just tender. Transfer the peppers to a plate and set aside. Arrange the salad leaves on individual plates.

3 Rinse the scallops and pat dry with kitchen paper. Season them with salt and pepper and arrange in one layer in the top of a steamer set over boiling water. Cover and steam over a high heat for about 3 minutes until tender. Drain on kitchen paper.

4 To serve, arrange the warm scallops on the salad leaves. Arrange the red peppers, olives and chives around the scallops. Whisk the dressing and spoon over the salad. Serve immediately.

Serves 4
Preparation time: 10–15 minutes
Cooking time: 8 minutes

baked mussels with parmesan and garlic

1.75 kg/3½ lb mussels, scrubbed and debearded (see
  page 109)
1 bouquet garni
125 ml/4 fl oz water
125 ml/4 fl oz dry white wine
2 tablespoons finely chopped shallot
1 garlic clove, crushed
2 tablespoons chopped parsley
75 g/3 oz fresh breadcrumbs
3 tablespoons grated Parmesan cheese
25 g/1 oz butter
salt and pepper

1 Put the mussels into a deep saucepan with the bouquet garni and salt and pepper. Add the water and wine, cover and cook over a moderate heat, shaking the pan occasionally, until the mussels open. Discard any that do not open, then strain them and reserve the cooking liquid.

2 Remove and discard the empty half of each mussel shell and arrange the remaining shells close together, mussel side up, in a shallow ovenproof dish. Sprinkle the mussels with the chopped shallot, garlic, parsley, breadcrumbs and Parmesan.

3 Put the reserved cooking liquid into a saucepan and bring to the boil. Boil rapidly until reduced to half its original volume. Pour the reduced liquid around the mussels and dot with butter. Bake in a preheated oven, 180°C (350°F), Gas Mark 4, for 15 minutes. Serve immediately.

Serves 4
Preparation time: 30 minutes
Cooking time: 30 minutes
Oven temperature: 180°C (350°F), Gas Mark 4

moules marinière

60 g/2½ oz butter
4 shallots, finely chopped
1 garlic clove, crushed
350 ml/12 fl oz dry white wine
1 bouquet garni
1.5 kg/3 lb mussels, scrubbed and debearded
  (see page 109)
2 tablespoons chopped parsley
salt and pepper
French bread, to serve

1 Melt the butter in a large saucepan. Add the shallots and garlic and fry over a low heat, stirring occasionally, until soft. Stir in the wine, add the bouquet garni and bring to the boil. Boil for 2 minutes, season to taste with salt and pepper, then add the mussels.

2 Cover and cook over a high heat, shaking the pan vigorously from time to time, until the mussel shells open. Remove from the pan with a slotted spoon and set aside. Discard any mussels that do not open.

3 Boil the liquid rapidly until reduced by half, then return the mussels to the pan and heat through, shaking the pan continuously, for 1 minute.

4 Sprinkle with the parsley and shake the pan again. Pile the mussels up in a warmed deep serving dish or in individual dishes and pour the liquid over the top. Serve immediately with crusty French bread.

Serves 4–6
Preparation time: 25 minutes
Cooking time: 20 minutes

mussels with bacon and tomato vinaigrette

1 kg/2 lb mussels, scrubbed and debearded
  (see page 109)
2 shallots, finely chopped
6 tablespoons dry white wine or water
6 smoked streaky bacon rashers, rinded
50 g/2 oz Parmesan cheese
basil or parsley sprigs, to garnish (optional)

Tomato vinaigrette:
6 tablespoons tomato juice
4 tablespoons extra virgin olive oil
2 tablespoons red wine vinegar
½ garlic clove, crushed
¼ teaspoon caster sugar
1 tablespoon finely shredded basil
salt and pepper

1 Start by making the vinaigrette. Whisk all the ingredients together in a small bowl or place in a screw-top jar, close the lid tightly and shake until combined. Set aside.

2 Place the mussels in a large saucepan with the shallots and white wine or water, cover and cook over a high heat for 3–4 minutes, or until the shells have opened. Drain, discarding the cooking liquid and any unopened mussels. Transfer the mussels and shallots to a serving bowl and leave to cool. Remove some of the shells, if liked, for ease of eating.

3 Meanwhile, cook the bacon under a preheated hot grill until crisp. Drain on kitchen paper. Crumble or snip into small pieces.

4 Pour the tomato vinaigrette over the mussel mixture, toss lightly, then scatter the bacon over the top. Adjust the seasoning to taste. Using a swivel vegetable peeler, shave the Parmesan over the top. Serve the salad scattered with basil or parsley, if liked.

Serves 4
Preparation time: 25 minutes
Cooking time: 8–9 minutes

grilled mussels

2 kg/4 lb mussels, scrubbed and debearded
  (see page 109)
200 ml/7 fl oz white wine
½ red pepper, cored, deseeded and chopped
2 garlic cloves, crushed
4 tablespoons finely chopped parsley
425 g/14 oz can tomatoes, drained and chopped
5 tablespoons fresh white breadcrumbs
2 tablespoons olive oil
1 tablespoon grated Parmesan cheese
salt and pepper

1 Put the cleaned mussels in a large saucepan, pour in the wine and bring to the boil, covered with a closely fitting lid.

2 Reduce the heat and cook the mussels for a few minutes, still covered, shaking the pan occasionally, until the mussels open. Discard any mussels that do not open. Remove the open mussels from the pan and remove and discard the top half of each shell.

3 In a bowl, mix together the chopped pepper, garlic, parsley, chopped tomatoes and 4 tablespoons of the breadcrumbs. Stir in 1 tablespoon of the olive oil and then season to taste with salt and pepper.

4 Add a little of this mixture to each of the mussels in their shells and place them in an ovenproof dish. Sprinkle with grated Parmesan, the remaining breadcrumbs and the remaining olive oil and bake in a preheated oven, 230°C (450°F), Gas Mark 8, for 10 minutes. Briefly place the mussels under a preheated hot grill for a crisp finish. Serve immediately.

Serves 4–6
Preparation time: 30 minutes
Cooking time: 15 minutes
Oven temperature: 230°C (450°F), Gas Mark 8

crispy giant prawns

Pacific prawns, also known as tiger prawns, are larger than Dublin Bay prawns and are only available frozen. Care should be taken in thawing them. If you are lucky enough to find uncooked ones, cook them in boiling salted water for 5 minutes; then use the cooking liquid in the sauce.

125 g/4 oz plain flour
1 tablespoon oil
150 ml/¼ pint beer or lager
2 egg whites
1 tablespoon chopped parsley
16 cooked peeled giant Pacific prawns
oil, for deep-frying
salt

Sauce:
8 tablespoons Mayonnaise (see page 145)
2 garlic cloves, crushed
2 tablespoons chopped thyme
1 teaspoon finely grated lemon rind
dash of Tabasco sauce

1 Sift the flour and salt into a bowl, then gradually beat in the oil and beer. Whisk the egg whites until very stiff, then fold them into the batter with the parsley. Drop in the prawns and coat well.

2 Heat the oil in a wok to 180–190°C (350–375°F) or until a cube of bread browns in 30 seconds. Deep-fry the prawns in batches for 2–3 minutes until golden brown and crisp. Drain on kitchen paper and keep hot while frying the remainder.

3 Mix all the sauce ingredients together, reserving a little of the lemon rind, and spoon into a bowl. Sprinkle the reserved lemon rind on top. Serve immediately with the hot prawns.

Serves 4
Preparation time: 15 minutes
Cooking time: 8–12 minutes

irish cockles and mussels with bacon

1.5 kg/3 lb mussels, scrubbed and debearded
   (see page 109)
150 ml/¼ pint water
175 g/6 oz cockles, washed and scrubbed
4 streaky bacon rashers, rinded
25 g/1 oz butter
½ onion, finely chopped
1 tablespoon finely chopped parsley
1 teaspoon finely chopped chives
salt and pepper
4 watercress sprigs, to garnish

1 Put the mussels in a large saucepan. Add the water, bring to the boil, cover and cook over a high heat, shaking the pan occasionally, for 5 minutes. Add the cockles and continue cooking for a further 3–5 minutes. Remove the cockles and mussels from the pan and discard any shells that remain closed. Remove the cockles and mussels from the shells.

2 Cut the bacon rashers in half widthways. Roll each piece neatly and secure with a wooden cocktail stick. Put in a pan of boiling water for a few minutes to remove the salt and set the rolls. Drain, dry and discard the cocktail sticks.

3 Melt the butter in a large frying pan. Add the bacon rolls and fry until browned. Remove from the pan and keep warm. Add the onion and fry until soft, then add the mussels, cockles and herbs and season to taste with salt and pepper. Toss in the butter to heat thoroughly. Divide evenly between 4 warmed serving plates, scatter over the bacon rolls and garnish with a sprig of watercress.

Serves 4
Preparation time: 30 minutes
Cooking time: 20 minutes

grilled prawns with garlic and herb butter

8 raw Dublin Bay prawns in the shell, weighing at least
   125 g/4 oz each
125 g/4 oz butter
1 garlic clove, crushed
4 tablespoons mixed herbs, such as parsley, tarragon and
   chervil, very finely chopped
salt and pepper

To garnish:
lemon wedges
sprigs of watercress and herbs

1 Cut the prawns in half lengthways, remove the gut and wash under cold running water. Dry with absorbent kitchen paper. Lay the prawns shell side down on a baking sheet.

2 Blend the butter, garlic and herbs together and season to taste with salt and pepper. Spread the herb butter over the prawns and cook under a preheated, very hot grill for 3–4 minutes.

3 Arrange on warmed plates and garnish with the lemon, sprigs of watercress and herbs. Serve immediately.

Serves 4
Preparation time: 5 minutes
Cooking time: 3–4 minutes

baked scallops with garlic and herbs

125 g/4 oz butter
50 g/2 oz fresh white breadcrumbs
1 garlic clove, finely chopped
1 tablespoon finely chopped parsley
1 tablespoon finely chopped coriander
8 large scallops, shelled, cleaned and both the white and
   coral sliced into rings
pepper

To garnish:
1 lemon, cut into 4 wedges
4 watercress sprigs

1 Butter 4 scallop shells or simi[...]
with half the butter. Combine the[...]
and herbs and season with pepper[...]
mixture evenly between the contain[...]
scallops on top and cover with the re[...]
mixture and the remaining butter cut in[...]

2 Set the shells or dishes on a baking she[...]
a preheated oven, 220°C (425°F), Gas Mar[...]
10–12 minutes. Be careful not to overcook t[...]
or they will become tough. The soft flesh, whe[...]
should be only just set. If, when the scallops are [...]ked,
the crumbs aren't golden in colour, quickly put the
dishes under a hot grill to finish.

3 Serve very hot, garnished with lemon wedges and
watercress sprigs.

Serves 4
Preparation time: 10 minutes
Cooking time: 10–12 minutes
Oven temperature: 220°C (425°F), Gas Mark 7

smoked salmon with potato cakes, soured cream and chives

250 g/8 oz potatoes, boiled and mashed
25 g/1 oz butter, melted
50 g/2 oz plain flour, plus extra for shaping
salt
snipped chives, to garnish

To serve:
250–300 g/8–10 oz smoked salmon, thinly sliced
2 tomatoes, deseeded and diced
4 tablespoons thick soured cream

1 First prepare the potato cakes. Put all the ingredients
into a bowl and mix gently with a wooden spoon to form
a light dough. Turn on to a lightly floured surface and roll
out to about 1 cm/½ inch thick. Cut into 4 circles using a
5 cm/2 inch plain cutter.

2 Warm a heavy-based frying pan over a gentle heat until
a light dusting of flour just begins to turn a very pale
fawn colour. Keep the pan at this temperature and add
the potato cakes. Cook for a few minutes until lightly
browned on each side.

[...]e salmon between 4 serving
[...]on one side. Allow the potato cakes to
[...]n place 1 on each plate beside the
[...]nge the tomato on top of each potato cake,
[...]oured cream and garnish with chives. Serve
[...]iately.

Serves 4
Preparation time: 30 minutes
Cooking time: 8 minutes

seafood escabèche

250 g/8 oz baby squid, cleaned
250 g/8 oz small raw Mediterranean prawns, peeled and
  deveined
16 large mussels, scrubbed and debearded
  (see page 109)
2 garlic cloves, chopped
1 small red chilli, deseeded and chopped
50 ml/2 fl oz dry sherry
1 tablespoon chopped basil, to garnish
bread, to serve

Marinade:
150 ml/¼ pint extra virgin olive oil
2 shallots, chopped
3 tablespoons white wine vinegar
pinch of sugar
1 tablespoon drained and chopped capers in brine
salt and pepper

1 First prepare the seafood. Cut the squid into rings and
the tentacles in half, if large, wash well. Wash and dry
the raw prawns.

2 Put the mussels into a pan with the garlic, chilli and
sherry, cover and steam for 4–5 minutes until all the
mussels are opened. Discard any that remain closed.
Remove the mussels with a slotted spoon and set aside.

3 Poach the prawns in the mussel liquid for 4–5 minutes
until cooked. Poach the squid for 2–3 minutes until
cooked. Remove with a slotted spoon and add to the
mussels. Reserve 2 tablespoons of the cooking liquid
and leave to cool.

4 Combine all the marinade ingredients and stir in the
reserved poaching liquid. Pour over the cold seafood,
toss well and chill for several hours.

5 Return the escabèche to room temperature for 1 hour, scatter over the basil and serve with bread.

Serves: 4
Preparation time: 25–30 minutes, plus chilling
Cooking time: 15 minutes

griddled tiger prawns with mint and lemon

750 g/1½ lb raw tiger prawns, peeled and deveined
1 large bunch of mint, chopped
2 garlic cloves, crushed
8 tablespoons lemon juice
sea salt and pepper
mint leaves, to garnish

1 Place the prawns in a glass mixing bowl. Add the mint, garlic and lemon juice, season to taste with salt and pepper and allow to marinate for at least 30 minutes or overnight.

2 Heat a griddle pan or nonstick frying pan. Place the prawns and marinade in the hot pan and cook for 2–3 minutes on each side. Serve garnished with mint leaves.

Serves 6
Preparation time: 10 minutes, plus marinating
Cooking time: 4–6 minutes

spicy butterflied prawns

500 g/1 lb raw tiger prawns
25 ml/1 fl oz orange juice
2 tablespoons lime juice
3 tablespoons olive oil
1 teaspoon white rum
1 garlic clove, crushed
1 teaspoon dried green peppercorns, crushed
salt

1 Remove the shells and tails from the prawns and slit them about halfway through along their backs so that they open up and lie flat. Remove the dark veins, then pat dry.

2 Combine all the remaining ingredients, with salt to taste, in a mixing bowl. Add the prawns and stir. Cover and leave to marinate in the refrigerator for at least 4 hours.

3 Thread the prawns on to skewers, inserting the point of the skewer at the tail end and pushing it through the prawn to come out at the head end. Reserve the marinade.

4 Cook the prawns under a very hot grill for 6–10 minutes, turning occasionally and basting with the marinade. Take care not to overcook them: the prawns are cooked when they turn opaque. Serve immediately.

Serves 4
Preparation time: 15 minutes, plus marinating
Cooking time: 6–10 minutes

marinated herring with horseradish cream

2 large herrings, filleted
8 tablespoons lemon juice
125 g/4 oz crème fraîche
1 tablespoon hot horseradish sauce
salt and pepper
1 tablespoon chopped dill, to garnish

Marinade:
150 ml/¼ pint white wine vinegar
150 ml/¼ pint water
75 g/3 oz caster sugar
1 garlic clove, sliced
1 small red onion, sliced
2 bay leaves
2 dill sprigs, bruised
1 teaspoon allspice berries, bruised
6 white peppercorns

1 Using a pair of tweezers, pull out as many of the tiny bones from the herring fillets as possible. Wash and dry well. Place the fillets, skin side down, in a ceramic dish and pour over the lemon juice. Cover and chill for 2 hours.

2 Meanwhile, prepare the marinade. Combine all the ingredients in a bowl and set aside. Stir occasionally to dissolve the sugar.

3 Drain the herrings and discard the juices. Cut the fish into bite-sized pieces, return to the dish and pour over the marinade. Cover and leave to marinate overnight in the refrigerator.

4 Remove the herring fillets from the marinade and allow them to return to room temperature for 1 hour. Discard the marinade.

5 Combine the crème fraîche and horseradish sauce in a small bowl, season to taste with salt and pepper and mix together well.

6 Arrange the herrings on a platter with the bowl of horseradish cream and garnish with chopped dill.

Serves 4
Preparation time: 25 minutes, plus marinating

spicy courgette fritters with smoked salmon

500 g/1 lb courgettes, grated
1 egg, beaten
2 tablespoons plain flour
1 chilli, deseeded and chopped
1 garlic clove, crushed
75 g/3 oz Cheddar cheese, grated
sea salt and pepper
dill sprigs, to garnish

To serve:
250 g/8 oz smoked salmon, thinly sliced
125 g/4 oz cream cheese

1 Heat a griddle pan or nonstick frying pan. Squeeze the excess moisture out of the grated courgettes – the best way to do this is to place all the courgettes in a clean tea towel and squeeze well.

2 Mix together the egg and flour until smooth, add all the other ingredients, mix well and season to taste with salt and pepper.

3 Spoon mounds of the mixture on to the griddle, flatten with a palette knife and cook the fritters for 4–5 minutes. Then turn and cook for a further 4–5 minutes. Do not disturb them while they are cooking as a crust needs to form on the cooking side, otherwise they will be difficult to turn.

4 Keep the cooked fritters warm and repeat until all the mixture has been used. Serve the fritters between layers of smoked salmon and cream cheese, garnished with sprigs of dill.

Serves 4
Preparation time: 10 minutes
Cooking time: 20 minutes

moroccan prawns with spices

500 g/1 lb raw tiger prawns in their shells
4 tablespoons olive oil
2 garlic cloves, crushed
1 teaspoon ground cumin
½ teaspoon ground ginger
1 teaspoon paprika
¼ teaspoon cayenne pepper
1 bunch of coriander, finely chopped
salt
lemon wedges, to serve

1 Peel and devein most of the prawns, leaving a few whole as they look attractive.

2 Heat the olive oil in a frying pan. Add the garlic and cook until it becomes aromatic. Stir in the cumin, ginger, paprika and cayenne pepper, heat for about 30 seconds, then add the prawns. Fry quickly, stirring, until they turn pink all over.

3 Stir in the coriander and season with salt. Heat for about 30 seconds, then serve the prawns with the cooking juices spooned over them and accompanied by lemon wedges.

Serves 4
Preparation time: 15 minutes
Cooking time: 3 minutes

seafood pancakes

125 g/4 oz flour
pinch of salt
2 eggs
300 ml/½ pint milk
butter, for frying and greasing
4 tablespoons grated Gruyère cheese

Filling:
250 g/8 oz monkfish, John Dory or cod fillets, skinned
150 ml/¼ pint dry white wine
4 scallops
50 g/2 oz butter
1 onion, finely chopped
125 g/4 oz mushrooms, chopped
25 g/1 oz flour
150 ml/¼ pint crème fraîche or double cream
125 g/4 oz cooked peeled prawns
1 teaspoon lemon juice
salt and pepper

1 First, make the crêpes. Sift the flour and salt into a mixing bowl and make a well in the centre. Break in the eggs and add some of the milk. Beat in the flour from the sides of the bowl to make a thick batter. Gradually beat in the remaining milk until the batter is really smooth.

2 Heat a little butter in a small frying pan and pour in sufficient batter to cover the base, tilting the pan to coat the base evenly. Cook until the underside is golden brown and then flip the crêpe over and cook the other side. Slide out on to a warmed plate and make the other crêpes in the same way. Keep warm.

3 To make the filling, put the fish in a saucepan with the wine and poach gently for 10 minutes. Add the scallops and cook for 2–3 minutes. Drain, reserving the liquor.

4 Melt the butter in a small saucepan. Add the onion and fry until golden. Add the mushrooms, fry for 2 minutes, then stir in the flour. Cook for 1 minute and add the reserved poaching liquid. Bring to the boil and cook, stirring, for 2 minutes. Add the cream, fish, scallops, prawns, lemon juice and salt and pepper.

5 Grease an ovenproof dish with butter. Place some of the seafood filling on each crêpe and roll them up. Arrange them in the dish and sprinkle the grated cheese over the top. Bake in a preheated oven, 200°C (400°F), Gas Mark 6, for 8–10 minutes until golden brown.

Serves 4–6
Preparation time: 20 minutes
Cooking time: 45 minutes
Oven temperature: 200°C (400°F), Gas Mark 6

pancake rolls with chicken and mushroom

250 g/8 oz plain flour
1 egg
about 300 ml/½ pint water
salt
oil, for deep-frying

Filling:
1 tablespoon oil
1 teaspoon finely chopped fresh root ginger
2 garlic cloves, crushed
250 g/8 oz chicken breast, skinned and diced
2 tablespoons soy sauce
1 tablespoon dry sherry
125 g/4 oz mushrooms, sliced
3 spring onions, chopped
50 g/2 oz cooked peeled prawns

1 Sift the flour and a pinch of salt into a bowl. Add the egg and beat in sufficient water to make a smooth batter. Use to make thin pancakes in a 20 cm/8 inch frying pan.

2 To make the filling, heat the oil in a preheated wok or frying pan. Add the ginger and garlic and fry for 30 seconds. Add the chicken and brown quickly. Stir in the soy sauce and sherry, then the mushrooms and spring onions. Increase the heat and cook for 1 minute. Remove from the heat, stir in the prawns and cool.

3 Place 2–3 tablespoons of the filling in the centre of each pancake. Fold in the sides and form into a tight roll, sealing the edge with a little flour and water paste.

4 Heat the oil in a deep-fryer or large saucepan to 180–190°C (350–375°F) or until a cube of bread browns in 30 seconds. Deep-fry the rolls, a few at a time, for 2–3 minutes. Drain on kitchen paper, then serve.

Serves 4–6
Preparation time: 10 minutes
Cooking time: 45 minutes

prawn toasts with ham and sesame seeds

1 teaspoon dry sherry
1 teaspoon salt
1 egg white
1 teaspoon cornflour
500 g/1 lb cooked peeled prawns, deveined and finely chopped
7 slices of white bread from a large sliced loaf, with the crusts removed
2 tablespoons sesame seeds
2 tablespoons chopped cooked ham
oil, for deep-frying
parsley sprigs, to garnish

1 Place the sherry, salt, egg white and cornflour in a bowl and mix until smooth. Stir in the prawns.

2 Divide this mixture between the bread slices. Sprinkle with the sesame seeds and ham and press the topping firmly into the bread, using the back of a spoon.

3 Heat the oil to 180–190°C (350–375°F) or until a cube of bread browns in 30 seconds. Deep-fry the toasts, a few at a time, with the prawn side down. When the edges of the bread turn golden, turn on to the other side. Fry until golden brown. Drain on absorbent kitchen paper and cut each slice of bread into 4 squares. Arrange on a serving plate, garnish with parsley and serve hot.

Serves 6–8
Preparation time: 20 minutes
Cooking time: 20 minutes

crab fritters with water chestnuts

375 g/12 oz crab meat, finely chopped
50 g/2 oz pork fat, minced
4 water chestnuts, peeled and finely chopped
1 egg white
2 tablespoons cornflour
1 tablespoon Chinese rice wine or dry sherry
sunflower oil, for deep-frying
salt and pepper

1 Place the crab meat in a bowl with the pork fat and water chestnuts and blend well. Add the egg white, cornflour, salt and pepper to taste and wine or sherry and mix together.

2 Heat the oil in a wok or deep saucepan to 180–190°C (350–375°F) or until a cube of bread browns in 30 seconds. Using a teaspoon, scoop up 1 spoonful of the crab mixture at a time and lower it into the hot oil.

3 Fry the balls until they are golden brown, remove with a slotted spoon and drain on absorbent kitchen paper. They should be crisp on the outside and tender inside. Serve hot.

Serves 4
Preparation time: about 10 minutes
Cooking time: 10–15 minutes

chinese barbecued spare ribs

1.5 kg/3 lb pork spare ribs
salt and pepper

Marinade:
4 tablespoons hoisin sauce
2 tablespoons clear honey
4 tablespoons soy sauce
4 tablespoons red wine vinegar
125 ml/4 fl oz Chicken Stock (see page 141)
¼ teaspoon Chinese five spice powder

1 Rub the spare ribs all over with a little salt, then sprinkle generously with pepper and place in a shallow ovenproof dish large enough to hold all the ribs in a single layer.

2 Make the marinade by mixing all the ingredients in a bowl or jug. Stir thoroughly, then pour the marinade over the ribs, cover and leave in a cool place for 4 hours, turning the ribs halfway through.

3 Drain the marinade into a jug and put the spare ribs into a hinged wire grill for ease of turning. Cook under a preheated grill or on the greased grill of a barbecue for 10 minutes, then turn and cook for 10 minutes more.

4 Baste with the marinade, turn the ribs again and cook for 15 minutes, then baste and turn again, cooking for a final 10 minutes.

Serves 4–6
Preparation time: 5 minutes, plus marinating
Cooking time: 45 minutes

minced meat samosas

2 tablespoons milk
oil, for deep-frying
chutney, to serve

Dough:
500 g/1 lb plain flour
1 teaspoon salt
175 g/6 oz soft margarine
150 ml/¼ pint water

Filling:
15 g/½ oz butter
1 small onion, chopped
½ teaspoon cumin seeds
250 g/8 oz minced beef
1 fresh green chilli, finely chopped
1 teaspoon salt
125 g/4 oz cooked peas
1 teaspoon chopped coriander leaves
pepper

1 To make the dough, sift the flour and salt into a large mixing bowl. Cut the margarine into small pieces and rub it into the flour with the fingertips, until the mixture resembles fine breadcrumbs. Stir in the water, a little at a time, until it is all amalgamated. Knead thoroughly until smooth. Cover with a damp cloth.

2 To make the filling, melt the butter in a saucepan. Add the onion and cumin seeds and fry over a moderate heat, stirring occasionally, for 5–7 minutes. Add the minced beef, chilli and salt and mix thoroughly. Reduce the heat and simmer for 10 minutes.

3 Stir in the peas and continue cooking over a moderate heat for 5 minutes, or until the liquid has evaporated. Remove the pan from the heat and mix in the coriander and a pinch of pepper. Leave to cool.

4 Divide the samosa dough into 12 equal portions and roll out each one to a thin circle, 18 cm/7 inches in diameter. Cut each circle in half with a sharp knife, then cover the semi-circles with a damp cloth while you fill them one at a time.

5 Brush the edges of each semi-circle with a little milk and spoon some filling on to the centre. Fold in the corners, overlapping them to form a cone. Fold over and seal the top to make a triangle.

6 Heat the oil to 180–190°C (350–375°F) or until a cube of bread browns in 30 seconds. Deep-fry in hot oil in batches, until crisp and golden. Drain on absorbent kitchen paper and serve hot with chutney.

Serves 6
Preparation time: 30 minutes
Cooking time: 30–40 minutes

vegetable samosas

1 quantity Samosa Dough (see above)
2 tablespoons milk
oil, for deep-frying
chutney, to serve

Filling:
1 tablespoon ghee or vegetable oil
pinch of asafoetida powder (optional)
2 teaspoons mustard seeds
500 g/1 lb potatoes, parboiled and diced

thai crab curry p244

szechuan prawns in chilli and tomato sauce p240

fresh sardines with pine nuts and anchovies p206

bouillabaisse p219

salmon wrapped in parma ham with fontina cheese and bay leaves   p225

scallop and prawn stir-fry   p242

seared skate wings with caperberries   p230

tuna livorno style   p201

125 g/4 oz cooked green peas
2 fresh green chillies, deseeded and chopped
1 teaspoon salt
1 teaspoon pomegranate seeds (optional)
1 teaspoon garam masala
2 tablespoons chopped coriander leaves

1 To make the filling, heat the ghee or oil in a frying pan. Add the asafoetida powder, if using, mustard seeds, potatoes, peas, chillies, salt and pomegranate seeds, if using. Stir over a moderate heat for 2 minutes. Cover the pan, reduce the heat and cook gently for 10 minutes.

2 Remove the pan from the heat and add the garam masala and chopped coriander. Stir well and then leave the filling to cool before using to stuff the samosas.

3 Roll out the samosa dough and prepare the semi-circles as described previously (see left). Use the vegetable filling to stuff the samosas and fold over, sealing the edges with milk. Remember to cover them with a damp cloth while you are assembling them.

4 Heat the oil for deep-frying to 180–190°C (350–375°F) or until a cube of bread browns in 30 seconds. Fry the samosas, a few at a time, until crisp and golden. Remove with a slotted spoon and drain on absorbent kitchen paper. Serve them hot with chutney.

Serves 6
Preparation time: 40 minutes
Cooking time: 30 minutes

spicy prawn kebabs

2 tablespoons oil
1 tablespoon lemon juice
2 garlic cloves, crushed
1 teaspoon paprika
½ teaspoon chilli powder
½ teaspoon salt
½ teaspoon turmeric
1 tablespoon finely chopped coriander leaves
12 giant Pacific prawns, peeled

1 Place all the ingredients in a shallow dish, stirring to coat the prawns thoroughly. Cover and chill for 2–3 hours, stirring occasionally.

2 Thread the prawns on to skewers or place in the grill pan, and cook under a preheated moderate grill for 3–4 minutes on each side, or until cooked. Spoon over the pan juices when turning.

Serves 4
Preparation time: 5 minutes, plus chilling
Cooking time: 6–8 minutes

prawn and egg sambal

500 g/1 lb cooked tiger prawn tails
4 hard-boiled eggs, shelled and quartered
300 ml/½ pint coconut milk
1 small onion, finely chopped
1 garlic clove, crushed
1 fresh green chilli, deseeded and chopped
2 tablespoons lemon juice
pinch of chilli powder
½ teaspoon salt
poppadoms, to serve (optional)

To garnish:
50 g/2 oz cooked green peas
chopped coriander leaves

1 Arrange the prawns and eggs in a shallow serving dish, then cover and chill in the refrigerator while you make the sauce.

2 Place the coconut milk, onion, garlic, chilli, lemon juice, chilli powder and salt in a food processor and purée until smooth and evenly mixed. Pour the mixture over the prawns and eggs, then cover and chill until required.

3 Serve the sambal well chilled, garnished with the peas and chopped coriander, and accompanied by poppadoms, if liked.

Serves 4
Preparation time: 15 minutes, plus chilling

crispy potato skins

6 large potatoes with unblemished skins
4 tablespoons olive oil
2 teaspoons coarse sea salt
2 teaspoons coarsely crushed black peppercorns
200 g/7 oz cream cheese
8 tablespoons single cream
3 tablespoons snipped chives
salt and pepper

1 Cut each potato into six pieces. Peel the potato pieces thickly and carefully. Put the skins in a bowl and drizzle with oil. (Use the potato flesh in another recipe.)

2 Drain the skins and arrange on a baking sheet. Sprinkle with coarse sea salt and crushed peppercorns. Bake in a preheated oven, 200°C (400°F), Gas Mark 6, turning occasionally, for 20–25 minutes.

3 Beat the cream cheese until smooth, then mix with the cream and chives. Season to taste with salt and pepper, spoon into a bowl, and serve with the hot potato skins.

Serves 8
Preparation time: 15 minutes
Cooking time: 20–25 minutes
Oven temperature: 200°C (400°F), Gas Mark 6

mushroom and tofu satay

500 g/1 lb ready-fried tofu, sliced
200 g/7 oz fresh shiitake mushrooms

Marinade:
125 ml/4 fl oz dark soy sauce
50 ml/2 fl oz water
15 g/½ oz palm sugar or light muscovado sugar
2 garlic cloves, chopped

Satay sauce:
2 fresh red chillies, deseeded and finely chopped
150 ml/¼ pint coconut milk
175 g/6 oz crunchy peanut butter
1 tablespoon dark soy sauce
1 teaspoon lemon juice
1 tablespoon coarsely crushed peanuts

To serve:
cucumber chunks
spring onions, finely sliced lengthways

1 Cut the sliced tofu into 3.5 cm/1½ inch lengths. Cut any large mushrooms in half.

2 Put all the marinade ingredients in a shallow bowl and stir to mix. Add the tofu and mushrooms and toss to coat on all sides. Leave to marinate for 1 hour.

3 Meanwhile, soak 8–12 wooden satay sticks in cold water for 20–30 minutes.

4 To make the satay sauce, put the chillies, coconut milk and peanut butter in a saucepan and heat gently, stirring, until smooth. Simmer over a low heat until thickened, then stir in the soy sauce and lemon juice. Transfer to a serving bowl, sprinkle with the crushed peanuts and set aside.

5 Remove the satay sticks from the water one at a time and carefully thread the tofu and mushrooms on to them. Cook under a hot grill for 1–2 minutes on each side until lightly browned.

6 Serve hot, garnished with cucumber chunks and sliced spring onions, with the sauce in a separate bowl.

Makes 8–12
Preparation time: 15 minutes, plus marinating
Cooking time: 10 minutes

camembert fritters

1 Camembert cheese, just ripe
15 g/½ oz butter
25 g/1 oz flour
5 tablespoons warm milk
1 tablespoon brandy or Calvados
¼ teaspoon freshly ground white pepper
1 egg
2 tablespoons water
1 tablespoon flour and 3 tablespoons dry breadcrumbs,
    for coating
oil, for frying
parsley sprigs, to garnish

1 Remove the rind from the Camembert cheese. Mash the cheese with a fork in a small bowl and beat well until it is really smooth.

2 Melt the butter in a saucepan. Stir in the flour and cook for 1–2 minutes without browning, then stir in the milk and brandy or Calvados, beating vigorously to make a smooth, thick sauce. Season with pepper and cool. Mix in the Camembert to make a firm croquette mixture.

3 Take small amounts of the cheese mixture and roll between floured hands to make cork-shaped croquettes. Beat the egg with the water and use to coat the croquettes.

4 Roll the croquettes at once in a mixture of flour and breadcrumbs and then deep-fry them quickly in hot oil until golden brown. Drain on absorbent kitchen paper and serve garnished with sprigs of parsley.

Serves 4
Preparation time: 15 minutes
Cooking time: 15–20 minutes

piedmontese peppers

2 small red peppers
2 large ripe plum tomatoes
2 garlic cloves, sliced
2 tablespoons balsamic vinegar
8 tablespoons extra virgin olive oil
8 anchovy fillets
4 large basil leaves
salt and pepper
bread, to serve

1 Cut each pepper lengthways through the stalk and discard the seeds. Place cut side up in a small roasting tin. Peel the tomatoes by immersing them in boiling water for 1 minute. Drain, peel and discard the skin. Cut the tomatoes in half and place one half in each pepper, cut side down.

2 Sprinkle the garlic slices over the tomatoes. Combine the vinegar and oil and drizzle over the tomato-stuffed peppers. Season well with salt and pepper.

3 Pour 2–3 tablespoons of water into the bottom of the tin. Bake in a preheated oven, 220°C (425°F), Gas Mark 7, for 30 minutes.

4 Remove from the oven and carefully arrange the anchovy fillets and basil leaves over the tomatoes and bake for a further 15–30 minutes until the peppers are golden and very tender. Cool slightly and serve with the pan juices and bread.

Serves 4
Preparation time: 15 minutes
Cooking time: 45 minutes–1 hour

bulgar stuffed tomatoes

50 g/2 oz bulgar wheat
4 beefsteak tomatoes
2 tablespoons olive oil, plus extra for drizzling
1 onion, finely chopped
2 tablespoons pine nuts
2 garlic cloves, crushed
1 teaspoon ground cumin
2 tablespoons raisins
2 tablespoons chopped parsley
1 tablespoon chopped mint
125 g/4 oz Cheddar cheese, grated
salt and pepper

1 Soak the bulgar in plenty of hot water for 30 minutes, drain well and squeeze out the excess liquid.

2 Cut a thin slice from the top of each tomato, discard the seeds, then scoop out and finely chop the flesh.

3 Heat the oil in a frying pan. Add the onion, pine nuts, crushed garlic and cumin and fry for 10 minutes until softened. Stir in the bulgar and the tomato pulp and fry for a further 5 minutes.

4 Remove the pan from the heat and stir in the raisins, parsley, mint and half the cheese and season to taste with salt and pepper. Spoon the mixture into the empty tomato shells and scatter over the remaining cheese.

5 Transfer the tomatoes to a small ovenproof dish, drizzle over a little extra oil and bake in a preheated oven, 190°C (375°F), Gas Mark 5, for 25–30 minutes until the tomatoes are very soft and the cheese crisp and golden.

Serves 4
Preparation time: 10 minutes, plus soaking
Cooking time: 40–45 minutes
Oven temperature: 190°C (375°F), Gas Mark 5

hot asparagus with balsamic vinegar and tomato dressing

500 g/1 lb young asparagus spears, trimmed
50 g/2 oz pine nuts, toasted
25 g/1 oz Parmesan cheese, shaved into thin slivers
sea salt flakes
pepper

Dressing:
2 tablespoons balsamic vinegar
1–2 garlic cloves, crushed
375 g/12 oz tomatoes, skinned, deseeded and chopped
5 tablespoons olive oil

1 To make the dressing, mix the balsamic vinegar, garlic, tomatoes and olive oil in a bowl and reserve.

2 Heat a griddle pan or nonstick frying pan, add the asparagus in a single layer and cook for 5 minutes on a medium heat, turning constantly.

3 Divide the asparagus between 4 warmed plates. Spoon over the balsamic vinegar and tomato dressing, top with the pine nuts and Parmesan slivers and sprinkle with sea salt and pepper. Serve immediately.

Serves 4
Preparation time: 15 minutes
Cooking time: 5 minutes

butter beans in tomato sauce

250 g/8 oz dried butter beans, soaked overnight in cold water
2 x 400 g/13 oz cans chopped tomatoes
300 ml/½ pint Vegetable Stock (see page 140)
2 garlic cloves, chopped
2 tablespoons extra virgin olive oil
1 tablespoon chopped oregano
2 bay leaves
1 teaspoon caster sugar
1 tablespoon lemon juice
2 tablespoons chopped dill
salt and pepper
crusty bread, to serve

1 Drain the soaked beans, wash well and set aside. Put the tomatoes, stock, garlic, olive oil, oregano, bay leaves and sugar in a large saucepan and bring to the boil.

2 Stir in the beans, return to the boil, cover and simmer over a low heat for 1½ hours, or until the beans are very tender. Remove the lid and simmer for a further 30 minutes until the sauce is reduced and thickened.

3 Stir in the lemon juice, chopped dill and season to taste with salt and pepper. Leave to cool slightly. Serve warm with some crusty bread.

Serves 6
Preparation time: 5 minutes, plus soaking
Cooking time: 2 hours

grilled mediterranean vegetables

1 small aubergine
1 large courgette
1 red pepper, cored and deseeded
1 red onion
3 garlic cloves
1 teaspoon cumin seeds
1 tablespoon chopped thyme
1 tablespoon balsamic vinegar
150 ml/¼ pint extra virgin olive oil
salt and pepper
1 tablespoon chopped basil, to garnish

1 First, prepare the vegetables. Cut the aubergine into 8 slices, the courgette into 5 mm/¼ inch thick diagonal slices, the pepper into thick strips and the onion into thick wedges. Place in a large bowl.

2 In a spice grinder or using a pestle and mortar, mash the garlic, cumin seeds and thyme to a paste. Transfer to a bowl and stir in the balsamic vinegar and 125 ml/4 fl oz of the oil and season with salt and pepper. Pour over the vegetables and toss well to coat.

3 Grill the vegetables under a preheated moderate grill, a few at a time, for 2–3 minutes on each side until they are charred and tender.

4 Transfer the vegetables to a warmed serving plate, drizzle over the remaining olive oil and scatter over the basil. Serve warm.

Serves 4
Preparation time: 10 minutes
Cooking time: about 20 minutes

roasted vine tomatoes with goats' cheese

500 g/1 lb cherry tomatoes on the vine
2 garlic cloves, sliced
2 thyme sprigs
6 tablespoons extra virgin olive oil
4 slices of bread, toasted
175 g/6 oz fresh goats' cheese, sliced
salt and pepper

1 Place the tomatoes, still attached to the vine, in a shallow roasting tin. Scatter over the garlic and thyme and drizzle over the oil. Season with salt and pepper.

2 Cook in a preheated oven, 230°C (450°F), Gas Mark 8, for 15–20 minutes until softened and browned. Spoon the tomatoes on to toasted bread, top with the goats' cheese and pour over the pan juices. Serve immediately.

Serves 4
Preparation time: 5 minutes
Cooking time: 15–20 minutes

haricot beans with lemon, rosemary and chilli

2 tablespoons extra virgin olive oil, plus extra to serve
1 small onion, finely chopped
2 garlic cloves, chopped
1 red chilli, deseeded and diced
1 teaspoon chopped rosemary
grated rind and juice of ½ lemon
425 g/14 oz can haricot beans, drained
2 tablespoons water
1 tablespoon chopped parsley
salt and pepper

1 Heat the oil in a frying pan. Add the onion, garlic, chilli, rosemary and lemon rind and fry for 10 minutes until softened, but not browned.

2 Stir in the haricot beans, lemon juice and water, bring to the boil, cover and simmer gently for 5 minutes.

3 Remove from the heat, season to taste with salt and pepper and leave to cool. Stir in the parsley and serve the beans drizzled with olive oil.

Serves 2–4
Preparation time: 5 minutes
Cooking time: 15 minutes

garlic and parsley baked field mushrooms

Field mushrooms are available from supermarkets, but if you cannot find them, use cultivated mushrooms, which come from the same family.

butter, for greasing
500 g/1 lb field mushrooms, stalks removed, then sliced
2 garlic cloves, crushed
75 g/3 oz butter, melted
2 tablespoons chopped parsley
6 tablespoons double cream
salt and pepper
hot French bread, to serve

1 Lightly grease 6 individual flameproof dishes, or one 600 ml/1 pint gratin dish.

2 Arrange the sliced mushrooms in the prepared dish or dishes. Add the crushed garlic to the butter and stir to incorporate. Pour the mixture over the mushrooms.

3 Mix together the parsley and cream in a bowl. Season with salt and pepper to taste and pour over the buttered mushrooms.

4 Bake in a preheated oven, 200°C (400°F), Gas Mark 6, for 10 minutes for individual dishes or 15–20 minutes for the large dish. Serve hot, with hot French bread to soak up the juices.

Serves 6
Preparation time: 10 minutes
Cooking time: 10–20 minutes
Oven temperature: 200°C (400°F), Gas Mark 6

burgundy mushrooms

3 tablespoons olive oil
1 onion, chopped
1 garlic clove, crushed
375 g/12 oz button mushrooms, trimmed
125 g/4 oz cooked smoked ham, cut into strips
1 teaspoon dried mixed herbs
150 ml/¼ pint red wine
salt and pepper
hot French bread, to serve

1 Heat the oil in a saucepan. Add the onion and garlic and fry over a low heat for 3 minutes until soft.

2 Add the mushrooms, ham, herbs, red wine and salt and pepper to taste. Bring to the boil, then turn off the heat and leave to marinate for about 30 minutes.

3 Divide the mixture between 4 large ramekin dishes. Bake in a preheated oven, 220°C (425°F), Gas Mark 7, for 15 minutes. Serve with hot French bread.

Serves 4
Preparation time: 10 minutes, plus marinating
Cooking time: 20 minutes
Oven temperature: 220°C (425°F), Gas Mark 7

coddled eggs

butter, for greasing
50 g/2 oz smoked salmon, cut into small pieces
4 eggs
4 tablespoons double cream
salt and pepper
chervil sprigs, to garnish

1 Grease 4 ramekin dishes and divide the smoked salmon between them.

2 Break an egg into each dish, on top of the smoked salmon pieces. Season with salt and pepper to taste and top each dish with 1 tablespoon cream.

3 Place the dishes in a roasting pan containing enough water to reach halfway up the ramekin dishes. Cook in a preheated oven, 180° (350°F), Gas Mark 4, for 10–15 minutes, or until set. Garnish with chervil and serve immediately.

Serves 4
Preparation time: 10 minutes
Cooking time: 10–15 minutes
Oven temperature: 180°C (350°F), Gas Mark 4

asparagus with green mayonnaise

2 bundles of fresh asparagus, about 500 g/1 lb in total, trimmed
Melba toast, to serve (optional)

Green mayonnaise:
3 egg yolks
1 tablespoon finely snipped chives
1 tablespoon finely chopped parsley
1 tablespoon lemon juice
300 ml/½ pint olive oil
salt and pepper

1 Scrape the lower half of each asparagus spear, then divide into 6 bundles. Tie each bunch firmly, finishing with a long-ended bow. (This makes it easier to remove the string later.) Cover the tips in loose cones of foil.

2 Cook the asparagus in a tall saucepan of boiling water, with the tips above the water level, for about 10 minutes until just tender. Do not overcook.

3 Carefully remove the bundles and drain on a wire rack.

4 To make the green mayonnaise, place the egg yolks, chives, parsley and lemon juice in a food processor or blender and process for 1–2 minutes. With the motor running, pour in the oil in a very thin stream until it is all incorporated. Season to taste with salt and pepper.

5 To serve, untie the bundles of asparagus and place 1 bundle on each plate. Serve the mayonnaise separately and accompany the dish with Melba toast, if liked.

Serves 6
Preparation time: 15 minutes
Cooking time: 10 minutes

courgette roulade

25 g/1 oz butter or margarine, plus extra for greasing
500 g/1 lb courgettes, grated
4 eggs, separated
1 teaspoon chopped savory
1 tablespoon chopped parsley
2 tablespoons grated Parmesan cheese
salt and pepper

Filling:
2 tablespoons vegetable oil
1 onion, chopped
175 g/6 oz mushrooms, sliced
1 tablespoon wholemeal flour
125 ml/4 fl oz milk

1 Grease a 30 x 20 cm/12 x 8 inch Swiss roll tin and line with greaseproof paper.

2 Melt the margarine in a frying pan. Add the courgettes and fry, stirring occasionally, for 7 minutes.

3 Place the courgettes in a bowl with the egg yolks, herbs and salt and pepper to taste and mix well. Whisk the egg whites until fairly stiff, fold 2 tablespoons into the courgette mixture to lighten it, then carefully fold in the rest, taking care not to knock out the air.

4 Turn the mixture into the prepared tin and spread evenly. Cook in a preheated oven, 200°C (400°F), Gas Mark 6, for 10–15 minutes until golden and risen.

5 Meanwhile, prepare the filling. Heat the oil in a saucepan. Add the onion and fry over a low heat for 3 minutes until softened. Add the mushrooms and fry for 3 minutes. Stir in the flour, then gradually stir in the milk. Season to taste with salt and pepper and simmer for 3 minutes.

6 Sprinkle the Parmesan cheese on a sheet of greaseproof paper. Turn the roulade out on to the paper and peel off the lining paper. Spread with the filling and roll up like a Swiss roll.

Serves 6
Preparation time: 25 minutes
Cooking time: 20 minutes
Oven temperature: 200°C (400°F), Gas Mark 6

griddled haloumi cheese with beefsteak tomatoes

Haloumi is a sheep's milk cheese with a firm texture similar to feta, which griddles very successfully.

2 packets of haloumi cheese
1 bag of mixed salad leaves
2 tablespoons olive oil
4 tablespoons lemon juice
1 bunch of marjoram, chopped
4 beefsteak tomatoes, skinned, cored and cut into wedges
75 g/3 oz pitted olives (optional)
sea salt and pepper

1 Heat a griddle pan or nonstick frying pan. Cut the haloumi into 16 slices and place on the griddle to cook for 3–4 minutes on each side.

2 Arrange the salad leaves on 4 serving plates.

3 Mix together the olive oil, lemon juice and marjoram, and season to taste with salt and pepper.

4 Arrange the haloumi and tomato wedges alternately on the salad leaves. Add the olives, if using, and spoon over the dressing. Serve immediately, while the cheese is still warm.

Serves 4
Preparation time: 15 minutes
Cooking time: 20 minutes

swordfish steaks in white wine and tomatoes

2 tablespoons olive oil
1 red onion, chopped
1 garlic clove, chopped
2 celery sticks, chopped
2 bay leaves
4 tomatoes, skinned and chopped
1 teaspoon sugar
300 ml/½ pint white wine
2 tablespoons chopped oregano
4 x 175g/6 oz swordfish steaks
salt and pepper

1 Heat the oil in a pan. Add the onion, garlic and celery and fry over a low heat for 5 minutes.

2 Add the bay leaves, tomatoes, sugar, white wine and oregano, season to taste with salt and pepper, mix well and bring to a gentle simmer.

3 Add the swordfish steaks and cook for 5 minutes, then turn them over and cook on the other side for a further 5 minutes. This dish can be served immediately, or in hot weather it is very good served at room temperature.

Serves 4
Preparation time: 10 minutes
Cooking time: 15 minutes

tuna steaks with sun-dried tomatoes

2 tablespoons olive oil
1 red onion, finely chopped
2 garlic cloves, crushed and chopped
1 rosemary sprig, chopped
75 g/3 oz plain flour
4 x 175 g/6 oz tuna steaks, skinned
oil, for frying
125 g/4 oz sun-dried tomatoes in oil, chopped
75 ml/3 fl oz red wine
1 tablespoon capers

75 g/3 oz black olives
handful of flat leaf parsley, chopped
salt and pepper
1 lemon, cut into 4 wedges, to serve

1 Heat the olive oil in a saucepan, add the onion, garlic and rosemary and fry over a low heat for 5 minutes.

2 Season the flour with salt and pepper. Dip the tuna steaks into the seasoned flour to coat evenly all over.

3 Heat the oil in a frying pan. Add the tuna steaks and cook for 4–5 minutes until golden. Turn over and cook on the other side for a further 4–5 minutes. Transfer the tuna steaks to a dish lined with kitchen paper and keep warm in the oven.

4 Add the sun-dried tomatoes to the onions and stir well. Increase the heat to high, add the red wine, capers, olives and parsley, season to taste with salt and pepper and simmer for 2 minutes. Serve the sauce with the tuna steaks and lemon wedges.

Serves 4
Preparation time: 5 minutes
Cooking time: 15 minutes

tuna livorno style

4 x 175 g/6 oz tuna steaks
50 g/2 oz plain flour
4 tablespoons olive oil
1 small onion, finely chopped
4 parsley sprigs, finely chopped
125 ml/4 fl oz dry white wine
1 tablespoon capers, drained
1 bay leaf, crumbled
¼ teaspoon ground cinnamon
salt and pepper
new potatoes and green salad, to serve

1 Coat the tuna steaks in flour. Heat the oil in a heavy-based pan, mix the onion and parsley together and add them to the pan. Sauté over a medium heat, stirring, until just golden, but not brown.

2 Add the tuna steaks and cook for 2 minutes on each side. Season to taste with salt and pepper and pour over the wine. Leave until this has evaporated a little, then add the capers, crumbled bay leaf and cinnamon. Cover and cook for 15 minutes, adding water if needed.

3 Serve the tuna steaks with the cooking juices poured over, accompanied by new potatoes and a green salad.

Serves 4
Preparation time: 5 minutes
Cooking time: 25 minutes

fresh tuna with anchovies and mushrooms

4–6 tablespoons oil
2–3 garlic cloves, crushed
1 large onion, finely chopped
150 g/5 oz button mushrooms, quartered or thickly sliced
6–8 anchovy fillets, chopped
2 tablespoons chopped parsley
1 tablespoon plain flour
300 ml/10 fl oz dry white wine
pinch of nutmeg
4 x 175 g/6 oz tuna steaks, about 1 cm/½ inch thick
pepper

1 Heat the oil in a pan. Add the garlic and onion and fry over a low heat until soft and lightly browned. Add the mushrooms and cook for 2–3 minutes, then add the anchovies, parsley and flour. Mix together well.

2 Stir in the wine, bring to the boil, stirring constantly, then simmer gently for 5–7 minutes.

3 Season to taste with pepper and a pinch of nutmeg. There should be no need to add salt because the anchovies are salty.

4 Place the tuna steaks in an oven-to-table dish and pour over the sauce. Cover with a lid or foil and cook in a preheated oven, 190°C (375°F), Gas Mark 5, for 40–45 minutes. Serve hot.

Serves 4
Preparation time: 15–20 minutes
Cooking time: 1 hour
Oven temperature: 190°C (375°F), Gas Mark 5

tuna with tomatoes, peppers and garlic

plain flour, for dusting
1 kg/2 lb tuna steaks, 2 cm/¾ inch thick
6 tablespoons olive oil
1 red pepper
1 green pepper
2 onions, sliced
2 large tomatoes, quartered
1 garlic clove, crushed
1 bouquet garni
200 ml/7 fl oz dry white wine
salt and pepper
2 tablespoons finely chopped basil, to garnish

1 Season the flour with salt and pepper and dust the tuna steaks with it. Heat half of the olive oil in a frying pan. Add the tuna stakes and fry over a low heat, turning once to seal both sides. Remove from the pan and transfer to an ovenproof dish.

2 Meanwhile, place the red and green peppers under a hot grill, turning occasionally until they are charred and blistered all over. Allow them to cool and then peel and slice them, discarding the seeds.

3 Heat the remaining olive oil. Add the onions and fry over a low heat until soft and golden brown. Add the peppers, tomatoes, garlic and bouquet garni. Season to taste with salt and pepper and then simmer gently for 20 minutes. Add the wine and bring to the boil. Remove from the heat.

4 Cover the tuna steaks with the sauce and bake in a preheated oven, 200°C (400°F), Gas Mark 6, for 20 minutes. Reduce the oven temperature to 160°C (325°F), Gas Mark 3, cover the dish and cook the tuna for a further 30 minutes. Serve sprinkled with chopped basil.

Serves 4–6
Preparation time: 20 minutes
Cooking time: about 1¼ hours
Oven temperature: 200°C (400°F), Gas Mark 6

tuna with spiced onion relish

4 x 175 g/6 oz tuna steaks
chilli powder, to taste
1 tablespoon ground coriander
2 tablespoons ground cumin
2 tablespoons grated fresh root ginger
4 tablespoons olive oil
1 kg/2 lb large onions, sliced
4 garlic cloves, crushed
100 ml/3½ fl oz Fish Stock (see page 142)
salt and cayenne pepper

1 Season the tuna sparingly with chilli powder. Cover and leave in a cool place for 1 hour.

2 Meanwhile, heat a dry heavy-based flameproof earthenware dish or frying pan. Add the coriander, cumin and ginger and season with salt and cayenne pepper, then dry-fry over a low heat for 30 seconds. Add the oil to the pan and heat for 30 seconds, then add the onions and garlic. Cover and cook gently for about 45 minutes until the onions are golden and very soft.

3 Add the stock to the pan and put the fish on the onions, bring to simmering point and cook gently until the fish flakes when tested with a fork.

4 Transfer the fish to a warmed serving dish with a slotted spoon. Boil the mixture in the pan until most of the liquid has evaporated, then add to the fish on the dish and serve.

Serves 4
Preparation time: 10 minutes, plus marinating
Cooking time: 1 hour

griddled tuna with shallot jus

4 x 100 g/3½ oz tuna steaks
flat leaf parsley sprigs, to garnish

Sauce:
4 shallots, finely chopped
300 ml/½ pint red wine
150 ml/¼ pint Marsala
salt and pepper

To serve:
mashed potatoes
lime wedges

1 Preheat a griddle pan or nonstick frying pan until it is very hot. Cook the tuna steaks, two at a time, for 3 minutes on each side. Remove from the pan and keep warm.

2 To make the sauce, mix the shallots, wine and Marsala in a saucepan, season to taste with salt and pepper and boil rapidly until reduced by half. Return the tuna steaks to the pan, add the shallot jus and simmer for 2 minutes. Garnish with the parsley and serve with mashed potatoes and lime wedges.

Serves 4
Preparation time: 5 minutes
Cooking time: 15 minutes

shark with tomatoes and chillies

4 tablespoons olive oil
3 garlic cloves, crushed
2 fresh red chillies, deseeded and finely chopped
500 g/1 lb ripe plum tomatoes, roughly chopped
1 glass of red wine, preferably Chianti
1 teaspoon chopped sage
4 shark steaks
salt and pepper
finely chopped flat leaf parsley, to garnish

1 Heat the oil in a large flameproof casserole. Add the garlic and chillies and cook over a low heat, stirring constantly, for about 5 minutes until softened.

2 Add the tomatoes, wine and sage and season to taste with salt and pepper. Bring to the boil, cover and simmer very gently, stirring occasionally, for 30 minutes.

3 Add the shark steaks to the sauce, cover and cook gently for 10–15 minutes until tender when pierced with a fork. Taste the sauce for seasoning, and adjust if necessary. Serve hot, sprinkled with chopped parsley.

Serves 4
Preparation time: 5 minutes
Cooking time: 45–50 minutes

roast monkfish with parma ham

4 x 175 g/6 oz monkfish fillets
4 rosemary sprigs
8 slices Parma ham
2 tablespoons olive oil, plus extra for brushing
1 red onion, chopped
1 garlic clove, chopped
6 tomatoes, skinned, deseeded and roughly chopped
1 teaspoon capers, roughly chopped
handful of flat leaf parsley
salt and pepper

1 Season the monkfish with salt and pepper to taste, place the rosemary sprigs on the fish and wrap the slices of Parma ham around them. Lightly oil an ovenproof dish and put the fish in it. Cook in a preheated oven, 220°C (425°F), Gas Mark 7, for 15 minutes.

2 Heat 1 tablespoon of the oil in a saucepan. Add the onion and garlic and fry over a low heat for 5 minutes.

3 Add the tomatoes and capers, mix well, then add the remaining olive oil and parsley. Season to taste with salt and pepper.

4 Serve the fish with some of the sauce spooned over one end.

Serves 4
Preparation time: 10 minutes
Cooking time: 15 minutes
Oven temperature: 220°C (425°F), Gas Mark 7

monkfish with tomatoes and garlic

4 x 175 g/6 oz monkfish steaks
3 tablespoons olive oil
1 tablespoon chopped oregano, to garnish

Marinade:
5 tablespoons olive oil
2 tablespoons lemon juice
1 tablespoon finely chopped parsley

Tomato sauce:
2 tablespoons olive oil
4 garlic cloves, chopped
750 g/1½ lb tomatoes, skinned and chopped
4 anchovy fillets, chopped
salt and pepper

1 Wash the monkfish steaks under cold running water and pat dry with kitchen paper. Put all the marinade ingredients in a bowl and mix together well.

2 Add the monkfish steaks to the marinade, turning them until they are thoroughly coated and glistening with oil. Cover the bowl and leave in a cool place to marinate for at least 1 hour.

3 Heat the olive oil in a large frying pan. Remove the fish steaks from the marinade, add them to the pan and fry gently until they are cooked and golden brown on both sides, turning the fish once during cooking. Remove the steaks from the pan, transfer to a warmed serving dish and keep warm.

4 While the fish steaks are cooking, make the tomato sauce. Heat the olive oil in a pan. Add the garlic and fry over a low heat until just golden. Add the tomatoes and anchovies and cook over a medium heat until the tomatoes are reduced to a thick pulpy consistency. Season to taste with salt and pepper.

5 Pour the sauce over the fish and sprinkle with oregano, to garnish.

Serves 4
Preparation time: 10–15 minutes, plus marinating
Cooking time: 20 minutes

baked monkfish with green pepper sauce

1.25 kg/2½ lb monkfish tail, skinned and filleted
1 teaspoon dried thyme
2 garlic cloves, cut into thin slivers
2 tablespoons lemon juice
200 ml/7 fl oz dry white vermouth
vegetable oil, for brushing
salt and pepper
2 tablespoons chopped parsley, to garnish

Pepper sauce:
3 tablespoons olive oil
2 green peppers, cored, deseeded and chopped
2 onions, finely chopped
3 courgettes, chopped
salt and pepper

1 Season the monkfish fillets with salt and pepper to taste and sprinkle 1 of them with thyme. Make small incisions in the flesh with a sharp knife and carefully insert the slivers of garlic. Sprinkle with lemon juice and place the other fillet on top of the garlic-studded fillet. Secure with string.

2 Lightly oil an ovenproof dish, place the fish in it and add the vermouth. Cover with foil and bake in a preheated oven, 190°C (375°F), Gas Mark 5, for 30 minutes. Remove the fish and keep warm, reserving the cooking liquid.

3 Meanwhile, make the sauce. Heat the olive oil in a heavy-based pan. Add the peppers and fry for about 5 minutes until softened. Add the onions and courgettes, season to taste with salt and pepper and cook over a low heat, stirring occasionally, for 15 minutes.

4 Add the reserved cooking liquid from the fish to the sauce, bring to the boil and cook, stirring well, for a few minutes.

5 Pour the sauce into an ovenproof dish and place the fish on top. Bake in the oven for 15 minutes, or until the fish is cooked. Remove the string and serve hot, sprinkled with chopped parsley.

Serves 4–6
Preparation time: 15 minutes
Cooking time: 45 minutes
Oven temperature: 190°C (375°F), Gas Mark 5

moroccan monkfish with mint

4 x 175 g/6 oz monkfish fillets
8 tablespoons extra virgin olive oil, plus extra for brushing
1 fresh red chilli, halved lengthways
4 tomatoes, deseeded and chopped
2 garlic cloves, crushed
1 shallot, finely chopped
3 tablespoons chopped mint

1 tablespoon chopped parsley
1 tablespoon lime juice
2 tablespoons red wine vinegar
salt and cayenne pepper

1 Brush the monkfish with olive oil, then season with salt and rub with the cut sides of the chilli. Cover and set aside for 1 hour.

2 Cook the monkfish under a preheated grill for about 4 minutes on each side until the flesh just flakes when tested with a fork.

3 Meanwhile, put 6 tablespoons of the oil, the tomatoes, garlic, shallot, mint and parsley into a small saucepan and heat until the garlic begins to sizzle and the tomatoes soften.

4 Whisk together the lime juice, vinegar and the remaining 2 tablespoons of olive oil, then slowly pour in the warm olive oil, whisking constantly. Season to taste with salt and cayenne pepper. Spoon the dressing over the fish and serve.

Serves 4
Preparation time: 10 minutes, plus marinating
Cooking time: 8 minutes

tunisian grilled sardines with tomato relish

16 fresh sardines, scaled, cleaned and gutted
coriander sprigs, to garnish (optional)

Marinade:
1 garlic clove
2 teaspoons coriander seeds, toasted
1 dried red chilli, deseeded and chopped
finely grated rind and juice of 1 lime
4 tablespoons virgin olive oil
salt

Tomato relish:
4 spring onions, white part only, chopped
2 tablespoons lime juice
250 g/8 oz well-flavoured tomatoes, skinned, deseeded and chopped
½ sun-dried tomato, chopped
½ dried red chilli, deseeded and chopped
3 tablespoons chopped coriander leaves

1 Wash the fish thoroughly, pat dry with kitchen paper and place in a shallow non-metallic dish.

2 To make the marinade, using a pestle and mortar pound together the garlic, coriander seeds and chilli with a pinch of salt. Add the lime rind and juice, then gradually work in the oil. Pour over the sardines, coat well with the mixture, then cover and leave for about 1 hour, turning the sardines 2–3 times.

3 Process all the relish ingredients in a food processor or blender. Place the sardines on a barbecue or under a hot grill and cook for 2–3 minutes on each side, basting with the marinade.

4 Serve the sardines with the relish and garnish with coriander sprigs, if liked.

Serves 4
Preparation time: 20 minutes, plus marinating
Cooking time: 6 minutes

spicy fried sardines

oil, for deep-frying
125 g/4 oz plain flour
750 g/1½ lb large, fresh sardines, scaled, cleaned and gutted
4 tablespoons olive oil
5 shallots, sliced
125 ml/4 fl oz white wine vinegar
4 garlic cloves, crushed and chopped
large handful of mint leaves, finely chopped
grated rind and juice of 1 lemon
½ teaspoon crushed dried chillies
salt and pepper

1 Heat the oil for deep-frying to 180–190°C (350–375°F) or until a cube of bread browns in 30 seconds. Season the flour with salt and pepper.

2 Dip the sardines into the seasoned flour and fry in the hot oil for 2 minutes, or until golden. Remove and place on a tray lined with kitchen paper to absorb the excess oil. Keep warm.

3 Heat 1 tablespoon of the olive oil in a saucepan. Add the shallots and fry over a low heat for 5 minutes, then add the vinegar and cook until nearly half of it has evaporated.

4 Transfer the sardines to a warmed serving dish. Add the remaining olive oil, the garlic, mint, lemon rind and juice and chillies to the shallot mixture and cook for 1 minute. Spoon the sauce over the sardines and season to taste with salt and pepper. This dish can be served hot or at room temperature.

Serves 4
Preparation time: 15 minutes
Cooking time: 10 minutes

4 Sprinkle the remaining breadcrumbs and the oil over the top and bake in a preheated oven, 180°C (350°F), Gas Mark 4, for 30 minutes. Sprinkle the lemon juice over the top just before serving. Serve hot, garnished with lemon wedges.

Serves 4
Preparation time: 30–35 minutes
Cooking time: 35 minutes
Oven temperature: 180°C (350°F), Gas Mark 4

fresh sardines with pine nuts and anchovies

75 ml/3 fl oz olive oil, plus extra for brushing
250 g/8 oz fresh white breadcrumbs
40 g/1½ oz sultanas, soaked in hot water and drained
40 g/1½ oz pine nuts
1 tablespoon chopped parsley
40 g/1½ oz can anchovies, drained and chopped
pinch of nutmeg
750 g/1½ lb fresh sardines, scaled, gutted and heads and
*   backbones removed*
about 12 bay leaves
4 tablespoons lemon juice
salt and pepper
lemon wedges, to garnish

1 Heat 4–5 tablespoons of oil in a frying pan. Add half the breadcrumbs and fry over a moderate heat, turning them frequently with a metal spatula, until they are a light golden brown.

2 Remove from the heat and add the sultanas, pine nuts, parsley, anchovies and nutmeg. Season to taste with salt and pepper.

3 Place a little of the mixture inside each sardine and press the sides together to close. Brush a large oven-to-table dish with oil. Arrange rows of sardines in a single layer in the dish and place half a bay leaf between each sardine.

mackerel with olives and tomatoes

4 x 375 g/12 oz mackerel, cleaned and gutted
2 tablespoons plain flour
4 tablespoons olive oil
1 garlic clove, crushed
3 anchovy fillets
250 g/8 oz canned plum tomatoes, drained and chopped
24 pitted black olives, halved
150 ml/¼ pint Fish Stock (see page 142)
1 tablespoon chopped parsley
salt and pepper

1 Lightly flour the mackerel. Heat the oil in a large pan. Add the garlic and anchovies and cook over a medium heat until the garlic is lightly browned. Add the fish and cook for a few minutes, turning once.

2 Add the tomatoes and olives. Continue to cook, adding fish stock from time to time, for about 30 minutes, until the fish is cooked and the sauce well thickened. Season to taste with salt and pepper and sprinkle with parsley just before the end of the cooking time.

3 Serve the fish with the sauce poured over it. This dish is delicious served with a country bread.

Serves 4
Preparation time: 10 minutes
Cooking time: 35–40 minutes

grilled mackerel with gooseberry and fennel sauce

4 x 275–375 g/9–12 oz mackerel, cleaned and gutted
fennel fronds and stalks (optional)
oil, for brushing
salt and pepper
boiled new potatoes, to serve

Sauce:
375 g/12 oz gooseberries, topped and tailed
125 ml/4 fl oz water
2 tablespoons sugar
25 g/1 oz butter
1 tablespoon finely chopped fennel

To garnish:
4 lemon wedges
4 fennel sprigs

1 Season the mackerel inside and out and stuff with the fennel fronds and stalks, if using. Cut 2–3 diagonal slits on each side of the backbone so that the heat can penetrate more quickly. Brush the fish and a baking sheet lightly with oil and set the prepared fish on top.

2 To make the sauce, combine the gooseberries with the water in a large saucepan. Bring to the boil, then add the sugar, butter and fennel. Cook gently for 6–7 minutes until the berries burst but still have texture.

3 Meanwhile, place the mackerel under a preheated moderate grill and cook for 4–7 minutes on each side, depending on the size, turning very carefully. Remove the herb stuffing and serve immediately, garnished with lemon wedges and sprigs of fennel. Accompany with the hot gooseberry sauce and boiled new potatoes.

Serves 4
Preparation time: 5–10 minutes
Cooking time: 15–20 minutes

herb stuffed herrings with mustard sauce

4 x 125 g/4 oz herrings, scaled, cleaned and gutted
boiled new potatoes, to serve

Stuffing:
75 g/3 oz butter
1 small onion, finely chopped
2 tablespoons finely chopped parsley
1 teaspoon finely chopped dill
2 hard-boiled eggs, finely chopped
grated rind of ½ lemon
50 g/2 oz breadcrumbs
salt and pepper

Sauce:
25 g/1 oz butter
25 g/1 oz plain flour
300 ml/½ pint milk
1 tablespoon lemon juice
1 tablespoon prepared English mustard
1 tablespoon finely chopped parsley

To garnish:
4 lemon wedges
4 flat leaf parsley sprigs

1 To make the stuffing, melt half the butter in a saucepan. Add the onion and fry over a low heat until soft. Use the remaining butter to grease an ovenproof dish and a sheet of foil.

2 Add the remaining stuffing ingredients to the onion and season to taste with salt and pepper. Divide the stuffing between the 4 fish, reshaping them carefully to make sure the stuffing will not fall out. Place each herring carefully in the dish, cover with the buttered foil and bake in a preheated oven, 160°C (325°F), Gas Mark 3, for 40–45 minutes.

3 Meanwhile, prepare the sauce. Melt the butter, stir in the flour, then gradually add the milk to form a smooth paste. Cook over a low heat, stirring constantly, for about 5 minutes until the sauce is thick and the flour cooked. Stir in the lemon juice, mustard and parsley and season to taste with salt and pepper.

4 Serve the herrings with lemon wedges, flat leaf parsley, the hot mustard sauce and boiled new potatoes.

Serves 4
Preparation time: 15–20 minutes
Cooking time: 45–50 minutes
Oven temperature: 160°C (325°F), Gas Mark 3

red mullet with almond chermoula

Chermoula is a distinctive Moroccan mixture of coriander, garlic, chillies and spices that is used in many ways, bringing character and flavour to dishes. Its most frequent use is as a marinade, either before cooking or afterwards, for fish, grilled or baked meat, poultry, and vegetable dishes. The food may also be cooked in chermoula.

50 g/2 oz coriander
large handful of mint, roughly chopped
40 g/1½ oz almonds
2 plump garlic cloves
pinch of dried chilli flakes
about 125 ml/4 fl oz virgin olive oil
lemon juice
4 x 300 g/10 oz red mullet, cleaned and gutted
salt and pepper

1 Put the coriander, mint, almonds, garlic and chilli into a food processor or blender. With the motor running, slowly pour in the oil to make a coarse or smooth paste, according to taste. Season to taste with salt and pepper and lemon juice.

2 With the point of a sharp knife, cut 2 deep slashes in both sides of each fish. Spread the chermoula over both sides of the fish, working it well into the slashes. Cover and leave in a cool place for 1 hour.

3 Put the mullet under a preheated grill and cook for 4–5 minutes on each side until the flesh just flakes when tested with a fork.

Serves 4
Preparation time: 10 minutes, plus marinating
Cooking time: 8–10 minutes

grilled red mullet with salsa verde

4 x 375 g/12 oz red mullet, scaled, gutted and cleaned

Salsa verde:
125 g/4 oz parsley, chopped
125 g/4 oz basil, chopped
5 anchovy fillets, roughly chopped
2 tablespoons capers
2 garlic cloves, crushed
juice and rind of 1 lemon
150 ml/¼ pint olive oil
salt and pepper

1 Make 3 slashes across the fish on each side and season with salt and pepper. Place under a preheated very hot grill and cook for 6–8 minutes on each side, or until cooked.

2 Meanwhile, to make the salsa verde, put the parsley, basil, anchovies, capers and garlic in a food processor or blender and process to a smooth paste. Add the lemon juice and rind and olive oil, season with salt and pepper and process again.

3 Remove the fish from the grill and put a spoonful of the salsa verde into each of the slashes on one side of the fish. Serve the remaining salsa separately in a small dish.

Serves 4
Preparation time: 10 minutes
Cooking time: 12–16 minutes

griddled red mullet with walnut and parsley pesto

4 x 150 g/5 oz red mullet fillets
sea salt and pepper

Walnut and parsley pesto:
50 g/2 oz walnut pieces, toasted
4 spring onions, chopped
1 garlic clove, chopped
2 tablespoons parsley, chopped
4 tablespoons extra virgin olive oil

To garnish:
1 lemon, cut into 4 wedges
parsley sprigs

1 First make the pesto. Place all the ingredients in a food processor or blender and process until fairly smooth. Season to taste with sea salt and pepper.

2 Heat a griddle pan or nonstick frying pan. Put on the fish, skin side down, and cook for 3 minutes on each side. The fish should be slightly charred on the outside and firm to the touch. Serve with a spoonful of the pesto and garnish with lemon wedges and parsley sprigs.

Serves 4
Preparation time: 10 minutes
Cooking time: 6 minutes

red mullet baked in foil

4 x 375 g/12 oz red mullet, scaled, cleaned and gutted
50 g/2 oz butter, diced
250 g/8 oz canned plum tomatoes, drained
1 tablespoon capers, drained
1 tablespoon roughly chopped basil
16 pitted black olives, chopped
salt and pepper

1 Season the fish with salt and pepper.

2 Grease a large sheet of foil with some of the butter. Put half the tomatoes in the centre, together with half the capers. Sprinkle with half the basil, half the remaining diced butter and half the olives. Put the fish on top and cover with the remaining ingredients.

3 Close the foil tightly, put the package on a baking sheet and bake in a preheated oven, 200°C (400°F), Gas Mark 6, for 35 minutes.

4 Transfer to a serving dish, open the foil slightly and serve.

Serves 4
Preparation time: 10 minutes
Cooking time: 35 minutes
Oven temperature: 200°C (400°F), Gas Mark 6

thai grilled mullet

1 large grey mullet, cleaned and gutted
1½ teaspoons chopped garlic
½ onion, chopped
5 mushrooms, wiped and sliced
2 tablespoons shredded fresh root ginger
1 celery stick, sliced
1 teaspoon pepper
1 tablespoon salted soya bean flavouring
1 tablespoon oyster sauce
250 ml/8 fl oz Thai Fish Stock (see page 143) or water

To serve:
1 lettuce, separated into leaves
3 lemon slices

1 Place the fish on a wooden board and score the skin 2–3 times with a sharp knife to allow the sauce to be absorbed during cooking. Rub the fish with garlic, pressing it well into the cuts. Transfer the fish to a shallow heatproof dish.

2 In a bowl, mix all the remaining ingredients well and pour over the fish. Place the fish under a preheated grill and cook for 20 minutes, turning the fish over halfway through the cooking time.

3 Just before serving, arrange a bed of lettuce on a shallow serving dish. Carefully transfer the fish to the dish, pour over the vegetable sauce and garnish with the lemon slices. Serve immediately.

Serves 4
Preparation time: 10–15 minutes
Cooking time: 20 minutes

grey mullet with red wine and garlic sauce

4 medium grey mullet or whiting, cleaned, gutted and
*   filleted*
flour, for coating
75 ml/3 fl oz olive oil

Red wine sauce:
2 tablespoons olive oil
2 onions, chopped
3 garlic cloves, crushed
2 tablespoons flour
500 ml/17 fl oz red wine
250 g/8 oz tomatoes, skinned and roughly chopped
2 tablespoons tomato purée
1 bouquet garni
salt and pepper

To garnish:
3 tablespoons capers
2 tablespoons chopped parsley

1 First make the sauce. Heat the olive oil in a large saucepan. Add the onions and garlic and fry over a low heat until soft and golden. Stir in the flour and cook gently for 1 minute, then add the red wine, stirring well. Bring to the boil.

2 Add the tomatoes, tomato purée and bouquet garni to the pan and season to taste with salt and pepper. Cook briskly, uncovered, for about 30 minutes, or until the sauce is thick and reduced.

3 Meanwhile, dust the fish fillets with flour. Heat the olive oil in a large frying pan. Add the fish and fry for 3–4 minutes each side until they are cooked and golden. Remove from the pan, drain and keep warm.

4 Pass the sauce through a sieve or process in a food processor or blender. Return to the pan and add the fish fillets. Heat through gently for 5–10 minutes. Add the capers and serve sprinkled with chopped parsley.

Serves 4
Preparation time: 15 minutes
Cooking time: 45–50 minutes

mexican red snapper with lime and coriander

1 kg/2 lb red snapper or other white fish, filleted and
*   skinned*
4 tablespoons lime or lemon juice
2 teaspoons salt
4 tablespoons olive oil
25 g/1 oz fresh breadcrumbs

1 garlic clove, crushed
6 tablespoons finely chopped coriander leaves
1 teaspoon grated lime or lemon rind
pepper
warmed tortillas, to serve (optional)

1 Rub the fish with half of the lime or lemon juice and 1 teaspoon of the salt and place, skin side down, in a lightly oiled, heavy-based frying pan. Add enough cold water to cover the fish and then simmer gently over a low heat for 5 minutes, turning once or twice during the cooking time.

2 Heat half of the olive oil in another pan. Add the breadcrumbs, garlic, the remaining salt and 4 tablespoons of the coriander. Cook over a low heat, stirring constantly, until the crumbs are golden brown. Spread over the fish and simmer for 7–10 minutes until the fish flakes easily.

3 Blend the remaining lime or lemon juice and oil together and pour over the fish. Cook for 2–3 minutes. Combine the remaining coriander with the grated lime or lemon rind and sprinkle over the fish. Season with pepper and serve hot with warmed tortillas if you want an authentic Mexican touch.

Serves 4
Preparation time: 10 minutes
Cooking time: 20 minutes

red snapper with spicy salsa

6 tomatoes, skinned, deseeded and chopped
1 bunch of spring onions, chopped
1 garlic clove, crushed
1 bunch of coriander, chopped
2 chillies, deseeded and diced
4 tablespoons lime juice
1 ripe avocado, peeled, stoned and diced
2 tablespoons olive oil
4 x 175 g/6 oz red snapper fillets
sea salt flakes and pepper

1 Combine all the ingredients, except the fish, in a bowl, cover and leave to marinate for 2–3 hours if possible. If you prefer a smooth salsa, place everything in a food processor or blender and process.

2 Heat a griddle pan or nonstick frying pan. Put on the snapper fillets, skin side down, and cook for 3–4 minutes. Turn and cook for a further 3 minutes, or until firm to the touch. Serve immediately with the spicy salsa.

Serves 4
Preparation time: 20 minutes, plus marinating
Cooking time: 5–10 minutes

caribbean spicy red snapper

4 small red snappers, scaled, cleaned and gutted
2 teaspoons salt
2 red chillies, deseeded and finely chopped
4 tablespoons lime juice
flour, for dusting
oil, for frying
1 onion, chopped
250 g/8 oz tomatoes, skinned and chopped
300 ml/½ pint water
salt and pepper

To serve:
lime wedges
hot pepper sauce
boiled rice

1 Slash the sides of each fish deeply 2 or 3 times, almost through to the bone.

2 Pound the salt and chopped chilli together in a mortar and sprinkle over the red snappers. Place the fish in a shallow bowl and pour the lime juice over the top. Cover and leave in a cool place for 1–2 hours to marinate.

3 Remove the fish from the bowl, reserving the marinade. Dust them well with flour. Heat the oil in a large frying pan. Add the fish and fry until crisp and golden on both sides, turning once during cooking. Remove and drain on absorbent kitchen paper. Keep the fish warm.

4 Pour off most of the oil. Add the onion to the pan and fry over a low heat until soft. Add the tomatoes and simmer gently until thickened. Add the water and reserved marinade and bring to the boil. Reduce the heat, add the fried fish and simmer for 5 minutes. Season to taste with salt and pepper and serve with lime wedges, hot pepper sauce and rice.

Serves 4
Preparation time: 10 minutes, plus marinating
Cooking time: 35–40 minutes

tarragon-infused sea bass fillets

4 x 175 g/6 oz sea bass fillets
large bunch of tarragon
2 tablespoons olive oil
4 tablespoons lemon juice
sea salt and pepper

1 Heat a griddle pan or nonstick frying pan. Put on the sea bass, skin side down, and cook for 3 minutes. Place a quarter of the tarragon on each fillet, pressing it into the fish. Turn the fish so that it is resting on the tarragon and cook for a further 3 minutes.

2 To serve, drizzle the fillets with olive oil and lemon juice and season to taste with salt and pepper. Serve with the charred tarragon.

Serves 4
Preparation time: 5 minutes
Cooking time: 6 minutes

sea bass with fennel

2 large fennel bulbs
6 tablespoons olive oil
8 tablespoons water
2 x 500 g/1 lb sea bass, cleaned and gutted
salt and pepper
fennel tops, to garnish

1 Cut the fennel bulbs lengthways into 1 cm/½ inch slices. Pour the oil into a large frying pan or wok, add the fennel and water and bring to the boil. Cover and simmer, stirring occasionally, for 30 minutes until the fennel is very tender.

2 Uncover the pan, season to taste with salt and pepper and boil until the water has evaporated and the fennel is golden brown. Transfer to a warmed plate and keep hot.

3 Season the fish with salt and pepper, add to the pan and baste with the hot oil. Cover and cook for 7–8 minutes. Turn the fish over, baste again and cook for a further 5–6 minutes.

4 Arrange the fish on a warmed serving dish, spoon the fennel and juices around and over the fish and serve immediately, garnished with fennel tops.

Serves 4
Preparation time: 5 minutes
Cooking time: 45–50 minutes

sea bass in sweet and sour sauce

1½ tablespoons plain flour
4 sea bass fillets
2 tablespoons olive oil
1 tablespoon butter
250 ml/8 fl oz dry white wine
2 tablespoons white wine vinegar
1 tablespoon sugar
2 tablespoons raisins
salt and pepper

1 Season the flour with salt and pepper. Cut the fish fillets on the diagonal into serving pieces, then coat in the seasoned flour.

2 Heat the oil and butter together in a large nonstick frying pan until foaming. Add as many pieces of fish as the pan will hold and fry over a medium heat for 1–2 minutes on each side until crispy and golden. Remove the fish pieces with a slotted spoon and set aside on a plate. Repeat with any remaining pieces of fish, if necessary.

3 Add the white wine, vinegar, sugar and raisins to the pan with salt and pepper to taste and stir over a moderate to high heat until reduced.

4 Return the fish to the pan, then shake the pan and spoon the sauce over the fish until the pieces are evenly coated. Serve immediately.

Serves 4
Preparation time: 10 minutes
Cooking time: about 10 minutes

deep-fried sea bass with garlic

oil, for deep-frying
625 g/1¼ lb sea bass, cleaned and gutted
15 garlic cloves
2 tablespoons oil
2 tablespoons palm sugar or light muscovado sugar
1 tablespoon light soy sauce

Sauce:
7 small green chillies
3 garlic cloves
5 tablespoons Thai fish sauce
3 tablespoons lime juice
1 teaspoon palm sugar or light muscovado sugar
15 g/½ oz coriander leaf, stalk and root, chopped

To garnish:
spring onion slivers
red chillies

1 Heat the oil for deep-frying in a preheated wok or frying pan to 180–190°C (350–375°F) or until a cube of bread browns in 30 seconds. Add the fish and fry for about 25 minutes. Turn it over carefully and cook for a further 10 minutes, or until really crispy. Remove the fish from the oil and drain on kitchen paper.

2 Meanwhile, make the sauce. Put the chillies into a mortar and pound for 1 minute, then add the garlic and pound together for 2 minutes, or until well broken down and combined with the chillies. Add the remaining sauce ingredients, one by one, pounding after each addition, then pour the sauce into a bowl and set aside.

3 Slice the garlic cloves. Heat the oil in a clean preheated wok or frying pan. Add the garlic and stir-fry for 3–5 minutes until golden and crispy. Turn off the heat and stir in the sugar and soy sauce.

4 Place the fish on a serving dish and top with the garlic. Garnish with the spring onion and chilli and serve with the sauce.

Serves 4
Preparation time: 15–20 minutes
Cooking time: 40 minutes

steamed pomfret with lemon grass

375 g/12 oz pomfret, cleaned and gutted
1 teaspoon salt
1 lemon grass stalk, cut into 3 pieces
15 small red and green chillies
1 coriander root, finely chopped
3 garlic cloves, finely sliced
3 tablespoons Thai fish sauce
2 tablespoons light soy sauce
ground dried chilli, to serve

1 Cut diagonal slashes on each side of the fish and rub the salt all over it to firm it up. Leave for 2 minutes, then wash off the salt.

2 Place the fish on a plate, arrange the lemon grass on top, put it into a steamer, and steam for 35–40 minutes.

3 Meanwhile, chop the chillies very finely and put them into a small bowl with the coriander, garlic, fish sauce and soy sauce and stir thoroughly.

4 To serve, pour the sauce over the fish and serve with the ground chilli on the side.

Serves 2
Preparation time: 5 minutes
Cooking time: 35–40 minutes

trout with parmesan and basil dressing

4 tablespoons olive oil, plus extra for brushing
4 x 200 g/7 oz trout fillets
large handful of basil leaves, roughly chopped
1 garlic clove, chopped
125 g/4 oz Parmesan cheese, freshly grated
salt and pepper

1 Lightly brush a baking sheet with oil and place under a preheated very hot grill to heat up.

2 Put the trout fillets on to the hot tray, sprinkle with salt and pepper and place under the grill for 5 minutes.

3 Put the basil and garlic into a bowl. Work in the olive oil using a hand-held blender.

4 Remove the fish from the grill and sprinkle with the grated Parmesan. Return to the grill and cook for a further 3–5 minutes until the Parmesan turns golden. Serve with the basil sauce drizzled over the golden trout fillets.

Serves 4
Preparation time: 10 minutes
Cooking time: 10 minutes

rainbow trout steamed in aromatic seasonings

1 tablespoon sesame oil
1 tablespoon light soy sauce
1 tablespoon dry sherry
2 x 500 g/1 lb rainbow trout, cleaned and gutted
4 garlic cloves, sliced
6 spring onions, shredded
5 cm/2 inch piece fresh root ginger, shredded
2 tablespoons dry white vermouth
2 tablespoons sunflower oil

1 Mix together the sesame oil, soy sauce and sherry and use to brush the inside and skin of the fish. Mix together the garlic, spring onions and ginger and place a fifth of this mixture inside each fish.

2 Place the fish on a heatproof plate, scatter over the remaining garlic mixture and pour over the vermouth and oil. Put the plate in a wok or steamer and steam vigorously for 15 minutes, or until the fish are tender.

3 Arrange on a warmed serving dish, pour over the juices and serve immediately.

Serves 4
Preparation time: 10 minutes
Cooking time: 15 minutes

griddled rainbow trout with ground almond dressing

4 x 275 g/9 oz rainbow trout, cleaned and gutted
125 g/4 oz ground almonds
6 tablespoons olive oil
4 tablespoons lemon juice
2 tablespoons chopped parsley
sea salt and pepper
parsley sprigs, to garnish

1 Rinse the trout and pat dry with kitchen paper. Heat a griddle pan or nonstick frying pan. Put on the trout and cook on each side for 8 minutes, carefully turning the fish with a palette knife. The skin should be charred.

2 Place the almonds in a small saucepan over a medium heat and stir constantly until lightly browned. Remove from the heat and add the oil, lemon juice and chopped parsley and season to taste with salt and pepper. Stir well and return to the heat for 2 minutes.

3 Serve the trout with the almond dressing poured over and garnish with sprigs of parsley.

Serves 4
Preparation time: 10 minutes
Cooking time: 15–20 minutes

baked trout with herb stuffing and cream sauce

75 g/3 oz butter
1 small onion, finely chopped
2 tablespoons finely chopped parsley
1 tablespoon finely chopped chives
3 teaspoons finely chopped dill
50 g/2 oz fine white breadcrumbs
finely grated rind of ½ lemon
2 teaspoons lemon juice
pinch of nutmeg
250 ml/8 fl oz single cream
4 x 300 g/10 oz rainbow or brown trout, cleaned and gutted
150 ml/¼ pint dry white wine
salt and pepper

To serve:
boiled potatoes
green vegetables or salad

1 Melt 50 g/2 oz of the butter in a large frying pan. Add the onion and cook until soft but not browned. Remove from the heat. Mix the herbs together and add half to the pan, together with the breadcrumbs, lemon rind, juice and nutmeg and season to taste with salt and pepper. Mix well and moisten with 1–2 tablespoons of the cream. Divide the stuffing between the fish.

2 Grease a large ovenproof baking dish with half the remaining butter. Lay the stuffed trout head to tail in the dish, dot with the remaining butter and pour over the wine. Bake in a preheated oven, 240°C (475°F), Gas Mark 9, for 20 minutes until slightly firm to the touch.

3 Pour the cooking liquid into a saucepan and boil rapidly until reduced by half. Add the remaining cream and herbs and return to the boil, adjusting the seasoning if necessary.

4 Arrange the fish on warmed individual serving plates, pour a little sauce over each one and serve with boiled potatoes and crisp green vegetables or salad.

Serves 4
Preparation time: 20 minutes
Cooking time: 30 minutes
Oven temperature: 240°C (475°F), Gas Mark 9

river trout sautéed with almonds

200 ml/7 fl oz milk
1 tablespoon plain flour
4 x 250 g/8 oz trout, scaled, cleaned and gutted
1 tablespoon oil
150 g/5 oz butter
125 g/4 oz flaked almonds
salt and pepper

To garnish:
lemon quarters
2 tablespoons finely chopped parsley

1 Put the milk in one dish and the flour in another. Dip each trout into the milk and then coat with flour. Shake gently to remove any excess flour.

2 Heat the oil and 125 g/4 oz of the butter in a large, heavy-based frying pan. Add the trout and cook gently for about 5 minutes on each side until cooked and golden brown. Take care that the butter does not burn. Remove and place on a warmed serving dish. Sprinkle with salt and pepper and keep the trout warm.

3 Wash the frying pan and dry it thoroughly. Add the remaining butter and heat gently until the butter starts to foam. Add the almonds and cook over a moderate heat, stirring constantly, for about 2 minutes until golden all over. Sprinkle the almonds and the butter in the pan over the trout and serve immediately, garnished with lemon quarters and sprinkled with parsley.

Serves 4
Preparation time: 10 minutes
Cooking time: 12 minutes

honey-grilled trout

4 rainbow trout, cleaned and gutted
75 g/3 oz butter
1 tablespoon chopped parsley
1½ tablespoons clear honey
2 tablespoons lemon juice
salt and pepper
brown bread and butter, to serve

To garnish:
parsley sprigs
lemon wedges

1 Pat the trout dry with kitchen paper. Remove the fins and trim the tails into a neat 'V' shape. Using a sharp knife, make 3 diagonal slashes on either side of each trout. Cream 25 g/1 oz of the butter with the parsley in a bowl and season to taste with salt and pepper. Put a pat of the seasoned butter inside each trout and place in a greased grill pan.

2 Put the remaining butter, the honey and lemon juice into a saucepan and heat gently until melted. Pour it over the trout, season to taste with salt and pepper and cook under a preheated moderately hot grill for 6–8 minutes on each side until cooked through, basting from time to time with the cooking juices.

3 Arrange the trout on a warmed serving dish, pour over the pan juices and garnish with the parsley sprigs and lemon wedges. Serve hot with brown bread and butter.

Serves 4
Preparation time: 10 minutes
Cooking time: 15–18 minutes

trout stuffed with couscous, almonds and herbs

4 tablespoons olive oil, plus extra for brushing
1 small onion, finely chopped
2 garlic cloves, crushed
125 g/4 oz couscous
300 ml/½ pint Fish or Vegetable Stock
   (see pages 142 and 140)
1 tablespoon chopped parsley
1 tablespoon chopped mint
4 x 375 g/12 oz trout, cleaned and gutted
50 g/2 oz flaked almonds
salt and pepper
warm bread, to serve

To garnish:
lemon wedges
mint sprigs

1 Heat 2 tablespoons of the oil in a frying pan. Add the onion and fry until softened, adding the garlic towards the end. Stir in the couscous, fish or vegetable stock, parsley and mint. Bring to the boil, then remove the pan from the heat and leave for 10–15 minutes until the liquid has been absorbed.

2 Season the trout with salt and pepper and fill the cavity of each one with a quarter of the couscous mixture. Brush a shallow ovenproof dish with oil and lay the trout in it. Mix the remaining oil with the almonds and spoon over the fish. Bake in a preheated oven, 200°C (400°F), Gas Mark 6, for 15–20 minutes until the fish flakes when tested with a fork.

3 Garnish with lemon wedges and mint sprigs and serve with warm bread.

Serves 4
Preparation time: 15 minutes, plus standing
Cooking time: 20–25 minutes
Oven temperature: 200°C (400°F), Gas Mark 6

baked sea bream with tarragon and lemon

1.25 kg/2½ lb sea bream, scaled, cleaned and gutted
25 g/1 oz butter
1 onion, sliced
3 small tomatoes, halved
2 tablespoons Fish Stock (see page 142)
100 ml/3½ fl oz water
4 tablespoons lemon juice
1 tablespoon fresh white breadcrumbs
1 tablespoon chopped tarragon
3 tablespoons olive oil

To garnish:
1 lemon, halved
tarragon sprigs

1 Place the fish in an ovenproof dish.

2 Melt the butter in a heavy-based frying pan. Add the onion and fry over a low heat for about 15 minutes, or until soft and golden brown.

3 Arrange the fried onion and halved tomatoes around the fish and then cover with the fish stock, water and lemon juice.

4 Sprinkle the breadcrumbs, chopped tarragon and olive oil on top. Bake in a preheated oven, 180°C (350°F), Gas Mark 4 for 40–45 minutes, basting occasionally. Serve garnished with lemon halves and tarragon.

Serves 6
Preparation time: 15 minutes
Cooking time: about 1 hour
Oven temperature: 180°C (350°F), Gas Mark 4

fragrant baked sea bream

1 tablespoon flaked almonds, lightly toasted and chopped
1 teaspoon paprika
1 teaspoon ground cinnamon
2 teaspoons ground cumin
pinch of crushed saffron threads
½ teaspoon cayenne pepper
2 garlic cloves, crushed
2 teaspoons caster sugar
750 g/1½ lb sea bream, cleaned and gutted
3 tablespoons lemon juice
4 tablespoons olive oil
salt and pepper
chopped coriander, to garnish

To serve:
coriander sprigs
tomato slices

1 Mix together the almonds, paprika, cinnamon, cumin, saffron, cayenne pepper, garlic and sugar and season with salt and pepper. Cut 3 slashes in both sides of the sea bream and place in a non-metallic dish. Rub the spice mixture over the fish, working it well into the slashes. Pour over the lemon juice and olive oil. Cover and leave in a cool place for 1 hour.

2 Put the fish and any marinade in a shallow earthenware ovenproof dish, cover with foil and bake in a preheated oven, 180°C (350°F), Gas Mark 4, for about 20–25 minutes, depending on the thickness of the fish, until the flesh flakes when tested with a fork.

3 Serve on a bed of coriander sprigs and tomato slices, garnished with chopped coriander.

Serves 2
Preparation time: 10 minutes, plus marinating
Cooking time: 20–25 minutes
Oven temperature: 180°C (350°F), Gas Mark 4

bream in a couscous jacket with tomato and mint

40 g/1½ oz fine couscous
25 g/1 oz blanched almonds, finely chopped
1 spring onion, thinly sliced
4 x 250 g/8 oz sea bream, scaled, cleaned and gutted
1 large egg, beaten
salt and pepper

Tomato and mint salad:
1 plump garlic clove, crushed
1 teaspoon lime juice
1 teaspoon white wine vinegar
5 tablespoons olive oil
2 large sun-ripened tomatoes, skinned, deseeded and
*   chopped*
25 g/1 oz mint, chopped

1 First make the salad. Stir together the garlic, lime juice, vinegar and half of the olive oil. Season to taste with salt and pepper, then add the tomatoes and half of the mint and gently toss together. Cover and refrigerate.

2 Mix together the couscous, almonds, spring onion, the remaining mint and season to taste with salt and pepper.

3 Dip each fish into the beaten egg, then coat evenly with the couscous mixture.

4 Heat the remaining olive oil in a large, nonstick frying pan. Add the fish in a single layer and fry for about 7 minutes on each side until the flesh flakes when tested with the point of a knife. Serve immediately with the tomato and mint salad.

Serves 4
Preparation time: 10 minutes
Cooking time: 14 minutes

sicilian fish stew with olives

75 ml/3 fl oz olive oil
1 onion, finely sliced
2 garlic cloves, crushed
2 carrots, cut into strips
400 g/13 oz can chopped tomatoes
125 g/4 oz black olives

1 bay leaf
4 slices of white bread
1 kg/2 lb mixed fish fillets and seafood (white fish, red
*   mullet, scallops, prawns), prepared or cut into chunks*
250 g/8 oz mussels, scrubbed and debearded
*   (see page 109)*
salt and pepper
2 tablespoons finely chopped parsley, to garnish
crusty bread, to serve

1 Heat 2 tablespoons of the olive oil in a heavy-based frying pan. Add the onion, garlic and carrots and fry over a low heat for about 5 minutes or until soft. Add the tomatoes with their juices, olives and bay leaf and season to taste with salt and black pepper. Simmer gently for 15 minutes.

2 Cut 4 large rounds from the slices of bread. Heat the remaining oil in a small frying pan. Add the bread rounds and fry until crisp and golden on both sides. Remove, drain on absorbent kitchen paper and keep warm.

3 Add the prepared fish and seafood to the stew and cook for 5 minutes. Add the mussels and simmer for 10 minutes, or until the shells open. Discard any that do not open. Remove and discard the bay leaf. Put a piece of fried bread in 4 warmed deep plates or large shallow soup bowls and ladle the fish stew over the top. Sprinkle with chopped parsley and serve immediately with plenty of crusty bread.

Serves 4
Preparation time: 30 minutes
Cooking time: 35 minutes

frittura mista

The Adriatic waters yield a variety of fish, so when Italian fishermen get just a few of each kind in their nets, they cook them all together in this typical sea food fry-up.

125–175 g/4–6 oz prepared squid, sliced
125–175 g/4–6 oz whitebait
125–175 g/4–6 oz large prawns
125–175 g/4–6 oz plaice fillets, skinned and cut into
*   1 cm/½ inch strips*
125 g/4 oz plain flour
salt and pepper
oil, for deep-frying

To garnish:
1–2 lemons, sliced or quartered
flat leaf parsley sprigs

1 Wash all the fish and dry well with absorbent kitchen paper. Season the flour with salt and pepper.

2 Heat the oil in a deep pan to 180–190°C (350–375°F), or until a cube of bread browns in 30 seconds. Toss the fish, a batch at a time, into the seasoned flour and deep-fry until golden brown. Drain well on absorbent kitchen paper, place on a warmed serving dish and keep hot.

3 Sprinkle the fish lightly with salt and garnish the dish with lemon slices and parsley just before serving.

Serves 4
Preparation time: 30–40 minutes
Cooking time: 15–20 minutes

4 Melt 25 g/1 oz of the remaining butter in a medium saucepan just before removing the fish from the oven, sprinkle in the flour and cook, stirring, for 1–2 minutes. Remove from the heat. Strain the cooking liquid from the fish and gradually stir it into the butter and flour mixture. Return to the heat and cook, stirring, for 2–3 minutes. Season to taste with salt and pepper. Pour the sauce evenly over the fish and leave to cool completely.

5 Spoon the potato over the fish, lightly smooth the surface, then mark the top in a pattern with a fork. Dot with the remaining butter. Bake in a preheated oven, 180°C (350°F), Gas Mark 4, for about 25 minutes until the fish is heated through and the topping is browned. Serve garnished with the chopped chives.

Serves 4
Preparation time: 15 minutes, plus cooling
Cooking time: 50 minutes
Oven temperature: 180°C (350°F), Gas Mark 4

classic fish pie

1 kg/2 lb potatoes, cut into chunks
750 g/1½ lb cod, hake or haddock, skinned, filleted and
*   cut into 4 equal pieces*
900 ml/1½ pints milk
75 g/3 oz butter
40 g/1½ oz plain flour
salt and pepper
1 tablespoon chopped chives, to garnish

1 Boil the potatoes in a large saucepan of salted water for about 15–20 minutes, or until tender.

2 Meanwhile, arrange the pieces of fish in a dish in 2 layers. Season to taste with salt and pepper and pour over 750 ml/1¼ pints of the milk. Cover closely with kitchen foil and bake in a preheated oven, 180°C (350°F), Gas Mark 4, for 25 minutes.

3 Drain the potatoes and pass them through a *mouli légumes* or sieve. Add 40 g/1½ oz of the butter and the remaining milk and beat until soft and creamy. Set aside to cool, but do not chill.

smoked fish pie

500 g/1 lb smoked haddock
450 ml/¾ pint milk
50 g/2 oz butter
1 onion, finely chopped
175 g/6 oz mushrooms, sliced
25 g/1 oz plain flour
1 teaspoon prepared English mustard
2 tablespoons finely chopped parsley
1 tablespoon lemon juice
2–3 eggs, hard-boiled and roughly chopped
salt and pepper

Topping:
875 g/1¾ lb potatoes, boiled and mashed
25 g/1 oz butter, melted
3–4 tablespoons milk
50 g/2 oz Cheddar cheese, grated

1 Put the haddock in a shallow saucepan and add the milk. Heat gently until simmering and cook for 5–10 minutes.

2 Meanwhile, melt the butter in a pan. Add the onion and fry until soft but not browned. Add the mushrooms and continue to fry until browning. Stir in the flour and cook gently for about 1 minute, then remove the pan from the heat.

3 When the fish is cooked, strain the liquor into a jug and gradually add to the onion and mushroom mixture, stirring well. Bring to the boil and simmer, stirring constantly, for 10 minutes until thick. Add the mustard, parsley, lemon juice and eggs and season to taste with salt and pepper. Flake the fish, remove the bones and add to the sauce. Pile into a deep ovenproof pie dish.

4 Mix the potatoes with the melted butter and milk, season well and pile roughly on top of the fish mixture, covering it evenly. Scatter over the cheese and bake in a preheated oven, 190°C (375°F), Gas Mark 5, for about 30 minutes until piping hot and crisp.

Serves 4–6
Preparation time: 20 minutes
Cooking time: 45–50 minutes
Oven temperature: 190°C (375°F), Gas Mark 5

bouillabaisse

200 ml/7 fl oz olive oil
2 onions, thinly sliced
2 leeks, trimmed and thinly sliced
3 tomatoes, skinned, deseeded and chopped
4 garlic cloves, crushed
1 fennel sprig
1 thyme sprig
1 bay leaf
1 orange rind strip without pith
750 g/1½ lb shellfish (crab, mussels, king prawns)
2 litres/3½ pints boiling water
2.5 kg/5 lb mixed skinless fish fillets (John Dory, monkfish, sea bass)
4 pinches of saffron powder
salt and pepper
slices of hot toast made from French bread, to serve

Rouille:
50 g/2 oz fresh white breadcrumbs
2 garlic cloves, finely chopped
1 red pepper, cored, deseeded, roasted and the flesh coarsely chopped
2 teaspoons tomato purée
250 ml/8 fl oz extra virgin olive oil

1 First make the rouille. Put the breadcrumbs in a small bowl, cover with cold water and set aside to soak for 5 minutes. Squeeze out the excess moisture and transfer to a food processor. Add the garlic, red pepper and tomato purée and process until smooth. With the motor running, gradually add the olive oil until fully incorporated. Set aside until required.

2 Heat the olive oil in a large saucepan. Add the onions, leeks, chopped tomatoes and garlic and fry over a low heat, stirring frequently, for a few minutes until soft. Stir in the fennel, thyme, bay leaf and orange rind.

3 Add the shellfish and boiling water and season to taste with salt and pepper. Increase the heat and boil for about 3 minutes to allow the oil and water to amalgamate.

4 Add the fish and reduce the heat. Continue cooking the fish over a medium heat for 12–15 minutes until cooked. The flesh should be opaque and tender but still firm – it should not be falling apart.

5 Taste the bouillabaisse when the fish is cooked and adjust the seasoning, if necessary. Stir in the saffron, then pour into a warm tureen or soup dishes. Serve immediately with slices of hot toasted French bread topped with a spoonful of rouille.

Serves 6–8
Preparation time: 30 minutes
Cooking time: 30 minutes

bourride

1 kg/2 lb firm white fish fillets, trimmed and cut into large pieces
500 g/1 lb firm potatoes, peeled and thickly sliced
2 egg yolks
6–8 slices French bread, toasted or fried
2 tablespoons chopped parsley, to garnish

Court bouillon:
600 ml/1 pint water
150 ml/¼ pint dry white wine
1 onion, sliced
1 leek, sliced
1 slice of lemon
1 parsley sprig
1 thyme sprig

1 fennel sprig
375 g/12 oz fish trimmings
1 teaspoon salt
6 black peppercorns

Aïoli:
4–5 garlic cloves, crushed
2 egg yolks
250 ml/8 fl oz extra virgin olive oil
1–2 tablespoons lemon juice
salt and pepper

1 First make the court bouillon. Put the water, wine, onion, leek, lemon, herbs, fish trimmings, salt and peppercorns into a large saucepan. Bring to the boil and then simmer for 45 minutes.

2 Meanwhile, make the aïoli. Put the garlic in a bowl with a pinch of salt and crush with the back of a spoon. Add the egg yolks and beat with an electric mixer for about 30 seconds until creamy. Gradually beat in the olive oil, adding it drop by drop until the mixture begins to thicken, then adding it in a thin continuous stream. Continue beating until thickened. Stir in lemon juice to achieve the desired consistency and season to taste with salt and pepper. Set aside until required.

3 Strain the court bouillon into a clean saucepan and add the pieces of fish and the potatoes. Cover the pan and bring to the boil. Reduce the heat and simmer gently for 15 minutes, or until the fish and potatoes are cooked. Remove with a slotted spoon and transfer to a deep dish or tureen.

4 Measure the court bouillon and, if necessary, make up to 600 ml/1 pint with water. Beat the egg yolks into 150 ml/¼ pint of the aïoli. Add a little of the court bouillon and blend well together. Return to the pan with the rest of the court bouillon and cook gently over a low heat, stirring constantly, until the sauce is thick enough to coat the back of a spoon. Pour the sauce over the fish and potatoes.

5 To serve, place 1–2 slices of French bread in each hot soup plate. Arrange some fish and potatoes in their sauce on top. Sprinkle with chopped parsley and serve the remaining aïoli separately.

Serves 4–6
Preparation time: 30 minutes
Cooking time: 1¼–1½ hours

caribbean seafood creole

4 tablespoons olive oil
2 onions, chopped
2 green peppers, cored, deseeded and chopped
2 garlic cloves crushed
500 lb/1 lb mixed seafood (cooked lobster meat, large prawns, crab meat)
4 tablespoons white wine
salt and pepper
chopped coriander, to garnish
boiled rice, to serve

Sofrito:
3 tablespoons olive oil
1 onion, chopped
3 garlic cloves, crushed
500 g/1 lb tomatoes, skinned and chopped
1 tablespoon chopped coriander

1 First make the sofrito. Heat the olive oil in a saucepan. Add the onion and garlic and fry over a low heat until soft and translucent. Add the tomatoes and coriander and season to taste with salt and pepper. Simmer over a very low heat for 20–30 minutes, until thickened.

2 Meanwhile, heat the olive oil in a large frying pan. Add the onions, green peppers and garlic and fry, stirring occasionally, until softened and golden, but do not allow them to brown.

3 Prepare the seafood, removing any shells from the lobster, prawns or crab meat. Add to the vegetables in the pan, together with the prepared sofrito. Simmer gently for 15 minutes.

4 Add the wine and stir well. Continue cooking for 5 minutes. Adjust the seasoning, if necessary, and serve garnished with coriander, accompanied by boiled rice.

Serves 4
Preparation time: 30 minutes
Cooking time: 40–50 minutes

italian fish casserole

3 tablespoons olive oil
2 red onions, finely diced
2 garlic cloves, chopped
½ teaspoon crushed dried chillies
200 g/7 oz prepared squid, cut into thin lengths
200 g/7 oz mussels, scrubbed and debearded
   (see page 109)
200 g/7 oz clams, cleaned
300 g/10 oz raw tiger prawns in their shells
150 ml/¼ pint Fish Stock (see page 142)
150 ml/¼ pint dry white wine
½ teaspoon saffron
8 tomatoes, skinned and deseeded
1 bay leaf
1 teaspoon sugar
500 g/1 lb red mullet fillets, cut into bite-sized pieces
handful of flat leaf parsley, chopped
salt and pepper

1 Heat the oil in a saucepan large enough to take all the
ingredients. Add the onion and garlic and fry over a low
heat for 5 minutes, then add the chillies and mix well.

2 Add the squid, mussels, clams and tiger prawns and
stir well. Add the fish stock, wine, saffron, tomatoes, bay
leaf and sugar and season to taste with salt and pepper.
Cover the pan and simmer gently for 5 minutes. Discard
any mussels or clams that do not open.

3 Add the red mullet, sprinkle with the parsley and
simmer for a further 5 minutes, then serve immediately.
This is a very simple dish to make but finger bowls are
needed at the table as it is very messy to eat.

Serves 4
Preparation time: 10 minutes
Cooking time: 20 minutes

mexican fish stew

3 tablespoons olive oil
1 large onion, chopped
2 garlic cloves, crushed
1 large red pepper, cored, deseeded and chopped
1 large yellow pepper, cored, deseeded and chopped
500 g/1 lb tomatoes, skinned and chopped
2 tablespoons finely chopped fresh root ginger
1 tablespoon chopped coriander
2 teaspoons chopped oregano
grated rind of 1 lime
dash of hot chilli sauce
2–4 dried red chillies, chopped
1.25 kg/2½ lb monkfish
300 ml/½ pint Fish Stock (see page 142)
12 scallops, halved
250 g/8 oz raw prawns
salt and pepper
torn coriander leaves, to garnish
warm tortillas, to serve

1 Heat the oil in a large heavy-based saucepan. Add the
onion, garlic and the red and yellow peppers and fry over
a low heat for about 10–15 minutes until they are tender.

2 Add the tomatoes, ginger, chopped coriander, oregano,
lime rind, chilli sauce and dried red chillies. Stir well to
mix thoroughly and then simmer the mixture gently over
a low heat for 10 minutes.

3 Cut the monkfish into chunks, removing any bone and
skin. Add the monkfish and stock to the saucepan and
bring to the boil. Reduce the heat and simmer gently for
20 minutes.

4 Stir in the scallops and prawns and cook gently for
2 further minutes until cooked. Season to taste with salt
and pepper. Serve the fish stew with warm tortillas and
garnished with torn coriander leaves.

Serves 6
Preparation time: 15 minutes
Cooking time: 45 minutes

fish and fennel tagine

4 tablespoons virgin olive oil
1 onion, chopped
3 garlic cloves, crushed
½ fennel bulb, thinly sliced
¼–½ teaspoon fennel seeds
500 g/1 lb ripe, well-flavoured tomatoes, chopped
1–2 teaspoons sun-dried tomato paste
4 x 175 g/6 oz cod or other fish steaks
½ bunch parsley, chopped
juice and grated rind of 1 lemon
salt and pepper
chopped parsley, to garnish

1 Heat 2 tablespoons of the oil in a frying pan. Add the onion, garlic, fennel and fennel seeds and fry until the onion is softened. Stir in the tomatoes and continue to cook for about 2 minutes, then add the tomato paste and simmer gently, uncovered, for about 15 minutes, stirring occasionally. Season to taste with salt and pepper, then set aside.

2 Heat the remaining oil in a frying pan. Add the fish and brown quickly on both sides. Transfer to kitchen paper to drain.

3 Lay the parsley in the bottom of a heavy flameproof earthenware dish that the fish will just fit in a single layer. Put the fish on top and sprinkle with the lemon juice and rind. Pour over the sauce and heat to simmering point. Cook very gently, uncovered, for 10–15 minutes until the fish just flakes when tested with the point of a sharp knife. Serve garnished with chopped parsley.

Serves 4
Preparation time: 10 minutes
Cooking time: 30–35 minutes

moroccan fish in golden marinade

6–8 sea bream fillets, scaled
3 tablespoons seasoned plain white flour
3 tablespoons virgin olive oil
chopped coriander or parsley, to garnish

Marinade:
3 tablespoons virgin olive oil
2 red onions, thinly sliced
1½ teaspoons cumin seeds, lightly crushed
½ teaspoon dried red chilli flakes
2 red peppers, cored, deseeded and sliced
large pinch of saffron threads, crushed and soaked in
   3 tablespoons water
finely shredded rind and juice of 1 orange
2–3 tablespoons lemon juice
caster sugar, to taste
salt and pepper

1 First make the marinade. Heat the oil in a frying pan. Add the onions and fry over a low heat for 2 minutes. Add the cumin seeds and chilli flakes and stir for about 45 seconds. Add the red peppers and fry, stirring occasionally, until soft, then add the saffron and its liquid, orange rind and juice and lemon juice. Allow to bubble for a few minutes, then add sugar, salt and pepper to taste. Leave to cool.

2 Coat the fish in the seasoned flour. Heat the oil in a large frying pan. Add the fish and fry for about 2–3 minutes on each side until browned and just cooked through.

3 Using a fish slice, transfer the fish to a shallow non-metallic dish. Leave to cool, then pour over the cooled marinade. Cover the dish, place in the refrigerator and leave the fish for 4–12 hours, turning it carefully 2–3 times during marinating.

4 Return the fish to room temperature about 30 minutes before serving, garnished with coriander or parsley.

Serves 4
Preparation time: 10 minutes, plus cooling and marinating
Cooking time: 10–12 minutes

grilled salmon steaks with herb butter

125 g/4 oz butter
2 tablespoons finely chopped mixed herbs such as
   parsley, dill, chervil, chives or fennel
squeeze of lemon juice
50 g/2 oz butter, melted
4 x 175 g/6 oz salmon steaks
salt and pepper

To garnish:
4 lemon wedges
watercress sprigs

To serve:
boiled new potatoes
steamed vegetables or green salad

1 Mix the butter, herbs and lemon juice in a bowl. Lay the butter on a piece of greaseproof paper and roll into a log shape about 2.5 cm/1 inch in diameter. Refrigerate until solid.

2 Brush a baking sheet with melted butter and lay the salmon steaks on top. Brush with half of the remaining butter and season well with salt and pepper. Cook under a preheated medium grill for about 4–5 minutes on each side. On turning each steak, brush with more melted butter and season again. Alternatively, the steaks can be cooked on a cast-iron griddle pan.

3 Cut the log of herb butter into 4 rounds. Transfer the cooked steaks carefully on to warmed plates and top each with a round of butter. Garnish with lemon wedges and sprigs of watercress and serve with boiled new potatoes, steamed vegetables or a green salad.

Serves 4
Preparation time: 15 minutes, plus chilling
Cooking time: 8–10 minutes

salmon with fennel

4 x 175 g/6 oz salmon steaks
6 tablespoons dry white vermouth
4 tablespoons dry white wine
pinch of dried mixed herbs
50 g/2 oz butter
2 teaspoons finely chopped shallots
1 fennel bulb, thinly sliced
3 small leeks, thinly sliced
6 tablespoons double cream
¼ teaspoon French mustard
salt and pepper
fennel tops, to garnish

1 Place the salmon steaks in a large saucepan or flameproof casserole, pour over the vermouth and wine and add the herbs. Bring to the boil over a low heat, cover and simmer very gently for 3–4 minutes.

2 Using a slotted spoon, transfer the salmon to a warmed serving plate, cover with foil and keep hot. Rub the cooking liquid through a strainer and set aside.

3 Melt the butter in a frying pan or preheated wok, add the shallots, fennel and leeks and stir-fry for 4–5 minutes without browning. Add the reserved cooking liquid, increase the heat and boil rapidly until it has reduced by just under half. Stir in the cream and mustard and season to taste with salt and pepper.

4 Spoon the sauce over the salmon and serve immediately, garnished with fennel tops.

Serves 4
Preparation: 10 minutes
Cooking time: 10–15 minutes

salmon steaks with teriyaki sauce

4 x 175 g/6 oz salmon steaks
4 baby gem lettuces, quartered lengthways

Teriyaki sauce:
1 tablespoon sunflower oil
1 tablespoon sesame oil
6 tablespoons teriyaki sauce
2 tablespoons rice or white wine vinegar
2 tablespoons lime juice
2 tablespoons clear honey

1 To make the sauce, place all the ingredients in a small saucepan and bring to the boil. Simmer fast for 10 minutes or until reduced to a thick, glossy sauce. Allow to cool for 5 minutes before using as it will be extremely hot.

2 Heat a griddle pan or nonstick frying pan over a moderate heat. Put on the salmon steaks and cook for 4 minutes on each side, until charred and firm.

3 Arrange the pieces of lettuce on 4 plates. Place the salmon steaks on top of the lettuce. Spoon the sauce over the salmon and let it run over the salad. Serve immediately.

Serves 4
Preparation time: 5 minutes
Cooking time: 15–20 minutes

creamy salmon kedgeree

50 g/2 oz butter
1 large onion, finely chopped
175 g/6 oz long grain rice, cooked until just tender
500 g/1 lb cooked salmon, boned and flaked
3 hard-boiled eggs, roughly chopped
2 tablespoons finely chopped parsley
150 ml/¼ pint single cream
salt and pepper
1 teaspoon finely chopped chives, to garnish

1 Melt half the butter in a large pan. Add the onion and fry until soft. Stir in the rice and season well with salt and pepper.

2 Add the salmon, eggs, parsley and cream, folding them carefully into the rice to prevent the fish and eggs from breaking up too much.

3 Pile the kedgeree into an ovenproof dish. Grease a sheet of foil with the remaining butter and use to cover the dish. Heat thoroughly in a preheated oven, 180°C (350°F), Gas Mark 4, for 15 minutes. When hot, serve sprinkled with the chives.

Serves 4
Preparation time: 10 minutes
Cooking time: 20–25 minutes
Oven temperature: 180°C (350°F), Gas Mark 4

roast fillet of salmon with saffron cream sauce

4 x 175 g/6 oz salmon fillets
oil, for frying and roasting
salt and pepper
1–2 tablespoons finely snipped chives, to garnish

Sauce:
150 ml/¼ pint Fish Stock (see page 142)
150 ml/¼ pint dry white wine
4 saffron strands
150 ml/¼ pint single cream

To serve:
steamed seasonal vegetables
boiled new potatoes

1 Season the salmon with salt and pepper. Heat a little oil in a large frying pan. Place the salmon in the pan, flesh side down. Cook for about 2 minutes over a high heat to brown.

2 Lightly oil a baking sheet and transfer the salmon to it, skin side down, season with salt and pepper and finish cooking in a preheated oven, 240°C (475°F), Gas Mark 9, for about 7–9 minutes, depending on the thickness of the fillet. The flesh should be opaque pink when cooked.

3 Meanwhile, make the sauce by combining the stock, wine and saffron in a saucepan. Bring to the boil, lower the heat and simmer until reduced by half. Add the cream, bring to the boil and boil continuously until the sauce thickens and coats the back of a spoon.

4 Serve the fish in the centre of a large plate with the sauce poured around and garnished with chives. Accompany with steamed seasonal vegetables and boiled new potatoes.

Serves 4
Preparation time: 5 minutes
Cooking time: 9–11 minutes
Oven temperature: 240°C (475°F), Gas Mark 9

salmon fish cakes

250 g/8 oz cooked, mashed potatoes
500 g/1 lb cooked salmon, boned and flaked
few drops Tabasco sauce or ½ teaspoon cayenne
  pepper (optional)
1–2 tablespoons lemon juice
2 tablespoons finely chopped parsley
1 large egg yolk, beaten
plain flour, for dusting
1 large egg, beaten
125–175 g/4–6 oz fresh white breadcrumbs
1 tablespoon oil
50 g/2 oz butter
salt and pepper

To serve:
Fresh Tomato Sauce (see page 147)
4 lemon wedges

1 Combine the potatoes, flaked fish, Tabasco sauce or cayenne pepper, if using, lemon juice and parsley in a large bowl and season well with salt and pepper. Mix well to combine. Bind with the egg yolk.

2 Turn the mixture on to a lightly floured surface and form into a thick roll about 28 cm/11 inches long and 5 cm/2 inches thick. Cut into 8 even-sized pieces and shape each into a neat cake 6 cm/2½ inches in diameter and 1.5 cm/¾ inch thick.

3 Dip the cakes in the beaten egg and coat evenly with breadcrumbs. Heat the oil and butter in a frying pan. Add the fish cakes and fry for about 5 minutes on each side until they are crisp, golden and very hot. Drain well on absorbent kitchen paper and serve with fresh tomato sauce and lemon wedges.

Serves 4
Preparation time: 20 minutes
Cooking time: 10 minutes

salmon wrapped in parma ham with fontina cheese and bay leaves

4 x 175 g/6 oz salmon fillets, skinned
4 thin slices of fontina cheese
4 or 8 bay leaves, depending on size
8 thin slices of Parma ham
sea salt and pepper
fresh pasta or mixed salad leaves, to serve

1 Heat a griddle pan or nonstick frying pan. Season the salmon fillets with salt and pepper.

2 Trim any rind from the cheese and cut the slices to fit on top of the salmon fillets. Place the cheese slices on the salmon fillets, top with the bay leaves and wrap the Parma ham around the salmon, securing the cheese and bay leaves.

3 Cook the prepared salmon fillets on the griddle for 4–5 minutes on each side, taking care when turning.

4 Serve with fresh pasta tossed in butter, or a leafy salad.

Serves 4
Preparation time: 10 minutes
Cooking time: 10 minutes

sole with parmesan

plain flour, for dusting
4 lemon sole fillets, skinned
75 g/3 oz butter
25 g/1 oz Parmesan cheese, grated
50 ml/2 fl oz Fish Stock (see page 142)
3 tablespoons Marsala or white wine
salt and pepper

To garnish:
grated Parmesan cheese
lemon wedges

1 Put some flour in a shallow bowl and season with salt and pepper. Dip the sole fillets into the seasoned flour to dust them lightly on both sides. Shake off any excess flour from the surface.

2 Melt the butter in a large frying pan. Add the floured sole and cook over a gentle heat until they are golden brown on both sides, turning them once during cooking.

3 Sprinkle the grated Parmesan over the sole, then cook very gently for a further 2–3 minutes until the cheese has melted.

4 Add the fish stock and the Marsala or white wine. Cover the pan and cook over a very low heat for 4–5 minutes until the sole are cooked and tender and the sauce reduced. Serve sprinkled with grated Parmesan and accompany with lemon wedges.

Serves 4
Preparation time: 5 minutes
Cooking time: 15–20 minutes

sole florentine

425 g/14 oz fresh spinach
25 g/1 oz butter
2 teaspoons olive oil
4 sole fillets, skinned
125 ml/4 fl oz dry white wine
125 ml/4 fl oz Fish Stock (see page 142)
freshly grated Parmesan cheese
salt and pepper

Cheese sauce:
50 g/2 oz butter
450 ml/¾ pint milk
50 g/2 oz plain flour
¼ teaspoon grated nutmeg
2–3 tablespoons single cream
50 g/2 oz Gruyère cheese, grated

1 Cook the spinach in a deep pan for 5 minutes in just the water remaining on the leaves after washing. Drain and mix with the butter.

2 Brush a flameproof dish with oil and place the sole in it. Cover with the wine and stock and season to taste with salt and pepper. Bake in a preheated oven, 180°C (350°F), Gas Mark 4, for 15 minutes.

3 Remove the fish and keep hot. Put the dish over a high heat to reduce the cooking juices down to about 2–3 tablespoons.

4 To prepare the cheese sauce, melt the butter in a small pan. Heat the milk in a separate pan. Stir the flour into the butter, then gradually add the hot milk, stirring vigorously to ensure no lumps form. Season with salt, pepper and nutmeg and stir well over a low heat until thick and cooked.

5 Add the reduced fish juices and cream and cook for a further 5 minutes to reduce the sauce a little more, then add the Gruyère.

6 Brush an ovenproof serving dish with the remaining oil and arrange the spinach in the base. Put the sole fillets on top, cover with the cheese sauce and top with Parmesan. Bake in a preheated oven, 200°C (400°F), Gas Mark 6, for approximately 10 minutes until the top is crisp and golden. Serve hot.

Serves 4
Preparation time: 20 minutes
Cooking time: 40 minutes
Oven temperature: 180°C (350°F), Gas Mark 4

sole with satay sauce

25 g/1 oz butter
1 shallot, very finely chopped
1 tablespoon chopped chives
1 tablespoon chopped tarragon
1 tablespoon chopped parsley
grated rind of ½ lemon
8 Dover or lemon sole fillets
1 egg, beaten
4–5 tablespoons fresh breadcrumbs
vegetable oil, for deep-frying
lime or lemon wedges, to garnish

Satay sauce:
1 teaspoon coriander seeds, crushed
1 teaspoon cumin seeds, crushed
1 teaspoon fennel seeds, crushed
2 garlic cloves, crushed
125 g/4 oz crunchy peanut butter
1 teaspoon dark soft brown sugar
2 fresh green chillies, deseeded and finely chopped
150 g/5 oz creamed coconut, dissolved in 450 ml/¾ pint hot water
3 tablespoons lemon or lime juice

1 First make the satay sauce: heat a wok or heavy-based frying pan, add the coriander, cumin and fennel seeds and dry-fry, stirring constantly, for 2 minutes.

2 Add the garlic, peanut butter, sugar, chillies and coconut milk, stir well and cook over a low heat for 7–8 minutes. Stir in the lemon or lime juice, set aside and keep warm.

3 Melt the butter in a pan, add the shallot and cook for 1 minute. Stir in the herbs and lemon rind. Cool slightly, then divide between the fish. Roll up each fillet and secure with wooden cocktail sticks.

4 Heat the oil to 180–190°C (350–375°F) or until a cube of bread browns in 30 seconds. Dip each fillet in the beaten egg, then coat in the breadcrumbs. Deep-fry for 4–5 minutes until golden. Drain on kitchen paper and arrange on a warmed serving dish. Serve with the satay sauce and lime or lemon wedges.

Serves 4
Preparation: 25 minutes
Cooking time: 20 minutes

sole véronique

125 g/4 oz black or white seedless grapes, skinned, plus
  extra to garnish
4 medium sole, skinned and filleted
225 ml/7½ fl oz Fish Stock (see page 142)
150 ml/¼ pint white wine
salt and freshly ground white pepper
fennel or dill leaves, to garnish

Cream sauce:
25 g/1 oz butter
20 g/¾ oz plain flour
150 ml/¼ pint double cream

To serve:
steamed mangetout
boiled new potatoes

1 Put 1 or 2 grapes on each fillet of sole, then roll up tightly. Secure the rolls with fine wooden cocktail sticks. Put them into an oblong casserole and cover with the stock and wine. Add any remaining skinned and deseeded grapes and season with salt and pepper. Cover and cook in a preheated oven, 200°C (400°F), Gas Mark 6, for 25 minutes, or until the fish is tender.

2 Lift the fish rolls and grapes from the stock. Remove the cocktail sticks from the rolls. Place the fish on a warmed dish, cover with kitchen foil so it does not dry and keep hot. Strain and reserve the liquid from the casserole dish.

3 To make the sauce, melt the butter in a pan. Stir in the flour, then blend in 225 ml/7½ fl oz of the reserved liquid. Stir as the sauce thickens, then gradually blend in the cream and any extra seasoning required. Heat gently without boiling, then add the skinned grapes. Spoon the sauce with the grapes on to heated plates. Arrange the fish rolls on top. Garnish with a few extra grapes – deseeded but not skinned – and the fennel or dill leaves. Serve with steamed mangetout and boiled new potatoes.

Serves 4
Preparation time: 25 minutes
Cooking time: 50 minutes
Oven temperature: 200°C (400°F), Gas Mark 6

cod and prawn bake in cheese sauce

450 ml/¾ pint milk
¼ onion
6 peppercorns
blade of mace
1 bay leaf
a few parsley stalks
50 g/2 oz butter
450 g/1 lb cod fillets, skinned
50 g/2 oz button mushrooms, sliced
125 g/4 oz cooked peeled prawns
30 g/1½ oz plain flour
1 tablespoon lemon juice
125 g/4 oz grated Cheddar cheese
salt and pepper

To serve:
country bread
salad

1 Put the milk into a saucepan with the onion, peppercorns, mace, bay leaf and parsley stalks. Bring to the boil, then remove from the heat and leave to infuse while preparing the remaining ingredients.

2 Melt the butter in another saucepan and use a little to brush the inside of a 1.6 litre/2¾ pint ovenproof pie dish. Cut the cod into finger-size strips, place in the pie dish and scatter the mushrooms and prawns on top.

3 Strain the milk through a sieve, then discard the contents of the sieve. Add the flour to the remaining butter in the saucepan, stirring to blend. Gradually stir in the strained milk to make a smooth sauce. Bring to the boil, stirring constantly until the sauce thickens. Season with salt, pepper and lemon juice and add two-thirds of the grated cheese. Stir until melted.

4 Pour the sauce over the fish, sprinkle with the remaining cheese, place on a baking sheet and cook in a preheated oven, 180°C (350°F), Gas Mark 4, for 20–25 minutes until golden brown. Serve with country bread and salad.

Serves 4
Preparation time: 15 minutes
Cooking time: 30–35 minutes
Oven temperature: 180°C (350°F), Gas Mark 4

roast cod and vegetables

3 tablespoons olive oil
750 g/1½ lb cod fillets, skinned
4 potatoes, unpeeled and quartered
6 tomatoes, halved
1 red onion, quartered
1 fennel bulb, cut into wedges
2 garlic cloves, crushed
75 g/3 oz black olives, pitted
25 g/1 oz green olives, pitted
25 g/1 oz capers
4 tablespoons lemon juice
salt and pepper
handful of flat leaf parsley, chopped, to garnish
warm focaccia bread, to serve

1 Lightly oil a large ovenproof dish. Put the cod, potatoes, tomatoes, onion and fennel into the dish in a single layer. Sprinkle with the garlic, olives, capers and lemon juice and season to taste with salt and pepper.

2 Drizzle with the remaining olive oil and roast in a preheated oven, 230°C (450°F), Gas Mark 8, for 25 minutes.

3 Garnish with flat leaf parsley and serve with warm focaccia bread.

Serves 4
Preparation time: 5 minutes
Cooking time: 25 minutes
Oven temperature: 230°C (450°F), Gas Mark 8

griddled cod steaks with mint pesto

4 x 175 g/6 oz cod steaks
1 lime, cut into wedges, to garnish
steamed green vegetables, to serve

Mint pesto:
6 tablespoons chopped mint
1 tablespoon chopped parsley
1 garlic clove, crushed and chopped
l tablespoon freshly grated Parmesan cheese

1 tablespoon double cream
1 teaspoon balsamic vinegar
3 tablespoons extra virgin olive oil
sea salt and pepper

1 Heat a griddle pan or nonstick frying pan. Put on the cod steaks and cook for 4 minutes on each side, until slightly charred and firm to the touch.

2 Place the pesto ingredients in a food processor or blender and process until smooth. Alternatively, pound the ingredients with a pestle and mortar.

3 Serve the cod steaks with a spoonful of pesto and with seasonal steamed green vegetables. Garnish with lime wedges.

Serves 4
Preparation time: 10 minutes
Cooking time: 8–10 minutes

saffron cod with vegetables

This Tuscan dish tastes particularly good accompanied by slices of grilled polenta. Quick-cooking polenta can be bought at Italian delicatessens and some supermarkets. It is very easy to prepare. Its attractive yellow colour gives the cod an extra lift.

½ teaspoon saffron threads
625 g/1¼ lb cod fillet
1 tablespoon plain flour
3 tablespoons olive oil
2 yellow peppers, cored, deseeded and sliced into slivers
2 tomatoes, quartered
1 small onion, finely chopped
1 garlic clove, finely chopped
1 tablespoon chopped parsley
salt and pepper
slices of polenta, to serve (optional)

1 Put the saffron threads to soak in a little hot water. Cut the cod into even-sized pieces and dust with flour. Heat the oil in a large shallow pan. Add the cod and cook over a moderate heat for a few minutes, turning once, until golden. Season to taste with salt and pepper, remove with a fish slice and keep warm.

2 Add the peppers, tomatoes, onion and garlic to the pan and fry over a low heat until golden. Season to taste with salt, reduce the heat, cover and simmer for about 15 minutes. Stir in the saffron liquid, cover and simmer for a further 10 minutes.

3 Add the pieces of cod and sprinkle with chopped parsley and simmer for a further 5 minutes until heated through and the vegetables are tender. Serve hot, accompanied by slices of polenta, if wished.

Serves 4
Preparation time: 10 minutes
Cooking time: 40 minutes

baked cod with potatoes and olives

butter, for greasing
375 g/12 oz potatoes, thinly sliced
1 teaspoon chopped thyme
4 x 200 g/7 oz cod fillets
2 tablespoons pitted black olives
2 tablespoons olive oil
salt and pepper

1 Grease a shallow ovenproof dish with butter. Arrange the potatoes in layers in the dish, sprinkling each layer with a little thyme and salt and pepper.

2 Place the pieces of cod on top of the potatoes, add the olives, drizzle with olive oil, season to taste with salt and pepper and add a little thyme.

3 Bake in a preheated oven, 220°C (425°F), Gas Mark 7, for 25 minutes. Check that the potatoes are soft before serving immediately.

Serves 4
Preparation time: 10 minutes
Cooking time: 25 minutes
Oven temperature: 220°C (425°F), Gas Mark 7

halibut in paper parcels

1 fennel bulb, sliced
4 x 200 g/7 oz halibut fillets
2 shallots, finely chopped
8 pitted black olives
a few sage leaves, torn
4 lemon slices
salt and pepper

1 Cut 4 sheets of greaseproof paper large enough to enclose the fish and vegetables.

2 Divide the fennel evenly among the sheets of greaseproof paper and put the fish on top. Sprinkle with the shallots, olives and sage, season to taste with salt and pepper and finish with a slice of lemon. The greaseproof paper can be folded over and rolled at the edges to seal, but a much easier way is to fold the paper and staple it.

3 Put the parcels on a baking sheet, and cook in a preheated oven, 200°C (400°F), Gas Mark 6, for 25 minutes.

4 Serve these parcels at the table so that everyone opens their own parcel and gets a waft of the delicious aroma that escapes when they are first opened.

Serves 4
Preparation time: 5 minutes
Cooking time: 25 minutes
Oven temperature: 200°C (400°F), Gas Mark 6

halibut with mixed baby tomatoes

500 g/1 lb mixed baby tomatoes (such as plum and
*   cherry)*
4 tablespoons olive oil
2 tablespoons balsamic vinegar
4 x 175 g/6 oz halibut fillets or steaks
1 bunch of green or purple basil
sea salt and pepper

1 Heat a griddle pan or nonstick frying pan. Put the whole tomatoes on the griddle and cook for about 6 minutes, rolling them around to cook all over. Some of the tomatoes will split and become very soft. Remove from the griddle, pour half the olive oil and balsamic vinegar over the tomatoes, season to taste with salt and pepper and keep warm.

2 Put the halibut fillets on the hot griddle pan and cook for about 4–6 minutes on each side, according to the thickness of the fish.

3 Add the basil leaves to the griddled tomato mix and place on 4 plates. Arrange the fish on top, drizzle with the remaining olive oil and balsamic vinegar, season to taste with salt and pepper and serve.

Serves 4
Preparation time: 5 minutes
Cooking time: 15 minutes

seared skate wings with caperberries

2 skate wings, weighing 300 g/10 oz each
1 teaspoon olive oil
2 tablespoons capers, or caperberries with their stalks, halved lengthways
1 tablespoon grated lemon rind
2 tablespoons lemon juice
salt and pepper
lemon wedges, to garnish
steamed ribbons of vegetables, to serve (optional)

1 Cut the skate wings in half and pat dry. Brush each side with a little oil. Heat a griddle pan or nonstick frying pan and sear the skate wings for 3 minutes on each side. If the wings are thick, cook them for a little longer.

2 Sprinkle the caperberries on top, together with the lemon rind and juice and cook for a few more seconds. Season and serve garnished with lemon wedges. Serve with steamed ribbons of vegetables, if liked.

Serves 4
Preparation time: 5 minutes
Cooking time: 6–8 minutes

haddock in chilli sauce

This dish looks very attractive when garnished with chilli flowers. To make chilli flowers, shred the chilli lengthways leaving 1 cm/½ inch attached at the stem end. Place in iced water for about 1 hour to open.

4 tablespoons oil
2 large onions sliced
3 garlic cloves, crushed
750 g/1½ lb haddock fillets, cut into chunks
2 tablespoons plain flour
1 teaspoon turmeric
4 green chillies (deseeded if liked), thinly sliced
2 tablespoons lemon juice
175 ml/6 fl oz thick coconut milk
salt
chilli flowers, to garnish (optional)

1 Heat the oil in a preheated wok or heavy-based frying pan. Add the onions and fry, stirring frequently, until soft and golden. Add the garlic and cook for 30 seconds. Remove the onions and garlic from the pan with a slotted spoon and set aside.

2 Toss the fish in the flour, add to the pan and brown quickly on all sides. Drain on kitchen paper.

3 Return the onions and garlic to the pan, stir in the turmeric and chillies and cook for 1 minute. Stir in the lemon juice, coconut milk and salt to taste and simmer, stirring constantly, for 10 minutes until the sauce has thickened.

4 Return the fish to the pan and heat for 2–3 minutes. Spoon into a warmed serving dish and garnish with chilli flowers, if using.

Serves 4
Preparation: 5 minutes
Cooking time: 25 minutes

haddock with soured cream and mushrooms

300 g/10 oz haddock fillet
15 g/½ oz butter
4 tablespoons water

Sauce:

15 g/½ oz butter
50 g/2 oz button mushrooms, sliced
125 ml/4 fl oz soured cream
¼ teaspoon paprika
salt and pepper
chopped parsley, to garnish

1 Place the haddock in a shallow 600 ml/1 pint ovenproof dish. Sprinkle with salt and pepper, dot with the butter and add the water.

2 Cover the ovenproof dish tightly with foil and cook in a preheated moderate oven, 160°C (325°F), Gas Mark 3, for 20 minutes.

3 Meanwhile, make the sauce. Melt the butter in a saucepan and fry the mushrooms for 1 minute. Stir in the soured cream and paprika and season to taste with salt and pepper. Heat through gently.

4 Drain the fish, pour over the sauce and garnish with chopped parsley.

Serves 2
Preparation time: 5 minutes
Cooking time: 20 minutes
Oven temperature: 160°C (325°F), Gas Mark 3

braised fish with black bean sauce

3 tablespoons salted black beans
2 tablespoons oil
2 spring onions, chopped
2.5 cm/1 inch piece fresh root ginger, chopped
1 small red pepper, cored, deseeded and chopped
2 celery sticks, chopped
2 tablespoons light soy sauce
2 tablespoons dry sherry
4 x 150 g/5 oz cod or haddock cutlets
shredded spring onion, to garnish

1 Soak the black beans in warm water for 10 minutes to remove some of the saltiness. Drain thoroughly.

2 Heat the oil in a preheated wok or deep frying pan. Add the spring onions, ginger, red pepper and celery and stir-fry for 1 minute. Stir in the soy sauce and sherry.

3 Place the fish on top of the vegetables and simmer for about 5–10 minutes, depending on the thickness of the fish, until almost tender. Spoon over the black beans and cook for 2 minutes.

4 Arrange the fish on a warmed serving dish and spoon the sauce over. Serve hot, garnished with the shredded spring onion.

Serves 4
Preparation time: 10 minutes, plus soaking
Cooking time: 10–15 minutes

fish steaks with soy sauce and ginger

500 g/1 lb fish steaks, such as cod, halibut,
   monkfish or hake
½ teaspoon salt
2 tablespoons sherry
4 tablespoons cornflour
1 egg white, lightly beaten
3 tablespoons sunflower oil
1 slice fresh root ginger, finely chopped
2 tablespoons light soy sauce
2 teaspoons sugar
125 ml/4 fl oz Thai Fish Stock (see page 143) or water
spring onion, to garnish

1 Cut the fish steaks into pieces about 5 x 4 cm/2 x 1½ inches and place them in a shallow dish. Mix together the salt, sherry and 1 tablespoon of the cornflour, pour over the fish and marinate for about 30 minutes.

2 Dip the fish pieces in egg white, then in the remaining cornflour.

3 Heat the oil in a preheated wok or frying pan. Add the fish pieces and fry until golden, stirring them gently to separate each piece. Add the ginger, soy sauce, sugar and stock or water. Cook for 3–4 minutes, or until the liquid has completely evaporated. Serve hot, garnished with spring onion.

Serves 4
Preparation time: about 15 minutes, plus marinating
Cooking time: 10 minutes

fish tandoori

50 ml/2 fl oz natural yogurt
2 tablespoons oil
2 tablespoons paprika
1 tablespoon ground cumin
1 teaspoon ground fennel seeds
1 teaspoon chilli powder
4 x 175 g/6 oz halibut steaks
salt

To garnish:
1 small lettuce, shredded
1 fennel bulb, sliced
lemon wedges

1 Put the yogurt in a bowl with the oil, paprika, cumin, fennel seeds, chilli powder and a little salt. Mix well together.

2 Place the halibut steaks in the bowl and rub well with the tandoori mixture. Cover the bowl and leave in a cool place to marinate for 4–5 hours.

3 Transfer the marinated fish to a shallow, ovenproof dish. Bake uncovered in a preheated oven, 180°C (350°F), Gas Mark 4, for 20–25 minutes.

4 Arrange the lettuce on a warmed serving dish and place the fish on top. Spoon over the juices and serve garnished with fennel and lemon wedges.

Serves 4
Preparation time: 15 minutes, plus marinating
Cooking time: 20–25 minutes
Oven temperature: 180°C (350°F), Gas Mark 4

fish curry with coconut milk

750 g/1½ lb cod fillet, skinned
2 tablespoons plain flour
4 tablespoons oil
2 onions, sliced
2 garlic cloves, crushed
1 teaspoon turmeric
4 green chillies, deseeded and finely chopped
2 tablespoons lemon juice
175 ml/6 fl oz thick coconut milk
salt

To garnish:
slices of red chilli
snipped chives

1 Cut the fish into 4 and coat with the flour. Heat the oil in a frying pan. Add the fish and fry quickly on both sides. Lift out with a slotted spoon and set aside.

2 Add the onion and garlic to the pan and fry for about 5 minutes until soft and golden. Add the turmeric, chillies, lemon juice, coconut milk and salt to taste and simmer for 10 minutes or until thickened.

3 Add the fish and any juices, spoon over the sauce and cook gently for 2–3 minutes until tender. Garnish with slices of chilli and snipped chives and serve at once.

Serves 4
Preparation time: 10 minutes
Cooking time: about 20 minutes

assam fish curry

4 tablespoons vegetable oil
3 tablespoons tamarind pulp, soaked in 250 ml/8 fl oz
  boiling water for 10 minutes
2 tomatoes, quartered
2 baby aubergines, quartered
2 large red chillies, quartered lengthways and deseeded
1 tablespoon soft brown sugar
½ teaspoon salt
625 g/1¼ lb skinless haddock or halibut, cut into
  5 cm/2 inch pieces
boiled rice, to serve

Spice paste:
5 small dried chillies soaked in cold water for
  10 minutes, then deseeded and chopped
8 shallots, chopped
3 lemon grass stalks, chopped
2 fresh red chillies, deseeded and chopped
2.5 cm/1 inch piece of fresh galangal, chopped
2 teaspoons dried shrimp paste
1 teaspoon turmeric
5 candlenuts or macadamia nuts (optional)

1 First, make the spice paste. Put the dried chillies, shallots, lemon grass, red chillies, galangal, shrimp paste, turmeric and candlenuts or macadamia nuts, if using, in a food processor or blender and process to a thick paste. Heat the oil in a large saucepan. Add the spice paste and fry over a gentle heat, stirring constantly, for about 5 minutes until softened.

2 Strain the tamarind pulp through a sieve, pressing it against the sieve to extract as much tamarind flavour as possible. Discard the pulp and add the strained tamarind liquid to the pan, together with the tomatoes, aubergines and chillies. Bring to the boil, then reduce the heat, cover and simmer gently for 12 minutes.

3 Add the sugar, salt and fish to the pan and stir gently to coat the fish in the sauce. Cover and cook the curry over a gentle heat for a further 7 minutes, or until the fish is cooked through. Taste and adjust the seasoning if necessary. Serve the curry hot with plain boiled rice.

Serves 4
Preparation time: about 20 minutes, plus soaking
Cooking time: 25–30 minutes

indian fish fritters

6 tablespoons vegetable oil
2 onions, chopped
1 tablespoon ground coriander
3 fresh green chillies, deseeded and chopped
1 teaspoon salt
1 teaspoon pepper
750 g/1½ lb cod fillets, skinned and cut into small pieces
2 tablespoons finely chopped coriander leaves

Batter:
125 g/4 oz chickpea or gram flour (besan)
½ teaspoon chilli powder
½ teaspoon salt
1 egg, beaten
7 tablespoons water

1 Heat 3 tablespoons of the oil in a pan. Add the onion and fry until just soft. Stir in the ground coriander, chillies, salt and pepper. Add the fish and fry for 2 minutes, then cover and cook over a very low heat for 2 minutes. Break up the mixture with a fork and add the chopped coriander. Remove from the heat and set aside while making the batter.

2 Sift the flour, chilli powder and salt into a bowl. Add the egg and water and beat well to make a smooth batter. Leave to stand for 30 minutes, then stir in the fish mixture.

3 Heat the remaining oil in a frying pan and drop in small spoonfuls of the batter mixture. Fry on both sides until golden. Drain thoroughly and keep warm while frying the remainder.

Serves 4
Preparation time: 20 minutes, plus standing
Cooking time: about 20 minutes

spicy fish cakes

500 g/1 lb cod fillet, skinned and cut into chunks
3 tablespoons Thai Red Curry Paste (see page 149)
1 egg
3 tablespoons Thai fish sauce
1–2 tablespoons rice flour
75 g/3 oz green beans, finely chopped
1 tablespoon finely shredded kaffir lime leaves
vegetable oil, for deep frying
coriander sprigs, to garnish
chilli sauce, to serve

1 Put the chunks of cod fillet and the red curry paste in a food processor or blender. Process until the fish is worked to a paste. Alternatively, pound together with a pestle in a mortar.

2 Transfer the fish mixture to a bowl and add the egg, fish sauce and sufficient flour to knead with your hands into a stiff mixture. Work in the beans and lime leaves with your hands.

3 Form the fish mixture into 16–20 balls, then, using your hands, flatten each ball into a round, about 1 cm/½ inch thick.

4 Heat the oil in a preheated wok or frying pan. Add the fish cakes, a few at a time, and fry for 4 minutes on each side until they are cooked and golden. Take care not to overcook them. Drain on kitchen paper and serve hot, garnished with coriander sprigs and with chilli sauce.

Serves 4–5
Preparation time: 20 minutes
Cooking time: about 30 minutes

fish java style

Laos is powdered dried galangal, a member of the ginger family, and is available from Chinese supermarkets.

3 tablespoons cornflour
1 teaspoon salt
750 g/1½ lb thick haddock fillets, skinned and
  cut into fingers
4–6 tablespoons oil
2 onions, sliced
3 garlic cloves, finely chopped
2.5 cm/1 inch piece of fresh root ginger, finely chopped
300 ml/½ pint water
1 teaspoon laos (optional)
2 tablespoons dark soy sauce
1 teaspoon sugar
¼ teaspoon grated nutmeg
2 tablespoons lemon juice

1 Mix the cornflour with the salt on a plate. Lightly roll the fish pieces in the mixture.

2 Heat half the oil in a preheated wok or heavy-based frying pan, add the fish and fry lightly. Lift them out and set aside on a plate.

3 Rinse out the pan and return to the heat with the remaining oil. Add the onions, garlic and ginger and fry until soft and golden. Stir in the water, laos, if using, soy sauce, sugar, nutmeg and lemon juice. Return the fish to the pan and simmer for 5–10 minutes or until the fish is cooked. Transfer to a warmed serving dish and serve immediately.

Serves 4
Preparation time: 15 minutes
Cooking time: 20–25 minutes

machi mussalam

1 kg/2 lb cod steaks
1 teaspoon salt
150 ml/¼ pint natural yogurt
4 tablespoons oil
2 onions, finely sliced
2.5 cm/1 inch piece of fresh root ginger, finely sliced

4 green chillies
2 garlic cloves
1 teaspoon fenugreek seeds
coriander leaves, to garnish (optional)

1 Sprinkle the fish with the salt and marinate it in the yogurt for at least an hour, turning once or twice.

2 Heat 1 tablespoon of the oil in a pan, add 1 of the onions and fry until crisp. Place this, together with the remaining onion, the ginger, chillies and garlic, in a blender or food processor and process to a smooth paste.

3 Heat the remaining oil in a large frying pan with a lid. Fry the fenugreek seeds for 30 seconds, then add the prepared paste and fry until it starts to brown.

4 Add the fish and yogurt, stir carefully and spoon the mixture over the fish. Cover and simmer for 5–10 minutes, or until cooked through. If the mixture seems to be drying out too fast, add 2 tablespoons water; if it is too liquid, uncover and allow to dry out.

5 Transfer to a warmed serving dish and garnish with coriander, if using.

Serves 6
Preparation time: 10 minutes, plus marinating
Cooking time: 15 minutes

steamed mussels in white wine sauce

50 g/2 oz butter
1 large onion, finely chopped
1–2 garlic cloves, finely chopped
1 small leek, finely sliced
2 kg/4 lb mussels, scrubbed and debearded
  (see page 109)
300 ml/½ pint dry white wine
150 ml/¼ pint water
25 g/1 oz plain flour
2 tablespoons finely chopped parsley
2 tablespoons double cream (optional)
salt and pepper
crusty bread, to serve

1 Melt half the butter in a large saucepan and gently fry the onion, garlic and leek until soft but not coloured. Add the mussels, wine and water, cover and bring to the boil.

2 Cook for 2–5 minutes until the mussels open, shaking the pan occasionally during cooking. Using a draining spoon, remove the mussels from the pan and divide between 4 large soup plates, discarding any that haven't opened during cooking. Keep warm.

3 Mix the remaining butter with the flour to form a paste and add to the pan, a little bit at a time, stirring to thicken the sauce. Bring to the boil, season to taste with salt and pepper and stir in the parsley. Add the cream to the sauce, if using. Pour the sauce over the mussels. Serve immediately with crusty bread.

Serves 4
Preparation time: 30 minutes
Cooking time: 10 minutes

mussels with fresh tomato and pepper sauce

1 red pepper
2 tablespoons olive oil
2 red onions, chopped
2 garlic cloves, chopped
6 tomatoes, skinned and chopped
½ teaspoon crushed dried chilli
125 ml/4 fl oz dry white wine
1 kg/2 lb mussels, scrubbed and debearded
  (see page 109)
2 tablespoons capers
large handful of flat leaf parsley, roughly chopped
salt and pepper
warm focaccia bread, to serve

1 Cut off the bottom of the pepper. Put the pepper on the chopping board and slice off 4–5 flat pieces, leaving the seeds and core intact. Place the pepper pieces under a hot grill and leave to blister and blacken, then peel off the skins and roughly chop the flesh.

2 Heat the oil in a large flameproof casserole. Add the onions and garlic and fry over a low heat for 5 minutes, but do not allow them to brown.

3 Add the pepper, tomatoes, chilli and white wine and simmer for 5 minutes to reduce and thicken the sauce.

4 Add the mussels and capers and season to taste with salt and pepper. Mix well, cover and bake in a preheated oven, 200°C (400°F), Gas Mark 6, for 8 minutes.

5 Remove the casserole from the oven. Discard any mussels that have not opened. Stir in the parsley and serve with warm focaccia bread.

Serves 4
Preparation time: 30 minutes
Cooking time: 25 minutes
Oven temperature: 200°C (400°F), Gas Mark 6

spicy indian steamed mussels

125 g/4 oz ghee or 2½ tablespoons vegetable oil
1 large onion, finely chopped
2 garlic cloves, finely chopped
2 teaspoons desiccated coconut
2 teaspoons salt
1 teaspoon turmeric
1 teaspoon chilli powder
1 teaspoon freshly ground black pepper
150 ml/¼ pint vinegar
1 kg/2 lb mussels, scrubbed and debearded
  (see page 109)
500 ml/17 fl oz natural yogurt
2 teaspoons garam masala
8 tablespoons lemon juice
coriander leaves, to garnish

1 Heat the ghee or oil in a large saucepan. Add the onion and garlic and fry over a low heat for 5 minutes, or until soft. Add the coconut and salt and continue frying until the coconut begins to brown. Stir in the turmeric, chilli powder and pepper and fry for 1 further minute.

2 Add the vinegar and mussels to the pan, cover and cook over a high heat, shaking the pan occasionally, for 5 minutes until the mussels open. Remove the pan from the heat. Discard any mussels that have not opened.

3 Remove the empty half shells from the mussels and discard. Arrange the mussels in layers in a warmed serving dish. Pour the cooking liquid into a blender or food processor, add the yogurt and garam masala and process for 1 minute. Return to the pan and heat through without boiling. Pour over the mussels and serve, sprinkled with lemon juice and coriander.

Serves 4
Preparation time: 20 minutes
Cooking time: 10–12 minutes

siamese pineapple and mussel curry

2 lemon grass stalks, roughly chopped
20 Thai basil leaves
1 kg/2 lb live mussels, scrubbed and debearded (see page 109)
2 tablespoons groundnut oil
2 tablespoons Thai Red Curry Paste (see page 149)
5 cm/2 inch piece of fresh galangal, finely chopped
1 large green chilli, thinly sliced
2 kaffir lime leaves, finely chopped
200 ml/7 fl oz coconut milk
1 tablespoon Thai fish sauce
1 teaspoon palm sugar or soft brown sugar
175 g/6 oz peeled fresh pineapple, cut into bite-sized pieces
Thai basil sprigs, to garnish (optional)

1 Pour about 2.5 cm/1 inch of water into a large saucepan. Add the lemon grass and Thai basil and bring the water to the boil. Tip in the mussels, cover and steam for 3–4 minutes, or until they have opened. Drain the mussels, discarding the lemon grass, Thai basil and any mussels which have not opened. Set the mussels on one side while preparing the sauce.

2 Heat the oil in a heavy-based saucepan. Add the curry paste, galangal, chilli and lime leaves and fry over a gentle heat, stirring, for about 4 minutes until fragrant. Stir in the coconut milk, fish sauce and sugar and cook for 1 further minute.

3 Reserve a few mussels in their shells to garnish and remove the remaining mussels from their shells. Add the shelled mussels and pineapple to the curry sauce. Stir gently and cook for 2–3 minutes to heat through. Serve hot, garnished with the reserved mussels and Thai basil, if using.

Serves 4
Preparation time: 30 minutes
Cooking time: 10–15 minutes

griddled squid and prawns with spicy chilli sauce

375 g/12 oz prepared squid, opened out
12 raw king or tiger prawns
fresh pasta, to serve

Chilli sauce:
2 red peppers
2 fresh red chillies
2 tablespoons sherry vinegar
3 tablespoons chopped oregano
5 tablespoons olive oil
2 shallots, finely chopped
2 tablespoons lemon juice
sea salt flakes and pepper

1 To make the sauce, heat a griddle pan or nonstick frying pan. Slice the base off the peppers, then slice down the sides into 4–5 flat pieces, leaving the seeds on the core. Slice the chillies into wide, flat pieces, discarding the seeds. Place the pepper, skin side down, on the griddle pan and cook until the skins are charred and blistered. Remove and cook the chillies in the same way. Place the peppers and chillies in a small dish, cover with clingfilm and leave to cool.

2 Peel the skins off the peppers and chillies and place the flesh in a food processor with the vinegar. Process until smooth, season to taste with salt and pepper and pour into a small saucepan.

3 Cut the squid in half, then score in a criss-cross pattern with a sharp knife. Heat the griddle pan and cook the prawns for 2 minutes on each side. Remove and cook the squid for 1–2 minutes on each side. It will curl up, so use a palette knife to hold it flat. Cut each piece in half once cooked.

4 Warm up the chilli sauce, adding the oregano, oil, shallots and lemon juice. Toss the prawns and squid in the warm chilli sauce and serve with fresh pasta.

Serves 4
Preparation time: 20 minutes
Cooking time: about 15 minutes

baby squid with spinach and tomatoes

2–3 tablespoons olive oil
1 onion, chopped
1–2 garlic cloves, crushed
1 fresh chilli, chopped
1 celery stick, chopped
2 tablespoons chopped parsley, plus extra to garnish
600 g/1¼ lb prepared baby squid, cut into
   1 cm/½ inch slices
2 teaspoons plain flour
125 g/4 oz mushrooms, quartered or thickly sliced
375 g/12 oz large tomatoes, skinned, deseeded and
   chopped
500 g/1 lb spinach, chopped
300 ml/½ pint dry white wine
salt and pepper

1 Heat the oil in a large pan. Add the onions, garlic, chilli and celery, and fry over a low heat until the onion is golden brown. Add the parsley and squid and cook gently for a further 10 minutes.

2 Stir in the flour, mix well and then add the mushrooms, tomatoes, spinach and white wine. Season to taste with salt and pepper.

3 Cover and simmer very gently for about 30 minutes, or until the squid is nearly cooked, then remove the lid and simmer until the sauce thickens and the squid is completely tender.

4 Check the seasoning and pour into a warmed serving dish. Serve hot, garnished with the extra chopped parsley.

Serves 4
Preparation time: 30–35 minutes
Cooking time: 50–55 minutes

pan-fried squid with chillies

1 kg/2 lb prepared small squid
4 tablespoons olive oil
3 garlic cloves, crushed
1 red chilli, finely chopped
4 tablespoons lemon juice
handful of flat leaf parsley, chopped
salt and pepper

1 Slit the squid down one side and lay them flat. Score the skin of each one with a fine criss-cross pattern.

2 Mix half the olive oil, the garlic, chilli and lemon juice in a bowl and add the squid. Mix well to coat all over, cover and marinate for 15 minutes.

3 Remove the squid from the marinade, reserving the marinade. Heat the remaining oil a large frying pan or a wok until it is just smoking. Add the squid, season with salt and pepper, stir well and cook over a high heat for 2–3 minutes. The squid will curl up, but just hold them flat for a few seconds to get a tasty browned outside.

4 Finally, add the strained marinade and the parsley to the pan, mix well and serve at once.

Serves 4
Preparation time: 15 minutes, plus marinating
Cooking time: 5 minutes

squid braised with red wine and garlic

500 g/1 lb prepared squid rings
1 red onion, thinly sliced into rings
2 garlic cloves, finely chopped
300 ml/½ pint full-bodied red wine
2 tablespoons red wine vinegar
salt and pepper
finely chopped flat leaf parsley, to garnish

1 Put the squid, onion and garlic in an ovenproof dish and season to taste with salt and pepper. Pour in the wine and wine vinegar and add enough water to cover the squid.

2 Cover the dish and cook in a preheated oven, 180°C (350°F), Gas Mark 4, for 45 minutes, or until tender.

3 Serve the squid straight from the dish, sprinkled with parsley.

Serves 4
Preparation time: 5 minutes
Cooking time: 45 minutes
Oven temperature: 180°C (350°F), Gas Mark 4

stir-fried squid with green pepper and ginger

sunflower oil, for deep-frying
250 g/8 oz prepared squid, cut into
*   5 x 4 cm/2 x 1½ inch pieces*
2 thin slices of fresh root ginger
125 g/4 oz green peppers, deseeded and sliced
1 teaspoon salt
1 tablespoon light soy sauce
1 teaspoon wine vinegar
1 teaspoon sesame oil
pepper

1 Heat the oil in a wok or frying pan to 180–190°C (350–375°F), or until a cube of bread browns in 30 seconds. Add the squid and deep-fry for about 30 seconds, stirring with chopsticks to prevent the pieces sticking together.

2 Pour off all but 1 tablespoon of oil from the wok. Add the ginger, green peppers and squid and stir-fry for 1 minute. Add the salt, soy sauce, vinegar and pepper and fry for 1 minute. Add the sesame oil and serve hot.

Serves 4
Preparation time: 20 minutes
Cooking time: 10 minutes

squid with vegetable tagine

4 tablespoons virgin olive oil
2 onions, chopped
3 garlic cloves, crushed
1 fresh red chilli, deseeded and chopped
2 anchovy fillets (optional)
1 aubergine, cut into 2.5 cm/1 inch cubes
2 tablespoons torn mint leaves
2 tablespoons chopped parsley
2 thyme sprigs
2 courgettes, sliced
2 red peppers, cored, deseeded and thickly sliced
4 well-flavoured tomatoes, deseeded and quartered
1 kg/2 lb prepared squid, cut into small squares
salt and pepper

1 Heat 2 tablespoons of the olive oil in a large frying pan. Add the onion, garlic and chilli and fry until softened, but not browned. Stir in the anchovy fillets, if using, mashing them thoroughly.

2 Add the aubergine to the pan and cook, stirring occasionally, for 5 minutes. Add the mint, parsley, thyme and courgettes. When the courgettes start to wilt add the peppers and tomatoes. Cook, stirring occasionally, until all the vegetables are tender.

3 Just before serving, heat the remaining oil in another large frying pan. Add the squid and fry over a high heat, stirring, for about 1 minute. Remove with a slotted spoon and add to the vegetables. Season to taste with salt and pepper and serve immediately.

Serves 6
Preparation time: 10 minutes
Cooking time: 25–30 minutes

squid with herbs

1 kg/2 lb prepared squid
4 tablespoons olive oil
3–4 garlic cloves, thickly sliced
2 tablespoons chopped thyme
1 tablespoon chopped parsley
2 tablespoons lemon juice
salt and pepper
crusty bread, to serve

To garnish:
lemon slices
tiny bunches of thyme

1 Cut the squid into slices and cut the tentacles in half if they are large. Heat the oil in a preheated wok or heavy-based frying pan. Add the garlic and cook gently until browned, then discard.

2 Season the squid to taste with salt and pepper. Increase the heat, add the squid to the wok and stir-fry briskly for just under 1 minute.

3 Sprinkle with the herbs and lemon juice. Serve immediately, garnished with lemon and thyme, and accompanied by crusty bread.

Serves 4
Preparation: 15 minutes
Cooking time: 5 minutes

king prawns in cream and mustard sauce

50 g/2 oz butter
24 peeled raw king prawns
2 tablespoons brandy
225 ml/7½ fl oz double cream
2–3 teaspoons French mustard
salt and white pepper
boiled rice, to serve

To garnish:
1 tablespoon chopped parsley
lemon wedges

1 Melt the butter in a frying pan. Add the prawns and cook for a few minutes. Warm the brandy, pour it over the prawns and set it alight.

2 When the flames have subsided, stir in the cream. Season to taste with the mustard, salt and pepper.

3 Simmer very gently for 4–5 minutes until the prawns are tender, making sure that they do not become tough. Pour into a hot serving dish and garnish with chopped parsley and lemon wedges before serving with rice.

Serves 4
Preparation time: 15 minutes
Cooking time: 10 minutes

tiger prawns with garlic and herbs

50 g/2 oz butter
2 tablespoons olive oil
750 g/1½ lb peeled raw tiger prawns
1 shallot, finely diced
2 garlic cloves, crushed
75 ml/3 fl oz dry white wine
125 g/4 oz flat leaf parsley, chopped
125 g/4 oz marjoram, chopped
salt and pepper

1 Melt the butter with the oil in a frying pan. Add the tiger prawns, shallot and garlic and fry over a low heat for 5 minutes, or until all the prawns have turned pink.

2 Add the white wine, parsley and marjoram and season to taste with salt and pepper. Mix well and serve immediately.

Serves 4
Preparation time: 10 minutes
Cooking time: 6 minutes

garlic prawns with chillies and limes

24 raw king prawns
6 garlic cloves, peeled
½ teaspoon sea salt
½ teaspoon whole black peppercorns
2 red chillies, deseeded and chopped
3 tablespoons olive oil
50 g/2 oz butter
4 tablespoons lime juice
3 tablespoons chopped coriander, to garnish

To serve:
lime wedges
1 avocado, sliced

1 Split the prawns carefully down the middle towards the tail end, without completely separating them. They should look rather similar to butterflies. Remove the dark vein running along the back of each prawn.

2 Crush the garlic cloves with the sea salt, peppercorns and the chopped chillies using a pestle and mortar until you have a thick aromatic paste.

3 Coat the prepared prawns with this garlic mixture and place them in a bowl. Scrape out any remaining garlic paste and spread over the prawns. Cover the bowl and leave in a cool place to marinate for at least 1 hour.

4 Heat the olive oil and butter in a large, heavy-based frying pan. Add the prawns and garlic paste and fry over a medium heat for 2–3 minutes until they turn pink.

5 Remove from the pan and keep warm. Add the lime juice to the pan and stir into the pan juices. Boil vigorously for a couple of minutes, then pour over the prawns. Garnish with coriander and serve with lime wedges and avocado slices.

Serves 4–6
Preparation time: 25 minutes, plus marinating
Cooking time: 5 minutes

oriental prawns with asparagus

175 g/6 oz fresh asparagus, cut into 2.5 cm/1 inch pieces
4 tablespoons dry sherry
1 teaspoon light soy sauce
500 g/1 lb cooked peeled prawns
2 tablespoons oil
2 garlic cloves, thinly sliced
2 teaspoons finely chopped fresh root ginger
4 spring onions, chopped
salt

1 Blanch the asparagus in boiling salted water for 2 minutes. Drain well and set aside.

2 Mix the sherry and soy sauce together in a large bowl. Stir in the prawns and marinate for 15 minutes.

3 Heat the oil in a preheated wok or heavy-based frying pan. Add the garlic, ginger and half the spring onions and stir-fry for about 1 minute. Add the prawns with their marinade and the asparagus and stir-fry for 1–2 minutes, until the ingredients are hot.

4 Transfer to a warmed serving dish and sprinkle with the remaining spring onions. Serve immediately.

Serves 4
Preparation: 5 minutes, plus marinating
Cooking time: 4–5 minutes

szechuan prawns in chilli and tomato sauce

250 g/8 oz raw prawns, peeled
1 egg white
2 teaspoons cornflour
sunflower oil, for deep-frying
1 spring onion, finely chopped
2 slices fresh root ginger, finely chopped
1 garlic clove, finely chopped
1 tablespoon Chinese rice wine or dry sherry
1 tablespoon tomato purée
1 tablespoon chilli sauce
tomato rose, to garnish
lettuce, to serve

1 Mix a pinch of salt with the prawns, add the egg white and dust with cornflour.

2 Heat the oil in a wok or deep pan to 180–190°C (350–375°F) or until a cube of bread browns in 30 seconds. Add the prawns, stirring to keep them separate, and deep-fry for 30 seconds over a moderate heat. Remove from the wok and drain.

3 Pour off all but 1 tablespoon of oil from the wok. Add the spring onion, ginger and garlic and stir-fry over a high heat for a few seconds. Add the prawns and stir-fry for 1 minute. Add the wine or sherry, tomato purée and chilli sauce, stirring until the sauce is well blended.

4 Line a serving dish with lettuce leaves and pour the prawns and sauce into the centre. Serve immediately, garnished with a tomato rose.

Serves 4
Preparation time: 20–25 minutes
Cooking time: 5 minutes

prawns in coconut sauce

16 large raw prawns, peeled
2 tablespoons vegetable oil
1 large onion, finely chopped
2 lemon grass stalks, chopped
2 fresh red chillies, deseeded and sliced
2.5 cm/1 inch piece of fresh root ginger, shredded
1 tablespoon ground cumin
1 tablespoon ground coriander
2 tablespoons Thai fish sauce
250 ml/8 fl oz thick coconut milk
3 tablespoons roasted peanuts, coarsely ground
2 tomatoes, skinned and chopped
1 teaspoon sugar
1 tablespoon lime juice
chopped coriander leaves, to garnish

1 With a sharp pointed knife, slit along the undersides of the prawns from head to tail.

2 Heat the oil in a preheated wok or frying pan. Add the onion and fry until soft and golden. Add the lemon grass, red chillies, ginger, cumin and coriander and stir-fry for 2 minutes.

3 Add the fish sauce and coconut milk to the wok. Stir well and then add the peanuts and chopped tomatoes. Cook over a low heat until the tomato is soft and the flavours of the sauce are well developed.

4 Stir in the prawns and simmer gently for 5 minutes, or until the prawns are pink and tender. Stir in the sugar, then transfer to a serving dish. Sprinkle with lime juice and garnish with coriander.

Serves 4
Preparation time: 20 minutes
Cooking time: 17–20 minutes

thai stir-fried prawns with garlic

1 tablespoon oil
50 g/2 oz onion, finely sliced
1 tablespoon finely chopped garlic
1 tablespoon pepper
50 g/2 oz broccoli stem, peeled and sliced
25 g/1 oz oyster mushrooms, torn
12 raw tiger prawns, peeled
1 teaspoon sugar
4–6 tablespoons Thai Fish Stock (see page 143)
4 tablespoons light soy sauce
coriander leaves, to garnish

1 Heat the oil in a wok, add the onion, garlic and pepper and stir-fry for 30 seconds. Add the broccoli stem and stir-fry for 1 minute. Add the mushrooms and stir-fry for 30 seconds, then add the prawns, sugar, 4 tablespoons of the stock and the soy sauce.

2 Stir-fry over a high heat for 1–2 minutes, adding more stock if the dish is drying out. Serve immediately, garnished with coriander leaves.

Serves 3–4
Preparation time: 15 minutes
Cooking time: 5 minutes

chilli prawns with cherry tomatoes

3 tablespoons vegetable oil
1 small onion, finely chopped
2.5 cm/1 inch piece of fresh root ginger, finely chopped
2 garlic cloves, crushed
1–2 fresh chillies or 1–2 teaspoons chilli powder
375 g/12 oz raw tiger prawns, peeled
6–8 cherry tomatoes, halved
2 tablespoons tomato purée
1 tablespoon red or white wine vinegar
pinch of caster sugar
½ teaspoon salt
coriander sprigs, to garnish

1 Heat the oil in a preheated wok or frying pan over moderate heat until hot. Add the onion, ginger, garlic and chillies or chilli powder and stir-fry for 2–3 minutes, or until soft but not browned.

2 Add the prawns, increase the heat to high and stir-fry for 1–2 minutes, or until they turn pink. Add the tomatoes, tomato purée, wine vinegar, sugar and salt and stir-fry for several minutes until the mixture is thick, taking care not to let the cherry tomatoes lose their shape. Taste and add more salt if necessary. Serve at once, garnished with sprigs of coriander.

Serves 4
Preparation time: 10 minutes
Cooking time: 10–15 minutes

prawn curry

50 g/2 oz ghee or 1 tablespoon vegetable oil
1 small onion, sliced
2 garlic cloves, sliced
2 teaspoons ground coriander
½ teaspoon ground ginger
1 teaspoon turmeric
½ teaspoon ground cumin
½ teaspoon chilli powder
2 tablespoons vinegar
500 g/1 lb cooked peeled prawns
200 ml/7 fl oz water
chopped coriander leaves, to garnish
boiled rice, to serve

1 Heat the ghee or oil in a large heavy-based saucepan. Add the onion and garlic and fry over a low heat for 4–5 minutes until golden and soft.

2 Mix together the ground coriander, ginger, turmeric, cumin and chilli powder in a small bowl. Mix in the vinegar to make a smooth paste.

3 Add the spice paste to the onion and garlic mixture in the pan and fry gently, stirring constantly with a wooden spoon, for 3 minutes.

4 Tip in the prawns and turn gently with a wooden spoon until they are well coated with the spices. Stir in the water and then simmer over a low heat for 2–3 minutes. Serve immediately, garnished with coriander leaves, with plain boiled rice.

Serves 4
Preparation time: 15 minutes
Cooking time: 12–15 minutes

seared scallops with basil and balsamic vinegar

3 tablespoons olive oil
16 large scallops, cleaned
2 shallots, finely chopped
4 tablespoons balsamic vinegar
large handful of basil leaves, torn
salt and pepper

1 Heat the oil in a large frying pan over a high heat until it is just smoking. Add the scallops and cook for 2 minutes on one side. Turn them over and add the shallots. Cook for 1 minute, then reduce the heat.

2 Add the balsamic vinegar and season to taste with salt and pepper. Turn the scallops to coat in the vinegar.

3 Sprinkle the basil over the scallops, quickly mix and serve immediately.

Serves 4
Preparation time: 10 minutes
Cooking time: 5 minutes

scallop and prawn stir-fry

4–6 fresh scallops
150 g/5 oz raw prawns, peeled
1 egg white
1 tablespoon cornflour
vegetable oil, for deep-frying
2 slices of fresh root ginger, finely shredded
2–3 spring onions, finely shredded
3 celery sticks, cut into small pieces
1 red pepper, cored, deseeded and cut into small pieces
1–2 carrots, cut into small pieces

2 tablespoons Chinese rice wine or dry sherry
1 tablespoon light soy sauce
2 teaspoons chilli bean paste (optional)
1 teaspoon salt
1 teaspoon sesame seed oil

1 Cut each scallop into 3–4 pieces. Leave the prawns whole if small, otherwise cut each one into 2 or 3 pieces. Put the seafood in a bowl with the egg white and about half of the cornflour and mix together.

2 Heat the oil in a wok or deep pan to 180–190°C (350–375°F) or until a cube of bread browns in 30 seconds. Deep-fry the scallops and prawns for 1 minute, stirring them all the time with chopsticks to keep the pieces separate. Scoop them out with a perforated spoon and drain on kitchen paper.

3 Pour off all but 2 tablespoons of oil from the wok. Increase the heat to high and add the ginger and spring onions. Add the celery, red pepper and carrots and stir-fry for about 1 minute. Return the scallops and prawns to the wok and stir in the rice wine or sherry, soy sauce and chilli bean paste, if using, and season with the salt.

4 Mix the remaining cornflour to a smooth paste with a little water, then add to the wok and blend all the ingredients until thickened. Sprinkle over the sesame seed oil and serve immediately.

Serves 4–6
Preparation time: 15 minutes
Cooking time: 10 minutes

sauté of scallops with mangetout

8 scallops with coral
3 tablespoons vegetable oil
6 spring onions, thinly sliced diagonally
2.5 cm/1 inch piece fresh root ginger, finely chopped
175 g/6 oz mangetout, trimmed
1 garlic clove, crushed
1 tablespoon sesame oil
2 tablespoons soy sauce
½ teaspoon caster sugar
pepper
spring onions, to garnish

1 Slice the scallops thickly, detaching the corals and keeping them whole. Set the corals aside.

2 Heat 2 tablespoons of the vegetable oil in a preheated wok or frying pan over a moderate heat. Add the spring onions and ginger and stir-fry for a few seconds. Add the mangetout and garlic and stir-fry for 2 minutes, then tip the vegetable mixture into a bowl and set aside.

3 Heat the remaining vegetable oil with the sesame oil over a moderate heat. Add the sliced scallops and stir-fry for 3 minutes. Return the spring onion, ginger and mangetout mixture to the wok, add the reserved corals, soy sauce and sugar and increase the heat to high. Toss for 1–2 minutes, or until all the ingredients are combined and piping hot. Season to taste with pepper and serve immediately, garnished with spring onions.

Serves 2
Preparation time: 15 minutes
Cooking time: about 10 minutes

singapore crab

2 tablespoons vegetable oil
2.5 cm/1 inch piece fresh root ginger, finely chopped
1 garlic clove, finely chopped
1 teaspoon hot chilli powder
6 tablespoons tomato ketchup
2 tablespoons red wine vinegar
1 tablespoon soft brown sugar
150 ml/¼ pint boiling Fish Stock (see page 142)
1 large cooked crab, chopped into serving pieces with claws and legs cracked open
salt

To serve:
cucumber curls or slices
prawn crackers
boiled rice

1 Heat the oil in a preheated wok or frying pan over a moderate heat. Add the ginger and garlic and stir-fry for 2–3 minutes until softened, taking care not to let them brown.

2 Add the chilli powder and stir well to combine, then add the ketchup, vinegar and sugar and bring to the boil. Add the boiling fish stock, then the pieces of crab. Stir-fry for about 5 minutes or until the crab is heated through. Season to taste with salt.

3 Serve hot, with cucumber curls, prawn crackers and boiled rice handed separately.

Serves 4
Preparation time: about 30 minutes
Cooking time: about 10 minutes

ginger and spring onion crab

2 tablespoons sherry
1 tablespoon Fish Stock (see page 142) or water
2 tablespoons cornflour
1 large cooked crab, chopped into serving pieces, with
  claws and legs cracked open
3 tablespoons vegetable oil
4 slices of fresh root ginger, finely chopped
4 spring onions, finely chopped
1 teaspoon salt
1 tablespoon soy sauce
2 teaspoons sugar

1 Mix 1 tablespoon of the sherry with the stock or water and cornflour. Pour over the crab and leave to marinate for a few minutes.

2 Heat the oil in a preheated wok or frying pan until it is very hot. Add the crab and fry briskly for about 1 minute, turning the pieces in the oil.

3 Add the ginger, spring onions, salt, soy sauce, sugar and the remaining sherry. Cook, stirring constantly, for about 5 minutes. Add a little water if the mixture becomes very dry. Serve immediately.

Serves 2–4
Preparation time: 20 minutes
Cooking time: 8–10 minutes

crab in black bean sauce

This dish looks particularly nice when garnished with spring onion flowers. To make them, trim the green tops from the onions, leaving only the white part. Shred the top ends of the onion pieces in vertical cuts, leaving 2.5 cm/1 inch of onion uncut at the base. Immerse in iced water until the shredded onion opens out and curls.

2 tablespoons vegetable oil
2 tablespoons salted black beans, coarsely chopped
2 garlic cloves, chopped
2 tablespoons finely chopped fresh root ginger
4 spring onions, chopped
250 g/8 oz lean pork, finely minced
1 large cooked crab, chopped into serving pieces
2 tablespoons dry sherry
300 ml/½ pint Chicken Stock (see page 141)
2 eggs, beaten
1–2 teaspoons sesame oil
spring onion flowers, to garnish

1 Heat the oil in a preheated wok or heavy-based frying pan. Add the black beans, garlic, ginger and spring onions and stir-fry briskly for 30 seconds.

2 Add the pork and brown quickly for 1 minute. Add the crab, sherry and stock and boil rapidly for 8–10 minutes.

3 Combine the eggs and sesame oil and stir into the wok. Stir for 30 seconds, until the egg has cooked into strands. Transfer to a warmed serving dish, garnish with spring onion flowers and serve immediately.

Serves 4
Preparation: 6 minutes
Cooking time: 12 minutes

thai crab curry

1 tablespoon oil
1½ teaspoons Thai Red Curry Paste (see page 149)
6 tablespoons coconut milk
1 lime leaf, torn
12 crab claws
150 ml/¼ pint Thai Fish Stock (see page 143)
2 tablespoons sugar
1 teaspoon salt
65 g/2½ oz canned bamboo shoots, drained and rinsed

To garnish:
½ large red chilli, sliced diagonally
coriander leaves

1 Heat the oil in a preheated wok or frying pan. Add the curry paste and stir-fry for 30 seconds, then add all the remaining ingredients. Stir well and simmer for about 10 minutes. If the liquid level reduces significantly, add more stock.

2 Turn into a bowl and serve, garnished with the chilli and coriander leaves.

Serves 3–4
Preparation time: 3 minutes
Cooking time: 12 minutes

thai-style crab cakes

65 g/2½ oz plain flour
½ teaspoon baking powder
1 egg, beaten
1 tablespoon Thai fish sauce
1 tablespoon lime juice
1½ teaspoons chilli sauce
150 g/5 oz crab meat
4 kaffir lime leaves, shredded
1 tablespoon chopped coriander leaves
½ tablespoon chopped mint
½ tablespoon chopped basil
salt and pepper
vegetable oil, for shallow frying

Dipping sauce:
50 ml/2 fl oz rice vinegar
50 g/2 oz caster sugar
¼ teaspoon crushed chilli flakes
½ teaspoon salt

1 Beat together the flour, baking powder, egg, fish sauce, lime juice and chilli sauce in a bowl until smooth. Stir in the crab meat, lime leaves and herbs and salt and pepper to taste. Set aside for 30 minutes to infuse the flavours.

2 Meanwhile, prepare the dipping sauce. Put all the ingredients in a small pan and heat gently until the sugar dissolves. Bring to the boil, then remove from the heat and allow to cool.

3 Heat a shallow layer of oil in a heavy-based frying pan. Whisk 2 tablespoons of cold water into the crab mixture and drop heaped teaspoons into the oil. Fry for 1 minute on each side until golden. Drain on kitchen paper and keep warm while frying the remainder. Serve hot with the dipping sauce.

Serves 2–4
Preparation time: 25 minutes, plus standing
Cooking time: 8–10 minutes

spicy crab and prawn purses

175 g/6 oz white crab meat
125 g/4 oz cooked peeled prawns
1 garlic clove, crushed
2 spring onions, chopped
1 tablespoon chopped coriander leaves
2 teaspoons chopped preserved stem ginger, plus
* 2 teaspoons ginger syrup from the jar*
¼ teaspoon chilli powder
1 tablespoon light soy sauce
grated rind and juice of 1 lime
4 tablespoons olive oil, plus extra for brushing
4 filo pastry sheets

Dipping sauce:
50 g/2 oz sugar
3 tablespoons rice or wine vinegar
½ teaspoon salt
1 teaspoon dried chilli flakes
2 tablespoons water

1 Place all the ingredients, except the pastry, in a bowl and stir well. Chill for 1 hour to let the flavours develop.

2 Meanwhile, place the ingredients for the dipping sauce in a small pan and heat gently until the sugar dissolves. Bring to the boil, remove from the heat and cool.

3 Cut the pastry into 12.5 cm/5 inch squares. Brush with oil and place a little crab mixture in the middle. Draw the edges up to a point and pinch together. Place on a greased baking sheet, brush them with oil and bake in a preheated oven, 190°C (375°F), Gas Mark 5, for 20–25 minutes until golden. Serve hot, with the sauce.

Makes 24
Preparation: 10 minutes, plus chilling
Cooking time: 20–25 minutes
Oven temperature: 190°C (375°F), Gas Mark 5

meat dishes

roast pork fillet with rosemary and fennel

1 large rosemary sprig
3 garlic cloves
750 g/1½ lb pork fillet, trimmed
4 tablespoons olive oil
2 fennel bulbs, cut into wedges
150 ml/¼ pint white wine
75 g/3 oz mascarpone cheese
salt and pepper
rosemary sprigs, to garnish

1 Break the rosemary into short pieces and cut the garlic into slices. Pierce the pork with a sharp knife and inset the pieces of rosemary and garlic evenly all over the fillet.

2 Heat 2 tablespoons of the olive oil in a frying pan. Add the pork fillet and fry, turning occasionally, for about 5 minutes or until browned all over.

3 Lightly oil a roasting tin, add the fennel and drizzle with olive oil. Place the pork fillet on top, season generously with salt and pepper and roast in a preheated oven, 230°C (450°F), Gas Mark 8, for 20 minutes.

4 Pour the wine into the frying pan and simmer until reduced by half. Add the mascarpone and season to taste with salt and pepper. Stir to mix well.

5 To serve, cut the pork into slices and arrange on a warmed serving dish with wedges of fennel. Pour the wine sauce into the roasting pan and place over a moderate heat. Using a wooden spoon stir all the tasty bits into the sauce, then spoon over the pork and fennel. Garnish with rosemary.

Serves 4
Preparation time: 15 minutes
Cooking time: 25 minutes
Oven temperature: 230°C (450°F), Gas Mark 8

loin of pork with citrus fruit

50 g/2 oz butter
1 small onion, finely chopped
1.25 kg/2½ lb loin of pork
4½ teaspoons Marsala wine
6 tablespoons orange juice
4 tablespoons lemon juice
125 ml/4 fl oz stock
12 black olives, pitted and chopped
salt and pepper
roast or mashed potatoes, to serve

1 Melt the butter in a large flameproof casserole over a medium heat. Add the onion and fry until golden, but not brown. Add the loin of pork and brown it on all sides.

2 Add the Marsala and when it has evaporated, add the orange and lemon juice. Season to taste with salt and pepper, cover and cook over a low heat for about 1½ hours. Add a little stock from time to time to make sure it does not dry out.

3 Halfway through the cooking time, add the olives to the pork, together with a little more pepper.

4 Serve the pork thinly sliced with the cooking juices poured over, accompanied with roast or mashed potatoes.

Serves 6
Preparation time: 5–10 minutes
Cooking time: 1¾ hours

loin of pork with juniper and bay

2 tablespoons olive oil
1.25 kg/2½ lb boned loin of pork
1 tablespoon juniper berries, coarsely crushed
2 cloves
10 bay leaves, fresh if possible, plus a sprig to garnish
2 large onions, chopped
300 ml/½ pint dry white wine
150–450 ml/¼–¾ pint Ham Stock (see page 142)
salt and pepper

1 Heat the olive oil in a heavy-based pan or flameproof casserole just large enough to hold the meat. Add the meat and brown on all sides.

2 Add the juniper berries, cloves, bay leaves and onions and stir into the oil. Season to taste with salt and pepper and pour in the white wine. Cover with a piece of greaseproof paper and a tight-fitting lid and cook over a very low heat for 1½ hours, or until tender. Avoid removing the lid too often, but check once or twice while the meat is cooking, adding a little stock if necessary. Remove the meat from the pan and place on a serving dish. Cover and keep hot.

3 Add sufficient stock to the pan to absorb all the browned residue. Bring to the boil, check the seasoning and strain the liquid. If liked, pour a little over the meat, serving the rest separately. Serve hot, garnished with a fresh bay sprig.

Serves 4–6
Preparation time: 10 minutes
Cooking time: 1½–1¾ hours

pork fillet with herbs and pistachios

1 tablespoon soya or sunflower oil
4 shallots or small onions, finely chopped
1 garlic clove, crushed and chopped
1 tablespoon wholemeal flour
150 ml/¼ pint dry white wine
750 g/1½ lb pork fillet, thinly sliced
2 tablespoons chopped sage leaves
2 tablespoons chopped chives
2 tablespoons chopped thyme
50 g/2 oz pistachio nuts, shelled and chopped
sea salt flakes and pepper
lemon wedges, to garnish

1 Heat the oil in a small saucepan. Add the shallots or onions and garlic and fry over a low heat for 3 minutes, but do not allow to brown. Sprinkle in the flour and stir. Stir in the wine, cook gently until the sauce is smooth and season to taste with salt and pepper. Then remove the pan from the heat.

2 Heat a griddle pan or nonstick frying pan. Add the sliced pork fillet, in batches. Cook each batch for 3 minutes on each side and keep warm.

3 Add the herbs and pistachio nuts to the sauce and heat through, stirring, for 1 minute. Serve the pork with the sauce, garnished with lemon wedges.

Serves 4–6
Preparation time: 20 minutes
Cooking time: 15–20 minutes

roast stuffed pork fillet

50 g/2 oz butter
1 large onion, finely chopped
175 g/6 oz fresh white breadcrumbs
grated rind of ½ lemon
pinch of dried thyme
4½ teaspoons finely chopped parsley
beaten egg, to bind
2 x 375 g/12 oz pork fillets
150 ml/¼ pint water
salt and pepper
apple sauce, to serve

Gravy:
1 tablespoon arrowroot
300 ml/½ pint Ham Stock (see page 142)

1 Melt half the butter in a pan. Add the onion and fry over a low heat until soft, but not browned. Stir in the breadcrumbs, lemon rind and herbs and season to taste with salt and pepper. Bind with a little beaten egg. Remove from the heat and leave to cool.

2 Slit the pork fillets lengthways without cutting right through them and flatten the meat until the fillets lie flat. Arrange the stuffing on top of one of the fillets turning in the ends. Lay the second fillet on top also tucking in the ends and wrapping the long sides around to enclose the stuffing. Tie at intervals with string.

3 Melt the remaining butter in an ovenproof dish. Add the fillets and brown them all over. Pour in the water, cover tightly and cook in a preheated oven, 180°C (350°F), Gas Mark 4, for 1–1¼ hours. Remove the string and transfer to a warmed serving dish.

4 Blend the arrowroot with the stock and stir into the cooking juices, then taste and adjust the seasoning if necessary. Serve the fillet carved in slices and accompanied by apple sauce.

Serves 4
Preparation time: 30 minutes
Cooking time: 1–1¼ hours
Oven temperature: 180°C (350°F), Gas Mark 4

catalan pork stew

150 ml/¼ pint olive oil
750 g/1½ lb lean pork cut into 2.5 cm/1 inch cubes
1 large onion, sliced
2 garlic cloves, crushed
500 g/1 lb tomatoes, skinned and chopped
1 green pepper, cored, deseeded and chopped
1½ teaspoons paprika
150 ml/¼ pint Chicken Stock (see page 141)
1 aubergine, sliced
2–3 tablespoons seasoned flour
salt and pepper
1 tablespoon chopped coriander leaves, to garnish
boiled rice, to serve

1 Heat 2 tablespoons of the oil in a large saucepan or flameproof casserole. Add the pork and fry over a low heat, turning occasionally, until golden brown on all sides. Remove from the pan with a slotted spoon.

2 Add the onion and garlic to the pan and cook until soft and golden. Return the meat to the pan and stir in the tomatoes, green pepper, paprika and stock. Season to taste with salt and pepper. Bring to the boil, cover with greaseproof paper and a lid and simmer gently for 1 hour, or until the meat is tender.

3 Dip the aubergine slices in seasoned flour. Heat some of the remaining oil in a large frying pan. Add the aubergine slices, a few at a time, and fry until they are golden brown on both sides, adding more oil as required. Remove with a slotted spoon and pat dry with kitchen paper.

4 Serve the stew with the fried aubergine, scattered with coriander, and plain boiled rice.

Serves 4
Preparation time: 20 minutes
Cooking time: 1¼ hours

pork and mushroom carbonnade

3 tablespoons sunflower oil
2 large onions, sliced
175 g/6 oz button mushrooms, quartered
750 g/1½ lb boneless pork, trimmed and cut into
  bite-sized pieces
1½ tablespoons plain flour
300 ml/½ pint light ale
300 ml/½ pint Chicken Stock (see page 141)
2 teaspoons soft light brown sugar
50 g/2 oz butter, softened
1½ teaspoons French mustard
40 g/1½ oz Cheddar cheese, grated
1 tablespoon chopped parsley
8 slices of French bread, about 2.5 cm/1 inch thick
salt and pepper

1 Heat 2 tablespoons of the oil in a flameproof casserole. Add the onions and mushrooms and fry over a low heat for 5 minutes. Remove from the casserole with a slotted spoon and set aside on a plate.

2 Heat the remaining oil in the casserole. Add the pork and fry over a moderately high heat, stirring, until the meat is sealed and browned on all sides.

3 Stir in the flour and cook for 1 minute. Stir in the ale and stock and bring to the boil. Remove the casserole from the heat and return the onions and mushrooms to it. Stir in the sugar and season with salt and pepper to taste. Cover and cook in a preheated oven, 180°C (350°F), Gas Mark 4, for 1¾ hours. Remove the casserole from the oven.

4 Mix the butter, mustard, cheese and parsley in a bowl and spread over the slices of French bread. Arrange the bread slices, cheese side up, on top of the casserole. Press the slices down into the gravy (they will rise again during cooking).

5 Return the casserole to the oven and cook, uncovered, for a further 30 minutes, until the bread topping is melted and golden. Serve at once.

Serves 4–6
Preparation time: 10–15 minutes
Cooking time: 2½ hours
Oven temperature: 180°C (350°F), Gas Mark 4

jamaica pork roast

2 kg/4 lb loin of pork
125 ml/4 fl oz dark rum
600 ml/1 pint Ham Stock (see page 142)
2 teaspoons arrowroot

Seasoning:
½ teaspoon ground cloves
½ teaspoon ground allspice
1 teaspoon ground ginger
2 garlic cloves, crushed
1 bay leaf, crumbled
salt and pepper

Basting sauce:
75 g/3 oz soft brown sugar
2 tablespoons lime juice
3 tablespoons rum

1 Mix all the seasoning ingredients together in a small bowl. With a sharp knife, cut through the fat on the pork loin in a diamond pattern. Rub the seasoning over the scored fat.

2 Place the loin of pork in a roasting tin. Pour the rum and 125 ml/4 fl oz of the stock over it. Roast in a preheated oven, 180°C (350°F), Gas Mark 4 for 1¾–2 hours.

3 Meanwhile, mix together the ingredients for the basting sauce and blend well. After 1 hour, remove the pork from the oven and baste with the sauce. Return to the oven for the remainder of the cooking time, adding more stock or a little water if necessary to moisten the meat.

4 When the meat is cooked, transfer it to a serving plate and keep warm. Pour off some of the fat from the tin and add the remaining basting sauce and stock. Stir well to scrape up any pork residue in the tin. Place over a moderate heat and bring to the boil, stirring. Mix the arrowroot with 1 tablespoon of water and stir into the gravy until thickened. Serve with the roast pork.

Serves 6
Preparation time: 10 minutes
Cooking time: 2 hours
Oven temperature: 180°C (350°F), Gas Mark 4

pork spare ribs with spicy chilli sauce

1 kg/2 lb lean pork spare ribs, cut into 5 cm/2 inch
  pieces
2 tablespoons sunflower oil
2 dried red chillies
2.5 cm/1 inch piece of fresh root ginger, finely chopped
1 garlic clove, thinly sliced
salt

Sauce:
4 tablespoons clear honey
4 tablespoons wine vinegar
2 tablespoons light soy sauce
2 tablespoons dry sherry
150 g/5 oz tomato purée
1 teaspoon chilli powder
2 garlic cloves, crushed

1 Mix all the sauce ingredients together and set aside. Sprinkle the spare ribs with salt.

2 Heat the oil in a preheated wok or frying pan. Add the red chillies and fry for 30 seconds to flavour it. Remove the chillies with a slotted spoon and discard. Add the ginger and garlic to the wok and stir-fry over a moderate heat for 30 seconds. Add the spare ribs and stir-fry for 5 minutes, until golden brown. Reduce the heat and cook gently for 10 minutes.

3 Add the sauce to the wok, cover and simmer gently for 25–30 minutes. Serve hot.

Serves 4–6
Preparation time: 15 minutes
Cooking time: 45 minutes

stir-fried pork with aubergine

175 g/6 oz boneless lean pork, shredded
2 spring onions, finely chopped
1 cm/½ inch piece of fresh root ginger, finely chopped
1 garlic clove, finely chopped
1 tablespoon soy sauce
1 teaspoon medium or dry sherry

1½ teaspoons cornflour
vegetable oil, for deep-frying
250 g/8 oz aubergine, cut into diamond-shaped chunks
1 tablespoon chilli sauce
3–4 tablespoons Chicken Stock (see page 141) or water
chopped spring onions, to garnish

1 Put the pork in a bowl with the spring onions, ginger, garlic, soy sauce, sherry and cornflour. Mix well, then leave to marinate for about 20 minutes.

2 Heat the oil in a wok or deep-fat fryer to 180–190°C (350–375°F) or until a cube of bread browns in 30 seconds. Lower the heat, add the aubergine and deep-fry for about 1½ minutes. Remove from the pan with a slotted spoon and drain on kitchen paper.

3 Pour off all but 1 tablespoon of oil from the pan. Add the pork and stir-fry for about 1 minute. Add the aubergine and chilli sauce and cook for about 1½ minutes, then moisten with the stock or water. Simmer until the liquid has almost evaporated. Serve hot, garnished with chopped spring onions.

Serves 3–4
Preparation time: 10 minutes, plus marinating
Cooking time: 10 minutes

sweet and sour pork

500 g/1 lb pork fillet, cut into 2.5 cm/1 inch cubes
1 teaspoon salt
pinch of pepper
½ teaspoon Chinese five-spice powder
2 tablespoons dry sherry
1 egg
3 tablespoons cornflour
vegetable oil, for deep-frying
2 tablespoons groundnut oil
1 garlic clove, crushed
1 onion, roughly chopped
1–2 green peppers, cored, deseeded and diced
250 g/8 oz canned pineapple chunks, with juice
3 tablespoons wine vinegar
50 g/2 oz sugar
4 tablespoons tomato ketchup
pineapple and cherries, to garnish

1 Bring a saucepan of water to the boil. Add the pork and boil until it changes colour. Drain the pork, cool and pat dry with kitchen paper.

2 Mix together the salt, pepper, five-spice powder, sherry, egg and cornflour. Add the pork and turn to coat well. Heat the vegetable oil to 180–190°C (350–375°F) or until a cube of bread browns in 30 seconds. Deep-fry the pork until brown. Drain on kitchen paper.

3 Heat the groundnut oil in a pan. Add the garlic and fry until golden. Add the onion and green pepper, and stir-fry for 1 minute. Stir in the pineapple juice, vinegar, sugar and tomato ketchup. Cook, stirring, until thickened. Add the pineapple and pork and stir until heated through. Serve hot, garnished with pineapple and cherries.

Serves 4–6
Preparation time: 10 minutes
Cooking time: 20–30 minutes

red-cooked pork with chestnuts

1.5–2 kg/3–4 lb belly pork
1¹/₂ teaspoons sugar
125 ml/4 fl oz water
5¹/₂ tablespoons soy sauce
250 g/8 oz chestnuts
5 tablespoons dry sherry
cooked shredded cabbage, to serve (optional)

1 Cut the pork through the skin, lean and fat, into 4 cm/1½ inch pieces. Combine the sugar, water and 4½ tablespoons of the soy sauce.

2 Put the pork pieces in a flameproof casserole and pour over just enough boiling water to cover. Bring back to the boil and simmer for 15 minutes, then drain off all the water. Pour in the soy sauce mixture. Stir the pork pieces in the sauce until well coated. Transfer to a preheated oven, 150°C (300°F), Gas Mark 2 and cook for 1 hour, stirring twice.

3 Meanwhile, cook the chestnuts in boiling water for 30 minutes. Drain, then remove the shells and skin.

4 Add the chestnuts to the pork, together with the sherry and the remaining soy sauce. Stir well and return to the oven for a further 1 hour. Serve hot, on a bed of cooked shredded cabbage, if liked.

Serves 10
Preparation time: 10 minutes
Cooking time: 2¼ hours
Oven temperature: 150°C (300°F), Gas Mark 2

pork in black bean sauce

1 tablespoon soy sauce
2 tablespoons dry sherry
1 tablespoon sugar
1 tablespoon plain flour
500 g/1 lb pork spare ribs, chopped into small pieces
3 tablespoons vegetable oil
1 garlic clove, crushed
2 spring onions, thinly sliced diagonally
2 tablespoons black or yellow bean sauce
5 tablespoons Chicken Stock (see page 141) or water
1 small green pepper, cored, deseeded and sliced
1 small red pepper, cored, deseeded and sliced

1 Mix together the soy sauce, sherry, sugar and flour in a large bowl. Add the pork spare ribs and leave in a cool place to marinate for 10–15 minutes.

2 Heat the oil in a preheated wok or frying pan. Add the pork spare ribs and stir-fry for a few minutes until they are golden. Remove with a slotted spoon and drain on kitchen paper.

3 Add the garlic, spring onions and black or yellow bean sauce to the wok and stir well. Add the pork spare ribs with the stock or water, and cook, covered, over a high heat for 5 minutes. If necessary, add a little more liquid. Replace the lid and cook for a further 5 minutes.

4 Add the sliced green and red peppers and stir well. Cook for 2 minutes and then remove from the heat. Transfer to a warm platter and serve immediately.

Serves 4
Preparation time: 10 minutes, plus marinating
Cooking time: 15–20 minutes

thai chilli pork

10 small shallots
25 g/1 oz large dried chillies, soaked for 20 minutes
24 coriander roots
6 tablespoons oil
250 g/8 oz minced pork
4 tomatoes, diced
3 tablespoons sugar
3 tablespoons Thai fish sauce
coriander leaves, to garnish

Salad:
½ cucumber, cut into chunks
1 little gem lettuce, separated into leaves
coriander sprigs

1 Put the shallots, chillies and coriander roots into a food processor or blender and process, adding a little water if the mixture seems very dry. Alternatively, pound them together using a pestle and mortar for 5–8 minutes until thoroughly amalgamated.

2 Heat the oil in a preheated wok or frying pan. Add the chilli paste and stir-fry for 30 seconds. Add the pork and tomatoes and cook, stirring, for 30 seconds, then add the sugar and fish sauce and continue to cook, stirring, for 4–5 minutes.

3 Turn the pork into a serving bowl, garnish with coriander and serve, with the salad arranged on a separate plate.

Serves 2
Preparation time: 10 minutes
Cooking time: 6–8 minutes

thai pork with lime

300 g/10 oz loin of pork, cut into
    2.5 x 1 cm/1 x ½ inch strips
2 tablespoons light soy sauce
½ teaspoon pepper
1 tablespoon oil
10 garlic cloves, chopped
15 small green chillies, chopped

4 tablespoons lime juice
4 tablespoons Thai fish sauce
1 tablespoon palm sugar or light muscovado sugar
15 g/½ oz mint leaves, finely chopped

1 Mix together the pork, soy sauce and pepper in a bowl.

2 Heat the oil in a preheated wok or frying pan. Add the pork mixture and stir-fry over a high heat for about 6 minutes until the pork is well cooked.

3 Transfer the pork to a mixing bowl or saucepan and add all the remaining ingredients. Mix thoroughly for 1–2 minutes, then turn into a serving dish.

Serves 2
Preparation time: 10–12 minutes
Cooking time: 6 minutes

pork in coconut milk

2 onions, quartered
8 dried red chillies
6 macadamia nuts
½ teaspoon terasi (dried shrimp paste)
2 tablespoons vegetable oil
750 g/1½ lb lean pork, cut into 2.5 cm/1 inch cubes
250 ml/8 fl oz water
1 teaspoon salt
250 ml/8 fl oz thick coconut milk
1 tablespoon sugar
2 tablespoons lemon or lime juice

To garnish:
dried red chilli strips
fresh coconut slices
coriander sprigs

1 Put the onions, chillies, macadamia nuts, terasi and 1 tablespoon water into a food processor or blender and process to a paste.

2 Heat the oil in a large saucepan. Add the spice paste and fry over a low heat, stirring, for 3–4 minutes. Add the pork and cook, stirring, until it changes colour and is well coated with the paste.

3 Pour in the water and add the salt. Cover and simmer gently for about 30 minutes until the pork is just tender.

4 Add the coconut milk and simmer, uncovered, for 10–15 minutes, stirring from time to time. Stir in the sugar and lemon or lime juice.

5 To serve, spoon the curry into individual bowls and garnish with dried chilli strips, fresh coconut and coriander sprigs.

Serves 4–6
Preparation time: 30 minutes
Cooking time: about 45 minutes

pork with tamarind

50 g/2 oz dried tamarind
300 ml/½ pint boiling water
75 g/3 oz ghee or butter
2 large onions, sliced
8 garlic cloves, sliced
750 g/1½ lb boneless lean pork, cubed
½ teaspoon paprika
½ teaspoon turmeric
1 teaspoon fenugreek seeds
25 g/1 oz piece of fresh root ginger, chopped
2 fresh green chillies
1 teaspoon salt
150 ml/¼ pint water
1½ teaspoons garam masala
2 bay leaves
6 cardamom pods
3 cloves
coriander sprigs, to garnish

1 Put the tamarind into a bowl and pour over the boiling water. Leave to soak for 30 minutes.

2 Melt the ghee or butter in a wok or heavy-based frying pan. Add the onions and garlic and fry for 5 minutes until soft. Add the pork and stir-fry to seal the meat on all sides.

3 Add the paprika, turmeric, fenugreek seeds, ginger, chillies and salt. Pour in the water, cover and cook for 20–30 minutes.

4 Mash the tamarind in the soaking water, then strain through a wire sieve set over a bowl, pressing the tamarind to extract as much pulp as possible.

5 Uncover the pan, bring to the boil and boil until nearly all the liquid has evaporated. Add the garam masala, bay leaves, cardamom pods, cloves and the tamarind pulp and cook over a very low heat for about 30 minutes, or until the pork is tender. Serve hot, garnished with the coriander sprigs.

Serves 4–6
Preparation time: 20 minutes, plus soaking
Cooking time: about 1¼ hours

cold baked ham

2.5–4 kg/5–8 lb gammon joint, either on the bone or
   boned and rolled
2 bay leaves
2 tablespoons demerara sugar
150 ml/¼ pint ginger ale

Glaze:
3 tablespoons ginger marmalade
6 tablespoons demerara sugar

1 Place the gammon in a large saucepan of cold water and leave to soak for 2–12 hours, depending on how salty it is.

2 Drain the gammon, then weigh and calculate the cooking time at 25 minutes per 500 g/1 lb, plus 20 minutes. For a joint over 3 kg/6 lb allow 20 minutes per 500 g/1 lb, plus 20 minutes.

3 Return the gammon to the pan and pour in enough fresh cold water to cover. Add the bay leaves and sugar and bring to the boil. Cover, lower the heat and simmer for half the estimated cooking time.

4 Remove the gammon from the pan and strip off the skin. Stand the gammon on a large sheet of foil in a roasting tin and score the fat diagonally in a trellis pattern. Mix together the marmalade and sugar and spread over the surface of the fat.

5 Pour the ginger ale around the joint and enclose in the foil, sealing the edges firmly. Cook in a preheated oven, 190°C (375°F), Gas Mark 5, for half the remaining cooking time.

6 Baste the gammon with the ginger ale, rewrap in the foil and cook until 20 minutes before the end of the cooking time. Fold back the foil, baste again and return to the oven.

7 Remove from the oven and leave the gammon to cool before serving.

Serves 10–15
Preparation time: 5 minutes, plus soaking and cooling
Cooking time: 2¼–3¼ hours
Oven temperature: 190°C (375°F), Gas Mark 5

griddled gammon with apricot salsa

4 x 175 g/6 oz gammon steaks

Apricot salsa:
250 g/8 oz fresh apricots, pitted and chopped
grated rind and juice of 1 lime
2 teaspoons fresh root ginger, finely diced
2 teaspoons clear honey
1 tablespoon olive oil
2 tablespoons chopped sage
4 spring onions, chopped
sea salt and pepper

1 Heat a griddle pan or nonstick frying pan. Add the gammon steaks, in batches, and cook for 4 minutes on each side. Keep warm until they are all cooked.

2 Mix together the apricots, lime rind and juice, ginger, honey, olive oil and sage in a small bowl. Crush the mixture with the back of a fork. Add the spring onions and season to taste with salt and pepper, mixing well. Serve the steaks immediately with the apricot salsa.

Serves 4
Preparation time: 20 minutes
Cooking time: 16–32 minutes

gammon steaks with parsley sauce

4 x 175 g/6 oz smoked gammon steaks, rinded
25 g/1 oz butter, melted
parsley sprigs, to garnish

Sauce:
150 ml/¼ pint soured cream
4 tablespoons chopped parsley
1 teaspoon French mustard
salt and pepper

1 Snip the fat at 1 cm/½ inch intervals around the gammon steaks. Brush the steaks on one side with butter. Place under a preheated moderate grill and cook for 5 minutes.

2 Turn the steaks, brush with more butter and cook for a further 3–5 minutes, or until cooked through. Transfer to a heated serving dish and keep warm in a low oven.

3 To make the sauce, combine all the ingredients in a small saucepan. Stir over a low heat until warmed through, but do not allow it to boil.

4 Pour the sauce over the gammon steaks, garnish with parsley sprigs and serve immediately.

Serves 4
Preparation time: 5 minutes
Cooking time: about 15 minutes

honey roast bacon with peaches

2 kg/4 lb boned collar of bacon, soaked overnight in cold water
1 bay leaf
1 small onion, quartered
400 g/13 oz can peach halves, drained, syrup reserved
2 tablespoons clear honey
about 40 whole cloves (optional)
1 tablespoon demerara sugar
¼ teaspoon ground cinnamon
watercress sprigs, to garnish

1 Drain the bacon and place, rind side down, in a large saucepan. Add the bay leaf and onion and pour in enough cold water to cover. Cover and bring to the boil, then lower the heat and simmer gently for 1½ hours.

2 Remove the bacon from the pan and allow to cool slightly. Strip off the skin, leaving the layer of fat, and place the bacon, fat side up, in a roasting tin. Using a sharp knife, score the fat into a diamond pattern. Mix 2 tablespoons of the reserved peach syrup with the honey and brush the mixture over the scored bacon fat. Stud each diamond with a clove, if using.

3 Roast the bacon in a preheated oven, 190°C (375°F), Gas Mark 5, for 25 minutes, until the topping is golden brown in colour.

4 Meanwhile, put the remaining peach syrup and the peach halves into a saucepan, stir in the sugar and cinnamon and simmer gently for 10 minutes.

5 Place the bacon on a warmed serving dish. Remove the peach halves from the sauce, arrange them around the base of the meat and garnish with watercress sprigs. Pour the peach sauce into a warmed sauceboat and serve separately.

Serves 6
Preparation time: 10 minutes, plus soaking
Cooking time: 2 hours
Oven temperature: 190°C (375°F), Gas Mark 5

bacon and onion pudding

625 g/1¼ lb lean boned collar of bacon, soaked overnight in cold water
50 g/2 oz butter, plus extra for greasing
2 onions, roughly chopped
2 carrots, thinly sliced
50 g/2 oz plain flour
300 ml/½ pint Chicken Stock (see page 141)
1½–2 tablespoons chopped parsley
pepper

Suet pastry:
250 g/8 oz self-raising flour
pinch of salt
125 g/4 oz shredded suet
150 ml/¼ pint cold water

1 Drain the bacon, trim the fat and cut the meat into 2.5 cm/1 inch pieces.

2 Melt the butter in a saucepan. Add the bacon, onions and carrots and cook over a low heat for 10 minutes.

3 Stir in the flour and cook, stirring constantly, for 1 minute. Gradually pour in the stock and bring to the boil, stirring. Lower the heat and simmer for 2 minutes. Add pepper to taste and stir in the parsley. Remove from the heat and leave to cool.

4 Make the suet pastry. Sift the flour with the salt into a mixing bowl. Stir in the suet, then add the water and mix to a soft dough. Knead gently on a lightly floured surface.

5 Cut off about a quarter of the dough and reserve for the lid. Roll out the remaining pastry to a circle 10 cm/4 inches larger than the top of a 1.2 litre/2 pint pudding basin. Grease the basin liberally with butter. Lightly dust the rolled out pastry with flour, then fold loosely in half and then into quarters. Lift the pastry into the basin, pointed end down, unfold and press neatly around the base and sides.

6 Spoon the cooled bacon mixture into the pastry-lined basin. Dampen the pastry edge. Roll out the reserved pastry to a circle large enough to cover the top of the pudding. Place on top and seal the edges together firmly.

7 Cover with pleated greased greaseproof paper and pleated foil and tie securely with string. Place the pudding in a large saucepan and pour in boiling water to come halfway up the sides of the basin. Boil the pudding for 2½–3 hours until cooked through, topping up with more boiling water as required. Serve hot.

Serves 4–6
Preparation time: 25 minutes, plus soaking
Cooking time: 2¾–3¼ hours

sausages with mustard mash

8 speciality sausages
2 onions, cut into wedges, roots left intact

Mustard mash:
1 kg/2 lb potatoes, quartered but left unpeeled
75 g/3 oz butter
1 tablespoon wholegrain mustard
3 teaspoons prepared English mustard

1 garlic clove, crushed
1 large bunch of parsley, chopped
dash of olive oil
sea salt and pepper

1 Heat a griddle pan or nonstick frying pan. Place the sausages on the griddle and cook for 10 minutes, turning to get an even colour. Add the onion wedges and cook for 6–7 minutes with the sausages.

2 Meanwhile, place the potatoes in a saucepan of cold water, bring to the boil and simmer for 15 minutes.

3 When the potatoes are cooked, drain well and return to the pan. Place over a low heat and allow any excess water to steam away, without colouring the potatoes. Remove from the heat and peel. Then mash them well, add the butter, mustards and garlic and season to taste with salt and pepper. Taste the potato and add more mustard if liked. Finally, add the parsley and a dash of olive oil and stir.

4 Serve the mash and sausages together with the griddled onion wedges.

Serves 4
Preparation time: 10 minutes
Cooking time: 25 minutes

milanese stew

300 g/10 oz pork rind
25 g/1 oz butter
3–4 tablespoons olive oil
2 large onions, sliced
2 large carrots, sliced
2 celery sticks, chopped
625 g/1¼ lb boneless pork, diced
150 ml/¼ pint dry white wine
1.5 litres/2½ pints Chicken Stock (see page 141)
250 g/8 oz Italian pork sausage or Continental sausage, cut into 2.5 cm/1 inch slices
750 g/1½ lb Savoy cabbage, shredded
salt and pepper

1 Place the pork rind in a pan, cover with water and season lightly with salt. Bring to the boil and cook for 10 minutes. Drain and cut the rind into 5 x 1 cm/2 x ½ inch strips.

2 Heat the butter and half the oil in another pan. Add the onion and fry over a low heat until soft, but not coloured. Add the carrots and celery, and cook, stirring frequently, for about 5 minutes.

3 Remove the vegetables from the pan. Heat the remaining oil and cook the pork until it is well sealed. Return the vegetables and pork rind to the pan and pour in the white wine and stock. Season to taste with salt and pepper.

4 Simmer gently for 1½–2 hours until the meat is almost tender. Add the sausage and cabbage, and continue cooking for a further 25–30 minutes. Taste and adjust the seasoning, if necessary, and transfer to a serving dish. Serve hot.

Serves 4–6
Preparation time: 20–25 minutes
Cooking time: 2½–3 hours

braised lamb with celery and onions

3 tablespoons olive oil
2 celery sticks, chopped
375 g/12 oz pickling onions
1 kg/2 lb boned leg or shoulder of lamb, cut into serving pieces
2–3 rosemary sprigs, cut into pieces
2 bay leaves
450 ml/¾ pint Chicken Stock (see page 141)
salt and pepper

1 Heat the oil in a flameproof casserole. Add the celery and onions and fry over a low heat for 5 minutes.

2 Add the meat, half the rosemary and the bay leaves and season to taste with salt and pepper. Fry over a moderate heat until the meat is browned on all sides.

3 Stir in the stock and just enough water to cover the meat. Cover the pan and simmer for 1 hour, or until the meat is tender.

malaysian beef and potato curry p281

pork spare ribs with spicy chilli sauce p250

lamb with couscous   p262

moroccan stuffed baked lamb   p260

sausages with mustard mash   p255

beef bourguignon   p275

roast beef with individual yorkshire puddings   p270

steak, kidney and oyster pudding   p269

4 Remove and discard the herbs. Garnish with the remaining rosemary and serve hot.

Serves 4
Preparation time: 20 minutes
Cooking time: 1½ hours

sardinian lamb with fennel and tomato

5 tablespoons olive oil
1 kg/2 lb boned leg of lamb, cut into serving pieces
1 onion, chopped
425 g/14 oz tomatoes, skinned and mashed
750 g/1½ lb fennel heads, quartered
salt and pepper

1 Heat the oil in a flameproof casserole. Add the meat and fry over a moderate heat until lightly browned on all sides.

2 Stir in the onion and fry for a further 5 minutes. Add the tomatoes and season with salt and pepper to taste.

3 Lower the heat, cover and simmer for 40 minutes, adding a little water if the casserole becomes too dry during cooking.

4 Meanwhile, cook the fennel in boiling salted water for 20 minutes. Drain and reserve 200 ml/7 fl oz of the cooking liquid.

5 Add the fennel and the reserved cooking liquid to the casserole and continue cooking for about 20 minutes until the meat is tender. The casserole should be fairly dry. Serve hot, sprinkled with pepper.

Serves 4
Preparation time: 20 minutes
Cooking time: 1¼ hours

lamb casserole with red wine and herbs

1.25 kg/2½ lb shoulder of lamb, boned and cubed
1 large onion, finely chopped
2 garlic cloves, crushed
2 large tomatoes, skinned, deseeded and quartered
1 bouquet garni, including thyme, parsley, rosemary, marjoram and bay leaf
rind of 1 orange, cut into thin strips
1 bottle of dry red wine
2 tablespoons olive oil
250 g/8 oz streaky bacon, rinded and diced
300 ml/½ pint Chicken Stock (see page 141)
250 g/8 oz plain flour
salt and pepper
boiled rice, to serve

To garnish:
75 g/3 oz small black olives
1 tablespoon chopped parsley

1 Trim any excess fat from the cubed lamb. Put the meat in a large casserole with the onion, garlic, tomatoes, bouquet garni, orange rind, salt to taste and 1 teaspoon pepper. Pour the wine over the top, add the oil and stir well. Cover and leave to marinate in the refrigerator for 4 hours.

2 Blanch the bacon in boiling water for 2 minutes and drain. Add to the casserole with the chicken stock so that the lamb is well covered with liquid. Season with a pinch of salt.

3 Mix the flour with a little water to form a paste, then roll into a thin strip. Press the paste between the casserole dish and lid to form a seal.

4 Cook in a preheated oven, 200°C (400°F), Gas Mark 6, for 1 hour, then reduce the temperature to 180°C (350°F), Gas Mark 4, and cook for a further 2 hours. Discard the strip of flour paste and remove the bouquet garni.

5 Sprinkle the casserole with black olives and garnish with parsley. Serve hot with plain boiled rice.

Serves 4–6
Preparation time: 15 minutes, plus marinating
Cooking time: 3 hours
Oven temperature: 200°C (400°F), Gas Mark 6

rack of lamb

2 lean best ends of neck of lamb, chined
750 g/1½ lb courgettes
200 g/7 oz can sweetcorn, drained
75 g/3 oz fresh wholemeal breadcrumbs
finely grated rind and juice of 1 small orange
4 tablespoons Quark or other soft cream cheese
375 g/12 oz baby corn cobs
1 tablespoon soya or sunflower oil
salt and pepper
rosemary sprigs, to garnish

1 Remove the skin and most of the fat from the surface of the meat, leaving just a thin, even layer of fat. Cut away the meat from the top 3.5 cm/1½ inches of the rib ends and scrape them well. Using a sharp knife, score the surface of the fat in a diamond pattern.

2 Grate 250 g/8 oz of the courgettes by hand or in a food processor and mix with the sweetcorn, breadcrumbs, orange rind and Quark or other soft cheese. Season the mixture with salt and pepper.

3 Shape the mixture into a long roll and place this along the curve of the bones of one joint; place the other joint over the first so that the bones interlock, forming 'crossed swords'. Fasten them firmly with string and wrap the tops of the bones with pieces of foil to prevent them from burning.

4 Place the joint on a rack in a roasting tin. Roast in a preheated oven, 180°C (350°F), Gas Mark 4, for 1¼ hours until the lamb is just tender and still slightly pink in the centre.

5 Meanwhile, cut the remaining courgettes into long sticks about the size of the baby corn cobs. Place the courgettes and corn cobs in a pan with the oil and the orange juice. Sprinkle them with pepper and cover the pan tightly. Cook over a fairly high heat, shaking the pan occasionally, until the vegetables are just tender.

6 Remove the meat from the oven and skim any fat from the juices. Place the meat in the centre of a warmed platter and arrange the vegetables around it. Garnish with sprigs of rosemary. Mix the cooking juices and serve separately as a sauce.

Serves 6
Preparation time: 40–50 minutes
Cooking time: 1¼ hours
Oven temperature: 180°C (350°F), Gas Mark 4

irish stew

1 kg/2 lb neck of lamb, cut into rings about
*   1.5 cm/¾ inch thick*
2 large onions, sliced
1 kg/2 lb floury potatoes, sliced
2 large carrots, sliced
2–3 tablespoons finely chopped parsley
400 ml/13 fl oz Chicken Stock (see page 141) or water
butter, for greasing
salt and pepper

1 Layer the meat and vegetables in a deep saucepan or flameproof casserole dish, finishing with a layer of potatoes. Sprinkle with half the parsley and season between each layer with salt and pepper. Pour over the stock or water and cover tightly with a piece of buttered greaseproof paper. Cover this with foil and a tightly fitting lid.

2 Bring to the boil, then reduce the heat and simmer very gently for 1½–2 hours either on the hob or in a preheated oven, 160°C (325°F), Gas Mark 3, until the meat is tender, the liquid well absorbed and the stew rich and pulpy.

3 If the potatoes are waxy in texture, they will not break down into the liquid. To thicken the juices, remove a few of these slices, mash them and return to the pan. Add the remaining parsley, taste and adjust the seasoning, if necessary, and serve immediately.

Serves 4
Preparation time: 20 minutes
Cooking time: 1½–2 hours
Oven temperature: 160°C (325°F), Gas Mark 3

lamb cutlets with rosemary and lemon

1 rosemary sprig, finely chopped
1 tablespoon olive oil
finely grated rind and juice of 1 lemon
8 lamb cutlets
salt and pepper

1 Mix the rosemary, olive oil and lemon rind and juice in a shallow dish and season with salt and pepper. Add the lamb cutlets and coat with the marinade. Leave to marinate for 10 minutes.

2 Place the cutlets on a grill pan, spoon over the marinade and cook under a preheated very hot grill for 5 minutes on each side.

Serves 4
Preparation time: 5 minutes, plus marinating
Cooking time: 10 minutes

parmesan breaded lamb chops

75 g/3 oz plain flour
8 lamb chops, trimmed
50 g/2 oz Parmesan cheese, freshly grated
50 g/2 oz fresh white breadcrumbs
2 eggs, beaten
2 tablespoons olive oil
salt and pepper
1 lemon, cut into 4 wedges, to garnish

1 Season the flour with salt and pepper. Dip the lamb chops into the seasoned flour, coating them evenly all over. Mix together the Parmesan and breadcrumbs and season with salt and pepper.

2 Dip the cutlets first in the beaten egg and then into the Parmesan mixture and coat all over, pressing the crumbs on to the lamb.

3 Heat the oil in a frying pan. Add the lamb chops and cook for 4 minutes on each side, or until golden. Take care when turning them over; a palette knife is best, so as not to loosen any of the cheesy crust from the chops.

4 Serve immediately, garnished with lemon wedges.

Serves 4
Preparation time: 10 minutes
Cooking time: 10 minutes

mediterranean lamb cakes with salsa verde

500 g/1 lb lean minced lamb
2 garlic cloves, crushed
1 tablespoon freshly grated Parmesan cheese
1 tablespoon chopped pitted olives
1 tablespoon chopped basil
finely grated rind of 1 lemon
1 tablespoon pine nuts, toasted and chopped
1 egg white
green salad, to serve

Salsa verde:
3 tablespoons chopped parsley
2 tablespoons chopped mint
1 tablespoon chopped chives
4 tablespoons olive oil
1 tablespoon chopped capers
3 garlic cloves, crushed
4 tablespoons lemon juice
1 small onion, chopped
1 ripe avocado, peeled, stoned and chopped
dash of Tabasco sauce
sea salt and pepper

1 Place the lamb, garlic, Parmesan, olives, basil, lemon rind, pine nuts and egg white in a bowl and mix well with a fork. Shape with wet hands into 8 even-sized patties.

2 Mix together all the salsa ingredients in a bowl. For a smooth salsa, process the ingredients in a blender or food processor. Taste and adjust the seasoning.

3 Heat a griddle pan or nonstick frying pan. Put on the lamb cakes and cook for 6–8 minutes on each side until charred and firm. Serve with the salsa and a green salad.

Serves 4
Preparation time: 25 minutes
Cooking time: 12–16 minutes

lamb brochettes

500 g/1 lb boned leg of lamb, cubed
8 dried apricots
8 button onions
1 tablespoon chopped mint
lemon wedges, to garnish

Marinade:
300 ml/½ pint natural yogurt
2 tablespoons finely chopped fresh root ginger
1 garlic clove, crushed
1 tablespoon lemon juice
½ teaspoon ground coriander
1 teaspoon ground cumin
pinch of cayenne pepper
salt and pepper

1 Mix all the ingredients for the marinade in a shallow dish large enough to hold all the lamb cubes in a single layer. Season to taste with salt and pepper. Add the lamb cubes and stir until they are well coated. Cover and leave to marinate in a cool place for 6 hours.

2 Meanwhile, put the apricots in a bowl and cover with boiling water. Set aside to soak.

3 Lift the lamb cubes out of the marinade with a slotted spoon. Drain the apricots. Thread the cubes of meat on to skewers alternately with the onions and apricots.

4 Cook the brochettes under a preheated moderately hot grill, turning frequently, for 12–15 minutes.

5 Meanwhile, pour the marinade into a small saucepan and warm gently. Stir in the mint.

6 Serve the brochettes garnished with lemon wedges. Serve the mint sauce separately.

Serves 4
Preparation time: 10 minutes, plus marinating
Cooking time: 12–15 minutes

moroccan stuffed baked lamb

2 kg/4 lb boned leg of lamb
1 onion, cut into thick wedges
3 tablespoons olive oil
8 tablespoons lemon juice

Stuffing:
50 g/2 oz couscous
150 ml/¼ pint boiling water
2 teaspoons coriander seeds
2 teaspoons cumin seeds
1 teaspoon ground cinnamon
3 tablespoons olive oil
50 g/2 oz pine nuts
50 g/2 oz flaked almonds
1 large onion, finely chopped
2 garlic cloves, crushed
1 teaspoon dried mint
4 tablespoons chopped coriander leaves
50 g/2 oz raisins
salt and pepper

1 First, make the stuffing. Put the couscous into a bowl, pour over the boiling water, stir and then leave until the water has been absorbed.

2 Heat a small heavy-based pan. Add the coriander and cumin seeds and heat until fragrant. Grind to a powder, then mix with the cinnamon.

3 Heat 1 tablespoon of the oil in a frying pan. Add the pine nuts and almonds and fry until browned. Transfer to kitchen paper to drain. Add the remaining oil to the pan. When it is hot, add the onion and fry until soft. Stir in the garlic and spice mixture and fry for 2 minutes, then add the nuts, mint, coriander and raisins and season to taste with salt and pepper.

4 Open out the lamb, skin side down, on a work surface. Season inside with pepper, then spread over the stuffing. If possible, tuck the flaps of the piece of lamb over the stuffing. Roll up the lamb into a neat sausage shape and tie securely with string.

5 Preheat the oven to its highest setting. Put the onion wedges into a roasting tin that the lamb will just fit. Put the lamb on the onion and pour over the oil and lemon juice. Bake for 15 minutes, then lower the oven heat to 220°C (425°F), Gas Mark 7 and bake for a further 25 minutes so the lamb is pink in the centre. Remove the lamb from the oven, cover and leave to stand in a warm place for about 15 minutes before carving.

Serves 8–10
Preparation time: 25 minutes, plus standing
Cooking time: 50 minutes–1 hour
Oven temperature: 220°C (425°F), Gas Mark 7

smothered lamb

2 tablespoons olive oil
500 g/1 lb large onions, sliced
5 garlic cloves, crushed
1 tablespoon cumin seeds
2 teaspoons coriander seeds
3 cloves
8 lamb cutlets or small chops
400 g/13 oz can chopped tomatoes
150 ml/¼ pint Chicken or Vegetable Stock
   (see pages 141 and 140) or water
2 tablespoons sun-dried tomato paste
large handful of coriander leaves
salt and pepper

1 Heat the oil in a large frying pan. Add the onions, season with salt and pepper and fry over a low heat until soft and golden. Stir in the garlic when the onions are nearly done.

2 Meanwhile, heat a small, dry heavy-based pan. Add the cumin and coriander seeds and the cloves and fry until fragrant. Grind to a powder. Add the ground spices to the cooked onion mixture and spread half of the onion mixture in a heavy flameproof casserole. Transfer the remainder to a bowl.

3 Brown the chops in the frying pan, then put them in the casserole. Cover with the remaining onions and pour over the tomatoes and their juice.

4 Stir the stock or water into the tomato paste, then add to the casserole. Cover and cook over a low heat for 1 hour until the lamb is tender. Uncover the casserole towards the end of cooking if there is too much liquid. Season with salt and pepper and stir in the coriander leaves just before serving.

Serves 4
Preparation time: 10 minutes
Cooking time: about 1¼ hours

lamb tagine with honeyed prunes

1 kg/2 lb boned shoulder of lamb, cut into
   4 cm/1½ inch cubes
2 Spanish onions, coarsely grated
3 plump garlic cloves, crushed
4 tablespoons olive oil
large pinch of dried chilli flakes
½ teaspoon ground ginger
½ teaspoon ground cumin
½ teaspoon paprika
pinch of crushed saffron threads
2 x 400 g/13 oz cans tomatoes
1 strip of orange rind
2 cinnamon sticks
bunch of coriander, chopped
24 large ready-to-eat prunes
3–4 tablespoons clear honey
75 g/3 oz blanched whole almonds, toasted
pepper
mint leaves, to garnish

1 Put the lamb into a bowl. Add the onions, garlic, oil, chilli flakes, ginger, cumin, paprika, saffron and plenty of pepper. Stir to coat the meat well. Cover and leave to marinate in a cool place for at least 2 hours, or in the refrigerator overnight.

2 Heat a large, heavy-based frying pan. Add the lamb, in batches, and brown evenly. Transfer to a tagine or heavy casserole. Put the marinade into the frying pan and cook, stirring, for 2–3 minutes, then stir into the lamb. Add the tomatoes, orange rind, cinnamon and half of the coriander. Mix well then cover and cook in a preheated oven, 160°C (325°F), Gas Mark 3, for 1¼ hours.

3 Meanwhile, put the prunes into a saucepan with the honey and just enough water to cover and simmer for 10 minutes.

4 Add the prunes and the cooking juices to the tagine and cook for 15 minutes, adding the remaining coriander after about 7 minutes.

5 Serve the tagine with the almonds scattered over and garnished with mint leaves.

Serves 6
Preparation time: 20 minutes, plus marinating
Cooking time: 1¾ hours
Oven temperature: 160°C (325°F), Gas Mark 3

lamb with couscous

500 g/1 lb boneless lean lamb, cut into large cubes
900 ml/1½ pints water
2 onions, quartered and thickly sliced
2 garlic cloves, crushed
pinch of saffron threads, crushed
1 teaspoon ground cinnamon
½ teaspoon paprika
1 fresh red chilli, deseeded and finely chopped
½ teaspoon ground ginger
250 g/8 oz small carrots, quartered lengthways
250 g/8 oz small turnips, quartered
250 g/8 oz kohlrabi or celeriac, cut into large chunks
500 g/1 lb couscous
2 teaspoons olive oil
250 g/8 oz courgettes, quartered lengthways
250 g/8 oz broad beans
4 tomatoes, quartered
large bunch of coriander, chopped
large bunch of parsley, chopped
40 g/1½ oz unsalted butter
salt and pepper

1 Put the lamb into a large saucepan. Add the water, the onions, garlic, saffron, cinnamon, paprika, chilli and ginger and season to taste with salt and pepper. Bring to the boil, remove the scum from the top, cover and simmer very gently for about 30 minutes. Add the carrots, turnips and kohlrabi or celeriac, cover and simmer for 15 minutes.

2 Put the couscous into a large bowl, pour over about 300 ml/½ pint water, stir well and leave for 10 minutes. Add another 300 ml/½ pint water and the oil and fork through the couscous to make sure the grains are separate, then leave for 10 minutes until swollen and tender, but still separate. Put into a steamer and place, uncovered, over a saucepan of boiling water for about 10 minutes.

3 Meanwhile, add the courgettes, broad beans, tomatoes, coriander and parsley to the lamb and cook for a further 5 minutes or until all the vegetables and the lamb are tender.

4 Fork through the couscous to separate the grains, then turn on to a large serving plate. Dot the butter over the top, stir in and season to taste with salt and pepper. Form into a mound with a large well in the centre and place the lamb in the well. Using a slotted spoon, lift the vegetables from the cooking broth and place on and around the lamb. Serve the remaining broth in a separate warm bowl.

Serves 4
Preparation time: 15 minutes, plus soaking
Cooking time: 1 hour

lamb shanks in red juices

about 4 tablespoons olive oil
2 lamb shanks
2 small aubergines, halved lengthways and thickly sliced
2 large onions, sliced
4 garlic cloves, crushed
1 cinnamon stick
400 g/13 oz can chopped tomatoes
2 tablespoons sun-dried tomato paste
2 teaspoons harissa
salt and pepper

1 Heat 2 tablespoons of the oil in a heavy flameproof casserole. Add the lamb and brown evenly. Remove to a plate with a slotted spoon.

2 Add the remaining oil to the casserole and brown the aubergines, in batches, adding more oil if necessary. Using a slotted spoon, transfer the aubergines to a plate.

3 Lower the heat slightly then add the onions and garlic to the casserole and cook until soft and lightly browned. Stir in the cinnamon stick, tomatoes, tomato paste and harissa, then return the lamb and aubergines to the casserole. Add enough water to come almost to the top of the shanks. Heat to just on simmering point, cover tightly and cook over a very low heat for 1½–2 hours until the lamb is very tender.

4 Lift the lamb on to a warmed plate. Remove as much fat as possible from the top of the cooking juices. Boil the juices in the casserole until thickened and the flavour concentrated to your liking, season well, then spoon around the lamb.

Serves 2
Preparation time: 5 minutes
Cooking time: about 2–2¼ hours

saffron stuffed shoulder of lamb

300 ml/½ pint water
10 saffron threads
40 g/1½ oz long-grain rice
125 g/4 oz butter
1 onion, finely chopped
6 ready-to-eat prunes, chopped
50 g/2 oz walnut halves, chopped
1 teaspoon chopped fresh or dried mint
1 egg, beaten
2 kg/4 lb shoulder of lamb, boned
2 garlic cloves, sliced lengthways
2 tablespoons plain flour
300 ml/½ pint Chicken Stock (see page 141)
150 ml/¼ pint wine
salt and pepper

1 Pour the water into a saucepan, add the saffron and a pinch of salt and bring to the boil. Add the rice, lower the heat and simmer for 15–20 minutes until all the water has evaporated and the rice is tender.

2 Meanwhile, melt 25 g/1 oz of the butter in a small saucepan. Add the onion and fry gently until translucent, but do not allow it to brown. Stir in the prunes, walnuts and mint.

3 Tip the saffron rice into a bowl, add the prune mixture, bind with the beaten egg and season to taste with salt and pepper.

4 Stuff the lamb with the mixture, then roll up and secure with butcher's string at 5 cm/2 inch intervals. Make diagonal slits in the skin on the top of the meat, and slip a slice of garlic into each one.

5 Place the plain flour in one end of the roasting tin and put in the meat with one of its cut edges resting on it. The flour will soak up the meat juices during cooking, both thickening and giving extra flavour to the gravy. Smear the remaining butter over the lamb and roast in a preheated oven, 180°C (350°F), Gas Mark 4, basting occasionally, for 2 hours.

6 Remove the meat to a serving platter and keep warm. Pour off two-thirds of the fat from the roasting tin into a small bowl, then place the roasting tin over a low heat. Stir well with a flat spoon to incorporate the flour and the fat and cook for 2–3 minutes. Pour in the stock and wine and bring to the boil. Lower the heat and simmer for 5 minutes. Season to taste with salt and pepper, strain and serve in a sauceboat with the meat.

Serves 6
Preparation time: 10 minutes
Cooking time: 2½ hours
Oven temperature: 180°C (350°F), Gas Mark 4

minted lamb with watercress stuffing

50 g/2 oz butter
1 onion, finely chopped
2 celery sticks, finely chopped
1 bunch of watercress, finely chopped
1½ tablespoons mint jelly
125 g/4 oz fresh white breadcrumbs
1 egg, beaten
1.75 kg/3½ lb shoulder of lamb, boned
1 tablespoon vegetable oil
salt and pepper
mint sprigs, to garnish

1 Melt half the butter in a saucepan. Add the onion and celery and cook over a low heat for 3 minutes. Add the watercress to the pan and cook for a further 3 minutes. Add the remaining butter and heat until melted. Remove from the heat, stir in 1½ teaspoons of the mint jelly, together with the breadcrumbs, egg and salt and pepper to taste. Leave to cool.

2 Use the mixture to stuff the cavity in the lamb. Shape the lamb into a neat round and tie securely with string. Weigh the joint and calculate the cooking time at 20 minutes per 500 g/1 lb, plus 30 minutes.

3 Heat the oil in a roasting tin, add the lamb and season with salt and pepper. Roast in a preheated oven, 190°C (375°F), Gas Mark 5, for all but 15 minutes of the calculated cooking time.

4 Remove the lamb from the oven, cut away the string and brush the meat with the remaining mint jelly. Return to the oven for a further 15 minutes. Transfer to a warmed serving dish, garnish with mint and serve hot. Alternatively, allow to cool and serve cold.

Serves 6–8
Preparation time: 15 minutes
Cooking time: about 2 hours
Oven temperature: 190°C (375°F), Gas Mark 5

oriental lamb

3 tablespoons vegetable oil
500 g/1 lb lamb fillet, cut into thin strips across the grain
3 spring onions, thinly sliced diagonally
1 garlic clove, crushed
1 small red pepper, cored, deseeded and cut lengthways
  into thin strips
1 small yellow pepper, cored, deseeded and cut
  lengthways into thin strips
2 courgettes, thinly sliced on the diagonal
225 g/7½ oz can water chestnuts, drained, rinsed and
  thinly sliced
pepper

Sauce:
2 teaspoons cornflour
4 tablespoons water
2 tablespoons soy sauce

1 First, prepare the sauce. Mix the cornflour to a thin paste with the water, then stir in the soy sauce. Cover and set aside.

2 Heat 2 tablespoons of the oil in a preheated wok or frying pan. Add the lamb strips, increase the heat to high and stir-fry for 3–4 minutes, or until the lamb is browned on all sides. Tip the lamb and its juices into a bowl and set aside.

3 Heat the remaining oil over a moderate heat. Add the spring onions, garlic and peppers and stir-fry for 3–4 minutes. Add the courgettes and stir-fry for a further 2 minutes.

4 Return the lamb and its juices to the wok, then add the water chestnuts. Stir the sauce to mix, pour into the wok and increase the heat to high. Toss for 2–3 minutes, or until all the ingredients are combined and the lamb is piping hot. season with pepper to taste and serve immediately.

Serves 4
Preparation time: 15 minutes
Cooking time: 15 minutes

braised lamb with soy and mandarin sauce

2 large oranges
4 lamb leg steaks
about 1 tablespoon oil
6 spring onions, shredded
150 ml/¼ pint Chicken Stock (see page 141)
25 g/1 oz brown sugar
salt and pepper

1 Thinly pare the rind from the oranges with a potato peeler. Shred the rind finely, blanch in boiling water for 5 minutes and drain.

2 Sprinkle the lamb with salt and pepper. Heat the oil in a preheated wok or frying pan. Add the lamb and fry until browned on both sides. Remove from the wok.

3 Add the onions to the wok and fry for 3 minutes. Place the lamb on top of the onions. Add the juice squeezed from the oranges, the stock, brown sugar, orange rind shreds and salt and pepper to taste. Cover with the lid and braise over a low heat for 40 minutes, or until the lamb is tender.

Serves 4
Preparation time: 15 minutes
Cooking time: 55 minutes

spring lamb stir-fried with garlic and sesame oil

375 g/12 oz lamb fillet
2 tablespoons dry sherry
2 tablespoons light soy sauce
1 tablespoon dark soy sauce
1 teaspoon sesame oil
2 tablespoons oil
6 garlic cloves, thinly sliced
2.5 cm/1 inch piece of fresh root ginger, chopped
1 leek, thinly sliced diagonally
4 spring onions, chopped

1 Cut the lamb into thin slices across the grain. Mix the sherry with the soy sauces and sesame oil. Add the lamb and toss to coat. Leave to marinate for 15 minutes.

2 Drain the lamb, reserving the marinade. Heat the oil in a preheated wok or deep frying pan. Add the meat and about 2 teaspoons of the marinade and fry briskly for about 2 minutes until well browned.

3 Add the garlic, ginger, leek and spring onions and fry for a further 3 minutes. Serve at once.

Serves 4
Preparation time: 10 minutes, plus marinating
Cooking time: 5 minutes

indian lamb kebabs

Mango powder, also known as aamchoor, *is a sour-tasting powder made from raw mangoes. It is sold in jars in specialist Indian food stores.*

750 g/1½ lb lean minced lamb
1 teaspoon grated fresh root ginger
1 large onion, finely chopped
25 g/1 oz chickpea or gram flour (besan)
2 fresh green chillies, finely chopped
1 teaspoon green mango powder
1 tablespoon salt
2 tablespoons lemon juice
1 egg
2 tablespoons chopped coriander leaves
50 g/2 oz melted ghee or 1 tablespoon vegetable oil
lime wedges, to garnish

Spices:
½ teaspoon poppy seeds, roasted and ground
1 teaspoon garam masala
1 tablespoon yellow or red chilli powder
½ teaspoon pepper
1 teaspoon black cumin seeds, roasted and ground
1 tablespoon ground coriander seeds

1 Mix the minced lamb, ginger, onion, chickpea or gram flour, chillies, mango powder, salt and lemon juice together with all the spices. Set aside for 30 minutes to allow the flavours to develop.

2 Work the egg and chopped coriander into the minced meat mixture. Continue kneading the mixture until it becomes sticky.

3 Divide the minced meat mixture into 18 equal-sized portions and then form each piece between your hands into a sausage shape. Thread the 'sausages' on to skewers. For longer kebabs, flatten them out on the skewers.

4 Cook under a preheated hot grill or over charcoal, turning frequently. Brush the kebabs with melted ghee or oil while they are cooking. Serve hot, garnished with lime wedges.

Serves 6
Preparation time: 30 minutes, plus standing
Cooking time: 20 minutes

roghan ghosht

4 tablespoons oil
2 onions, finely chopped
750 g/1½ lb boned leg of lamb, cubed
300 ml/½ pint natural yogurt
2 garlic cloves
2.5 cm/1 inch piece of fresh root ginger
2 fresh green chillies
1 tablespoon coriander seeds
1 teaspoon cumin seeds
1 teaspoon chopped mint leaves
1 teaspoon chopped coriander leaves
6 cardamoms
6 cloves
2.5 cm/1 inch piece of cinnamon stick
125 g/4 oz flaked almonds
salt

1 Heat 2 tablespoons of the oil in a pan. Add half of the onions and fry until golden. Add the lamb and all but 2 tablespoons of the yogurt, stir well, cover and simmer for 20 minutes.

2 Place the garlic, ginger, chillies, coriander seeds, cumin seeds, mint, fresh coriander and the remaining yogurt in a blender or food processor and process to a paste.

3 Heat the remaining oil in a large saucepan. Add the cardamoms, cloves and cinnamon and fry, stirring, for 1 minute. Add the remaining onion and the prepared paste and fry, stirring constantly, for 5 minutes.

4 Add the lamb and yogurt mixture and season to taste with salt. Stir well and bring to simmering point. Cover and cook for 30 minutes. Add the almonds and cook for a further 15 minutes until the meat is tender.

Serves 4
Preparation time: 30 minutes
Cooking time: 1¼ hours

lamb dhansak

50 g/2 oz red lentils
50 g/2 oz chickpeas
50 g/2 oz moong dhal
750 g/1½ lb lamb fillet, cut into 5 cm/2 inch cubes
300 g/10 oz aubergine, cubed
250 g/8 oz pumpkin, cubed
125 g/4 oz potato, cubed
2 onions, roughly chopped
2 tomatoes, skinned and chopped
75 g/3 oz fresh spinach
3 tablespoons ghee or vegetable oil
1 large onion, thinly sliced
2 tablespoons tomato purée
salt and pepper
deep-fried onion slices, to garnish
boiled rice, to serve

Masala mixture:
3 fresh red chillies, deseeded and chopped
3 fresh green chillies, deseeded and chopped
6 garlic cloves, crushed
2.5 cm/1 inch piece of fresh root ginger, finely chopped
25 g/1 oz coriander leaves
15 g/½ oz mint leaves
4 tablespoons water

Dry spice mixture:
2 teaspoons turmeric
1 teaspoon black mustard seeds
½ teaspoon ground cinnamon
¼ teaspoon fenugreek powder
2 tablespoons ground cumin
4 cardamoms, crushed

1 Soak the lentils, chickpeas and moong dhal overnight in separate bowls of cold water.

2 The next day, drain the pulses and place them in a large saucepan with the lamb. Pour over enough boiling water to cover the lentils and meat and season generously with salt. Bring to the boil, skim any scum from the surface, then cover and simmer, stirring occasionally, for about 20 minutes.

3 Tip all the prepared vegetables into the pan, stir and continue cooking for a further 40 minutes until the lentils and vegetables are cooked and the lamb is tender. Drain the liquid from the pan and reserve. Remove the pieces of meat with a slotted spoon. Set the meat aside and tip the vegetables and lentils into a blender or food processor. Process to a thick purée.

4 Heat the ghee or oil in a large heavy-based sauté pan and fry the onion over a low heat for 5 minutes until it is softened and golden.

5 Place all the masala ingredients in a food processor and process to a paste. Add this paste to the softened onion and cook gently for a further 3 minutes. Stir in the dry spice mixture and cook, stirring, for 3 minutes.

6 Add the lamb and vegetable purée to the pan, together with the tomato purée and reserved cooking liquid. Season, cover and simmer for 30 minutes until thick. If it becomes too dry, add a little water. Taste and adjust the seasoning if necessary. Transfer to a warmed serving dish, garnish with fried onions and serve with rice.

Serves 6
Preparation time: 30 minutes, plus soaking
Cooking time: 1¾ hours

balti lamb madras

1 tablespoon vegetable oil
1 onion, chopped
2 garlic cloves, crushed
2 fresh green chillies, deseeded and sliced
2 teaspoons chilli powder
2 teaspoons garam masala
500 g/1 lb lean lamb, cut into 3.5 cm/1½ inch cubes
1 tablespoon vinegar
1 teaspoon salt
2 tomatoes, skinned, deseeded and chopped
1 tablespoon coconut flakes, to garnish

1 Heat the oil in a preheated wok or heavy-based frying pan. Add the onion, garlic, chillies and chilli powder and stir-fry for 2 minutes. Add the garam masala, cubed lamb, vinegar, salt and chopped tomatoes. Stir the mixture thoroughly.

2 Cover the wok and cook over a moderate heat for 30–40 minutes until the lamb is tender, adding a little water if it appears to be sticking to the base of the wok.

3 Transfer to a warmed serving dish, scatter with the coconut flakes and serve immediately.

Serves 4
Preparation time: 10 minutes
Cooking time: 35–45 minutes

lamb with yogurt

4 tablespoons oil
3 onions, finely chopped
6 cardamom pods
5 cm/2 inch piece of cinnamon stick
4½ teaspoons ground coriander
2 teaspoons ground cumin
½ teaspoon turmeric
½ teaspoon ground cloves
1–2 teaspoons chilli powder
½ teaspoon grated nutmeg
1 tablespoon paprika
300 g/10 oz natural yogurt
750 g/1½ lb boned leg of lamb, cubed
1 large tomato, skinned and chopped
salt
fennel sprigs, to garnish

1 Heat the oil in a large saucepan. Add the onions, cardamom and cinnamon and fry for about 5 minutes.

2 Stir in the coriander, cumin, turmeric, cloves, chilli powder and nutmeg and fry until dry, then add 2 tablespoons water and cook, stirring, for 5 minutes, adding a little more water if necessary.

3 Add the paprika and gradually stir in the yogurt. Add the lamb, tomato and salt to taste and mix well. Bring to simmering point, cover and cook for 1 hour or until tender. Garnish with the fennel sprigs to serve.

Serves 4
Preparation time: 15 minutes
Cooking time: 1¼ hours

malabar lamb curry

3 tablespoons oil or ghee
2 onions, finely chopped
1 teaspoon turmeric
1 tablespoon ground coriander
1 teaspoon ground cumin
2 teaspoons chilli powder
½ teaspoon ground cloves
12 curry leaves
750 g/1½ lb boned leg of lamb, cubed
1 tablespoon coarsely grated coconut
300 ml/½ pint water
1 teaspoon salt

1 Heat the oil or ghee in a saucepan. Add the onions and fry until golden. Stir in the turmeric, coriander, cumin, chilli powder, cloves and curry leaves and fry for 1–2 minutes.

2 Add the lamb and coconut and fry, stirring, until well browned. Pour in the water and add the salt. Cover and simmer for 45 minutes or until the lamb is tender.

3 Transfer to a warmed serving dish and serve immediately.

Serves 4
Preparation time: 5 minutes
Cooking time: 55 minutes

fillet steak wrapped in parma ham

handful of chopped marjoram
2 garlic cloves, finely chopped
4 x 175 g/6 oz fillet steaks
8 slices of Parma ham
125 g/4 oz buffalo mozzarella, cut into 4 slices
salt and pepper

1 Mix together the marjoram and garlic and season with salt and pepper. Coat the steaks with the herb mixture, then wrap them in the Parma ham. Make sure that all the steak is covered with the ham.

2 Put the steaks on a greased grill rack and place under a preheated very hot grill, as close to the heat as possible without burning them. Cook on each side for 3 minutes if you like your steak rare, 5–6 minutes for medium and 8 minutes for well done.

3 Place the slices of mozzarella on the steaks, return to the grill and cook until the mozzarella is melting and just turning golden.

4 Remove the steaks from the grill and leave to rest for 5 minutes before serving. This allows the meat to relax.

Serves 4
Preparation time: 10 minutes
Cooking time: 8 minutes

fillet steak baked in pastry

40 g/1½ oz butter
1 tablespoon oil
2 small onions, finely chopped
1 garlic clove, crushed
125 g/4 oz mushrooms, finely chopped
pinch of ground nutmeg
4 x 175 g/6 oz fillet steaks, trimmed
250 g/8 oz frozen puff pastry, defrosted
1 tablespoon plain flour, for dusting
1 egg, beaten
4 slices of ham
salt and pepper
chervil or parsley sprigs, to garnish

1 Heat 25 g/1 oz of the butter and the oil in a frying pan. Add the onions and garlic and fry over a low heat until soft. Add the mushrooms and nutmeg, season to taste with salt and pepper and stir over a gentle heat.

2 Melt the remaining butter in a clean frying pan. Add the fillet steaks and then sear quickly on both sides. Remove from the pan, cool quickly and keep chilled until required.

3 Roll out the pastry on a lightly floured surface and cut into 8 rounds large enough to half cover the steaks. Brush a 2.5 cm/1 inch border around the edge of each pastry round with beaten egg. Cut the ham into 8 rounds the same size as the steaks.

4 Place 1 piece of ham on each of 4 pastry rounds. Cover the ham with a portion of the mushroom mixture, a fillet steak, another portion of mushrooms and another round of ham. Top with a pastry round. Seal the edges of the pastry between your fingers and then with a fork.

5 Cut any pastry trimmings into leaves and use to decorate. Brush with beaten egg and cook in a preheated oven, 220°C (425°F), Gas Mark 7, for 20 minutes until golden brown. Garnish with chervil or parsley sprigs.

Serves 4
Preparation time: 30 minutes
Cooking time: 30–35 minutes
Oven temperature: 220°C (425°F), Gas Mark 7

thin steak on a bed of hot leaves

4 x 175 g/6 oz entrecôte steaks
8 tablespoons olive oil
4 tablespoons lemon juice
2 tablespoons red wine vinegar
250 g/8 oz mixed hot salad leaves
sea salt and pepper

1 Spread out a piece of greaseproof paper, place a steak in the middle and cover with another piece of paper. Using a rolling pin or meat mallet, gently beat the steak until it is at least twice its original size. Repeat with the other steaks.

2 Mix together the olive oil, lemon juice, red wine vinegar and seasoning. Pour over the leaves and toss well. Divide the salad leaves between 4 large plates.

3 Heat a griddle pan or nonstick frying pan until very hot. Season the steaks on both sides, place on the griddle and flash-cook on both sides just long enough to sear the meat. Place the steaks on the salad leaves and serve immediately.

Serves 4
Preparation time: 15 minutes
Cooking time: 10 minutes

steak, kidney and oyster pudding

Pastry:
butter, for greasing
250 g/8 oz suet, shredded
500 g/1 lb plain flour, plus extra for dusting
50 g/2 oz fresh white breadcrumbs
pinch of salt
300 ml/½ pint cold water

Filling:
2 tablespoons plain flour, seasoned
1.5 kg/3 lb rump steak trimmed and cut into
*   2.5 cm/1 inch cubes*
500 g/1 lb ox kidney, chopped
1 small onion, grated
2 teaspoons Worcestershire sauce
2 teaspoons chopped parsley
6 oysters, fresh or canned
600 ml/1 pint Beef Stock (see page 141)
salt and pepper

1 Grease a 2.4 litre/4 pint pudding basin. To make the pastry, mix together all the dry ingredients, then add the water slowly, to make a smooth, pliable dough.

2 Turn the dough on to a floured surface and roll out. Reserve enough to cover the top of the pudding. Cut a strip long enough to line the basin sides, plus a round for the bottom. Press to seal the edges together.

3 To make the filling, sift the flour on to a plate, then roll the meat and onion in it and put into the lined basin.

4 Add salt, pepper, the Worcestershire sauce, parsley and oysters and mix in carefully. Add the stock, which should not come higher than 2.5 cm/1 inch from the top. Roll out the remaining suet crust to fit the top. Moisten the edge and lay it on, pressing down at the rim.

5 Cover with buttered greaseproof paper or aluminium foil pleated across the middle to allow the pudding to rise. Tie securely and place in the top of a steamer or in a deep saucepan.

6 Pour in boiling water. If the pudding is in a saucepan, do not let the water come above the rim of the basin. Put the lid on the saucepan or steamer and cook for 4–5 hours, topping up the water as necessary. Longer cooking will only improve the pudding. To serve, remove the paper or foil and wrap the basin in a napkin or folded tea towel.

Serves 6–8
Preparation time: 45 minutes
Cooking time: 4–5 hours

roast beef with individual yorkshire puddings

1 roasting joint of beef
Dijon or French mustard
1 quantity Basic Batter (see page 126)
pepper

1 Check the weight of the joint, and calculate cooking time. Place the meat in a roasting tin, season with pepper and coat with mustard.

2 To fast-roast the beef, preheat the oven to 220°C (425°F), Gas Mark 7. Allow 15 minutes per 500 g/1 lb plus 15 minutes for rare beef; 20 minutes per 500 g/1 lb plus 20 minutes for medium-cooked beef; 25 minutes per 500 g/1 lb plus 25 minutes for well-cooked beef. Reduce the heat to 190°C (375°°F), Gas Mark 5, after the first hour's cooking.

3 To slow-roast the beef, preheat the oven to 180°C (350°F), Gas Mark 4. Allow 25 minutes per 500 g/1 lb plus 25 minutes for medium-cooked beef and 35 minutes per 500 g/1 lb plus 35 minutes for well-cooked beef. Reduce the heat to 160°C (325°F), Gas Mark 3 after 1½ hours. (Slow-roasting is not recommended for cooking rare beef.)

4 When it is cooked, remove the beef from the oven to rest. Heat the oven to 230°C (450°F), Gas Mark 8. Grease 12 deep patty tins and heat well in the oven. Beat the batter and pour it into the patty tins. Cook for 10–12 minutes until well risen. Reduce the oven temperature to the original setting. Return the meat. Continue cooking for 8–15 minutes at the higher temperature or 15–20 minutes at the lower temperature.

5 Remove the meat and puddings. Transfer to a serving dish and serve with gravy made from the meat juices.

Makes 12 Yorkshire puddings
Preparation time: 20–25 minutes
Cooking time and oven temperature: see above

beef and guinness stew

50 g/2 oz plain flour
1 kg/2 lb topside of beef, cut into 2.5cm/1 inch cubes
2 tablespoons oil
1 large onion, sliced
1 large carrot, thickly sliced
300 ml/½ pint Guinness
750 ml/1¼ pints water
1 bay leaf
125 g/4 oz pitted prunes, soaked in water
salt and pepper
2 tablespoons finely chopped parsley, to garnish
baked potatoes, to serve

1 Season the flour with salt and pepper and toss the meat in the flour. Heat the oil in a large saucepan or casserole. Add the beef cubes and fry until browned all over. Add the onion and cook for a few minutes, then stir in any remaining flour.

2 Add the carrot, Guinness and water, stirring well to combine. Bring to the boil, add the bay leaf, cover and simmer gently for 1½–2 hours until the meat is tender. Alternatively cook in a preheated oven, 160°C (325°F), Gas Mark 3, for the same length of time. Half an hour before the end of the cooking time, add the prunes.

3 Remove the bay leaf, taste and adjust the seasoning if necessary, sprinkle with the parsley and serve with baked potatoes.

Serves 4
Preparation time: 20–30 minutes
Cooking time: 1½–2 hours
Oven temperature: 160°C (325°F),Gas Mark 3

irish meatloaf

50 g/2 oz butter
25 g/1 oz fresh white breadcrumbs, toasted in the oven
  until dry and golden brown
1 small onion, finely chopped
500 g/1 lb minced beef
125 g/4 oz white breadcrumbs
1 tablespoon tomato ketchup
1 teaspoon Worcestershire sauce
1 teaspoon crushed juniper berries
1 tablespoon finely chopped chives
1 tablespoon finely chopped parsley
1 teaspoon finely chopped oregano
1 egg, beaten
salt and pepper
Quick Tomato Sauce (see page 147), to serve

1 Grease a 19 x 9 x 5.5 cm/7½ x 3¾ x 2¼ inch loaf tin
with half the butter and dust with the browned
breadcrumbs.

2 Heat the remaining butter in a saucepan. Add the
onion and fry until soft, then add the beef and continue
to cook until browning. Stir in the remaining ingredients
and pack tightly into the prepared tin.

3 Cover the tin with foil and bake in a preheated oven,
190°C (375°F), Gas Mark 5, for 1–1½ hours until firm to
the touch. Leave to rest for 10–15 minutes before
turning out.

4 Serve cut in slices either hot or cold. Quick tomato
sauce is a tasty accompaniment.

Serves 4
Preparation time: 15–20 minutes
Cooking time: 1–1¼ hours
Oven temperature: 190°C (375°F), Gas Mark 5

mustard beef casserole

750 g/1½ lb lean braising steak, cubed
1 tablespoon seasoned wholemeal flour
2 tablespoons sunflower oil
1 large onion, sliced
4 carrots, sliced
300 ml/½ pint beer
4 tablespoons Beef Stock (see page 141)

3 teaspoons wholegrain mustard
1 teaspoon softened butter or margarine
½ French bread stick, sliced
salt and pepper
chopped fresh parsley, to garnish

1 Toss the meat in the seasoned flour. Heat the oil in a
flameproof casserole, add the onion and fry gently for
5 minutes. Add the meat and cook until browned.

2 Stir in the carrots, then add the beer and stock. Stir in
2 teaspoons of the mustard and season to taste with salt
and pepper. Bring to the boil, cover and cook in a
preheated oven, 180°C (350°F), Gas Mark 4, for
1½ hours.

3 Meanwhile, blend the remaining mustard with the
softened butter or margarine in a small bowl. Spread the
mustard mixture over the slices of bread. Remove the
casserole from the oven and place the bread on top,
mustard side up. Return to the oven and cook,
uncovered, for 20 minutes. Garnish with the parsley
and serve.

Serves 4
Preparation time: 10 minutes
Cooking time: about 2 hours
Oven temperature: 180°C (350°F), Gas Mark 4

beef wellington

1 kg/2 lb fillet of beef, trimmed
40 g/1½ oz butter, softened
1 onion, finely chopped
250 g/8 oz mushrooms, chopped
400 g/13 oz frozen puff pastry, defrosted
beaten egg, to glaze
salt and pepper
watercress sprigs, to garnish

1 Pat the beef dry with kitchen paper and spread with
15 g/½ oz of the butter. Place in a roasting tin and roast
in a preheated oven, 190°C (375°F), Gas Mark 5,
basting occasionally, for 40 minutes. Remove and cool.

2 Melt the remaining butter in a saucepan. Add the
onion and cook gently for 5 minutes until softened. Add
the mushrooms and cook for about 15 minutes until
most of the liquid has evaporated. Remove from the
heat, season to taste with salt and pepper and leave
until cold.

3 Roll out the pastry to a rectangle large enough to enclose the fillet of beef. Carefully place the pastry on a baking sheet. Spread half the mushroom mixture down the centre of the pastry. Place the beef on top, then top with the remaining mushroom mixture. Brush the edges of the pastry with egg and wrap the pastry around the meat, pressing the long edges together firmly and tucking in the short ends to seal. Use the trimmings to make pastry leaves to decorate.

4 Brush the pastry all over with beaten egg, then cook in a preheated oven, 230°C (450°F), Gas Mark 8, for about 40 minutes; cover with foil for the last 10 minutes so the pastry stays golden brown. Transfer to a serving dish, garnish with watercress sprigs, then slice and serve.

Serves 4–6
Preparation time: 15 minutes
Cooking time: 1¾ hours
Oven temperature: 190°C (375°F), Gas Mark 5

beef with celery

2 tablespoons vegetable oil
500 g/1 lb braising steak, cut into 2.5 cm/1 inch cubes
15 g/½ oz butter or margarine
2 onions, chopped
1 carrot, diced
1 tablespoon plain flour
300 ml/½ pint Beef Stock (see page 141)
4 celery sticks, sliced into 2.5 cm/1 inch lengths
½ teaspoon dried mixed herbs
1 tablespoon soured cream
50 g/2 oz walnuts, chopped
salt and pepper

1 Heat the oil in a large frying pan. Add the beef and fry over a moderately high heat, turning occasionally, for 3–4 minutes to seal. Using a slotted spoon, transfer the meat to a casserole.

2 Add the butter or margarine to the oil remaining in the frying pan. When melted, add the onions and carrot and fry gently for 5 minutes until softened. Sprinkle in the flour and cook, stirring, for a further 1–2 minutes, then gradually add the stock and season with plenty of salt and pepper.

3 Pour the contents of the pan over the meat and stir in the celery and herbs. Cover and cook in a preheated oven, 150°C (300°F), Gas Mark 2, for 1½–1¾ hours, or until the beef is tender.

4 Just before serving, swirl the soured cream over the top and sprinkle with the walnuts.

Serves 4
Preparation time: 10 minutes
Cooking time: 1¾–2 hours
Oven temperature: 150°C (300°F), Gas Mark 2

pot-roast of beef

4 tablespoons vegetable oil
25 g/1 oz butter
1.25–1.5 kg/2½–3 lb topside or silverside of beef
2 large onions, quartered
2 large carrots, cut into 1 cm/½ inch slices
1 bouquet garni or 2 sprigs each of thyme, parsley and marjoram
4 black peppercorns
½ teaspoon salt
150 ml/¼ pint red wine mixed with 450 ml/¾ pint water
2 teaspoons cornflour

1 Heat the oil and butter in a flameproof casserole. Add the beef and turn until browned.

2 Reduce the heat and pack the vegetables all around the beef. Add the herbs, peppercorns and salt. Pour in the wine and water. Cover the casserole closely with foil, then the lid and cook in a preheated oven, 150°C (300°F), Gas Mark 2, for 3 hours until the beef is tender and cooked through.

3 Transfer the beef to a warmed serving dish. Discard the herbs. Lift out the vegetables with a slotted spoon and place around the beef. Keep hot while making the sauce.

4 Bring the cooking liquid in the casserole to the boil. Mix the cornflour with a little water to make a smooth paste, pour a little of the boiling gravy on to it, stirring well and pour back into the boiling gravy in the casserole, stirring constantly. If the sauce is too thick, thin with a little stock or water and return to the boil. Pour the sauce over the beef and vegetables and serve.

Serves 6
Preparation time: 30 minutes
Cooking time: about 3¼ hours
Oven temperature: 150°C (300°F), Gas Mark 2

braised beef with cheese dumplings

4 tablespoons vegetable oil
2 onions, sliced
750 g/1½ lb stewing beef, cubed
4 teaspoons plain flour
1 teaspoon brown sugar
pinch of cinnamon
300 ml/½ pint brown ale
salt and pepper

Dumplings:
125 g/4 oz self-raising flour
50 g/2 oz suet, shredded, or margarine, melted
25 g/1 oz Cheddar cheese, grated
2–3 tablespoons water
salt and pepper

1 Heat the oil in a frying pan. Add the onions and fry over a low heat until soft, then transfer to a casserole. Brown the beef quickly on all sides in the pan, then add the flour and let it cook for 1 minute, stirring.

2 Add the sugar and cinnamon and gradually pour in the brown ale. Stir well, then season with salt and pepper to taste.

3 Put the meat and gravy into the casserole, cover and cook in a preheated oven, 180°C (350°F), Gas Mark 4, for 30 minutes. Then reduce the oven temperature to 160°C (325°F), Gas Mark 3, and continue cooking for 1 further hour.

4 To make the dumplings, mix the dry ingredients together, season with salt and pepper and gradually add the water. Add a little more if needed to make a fairly slack dough. Flour the hands and break the dough into 8 small pieces, then roll into little balls with the palms of the hands. Chill until required.

5 Test the meat with a fork after 1½ hours' cooking time. If necessary, cook for a further 30 minutes. If the casserole is dry, add some water or beer.

6 Place the dumplings on top of the casserole about 20 minutes before the meat is ready and cook, uncovered, for about 20–30 minutes until they are risen. Alternatively, poach the dumplings, about 4 at a time, in a saucepan of boiling salted water for about 15 minutes. Drain well and serve with the meat.

Serves 4–6
Preparation time: 30 minutes
Cooking time: about 2 hours
Oven temperature: 180°C (350°F), Gas Mark 4

beef braised in red wine

1.5 kg/3 lb beef topside or rolled silverside
25 g/1 oz bacon fat or dripping
1 onion, finely chopped
1 rosemary sprig
salt and pepper
puréed potatoes and carrots, to serve

Marinade:
1 onion, sliced
1 carrot, sliced
1 celery stick, sliced
2 garlic cloves, crushed
2 bay leaves
6 peppercorns
600 ml/1 pint Barolo or other red wine

1 First, marinate the beef. Put the meat in a deep bowl and add the onion, carrot, celery, garlic, bay leaves, peppercorns and red wine. Cover the bowl and place in the refrigerator to marinate for 24 hours, turning the beef several times. Lift the meat out of the marinade and dry it carefully. Reserve the marinade.

2 Heat the bacon fat or dripping in a large flameproof casserole. Add the chopped onion and fry over a low heat for about 5 minutes, or until it is soft and golden. Add the beef, increase the heat and brown quickly on all sides.

3 Strain the reserved marinade into the casserole and bring to the boil. Add the rosemary and season to taste with salt and pepper. Lower the heat, cover tightly and simmer gently for at least 3 hours, or until the meat is tender. Turn the meat once halfway through cooking.

4 Transfer the meat to a carving dish or board and slice fairly thickly. Arrange the slices on a warmed serving dish. If the sauce is too thin, reduce a little by rapid boiling. Remove and discard the rosemary and pour the sauce over the meat. Serve immediately with puréed potatoes and carrots.

Serves 6
Preparation time: 10 minutes, plus marinating
Cooking time: 3–3½ hours

stuffed beef olives

1 kg/2 lb beef topside
125 g/4 oz pecorino cheese, grated
2 slices of Parma ham, chopped
3 garlic cloves, crushed
3 tablespoons chopped parsley
1 tablespoon chopped basil
3 tablespoons olive oil
salt and pepper
torn basil leaves, to garnish

Tomato sauce:
1 onion, chopped
2 garlic cloves, crushed
1 kg/2 lb tomatoes, skinned and chopped
1 tablespoon tomato purée
125 ml/4 fl oz red wine

1 Cut the beef into thin slices and place between 2 sheets of greaseproof paper. Flatten them with a rolling pin and then season with salt and pepper.

2 To make the filling, put the grated pecorino in a bowl with the chopped ham, garlic, parsley and basil. Mix well together and spread a little of this mixture on to each slice of beef. Roll up, folding in the sides, and secure with cotton or fine string.

3 Heat the olive oil in a large saucepan. Add the beef rolls and fry over a low heat until they are slightly brown all over, turning as necessary. Remove from the pan and keep warm.

4 Finally, make the sauce. Add the onion and garlic to the oil in the pan and sauté until soft. Add the tomatoes, tomato purée and wine and season to taste with salt and pepper. Bring to the boil and then add the beef rolls. Cover and simmer gently for 1½–2 hours or until tender. Remove the string from the beef rolls and serve with the sauce, sprinkled with basil.

Serves 6
Preparation time: 10–15 minutes
Cooking time: about 2 hours

provençal beef stew

1 kg/2 lb lean chuck or stewing steak, cut into cubes
2 large onions, sliced
3 carrots, sliced
1 strip orange rind, without pith
1 bay leaf
4–5 peppercorns
300 ml/½ pint red wine
50 g/2 oz dripping or lard
3 garlic cloves, crushed
300 ml/½ pint Beef Stock (see page 141)
salt and pepper
2 tablespoons finely chopped parsley, to garnish

1 Put the cubes of beef in a deep bowl with 1 sliced onion, the carrots, orange rind, bay leaf and peppercorns. Pour the red wine over the top, cover the bowl and leave to marinate in the refrigerator overnight. The following day, remove the meat and vegetables and drain well. Reserve the marinade and vegetables.

2 Heat the dripping or lard in a flameproof casserole. Add the meat and brown on all sides, stirring occasionally. Remove from the pan with a slotted spoon and keep warm. Add the remaining onion and the garlic to the casserole, and cook over a low heat until light golden brown.

3 Return the meat to the pan, together with the wine marinade, including the marinated vegetables, orange peel and bay leaf. Discard the peppercorns. Add the stock, season to taste with salt and pepper and bring to the boil.

4 Cover the casserole and cook in a preheated oven, 160°C (325°F), Gas Mark 3, for 2–2½ hours until tender. Discard the bay leaf, and remove the meat from the casserole and keep warm. Boil the sauce until reduced by half. Return the meat to the casserole or place in another dish and pour the sauce over the top. Sprinkle with parsley and serve.

Serves 6
Preparation time: 20 minutes, plus marinating
Cooking time: 2¼–2¾ hours
Oven temperature: 160°C (325°F), Gas Mark 3

beef bourguignon

1 large onion, thinly sliced
a few parsley sprigs
a few thyme sprigs
1 bay leaf, crumbled
1 kg/2 lb chuck steak or top rump cut into
  2.5 cm/1 inch cubes
2 tablespoons marc or brandy
400 ml/14 fl oz red Burgundy wine
2 tablespoons olive oil
50 g/2 oz butter
150 g/5 oz lean bacon, rinded and roughly chopped
24 small pickling onions
500 g/1 lb button mushrooms, halved
25 g/1 oz plain flour
300 ml/½ pint Beef Stock (see page 141)
1 garlic clove, crushed
1 bouquet garni
salt and pepper

1 Put a few onion slices in a deep bowl with a little parsley, thyme and some crumbled bay leaf. Place a few pieces of beef on top and continue layering in this way until all the onion, beef and herbs are used. Mix together the marc or brandy with the wine and oil and pour over the beef. Cover and leave to marinate for at least 4 hours.

2 Melt the butter in a flameproof casserole. Add the bacon and fry over a moderate heat until golden brown. Remove and set aside. Add the small onions and fry until golden on all sides. Add the mushrooms and fry, stirring, for 1 minute. Drain and set aside.

3 Remove the beef from the marinade, then strain the marinade and set aside. Add the beef to the casserole and fry briskly until browned on all sides. Sprinkle in the flour and cook, stirring, for 1 minute. Gradually stir in the strained marinade, then add the stock, garlic and bouquet garni. Season to taste with salt and pepper, cover and simmer gently for 2 hours.

4 Skim off any fat on the surface and add the bacon, onions and mushrooms to the casserole. Cover and simmer for 30 minutes, or until the beef is tender. Discard the bouquet garni and serve immediately.

Serves 4–6
Preparation time: 30 minutes, plus marinating
Cooking time: 2¾ hours

beef pepperpot

2 tablespoons plain flour
1 teaspoon paprika
750 g/1½ lb braising steak, cut into 2.5 cm/1 inch cubes
2 tablespoons vegetable oil
12 small onions or shallots
125 g/4 oz button mushrooms, quartered
1 garlic clove, crushed (optional)
200 g/7 oz canned tomatoes
450 ml/¾ pint Beef Stock (see page 141)
1 red pepper, cored, deseeded and cut into
  1 cm/½ inch strips
1 green pepper, cored, deseeded and cut into
  1 cm/½ inch strips
salt and pepper
boiled rice, to serve

1 Spread the flour out on a plate, season with the paprika, salt and pepper and use to coat the beef cubes, reserving any excess seasoned flour.

2 Heat the oil in a flameproof casserole. Add the onions or shallots, mushrooms and garlic, if using, and fry over a moderate heat, stirring frequently, for 5 minutes. Remove the vegetables from the casserole with a slotted spoon and set aside on a plate.

3 Add the beef to the casserole and fry over a moderately high heat to seal and brown on all sides.

4 Return the onion, garlic and mushrooms to the casserole, stir in the reserved flour and cook for 1 minute. Stir in the tomatoes, together with their can juice, breaking them up with a wooden spoon. Stir in the stock and bring to the boil.

5 Cover the casserole and cook in a preheated oven, 160°C (325°F), Gas Mark 3, for 1½ hours. Stir in the red and green pepper strips, cover again and cook for a further 30 minutes. Serve hot with plain boiled rice.

Serves 4–6
Preparation time: 10 minutes
Cooking time: 2¼ hours
Oven temperature: 160°C (325°F), Gas Mark 3

beef tacos

500 g/1 lb steak, minced
75 g/3 oz onion, chopped
65 g/2½ oz green pepper, cored, deseeded and chopped
1 garlic clove, crushed
1 teaspoon dried oregano
½ teaspoon hot paprika
¼ teaspoon ground cumin
¼ teaspoon dried hot red chilli flakes
125 ml/4 fl oz tomato purée
12 tortillas
vegetable oil, for frying
salt and pepper

To serve:
1 lettuce, shredded
2 tomatoes, finely chopped
2 tablespoons grated Cheddar cheese
1 avocado, diced
150 ml/¼ pint soured cream

1 Dry-fry the minced steak in a frying pan until brown and crumbly, stirring occasionally and breaking it up with a wooden spoon.

2 Add the onion, green pepper and garlic and cook, stirring occasionally, until softened. Stir in the herbs and spices and season to taste with salt and pepper. Add the tomato purée and mix well. Cover and cook gently for 10 minutes, stirring occasionally.

3 Place a little of the mixture on each tortilla and roll up. Secure with a cocktail stick. Heat the oil in a frying pan and then fry the rolls quickly until golden. Serve with your choice of accompaniments.

Serves 4–6
Preparation time: 30 minutes
Cooking time: 30 minutes

chile verde

5 tablespoons olive oil
1 kg/2 lb stewing steak, cubed
3 green peppers
3 garlic cloves, crushed
4 fresh green chillies, deseeded and finely sliced
475 g/15 oz canned chopped tomatoes
2 teaspoons brown sugar
¼ teaspoon ground cloves
¼ teaspoon ground cinnamon
2 teaspoons ground cumin
4 tablespoons lime juice
325 ml/11 fl oz Beef Stock (see page 141) or red wine
salt and pepper
3 tablespoons chopped coriander, to garnish

1 Heat 3 tablespoons of the olive oil in a large heavy-based casserole. Add the stewing steak, in batches, and cook over a medium heat, turning frequently, until lightly browned. Remove from the pan with a slotted spoon and keep warm. Pour off the meat juices and reserve.

2 Cut the green peppers into 2.5cm/1 inch squares. Heat the remaining oil in the casserole and sauté the green pepper and garlic over a low heat for 5 minutes until the pepper is cooked and tender.

3 Return the meat to the pan and add the chilli, chopped tomatoes, brown sugar, cloves, cinnamon, cumin, lime juice and beef stock or wine. Bring to the boil, stirring continuously. Cover the casserole and cook in a preheated oven, 190°C (375°F), Gas Mark 5, for 1¾ hours.

4 Remove the casserole from the oven, uncover and simmer over a low heat for 20 minutes, or until the sauce has reduced and thickened. Season to taste with salt and pepper. Serve immediately, garnished with chopped coriander.

Serves 4
Preparation time: 10 minutes
Cooking time: 2½ hours
Oven temperature: 190°C (375°F), Gas Mark 5

stir-fried beef

375 g/12 oz rump steak
1 tablespoon light soy sauce
1 tablespoon dark soy sauce
1 tablespoon soft brown sugar
1 teaspoon sesame oil
1 tablespoon Chinese rice wine or dry sherry
2 tablespoons white sesame seeds
2 tablespoons sunflower oil
1 garlic clove, thinly sliced
2 celery sticks, diagonally sliced
2 carrots, thinly sliced
50 g/2 oz button mushrooms, sliced

1 Cut the steak into thin slices across the grain and place in a shallow dish. Combine the soy sauces, sugar, sesame oil and wine or sherry. Pour over the meat, toss to coat well and leave to marinate for 15 minutes.

2 Dry-fry the sesame seeds in a heavy-based pan until they are golden.

3 Heat the oil in a preheated wok or frying pan. Add the garlic, celery and carrots and stir-fry briskly for 1 minute. Remove from the wok. Increase the heat, add the beef and stir-fry for about 3 minutes until well browned. Return the vegetables to the wok, add the mushrooms and cook for a further 30 seconds. Sprinkle with the toasted sesame seeds and serve at once.

Serves 4
Preparation time: 10 minutes, plus marinating
Cooking time: 6 minutes

spiced beef with leeks and celery

500 g/1 lb rump or sirloin steak
2 leeks
3 celery sticks
6 tablespoons vegetable oil
1 garlic clove, crushed with a pinch of salt
1 teaspoon red wine vinegar
1 teaspoon soy sauce
1 tablespoon sesame oil
1 tablespoon hot soy bean paste

1 Cut the beef into small, thin slivers. Cut the leeks and celery into matchstick pieces.

2 Heat 3 tablespoons of the oil in a preheated wok or large frying pan over a high heat. Add the leeks and celery, stir-fry for 1 minute and remove.

3 Add the remaining oil to the pan. Add the steak and stir-fry until it has browned and all the moisture in the pan has evaporated. Stir in the garlic, vinegar, soy sauce, sesame oil and soy bean paste. Add the vegetables and stir-fry for 1 minute. Serve immediately.

Serves 4–6
Preparation time: 10 minutes
Cooking time: 10 minutes

ginger beef with peppers

500 g/1 lb lean fillet steak, thinly sliced
2 teaspoons soy sauce
2 tablespoons sesame oil
2.5 cm/1 inch piece of fresh root ginger, sliced
2 teaspoons vinegar
1 tablespoon water
1 teaspoon salt
1 teaspoon cornflour
1 garlic clove, crushed
pinch of Chinese five-spice powder
1 red pepper, cored, deseeded and cut into chunks
1 green pepper, cored, deseeded and cut into chunks
slivers of fresh red chilli, deseeded, to garnish

1 Put the slices of fillet steak into a bowl and add the soy sauce, 1 teaspoon of the sesame oil, the sliced ginger, vinegar, water, salt and cornflour. Stir well to mix until the slices are thoroughly coated. Cover and leave to marinate in the refrigerator for at least 20 minutes.

2 Heat the remaining sesame oil in a preheated wok or frying pan. Add the garlic and five-spice powder and stir-fry for 30 seconds. Add the marinated steak slices. Stir-fry quickly until the meat is browned on the outside yet still pink and tender on the inside. Remove with a slotted spoon and set aside.

3 Add the red and green peppers to the wok and stir-fry briskly for 2–3 minutes, tossing them in the oil.

4 Add the steak and any remaining marinade. Stir-fry for 1 minute until the meat is heated through. Transfer to a warmed serving dish and serve garnished with thin slivers of chilli.

Serves 3–4
Preparation time: 10 minutes, plus marinating
Cooking time: 5 minutes

szechuan pepper beef

1 tablespoon Szechuan peppercorns
3 tablespoons vegetable oil
500 g/1 lb rump or fillet steak, cut into thin strips across the grain
1 large red pepper, cored, deseeded and cut lengthways into thin strips
2 red chillies, deseeded and finely chopped
2.5 cm/1 inch piece of fresh root ginger, cut into matchstick strips
2 garlic cloves, crushed

Sauce:
2 teaspoons cornflour
4 tablespoons water
3 tablespoons soy sauce
2 teaspoons dark soft brown sugar

1 First prepare the sauce. Mix the cornflour to a thin paste with the water, then stir in the soy sauce and sugar. Set aside.

2 Dry-fry the Szechuan peppercorns in a preheated wok or frying pan over a low heat for 1–2 minutes. Remove from the wok and crush using a mortar and pestle. Set aside.

3 Heat half of the oil in the wok over a moderate heat. Add the beef strips and crushed peppercorns, increase the heat to high and stir-fry for 3–4 minutes or until the beef is browned on all sides. Tip the beef and its juices into a bowl and set aside.

4 Heat the remaining oil over a moderate heat. Add the red pepper, chillies, ginger and garlic and stir-fry for 2–3 minutes until softened, taking care not to let the ingredients brown.

5 Return the beef and its juices to the wok and stir to mix with the vegetables. Stir the sauce to mix, then pour over the beef and vegetables. Increase the heat to high and toss until the beef is hot and all the ingredients are evenly combined. Serve at once.

Serves 3–4
Preparation time: 15 minutes
Cooking time: 12 minutes

beef in oyster sauce

2 tablespoons oyster sauce
1 tablespoon dry sherry
1 tablespoon cornflour
250 g/8 oz beef steak, cut into fairly thick slices
125 g/4 oz button mushrooms, or 3–4 Chinese dried mushrooms soaked in warm water for 20 minutes
4 tablespoons vegetable oil
1 cm/½ inch piece of fresh root ginger, chopped
2 spring onions, chopped
175 g/6 oz broccoli, divided into small florets
125 g/4 oz bamboo shoots, sliced
1 carrot, sliced
1 teaspoon salt
1 teaspoon sugar
2 tablespoons Chicken Stock (see page 141) or water

1 In a bowl, mix together the oyster sauce, sherry and cornflour. Add the beef slices, turn to coat, cover and leave to marinate in the refrigerator for 20 minutes.

2 If using Chinese dried mushrooms, drain and squeeze dry, discard the stalks and finely slice the caps.

3 Heat half of the oil in a preheated wok or frying pan. Add the beef and stir-fry for 10–15 seconds. Remove with a slotted spoon and set aside.

4 Heat the remaining oil, then add the ginger, spring onions, mushrooms, broccoli, bamboo shoots and carrot. Add the salt and sugar and stir-fry for 1½ minutes. Add the beef, stir well and moisten with a little stock or water. Heat through and serve at once.

Serves 4
Preparation time: 15 minutes, plus marinating
Cooking time: 5 minutes

stir-fried orange beef

350 g/12 oz rump steak
2 teaspoons sesame oil
2 tablespoons dark soy sauce
1 tablespoon dry sherry
1 cm/½ inch piece of fresh root ginger, finely chopped
2 teaspoons cornflour
4 tablespoons oil
2 dried red chillies, crumbled
shredded rind of 1 orange
½ teaspoon roasted Szechuan peppercorns, finely ground
1 teaspoon light soft brown sugar
salt

To garnish:
orange slices
parsley sprigs

1 Cut the beef into thin slices 5 cm/2 inches long, cutting across the grain.

2 Combine half the sesame oil, half the soy sauce, the sherry, ginger and cornflour in a dish. Add the meat and toss until well coated. Leave to marinate for 15 minutes, then drain well.

3 Heat the oil in a preheated wok or heavy-based frying pan and quickly brown the meat on all sides for 2 minutes. Drain on kitchen paper.

4 Pour off all but 1 tablespoon of oil from the pan. Return the pan to the heat, add the chillies and stir-fry for 30 seconds. Return the meat to the pan and add the orange rind, Szechuan pepper, sugar, the remaining soy sauce and salt to taste. Stir-fry for 4 minutes then sprinkle with the remaining sesame oil. Serve immediately, garnished with the orange slices and parsley sprigs.

Serves 4
Preparation: 5 minutes, plus marinating
Cooking time: 7 minutes

spicy beef in yogurt

500 g/1 lb braising or stewing steak, thinly sliced
1 teaspoon salt
300 ml/½ pint natural yogurt
175 g/6 oz ghee or 3 tablespoons vegetable oil
1 large onion, sliced
3 garlic cloves, sliced
1½ teaspoons ground ginger
2 teaspoons ground coriander
2 teaspoons chilli powder
½ teaspoon ground cumin
1½ teaspoons turmeric
1 teaspoon garam masala
boiled rice, to serve

1 Place the beef between 2 sheets of greaseproof paper and beat until thin with a rolling pin or meat mallet.

2 Rub the beef with the salt and then cut into serving-sized pieces. Place in a bowl and cover with the yogurt. Cover and leave to marinate overnight in the refrigerator.

3 Heat the ghee or vegetable oil in a heavy-based saucepan. Add the onion and garlic and fry over a low heat for 4–5 minutes until soft. Add the spices and fry, stirring constantly, for a further 3 minutes.

4 Add the beef and yogurt marinade to the pan and stir well. Cover the pan with a tightly-fitting lid and then simmer for 1½ hours, or until the meat is tender. Serve with rice.

Serves 4
Preparation time: 15 minutes, plus marinating
Cooking time: 1¾ hours

kofta with yogurt

500 g/1 lb minced beef
75 g/3 oz fresh breadcrumbs
2 fresh green chillies, finely chopped
1 onion, finely chopped
2.5 cm/1 inch piece of fresh root ginger, finely chopped
2 teaspoons ground coriander
1 egg, lightly beaten
oil, for frying
600 g/1 pint natural yogurt
salt
2 tablespoons finely chopped coriander leaves,
   to garnish

1 Mix together the minced beef, breadcrumbs, chillies, onion, ginger, ground coriander, salt to taste and egg, and shape the mixture into walnut-sized balls.

2 Heat the oil in a large pan. Add the meatballs and fry until well browned and cooked through. Drain carefully.

3 Pour the yogurt into a serving bowl and add the meatballs while still hot. Sprinkle with chopped coriander and serve warm.

Serves 4
Preparation time: 15 minutes
Cooking time: 15 minutes

balti kheema

2 tablespoons vegetable oil
500 g/1 lb green peppers, cored, deseeded and sliced
500 g/1 lb onions, sliced
2 teaspoons salt
2 teaspoons pepper
½ teaspoon ground cumin
2 teaspoons garam masala
pinch of ground cinnamon
1½ teaspoons chilli powder
750 g/1½ lb minced lamb
red onion rings, to garnish
poppadums, to serve

1 Heat the oil in a preheated Balti pan, wok or heavy-based frying pan. Add the peppers and stir-fry for about 1 minute. Remove the peppers with a slotted spoon and keep warm.

2 Add the onions to the oil and fry until they are golden brown. Add the salt, pepper, cumin, garam masala, cinnamon and chilli powder and stir-fry for 2 minutes.

3 Add the minced lamb and cook gently for about 20 minutes, stirring frequently to make sure that it does not stick to the base of the pan.

4 Return the green peppers to the pan and heat through over a low heat for a further 10 minutes. Garnish with onion rings and serve with poppadums.

Serves 4–6
Preparation time: 15 minutes
Cooking time: 35 minutes

thai red beef curry

3 tablespoons groundnut oil
3 tablespoons Thai red curry paste (see page 149)
½ teaspoon ground coriander
½ teaspoon ground cumin
4 Kaffir lime leaves, shredded
500 g/1 lb fillet of beef, cut into thin strips
400 ml/14 fl oz coconut milk
2 tablespoons crunchy peanut butter
2 teaspoons Thai fish sauce
1 tablespoon soft brown sugar
coriander sprigs, to garnish (optional)
steamed rice, to serve

1 Heat the oil in a heavy-based saucepan. Add the red curry paste, ground coriander and cumin and the lime leaves. Cook over a low heat, stirring frequently, for 3 minutes.

2 Add the beef strips to the pan, stir to coat them evenly in the curry paste and cook gently, stirring frequently for 5 minutes.

3 Add half of the coconut milk to the pan, stir to combine and simmer gently for 4 minutes until most of the coconut milk has been absorbed.

4 Stir in the remaining coconut milk with the peanut butter, fish sauce and sugar. Simmer gently for 5 minutes until the sauce is thick and the beef is tender. Garnish with coriander sprigs, if using, and serve immediately with steamed rice.

Serves 4
Preparation time: 5–10 minutes
Cooking time: about 20 minutes

malaysian beef and potato curry

2 tablespoons groundnut oil
5 shallots, chopped
2 garlic cloves, crushed
5 cm/2 inch piece of fresh root ginger, grated
2 tablespoons hot curry powder
1 teaspoon ground cinnamon
1 teaspoon ground cumin
1 teaspoon ground coriander
¼ teaspoon ground cardamom
4 curry leaves
1 star anise
4 cloves
375 g/12 oz sirloin steak, cut into 1 cm/½ inch strips
300 g/10 oz potatoes, peeled and cut into medium chunks
2 large red chillies, deseeded and finely chopped
½ teaspoon salt
300 ml/½ pint coconut milk
2 tablespoons lime juice
1 teaspoon soft brown sugar
sliced red chillies, to garnish

1 Heat the oil in a saucepan. Add the shallots, garlic and ginger, and fry over a low heat, stirring frequently, for 5 minutes until softened.

2 Add the curry powder, cinnamon, cumin, coriander, cardamom, curry leaves, star anise and cloves and fry for 1 minute.

3 Add the beef and stir well to coat it in the spice mixture. Add the potatoes, chillies, salt and coconut milk. Stir to combine, bring to the boil, then reduce the heat, cover the pan and simmer gently, stirring occasionally, for 40 minutes until the beef is tender and the potatoes are cooked.

4 Stir in the lime juice and brown sugar and cook, uncovered, for 2 minutes. Taste and adjust the seasoning, if necessary, and serve hot, garnished with sliced red chillies.

Serves 4
Preparation time: 20 minutes
Cooking time: 50 minutes

breaded veal escalopes with parma ham and parmesan

4 x 175 g/6 oz veal escalopes
75 g/3 oz plain flour
2 eggs, beaten
175 g/6 oz fresh breadcrumbs
75 g/3 oz butter
50 g/2 oz Parma ham
50 g/2 oz Parmesan cheese, freshly grated
salt and pepper
handful of flat leaf parsley, chopped, to garnish
1 lemon, cut into 4 wedges, to serve

1 Place the veal escalopes between 2 sheets of greaseproof paper and flatten them by pounding with a rolling pin or meat mallet.

2 Season the flour with salt and pepper. Dip the escalopes first in the flour, then in the egg and finally in the breadcrumbs, coating them evenly.

3 Melt the butter in a large frying pan. When it is foaming, add the escalopes and cook for 1–2 minutes on each side or until golden.

4 Arrange the escalopes on a grill pan. Put a piece of Parma ham on each one and sprinkle with the grated Parmesan. Place the escalopes under a preheated very hot grill and cook for 4–5 minutes until the Parmesan is golden.

5 Garnish the escalopes with chopped parsley and serve with lemon wedges.

Serves 4
Preparation time: 10 minutes
Cooking time: 10 minutes

veal escalopes with lemon and pine nuts

75 g/3 oz plain flour
4 x 175 g/6 oz veal escalopes
50 g/2 oz butter
1 tablespoon olive oil
75 g/3 oz pine nuts
grated rind and juice of 1 lemon
75 ml/3 fl oz Chicken Stock (see page 141)
handful of parsley, finely chopped
salt and pepper

1 Season the flour with salt and pepper. Dip the escalopes into the seasoned flour, coating them evenly all over.

2 Heat the butter and oil in a frying pan. When it is foaming, add the escalopes and cook for about 3 minutes on each side until golden.

3 Sprinkle the pine nuts into the pan and stir until golden. Add the lemon rind and juice, chicken stock and parsley and season to taste with salt and pepper. Bring to the boil and mix well. Serve immediately.

Serves 4
Preparation time: 10 minutes
Cooking time: 10 minutes

veal chops with gremolata

4 thin veal chops
75 g/3 oz seasoned flour
50 g/2 oz butter
1 tablespoon olive oil
2 onions, chopped
2 garlic cloves, crushed
2 celery sticks, chopped
1 carrot, chopped
2 bay leaves
6 tomatoes, skinned, deseeded and chopped
125 ml/4 fl oz Chicken Stock (see page 141)
125 ml/4 fl oz dry white wine
salt and pepper

Gremolata:
2 tablespoons finely chopped parsley
1 tablespoon finely chopped sage
finely grated rind of 3 lemons
3 large garlic cloves, crushed and chopped

1 Coat both sides of the veal chops with seasoned flour. Melt the butter and oil in a flameproof casserole, add the chops and brown well on each side. Remove from the casserole and keep warm.

2 Add the onions, garlic, celery and carrot to the pan and fry over a low heat for 3 minutes. Add the bay leaves, tomatoes, stock and wine and season to taste with salt and pepper. Mix well and bring to the boil. Return the chops to the casserole and turn to coat them in the sauce. Cover and cook in a preheated oven, 200°C (400°F), Gas Mark 6, for 20 minutes.

3 Meanwhile, make the gremolata. Mix together the parsley, sage, lemon rind and garlic.

4 To serve, transfer the chops to a warmed serving plate and keep them warm. Boil the sauce to reduce, if necessary, then pour it over the chops and spoon some of the gremolata over each one.

Serves 4
Preparation time: 10 minutes
Cooking time: 30 minutes
Oven temperature: 200°C (400°F), Gas Mark 6

veal chops with savoury butter

2 garlic cloves
150 g/5 oz butter, diced
3 anchovy fillets, chopped
1 tablespoon chopped parsley
1 lemon
12 veal chops
125 ml/4 fl oz dry white wine
6 tablespoons olive oil
½ teaspoon chopped rosemary
salt and pepper
lettuce leaves, to garnish

1 Finely chop 1 garlic clove and mix with the diced butter and anchovies in a small bowl. Add the chopped parsley and season with a squeeze of lemon juice and pepper to taste. Work the mixture together and form it into a 2 cm/¾ inch diameter cylinder. Wrap in foil and put in the refrigerator to harden.

2 Flatten the veal with a mallet. Make a marinade using the wine, half the oil, the rosemary, the other garlic clove, crushed, the remaining lemon juice and salt and pepper to taste. Marinate the veal for 3 hours.

3 Drain the chops and cook under a hot grill, using the remaining oil to baste them. Serve topped with slices of anchovy butter and lettuce leaves.

Serves 6
Preparation time: 15 minutes, plus marinating
Cooking time: 15 minutes

veal with aubergine

4 aubergines, thinly sliced
1 carrot, chopped
1 celery stick, chopped
½ onion, chopped
875 g/1¾ lb boned loin of veal
250 ml/8 fl oz olive oil
½ teaspoon chopped sage
½ teaspoon chopped rosemary
125 ml/4 fl oz wine vinegar
2 garlic cloves, finely chopped
½ teaspoon chopped basil leaves
salt and pepper

1 Cook the aubergines under a hot grill without adding any fat.

2 Meanwhile, put the carrot, celery and onion into a pan with the veal, season with salt and pour over water to cover. Bring to the boil, lower the heat and simmer gently for 2 hours, or until the meat is cooked.

3 Remove the veal from the pan. Put 1 tablespoon of the oil in another pan with the sage and rosemary and lightly brown the veal. Pour over half the vinegar and cook until it evaporates. Remove the meat and leave to cool.

4 While the veal is cooking, arrange layers of aubergine slices in a shallow dish and season with a little of the garlic, the basil, the remaining oil and vinegar and salt and pepper. Continue until the aubergine is used up and pour over any remaining oil. Leave to marinate for 1 hour, or longer if convenient.

5 To serve, slice the veal and arrange the slices on a plate alternately with slices of aubergine. Strain the marinade over the dish.

Serves 6
Preparation time: 40 minutes, plus marinating
Cooking time: about 2 hours

scallopine alla milanese

4 x 125 g/4 oz veal escalopes
1–2 eggs, beaten
dried breadcrumbs, for coating
75 g/3 oz butter
salt and pepper
green beans, to serve

To garnish:
lemon twists
parsley sprigs

1 Beat the veal lightly with a mallet to flatten. Dip into the beaten egg and coat with breadcrumbs.

2 Melt the butter in a large frying pan. Add the veal and fry for 2–3 minutes on each side until tender and golden.

3 Transfer the cooked veal to a warmed serving dish and sprinkle with salt and pepper to taste. Garnish with lemon twists and chopped parsley and serve immediately with fresh green beans.

Serves 4
Preparation time: 10 minutes
Cooking time: 8–10 minutes

venetian calves' liver

50 g/2 oz butter
2 tablespoons olive oil
2 onions, finely sliced
4 x 175 g/6 oz pieces thinly sliced calves' liver
125 ml/4 fl oz red wine
1 tablespoon finely chopped parsley
salt and pepper

1 Heat half of the butter and half of the oil in a large frying pan. Add the onions and fry over a low heat for 10 minutes, but do not allow to brown. Remove the onions and set aside.

2 Season the liver on both sides with salt and pepper to taste. Add the remaining oil and butter to the pan. When it is foaming, add the liver and cook on a high heat for 2 minutes on each side, or longer if you do not like your liver pink in the middle. Remove the liver and place on a warmed serving plate.

3 Heat the frying pan for a few seconds, then add the wine and return the onions to the pan. Boil rapidly to reduce for 1 minute, then stir in the parsley and pour the sauce over the liver. Serve immediately.

Serves 4
Preparation time: 10 minutes
Cooking time: 15 minutes

calves' liver and bacon with roasted tomato chutney

3 tablespoons olive oil
750 g/1½ lb tomatoes, halved and green cores removed
1 red onion, sliced
1 garlic clove, chopped
50 g/2 oz raisins
50 g/2 oz brown sugar
3 tablespoons white wine vinegar
1 teaspoon chopped rosemary
1 teaspoon black mustard seeds
8 smoked streaky bacon rashers, rinded
4 slices of calves' liver, about 125 g/4 oz each
sea salt and pepper
rosemary sprigs, to garnish

1 Spoon 2 tablespoons of the olive oil into a roasting tin and heat in a preheated oven, 220°C (425°F), Gas Mark 7. Add the tomatoes, turn them in the oil to coat well and place the tin at the top of the oven. Roast for about 40 minutes, or until the tomatoes begin to darken around the edges.

2 Heat the remaining olive oil in a frying pan. Add the onion and garlic. Fry over a low heat for 5 minutes, then add the raisins, brown sugar, vinegar, rosemary, mustard seeds and seasoning. Mix well and simmer for 2 minutes. Mix in the roasted tomatoes, then remove from the heat.

3 Heat a griddle pan or nonstick frying pan. Put on the bacon and cook for about 2 minutes on each side until crispy. Keep warm. Place the liver on the griddle and cook for 2 minutes on each side for pink, or 4 minutes for well done. Serve at once with the bacon and roasted tomato chutney, garnished with rosemary sprigs.

Serves 4
Preparation time: 10 minutes
Cooking time: about 1 hour
Oven temperature: 220°C (425°F), Gas Mark 7

lambs' kidneys in burgundy

25 g/1 oz butter
1 tablespoon olive oil
1 onion, finely chopped
125 g/4 oz mushrooms, chopped
125 g/4 oz unsmoked bacon, diced
8 lambs' kidneys
300 ml/½ pint Burgundy or other dry red wine
1 garlic clove, crushed
1 bouquet garni
1 tablespoon plain flour
salt and pepper
1 tablespoon chopped parsley, to garnish

1 Heat half of the butter and all of the oil in a heavy frying pan. Add the onion, mushrooms and bacon, and fry over a low heat until golden. Remove them from the pan with a slotted spoon and keep warm.

2 Remove the membrane surrounding the kidneys and trim away the fat. Split the kidneys in half lengthways and, using a sharp knife, remove the central white cores. Add the prepared kidneys to the pan and cook them over high heat to seal them. Reduce the heat and cook gently for 3–4 minutes. Remove from the pan and keep them warm.

3 Add the red wine to the frying pan together with the onion, mushroom and bacon mixture. Season to taste with salt and pepper and stir in the garlic and bouquet garni. Simmer gently for 10 minutes.

4 Mix the remaining butter with the flour to make a paste and add to the sauce, a little at a time, stirring all the time until it thickens. Pour the sauce over the kidneys and serve sprinkled with parsley.

Serves 4
Preparation time: 15 minutes
Cooking time: 25 minutes

chilli liver

125 g/4 oz red kidney beans, soaked overnight
2 tablespoons vegetable oil
1 onion, sliced
50 g/2 oz mushrooms, finely chopped
375 g/12 oz lambs' liver, finely chopped
1 garlic clove, crushed
½–1 teaspoon chilli powder
2 teaspoons wholemeal flour
400 g/13 oz can chopped tomatoes
1 teaspoon cumin seeds
salt and pepper
parsley sprigs, to garnish

1 Drain the beans, rinse, place in a saucepan and cover with cold water. Bring to the boil and boil rapidly for 10 minutes, then reduce the heat and simmer for 35–45 minutes until tender. Drain and rinse thoroughly under cold running water.

2 Heat the oil in a saucepan. Add the onion and fry gently for 5 minutes until soft. Add the mushrooms and cook for 1 minute. Add the liver and garlic. Cook, stirring, for 5 minutes.

3 Stir in the chilli powder and flour and cook, stirring constantly, for 1 minute. Stir in the tomatoes. Season to taste with salt and pepper, then stir in the cumin.

4 Bring to the boil, add the beans, then cover and simmer for 20 minutes. Transfer to a warmed serving dish and garnish with parsley sprigs.

Serves 4
Preparation time: 5 minutes, plus soaking
Cooking time: 1½ hours

liver with herbs

2 tablespoons wholemeal flour
500 g/1 lb lambs' liver, sliced
2 tablespoons oil
2 onions, chopped
150 ml/¼ pint red wine
150 ml/¼ pint Chicken Stock (see page 141)
2 tablespoons tomato purée
1 teaspoon chopped thyme
2 tomatoes, skinned, deseeded and sliced
salt and pepper
chopped parsley, to garnish

1 Season the flour with salt and pepper and spread it out on a plate. Toss the liver in the seasoned flour, coating well all over.

2 Heat the oil in a frying pan. Add the liver and fry gently for 2 minutes on each side. Remove from the pan.

3 Add the onions to the pan and fry gently until softened. Stir in the wine, stock, tomato purée and thyme and season to taste with salt and pepper. Bring to the boil. Return the liver to the pan, cover and simmer for 15 minutes. Add the tomatoes and cook for a further 5 minutes, or until tender.

4 Arrange the liver on a warmed serving dish. Pour the sauce over the liver. Sprinkle with chopped parsley and serve immediately.

Serves 4
Preparation time: 5 minutes
Cooking time: 25–30 minutes

poultry & game

chicken with wild mushrooms

50 g/2 oz dried wild mushrooms, or 250 g/8 oz fresh
    mushrooms, sliced
50 g/2 oz plain flour
4 boneless, skinless chicken breasts
50 g/2 oz butter
1 tablespoon olive oil
2 shallots, diced
2 garlic cloves, chopped
125 ml/4 fl oz white wine
125 g/4 oz mascarpone cheese
handful of chives, snipped
salt and pepper

1 If using dried mushrooms, put them into a bowl and just cover with hot water. Leave to soak for 15 minutes.

2 Meanwhile, season the flour with salt and pepper and toss the chicken in the seasoned flour to cover all over.

3 Heat the butter and oil in a frying pan. Add the chicken and cook for 4 minutes on each side until coloured. Remove the chicken and keep warm.

4 Add the shallots and garlic to the pan and fry over a low heat for 5 minutes. Add the wine and mix well to include any tasty brown bits from the pan.

5 Add the mascarpone and the mushrooms to the pan; if using dried mushrooms, add the soaking liquid. Mix well to melt the mascarpone. If the mixture is very runny, turn up the heat to evaporate some of the liquid. If you are using fresh mushrooms, add a little extra liquid, but remember that mushrooms make their own liquid as they cook.

6 Return the chicken to the pan and simmer gently for 10 minutes, turning it from time to time. Finally stir the snipped chives into the pan, season to taste with salt and pepper and serve immediately.

Serves 4
Preparation time: 10 minutes
Cooking time: 25 minutes

roman chicken

4 tablespoons olive oil
2 red onions, sliced
2 garlic cloves, sliced
2 red peppers, cored, deseeded and sliced
2 yellow peppers, cored, deseeded and sliced
½ teaspoon crushed dried chillies
8 boneless chicken thighs
100 ml/3½ fl oz white wine
large handful of basil, roughly torn
salt and pepper

1 Heat the olive oil in a large frying pan. Add the onions, garlic, red and yellow peppers and chillies and cook over a low heat for 5 minutes.

2 Add the chicken thighs, pushing them down to the bottom of the pan, to seal on the outside. Cook for a further 5 minutes.

3 Add the wine and season with salt and pepper to taste. Cover the pan and cook over a low heat for about 15 minutes. Check occasionally that the chicken and sauce do not stick to the base of the pan and add a little more wine, if necessary.

4 Stir in the basil just before serving.

Serves 4
Preparation time: 5 minutes
Cooking time: 25 minutes

chicken with rosemary and garlic

2 tablespoons olive oil
2 tablespoons white wine vinegar
2 tablespoons chopped rosemary
3 garlic cloves, crushed
1 teaspoon paprika
pared rind of 1 lemon
4 boneless, skinless chicken breasts, cut into
*   long thin strips*
handful of flat leaf parsley, chopped
salt and pepper

1 Mix together the olive oil, vinegar, rosemary, garlic, paprika and lemon rind in a bowl and season to taste with salt and pepper. Add the chicken and mix well, then leave to marinate for 10 minutes. Alternatively, this could be done the night before.

2 Heat a large nonstick pan, add the chicken and the marinade, mix well and cook over a moderate heat, stirring constantly, for 15 minutes.

3 To serve, stir in the chopped parsley and serve hot.

Serves 4
Preparation time: 10 minutes, plus marinating
Cooking time: 15 minutes

roast chicken with bread sauce and gravy

1.5–2 kg/3–4 lb oven-ready chicken with giblets
1 lemon
1 bouquet garni
4 tablespoons olive oil
salt and pepper

Bread sauce:
600 ml/1 pint milk
1 small onion, grated
pinch of ground cloves
pinch of ground bay leaves
75 g/3 oz fresh white breadcrumbs
25 g/1 oz butter
ground nutmeg

Gravy:
2 tablespoons plain flour
300 ml/½ pint Chicken Stock (see page 141), made with
*   the giblets, or wine*

1 Remove the giblets from the chicken and reserve to make the gravy stock. Put the lemon and the bouquet garni inside the chicken cavity and truss the chicken securely. Brush a roasting tin with a little of the oil. Place the chicken in the tin, pour over the remaining olive oil and sprinkle with salt and pepper to taste.

2 Roast the chicken in a preheated oven, 180°C (350°F), Gas Mark 4, for 1½–1¾ hours, or until the juices run clear when pricked with a fork.

3 Prepare the bread sauce 15 minutes before the chicken is cooked. Pour the milk into a pan and add the onion, cloves and bay leaves. Heat until the milk has almost reached boiling point. Stir in the breadcrumbs and butter. Remove from the heat and leave for 5 minutes. Add nutmeg and salt to taste.

4 To make the gravy, remove the chicken from the oven and place on a serving dish in a warm place. Pour off all but 2 tablespoons of fat from the pan, leaving the residue. Add the flour to the pan and stir over low heat until it is bubbling and golden. Gradually stir in the chicken stock or wine. Add salt and pepper to taste.

5 Serve the chicken accompanied by the bread sauce and gravy.

Serves 4–6
Preparation time: 30 minutes
Cooking time: 1½–1¾ hours
Oven temperature: 180°C (350°F), Gas Mark 4

chicken and fennel with dill dressing

8 chicken thighs, boned
2 fennel heads, sliced
4 tablespoons olive oil
1 tablespoon balsamic vinegar
1 bunch of dill, chopped
sea salt and pepper

1 Heat a griddle pan or nonstick frying pan. Put on the chicken and cook for 6–8 minutes on each side. Remove and keep warm.

2 Add the fennel to the pan and cook for 4 minutes on each side. Remove from the pan and keep warm. Return the chicken to the pan and cook for another 3 minutes on each side to give a good crust to the skin.

3 Mix together the oil, vinegar, dill and seasoning. Serve the chicken and fennel with the dressing poured over. This dish can be served either hot or at room temperature, as you prefer.

Serves 4
Preparation time: 10 minutes
Cooking time: about 30 minutes

black olive chicken rolls

3 garlic cloves, crushed
2 tablespoons capers
4 anchovy fillets, chopped
1 teaspoon thyme leaves
1 shallot, chopped
175 g/6 oz pitted black olives
1 tablespoon olive oil, plus extra for brushing
4 small boneless, skinless chicken breasts
salt and pepper
cooked pasta, tossed in olive oil, parsley and freshly grated Parmesan cheese, to serve

1 Put the garlic, capers, anchovies, thyme, shallot, olives and olive oil into a food processor or blender and process.

2 Place each chicken breast between 2 sheets of greaseproof paper and flatten until it is about 2½ times its original size by pounding with a rolling pin or meat mallet. Season the chicken breasts with salt and pepper and spread each with a thin layer of the olive paste.

3 Brush an ovenproof dish with olive oil. Roll up the chicken breasts and secure with 2 wooden cocktail sticks. Cut each chicken roll in half and place in the prepared dish. Cover with foil and cook in a preheated oven, 200°C (400°F), Gas Mark 6, for 20 minutes, or until cooked. Serve with pasta tossed in olive oil, parsley and Parmesan.

Serves 4
Preparation time: 15 minutes
Cooking time: 20 minutes
Oven temperature: 200°C (400°F), Gas Mark 6

tequila chicken in pine nut sauce

4 tablespoons sunflower or corn oil
4 chicken portions, preferably leg joints, skinned
2 garlic cloves, chopped
4 tomatoes, skinned and chopped
300 ml/½ pint Chicken Stock (see page 141)
dash of Tabasco sauce or a pinch of chilli powder

carnival chicken with sweet potato mash   p296

chicken with coconut milk   p301

saffron chicken with apricots   p293

chicken tikka masala   p304

coconut grilled chicken p298

roast turkey with juniper and pomegranate p308

devilled chicken p290

turkey breasts with parmesan, egg and spinach p308

2 ginger nut biscuits
50 g/2 oz seedless raisins
2 tablespoons tequila or dry sherry
3 tablespoons pine nuts
salt and pepper

1 Heat 2 tablespoons of the oil in a heavy-based frying pan. Add the chicken and cook steadily for 10 minutes, turning over once or twice. Remove from the pan with a slotted spoon.

2 Heat the remaining oil. Add the garlic and tomatoes and cook for a few minutes.

3 Meanwhile, blend the chicken stock with the Tabasco sauce or chilli powder and pour over the ginger nut biscuits. When these are slightly softened, mash them with the liquid, or sieve, or blend in a blender. Pour this mixture into the pan and stir to blend with the garlic and tomatoes. Add the chicken joints and raisins.

4 Cover the pan and cook for about 10 minutes until the chicken is tender. Finally, add the tequila or sherry, the pine nuts and any seasoning required. Heat through for 2 minutes, then serve.

Serves 4
Preparation time: 30 minutes
Cooking time: 35 minutes

coq au vin

2 tablespoons olive oil
50 g/2 oz butter
2.5 kg/5 lb oven-ready chicken, cut into 12 serving
  pieces
24 small pickling onions, peeled
125 g/4 oz smoked bacon, rinded and diced
1 tablespoon plain flour
1 bottle good red wine
1 bouquet garni
2 garlic cloves
pinch of sugar
freshly grated nutmeg
24 button mushrooms
1 tablespoon brandy
3–4 slices of bread
vegetable oil, for frying
salt and pepper
2 tablespoons chopped parsley, to garnish

1 Heat the olive oil and butter in a large flameproof casserole. Add the chicken pieces and fry over a low heat, turning occasionally, until golden on all sides. Remove with a slotted spoon and keep warm.

2 Pour off a little of the fat from the casserole, then add the onions and bacon. Fry over a low heat until lightly coloured, then sprinkle in the flour and stir well.

3 Pour in the wine and bring to the boil, stirring. Add the bouquet garni, unpeeled garlic cloves, sugar and nutmeg, and salt and pepper to taste. Return the chicken to the casserole, lower the heat, cover and simmer for 15 minutes.

4 Add the mushrooms and continue cooking gently for a further 45 minutes, or until the chicken is cooked and tender. Remove the chicken with a slotted spoon and arrange the pieces on a warm serving platter. Keep hot.

5 Pour the brandy into the sauce and boil, uncovered, for 5 minutes until thick and reduced. Remove and discard the bouquet garni and garlic cloves.

6 Remove the crusts from the bread and cut into pieces. Fry in oil until crisp and golden on both sides. Remove and pat with absorbent kitchen paper. Pour the sauce over the chicken and serve with the bread croûtes. Sprinkle with chopped parsley.

Serves 6–8
Preparation time: 15–20 minutes
Cooking time: 1½ hours

basque chicken

4 tablespoons olive oil
175 g/6 oz smoked ham or streaky bacon, rinded and
  diced
4 large chicken portions
4 onions, sliced
3 garlic cloves, crushed
2 green peppers, cored, deseeded and diced
¼ teaspoon dried marjoram
400 g/13 oz fresh or canned tomatoes, skinned and
  chopped
150–300 ml/¼–½ pint Chicken Stock (see page 141)
salt and pepper
2 tablespoons chopped parsley, to garnish

1 Heat the olive oil in a sauté pan or deep frying pan. Add the diced ham or bacon and fry over a low heat, stirring occasionally, until lightly browned. Remove the ham from the pan with a slotted spoon and keep warm.

2 Add the chicken portions to the pan and cook, turning occasionally, until they are uniformly brown all over. Remove with a slotted spoon and keep warm.

3 Add the onions and garlic to the pan and cook gently until soft and golden. Add the peppers and marjoram, cover and cook gently for 10 minutes.

4 Add the tomatoes and stock (300 ml/½ pint if using fresh tomatoes;150 ml/¼ pint if using canned tomatoes in juice). Season to taste with salt and pepper. Return the chicken and ham or bacon to the pan, cover and cook gently for 40–45 minutes, or until the chicken is cooked through and tender.

5 Remove the chicken and transfer to a serving dish. Boil the sauce gently to reduce it, if necessary, until it is thick enough to coat the back of a spoon. Adjust the seasoning and pour over the chicken. Sprinkle with chopped parsley and serve.

Serves 4
Preparation time: 20 minutes
Cooking time: 1 hour

chicken stuffed with spinach and ricotta

4 boneless, skinless chicken breasts
125 g/4 oz ricotta cheese
125 g/4 oz cooked spinach, squeezed dry
¼ teaspoon grated nutmeg
8 slices of Parma ham
2 tablespoons olive oil
salt and pepper

1 Make a long horizontal slit through the thickness of each chicken breast without cutting right through.

2 Crumble the ricotta into a bowl. Chop the spinach and add to the ricotta with the nutmeg. Season to taste with salt and pepper and mix well.

3 Divide the stuffing between the 4 chicken breasts and wrap each one in 2 pieces of Parma ham, winding it around the chicken to totally cover the meat.

4 Heat the oil in a shallow ovenproof casserole. Add the chicken breasts and cook over a low heat for 4 minutes on each side, or until the ham starts to brown. Transfer the pan to a preheated oven, 200°C (400°F), Gas Mark 6, and cook for 15 minutes. The ham should be browned and slightly crunchy on the outside and the chicken moist and soft.

Serves 4
Preparation time: 10 minutes
Cooking time: 25 minutes
Oven temperature: 200°C (400°F), Gas Mark 6

devilled chicken

2 poussins
125 ml/4 fl oz olive oil
6 tablespoons lemon juice
2 tablespoons mixed peppercorns, coarsely crushed in a mortar
coarse sea salt or rock salt
lemon wedges, to garnish

1 First, spatchcock the poussins. Place 1 bird, breast side down, on a work surface and cut along each side of the backbone with poultry shears. Discard the backbone or use it in the stockpot. Put the bird, breast side up, on a board and press hard with your hand on the breastbone to break it. To keep the bird flat during cooking, push 2 metal skewers through the bird, 1 through the wings with the breast in between, the other through the thighs. Repeat with the other poussin.

2 Put the poussins in a non-metallic dish and slash them all over with the point of a small sharp knife.

3 Whisk together the oil, lemon juice and crushed peppercorns and brush all over the poussins, working the marinade into the cuts in the meat. Cover and leave to marinate for at least 4 hours, preferably overnight, in the refrigerator.

4 Prepare a barbecue and let it burn until the flames have died down and the coals are grey or heat a grill. Sprinkle the skin of the poussins with salt, then place them, skin side down, on the grill. Cook for 15 minutes, then turn over and cook for 10 minutes more.

5 Remove the poussins from the grill and cut each bird in half lengthways with poultry shears. Serve hot, warm or cold, with lemon wedges.

Serves 4
Preparation time: 10 minutes, plus marinating
Cooking time: 25 minutes

hunter's chicken with polenta

4 tablespoons olive oil
1 oven-ready chicken, jointed
1 onion, chopped
5 plum tomatoes, skinned and chopped
300 ml/½ pint dry white wine
1 rosemary sprig
1 tablespoon chopped thyme
15 g/½ oz plain flour
15 g/½ oz butter
salt and pepper
2 tablespoons chopped parsley, to garnish

Polenta:
750 ml/1¼ pints water
250 ml/8 fl oz milk
1 teaspoon salt
250 g/8 oz pre-cooked polenta
50 g/2 oz butter

1 Heat the oil in a large frying pan. Add the chicken joints and fry until golden all over, turning occasionally. Remove and keep warm.

2 Add the onion to the pan and cook gently until golden. Add the tomatoes, wine, rosemary, thyme and salt and pepper. Bring to the boil, stirring, and then reduce the heat to a simmer. Return the chicken to the pan and simmer, covered, for 20–30 minutes until the chicken is cooked through.

3 Meanwhile, cook the polenta. Bring the water and milk to the boil in a large pan, add the salt, then sprinkle in the polenta in a thin, steady stream, stirring all the time. Cook over a medium heat, stirring constantly, for 8 minutes, or according to the packet instructions. Remove from the heat, beat in the butter until melted and season with pepper.

4 Remove the chicken and arrange on a warm serving dish. Blend the flour with the butter and add to the sauce. Bring to the boil, stirring constantly until the sauce thickens slightly. Pour over the chicken, sprinkle with parsley and serve with the polenta.

Serves 4
Preparation time: 15 minutes
Cooking time: 30–40 minutes

chicken cacciatore

4 tablespoons olive oil
4 slices pancetta or unsmoked bacon, chopped
1 large chicken, about 1.5 kg/3 lb, cut into 4 portions
2 garlic cloves, crushed
2 red onions, roughly chopped
500 g/1 lb tomatoes, skinned and chopped
250 g/8 oz mushrooms, sliced
1 rosemary sprig
1 bay leaf
150 ml/¼ pint dry white wine
300 ml/½ pint Chicken Stock (see page 141)
salt and pepper
1 tablespoon chopped parsley, to garnish

1 Heat the oil in a large frying pan. Add the pancetta or bacon and fry, stirring occasionally, for 2–3 minutes until browned. Remove and keep warm.

2 Put the chicken portions in the pan and fry in the oil, turning occasionally, until they are golden brown all over. Remove the chicken from the pan and keep warm.

3 Add the garlic, onions, tomatoes and mushrooms and cook gently over a low heat, stirring occasionally, for 5 minutes. Return the chicken and pancetta or bacon to the frying pan.

4 Add the herbs, then pour in the wine and chicken stock. Simmer gently for about 1 hour until the chicken is tender and the sauce reduced. Season to taste with salt and pepper.

5 Serve hot, garnished with the chopped parsley.

Serves 4
Preparation time: 15 minutes
Cooking time: 1¼ hours

chicken with olives

175 g/6 oz black olives, pitted and chopped
1 tablespoon chopped parsley
1 tablespoon chopped chervil
1 tablespoon chopped tarragon
1 tablespoon chopped watercress
3 garlic cloves, chopped
150 g/5 oz butter, melted
4 chicken portions
3 tablespoons olive oil
1 bouquet garni
salt and pepper

1 Mix half of the black olives with all the fresh herbs, the watercress, garlic and melted butter. Season to taste with salt and pepper.

2 Rub the prepared herb, olive and butter mixture all over the chicken portions and transfer them to a large ovenproof dish. Prick the skin of the chicken all over with a sharp knife, then sprinkle with the olive oil. Add the bouquet garni to the dish.

3 Roast the chicken in a preheated oven, 200°C (400°F), Gas Mark 6, for 35–40 minutes.

4 Remove and discard the bouquet garni and serve the chicken garnished with the remaining olives.

Serves 4
Preparation time: 10 minutes
Cooking time: 35–45 minutes
Oven temperature: 200°C (400°F), Gas Mark 6

provençal chicken with fragrant herbs

1.5–2 kg/3–4 lb chicken
4 tablespoons lemon juice
3 tablespoons olive oil
25 g/1 oz butter, melted
pinch of herbes de Provence
1 lemon, peeled and sliced
salt and pepper
lemon slices, to garnish
boiled rice or vegetables, to serve

1 Place the chicken in a roasting tin and brush it all over with the lemon juice.

2 Mix 2 tablespoons of olive oil with the butter, salt, pepper and herbs. Coat the chicken with this sauce.

3 Place the lemon slices inside the chicken, then roast in a preheated oven, 180°C (350°F), Gas Mark 4, for 1½–1¾ hours.

4 Sprinkle the chicken with the remaining olive oil just before carving. Serve the chicken garnished with lemon slices and accompanied by plain boiled rice or vegetables.

Serves 4
Preparation time: 10 minutes
Cooking time: 1½–1¾ hours
Oven temperature: 180°C (350°F), Gas Mark 4

chicken tagine with almonds & saffron

2 tablespoons olive oil
4 large chicken breasts
2 onions, very finely chopped
2 celery sticks, finely chopped
2 small carrots, very finely chopped
1 garlic clove, crushed
150 ml/¼ pint Chicken Stock (see page 141)
large pinch of saffron threads
50 g/2 oz almonds, freshly ground
salt and pepper
roughly chopped coriander leaves, to garnish

1 Heat the oil in a heavy flameproof casserole. Add the chicken and brown evenly. Transfer to kitchen paper to drain.

2 Add the onions, celery, carrots and garlic to the casserole and cook gently for 5–7 minutes until lightly coloured. Add the stock and saffron. Stir in the almonds, season to taste with salt and pepper and bring gently to the boil.

3 Return the chicken to the casserole and add enough water almost to cover. Heat to simmering point, then cover the casserole tightly and cook over a very low heat for about 30–40 minutes until the chicken juices run clear when the thickest part is pierced with the point of a sharp knife.

4 Remove the chicken to a warm serving platter, cover and keep warm. Boil the cooking liquid to reduce it to the right consistency and flavour. Scatter over the coriander leaves and serve.

Serves 4
Preparation time: 15 minutes
Cooking time: 1–1¼ hours

moroccan red chicken

25 g/1 oz unsalted butter
4 chicken portions
1 onion, chopped
1 teaspoon black peppercorns, crushed
2 teaspoons paprika
1 teaspoon cumin seeds
5 cm/2 inch cinnamon stick
1 tablespoon chopped coriander
4 tablespoons lemon juice
salt

1 Heat the butter in a heavy flameproof casserole. Add the chicken, in batches, and brown evenly. Remove to kitchen paper to drain.

2 Add the onion to the casserole and fry gently until softened and translucent. Add the peppercorns, paprika, cumin and cinnamon, then return the chicken pieces to the pan. Pour in enough water to just cover the chicken, cover the casserole tightly and simmer gently for about 1 hour, turning the chicken a couple of times.

3 Transfer the chicken to a warm platter. Boil the cooking juices hard until reduced by half, then strain the juices and stir in the coriander and lemon juice. Season with salt to taste. Pour the juices over the chicken and serve.

Serves 4
Preparation time: 5 minutes
Cooking time: about 1¼ hours

saffron chicken with apricots

400 g/13 oz can chopped tomatoes
1 small onion, chopped
1 garlic clove, crushed
175 g/6 oz whole dried apricots
1.75 kg/3½ lb oven-ready chicken, jointed
2 teaspoons ground cinnamon, plus extra for flavouring
pinch of crushed saffron threads
3 tablespoons lemon juice, plus extra for flavouring
2 teaspoons orange flower water
1 tablespoon olive oil
50 g/2 oz dried apricots, sliced
3 tablespoons flaked almonds
2 tablespoons raisins
salt and pepper
salad, to serve

1 Make up the can of tomatoes to 450 ml/¾ pint with water and pour half of it into a heavy-based casserole, then add the onion, garlic and the whole dried apricots. Put the chicken into the casserole.

2 Mix the remaining tomato mixture with the cinnamon, saffron and lemon juice and pour over the chicken. Heat to simmering point, then cover the casserole tightly and simmer over a very low heat for about 35 minutes.

3 Transfer the chicken to a warm serving platter, cover and keep warm.

4 Pour the contents of the casserole into a food processor or blender and process to a purée. Strain the purée, if you like. Pour the purée into a saucepan and add the orange flower water and season to taste with salt and pepper.

5 Heat the oil in another saucepan. Add the sliced dried apricots, the almonds and raisins. Toss to warm through, then flavour with lemon juice and cinnamon.

6 Pour the sauce over the chicken and scatter with the almond mixture. Serve with a salad.

Serves 4
Preparation time: 20 minutes
Cooking time: 45 minutes

chicken with almonds

1 lemon, halved
4 chicken quarters
½ teaspoon ground ginger
½ teaspoon ground cinnamon
pinch of saffron threads, toasted and crushed
1 Spanish onion, finely chopped
125 g/4 oz blanched almonds, chopped
large bunch of parsley, finely chopped
salt and pepper

1 Squeeze the lemon over the chicken, rub in the juice and season with salt and pepper. Mix together the ginger, cinnamon and saffron and spread over the chicken. Cover and leave at room temperature for about 1 hour.

2 Put the chicken quarters into a heavy flameproof casserole in which they just fit. Add the onion and almonds and sufficient water almost to cover. Bring just to simmering point, cover and simmer over a very low heat for about 45–60 minutes, turning the chicken occasionally. Add the parsley and cook for a further 5 minutes.

3 Transfer the chicken to a warm plate, cover and keep warm. Boil the cooking juices in the casserole to give a well-flavoured sauce, adjusting the levels of the spices and salt and pepper, if necessary. Return the chicken to the casserole and turn in the sauce to coat completely.

Serves 4
Preparation time: 10 minutes, plus marinating
Cooking time: 1¼–1½ hours

cuban chicken with pineapple

2 kg/4 lb chicken, cut into 6 pieces
grated rind and juice of 1 lime
flour, for dusting
2 tablespoons olive oil
15 g/½ oz butter
1 onion, chopped

1 garlic clove, crushed
1 fresh red chilli, deseeded and finely chopped
2 tomatoes, skinned and chopped
3 tablespoons raisins
1 teaspoon brown sugar
salt and pepper

Sauce:
1 ripe pineapple, peeled and cored
2 tablespoons rum

1 Put the chicken pieces in a large bowl. Rub them all over with the lime juice and grated rind, and sprinkle with salt and pepper. Set aside for 30 minutes for the chicken to absorb the flavour of the lime.

2 Dust the chicken pieces lightly with flour. Heat the oil and butter in a large, heavy frying pan. Add the chicken to the hot oil and fry gently over a low heat until it is tender and golden brown. Turn the chicken frequently to cook it on both sides.

3 Add the onion, garlic and chilli and fry over a low heat for 5 minutes. Add the tomatoes, raisins and brown sugar, mix well and cook for a further 10 minutes.

4 Meanwhile, chop and crush the pineapple and then process to a pulp with all its juice in a blender or food processor. Transfer to a pan and simmer over a low heat until reduced to a quarter of its original volume. Stir in the rum, then pour the pineapple sauce over the chicken and serve.

Serves 6
Preparation time: 15 minutes, plus marinating
Cooking time: 40 minutes

jamaican jerked chicken

25 g/1 oz allspice berries
5 cm/2 inch cinnamon stick
1 teaspoon freshly grated nutmeg
1 fresh red chilli, deseeded and finely chopped
4 spring onions, thinly sliced
1 bay leaf, crumbled
1 tablespoon dark rum
6 chicken joints
salt and pepper
boiled rice, to serve

Pineapple chutney:
2 fresh pineapples, peeled and chopped
2.5 cm/1 inch piece of fresh root ginger, finely chopped
1 onion, finely chopped
1 fresh red chilli, deseeded and finely chopped
125 ml/4 fl oz vinegar
250 g/8 oz dark brown sugar

1 First, make the jerked seasoning. Pound the allspice berries, cinnamon and nutmeg in a mortar or grind them to a powder in an electric grinder. Add the chilli, spring onions, bay leaf and salt and pepper to the mortar and continue pounding to a thick paste.

2 Stir the rum into the paste and mix well. Slash the chicken deeply on the skin side 2 or 3 times and rub the jerked seasoning paste all over the chicken pieces. Cover and chill in the refrigerator for 1–2 hours.

3 Meanwhile, make the pineapple chutney. Put all the ingredients in a saucepan and stir well. Place over a moderate heat and stir until the sugar has completely dissolved. Bring to the boil and then reduce the heat a little. Cook vigorously, stirring occasionally, until the chutney thickens.

4 Pour the chutney into sterilized glass jars and seal. If wished, it can be made in advance and kept for 2–3 weeks in the refrigerator.

5 Roast the jerked chicken in a preheated oven, 200°C (400°F), Gas Mark 6, for 20–30 minutes, or cook under a hot grill. Serve with the pineapple chutney and plain boiled rice.

Serves 6
Preparation time: 20 minutes, plus marinating
Cooking time: 20–30 minutes
Oven temperature: 200°C (400°F), Gas Mark 6

grilled chicken creole

6 boneless, skinless chicken breasts
salt and pepper
boiled rice, to serve

Creole seasoning:
2 spring onions, finely chopped
½ red onion, finely chopped
2 garlic cloves, crushed
1 fresh red chilli, deseeded and finely chopped

3 chives, snipped
a few thyme sprigs, chopped
a few parsley sprigs, chopped
3 allspice berries, crushed
2 tablespoons lime juice
2 tablespoons olive oil

Avocado sauce:
1 large ripe avocado
1 tablespoon finely chopped onion
½ garlic clove, crushed
cayenne pepper
lime juice (optional)

1 First, prepare the Creole seasoning. Put the spring onions, onion, garlic, chilli, herbs and allspice berries in a bowl. Add the lime juice and olive oil and stir well to mix thoroughly together.

2 Slash the chicken breasts 2 or 3 times on both sides and season lightly with salt and pepper. Rub the seasoning over both sides of each chicken breast, pressing it into the slashes. Cover and chill in the refrigerator for 2–3 hours.

3 Put the chicken breasts on a grill rack and cook under a preheated hot grill, turning once, until cooked on both sides. Take care that the herbs do not burn. Alternatively, cook them in a preheated oven, 200°C (400°F), Gas Mark 6, for about 20 minutes.

4 While the chicken is cooking, make the avocado sauce. Mash the avocado to a smooth paste and beat in the onion, garlic and cayenne pepper to taste. Add a little lime juice, if wished, to prevent the sauce from discolouring. Serve with the chicken and rice.

Serves 4
Preparation time: 10 minutes, plus marinating
Cooking time: 15–20 minutes
Oven temperature: 200°C (400°F), Gas Mark 6

mexican orange chicken

1 teaspoon salt
¼ teaspoon ground cinnamon
pinch of ground cloves
4 skinless chicken portions
2 tablespoons oil
1 onion, chopped
2 garlic cloves, crushed

150 ml/¼ pint fresh orange juice
150 ml/¼ pint Chicken Stock (see page 141)
2 tablespoons raisins
2 green chillies, deseeded and sliced
50 g/2 oz slivered almonds
3 oranges, peeled and thinly sliced
2 tablespoons chopped coriander

1 Mix together the salt, ground cinnamon and cloves and rub this spicy mixture all over the chicken portions to flavour them.

2 Heat the oil in a large frying pan. Add the chicken and fry, turning occasionally, until all the chicken pieces are browned all over. Remove from the pan and pour off any excess fat. Keep the chicken warm.

3 Add the onion and garlic to the pan and fry over a low heat until tender and golden. Return the chicken to the pan and stir in the orange juice, stock, raisins and chillies. Cover the pan and simmer for 1 hour, or until the chicken is cooked and tender.

4 Add the almonds and the orange slices and stir gently. Heat through over a low heat for about 5 minutes. Serve the orange chicken sprinkled with chopped coriander.

Serves 4
Preparation time: 15 minutes
Cooking time: 1½ hours

carnival chicken with sweet potato mash

4 skinless chicken breasts
flat leaf parsley sprigs, to garnish

Marinade:
100 ml/3½ fl oz sweet sherry
1 teaspoon Angostura bitters
1 tablespoon light soy sauce
1 tablespoon chopped fresh root ginger
pinch of ground cumin
pinch of ground coriander
1 teaspoon dried mixed herbs
1 small onion, finely chopped
75 ml/3 fl oz Chicken Stock (see page 141)

Sweet potato mash:
2 sweet potatoes
2 tablespoons fromage frais (optional)
salt and pepper

1 Place the chicken breasts in a non-metallic dish. Mix together all the marinade ingredients in a bowl. Spoon the marinade over the chicken, making sure all the pieces are well coated. Cover and leave to marinate in the refrigerator overnight.

2 Place the chicken breasts on a grill pan and cook under a preheated moderate grill for 20 minutes, turning them over halfway through cooking.

3 Meanwhile, boil the sweet potatoes in their skins for 20 minutes until soft. Drain well and peel. Mash the potato and let it dry off slightly, then stir in the fromage frais, if using. Season to taste with salt and pepper and serve with the chicken. Garnish with the parsley.

Serves 4
Preparation time: 15–20 minutes, plus marinating
Cooking time: 20 minutes

stewed chicken with chestnuts and ginger

6 tablespoons soy sauce
1 tablespoon dry sherry
1 kg/2 lb chicken, boned and cut into 3.5 cm/1½ inch pieces
2 tablespoons oil
1 cm/½ inch piece of fresh root ginger, chopped
4 spring onions, chopped
500 g/1 lb chestnuts, peeled and skinned
450 ml/¾ pint water
1 tablespoon sugar

1 Mix together the soy sauce and sherry in a dish and add the chicken. Leave to marinate for 15 minutes.

2 Heat the oil in a large pan. Add the chicken mixture, ginger and half the spring onions and stir-fry until the chicken is golden.

3 Add the chestnuts, water and sugar. Bring to the boil, cover and simmer for 40 minutes, or until tender. Serve hot, garnished with the remaining spring onions. Stir in a little cornflour paste to thicken the sauce, if liked.

Serves 3–4
Preparation time: 10 minutes, plus marinating
Cooking time: 50 minutes

4 Add the soy sauce and stir, then return the batter-coated chicken to the pan and stir again over a high heat. Serve, garnished with the spring onion and coriander sprigs.

Serves 2
Preparation time: 10 minutes
Cooking time: 12–14 minutes

stir-fried chicken with pineapple

oil, for deep-frying
50 g/2 oz tempura flour or self-raising flour
75 ml/3 fl oz water
125 g/4 oz skinless, boneless chicken, cut into
   bite-sized pieces
1 tablespoon vegetable oil
150 g/5 oz fresh pineapple, cut into chunks
1 tomato, cut into 8 pieces
1 tablespoon tomato purée
1 tablespoon palm sugar or light muscovado sugar
50 g/2 oz cashew nuts
4½ teaspoons light soy sauce

To garnish:
1 spring onion, diagonally sliced
coriander sprigs

1 Heat the oil in a preheated wok or frying pan to 180–190°C (350–375°F) or until a cube of bread browns in 30 seconds. Meanwhile, thoroughly mix together the flour and water to make a coating batter.

2 Coat half the chicken pieces in the batter and deep-fry them until they are golden brown. Remove from the oil and drain on kitchen paper. Repeat the process with the rest of the chicken.

3 Pour off the oil, wipe the wok clean with kitchen paper, then heat the vegetable oil in it. Add the pineapple, tomato, tomato purée, sugar and cashew nuts and stir-fry for 2 minutes.

oriental chicken with turmeric

100 g/3½ oz creamed coconut, roughly chopped
50 g/2 oz macadamia nuts, roughly chopped
1 garlic clove, roughly chopped
3 tablespoons vegetable oil
1 onion, finely chopped
8 chicken thighs, boned, skinned and cut into large
   chunks
1 tablespoon turmeric
thinly pared rind and juice of 1 lemon
salt and pepper
flat leaf parsley sprigs, to garnish

1 Put the chopped coconut into a measuring jug, pour in boiling water up to the 300 ml/½ pint mark and stir until the coconut is dissolved. Set aside.

2 Pound half of the macadamia nuts to a paste with the garlic using a mortar and pestle or process in a food processor.

3 Heat the oil in a preheated wok or frying pan over a moderate heat. Add the onion, together with the nut and garlic paste, and stir-fry for 2–3 minutes until the onion is softened, taking care not to let it brown.

4 Add the chicken pieces, increase the heat to high and stir-fry for 1–2 minutes until the chicken is lightly coloured on all sides. Stir in the turmeric and season with salt and pepper to taste. Add the coconut milk and bring to the boil, stirring constantly.

5 Lower the heat, add the lemon rind and juice and simmer, stirring frequently, for about 10 minutes, or until the chicken is tender and the sauce thickened. Remove and discard the lemon rind. Taste for seasoning and serve hot, sprinkled with the remaining chopped macadamia nuts and flat leaf parsley sprigs.

Serves 3–4
Preparation time: 20 minutes
Cooking time: about 20 minutes

coconut grilled chicken

4 boneless chicken breasts

Marinade:
425 ml/14 fl oz coconut milk
4 garlic cloves, crushed
4 small green or red chillies, deseeded and chopped
2.5 cm/1 inch piece of fresh root ginger, sliced
grated rind and juice of 1 lime
2 tablespoons palm sugar or light muscovado sugar
3 tablespoons light soy sauce
1 tablespoon Thai fish sauce
25 g/1 oz coriander leaves, stalks and roots

To garnish:
red chilli, finely diced
spring onion slivers

1 To make the marinade, blend together all the ingredients.

2 Make 3 diagonal cuts on each side of the chicken breasts, place them in a dish and pour over the marinade. Cover and leave them in the refrigerator for 2 hours.

3 Arrange the chicken pieces in the grill pan, making sure they are fairly thickly spread with the marinade. Cook under a preheated grill for about 15 minutes, turning occasionally. The skin side will take a little longer than the other side.

4 Meanwhile, heat the remaining marinade in a saucepan, adding a little chicken stock or water if it is too thick.

5 When the chicken is cooked, cut it into slices and arrange on a serving dish. Serve garnished with spring onion slivers and diced chilli, with the sauce in a separate bowl.

Serves 4
Preparation time: 10 minutes, plus marinating
Cooking time: 15 minutes

steamed chicken with chinese cabbage

1.5 kg/3 lb oven-ready chicken
2 teaspoons salt
6–8 dried shiitake mushrooms
750 g/1½ lb Chinese cabbage
5 slices of fresh root ginger
2 chicken stock cubes

1 Bring a large saucepan of water to the boil. Add the salt and immerse the chicken in the water. Skim off all scum that rises to the surface and boil for 5–6 minutes. Drain the chicken.

2 Meanwhile, soak the mushrooms in boiling water and leave to stand for 20 minutes. Drain and discard the stems. Cut the cabbage into 5 cm/2 inch slices.

3 Place the mushroom caps and ginger in a large, deep, heatproof bowl. Put the chicken on top of the mushrooms and pour in just enough water to cover it. Cover the top of the bowl tightly with kitchen foil. Place the bowl in a large saucepan of water, which should not come more than halfway up the sides of the bowl. Bring the water to the boil, then simmer for 1 hour, topping up with boiling water if necessary.

4 Lift out the chicken. Place the sliced cabbage in the bottom of the bowl and sprinkle with the crumbled stock cubes. Replace the chicken. Tightly cover the bowl again with foil and simmer gently for a further 1 hour. Arrange the vegetables and chicken on a warm platter to serve.

Serves 4–6
Preparation time: 10 minutes, plus soaking
Cooking time: 2¼ hours

spicy chicken and peanuts

125 g/4 oz unsalted peanuts
375 g/12 oz boneless, skinless chicken breasts
2 tablespoons oil
1 dried red chilli
2 tablespoons dry sherry
1 tablespoon dark soy sauce
pinch of sugar
1 garlic clove, crushed
2 spring onions, chopped
2.5 cm/1 inch piece of fresh root ginger, finely chopped
1 teaspoon wine vinegar
2 teaspoons sesame oil
sliced red chilli, to garnish

1 Immerse the peanuts in a bowl of boiling water for about 2 minutes. Drain well, remove the skins and place on kitchen paper to dry thoroughly. Cut the chicken into 2.5 cm/1 inch cubes.

2 Heat the oil in a preheated wok or heavy-based frying pan. Crumble the chilli into the pan, add the chicken and peanuts and stir-fry for 1 minute. Remove from the pan.

3 Add the sherry, soy sauce, sugar, garlic, spring onions, ginger and vinegar to the pan. Bring to the boil, then simmer for 30 seconds. Return the chicken, chilli and peanuts to the pan and cook for 2 minutes. Sprinkle over the sesame oil.

4 Pile on to a warm serving dish, garnish with red chilli and serve immediately.

Serves 4
Preparation: 10 minutes
Cooking time: about 5 minutes

chicken and leeks

½ cucumber
375 g/12 oz boneless, skinlesss chicken breasts
2 tablespoons oil
3 leeks, thinly sliced diagonally
4 garlic cloves, thinly sliced
1 tablespoon light soy sauce
1 tablespoon dry sherry
1 dried red chilli, crumbled
1 tablespoon chopped coriander leaves
salt
coriander leaves, to garnish

1 Peel the cucumber, cut in half and remove the seeds with a teaspoon. Cut the flesh into 2.5 cm/1 inch cubes, place in a colander and sprinkle with salt. Set aside for 20 minutes, then rinse well and drain.

2 Meanwhile, cut the chicken into 2.5 cm/1 inch cubes.

3 Heat the oil in a preheated wok or heavy-based frying pan. Add the leeks and garlic and cook briskly for 30 seconds. Add the chicken and brown quickly for 1 minute. Add the soy sauce, sherry and chilli and cook for a further 30 seconds. Stir in the cucumber and cook for 30 seconds.

4 Transfer to a warm serving dish, sprinkle with the chopped coriander, garnish with coriander leaves and serve immediately.

Serves 4
Preparation: 20 minutes, plus standing
Cooking time: 2½ minutes

ginger chicken with honey

5 spring onions, sliced into 1 cm/½ inch pieces
50 g/2 oz piece of fresh root ginger, finely chopped
2 tablespoons vegetable oil
375 g/12 oz boneless, skinlesss chicken breasts, thinly sliced
3 chicken livers, chopped
2 tablespoons dried Chinese black mushrooms, soaked in warm water for 20 minutes
1 onion, sliced
3 garlic cloves, crushed
2 tablespoons soy sauce
1 tablespoon clear honey

1 Put the spring onions into a bowl, cover with cold water and leave to soak until required. Mix the chopped ginger with a little cold water, then drain and squeeze to remove its heat. Rinse under cold running water and drain well.

2 Heat the oil in a preheated wok or frying pan over moderate heat. Add the chicken and chicken livers and stir-fry for 5 minutes. Remove with a slotted spoon and set aside.

3 Drain the mushrooms and squeeze them dry. Discard the stalks. Add the onion to the wok and fry over a low heat until soft. Add the garlic and mushrooms and stir-fry for 1 minute. Return the cooked chicken pieces and chicken livers to the wok.

4 Mix the soy sauce and honey, stirring until blended. Pour over the chicken and stir well. Add the drained ginger and stir-fry for 2–3 minutes. Add the drained spring onions, mix well, then transfer to a serving dish. This dish tastes even better if it is cooked the day before and then reheated.

Serves 4
Preparation time: 15 minutes, plus soaking
Cooking time: 15 minutes

3 Heat the oil in a preheated wok or frying pan. With a fork, lift the strips of chicken one at a time out of the egg white mixture and drop into the hot oil. Shallow-fry, in batches, for about 3–4 minutes, or until golden. Remove with a slotted spoon and drain on kitchen paper. Keep the chicken hot.

4 Pour off all but 1 tablespoon of the oil from the wok. Add the spring onions and garlic and stir-fry over a moderate heat for 30 seconds. Stir the sauce, pour it into the wok and stir to mix. Increase the heat to high and bring to the boil, stirring constantly.

5 Return the chicken to the wok and stir-fry for 1–2 minutes, or until evenly coated in the sauce. Serve at once, garnished with lemon slices.

Serves 2
Preparation time: 20 minutes
Cooking time: about 15 minutes

chinese lemon chicken

1 egg white
2 teaspoons cornflour
pinch of salt
250 g/8 oz boneless, skinless chicken breasts, cut into thin strips across the grain
300 ml/½ pint vegetable oil
½ bunch of spring onions, shredded
1 garlic clove, crushed
lemon slices, to garnish

Sauce:
2 teaspoons cornflour
Chicken Stock (see page 141) or water
finely grated rind of ½ lemon
2 tablespoons lemon juice
1 tablespoon soy sauce
2 teaspoons Chinese rice wine or dry sherry
2 teaspoons caster sugar

1 First prepare the sauce. Mix the cornflour to a thin paste with a little stock or water, then stir in the remaining sauce ingredients. Set aside.

2 Lightly beat the egg white in a shallow dish with the cornflour and a pinch of salt. Add the strips of chicken and turn to coat. Set aside.

stir-fried chicken with celery

250 g/8 oz boneless, skinless chicken breasts, shredded
½ teaspoon salt
1 egg white
1 tablespoon cornflour
4 tablespoons vegetable oil
2.5 cm/1 inch piece of fresh root ginger, cut into thin strips
2 spring onions, cut into thin strips
1 small celery stick, cut into strips
1 green pepper, cored, deseeded and cut into thin strips
2 tablespoons soy sauce
1 tablespoon dry sherry

1 Place the chicken in a bowl. Add the salt, egg white and cornflour and mix thoroughly.

2 Heat the oil in a preheated wok or frying pan. Add the chicken shreds and stir-fry over a moderate heat until the chicken is lightly and evenly coloured. Remove the chicken with a slotted spoon and set aside.

3 Increase the heat and, when the oil is very hot, add the ginger and spring onions followed by the celery and green pepper. Stir-fry for about 30 seconds over a high heat.

4 Return the chicken shreds to the wok, together with the soy sauce and sherry. Mix well and cook, stirring constantly, for a further 1–1½ minutes. Transfer to a serving dish and serve immediately.

Serves 3–4
Preparation time: 15 minutes
Cooking time: 7–8 minutes

stir-fried lemon chicken with vegetables

375 g/12 oz boneless, skinless chicken breasts
2 tablespoons Chinese rice wine or dry sherry
4 spring onions, chopped
2.5 cm/1 inch piece of fresh root ginger, finely chopped
2 tablespoons sunflower oil
1–2 garlic cloves, sliced
2 celery sticks, sliced diagonally
1 small green pepper, cored, deseeded and sliced
  lengthways
2 tablespoons light soy sauce
2 tablespoons lemon juice
shredded rind of 2 lemons
¼ teaspoon chilli powder

To garnish:
lemon slices
parsley sprig

1 Cut the chicken into 7 cm/3 inch strips. Mix the wine or sherry with the spring onions and ginger. Add the chicken and toss well to coat the pieces. Set aside to marinate for 15 minutes.

2 Heat the oil in a preheated wok or frying pan. Add the garlic, celery and green pepper and stir-fry for 1 minute. Add the chicken in its marinade and cook for a further 2 minutes.

3 Stir in the soy sauce, lemon juice and rind and the chilli powder, and cook for a further 1 minute. Transfer to a warm serving dish and garnish with lemon slices and a sprig of parsley.

Serves 4
Preparation time: 10 minutes, plus marinating
Cooking time: 4 minutes

cashew chicken with garlic, wine and ginger

375 g/12 oz boneless, skinless chicken breasts
1 egg white, lightly beaten
4 tablespoons Chinese rice wine or dry sherry
2 teaspoons cornflour
3 tablespoons sunflower oil
4 spring onions, chopped
2 garlic cloves, chopped
2.5 cm/1 inch piece of fresh root ginger, finely chopped
1 tablespoon light soy sauce
125 g/4 oz unsalted cashew nuts

1 Cut the chicken into 1 cm/½ inch cubes. Mix together the egg white, half the wine or sherry and the cornflour. Place the chicken cubes in this mixture and toss until evenly coated.

2 Heat the oil in a preheated wok or frying pan. Add the spring onions, garlic and ginger and stir-fry for 30 seconds. Add the chicken and cook for 2 minutes.

3 Pour in the remaining wine or sherry and the soy sauce and stir well. Add the cashews and cook for a further 30 seconds. Serve at once.

Serves 4
Preparation time: 10 minutes
Cooking time: 4 minutes

chicken with coconut milk

about 3 tablespoons oil
4 boneless, skinless chicken breasts, cut into 3 or 4 pieces
6 cardamom pods
6 cloves
5 cm/2 inch cinnamon stick
1 large onion, finely sliced
2 garlic cloves
3.5 cm/1½ inch piece of fresh root ginger, chopped
3 green chillies, deseeded
4 tablespoons lemon juice
1 teaspoon turmeric
50 g/2 oz creamed coconut
150 ml/¼ pint hot water
salt
strips of red pepper, to garnish

1 Heat the oil in a heavy-based saucepan. Add the chicken and fry quickly all over. Remove with a slotted spoon and set aside.

2 Add a little more oil to the pan, if necessary, and fry the cardamom, cloves and cinnamon for 1 minute. Add the onion and fry over a low heat for about 5 minutes until softened.

3 Place the garlic, ginger, chillies and lemon juice in a food processor or blender and process to a smooth paste. Add to the pan, together with the turmeric, and cook for 5 minutes.

4 Melt the coconut in the hot water and add to the pan. Season to taste with salt. Simmer for 2 minutes, then add the chicken pieces and any juices. Simmer for 15–20 minutes until tender.

5 Transfer to a warm serving dish, garnish with red pepper strips and serve immediately.

Serves 4
Preparation time: 10 minutes
Cooking time: 35–40 minutes

chicken korma

175 ml/6 fl oz natural yogurt
2 teaspoons turmeric
3 garlic cloves, sliced
1.5 kg/3 lb oven-ready chicken, skinned and cut into 8 pieces
125 g/4 oz ghee or 4 tablespoons vegetable oil
1 large onion, sliced
1 teaspoon ground ginger
5 cm/2 inch cinnamon stick
5 cloves
5 cardamom pods
1 tablespoon crushed coriander seeds
1 teaspoon ground cumin
½ teaspoon chilli powder
1 teaspoon salt
4½ teaspoons desiccated coconut

To garnish:
2 teaspoons toasted almonds
coriander leaves

1 Put the yogurt, turmeric and one of the garlic cloves into a food processor or blender and process the mixture to a smooth purée.

2 Place the chicken pieces in a shallow dish and pour the yogurt mixture over them. Cover the dish and leave to marinate in the refrigerator overnight.

3 Heat the ghee or oil in a large, heavy-based saucepan. Add the onion and remaining garlic and fry over a low heat for 4–5 minutes until soft. Add the spices and salt and fry, stirring constantly, for a further 3 minutes.

4 Add the chicken pieces with the yogurt marinade and coconut and mix well. Cover the pan with a tightly fitting lid and simmer gently for 45 minutes, or until the chicken is cooked and tender. Transfer to a warm serving dish and scatter with the almonds and coriander leaves.

Serves 4
Preparation time: 15 minutes, plus marinating
Cooking time: 55 minutes

chicken with cashews

4 boneless, skinless chicken breasts
2 tablespoons vegetable oil
1 bunch of spring onions, thinly sliced diagonally
2 garlic cloves, crushed
125 g/4 oz cashews
pepper
boiled rice, to serve

Sauce:
2 teaspoons cornflour
6 tablespoons Chicken Stock (see page 141) or water
3 tablespoons soy sauce
2 tablespoons Chinese rice wine or dry sherry
2 teaspoons dark soft brown sugar

1 First prepare the sauce. Place the cornflour in a bowl, add 1 tablespoon of the stock or water and work to a paste. Stir in the remaining stock or water, the soy sauce, rice wine or sherry and sugar. Set aside.

2 Cut the chicken breasts into thin strips across the grain. Heat the oil in a preheated wok or frying pan over a moderate heat. Add the chicken strips, increase the heat to high and stir-fry for 3–4 minutes until lightly coloured on all sides. Add the spring onions and garlic and stir-fry for a further 1 minute.

3 Stir the sauce to mix, then pour into the wok. Bring to the boil, stirring constantly. Add the cashews and toss to combine with the chicken and spring onions. Season with pepper to taste and serve immediately with rice.

Serves 3–4
Preparation time: 10 minutes
Cooking time: 10–15 minutes

tandoori chicken

8 skinless chicken quarters
8 tablespoons lemon juice
2 teaspoons salt

Marinade:
10 cloves
2 teaspoons coriander seeds
2 teaspoons cumin seeds
seeds of 10 cardamom pods
2 onions, chopped
4 garlic cloves, chopped
7 cm/3 inch piece of fresh root ginger, chopped
2 teaspoons chilli powder
2 teaspoons pepper
1½ teaspoons turmeric
350 ml/12 fl oz natural yogurt
few drops of red food colouring (optional)

1 Score each piece of chicken several times with a sharp knife. Place in a large non-metallic dish and sprinkle with the lemon juice and salt. Rub this mixture in well, then cover and leave in a cool place for 1 hour.

2 Meanwhile, prepare the marinade. Spread the cloves, coriander, cumin and cardamom seeds on a baking tray and roast in a preheated oven, 200°C (400°F), Gas Mark 6, for 10–15 minutes. Leave to cool, then grind them coarsely in a mortar.

3 Put the onions, garlic and ginger in a blender or food processor and sprinkle with the chilli powder, pepper and turmeric. Add the yogurt and ground roasted spices and strain in the lemon juice from the chicken. Process until smooth, adding some red food colouring, if wished.

4 Place the chicken pieces in a single layer in a large roasting pan and pour over the marinade. Cover the pan and leave in the refrigerator to marinate for at least 24 hours, turning occasionally. Cook in a preheated oven, 200°C (400°F), Gas Mark 6, for 20 minutes and then place under a hot grill until crisp. Serve hot or cold.

Serves 8
Preparation time: 30 minutes, plus standing and marinating
Cooking time: 40 minutes
Oven temperature: 200°C (400°F), Gas Mark 6

chicken matsaman curry

3 tablespoons vegetable oil
4 chicken drumsticks
350 ml/12 fl oz coconut milk
4½ teaspoons matsaman curry paste
3 new potatoes, scrubbed or peeled
1 onion, quartered
½ teaspoon lemon juice
4½ teaspoons Thai fish sauce
1½ teaspoons sugar
25 g/1 oz roasted peanuts

1 Heat the oil in a large saucepan. Add the chicken drumsticks and brown on all sides. Stir the coconut milk into the pan and bring to the boil. Add the curry paste. Lower the heat and simmer for 2 hours.

2 Stir in the potatoes, onion, lemon juice, fish sauce, sugar and peanuts, cover the pan and simmer for a further 20 minutes. Serve immediately.

Serves 4
Preparation time: 15 minutes
Cooking time: about 2½ hours

indian chicken and lentils

500 g/1 lb dried split peas or lentils
1.2 litres/2 pints water
175 g/6 oz ghee or 5 tablespoons vegetable oil
2 large onions, sliced
4 garlic cloves, sliced
6 cloves
6 cardamoms
1½ teaspoons ground ginger
2 teaspoons garam masala
2½ teaspoons salt
1.5 kg/3 lb oven-ready chicken, skinned, boned and cut
  into 8 pieces
500 g/1 lb frozen leaf spinach
4 large tomatoes, skinned and chopped

1 Place the split peas or lentils in a large saucepan. Add the water and bring to the boil. Cover the pan, lower the heat and simmer for 15 minutes.

2 Heat the ghee or oil in a large, heavy-based saucepan. Add the onions and garlic and fry for 4–5 minutes until soft. Add the spices and salt and fry, stirring constantly, for 3 minutes. Add the chicken and brown on all sides, then remove and drain on absorbent kitchen paper.

3 Add the spinach and tomatoes to the saucepan and fry over a low heat, stirring occasionally, for 10 minutes.

4 Mash the peas or lentils in their cooking water and then stir them into the spinach mixture. Return the chicken to the pan, cover with a tightly-fitting lid and simmer gently for 45 minutes, or until the chicken is cooked and tender.

Serves 4
Preparation time: 30 minutes
Cooking time: 1¼ hours

white chicken curry

3 tablespoons oil
2 onions, thinly sliced
8 long green chillies, thinly sliced lengthways
2.5 cm/1 inch piece of fresh ginger, thinly sliced
1 teaspoon salt

75 g/3 oz creamed coconut, melted in
  450 ml/¾ pint hot water
4 chicken thighs and 4 chicken legs, skinned
3 tablespoons lime juice

1 Heat the oil in a saucepan. Add the onions and fry gently for 3 minutes, but do not let them colour. Add the chillies, ginger and salt. Stir well, then pour in the coconut mixture.

2 Add the chicken and simmer gently for 30 minutes, or until cooked through. Stir occasionally and if there is any hint of the sauce catching, add a little water.

3 When ready, remove from the heat, stir in the lime juice and serve immediately.

Serves 4
Preparation time: 5 minutes
Cooking time: 35 minutes

chicken tikka masala

Chicken tikka:
500 g/1 lb boneless, skinless chicken breasts, cubed
1 teaspoon finely chopped fresh root ginger
1 teaspoon finely chopped garlic
1 teaspoon chilli powder
¼ teaspoon turmeric
1 tablespoon ground coriander
1 teaspoon salt
150 ml/¼ pint natural yogurt
4 tablespoons lemon juice
3 tablespoons chopped coriander leaves
1 tablespoon lime juice

Masala sauce:
50 g/2 oz ghee or 2 tablespoons vegetable oil
2 onions, thinly sliced
2.5 cm/1 inch piece of fresh root ginger, finely chopped
2 garlic cloves, crushed
6 cardamoms, bruised
2 teaspoons garam masala
2 teaspoons ground coriander
½–1 teaspoon chilli powder
300 ml/½ pint double cream
2 tablespoons tomato purée
4 tablespoons hot water
½ teaspoon sugar
½ teaspoon salt

To garnish:
coriander leaves
lime slices

To serve:
boiled rice
chapatis or naan bread

1 First, prepare the chicken. Mix together the chicken, ginger, garlic, chilli powder, turmeric, ground coriander, salt, yogurt, lemon juice and 1 tablespoon of the chopped coriander in a large, non-metallic dish. Cover and leave to marinate in the refrigerator for at least 6 hours or overnight.

2 To make the masala sauce, heat the ghee or vegetable oil in a large flameproof casserole. Add the onions, ginger and garlic and fry over a low heat, stirring frequently, for about 5 minutes until soft but not browned.

3 Add the spices and fry, stirring, for 1–2 minutes until fragrant, then add the cream, tomato purée, water, sugar and salt. Bring to the boil over a moderate heat, stirring, then lower the heat and simmer gently, stirring occasionally, for 10–15 minutes. Remove the pan from the heat and leave to stand while cooking the chicken.

4 Remove the chicken from the marinade and thread on wooden skewers. Cook under a preheated grill, turning frequently, for 6–8 minutes until tender and cooked through.

5 Remove the cubes of chicken from the skewers and tip it into the masala sauce. Place over a low heat and simmer, stirring, for about 5 minutes. Add the remaining chopped coriander leaves and the lime juice. Taste and adjust the seasoning if necessary.

6 Serve immediately, garnished with coriander leaves and slices of lime and accompanied by plain boiled rice, chapatis or naan bread.

Serves 4
Preparation time: 20 minutes, plus marinating
Cooking time: 40–45 minutes

kashmiri chicken

50 g/2 oz ghee or 2 tablespoons vegetable oil
3 large onions, finely sliced
10 peppercorns
10 cardamoms
5 cm/2 inch piece of cinnamon stick
5 cm/2 inch piece of fresh root ginger, finely chopped
2 garlic cloves, finely chopped
1 teaspoon chilli powder
2 teaspoons paprika
1.5 kg/3 lb skinless chicken pieces
250 ml/8 fl oz natural yogurt
salt

1 Heat the ghee or vegetable oil in a deep frying pan. Add the onions, peppercorns, cardamoms and cinnamon and fry until the onions are golden. Add the ginger, garlic, chilli powder, paprika and salt to taste and fry, stirring occasionally, for 2 minutes.

2 Add the chicken pieces and fry until browned. Gradually add the yogurt, stirring constantly. Cover and cook gently for about 30 minutes.

Serves 6
Preparation time: 20 minutes
Cooking time: 40 minutes

balti chicken with green pepper

6 tablespoons vegetable oil
1 onion, chopped
½ teaspoon ground turmeric
1 teaspoon ground coriander
1 teaspoon ground cumin
1 teaspoon chilli powder
2 tablespoons water
750 g/1½ lb boneless, skinless chicken meat, cubed
1 kg/2 lb tomatoes, chopped
1 large green pepper, cored, deseeded and diced
4–6 garlic cloves, chopped
2 fresh green chillies, chopped
salt

To garnish:
2 tomatoes, quartered
coriander sprigs

1 Heat the oil in a large wok or heavy-based saucepan. Add the onion and fry until soft. Mix the turmeric, coriander, cumin and chilli powder with the water. Stir this spice mixture into the onions and cook for about 3–4 minutes, until the liquid has evaporated.

2 Add the chicken and fry on all sides, then add the tomatoes and salt to taste. Cover and cook for about 15 minutes.

3 Stir in the green pepper, garlic and chillies. Cook, uncovered, until all the tomato juices have evaporated and the chicken is cooked through. Serve hot, garnished with the tomatoes and sprigs of coriander.

Serves 4–6
Preparation time: 20 minutes
Cooking time: 30–40 minutes

3 Place the coriander leaves and green chillies in a blender or food processor and process to a paste. Add this paste to the pan, reduce the heat to very low and cook, stirring constantly, for a further 10 minutes.

4 Add the chicken pieces to the pan, turn them in the spice mixture to coat them evenly, then add the stock, coconut milk and salt. Bring to the boil, reduce the heat, cover and simmer, stirring and turning the chicken occasionally, for about 50 minutes, or until the juices from the chicken run clear when tested with a skewer. Stir in the lemon juice and taste and adjust the amount of salt, if necessary.

5 Transfer the cooked chicken pieces to a serving dish and keep them warm. Increase the heat and boil the curry sauce for 5–8 minutes to thicken it. Pour it over the chicken and garnish with coriander leaves.

Serves 6
Preparation time: 20 minutes
Cooking time: 1 hour 20 minutes

bangalore chicken curry

3 tablespoons ghee or vegetable oil
2 onions, thinly sliced
6 garlic cloves, chopped
1 teaspoon turmeric
¾ teaspoon ground coriander
¾ teaspoon ground cumin
40 g/1½ oz coriander leaves
3 large fresh green chillies, deseeded and chopped
1.75 kg/3½ lb chicken, cut into 8 pieces
150 ml/¼ pint Chicken Stock (see page 141)
300 ml/½ pint coconut milk
1 teaspoon salt
1 tablespoon lemon juice
coriander leaves, to garnish

1 Heat the ghee or oil in a large heavy-based frying pan. Add the onions and fry over a medium heat, stirring frequently, for about 5 minutes until they are softened and golden.

2 Stir in the garlic, turmeric, ground coriander and cumin and cook, stirring, for a further 3 minutes.

poussins with herb sauce

2 tablespoons oil
4 x 400 g/13 oz poussins
grated rind and juice of 1 lemon
2 tablespoons Chicken Stock (see page 141) or water
2 tablespoons chopped mixed herbs, such as parsley,
  chives, thyme and marjoram
150 ml/¼ pint double cream
salt and pepper
watercress, to garnish

1 Heat the oil in a large saucepan. Add the poussins and brown lightly all over.

2 Add the lemon rind and juice, stock and salt and pepper to taste. Cover and simmer for about 20–25 minutes until tender and cooked through. Place on a warm serving dish and keep hot.

3 Add the herbs and cream to the pan and heat gently. Check the seasoning. Pour the sauce around the poussins and garnish with watercress to serve.

Serves 4
Preparation time: 5 minutes
Cooking time: 40–45 minutes

spatchcock poussin with chilli jam

125 g/4 oz red chillies, cored, deseeded and roughly
  chopped
1 onion, chopped
5 cm/2 inch piece of fresh root ginger, peeled and diced
125 ml/4 fl oz white vinegar
500 g/1 lb sugar
2 poussins

1 First make the chilli jam. Place the chillies in a food
processor or blender with the onion, ginger and vinegar.
Process until finely chopped.

2 Place the chilli mixture in a saucepan and add the
sugar. Bring to the boil, then simmer for 10 minutes. The
mixture should be thick, sticky and jam-like.

3 Place 1 poussin on a board, breast downwards. Cut
along the backbone on both sides with poultry shears or
a sharp knife and remove. Open out the poussin and
place, skin side up, on a chopping board. Beat gently
with a meat mallet or rolling pin to flatten, but avoid
splintering the bones and tearing the skin. Fold the
wing tips under the wings, so that they lie flat. Insert
2 skewers, criss-cross fashion, to hold it flat. Repeat with
the other poussin.

4 Heat a griddle pan or nonstick frying pan. Put on the
poussins, flesh side down. Cook for 15 minutes on each
side over a moderate heat until charred and cooked
through. To test, insert a sharp knife in the thickest part
of the thigh – the juices should run clear. To serve, cut
each poussin in half, and serve with the chilli jam.

Serves 4
Preparation time: 35 minutes
Cooking time: 45 minutes

tangy chicken livers with broccoli

2 tablespoons sesame oil
25 g/1 oz butter
2 garlic cloves, crushed
250 g/8 oz mushrooms, thinly sliced
500 g/1 lb chicken livers, trimmed and roughly chopped
125 g/4 oz broccoli, chopped
1 tablespoon grated orange rind
4 tablespoons orange juice
2 tablespoons dry sherry
pinch of ground ginger
salt and pepper
2 tablespoons chopped parsley, to garnish

1 Heat the oil and butter in a large frying pan. Add the
garlic and fry gently, stirring, for 1 minute until the garlic
has softened. Add the mushrooms and chicken livers
and cook, stirring occasionally, for 5 minutes until the
chicken livers are browned on all sides.

2 Add the broccoli, orange rind and juice, sherry and
ground ginger. Season the mixture with a little salt and
plenty of pepper. Bring to the boil, reduce the heat,
cover and simmer for 5–6 minutes, or until the broccoli
is just tender but still crisp.

3 Adjust the seasoning to taste and transfer to a serving
dish. Garnish with the parsley and serve immediately.

Serves 4
Preparation time: 10 minutes
Cooking time: 11–12 minutes

chicken livers with marsala and oregano

75 g/3 oz butter
50 g/2 oz pancetta or bacon, diced
1 shallot, diced
1 garlic clove, chopped
500 g/1 lb chicken livers, trimmed
175 ml/6 fl oz Marsala
1 tablespoon chopped oregano
salt and pepper
buttered tagliatelle, to serve

1 Melt half of the butter in a large frying pan. Add the pancetta, shallot and garlic and fry over a low heat for 5 minutes without allowing to colour, then remove from the pan and reserve.

2 Melt the remaining butter in the pan. Add the chicken livers and cook over a high heat for 3 minutes until the chicken livers are evenly brown on the outside. Chicken livers are best when browned on the outside but still pink in the middle.

3 Return the shallot mixture to the pan and mix well. Add the Marsala and oregano and season to taste with salt and pepper. Bring to the boil. Serve immediately with buttered tagliatelle.

Serves 4
Preparation time: 5 minutes
Cooking time: 10 minutes

turkey breasts with parmesan, egg and spinach

2 eggs
50 g/2 oz Parmesan cheese, grated
3–4 tablespoons olive oil
300 g/10 oz spinach, chopped
pinch of nutmeg
4 lean streaky bacon rashers, rinded
2 x 250 g/8 oz turkey breast fillets
25 g/1 oz butter
300 ml/10 fl oz dry white wine
½ teaspoon chopped rosemary
salt and pepper
steamed spinach, to serve

1 Whisk 1 of the eggs with half the Parmesan and season well. Heat a scant tablespoon of oil in a 15 cm/6 inch frying pan. Add the egg mixture and cook until golden brown, then turn over and cook on the reverse side. Make another omelette in the same way.

2 Heat 1 tablespoon of the remaining oil in another pan. Add the spinach and cook over a moderate heat until it softens. Season with nutmeg, salt and pepper.

3 Place an omelette, half the spinach and 2 rashers of streaky bacon on each prepared turkey fillet. Roll up towards the pointed end and secure with cocktail sticks and string.

4 Melt the butter and 1 tablespoon of oil in a flameproof casserole. Add the turkey and brown on all sides. Pour in the wine, add the rosemary and season to taste with salt and pepper.

5 Cover and cook in a preheated oven, 180°C (350°F), Gas Mark 4, for 1–1¼ hours until the turkey is tender. Take the turkey fillets from the pan and remove the cocktail sticks and strings. Cut into thick slices and arrange on a dish. Pour over the cooking liquid and serve hot with steamed spinach.

Serves 4–6
Preparation time: 40–45 minutes
Cooking time: 1¼–1½ hours
Oven temperature: 180°C (350°F), Gas Mark 4

roast turkey with juniper and pomegranate

2 kg/4 lb oven-ready turkey with giblets
50 g/2 oz butter, diced
150 ml/¼ pint olive oil
4 juniper berries
1 rosemary sprig, plus extra to garnish
200 ml/7 fl oz dry white wine
juice of 2 pomegranates
2 tablespoons lemon juice
4 tablespoons Chicken Stock (see page 141)
salt and pepper

1 Sprinkle the turkey inside and out with salt, then place one-third of the butter in the cavity. Sew the opening with trussing thread or string. Brush a roasting tin with a little oil and place the turkey in it.

2 Top with the remaining butter, 7 tablespoons of the remaining oil, the juniper berries and the rosemary, then pour in the wine. Roast in a preheated oven, 180°C (350°F), Gas Mark 4, basting the turkey occasionally with the wine and cooking juices, for 1½ hours.

3 Add half the pomegranate juice and cook for a further 1 hour, or until the turkey is almost tender.

4 Meanwhile, finely chop the turkey liver and gizzard. Heat the remaining oil in a heavy-based pan. Add the liver and gizzard and fry until browned. Remove from the heat and set aside.

5 Add the juice of the remaining pomegranate to the turkey and season to taste with salt and pepper. Roast for a further 10 minutes, then lift out the turkey and cut into serving pieces. Arrange them in an ovenproof serving dish.

6 Skim off the fat from the cooking juices and place the pan over a moderate heat. Add the lemon juice and stock and boil until reduced by about half. Strain and stir into the giblet mixture. Pour this sauce over the turkey pieces and return to the oven for a further 7–8 minutes. Serve immediately, garnished with a sprig of rosemary.

Serves 8
Preparation time: 30 minutes
Cooking time: 2¾ hours
Oven temperature: 180°C (350°F), Gas Mark 4

turkey with chestnut and apple stuffing

500 g/1 lb chestnuts
4 shallots, finely chopped
1 tablespoon chopped parsley
1 small egg, beaten
500 g/1 lb dessert apples, peeled, cored and chopped
250 g/8 oz belly of pork, finely chopped
6 kg/12 lb oven-ready turkey
50 g/2 oz butter
150 ml/¼ pint Madeira
salt and pepper

To garnish:
apple rings
watercress

1 Cook the chestnuts in boiling water for 15 minutes. Drain, cool, skin and chop. Mix with the shallots, parsley and egg and season to taste with salt and pepper.

2 Place the apples in a pan and cook, stirring, for 5 minutes. Mix them into the stuffing, together with the pork. Put the stuffing into the neck cavity of the turkey, then sew up the opening.

3 Place the turkey in a roasting pan, rub the skin with the butter and season liberally with salt and pepper. Roast in a preheated oven, 180°C (350°F), Gas Mark 4, basting occasionally, for 3½–4 hours.

4 Transfer the turkey to a warm serving dish. Add the Madeira to the roasting pan, place over a high heat and boil for 3 minutes. Spoon over the turkey and serve, garnished with apple rings and watercress.

Serves 10
Preparation time: 15 minutes, plus cooling
Cooking time: 4–4½ hours
Oven temperature: 180°C (350°F), Gas Mark 4

turkey crumble

2 carrots, thinly sliced
1 leek, sliced
40 g/1½ oz butter, plus extra for greasing
1 onion, finely chopped
40 g/1½ oz plain flour
250 ml/8 fl oz Chicken Stock (see page 141)
375 g/12 oz can sweetcorn with peppers, drained and juice reserved
250 g/8 oz cooked turkey, cut into chunks
salt and pepper

Topping:
75 g/3 oz wholemeal flour
50 g/2 oz chilled butter
75 g/3 oz wholemeal breadcrumbs
25 g/1 oz grated Cheddar cheese
1 tablespoon chopped parsley

1 Boil the carrots in lightly salted water for 10 minutes. Add the leek and cook for a further 5–8 minutes. The vegetables should retain a slight 'bite'. Drain and refresh under cold water. Drain again and set aside.

2 Melt the butter in a large saucepan over a moderate heat. Add the onion and cook until softened but not browned. Add the flour and cook, stirring, for 2 minutes. Remove from the heat and gradually stir in the stock and reserved can juices. Return to the heat and cook, stirring constantly, until the sauce has thickened and is almost boiling. Season to taste with salt and pepper. Add the cooked turkey, leeks, carrots and sweetcorn and mix well. Grease an ovenproof dish, transfer the turkey and vegetable mixture to it and set aside.

3 To make the topping, place the flour in a bowl. Add the butter and rub in lightly with the fingertips until the mixture resembles fine breadcrumbs. Season lightly and stir in the breadcrumbs, cheese and parsley. Spoon the topping over the turkey and vegetable mixture and bake in a preheated oven, 190°C (375°F), Gas Mark 5, for 35–40 minutes, or until the topping is crisp and light golden brown.

Serves 6
Preparation time: 20 minutes
Cooking time: about 1 hour
Oven temperature: 190°C (375°F), Gas Mark 5

turkey au gratin

500 g/1 lb cooked turkey, chopped
25 g/1 oz butter
125 g/4 oz blanched almonds
50 g/2 oz Parmesan cheese, grated
4 tablespoons chopped parsley
75 g/3 oz brown breadcrumbs

Sauce:
25 g/1 oz butter or margarine
25 g/1 oz plain flour
600 ml/1 pint milk
50 g/2 oz Cheddar cheese, grated
1 garlic clove, crushed
salt and pepper

1 Arrange the turkey in a shallow ovenproof dish. Melt the butter in a saucepan, add the almonds and toss until golden. Sprinkle the nuts and butter over the turkey.

2 To make the sauce, melt the butter in a saucepan. Sprinkle in the flour and cook, stirring, for 1–2 minutes. Gradually add the milk, a little at a time, stirring after each addition, then simmer for 2 minutes. Add the grated Cheddar and garlic, season to taste with salt and pepper, and stir until the cheese has melted.

3 Pour the sauce over the turkey. Mix together the Parmesan, parsley and breadcrumbs and sprinkle evenly over the turkey. Bake in a preheated oven, 160°C (325°F), Gas Mark 3, for 30–40 minutes until golden.

Serves 4
Preparation time: 15 minutes
Cooking time: 35–45 minutes
Oven temperature: 160°C (325°F), Gas Mark 3

glazed spiced roast turkey

175 g/6 oz blanched almonds, very finely chopped
2 tablespoons sesame seeds
1 tablespoon ground cumin
1 tablespoon ground coriander
2 tablespoons ground cinnamon
2 teaspoons ground ginger
1 teaspoon ground cloves
5 kg/10 lb oven-ready turkey with giblets
5 whole cloves
1 onion, peeled
25 g/1 oz butter, softened
500 ml/17 fl oz Chicken Stock (see page 141)
125 ml/4 fl oz clear honey
2 cinnamon sticks
salt and pepper

1 Spread the almonds and sesame seeds on a baking sheet, then put it in a preheated oven, 180°C (350°F), Gas Mark 4, for 8–10 minutes, stirring the mixture occasionally, until it is evenly browned. Remove from the oven and set aside.

2 Meanwhile, mix together the cumin, coriander, cinnamon, ginger and ground cloves and season to taste with salt and pepper. Rub the spice mixture over the skin of the turkey and in the cavity. Stick the whole cloves into the onion, put it in the cavity, then sew up the opening with fine string.

3 Put the turkey on a rack in a roasting tin and spread the butter over the skin. Stir half of the stock into the honey. Cut the giblets into pieces and put them into the roasting tin, together with the cinnamon sticks. Pour the honey mixture over the bird, then roast for 2½–3 hours until the juices run clear when the thickest part is pierced with a fine skewer. Turn the bird first on one side, then the other at regular intervals, and baste frequently with the honey and stock mixture. When it begins to brown, add the remaining stock.

4 About 30 minutes before the turkey is due to be served, remove it from the roasting tin. Strain the cooking juices into a heatproof jug. Skim off the fat. If there is more than about 250 ml/8 fl oz of glaze left in the jug, boil the juices to reduce them. Stir in the almond mixture.

5 Return the turkey to the roasting tin. Spread with the glaze, then continue the cooking, basting frequently, until the skin is a rich golden brown and crisp.

6 Transfer the bird to a warm carving dish, spoon over any remaining glaze, cover and leave in a warm place for 10–15 minutes before carving.

Serves 8–10
Preparation time: 10 minutes
Cooking time: 2¾–3½ hours
Oven temperature: 180°C (350°F), Gas Mark 4

turkey breasts in cider

2 tablespoons plain flour
500 g/1 lb turkey breast, cut into 2.5 cm/1 inch squares
2 tablespoons sunflower oil
2 small onions, sliced
400 ml/14 fl oz dry cider
3 large red peppers, cored, deseeded and sliced
2 tablespoons single cream
salt and pepper
chopped parsley, to garnish

1 Put the flour in a polythene bag and season with salt and pepper. Add the turkey and shake well to coat.

2 Heat the oil in a large frying pan. Add the onions and fry for 5 minutes over a low heat until softened. Add the turkey pieces to the pan, reserving any excess flour, and fry over a moderate heat, turning frequently, for 4–5 minutes until golden brown. Using a slotted spoon, transfer the turkey and onions to a plate.

3 Add any reserved seasoned flour to the pan and cook for 1 minute, stirring constantly. Gradually pour in the cider, season to taste with salt and pepper and bring to the boil, stirring.

4 Return the turkey and onions to the pan, together with the red peppers. Reduce the heat and simmer for 15–20 minutes, or until the turkey is cooked through.

5 Remove from the heat, stir in the cream, transfer to a warm serving dish, garnish with parsley and serve immediately.

Serves 4
Preparation time: 5 minutes
Cooking time: 25–30 minutes

oriental turkey parcels

1 tablespoon soy sauce
1 tablespoon dry sherry
1 tablespoon sesame oil
500 g/1 lb turkey breast, cut into 16 equal pieces
4 spring onions, each cut into 4 pieces
5 cm/2 inch piece of fresh root ginger, shredded
½ red pepper, cored, deseeded and shredded
1 celery stick, shredded
4 tablespoons oil

1 Mix the soy sauce, sherry and sesame oil together, add the turkey and toss well to coat. Leave to marinate for 15–20 minutes.

2 Cut out 16 pieces of foil large enough to enclose the pieces of turkey generously. Brush the foil with oil, place a piece of turkey in the centre of each and top with a piece of spring onion, ginger, pepper and celery. Fold the foil over to enclose the turkey and seal the edges well.

3 Heat the oil in a preheated wok or heavy-based frying pan. Add the foil parcels and fry for about 2 minutes each side. Remove from the pan and leave to drain.

4 Reheat the oil to very hot and return the turkey parcels to the pan for 1 minute. Drain well and serve immediately in the silver parcels.

Serves 4
Preparation: 15 minutes, plus marinating
Cooking time: 5 minutes

stir-fried turkey with pine nuts and green peppers

3 tablespoons rapeseed oil
50 g/2 oz pine nuts
1 onion, thinly sliced
2.5 cm/1 inch piece of fresh root ginger, very thinly sliced
2 green peppers, cored, deseeded and cut lengthways
  into thin strips
500 g/1 lb cooked turkey, cut diagonally into thin strips
salt and pepper
Chinese noodles, to serve

Sauce:

2 teaspoons cornflour
2 tablespoons water
2 tablespoons soy sauce
2 tablespoons rice wine or dry sherry
1 tablespoon wine vinegar
1 garlic clove, crushed
1 teaspoon soft dark brown sugar

1 To make the sauce, blend the cornflour and water, add the remaining sauce ingredients and set aside.

2 Heat 1 tablespoon of the oil in a preheated wok or frying pan. Add the pine nuts and toss for 1–2 minutes until golden brown. Remove and drain on kitchen paper.

3 Add the remaining oil to the pan, then the onion, ginger and green peppers and stir-fry over a low heat for 3–4 minutes until softened, but not coloured. Remove and set aside.

4 Add the turkey to the pan and stir-fry for 1–2 minutes until heated through.

5 Whisk the sauce, add to the wok and bring to the boil, stirring until it has thickened. Add the pepper mixture and toss to mix, then add the pine nuts and toss again. Season to taste with salt and pepper and serve with Chinese noodles.

Serves 4
Preparation time: 15 minutes
Cooking time: 10–15 minutes

stir-fried turkey in sweet and sour sauce

1 tablespoon sunflower oil
1 onion, finely chopped
500 g/1 lb turkey breast, cut into cubes
½ yellow or red pepper, cored, deseeded and sliced
3 mushrooms, sliced
spring onion, to garnish

Sauce:

4½ teaspoons light soy sauce
4½ teaspoons tomato purée
2 teaspoons cornflour
300 ml/½ pint water
3 tablespoons unsweetened pineapple juice
2 tablespoons wine vinegar
1½ teaspoons brown sugar

1 First, make the sauce. Place all the ingredients in a small pan and mix well. Bring to the boil, then simmer, stirring, until thickened. Keep warm.

2 Heat the oil in a preheated wok or frying pan. Add the onion and stir-fry for 2 minutes. Add the turkey and stir-fry for 2–3 minutes. Add the pepper and mushrooms and cook for 2–3 minutes.

3 Transfer to a warm serving dish and pour over the sauce. Garnish with spring onion and serve hot.

Serves 4
Preparation time: 6 minutes
Cooking time: 10–15 minutes

turkey and orange stir-fry

350 g/12 oz turkey breast, cut into 4 cm/1½ inch pieces
grated rind and juice of 2 oranges
1 tablespoon cornflour
1 tablespoon sunflower oil
1 teaspoon sesame oil
½ red pepper, cored, deseeded and cut into neat strips
½ green pepper, cored, deseeded and cut into neat strips
3 celery sticks, diced
125 g/4 oz carrots, cut into matchstick slices
salt and pepper
boiled rice, to serve

Marinade:

1 tablespoon soy sauce
2 tablespoons orange juice

1 First, make the marinade. Mix the soy sauce and orange juice together in a shallow dish. Place the turkey pieces in the marinade and leave for 30 minutes.

2 Measure the orange juice and add sufficient water to make up to 150 ml/¼ pint. Blend the cornflour with this and add a little salt and pepper. Lift the turkey from the marinade and drain well. Reserve the marinade.

3 Heat the 2 oils in a preheated wok or heavy-based frying pan. Add the turkey pieces and stir-fry for 4–5 minutes. Add the orange rind, peppers, celery and carrots. Continue stir-frying for a further 3 minutes.

4 Pour in the cornflour and orange juice mixture, together with any marinade that may be left. Stir as the liquid comes to the boil and thickens slightly.

5 Serve immediately with plain boiled rice.

Serves 4
Preparation time: 25–30 minutes, plus marinating
Cooking time: 9–10 minutes

duck with oranges

25 g/1 oz butter
3 tablespoons olive oil
2 kg/4 lb oven-ready duck, trussed with thread or string
pared rind and juice of 2 oranges
4 garlic cloves, crushed
125 g/4 oz raw country ham, cut into thin strips
600 ml/1 pint dry white wine
200 ml/7 fl oz Chicken Stock (see page 141)
1 bouquet garni
1 tablespoon wine vinegar
salt and pepper
2 oranges, cut into thin rings, to serve

Beurre manié:
1 tablespoon flour
25 g/1 oz butter, softened

1 Heat the butter and oil in a deep flameproof casserole. Add the duck and fry over a moderate heat, turning the duck as necessary, until it is golden brown all over.

2 Using a sharp knife, cut the pared orange rind into fine strips and plunge them into a small pan of boiling water. Blanch for 5 minutes, then remove and drain. Dry thoroughly on absorbent kitchen paper and set aside.

3 Add the garlic and strips of ham to the casserole and fry for 1–2 minutes. Pour in the white wine and stock, bring to the boil and simmer for a few minutes until slightly reduced. Add the bouquet garni, salt and pepper to taste and orange juice.

4 Cover the casserole. Reduce the heat and simmer gently for 1½ hours, or until the duck is cooked. Baste occasionally during cooking.

5 To make the beurre manié, blend the flour and butter. Remove the cooked duck from the casserole, cut into serving pieces and keep warm. Boil the cooking liquid for about 10 minutes until reduced. Add the vinegar, strips of orange rind and the beurre manié, in small pieces at a time, stirring all the time until the sauce thickens. Carve the duck and serve with the orange sauce, garnished with orange rings.

Serves 6
Preparation time: 20 minutes
Cooking time: 1¾ hours

marinated grilled duck

4 duck breast and wing portions
150 ml/¼ pint natural yogurt
salt and pepper
watercress sprigs, to garnish
brown rice, to serve

Marinade:
1 teaspoon soy sauce
150 ml/¼ pint red wine vinegar
1 onion, chopped
12 juniper berries, crushed
2 teaspoons fennel seeds
1 garlic clove, crushed

1 Put the duck portions in a large clear plastic bag. Add all the marinade ingredients, exclude any air and seal. Leave for 8 hours, turning occasionally.

2 Drain the duck, reserving the marinade. Place the duck, skin side down, in a roasting pan. Cook in a preheated oven, 220°C (425°F), Gas Mark 7, basting once with the reserved marinade, for 30 minutes. Turn and cook, basting again, for a further 30 minutes. Transfer to a warm dish and keep hot.

3 Place 6 tablespoons of the remaining marinade in a small saucepan, cover and heat gently for 5 minutes. Strain, whisk into the yogurt and season to taste with salt and pepper.

4 Serve the duck on a bed of brown rice, garnished with watercress and topped with the sauce.

Serves 4
Preparation time: 10 minutes, plus marinating
Cooking time: about 1 hour
Oven temperature: 220°C (425°F), Gas Mark 7

crispy roast duck with kumquats

2 kg/4 lb oven-ready duckling
3 tarragon sprigs
250 g/8 oz kumquats
1 tablespoon orange juice
3 tablespoons sherry
1 tablespoon clear honey
salt and pepper
green beans, to serve

1 Dry the duckling thoroughly inside and out with kitchen paper, then season the cavity with salt and pepper. Tuck the tarragon sprigs and 4 of the kumquats inside the duckling, then place it on a rack over a roasting tin. With a needle, prick the duckling in several places to release the fat during cooking. Rub the skin with salt and roast in the centre of a preheated oven, 190°C (375°F), Gas Mark 5, for 1½ hours or until the skin is crisp and golden.

2 A few minutes before the duckling is cooked, cut the remaining kumquats lengthways in half and place in a pan with the orange juice, sherry and honey. Bring to the boil and simmer, stirring constantly, for 2 minutes.

3 To serve, carve the duckling into quarters, place on a warm serving dish, spoon over the kumquats and serve with green beans.

Serves 4
Preparation time: 15 minutes
Cooking time: about 1½ hours
Oven temperature: 190°C (375°F), Gas Mark 5

duck breasts with balsamic vinegar

1 tablespoon oil
4 boneless duck breasts
4 tablespoons balsamic vinegar
75 g/3 oz cranberries
50 g/2 oz brown sugar
salt and pepper

1 Heat the oil in a frying pan. Add the duck breasts, skin side down, and cook over a moderate heat for 5 minutes. Reduce the heat and cook for a further 10 minutes. Drain the excess oil from the duck skin.

2 Turn the duck breasts over and add the balsamic vinegar, together with the cranberries and sugar. Season to taste with salt and pepper and cook for a further 10 minutes.

3 Serve the duck breasts with the sauce spooned over. The cranberries will have broken down and made a delicious sauce with the vinegar and duck juices, and the duck breasts should be pink and juicy in the middle.

Serves 4
Preparation time: 5 minutes
Cooking time: 25 minutes

roast heather honey duck with walnut stuffing

2.5 kg/5 lb oven-ready duckling
2 tablespoons lemon juice
2 tablespoons clear heather honey
2 tablespoons plain flour
300 ml/½ pint Chicken Stock (see page 141)
salt and pepper

Stuffing:
1 tablespoon vegetable oil or duck fat
1 onion, finely chopped
125 g/4 oz walnuts, chopped
125 g/4 oz fresh white breadcrumbs
grated rind of 1 lemon
1 tablespoon chopped parsley
1 teaspoon chopped marjoram
1 egg, beaten

To serve:
roasted root vegetables
boiled cabbage

1 First, make the stuffing. Heat the oil in a pan. Add the onion and fry until soft. Stir in the walnuts, breadcrumbs, lemon rind, parsley and marjoram and season to taste with salt and pepper. Bind with the egg.

2 Prick the duck all over with a fine skewer. Fill the body cavity with the stuffing. Truss the duck, and set on a wire rack in a roasting tin. Mix the lemon juice and honey together and brush over the duck. Season to taste with salt and pepper.

3 Cook in a preheated oven, 220°C (425°F), Gas Mark 7, for 10 minutes, then reduce the temperature to 190°C (375°F), Gas Mark 5 and cook for 25 minutes per 500 g/1 lb, allowing 10–15 minutes resting time at the end. Baste frequently during the cooking, brushing with any remaining lemon and honey mixture.

4 Remove from the oven and drain off all but 1 tablespoon of fat from the pan. Stir in the flour, blending with the cooking juices, add the stock and boil to thicken for the gravy. Serve with roasted root vegetables and boiled cabbage.

Serves 4
Preparation time: 20 minutes
Cooking time: 2–2½ hours
Oven temperature: 220°C (425°F), Gas Mark 7

duck with peppercorns

2 x 1 kg/2 lb oven-ready ducklings
25 g/1 oz butter
4 shallots, finely chopped
150 ml/¼ pint dry white wine
4 tablespoons brandy

4 tablespoons whole green peppercorns or 1 tablespoon
*   black peppercorns, coarsely crushed*
400 ml/14 fl oz double cream
salt and pepper

1 Prick the skin of the ducklings with a fork and season liberally with salt and pepper. Place in a roasting tin and cook in a preheated oven, 200°C (400°F), Gas Mark 6, for about 1¼ hours until tender.

2 Meanwhile, melt the butter in a pan. Add the shallots and cook until transparent. Stir in the wine and brandy, bring to the boil and boil for 5 minutes.

3 Cut the ducklings into pieces, arrange on a warm serving dish and keep hot. Add the peppercorns and cream to the sauce and season with salt to taste. Cook for 3–5 minutes until thickened. Spoon the sauce over the ducklings and serve immediately.

Serves 6
Preparation time: 5 minutes
Cooking time: about 1¼ hours
Oven temperature: 200°C (400°F), Gas Mark 6

braised duck with shiitake mushrooms

4 dried shiitake mushrooms
2 kg/4 lb oven-ready duck, cut into individual portions
5 tablespoons light soy sauce
4 tablespoons sunflower oil
3 spring onions, chopped
2.5 cm/1 inch piece of fresh root ginger, chopped
3 star anise
1 teaspoon black peppercorns
2 teaspoons Chinese rice wine or dry sherry
125 g/4 oz canned bamboo shoots, drained, rinsed and
*   sliced*
2 tablespoons cornflour
2 tablespoons water

1 Soak the mushrooms in boiling water for 20 minutes. Drain and discard the stems.

2 Rub the duck with a little soy sauce. Heat the oil in a preheated wok or large frying pan, add the duck and fry until it is golden all over.

3 Transfer the duck to a saucepan. Add the spring onions, ginger, star anise, peppercorns, wine or sherry, the remaining soy sauce and enough cold water to cover. Bring to the boil, reduce the heat and simmer for 1½–2 hours. Add the mushrooms and bamboo shoots 20 minutes before the end of the cooking time.

4 Mix the cornflour with the water and stir this mixture into the pan. Continue to cook until the sauce has thickened. Transfer to a warm serving dish and serve hot.

Serves 4
Preparation time: 20 minutes, plus soaking
Cooking time: 1½–2 hours

duck with spiced orange sauce

2 tablespoons vegetable oil
750 g/1½ lb skinless duck breast, cut into thin strips across the grain
seeds of 6 cardamom pods, crushed
pepper
orange segments, to garnish
boiled or steamed rice, to serve

Sauce:
1 tablespoon cornflour
4 tablespoons water
6 tablespoons fresh orange juice
1 tablespoon Chinese rice wine or dry sherry
1 tablespoon soy sauce
1 teaspoon dark soft brown sugar
1 teaspoon Chinese five-spice powder

1 First prepare the sauce. Mix the cornflour to a thin paste with the water, then stir in the orange juice, rice wine or sherry, soy sauce, sugar and five-spice powder. Set aside.

2 Heat the oil in a preheated wok or frying pan over a moderate heat. Add the duck strips and crushed cardamom seeds, increase the heat to high and stir-fry for 3–4 minutes, or until lightly coloured on all sides.

3 Stir the sauce to mix, then pour into the wok and bring to the boil, stirring constantly. Stir-fry for a further 1–2 minutes until the duck is tender and coated in the sauce. Season with pepper to taste and serve immediately with plain boiled or steamed rice and garnished with orange segments.

Serves 3–4
Preparation time: 10 minutes
Cooking time: 5–10 minutes

stir-fried duck with bamboo shoots and almonds

500 g/1 lb boneless duck
2 slices of fresh root ginger, shredded
1 garlic clove, crushed
3 tablespoons oil
3–4 dried Chinese mushrooms (optional)
4 spring onions, sliced
125 g/4 oz canned bamboo shoots, drained, rinsed and sliced
3 tablespoons soy sauce
2 tablespoons dry sherry
2 teaspoons cornflour
25 g/1 oz flaked almonds, toasted

1 Cut the duck into small chunks and place in a bowl with the ginger and garlic. Pour over 1 tablespoon of the oil and leave to marinate for 30 minutes.

2 Meanwhile, soak the mushrooms, if using, in warm water for 15 minutes. Squeeze dry, discard the hard stalks, then slice the mushroom caps.

3 Heat the remaining oil in a preheated wok or deep frying pan. Add the spring onions and stir-fry for 30 seconds. Add the duck and cook for 2 minutes. Add the mushrooms, bamboo shoots, soy sauce and sherry, and cook for 2 minutes. Blend the cornflour with 1 tablespoon water and stir into the pan. Cook for 1 minute, stirring, until thickened. Serve hot, sprinkled with the almonds.

Serves 4–6
Preparation time: 15 minutes, plus marinating
Cooking time: 5–6 minutes

barbecued duck with ginger and sesame seeds

4 boneless, skinless duck breasts
2 tablespoons brown sugar
1 teaspoon salt
4 tablespoons light soy sauce
1 tablespoon sesame oil
1 cm/½ inch piece of fresh root ginger, finely chopped
1 teaspoon sesame seeds

1 Cut each duck breast into 8 even-sized pieces. Mix the remaining ingredients in a large bowl and add the duck. Stir, cover and marinate for 3–4 hours in a cool place or overnight in the refrigerator. Spoon the marinade over the duck several times to coat the pieces evenly.

2 Remove the duck from the marinade with a slotted spoon and thread on to 8 bamboo skewers or 4 large metal skewers.

3 Place the skewers on a moderately hot barbecue or under a preheated grill and cook the small skewers for 8–10 minutes, the larger ones for 10–12 minutes. Turn the skewers several times during cooking and baste with the remaining marinade. Serve the duck hot or cold, either on or off the skewers.

Serves 4
Preparation time: 15 minutes, plus marinating
Cooking time: 8–12 minutes

green duck curry

2–2.5 kg/4–5 lb oven-ready duckling with giblets
coarse salt, for sprinkling
500 ml/17 fl oz thick coconut milk
4 kaffir lime leaves, plus extra to garnish
7½ teaspoons Thai Green Curry Paste (see page 149)
500 ml/17 fl oz thin coconut milk
2–3 fresh green chillies, deseeded and sliced
Thai fish sauce, to taste
sliced red chillies, to garnish

1 Sprinkle the skin of the duck generously with coarse salt. Set aside for 15 minutes.

2 Brush off the salt and chop the duck into 5 cm/2 inch pieces. Heat a wok or frying pan over a medium-high heat. Add a few pieces of duck and brown them thoroughly. Remove with a slotted spoon and drain on kitchen paper. Brown the remaining duck pieces in the same way. Discard the rendered fat from the wok and wipe it clean.

3 Reduce the heat to moderate. Skim the coconut cream from the top of the thick coconut milk and bring to the boil in the wok, then add the lime leaves and curry paste. Reduce the heat and cook, stirring constantly, until the oil begins to separate. Add the duck pieces, turn to cover evenly with the sauce, then cook gently for 5 minutes.

4 Add both the thick and thin coconut milks, bring just to the boil, then reduce the heat to very low. Simmer, stirring occasionally, for about 1–1¼ hours until the duck is tender.

5 Remove from the heat, transfer to a bowl and allow to cool. Cover and chill overnight.

6 Skim the excess fat from the curry, then return to the wok, stir in the chillies and season with Thai fish sauce to taste. Simmer for 5 minutes, or until heated through. Transfer to a warm serving dish, garnish with sliced red chillies and shredded lime leaves and serve immediately.

Serves 4–6
Preparation time: 15 minutes, plus standing and chilling
Cooking time: 1½–1¾ hours

balinese duck curry

4 tablespoons vegetable oil
1.5 kg/3 lb oven-ready duck, cut into 4 portions
1 lemon grass stalk, halved lengthways
4 kaffir lime leaves, bruised
1 teaspoon salt
300 ml/½ pint water
2 teaspoons soft brown sugar
2 green chillies, sliced, to garnish

Spice paste:

8 shallots, chopped
4 garlic cloves, chopped
6 large green chillies, deseeded and chopped
5 cm/2 inch piece of fresh root ginger, chopped
2.5 cm/1 inch piece of fresh galangal, chopped
2 teaspoons turmeric
¼ teaspoon pepper
6 candlenuts or macadamia nuts (optional)

1 First make the spice paste. Put the shallots, garlic, green chillies, ginger, galangal, turmeric, pepper and candlenuts or macadamia nuts, if using, into a food processor or blender and process to a thick paste.

2 Heat the vegetable oil in a large frying pan. Add the paste and fry over a low heat, stirring constantly, for about 3 minutes, or until softened and fragrant.

3 Add the duck portions, lemon grass, lime leaves and salt to the pan. Stir to coat the duck evenly in the spice mixture and fry for a further 4 minutes to seal the meat. Add the water, stir well and bring to the boil. Reduce the heat, cover the pan and simmer, stirring from time to time, for 45 minutes until the duck is tender.

4 Remove the lid from the pan, stir in the sugar and increase the heat to moderate. Cook, stirring frequently, for a further 30 minutes until the duck is cooked and the sauce is thick.

5 Skim off any surplus fat from the surface of the curry. Taste and adjust the seasoning if necessary. Serve hot, garnished with sliced chillies.

Serves 4
Preparation time: 25 minutes
Cooking time: 1½ hours

thai chilli fried duck

¼ roast duck
2 tablespoons oil
3 large garlic cloves, finely chopped
½ onion, sliced
25 g/1 oz carrot, sliced
50 g/2 oz mixed green, red and yellow peppers, cored deseeded and sliced
3 baby corn cobs, diagonally sliced

1 broccoli floret, chopped
4 sugar snap peas or mangetout
2 small green chillies, finely sliced
1 teaspoon palm sugar or light muscovado sugar
2 tablespoons light soy sauce
3 tablespoons Chicken Stock (see page 141)
basil leaves, to garnish

1 Take the skin and meat off the duck, chop into bite-sized pieces and set aside.

2 Heat the oil in a preheated wok or frying pan. Add the garlic and stir-fry for 10 seconds. Add the duck, stir briefly and then add the onion, carrot, mixed peppers, corn cobs, broccoli and sugar snap peas or mangetout. Stir-fry vigorously for 20 seconds, add the chilli and cook, stirring, for 45 seconds.

3 Finally, add the sugar, light soy sauce and chicken stock, mixing them thoroughly with the contents of the wok for 3 minutes.

4 Turn on to a serving dish and garnish with basil leaves.

Serves 2
Preparation time: 15 minutes
Cooking time: 6 minutes

roast goose with apple and whiskey stuffing

6 kg/12 lb oven-ready goose
1 Cox's apple, peeled, cored and grated
2 tablespoons Irish whiskey
25 g/1 oz butter
1 onion, finely chopped
250 g/8 oz coarse white breadcrumbs
2 tablespoons finely chopped parsley
1 tablespoon finely chopped sage
pinch of grated lemon rind
1 small egg, beaten
salt and pepper

To serve:
roast potatoes
braised red cabbage

1 Truss the goose, prick the bird all over with a fine skewer and set on a wire rack in a roasting tin. Season with salt and pepper. Cook in a preheated oven, 240°C (475°F), Gas Mark 9, for 30 minutes, then reduce the heat to 190°C (375°F), Gas Mark 5 for 3½–4½ hours. Pour off the fat several times during the cooking. Reserve for future use.

2 Soak the grated apple in the whiskey. Melt the butter in a pan. Add the onion and fry until soft. Add the soaked apple, breadcrumbs, herbs and lemon rind and season to taste with salt and pepper. Bind with the egg.

3 Grease a 900 ml/1½ pint soufflé dish with goose fat and fill with the stuffing. Cover with foil and cook with the goose for 45 minutes. Some of the stuffing could also be used to stuff small Cox's apples which can be baked for 30 minutes with the goose.

4 Rest the goose for 15–20 minutes in a warm place before carving. Serve the goose with roast potatoes and braised red cabbage, accompanied by the stuffing.

Serves 6
Preparation time: 30 minutes
Cooking time: 4–5 hours
Oven temperature: 240°C (475°F), Gas Mark 9

irish roast pheasant

50 g/2 oz butter
875 g/1¾ lb oven-ready pheasant, with giblets
1 small onion, quartered
1 celery stick, chopped
1 small carrot, sliced
65 ml/2½ fl oz red wine
450 ml/¾ pint water
1 bay leaf
6 peppercorns
2 tablespoons plain flour
salt and pepper
watercress, to garnish

To serve:
Brussels sprouts
roasted root vegetables
roast potatoes
game chips

1 Melt half the butter in a pan. Fry the giblets, together with the onion, celery and carrot, until browned. Add the red wine and boil over a high heat to reduce by half. Add the water, bay leaf and peppercorns, then simmer while preparing and roasting the pheasant. This stock will be used to make the gravy.

2 Spread the remaining butter over the pheasant, season with salt and pepper and set the bird in a roasting tin. Roast in a preheated oven, 220°C (425°F), Gas Mark 7, for 20–25 minutes per 500 g/1 lb. Baste several times during cooking. Once the bird is cooked, cover loosely and rest for 10 minutes before carving.

3 Meanwhile, strain the stock and boil quickly to reduce to 200 ml/7 fl oz. Remove the pheasant and drain all but 1 tablespoon of fat from the roasting tin, add the flour and stir well to mix with the sediment. Blend in the stock. Boil, strain and keep warm.

4 Serve the pheasant garnished with watercress and accompanied by Brussels sprouts, roasted root vegetables, roast potatoes, game chips and gravy.

Serves 2
Preparation time: 20 minutes
Cooking time: 35–45 minutes
Oven temperature: 220°C (425°F), Gas Mark 7

burgundy pheasants

2 plump oven-ready pheasants with giblets
1 small thyme sprig or a pinch of dried thyme
50 g/2 oz butter
300 ml/½ pint red Burgundy
1 tablespoon arrowroot or cornflour
2 tablespoons redcurrant jelly
2 tablespoons drained cocktail onions
2 tablespoons stuffed green olives (optional)
salt and pepper

To garnish:
redcurrants
parsley sprigs

To serve:
bacon rolls
game chips
fried crumbs
small sausages

1 Put the pheasant giblets into a pan with enough water to cover, add a little salt and pepper and thyme. Cover the pan and simmer for 45 minutes. Strain the liquid and boil briskly until reduced to 300 ml/½ pint of stock.

2 Meanwhile, put half the butter inside the birds and spread the remainder over the skin. Put them into a roasting tin and cover lightly with kitchen foil to keep from drying out. Roast in a preheated oven, 200°C (400°F), Gas Mark 6, for 40 minutes. Take the roasting tin out of the oven about 10 minutes before the birds are cooked. Lift them on to a dish and pour out all the fat, straining 1 tablespoon into a pan for the sauce. Replace the birds and pour 3 tablespoons of the wine over them. Return to the oven while you make the sauce.

3 To make the sauce, blend the arrowroot or cornflour with the remaining wine and add to the fat in the pan, together with the redcurrant jelly and giblet stock. Bring to the boil, stirring constantly until the sauce thickens slightly and the jelly dissolves.

4 Lift the pheasants on to a warm dish. Strain the juices from the roasting tin into the sauce. Boil for a few minutes, then add the onions and olives, if using, and any extra seasoning required. Heat for 2–3 minutes.

5 Pour the sauce over the pheasants and garnish with redcurrants and sprigs of parsley. Serve with accompaniments such as bacon rolls, game chips, fried crumbs and small sausages.

Serves 4–6
Preparation time: 20 minutes
Cooking time: 50 minutes
Oven temperature: 200°C (400°F), Gas Mark 6

pigeons in honey

1 teaspoon coriander seeds, lightly crushed
2 tablespoons clear honey
2 onions, sliced
300 ml/½ pint dry cider
300 ml/½ pint chilli vinegar
4 oven-ready wood pigeons, halved lengthways
25 g/1 oz butter
2 tablespoons vegetable oil
salt and pepper
chopped parsley, to garnish

To serve:
sautéed mushrooms
celery julienne

1 Mix the coriander, honey, onion, cider and vinegar in a large non-metallic bowl. Add the pigeons and leave to marinate for 8 hours or overnight. Drain, reserving the marinade, and dry well.

2 Heat the butter and oil in a large flameproof casserole. Add the pigeons in 2 batches, seasoning them with salt and pepper, and brown on both sides. Put all the birds in the casserole and pour over the marinade. Cover and cook in a preheated oven, 160°C (325°F), Gas Mark 3, for 1–1¼ hours until tender.

3 Serve garnished with parsley, and accompanied by sautéed mushrooms and a celery julienne.

Serves 4
Preparation time: 5 minutes, plus marinating
Cooking time: 1¼–1½ hours
Oven temperature: 160°C (325°F), Gas Mark 3

braised breast of wood pigeon

75 g/3 oz plain flour
8 skinless wood pigeon breasts
2 tablespoons olive oil
1 red onion, chopped
2 garlic cloves, chopped
3 celery sticks, chopped
250 ml/8 fl oz red wine
grated rind of 1 orange
1 thyme sprig
1 rosemary sprig
1 bay leaf
½ teaspoon ground cinnamon
2 teaspoons juniper berries, crushed
200 g/7 oz redcurrant jelly
handful of flat leaf parsley, chopped
salt and pepper

1 Season the flour with salt and pepper. Dip the wood pigeon breasts into the seasoned flour and coat evenly.

2 Heat the oil in a wide saucepan. Add the pigeon breasts and cook for 2 minutes on each side. Remove from the pan.

griddled leeks, asparagus and peppers with balsamic vinegar   p363

baked aubergines with anchovy and pecorino stuffing   p330

honey-glazed turnips   p361

braised courgettes   p365

leek filo tarts   p335

vegetable pie with potato pastry   p334

vegetables in malaysian coconut sauce   p355

roasted parsnips dressed with lemon and garlic   p361

3 Add the onion, garlic and celery and fry over a low heat for 5 minutes. Increase the heat and pour in the red wine, stirring well to incorporate any tasty brown bits from the pan.

4 Add the orange rind, thyme, rosemary, bay leaf, cinnamon, juniper berries and redcurrant jelly and season to taste with salt and pepper. Return the pigeon breasts to the pan and baste well with the sauce. Simmer for 10 minutes.

5 Remove the pigeon from the pan and keep warm. Increase the heat and reduce the liquid to make a rich glaze. Return the pigeon breasts to the pan, add the parsley and serve.

Serves 4
Preparation time: 10 minutes
Cooking time: 20 minutes

pigeon with kumquats

3 tablespoons olive oil
6 young oven-ready pigeons
250 g/8 oz button onions, peeled
1 cinnamon stick
1 bay leaf
1 teaspoon grated fresh root ginger
large pinch of saffron threads, toasted and crushed
900 ml/1½ pints Chicken Stock (see page 141)
250 g/8 oz kumquats, halved
2 tablespoons clear honey
salt and pepper
lightly toasted almonds, to garnish

1 Heat the oil in a large, heavy flameproof casserole. Add the pigeons, in batches, and cook until browned. Using a slotted spoon, transfer them to a dish.

2 Stir the onions into the casserole and fry over a low heat until golden. Stir in the cinnamon, bay leaf, ginger, saffron and stock, season to taste with salt and pepper and bring to the boil.

3 Return the pigeons to the casserole with any juices that have collected in the dish, cover and cook gently, turning the pigeons occasionally, for about 45 minutes until they become tender.

4 Add the kumquats and honey, cover and cook for a further 30–45 minutes until the pigeons are very tender. Using a slotted spoon, transfer them to a large warm serving platter, cover and keep warm.

5 Boil the cooking liquid until slightly thickened. Remove and discard the cinnamon and bay leaf. Pour the liquid over the pigeons, scatter over the almonds and serve.

Serves 6
Preparation time: 10 minutes
Cooking time: about 1¾ hours

stewed pigeons in wine

6 streaky bacon rashers, rinded
3 young oven-ready pigeons
50 g/2 oz butter
2 tablespoons brandy
150 ml/¼ pint dry white wine
10 pickling onions
6 tablespoons Beef Stock (see page 141)
125 g/4 oz button mushrooms
1 tablespoon chopped parsley
salt and pepper

To garnish:
12–16 green olives
thyme sprigs

1 Wrap 2 rashers of bacon around each pigeon and secure with string. Melt the butter in a pan, add the pigeons and cook for 10 minutes until browned all over.

2 Pour over the brandy and wine, bring to the boil and cook for 2 minutes. Add the onions and stock and season to taste with salt and pepper. Cover and simmer for 1 hour.

3 Add the mushrooms and parsley and cook for 5 minutes. Transfer to a warm serving dish, garnish with olives and thyme and serve immediately.

Serves 6
Preparation time: 10 minutes
Cooking time: about 1¼ hours

guinea fowl with raspberries

1 oven-ready guinea fowl
25 g/1 oz butter
2 rosemary sprigs
175 g/6 oz fresh raspberries
1 tablespoon oil
4 tablespoons raspberry vinegar
4 tablespoons double cream
salt and pepper

To garnish:
50 g/2 oz fresh raspberries
parsley sprigs
bay leaves

1 Season the guinea fowl well inside and out. Put half the butter, the rosemary and one-third of the raspberries in the body cavity.

2 Heat the remaining butter and the oil in a pan. Add the guinea fowl and brown on all sides. Add the vinegar.

3 Lay the guinea fowl on its side and cook for 20–25 minutes, then turn on to the other side and cook for a further 20–25 minutes. Transfer to a warm serving dish and keep hot.

4 Add the cream and salt and pepper to taste to the pan, stirring well to dissolve the sediment. Add the remaining raspberries and heat through, without stirring. Spoon the raspberry sauce around the guinea fowl. Garnish with the raspberries and herbs.

Serves 2–4
Preparation time: 10 minutes
Cooking time: about 1 hour

grilled guinea fowl with fresh herb sauce

4 boneless guinea fowl breasts
2 tablespoons olive oil
salt and pepper

Herb sauce:
3 garlic cloves, crushed
4 anchovy fillets, chopped
large handful of flat leaf parsley
handful of rocket leaves
handful of sorrel leaves
handful of basil leaves
2 tablespoons lemon juice
125 ml/4 fl oz extra virgin olive oil

1 Put the guinea fowl breasts, skin side up, on a lightly oiled grill pan, brush with a little olive oil and season with salt and pepper. Place the pan under a preheated grill and cook the guinea fowl for about 10 minutes on each side.

2 Meanwhile, make the herb sauce. Put the garlic, anchovies, parsley, rocket, sorrel, basil and lemon juice into a food processor or blender and process for 1 minute. With the motor running, slowly drizzle in the olive oil; the sauce should be thick and bright green with a strong fresh aroma. Finally, season with salt and pepper and process again.

3 The guinea fowl is ready when the skin is crunchy and dark brown. Serve with a little herb sauce on each plate and the remainder in a small dish.

Serves 4
Preparation time: 10 minutes
Cooking time: 20 minutes

sautéed guinea fowl with tomatoes

1.5 kg/3 lb guinea fowl, jointed
50 g/2 oz butter
2–3 tablespoons olive oil
500 g/1 lb tomatoes, skinned, deseeded and sliced or
*   400 g/13 oz can tomatoes, drained*
salt and pepper
1 tablespoons chopped parsley, to garnish
roast potatoes, to serve

1 Season the guinea fowl with salt and pepper. Heat the butter and oil in a flameproof casserole. Add the pieces of guinea fowl and brown well on all sides over a moderate heat.

2 Lower the heat, cover with a tight-fitting lid and cook over a gentle heat, turning the pieces of guinea fowl from time to time, for 25–35 minutes, or until the meat is tender.

3 Drain off most of the fat from the pan and add the tomatoes. Cook until they thicken slightly and then season to taste with salt and pepper. Pour into a serving dish, sprinkle over the parsley and serve hot with small roast potatoes.

Serves 4
Preparation time: 15–20 minutes
Cooking time: 40–45 minutes

griddled and roasted guinea fowl

1.75 kg/3½ lb guinea fowl, cut into 8 portions
2 tablespoons Dijon mustard
grated rind and juice of 2 lemons
vegetable oil, for brushing
sea salt and pepper

1 Heat a griddle pan or nonstick frying pan. Put on the guinea fowl joints and cook for about 6 minutes on each side. The skin should be quite charred, which will give the guinea fowl a good flavour.

2 Mix the mustard, lemon rind and juice together and season to taste with salt and pepper.

3 Brush a roasting tin with a little oil. Remove the guinea fowl from the pan and place in the roasting tin. Brush the joints with the mustard mixture, then roast in a preheated oven, 200°C (400°F), Gas Mark 6, for 20 minutes. To test, insert a sharp knife into the thickest part of each joint – the juices should run clear.

Serves 4
Preparation time: 10 minutes
Cooking time: about 40 minutes
Oven temperature: 200°C (400°F), Gas Mark 6

quail with artichoke hearts

75 g/3 oz plain flour
4 oven-ready quail
2 tablespoons olive oil
1 onion, chopped
2 celery sticks, chopped
2 garlic cloves, crushed
300 ml/½ pint white wine
handful of sage, chopped
400 g/13 oz jar prepared artichoke hearts, drained
salt and pepper
pasta tossed in butter, to serve

1 Sprinkle the flour on a plate and season with salt and pepper. Dip the quail in the seasoned flour, making sure they are evenly coated.

2 Heat the oil in a large saucepan. Add the quail and brown all over. Remove from the pan and keep warm.

3 Add the onion, celery and garlic and fry over a low heat for 3 minutes, then pour in the wine, scraping any browned bits from the base of the pan.

4 Return the quail to the pan, add the sage and artichoke hearts and season to taste with salt and pepper. Cover the pan and simmer for 20 minutes, turning the quail from time to time. Serve with fresh pasta tossed in butter.

Serves 4
Preparation time: 5 minutes
Cooking time: 30 minutes

ostrich and wild mushroom daube

500 g/1 lb lean ostrich meat, diced
1 onion, diced
2 celery sticks, chopped
1 carrot, cut into chunks
300 ml/½ pint Chicken Stock (see page 141)
300 ml/½ pint red wine

2 bay leaves
1 tablespoon tomato purée
125 g/4 oz wild mushrooms
2 tablespoons torn flat leaf parsley
salt and pepper

1 Put the ostrich meat, onion, celery and carrot into a large flameproof casserole. Add the stock, wine, bay leaves and tomato purée and stir. Season to taste with salt and pepper. Cover the casserole and simmer gently for 1¼ hours.

2 About 15 minutes before the end of cooking time, stir in the mushrooms and simmer until they are tender. Stir in the torn parsley and serve hot.

Serves 4
Preparation time: 10 minutes
Cooking time: 1¼ hours

hare casserole

300 ml/½ pint dry red wine
4 tablespoons olive oil
1 garlic clove, crushed
1 bay leaf
1 kg/2 lb boneless hare, cut into cubes
25 g/1 oz butter
2 large carrots, sliced
150 ml/¼ pint Beef Stock (see page 141)
250 g/8 oz baby onions
250 g/8 oz button mushrooms
salt and pepper

1 Mix together the wine, oil, garlic, bay leaf and salt and pepper in a shallow dish. Add the hare and leave to marinate overnight.

2 Drain the hare, reserving the marinade, and pat dry with kitchen paper. Melt the butter in a flameproof casserole. Add the hare cubes and brown on all sides. Stir in the reserved marinade, carrots and stock and bring to the boil. Cover and cook in a preheated oven, 180°C (350°F), Gas Mark 4, for 2 hours.

3 Meanwhile, blanch the onions in boiling water for 5 minutes, then drain and peel, when cool enough to handle.

4 Remove the casserole from the oven, add the onions and mushrooms and stir well. Cook, uncovered, for a further 30 minutes, or until the hare is tender. Discard the bay leaf before serving.

Serves 4
Preparation time: 10 minutes, plus marinating
Cooking time: 2 hours 40 minutes
Oven temperature: 180°C (350°F), Gas Mark 4

rabbit with mustard sauce

4 rabbit quarters
1 tablespoon vinegar
25 g/1 oz butter
250 g/8 oz unsmoked streaky bacon, rinded and diced
2 onions, chopped
15 g/½ oz plain wholemeal flour
450 ml/¾ pint Chicken Stock (see page 141)
1 bouquet garni
150 ml/¼ pint double cream
2 tablespoons French mustard
salt and pepper
chopped parsley, to garnish

1 Soak the rabbit quarters overnight in water with the vinegar added. Drain, rinse and pat dry with kitchen paper.

2 Melt the butter in a flameproof casserole. Add the rabbit quarters and brown on all sides. Remove the rabbit and set aside.

3 Add the bacon and onions to the casserole and fry until golden brown. Sprinkle over the flour and cook, stirring, for 2 minutes. Gradually stir in the stock and bring to the boil. Season, then return the rabbit to the casserole and add the bouquet garni. Cover and cook in a preheated moderate oven, 180°C (350°F), Gas Mark 4, for 1½ hours.

4 Remove the rabbit from the casserole. Discard the bouquet garni. Mix the cream with the mustard and stir into the cooking liquid. Cook, stirring, over a low heat, but do not allow the sauce to boil. Return the rabbit to the casserole and reheat. Serve garnished with parsley.

Serves 4
Preparation time: 15 minutes, plus marinating
Cooking time: 2 hours
Oven temperature: 180°C (350°F), Gas Mark 4

pan-cooked rabbit with sage

2 tablespoons olive oil
1 rabbit, cut into 8 pieces
handful of chopped sage
1 large rosemary sprig
150 ml/¼ pint dry white wine
1 tablespoon Dijon mustard
salt and pepper
handful of flat leaf parsley, chopped, to garnish

1 Heat the oil in a large frying pan. Add the rabbit pieces and brown all over.

2 Season well with salt and pepper. Add the sage, rosemary, wine and mustard, mix thoroughly and coat the rabbit in the wine sauce.

3 Simmer the rabbit for 20 minutes, turning frequently so that it cooks evenly.

4 Serve hot, sprinkled generously with the roughly chopped parsley.

Serves 4
Preparation time: 5 minutes
Cooking time: 30 minutes

italian sweet and sour rabbit

75 g/3 oz plain flour
1 rabbit, cut into 8 pieces
2 tablespoons olive oil
1 onion, diced
1 garlic clove, crushed
300 ml/½ pint red wine
1 rosemary sprig
4 tablespoons balsamic vinegar
1 tablespoon brown sugar
2 tablespoons sultanas
2 tablespoons pine nuts, toasted
2 tablespoons black olives, pitted and roughly chopped
salt and pepper

1 Season the flour with salt and pepper. Coat the rabbit evenly all over in the seasoned flour.

2 Heat the olive oil in a large frying pan. Add the rabbit pieces, turning to brown them all over, then remove with a slotted spoon and set aside.

3 Add the onion and garlic and fry over a low heat for 5 minutes until softened, but do not allow to brown.

4 Return the rabbit to the pan, pour in the red wine, add the rosemary, vinegar, sugar and sultanas and season to taste with salt and pepper. Simmer for 20 minutes, turning the rabbit to coat it in the sauce and cook evenly.

5 Just before serving, add the pine nuts and olives and stir to mix well.

Serves 4
Preparation time: 10 minutes
Cooking time: 35 minutes

rabbit casserole

250 g/8 oz fennel bulbs, quartered
3 garlic cloves
1.25 kg/2½ lb oven-ready rabbit, with liver
125 g/4 oz bacon or raw ham
7 tablespoons olive oil
125 g/4 oz fresh breadcrumbs, soaked in a little milk and squeezed dry
salt and pepper
fennel slivers, to garnish

1 Cook the fennel and 2 cloves of garlic in a large pan of boiling salted water for 15 minutes. Drain thoroughly, reserving the cooking liquid, but discarding the garlic. Chop the fennel finely and set aside.

2 Mince the liver together with the bacon or raw ham and the remaining garlic. Heat 2 tablespoons of oil in a flameproof casserole. Add the fennel and liver mixture and cook over a low heat for 10 minutes, then mix with the breadcrumbs and salt and pepper to taste. Stuff the rabbit with this mixture, then sew up the opening with trussing thread or string.

3 Place the rabbit in a roasting tin and sprinkle with the remaining oil and season with salt and pepper to taste. Cover with foil and roast in a preheated oven, 180°C (350°F), Gas Mark 4, for 1½ hours, or until the rabbit is tender, basting occasionally with the fennel cooking liquid. Transfer the rabbit to a serving platter garnished with chopped fennel. Serve hot.

Serves 4
Preparation time: 15–20 minutes
Cooking time: 2 hours
Oven temperature: 180°C (350°F), Gas Mark 4

butterfly venison steaks

4 x 125 g/4 oz venison fillet steaks
40 g/1½ oz butter
1 tablespoon olive oil
2 tablespoons brandy
salt and white pepper

Horseradish butter:
25 g/1 oz butter, softened
2 tablespoons chopped chives
2 teaspoons grated horseradish

1 First, make the horseradish butter. Mix all the ingredients together and shape into a roll. Wrap in foil and chill until firm, then slice and cut into shapes.

2 Cut the venison steaks almost in half horizontally and open out flat to form a 'butterfly' shape, pressing them with the hand to flatten. Sprinkle each steak with salt and pepper.

3 Heat the butter and oil in a heavy-based frying pan. Add the steaks and fry for 15 seconds on each side, pressing down firmly. Transfer to a warm serving dish and keep hot.

4 Remove the pan from the heat and pour in the brandy, stirring to dissolve the sediment. Pour over the steaks, top each one with a portion of horseradish butter and serve immediately.

Serves 4
Preparation time: 10 minutes
Cooking time: 30 seconds

venison with brandy and redcurrant sauce

625–750 g/1¼–1½ lb venison, diced
2 tablespoons olive oil
125 g/4 oz streaky bacon, rinded and diced
2–3 tablespoons seasoned flour
6–8 tablespoons redcurrant jelly
2 tablespoons grappa or brandy
salt and pepper

Marinade:
1 carrot, sliced
1 celery stick, sliced
1 onion, sliced
2 garlic cloves, crushed
6–8 parsley stalks
1 rosemary or thyme sprig
2 bay leaves
4 juniper berries
8 peppercorns
600 ml/1 pint red wine

1 Place the venison and the marinade ingredients in a non-metallic bowl, cover and refrigerate for at least 24 hours, turning the venison from time to time. Remove the meat from the marinade, reserving the marinade, and drain until dry.

2 Heat the oil in a pan. Add the bacon and fry until golden brown. Remove from the pan. Toss the venison in the seasoned flour, then add to the pan and brown it on all sides in the hot oil.

3 Add the bacon and the marinade. Season lightly with salt and pepper, cover and simmer over a low heat or cook in a preheated oven, 180°C (350°F), Gas Mark 4, for 1½–2 hours.

4 Remove the venison from the pan, cover and keep hot. Strain the cooking liquid into a clean pan and whisk in 2 tablespoons of redcurrant jelly. Boil until the sauce reduces to a thin coating consistency. Pour over the meat and keep hot.

5 Melt the remaining redcurrant jelly in a pan and whisk until smooth. Add the grappa or brandy and boil for about 1 minute. Serve in a warmed sauce boat.

Serves 4–6
Preparation time: 20 minutes, plus marinating
Cooking time: 1¾–2¼ hours
Oven temperature: 180°C (350°F), Gas Mark 4

venison stew

1–2 tablespoons vegetable oil
1 onion, finely chopped
750 g–1 kg/1½–2 lb boneless lean venison, cut into 2.5 cm/1 inch cubes
25 g/1 oz plain flour
300 ml/½ pint Guinness
750 ml/1¼ pints Beef Stock (see page 141) or water
1 bay leaf
1 marjoram sprig
12–18 pickling onions
125–175 g/4–6 oz celery, cut in 2.5 cm/1 inch lengths
2 tablespoons finely chopped parsley
salt and pepper

1 Heat half the oil in a large frying pan. Add the onion and fry over a low heat until soft and beginning to brown. Transfer to a large flameproof casserole.

2 Heat the remaining oil in a pan. Add the meat, in batches, and fry until browned. Mix with the onions. Stir in the flour and add the Guinness, stock, bay leaf and marjoram and season to taste with salt and pepper. Bring to the boil, then reduce the heat and simmer gently for 1–1½ hours until the meat is almost tender. The stew can also be cooked in a preheated oven, 150°C (300°F), Gas Mark 2, for the same length of time. Add the pickling onions and celery 15–30 minutes before the end of the cooking time.

3 Taste and adjust the seasoning, if necessary, stir in the parsley and serve immediately.

Serves 4–6
Preparation time: 15 minutes
Cooking time: 1½–2 hours
Oven temperature: 150°C (300°F), Gas Mark 2

game pie

25 g/1 oz butter
1 large onion, finely chopped
2 partridges or 1 pheasant, cleaned and jointed
250 g/8 oz lean steak, cut into 2.5 cm/1 inch pieces
2 bacon rashers, rinded and cut into 1 cm/½ inch strips
125 g/4 oz mushrooms
1 thyme sprig
1 bay leaf
600 ml/1 pint Beef Stock (see page 141)
300 g/10 oz Shortcrust or Flaky Pastry dough (see pages 124 and 125)
1 egg, beaten
salt and pepper

1 Melt the butter in a frying pan. Add the onion and cook until soft. Add the game joints and brown on all sides. Remove from the pan and reserve. Add the steak to the pan and brown lightly.

2 Spread the steak on the base of a large pie dish and arrange the game joints on top. Sprinkle the onion, bacon, mushrooms and herbs on top. Season to taste with salt and pepper and just cover with stock. Cover with kitchen foil and cook in a preheated oven, 150°C (300°F), Gas Mark 2, for about 1½–2 hours until the meat is tender.

3 Remove the dish from the oven and allow to cool. Increase the oven temperature to 200°C (400°F), Gas Mark 6. Add a little more stock to bring the liquid 1 cm/½ inch from the top of the meat.

4 Roll out the pastry and cut out a lid 2.5 cm/1 inch wider than the dish. Cut a strip from around the edge of the pastry and lay it around the rim of the dish. Moisten with water, then lay on the pastry lid, pressing it down firmly. Knock back the edges and mark with a knife in ridges. Brush with beaten egg. Roll out the trimmings and use to make leaves or other decorations. Place on the lid and brush with egg again. Return to the oven and bake for 20 minutes.

5 Reduce the oven temperature to 150°C (300°F), Gas Mark 2, place the pie on a lower shelf in the oven and bake for a further 15–20 minutes.

Serves 6
Preparation time: 30 minutes, plus cooling
Cooking time: 2¼–2¾ hours
Oven temperature: 150°C (300°F), Gas Mark 2

vegetable dishes

aubergine, tomato and mozzarella mountains

1 aubergine, cut into 8 slices
2 tablespoons olive oil
2 beef tomatoes, skinned, then cut into 8 slices
250 g/8 oz buffalo mozzarella, cut into 8 slices
1 quantity Pesto (see page 146)
salt and pepper
mint sprigs, to garnish

1 Arrange the aubergine slices on a preheated griddle or under a preheated hot grill and cook until browned on both sides.

2 Lightly oil a baking sheet. Place four of the aubergine slices on the baking sheet. Put a tomato slice and a mozzarella slice on each one, then make a second layer of aubergine, tomato and mozzarella, sprinkling each layer with salt and pepper as you go. Skewer with a cocktail stick through the centre to hold the stacks together.

3 Place the stacks in a preheated oven, 190°C (375°F), Gas Mark 5, and cook for 10 minutes.

4 Transfer the stacks to individual serving plates and carefully remove the cocktail sticks. Drizzle with a little olive oil and top with a generous spoonful of pesto. Garnish with mint sprigs, and serve warm or at room temperature.

Serves 4
Preparation time: 10 minutes
Cooking time: 10 minutes
Oven temperature: 190°C (375°F), Gas Mark 5

baked aubergine and gorgonzola

4 tablespoons olive oil
1 red onion, chopped
2 garlic cloves, chopped
400 g/13 oz can chopped tomatoes
1 red chilli, diced

handful of basil, roughly torn
2 aubergines, thickly sliced
125 g/4 oz Gorgonzola cheese
salt and pepper

1 Heat 1 tablespoon of the olive oil in a saucepan, add the onion and garlic and sauté for 3 minutes. Add the tomatoes and chilli and simmer for about 8–10 minutes until the sauce has reduced. Add the basil and season well with salt and pepper.

2 Heat the remaining olive oil in a large frying pan, and then fry the aubergine slices until golden on each side.

3 Place a layer of aubergines in a shallow ovenproof dish and spoon over half of the sauce. Make another layer of aubergines, then add the rest of the sauce and finally crumble over the Gorgonzola. Bake in a preheated oven, 190°C (375°F), Gas Mark 5, for 15 minutes.

Serves 4
Preparation time: 5 minutes
Cooking time: 25 minutes
Oven temperature: 190°C (375°F), Gas Mark 5

stuffed aubergines

2 aubergines
4 tablespoons olive oil
2 tablespoons pine nuts
8 tomatoes, skinned and chopped
2 garlic cloves, chopped
4 anchovy fillets, chopped
1 tablespoon capers, chopped
handful of basil, chopped
handful of flat leaf parsley, chopped
75 g/3 oz pecorino cheese, grated
50 g/2 oz white breadcrumbs
salt and pepper

1 Halve the aubergines lengthways and scoop out the flesh without breaking the skin. Roughly chop the flesh.

2 Heat the olive oil in a frying pan, add the aubergine shells and sauté on each side for 3–4 minutes. Place them in a lightly oiled baking dish and then sauté the flesh until golden brown.

3 Toast the pine nuts in a dry frying pan over moderate heat until browned, stirring constantly.

4 Mix together the chopped tomato, garlic, anchovies, capers, basil, parsley, half of the pecorino cheese, the pine nuts, breadcrumbs and aubergine flesh, and season with salt and pepper. Spoon the mixture into the sautéed aubergine shells, piling it high. Sprinkle with the remaining cheese, then place in a preheated oven, 200°C (400°F), Gas Mark 6, and cook for 20 minutes. Serve hot or cold.

Serves 4
Preparation time: 15 minutes
Cooking time: 25 minutes
Oven temperature: 200°C (400°F), Gas Mark 6

sicilian aubergines

4 tablespoons olive oil
2 red onions, sliced
2 garlic cloves, chopped
2 celery sticks, chopped
1 aubergine, cut into small dice
1 yellow pepper, cored, deseeded and cut into thin strips
1 red pepper, cored, deseeded and cut into thin strips
150 ml/¼ pint passata
2 tablespoons red wine vinegar
6 anchovy fillets, cut into long strips
50 g/2 oz capers, roughly chopped
125 g/4 oz black olives, pitted
75 g/3 oz pine nuts
handful of flat leaf parsley, chopped
pepper

1 Heat the olive oil in a heavy-based saucepan, add the onions, garlic and celery and sauté for 3 minutes. Add the aubergine and yellow and red peppers, turn up the heat and cook for a further 5 minutes, stirring constantly.

2 Add the passata and vinegar and bring to the boil, then reduce the heat so that the mixture just simmers for 10 minutes. Add the anchovies, capers and olives, and simmer the mixture for a further 5 minutes.

3 Meanwhile, toast the pine nuts in a dry frying pan until browned, stirring constantly.

4 Season the aubergine mixture with pepper, add the pine nuts and chopped parsley, and mix well. Serve hot or at room temperature.

Serves 4
Preparation time: 15 minutes
Cooking time: 25 minutes

baked aubergines with anchovy and pecorino stuffing

625 g/1¼ lb small round aubergines
125 ml/4 fl oz oil
1 onion, finely chopped
4 anchovy fillets, drained and finely chopped
600 g/1½ lb plum tomatoes, skinned, deseeded and
  chopped
1 heaped tablespoon capers, finely chopped
6 basil leaves, torn, plus extra to garnish
50 g/2 oz pecorino cheese, grated
pepper

1 Cut the tops off the aubergines. Slit the flesh into wedge shapes, making cuts from the top to just over halfway down the sides with a sharp knife. Sprinkle with salt and leave upside down in a colander for 30 minutes to drain. Rinse well.

2 Heat one-third of the oil in a shallow frying pan, add the onion and fry over moderate heat until golden. Add the anchovies and cook until they are softened.

3 Stir in the tomatoes, capers and basil, and season with pepper. Continue cooking until the sauce has thickened. Remove from the heat and add the pecorino.

4 Dry the aubergines on kitchen paper and put them into a baking dish. Open them out a little, fill with the sauce, trickle the remaining oil over the top, and put in a preheated oven, 180°C (350°F), Gas Mark 4, for 30 minutes. Garnish with basil and serve immediately.

Serves 4
Preparation time: 15 minutes, plus draining
Cooking time: 45 minutes
Oven temperature: 180°C (350°F), Gas Mark 4

melanzane parmigiana

6 aubergines, thickly sliced lengthways
2 tablespoons olive oil
1 quantity Fresh Tomato Sauce (see page 147)
250 g/8 oz Cheddar cheese, grated
50 g/2 oz Parmesan cheese, grated
salt

1 Sprinkle the aubergine slices with salt and leave to drain in a colander for 30 minutes. Rinse well under cold running water, drain and pat dry on kitchen paper.

2 Brush the aubergine slices with oil and place on 2 large baking sheets. Roast the aubergines at the top of a preheated oven, 200°C (400°F), Gas Mark 6, for 10 minutes on each side until golden and tender.

3 Meanwhile, reheat the tomato sauce and keep warm.

4 Spoon a little of the tomato sauce into a lasagne dish and top with a layer of aubergines and some of the Cheddar. Continue with the layers, finishing with the Cheddar. Sprinkle over the Parmesan and bake for 30 minutes until the cheese is bubbling and golden.

Serves 6
Preparation time: 10 minutes, plus draining
Cooking time: 50 minutes
Oven temperature: 200°C (400°F), Gas Mark 6

peppers with brown rice and walnut stuffing

4 red or yellow peppers, halved lengthways, cored and
  deseeded
Parmesan shavings, to garnish

Stuffing:
2 tablespoons sunflower oil
1 onion, chopped
1 large garlic clove, crushed
50 g/2 oz brown rice
1 bay leaf
450 ml/¾ pint tomato juice

1 teaspoon dried basil
50 g/2 oz Cheddar cheese, grated
125 g/4 oz walnuts, chopped
salt and pepper

1 First make the stuffing. Heat the oil in a saucepan, add the onion and garlic and cook for 10 minutes, stirring.

2 Add the rice, bay leaf and half of the tomato juice. Cover and simmer for 40 minutes, or until the rice is just tender.

3 Discard the bay leaf. Stir in the basil, cheese and walnuts, and season to taste with salt and pepper.

4 Fill the peppers with heaped spoonfuls of the stuffing and place in a greased casserole dish. Pour the remaining tomato juice around the peppers and bake in a preheated oven, 180°C (350°F), Gas Mark 4, for about 30–40 minutes. Garnish with a generous amount of Parmesan shavings and serve immediately.

Serves 4
Preparation time: 10 minutes
Cooking time: 1¼–1½ hours

peperonata

100 ml/3½ fl oz olive oil
375 g/12 oz onions, finely sliced
2 garlic cloves, crushed
500 g/1 lb red and yellow peppers, cored, deseeded and
  quartered
500 g/1 lb ripe tomatoes, skinned and chopped,
  or 400 g/13 oz can chopped tomatoes
salt and pepper

1 Heat the oil in a heavy-based pan, add the onions and garlic and fry gently until they are lightly coloured.

2 Add the peppers, cover and cook over a gentle heat for 10–12 minutes.

3 Add the tomatoes and season well with salt and pepper. Cook, uncovered, until the peppers are tender and the liquid has reduced to a thick sauce. If canned tomatoes are used, raise the heat toward the end of the cooking time to evaporate the extra liquid.

4 Check the seasoning and pour into a serving dish. Serve hot or cold.

Serves 4
Preparation time: 20 minutes
Cooking time: 40–45 minutes

ratatouille

4 tablespoons olive oil
3 onions, finely chopped
3 garlic cloves, finely chopped
750 g/1½ lb tomatoes, skinned and chopped
5 courgettes, sliced
2 large aubergines, sliced
salt and pepper
2 tablespoons chopped parsley

1 Heat the oil in a frying pan, add the onions and garlic and fry gently for 5 minutes. Add the tomatoes and cook for a few minutes until the juice starts to flow.

2 Add the courgettes and aubergines and stir them all together to mix well. Add a little salt and pepper. Cover the pan and simmer for about 30 minutes, or until the vegetables are softened.

3 Taste and adjust the seasoning if necessary, then stir in some of the chopped parsley. Serve hot or cold, with some more parsley sprinkled on the top.

Serves 6–8
Preparation time: 15–20 minutes
Cooking time: 45 minutes

mediterranean suet parcel

500 g/1 lb self-raising flour
1 teaspoon salt
175 g/6 oz vegetable suet
150 ml/¼ pint natural yogurt
200 ml/7 fl oz milk
1 egg yolk, beaten, to glaze
Mushroom Gravy (see page 147), to serve

Filling:
2 aubergines, thickly sliced lengthways
2 tablespoons olive oil
2 large red peppers, cored, deseeded and quartered
4 firm ripe tomatoes, sliced
12 large basil leaves
175 g/6 oz mozzarella cheese, thinly sliced

1 Sift the flour and salt into a large bowl, stir in the suet and gradually work in the yogurt and milk to form a stiff dough. Knead lightly until smooth, wrap and leave to rest while preparing the filling.

2 Brush the aubergine slices with a little oil and place under a preheated hot grill for 5–6 minutes on each side until golden and tender. Grill the pepper quarters, skin side up, for 6–8 minutes until blistered and blackened. Put them in a polythene bag until they are cool, then peel off the skin.

3 On a lightly floured surface, roll out the dough to a 35 cm/14 inch square. Arrange the aubergines, peppers and tomatoes, basil and cheese in layers, diagonally in the centre of the pastry, forming a 20 cm/8 inch square.

4 Dampen the edges of the pastry with a little water and draw up the 4 corners, pressing together in the middle to seal in the filling.

5 Transfer the parcel to a baking sheet, brush with the beaten egg yolk and place in a preheated oven, 200°C (400°F), Gas Mark 6, for 30 minutes. Reduce the temperature to 180°C (350°F), Gas Mark 4, and bake for a further 15 minutes until puffed up and golden. Leave to rest for 5 minutes, then serve the parcel hot, with mushroom gravy.

Serves 6
Preparation time: 40 minutes, plus making the gravy
Cooking time: 1 hour
Oven temperature: 200°C (400°F), Gas Mark 6

vegetable moussaka

50 g/2 oz butter or margarine
3 tablespoons sunflower or corn oil
2 aubergines, thinly sliced
4 potatoes, thinly sliced
3 large onions, chopped
2 garlic cloves, chopped
3 large tomatoes, skinned and sliced
salt and pepper
1 tablespoon chopped parsley, to garnish (optional)

Cheese sauce:
50 g/2 oz butter or margarine
40 g/1 1/2 oz wholemeal flour
600 ml/1 pint milk
250 g/8 oz Cheddar cheese, grated
1/2–1 teaspoon mixed spice or grated nutmeg
1 teaspoon French mustard

1 Heat half the butter and oil in a pan, add the aubergines and potato slices and cook for 10 minutes, turning over once or twice. Remove from the pan.

2 Heat the rest of the butter and oil, add the onions, garlic and tomatoes, and cook for 10 minutes without browning. Add half the aubergines and potatoes, mix and season to taste with salt and pepper.

3 To make the sauce, melt the butter in a saucepan, add the flour and stir over the heat for 1–2 minutes, then gradually blend in the milk. Stir until a smooth sauce is formed. Remove from the heat, add approximately 175 g/6 oz of the cheese and season with salt, pepper, mixed spice or nutmeg and mustard.

4 Spoon half of the mixed vegetables into a casserole, add half of the sauce and the remainder of the mixed vegetables. Top with a neat layer of aubergines and potatoes, then the rest of the sauce.

5 Cover the casserole with a lid or foil; make sure this does not touch the sauce. Bake for 1 1/4 hours in a preheated oven, 160°C (325°F), Gas Mark 3. Remove the lid, add the remaining cheese, return to the oven, raising the heat slightly, and cook for a further 10 minutes, or until the cheese topping has melted. Garnish with chopped parsley, if liked.

Serves 4
Preparation time: 15 minutes
Cooking time: about 2 hours
Oven temperature: 160°C (325°F), Gas Mark 3

mediterranean vegetables with fresh herbs

4 tablespoons olive oil
1 garlic clove, crushed
3 large onions, sliced
3 large green peppers, cored, deseeded and sliced
400 g/13 oz can tomatoes
3 tablespoons chopped parsley or chervil
2 tablespoons chopped basil
2 tablespoons chopped thyme
1–2 tablespoons capers
10–12 black olives, pitted
salt and pepper

1 Heat the oil in a pan, add the garlic and onions, and fry very gently for 10 minutes, stirring occasionally.

2 Add the green peppers and cook gently, stirring, for 1 minute.

3 Add the tomatoes and their juice, then the herbs, and season to taste with salt and pepper. Bring to the boil, then lower the heat, cover and simmer for 30 minutes, stirring occasionally until the vegetables are very soft. Remove from the heat.

4 Stir in the capers and black olives, then taste and adjust the seasoning. Serve warm, or chilled as a starter.

Serves 4
Preparation time: 20 minutes
Cooking time: 45 minutes

stir-fried summer vegetables

2 tablespoons vegetable oil
4 spring onions, trimmed and cut into 5 cm/2 inch lengths
2 garlic cloves, thinly sliced
1 cm/¹⁄₂ inch slice of fresh root ginger, shredded
125 g/4 oz green beans, halved

¹⁄₂ small cauliflower, broken into small florets
125 g/4 oz mangetout
3 celery sticks, diagonally sliced
50 g/2 oz courgettes, diagonally sliced
1 red pepper, cored, deseeded and thinly sliced
1 green pepper, cored, deseeded and thinly sliced
1 yellow pepper, cored, deseeded and thinly sliced
2 tablespoons soy sauce
1 teaspoon sesame seed oil
pepper

1 Heat the oil in a wok or large frying pan, add the spring onions, garlic and ginger, and stir-fry for 30 seconds without browning.

2 Add all the remaining vegetables, then pepper to taste, and toss well. Stir-fry for 2 minutes.

3 Stir in the soy sauce and sesame seed oil and serve immediately.

Serves 6
Preparation time: 35 minutes
Cooking time: 3 minutes

winter vegetable casserole with cheese topping

2 tablespoons olive oil
3 large onions, quartered
2 garlic cloves, thinly sliced
400 g/13 oz can tomatoes
150 ml/¹⁄₄ pint dry white wine
1 small or ¹⁄₂ large celeriac, peeled and diced
4 celery sticks, trimmed and cut into 5 cm/2 inch lengths
6 carrots, quartered
1 green pepper, cored, deseeded and sliced
2 leeks, cut into 5 cm/2 inch lengths
a few cauliflower florets
1 tablespoon tomato purée
2 teaspoons dried mixed herbs
salt and pepper

Cheese topping:
175 g/6 oz plain flour
pinch of salt
75 g/3 oz butter
2 tablespoons freshly grated Parmesan cheese
125 g/4 oz mature Cheddar cheese, grated
2 tablespoons chopped parsley

1 Heat the oil in a large pan, add the onion and garlic, and fry gently for 5 minutes without browning, taking care not to break up the onions.

2 Stir in the tomatoes with their juice, and the wine, then add the celeriac, celery, carrots and salt and pepper to taste. Cover and simmer for 20 minutes. Stir in the green pepper, leeks, cauliflower, tomato purée and herbs, and simmer for a further 10 minutes. Pour the mixture into an ovenproof dish.

3 To make the cheese topping, sift the flour and salt in a bowl. Rub in the butter until the mixture resembles fine breadcrumbs. Stir in the cheeses and parsley, then sprinkle over the vegetable mixture. Bake the casserole in a preheated oven, 200°C (400°F), Gas Mark 6, for 35–40 minutes, until golden brown. Serve hot.

Serves 4–6
Preparation time: 20 minutes
Cooking time: about 1¼ hours
Oven temperature: 200°C (400°F), Gas Mark 6

vegetable pie with potato pastry

Pastry:
250 g/8 oz self-raising flour
175 g/6 oz butter or soft margarine
1 teaspoon salt
250 g/8 oz cold mashed potato
1 tablespoon milk
1 egg yolk, beaten, to glaze

Filling:
250 g/8 oz mixed vegetables (carrots, broccoli, cauliflower, parsnips, courgettes), diced
2 tablespoons olive oil
125 g/4 oz mushrooms, sliced
1 large or 2 medium onions, thinly sliced
150 ml/¼ pint Classic White Sauce (see page 144)
75 g/3 oz Cheddar cheese, grated
salt and pepper

1 To make the pastry, place the flour in a bowl and rub in the butter or margarine until the mixture resembles breadcrumbs. Mix in the salt and work the mashed potato into this mixture, adding the milk a little at a time.

2 Knead on a floured board until the dough is smooth and fairly soft. Roll out the pastry and use it to line a large, shallow ovenproof dish. Line the pastry case with greaseproof paper and fill with baking beans or dried beans. Bake in a preheated oven, 200°C (400°F), Gas Mark 6, for 10 minutes. Lift out the paper and beans and bake for a further 5 minutes or until it is light golden brown.

3 Meanwhile, cook the mixed vegetables in salted boiling water until just tender and allow to cool. Heat half of the oil in a frying pan, add the mushrooms, fry lightly and allow to cool. Add the remaining oil to the pan, fry the onions lightly and allow to cool. Mix the cooled vegetables into the white sauce and season to taste with salt and pepper.

4 Remove the pastry from the oven, allow to cool a little and then fill with the vegetable mixture, spreading with a palette knife so that it is smooth and flat. Sprinkle with the grated Cheddar. Brush the edges of the pastry with the beaten egg yolk and return to the oven for 15 minutes or until the cheese is melted and beginning to brown. Serve hot.

Serves 4
Preparation time: 30 minutes, plus cooling
Cooking time: 30 minutes
Oven temperature: 200°C (400°F), Gas Mark 6

rich vegetable pie in flaky pastry

4 tablespoons olive oil
500 g/1 lb button mushrooms, halved
2 garlic cloves, crushed
250 g/8 oz baby onions, halved
250 g/8 oz parsnips, chopped
250 g/8 oz carrots, chopped
2 tablespoons chopped thyme
1 tablespoon chopped sage
300 ml/½ pint full-bodied dry red wine
400 g/13 oz can chopped tomatoes
150 ml/¼ pint Vegetable Stock (see page 140)
2 tablespoons tomato purée
2 tablespoons dark soy sauce
1 quantity Flaky Pastry (see page 125)
1 egg yolk, beaten, to glaze
salt and pepper

1 Heat half the oil in a frying pan, add the mushrooms and garlic, and stir-fry for 3–4 minutes until golden. Remove from the pan and set aside.

2 Add the remaining oil to the pan and fry the onions, parsnips, carrots and herbs for 10 minutes. Add the wine and boil rapidly for 3 minutes. Stir in the tomatoes, stock, tomato purée and soy sauce. Bring to the boil, cover and simmer for 30 minutes.

3 Add the mushrooms, season to taste, transfer to a 1.8 litre/3 pint pie dish and set aside.

4 On a lightly floured surface, roll out the pastry to a little larger than the pie dish. Cut 4 strips, 2.5 cm/1 inch wide, from around the edge of the pastry and press on to the rim of the dish, wetting the rim as you go.

5 Lay the remaining pastry over the pie, trim the edges and press together, wetting the pastry to seal. Flute the edges and use any trimmings to decorate the pie.

6 Brush the pastry with beaten egg yolk and bake in a preheated oven, 220°C (425°F), Gas Mark 7, for 20 minutes, then reduce the temperature to 200°C (400°F), Gas Mark 6, and bake for a further 15 minutes. Serve hot.

Serves 6
Preparation time: 30 minutes, plus making pastry and chilling
Cooking time: about 1¼ hours
Oven temperature: 220°C (425°F), Gas Mark 7

filo pie with seaweed filling

There are several varieties of edible seaweed. Dulse seaweed is cold dried and is similar to Japanese nori, which could be used instead.

4 tablespoons olive oil, plus extra for brushing
1 onion, finely chopped
1 garlic clove, crushed
2 teaspoons grated fresh root ginger
175 g/6 oz button mushrooms
50 g/2 oz dried dulse seaweed
1 tablespoon dark soy sauce
1 tablespoon lemon juice
2 tablespoons chopped coriander leaves
50 g/2 oz fresh white breadcrumbs
50 g/2 oz pine nuts

2 tablespoons sesame seeds
12 sheets of filo pastry, defrosted if frozen
pepper
Mushroom Gravy (see page 147), to serve

1 Heat half the oil in a large frying pan, add the onion, garlic and ginger, and fry gently for 5 minutes. Add the mushrooms and fry for a further 5 minutes, stirring frequently.

2 Using a pair of scissors, cut the seaweed into small pieces. Add to the pan with the soy sauce, lemon juice and coriander. Stir over a low heat until the seaweed is softened, then remove from the heat.

3 In another pan, heat the remaining oil and stir-fry the breadcrumbs, pine nuts and sesame seeds for 4–5 minutes until evenly browned. Remove from the heat.

4 Keeping the remaining pastry covered with a clean, damp tea towel, take 1 sheet at a time and trim to fit into an oiled 20 x 30 cm/8 x 12 inch roasting tin. Press into the base and brush with oil. Sprinkle with 2 teaspoons of the breadcrumb mixture.

5 Repeat with 5 more sheets of pastry; and half the breadcrumb mixture. Spread over the seaweed mixture and then repeat the layers of pastry and breadcrumbs, ending with a layer of pastry.

6 Brush liberally with oil, mark into 6 portions with a sharp knife and place in a preheated oven, 190°C (375°F), Gas Mark 5, for 30 minutes until crisp and golden, covering with foil if the top becomes too brown. Serve hot with the gravy.

Serves 6
Preparation time: 25 minutes
Cooking time: 45 minutes
Oven temperature: 190°C (375°F), Gas Mark 5

leek filo tarts

8 sun-dried tomatoes
2 leeks, sliced into rings
300 ml/½ pint white wine
2 tablespoons skimmed milk
1 small egg, separated
50 g/2 oz low-fat soft cheese
12 x 15 cm/6 inch squares of filo pastry
salt and pepper

To serve:
tomatoes
sliced red onion

1 Put the sun-dried tomatoes into a small bowl and pour over enough boiling water to cover. Set aside for 20 minutes.

2 Meanwhile, put the leeks into a saucepan with the white wine, bring to the boil and simmer until all of the wine has evaporated. Remove the leeks from the heat and stir in the milk, egg yolk and soft cheese, and season well with salt and pepper.

3 Brush a pastry square with a little egg white and use it to line the base and sides of a 10 cm/4 inch tart case. Brush two more squares and lay these on top, each at a slightly different angle from the first, allowing the edges to flop over the rim. Line three more tart cases in the same way, using up all the pastry squares.

4 Half-fill each pastry case with a spoonful of the cooked leek mixture. Lay two rehydrated tomatoes on top of each tart and then cover with the remaining leeks. Season well and cook in a preheated oven, 200°C (400°F), Gas Mark 6, for 20 minutes, covering with aluminium foil after 10 minutes. Serve with tomatoes and sliced red onion.

Serves 4
Preparation time: 20 minutes, plus soaking
Cooking time: 30 minutes
Oven temperature: 200°C (400°F), Gas Mark 6

roasted autumn vegetables with garlic sauce

Cut the vegetables into similar-sized pieces so they cook evenly.

1 large garlic head
2 large onions, cut into wedges
8 small carrots, quartered
8 small parsnips, quartered
12 small potatoes, halved if large
2 fennel heads, thickly sliced
4 rosemary sprigs
4 thyme sprigs
6 tablespoons olive oil
salt and pepper

Garlic sauce:
1 large slice of day-old bread (about 75 g/3 oz)
4 tablespoons milk
75 ml/3 fl oz olive oil

1 Blanch the whole head of garlic in boiling water for 5 minutes. Drain and pat dry on kitchen paper.

2 Put all the vegetables and herbs in a large roasting pan, placing the garlic in the middle. Season well with salt and pepper and stir in the oil to coat the vegetables. Cover the pan with foil and place in a preheated oven, 220°C (425°F), Gas Mark 7, for 50 minutes. Remove the foil and bake for a further 30 minutes.

3 Remove the head of garlic. Carefully peel and discard the skin, and mash the garlic flesh with a fork. Put the bread in a bowl, add the milk and soak for 5 minutes.

4 Place the bread and garlic flesh in a liquidizer and process to form a smooth paste. Gradually blend in the oil until evenly combined; season to taste.

5 Serve the roasted vegetables accompanied by the garlic sauce to dip.

Serves 4–6
Preparation time: 25 minutes
Cooking time: about 1½ hours
Oven temperature: 220°C (425°F), Gas Mark 7

herb roulade with spinach and ricotta

25 g/1 oz butter
40 g/1½ oz plain four
1 teaspoon Dijon mustard
200 ml/7 fl oz semi-skimmed milk
50 g/2 oz cheese, grated
4 eggs, separated
4 tablespoons chopped mixed herbs (basil, chervil, chives, tarragon, thyme)
salt and pepper
Fresh Tomato Sauce (see page 147), to serve

Filling:
175 g/6 oz ricotta or curd cheese
2 tablespoons olive oil, plus extra for oiling
1 leek, finely chopped
500 g/1 lb frozen leaf spinach, defrosted
1/4 teaspoon freshly grated nutmeg

1 Grease a 23 x 33 cm/9 x 13 inch Swiss roll tin and line with nonstick baking paper. Melt the butter in a saucepan, stir in the flour and mustard, and cook over a low heat for 1 minute, then gradually add the milk, stirring until evenly blended. Bring the sauce slowly to the boil, stirring constantly until it thickens. Cook over a low heat for 2 minutes.

2 Remove the pan from the heat, leave to cool slightly, then beat in the cheese, egg yolks, herbs, salt and pepper. Whisk the egg whites until stiff and fold into the sauce until evenly incorporated.

3 Pour the mixture into the prepared tin and place in a preheated oven, 200°C (400°F), Gas Mark 6, for 12–15 minutes until risen and firm to the touch. Remove from the oven and set aside to cool. Reduce the temperature to 190°C (375°F), Gas Mark 5.

4 Meanwhile, prepare the filling. Beat the cheese and half the oil together until smooth and season with salt and pepper.

5 Heat the remaining oil in a frying pan and fry the leek for 5 minutes. Drain the spinach in a colander, pressing with a wooden spoon to squeeze out the excess moisture, and chop finely. Add to the leeks, season with nutmeg and cook gently for 5 minutes.

6 To assemble the roulade, turn it out of the tin and carefully peel away the paper. Spread the softened cheese and then the spinach mixture on the roulade. Roll up from a short end and place on the oiled Swiss roll tin. Brush with oil and bake for 20–25 minutes. Serve hot, in slices, with fresh tomato sauce.

Serves 6
Preparation time: 40 minutes
Cooking time: 40–50 minutes
Oven temperature: 200°C (400°F), Gas Mark 6

cashew nut roll

40 g/1 1/2 oz butter
40 g/1 1/2 oz plain flour
250 ml/8 fl oz milk
4 small eggs, separated
125 g/4 oz cashew nuts, lightly toasted and coarsely ground
pepper

Filling:
500 g/1 lb tomatoes, skinned and roughly chopped
2 celery sticks, chopped
2 shallots, chopped
1/2 teaspoon dried oregano
2 tablespoons tomato purée
125 g/4 oz cashew nuts, lightly toasted and coarsely chopped

To garnish:
freshly grated Parmesan cheese
coriander sprigs

1 Melt the butter in a small saucepan, stir in the flour and cook for 1 minute. Gradually blend in the milk, and cook until the mixture thickens. Remove the saucepan from the heat and stir in the egg yolks and ground cashew nuts. Season with pepper.

2 Whisk the egg whites stiffly and stir a spoonful of egg white into the sauce mixture. Fold in the remaining egg whites. Spread the mixture in a greased and lined 23 x 33 cm/9 x 13 inch Swiss roll tin. Bake in a preheated oven, 190°C (375°F), Gas Mark 5, for 15–20 minutes until set and golden.

3 Meanwhile, make the filling. Place the tomatoes, celery, shallots, oregano and tomato purée in a saucepan and simmer gently for 5–10 minutes until the mixture is thick and pulpy. Stir in the chopped cashew nuts, reserving a few for garnish.

4 Turn out the roll on to a hot, clean, damp tea towel covered with a sheet of greaseproof paper. Trim the edges. Spread the filling over the roll and roll up from a short side, using the tea towel to help you roll.

5 Sprinkle with the Parmesan and reserved nuts, and garnish with coriander sprigs. Serve hot in slices.

Serves 6
Preparation time: 15 minutes
Cooking time: 20 minutes
Oven temperature: 190°C (375°F), Gas Mark 5

feta and roasted vegetable pie

Pastry:
125 g/4 oz self-raising flour
50 g/2 oz oatmeal
75 g/3 oz chilled butter, diced
about 2 tablespoons iced water

Filling:
1 aubergine, sliced
1 red pepper, cored, deseeded and cut into thick strips
1 onion, cut into wedges
2 courgettes, cut into sticks
3 tomatoes, halved
2 garlic cloves, chopped
3 tablespoons olive oil
2 teaspoons chopped rosemary
125 g/4 oz feta cheese, crumbled
2 tablespoons freshly grated vegetarian Parmesan cheese
salt and pepper

1 Mix the flour and oatmeal in a bowl and rub in the butter until the mixture resembles breadcrumbs. Add enough of the measured water to mix to a firm dough. Turn out on to a lightly floured surface and knead briefly.

2 Roll out the pastry and use to line a 23 cm/9 inch pie plate. Line the pastry case with greaseproof paper and fill with baking beans or dried beans. Bake in a preheated oven, 200°C (400°F), Gas Mark 6, for 15 minutes. Lift out the paper and beans and bake for a further 5 minutes or until it is light golden brown.

3 Meanwhile, prepare the filling. Arrange the vegetables in a roasting tin. Add the garlic, oil and rosemary, and season to taste with salt and pepper. Turn the vegetables to coat them evenly with the oil. Roast at 200°C (400°F), Gas Mark 6 for 35 minutes, or until tender, turning them occasionally.

4 Remove the cooked vegetables with a slotted spoon and arrange in the pastry case. Scatter the feta cheese over the top and sprinkle with the Parmesan. Return the pie to the oven for 10 minutes until the top is crisp and golden. Serve warm or cold.

Serves 6
Preparation time: 25 minutes
Cooking time: 55 minutes
Oven temperature: 200°C (400°F), Gas Mark 6

winter vegetable platter with rouille

selection of winter vegetables (potatoes, parsnips, kohlrabi, baby turnips, leeks, Jerusalem artichokes, celeriac, carrots)
olive oil
sea salt
herb sprigs, to garnish

Rouille:
1 red pepper, cored, deseeded and chopped
2 garlic cloves, chopped
2 red chillies, deseeded and chopped
6 tablespoons olive oil
25 g/1 oz fresh white breadcrumbs
salt and pepper

1 First prepare the rouille. Put the pepper, garlic, chillies and olive oil in a liquidizer or food processor, and process until fairly smooth. Clean down the sides of the container with a spatula occasionally to make sure you blend all the ingredients evenly. Add the breadcrumbs, and salt and pepper to taste, and process again to form a thick paste. Transfer to a small bowl, cover and chill until ready to serve.

2 Prepare the vegetables according to type and size (the dish will look more attractive if all the vegetables are of a similar size, or are cut into similarly-sized pieces. Boil or steam the vegetables until just tender. Drain and refresh under cold running water, then drain thoroughly.

3 Arrange the vegetables on a large serving platter. Drizzle with olive oil and sprinkle with sea salt. Garnish with sprigs of herbs and serve with the rouille.

Serves 4–6
Preparation time: 30 minutes
Cooking time: 20–30 minutes

sweet potato and pea tagine

4 tablespoons lemon juice
3–4 teaspoons clear honey
1 teaspoon ground cinnamon
¼ teaspoon chilli powder, or to taste
2 tablespoons olive oil
750 g/1½ lb sweet potatoes, cut into 1 cm/½ inch cubes
1 onion, finely chopped
2 garlic cloves, finely chopped
4 tablespoons water
salt

1 Mix together 1 tablespoon of the lemon juice and all of the honey, cinnamon and chilli powder. Set aside.

2 Heat the oil in a large, heavy frying pan, add the sweet potatoes and cook for 10 minutes, stirring occasionally. Add the onion, garlic, salt, the remaining lemon juice and the measured water. Cook for about 5 minutes, stirring occasionally, until the onion begins to brown. Add the spiced honey mixture and cook for 2 minutes, stirring, then serve.

Serves 4
Preparation time: 10 minutes
Cooking time: 17 minutes

potato and leek bake

1.25 kg/2½ lb potatoes, peeled
500 g/1 lb leeks, trimmed and sliced
1 garlic clove, crushed (optional)
150 ml/¼ pint single cream
50 g/2 oz Cheddar cheese, grated
25 g/1 oz fresh breadcrumbs
salt and pepper
parsley sprigs, to garnish (optional)

1 Place the potatoes in a saucepan of salted boiling water and parboil for 3 minutes. Drain and slice.

2 Place the leeks and garlic, if using, in a greased ovenproof dish and season with pepper. Arrange the potatoes on the top and pour the cream over. Cover with foil and bake in a preheated oven, 190°C (375°F), Gas Mark 5, for 45 minutes until the potatoes are tender.

3 Sprinkle with the cheese and breadcrumbs and cook under a preheated moderate grill until the top is browned. Garnish with parsley sprigs, if liked, and serve at once.

Serves 6
Preparation time: 20 minutes
Cooking time: 50 minutes
Oven temperature: 190°C (375°F), Gas Mark 5

mixed baked beans

425 g/14 oz can red kidney beans
425 g/14 oz can haricot beans
425 g/14 oz can aduki beans
250 ml/8 fl oz passata
1 tablespoon molasses or black treacle
½ tablespoon wholegrain mustard
1 tablespoon Worcestershire sauce or dark soy sauce
pinch of ground cloves
½ teaspoon salt
1 large onion, finely chopped
2 carrots, diced
2 celery sticks, chopped
2 bay leaves
4 tablespoons chopped parsley
grated Cheddar cheese, to garnish (optional)

1 Drain the liquid from the beans and pour half into a bowl, discarding the rest. Whisk the passata, molasses, mustard, Worcestershire or soy sauce, cloves and salt in the liquid until evenly combined.

2 Put the beans and all the remaining ingredients except the parsley in a casserole dish and stir in the liquid. Cover with a tight-fitting lid. Place in a preheated oven, 180°C (350°F), Gas Mark 4, for 2 hours. Stir in the parsley, sprinkle with the Cheddar, if liked, and serve.

Serves 6–8
Preparation time: 15 minutes
Cooking time: 2 hours
Oven temperature: 180°C (350°F), Gas Mark 4

green lentil and vegetable tagine with couscous

125 g/4 oz green lentils, rinsed
600 ml/1 pint water
4 tablespoons olive oil
2 small onions, cut into wedges
2 garlic cloves, chopped
1 tablespoon ground coriander
2 teaspoons ground cumin
1 teaspoon turmeric
1 teaspoon ground cinnamon
12 new potatoes, halved if large
2 large carrots, thickly sliced
250 g/8 oz couscous
2 courgettes, sliced
175 g/6 oz button mushrooms
300 ml/½ pint tomato juice
1 tablespoon tomato purée
125 g/4 oz ready-to-eat dried apricots, chopped
2 tablespoons chilli sauce, plus extra to serve (optional)

1 Put the lentils in a saucepan with the measured water, bring to the boil, cover and simmer for 20 minutes.

2 Meanwhile, heat half the oil in a large saucepan, add the onions, garlic and spices and fry for 5 minutes. Add the potatoes and carrots and fry for a further 5 minutes. Add the lentils with their cooking liquid, cover and simmer gently for 15 minutes.

3 Rinse the couscous several times under cold running water to moisten all the grains and spread out on a large baking sheet. Sprinkle over a little water and then leave to soak for 15 minutes.

4 Heat the remaining oil in a frying pan, add the courgettes and mushrooms and fry for 4–5 minutes, until lightly golden. Add to the lentil mixture with the tomato juice, tomato purée, dried apricots and chilli sauce, and return to the boil. Cook for a further 10 minutes until the vegetables and lentils are tender.

5 Steam the couscous according to the packet instructions or over the stew in a double boiler for 6–7 minutes. Transfer to a large warmed platter, spoon on the vegetable and lentil tagine, and serve the juices separately, with extra chilli sauce if liked.

Serves 4–6
Preparation time: 40–45 minutes, plus soaking
Cooking time: 45 minutes

borlotti bean goulash

2 tablespoons olive oil
1 onion, chopped
2 carrots, sliced
1 teaspoon caraway seeds
2 red peppers, cored, deseeded and diced
250 g/8 oz sweet potato, cubed
2 tablespoons paprika
1 teaspoon cayenne pepper
600 ml/1 pint Vegetable Stock (see page 140)
2 tablespoons tomato purée
425 g/14 oz can borlotti beans, drained

Dumplings:
75 g/3 oz self-raising flour
½ teaspoon salt
50 g/2 oz suet
15 g/½ oz Cheddar cheese, grated
½ teaspoon celery salt
4–5 tablespoons iced water
pepper

1 Heat the oil in a large flameproof casserole, add the onion, carrots and caraway seeds, and fry for 5 minutes. Add the peppers, sweet potato, paprika and cayenne and fry for a further 3 minutes.

2 Stir in the stock, tomato purée and beans, bring to the boil, cover and cook over a low heat for 30 minutes.

3 Meanwhile, make the dumplings. Sift the flour and salt into a bowl and stir in the suet, cheese, celery salt and a little pepper. Working quickly and lightly, gradually mix in just enough of the measured water to form a firm dough. Shape into 12 small balls.

4 Add the dumplings to the goulash, cover and cook over a gentle heat for a further 20 minutes until the vegetables are tender and the dumplings light and fluffy.

Serves 4
Preparation time: 25 minutes
Cooking time: 1 hour

spicy beanburgers and mango salsa

1 tablespoon sunflower oil
½ large red onion, finely chopped
1 garlic clove, crushed
1 teaspoon grated fresh root ginger
1 teaspoon ground cumin
1 teaspoon ground coriander
2 teaspoons chilli powder
425 g/14 oz can red kidney beans, drained
75 g/3 oz fresh wholemeal breadcrumbs
2 tablespoons chopped coriander sprigs
2 tablespoons dark soy sauce
wholemeal flour, to dust
vegetable oil, for shallow-frying
salt and pepper
4 coriander sprigs, to garnish

Mango salsa:
½ small ripe mango, peeled, stoned and finely chopped
1 ripe tomato, skinned, deseeded and diced
1 red chilli, deseeded and finely chopped
1 tablespoon chopped coriander leaves
1 tablespoon chopped red onion
1 tablespoon lime juice
pinch of sugar
1 tablespoon olive oil

1 Heat the oil in a frying pan, add the onion, garlic, ginger and spices, and fry for 10 minutes. Remove from the heat and leave to cool slightly.

2 Put the onion mixture into a food processor with the beans, breadcrumbs, coriander and soy sauce and blend until smooth. Season to taste with salt and pepper.

3 To make the salsa, stir all the ingredients together. Cover and set aside for the flavours to develop.

4 With wet hands, form the bean mixture into 8 small burgers and coat lightly in flour. Heat 1 cm/½ inch oil in a frying pan and fry the burgers in batches for 2–3 minutes on each side until crisp and golden. Drain on kitchen paper and keep warm while cooking the rest. Serve immediately with a spoonful of salsa, garnished with coriander sprigs.

Serves 4
Preparation time: 45 minutes
Cooking time: 20 minutes

bean tagine

500 g/1 lb red or white kidney beans, soaked overnight and drained
2 celery sticks, halved
2 bay leaves
4 parsley sprigs
4 tablespoons olive oil
500 g/1 lb onions, chopped
5 garlic cloves, crushed
2 red chillies, deseeded and chopped
4 red peppers, cored, deseeded and chopped
1 tablespoon paprika
large handful of mixed chopped mint, coriander and parsley
salt and pepper
mint leaves, to garnish
harissa, to serve (optional)

Sauce:
1 kg/2 lb canned chopped tomatoes
2 tablespoons olive oil
4 parsley sprigs
1 tablespoon sugar

1 Boil the beans in unsalted water for 10 minutes, then drain. Tie the celery, bay leaves, and parsley together with kitchen string. Cover the beans with fresh water, add the celery and herbs, and simmer for about 1 hour, until the beans are just tender. Drain, reserving the cooking liquid, and discard the celery and herbs.

2 Meanwhile, make the sauce. Empty the tomatoes and their juice into a saucepan, add the olive oil, parsley and sugar and bring to a boil, then simmer, uncovered, for about 20 minutes, until thick.

3 Heat the oil in a heavy flameproof casserole, add the onions, garlic, chillies, red peppers and paprika, and fry gently for 5 minutes. Stir in the beans, the sauce, and enough of the reserved cooking liquid to just cover the beans. Season with salt and pepper, cover, and cook in a preheated oven, 150°C (300°F), Gas Mark 2, for 1½ hours, stirring occasionally.

4 Just before serving, stir in the mint, parsley and coriander. Garnish with mint leaves and serve with a bowl of harissa, if liked.

Serves 8
Preparation time: 15 minutes, plus soaking
Cooking time: 2½–2¾ hours
Oven temperature: 150°C (300°F), Gas Mark 2

vegetable crusted cassoulet

125 g/4 oz dried haricot beans, soaked overnight
1.2 litres/2 pints cold water
15 g/½ oz dried ceps
150 ml/¼ pint boiling water
6 tablespoons olive oil
2 garlic cloves, chopped
250 g/8 oz baby onions, halved
175 g/6 oz mixed mushrooms, sliced
1 tablespoon each chopped thyme, rosemary and sage
2 carrots, diced
2 celery sticks, sliced
1 red pepper, cored, deseeded and diced
150 ml/¼ pint red wine
4 tablespoons tomato purée
1 tablespoon dark soy sauce
salt and pepper

Crust:
½ small French stick, thinly sliced
2 tablespoons olive oil
1 garlic clove, crushed
2 tablespoons chopped thyme
25 g/1 oz Parmesan cheese, freshly grated

1 Drain the beans and place in a saucepan with the measured cold water. Bring to the boil and boil rapidly for about 10 minutes. Lower the heat, cover and simmer gently for 45 minutes. Drain the beans and reserve 300 ml/½ pint of the cooking liquid.

2 Meanwhile, soak the dried ceps in the measured boiling water for 20 minutes, then drain, reserving the liquid. Slice the ceps.

3 Heat half the oil in a frying pan, add the garlic and onions and fry for 5 minutes. Add the mushrooms and herbs, and stir-fry for a further 5 minutes until the mushrooms are golden. Remove from the pan with a slotted spoon and set aside.

4 Heat the remaining oil in the frying pan, add the carrots, celery and pepper and fry for 5 minutes. Add the wine and boil rapidly for 3 minutes. Stir in the beans with the reserved cooking liquid, the mushroom mixture, ceps and their liquid, tomato purée and soy sauce and season to taste with salt and pepper. Spoon into 4 small dishes or 1 large gratin dish.

5 Layer the sliced bread over the casserole. Mix together the oil, garlic and thyme, brush over the bread and scatter with the Parmesan. Cover loosely with foil and place in a preheated oven, 190°C (375°F), Gas Mark 5, for 30 minutes. Remove the foil and bake for a further 20 minutes until the crust is golden.

Serves 6
Preparation time: 40 minutes, plus soaking
Cooking time: 1½–1¾ hours
Oven temperature: 190°C (375°F), Gas Mark 5

green lentils with pancetta and plum tomatoes

If you cannot get pancetta, use a mixture of smoked streaky bacon and Italian salami.

175 g/6 oz green lentils
3 tablespoons olive oil
175 g/6 oz pancetta, cut into short, thin strips
375 g/12 oz plum tomatoes, sliced
½ red onion, chopped
2 tablespoons chopped parsley
salt and pepper

Dressing:
4 tablespoons olive oil
2 tablespoons red wine vinegar
pinch of sugar
1 garlic clove, crushed

1 Put the lentils in a sieve and rinse under cold running water. Tip into a saucepan, cover with fresh water and bring to the boil. Boil rapidly for 10 minutes, then skim off any foam. Lower the heat, cover and simmer for 15–20 minutes, or until the lentils are just tender. Drain, rinse under cold running water, then drain again thoroughly. Transfer to a shallow serving bowl.

2 Heat the oil in a large frying pan, add the pancetta and cook over a moderately high heat until it is beginning to crisp. Remove the pan from the heat.

3 Add the tomatoes and onion to the lentils with the pancetta and parsley. Season with salt and pepper.

4 Just before serving, whisk all the dressing ingredients in a small bowl until blended or place them in a screw-top jar and shake well to combine. Pour the dressing over the salad and toss to mix.

Serves 4
Preparation time: 20 minutes
Cooking time: 25–30 minutes

chickpeas with tomatoes and spinach

3 aubergines, cut into 2.5 cm/1 inch pieces
about 4 tablespoons olive oil
1 onion, chopped
4 garlic cloves, crushed
1 cm/½ inch piece of fresh root ginger, grated
1 red chilli, deseeded and chopped
2 teaspoons ground cumin
2 teaspoons ground coriander
2 x 400 g/13 oz cans chickpeas, drained and rinsed
2 x 400 g/13 oz cans chopped tomatoes
125 ml/4 fl oz water
500 g/1 lb small spinach leaves
salt and pepper

1 Put the aubergines into a colander, sprinkle with salt and leave to drain for 1 hour, then rinse them well and dry thoroughly.

2 Heat the oil in a large frying pan, add the aubergines in batches and cook until browned on the outside and tender inside. Remove with a slotted spoon and drain on kitchen paper.

3 If necessary, add a little extra oil to the pan. When it is hot, add the onion and fry until soft and golden, adding the garlic, ginger and chilli when it is almost done. Stir in the cumin and coriander for 30 seconds then return the aubergines to the pan and add the chickpeas, the tomatoes and their juice and the measured water. Simmer gently for 15 minutes.

4 Add the spinach, and more water if necessary, bring to the boil and cook for 1–2 minutes until the spinach wilts. Season to taste and serve.

Serves 4
Preparation time: 10 minutes, plus draining
Cooking time: 30–40 minutes

vegetable tagine

1 tablespoon olive oil
1 red onion, cut into wedges
2 garlic cloves, crushed
3 celery sticks, sliced
3 carrots, thinly sliced
2 teaspoons harissa
about 625 g/1¼ lb small aubergines, chopped
2 large tomatoes, chopped
250 ml/8 fl oz water
125 g/4 oz small okra, trimmed
salt
chopped coriander leaves, to garnish

1 Heat the oil in a saucepan, add the onion, garlic, celery and carrots, and cook until beginning to brown. Add the harissa and stir for 1 minute.

2 Add the aubergines, tomatoes and the measured water to the pan. Bring to the boil then cover the pan and simmer gently for about 25 minutes.

3 Stir the okra into the pan, cover and cook for 15–20 minutes until it is tender. If necessary, uncover the pan towards the end of cooking so the consistency of the sauce at the end of the cooking is quite thick. Add salt to taste. Garnish with chopped coriander, and serve.

Serves 4
Preparation time: 15 minutes
Cooking time: 40–45 minutes

curried parsnip and cheese soufflés

250 g/8 oz parsnips, chopped
40 g/1¹/₂ oz ground almonds
25 g/1 oz butter, plus extra for greasing
25 g/1 oz plain flour
2 teaspoons hot curry paste
200 ml/7 fl oz milk
40 g/1¹/₂ oz Gruyère or Cheddar cheese, grated
3 eggs, separated
2 tablespoons chopped coriander leaves
salt and pepper

1 Steam the parsnips for 15–20 minutes until tender. Mash well and set aside to cool.

2 Toast the ground almonds in a dry frying pan over moderate heat until golden.

3 Melt the butter in a small saucepan, add the flour and cook for 1 minute, stirring. Stir in the curry paste and gradually add the milk, stirring constantly until smooth. Slowly bring to the boil, stirring constantly until thickened. Cook over a low heat for 2 minutes.

4 Remove the pan from the heat and stir in the cheese until melted. Cool slightly, then beat in the egg yolks with the cooled mashed parsnip, coriander, half the toasted ground almonds, and salt and pepper to taste.

5 Whisk the egg whites until stiff and carefully fold into the parsnip mixture until evenly incorporated.

6 Grease 6 large ramekin dishes and line with the remaining toasted ground almonds. Spoon in the soufflé mixture and place the ramekin dishes in a large roasting pan. Add enough boiling water to come two-thirds of the way up the sides of the ramekin dishes and place the roasting pan in a preheated oven, 200°C (400°F), Gas Mark 6, for 25 minutes until risen and golden. Serve the soufflés immediately.

Serves 6
Preparation time: 25 minutes
Cooking time: 45–50 minutes
Oven temperature: 200°C (400°F), Gas Mark 6

stuffed courgettes

6 courgettes, trimmed
25 g/1 oz crustless white bread
milk, for soaking
125 g/4 oz ricotta or soft curd cheese
¹/₄ teaspoon dried oregano
1 garlic clove, crushed
40 g/1¹/₂ oz Parmesan cheese, freshly grated
1 egg yolk
salt and pepper

1 Cook the courgettes in a large saucepan of salted boiling water for 5 minutes. Drain well. Soak the bread in a little milk until soft and then squeeze dry.

2 Halve the courgettes lengthways and carefully scoop out the centres using a teaspoon. You should be left with long boat-shaped cases that are ready for filling.

3 Chop the courgette centres finely and place in a bowl. Add the bread, ricotta or soft curd cheese, oregano, garlic, Parmesan, egg yolk, salt and pepper. Mix thoroughly. The consistency should be fairly soft. If it is too stiff, add a little milk.

4 Arrange the courgette cases close together in a single layer in a well-oiled shallow baking tray or ovenproof dish. Fill the cases with the cheese mixture and bake in a preheated oven, 190°C (375°F), Gas Mark 5, for 35–40 minutes until the courgettes are tender and the filling is golden brown. Serve immediately.

Serves 4
Preparation time: 20 minutes
Cooking time: 40–45 minutes
Oven temperature: 190°C (375°F), Gas Mark 5

courgette, sun-dried tomato and ricotta flan

1 quantity Shortcrust Pastry (see page 124)
2 tablespoons olive oil
1 small onion, thinly sliced
2 courgettes, thinly sliced
50 g/2 oz drained sun-dried tomatoes in oil, sliced

250 g/8 oz ricotta or curd cheese
2 tablespoons milk
2 eggs, beaten
4 tablespoons chopped herbs (basil, rosemary,
   sage, thyme)
12 black olives, pitted and halved
salt and pepper

1 On a lightly floured surface, roll out the pastry and use to line a 23 cm/9 inch flan tin. Prick the base and chill for a further 20 minutes. Line the pastry case with greaseproof paper and fill with baking beans or dried beans. Bake in a preheated oven, 200°C (400°F), Gas Mark 6, for 10 minutes. Lift out the paper and beans and bake for a further 10 minutes or until it is light golden brown.

2 Heat the oil in a frying pan, add the onion and courgettes and fry gently for 5–6 minutes until lightly golden. Scatter over the base of the pastry case and top with the sun-dried tomatoes.

3 Beat the ricotta, milk, eggs, herbs and salt and pepper together and spread over the courgette mixture. Scatter over the olives and bake for 30–35 minutes until firm and golden.

Serves 6–8
Preparation time: 30 minutes, plus chilling
Cooking time: about 1 hour
Oven temperature: 200°C (400°F), Gas Mark 6

griddled butternut squash with parmesan

1 kg/2 lb butternut squash, peeled, deseeded and cut into
   small wedges or slices
75 g/3 oz butter
150 g/5 oz Parmesan cheese
sea salt flakes and pepper

1 Heat a griddle pan or nonstick frying pan, add the squash in batches and cook for about 10 minutes on each side. As the squash is cooked, place on a large plate and keep warm.

2 Melt the butter in a small pan and heat until it just begins to brown, to give a rich, nutty flavour. Pour the butter over the cooked squash and season with salt and pepper. Using a mandoline or vegetable peeler, shave the Parmesan directly on to the squash and serve at once, or just warm, but before the butter hardens.

Serves 4
Preparation time: 10 minutes
Cooking time: 40 minutes

asparagus, walnut and parmesan flan

1 quantity Shortcrust Pastry (see page 124)
10 garlic cloves, peeled
2 tablespoons olive oil
375 g/12 oz asparagus
40 g/1½ oz walnuts, toasted and chopped
200 ml/7 fl oz single cream or milk
3 eggs, lightly beaten
75 g/3 oz Parmesan cheese, grated
salt and pepper

1 On a lightly floured surface, roll out the pastry and use to line a deep, 23 cm/9 inch flan tin. Prick the base with a fork and chill for 20 minutes.

2 Meanwhile, cook the garlic cloves in boiling water for 10 minutes, drain and pat dry. Mash with 1 tablespoon of the oil to form a paste.

3 Line the pastry case with greaseproof paper and fill with baking beans or dried beans. Bake in a preheated oven, 200°C (400°F), Gas Mark 6, for 10 minutes. Lift out the paper and beans and bake for a further 10 minutes or until it is light golden brown. Reduce the oven temperature to 190°C (375°F), Gas Mark 5.

4 Heat the remaining oil and stir-fry the asparagus for 5 minutes. Scatter the asparagus over the pastry case together with the walnuts. Beat together the cream or milk, garlic paste, eggs, Parmesan, salt and pepper. Pour over the asparagus and bake for 25 minutes until set and golden brown.

Serves 6–8
Preparation time: 25 minutes, plus chilling
Cooking time: 50 minutes
Oven temperature: 200°C (400°F), Gas Mark 6

grilled asparagus with walnut sauce

To serve as a starter, transfer the grilled asparagus to individual gratin dishes, spread over the sauce and return to the grill.

1 kg/2 lb asparagus

Walnut sauce:
50 g/2 oz walnuts
2 large spring onions, very finely chopped
1 garlic clove, crushed
1 teaspoon grated lemon rind
1 tablespoon chopped basil
1 tablespoon chopped parsley
4 tablespoons walnut oil, plus extra for brushing
50 ml/2 fl oz milk
25 g/1 oz vegetarian Parmesan cheese, grated (optional)

1 First make the sauce. Fry the walnuts in a dry frying pan over moderate heat, stirring, until toasted. Grind them with the spring onions, garlic, lemon rind and herbs. Whisk in the oil and then the milk to form a smooth sauce of a fairly thick pouring consistency.

2 Brush the asparagus with oil and place under a preheated hot grill for 5–6 minutes, turning frequently until golden and tender.

3 Transfer the asparagus to a warmed gratin dish, pour over the sauce and then sprinkle over the cheese, if using. Return to the grill for 1–2 minutes until bubbling. Serve at once.

Serves 4–6
Preparation time: 15 minutes
Cooking time: 10–15 minutes

stuffed artichokes

4 globe artichokes
2 tablespoons lemon juice
1 onion, thinly sliced
2 carrots, thinly sliced
1 bay leaf
250 ml/8 fl oz dry white wine
250 ml/8 fl oz water
1 tablespoon arrowroot dissolved in 3 tablespoons of water
salt and pepper

Stuffing:
2 tablespoons olive oil
1 onion, finely chopped
2 garlic cloves, crushed
125 g/4 oz raw ham or streaky bacon, chopped
2 tablespoons chopped parsley
50 g/2 oz fresh breadcrumbs
salt and pepper

1 Remove the stalks and the leaves at the base of each artichoke. Cut off the ends of the leaves. Sprinkle with lemon juice to prevent them discolouring and set aside until you are ready to cook them. Put them in a large saucepan of salted boiling water, simmer for 10–15 minutes and then drain upside-down. Remove the fibrous choke in the centre of each artichoke with a small spoon.

2 To make the stuffing, heat the oil in a saucepan, add the onion and garlic, and fry over low heat until soft and golden. Remove from the heat and add the ham or bacon, parsley and breadcrumbs. Stir well and season to taste.

3 Fill the hollow centre of each prepared artichoke with the stuffing. Put the onion and carrots in a flameproof casserole and place the artichokes on top. Add the bay leaf and pour over the wine and measured water, and add a little salt and pepper. Bring to the boil, then reduce the heat and simmer gently for 45 minutes.

4 Remove the artichokes and keep warm. Strain the cooking liquid into a small saucepan and add the dissolved arrowroot. Heat gently, stirring all the time, until the sauce has a creamy consistency. Season to taste with salt and pepper, and serve hot with the artichokes.

Serves 4
Preparation time: 40 minutes
Cooking time: 1–1¼ hours

mushroom crêpes

oil, for frying
½ quantity Crêpe Batter (see page 127)
flat leaf parsley sprigs, to garnish

Filling:
300 g/10 oz chestnut mushrooms, chopped
1 bunch of spring onions, finely chopped
1 garlic clove, chopped
400 g/13 oz can chopped tomatoes, drained
2 tablespoons chopped oregano

1 Pour a few drops of oil in a frying pan. Heat the pan and pour in a ladleful of batter and cook for 1 minute. Carefully flip the crêpe and cook the second side. Slide out of the pan on to greaseproof paper. Make 3 more crêpes in the same way, adding a few more drops of oil to the pan between each, and stack in between greaseproof paper.

2 To make the filling, put all the ingredients into a small saucepan and cook for 5 minutes, stirring occasionally. Divide the filling between the crêpes, reserving a little of the mixture to serve, and roll up.

3 Transfer the crêpes to an ovenproof dish and cook in a preheated oven, 180°C (350°F), Gas Mark 4, for 20 minutes. Garnish with parsley and serve with the remaining filling.

Serves 4
Preparation time: 20–25 minutes
Cooking time: 35 minutes
Oven temperature: 180°C (350°F), Gas Mark 4

spinach tart

Pastry:
175 g/6 oz plain flour
¼ teaspoon baking powder
pinch of salt
125 g/4 oz chilled butter, diced
1 egg yolk

Filling:
50 g/2 oz butter
1 onion, finely chopped
250 g/8 oz frozen leaf spinach, defrosted and drained
¼ teaspoon grated nutmeg
250 g/8 oz mascarpone cheese
50 g/2 oz hard pecorino cheese, grated
1 egg, plus 2 egg yolks
salt and pepper

1 To make the pastry, sift the flour, baking powder and a pinch of salt together. Make a well in the centre, add the butter and egg yolk and gradually work the flour into the butter and egg yolk with your fingertips.

2 Gather the dough together, then roll it out gently to a rough round on a floured surface. Lift the round into a 23 cm/9 inch fluted tart tin with a removable base and press the pastry into the corners and up the sides. Trim the top edge with a knife, then chill in the refrigerator for 30 minutes.

3 Meanwhile, make the filling. Melt the butter in a small pan, add the onion and cook gently for about 5 minutes, stirring frequently, until softened but not coloured. Add the spinach and nutmeg, season to taste with salt and pepper, and stir well to mix. Transfer to a bowl and leave to cool.

4 Line the pastry case with greaseproof paper and fill with baking beans or dried beans. Bake in a preheated oven, 190°C (375°F), Gas Mark 5, for 15 minutes. Lift out the paper and beans and set the pastry case aside. Reduce the oven temperature to 160°C (325°F), Gas Mark 3.

5 Place the mascarpone into a large bowl and whisk in the pecorino, egg and egg yolks. Add the cooled spinach and salt and pepper to taste, blend well together, then spoon into the pastry case. Bake in the oven for 30 minutes, covering the edge of the pastry with foil if it shows signs of overbrowning.

6 Leave the tart to stand for 10–15 minutes before serving, or serve cold.

Serves 4–6
Preparation time: 30 minutes, plus chilling and cooling
Cooking time: 50 minutes
Oven temperature: 190°C (375°F), Gas Mark 5

spinach and chickpea flan

1 quantity Shortcrust Pastry (see page 124)
175 g/6 oz spinach
2 tablespoons olive oil
1 small onion, thinly sliced
2 garlic cloves, crushed
1 teaspoon turmeric
200 g/7 oz canned chickpeas, drained
2 eggs, lightly beaten
200 ml/7 fl oz single cream
pinch of grated nutmeg
salt and pepper

1 Roll out the pastry on a lightly floured surface, and use to line a deep, 20 cm/8 inch flan tin. Prick the base; chill for 20 minutes. Line the pastry case with greaseproof paper and fill with baking beans or dried beans. Bake in a preheated oven, 200°C (400°F), Gas Mark 6, for 10 minutes. Lift out the paper and beans and bake for a further 10 minutes or until it is light golden brown.

2 Place the spinach in a large saucepan with just the water left on the leaves. Heat gently for 3–4 minutes until the spinach wilts. Drain in a colander, pressing down firmly with a wooden spoon to squeeze out excess moisture, and chop finely.

3 Heat the oil in a saucepan, add the onion, garlic and turmeric, and fry for 5 minutes. Stir in the chickpeas and spinach, remove from the heat and spread over the pastry case.

4 Beat the eggs, cream, nutmeg, salt and pepper together and pour into the pastry case. Bake for 35–40 minutes until firm and golden, and serve.

Serves 6–8
Preparation time: 25 minutes, plus chilling
Cooking time: 1 hour
Oven temperature: 200°C (400°F), Gas Mark 6

braised chinese vegetables

2–3 tablespoons dried wood ears or 5–6 dried Chinese mushrooms, soaked in water for 20–25 minutes
250 g/8 oz firm tofu
4 tablespoons vegetable oil
125 g/4 oz carrots, sliced
125 g/4 oz mangetout, trimmed
125 g/4 oz Chinese leaves, sliced
125 g/4 oz canned sliced bamboo shoots or whole baby corns
1 teaspoon sugar
1 tablespoon light soy sauce
1 teaspoon cornflour mixed to a smooth paste with 1 tablespoon cold water
salt
1 teaspoon sesame seed oil, to finish (optional)

1 Drain the mushrooms, discard the hard stalks, then rinse and cut the flesh into small slices.

2 Cut the tofu into about 24 small pieces, then put them in a saucepan of lightly salted boiling water for 2–3 minutes, so that they become firm. Remove with a slotted spoon and drain.

3 Heat about half of the oil in a flameproof casserole or heavy-based saucepan until hot. Add the tofu and fry until lightly browned on both sides. Remove the tofu, then heat the remaining oil in the pan. Add the vegetables and stir-fry for about 1–2 minutes. Return the tofu to the pan, add 1 teaspoon of salt, the sugar and soy sauce and stir well. Cover, reduce the heat and braise for 2–3 minutes.

4 Pour the cornflour paste over the vegetables and stir. Increase the heat to high to thicken the sauce, then sprinkle in the sesame seed oil, if using, and serve.

Serves 4
Preparation time: 15 minutes, plus soaking
Cooking time: 7–10 minutes

crispy vegetables with spicy avocado dip

125 g/4 oz plain flour
pinch of salt
1 tablespoon sunflower oil
150 ml/¼ pint water
2 egg whites, stiffly whisked
500 g/1 lb mixed vegetables (cauliflower or broccoli florets, green beans, whole mushrooms, mangetout and strips of courgette)
oil, for deep-frying

Dip:
1–2 garlic cloves, chopped
4 tomatoes, skinned, deseeded and chopped
1 teaspoon chilli powder
2 avocados, peeled and stoned
1 tablespoon chopped coriander leaves
pinch of ground coriander (optional)

1 First make the dip. Place all the ingredients in a food processor or blender and work to a smooth purée. Spoon into a serving dish and chill.

2 To make the batter, sift the flour and salt into a mixing bowl. Gradually beat in the oil and water, then fold in the egg white.

3 Heat the oil in a wok or frying pan to 180–190°C (350–375°F), or until a cube of bread browns in 30 seconds. Dip the vegetables in the batter, then deep-fry in batches for 2–3 minutes, until golden. Make sure the oil comes back to full heat after each batch.

4 Drain the vegetables on kitchen paper and serve with the dip.

Serves 6
Preparation time: 15 minutes
Cooking time: 20 minutes

artichoke and red pepper stir-fry

If you are short of time, omit roasting the red pepper, but stir-fry it for a few minutes longer to soften it.

1 large red pepper
2 tablespoons olive oil
1 onion, finely chopped
2.5 cm/1 inch piece of fresh root ginger, finely chopped
1 garlic clove, crushed
300 g/10 oz can artichoke hearts, drained and sliced
1 tablespoon balsamic vinegar
salt and pepper
few basil leaves, to garnish

1 Roast the red pepper under a hot grill, turning it frequently until the skin is blistered and blackened on all sides. Place it in a polythene bag until cool, then peel off the skin. Core and deseed the pepper and cut the flesh lengthways into thin strips, then set aside.

2 Heat the oil in the wok over moderate heat. Add the onion, ginger and garlic, and stir-fry for 2–3 minutes or until softened without browning. Add the artichokes and pepper strips, increase the heat to high and toss until piping hot. Sprinkle over the balsamic vinegar and add salt and pepper to taste. Garnish with the basil leaves and serve immediately.

Serves 4
Preparation time: 10 minutes
Cooking time: about 15 minutes

stir-fried mushrooms

50 g/2 oz dried shiitake mushrooms, soaked in warm
*   water for 20 minutes*
1 tablespoon oil
1 teaspoon finely chopped fresh root ginger
2 spring onions, finely chopped
1 garlic clove, crushed
250 g/8 oz button mushrooms
250 g/8 oz can straw mushrooms, drained
1 teaspoon chilli bean sauce or chilli powder
2 teaspoons dry sherry
2 teaspoons dark soy sauce
1 tablespoon Chicken Stock (see page 141) or water
pinch of sugar
pinch of salt
1 teaspoon sesame oil

1 Drain the mushrooms and squeeze them dry. Discard the hard stalks.

2 Heat the oil in the wok over moderate heat, add the ginger, spring onions and garlic, and stir-fry briskly for 5–10 seconds.

3 Add the dried mushrooms and button mushrooms and cook for 5 minutes, stirring all the time.

4 Add the straw mushrooms, chilli bean sauce or chilli powder, sherry, soy sauce, stock, sugar, salt and sesame oil. Mix well, stir-fry for 5 minutes, and serve immediately.

Serves 4
Preparation time: 5 minutes, plus soaking
Cooking time: 10 minutes

stir-fried green beans

3 tablespoons vegetable oil
2 garlic cloves, crushed
2 shallots, thinly sliced
1 slice of fresh root ginger, chopped
1 fresh red chilli, deseeded and finely chopped
½ teaspoon salt
500 g/1 lb green beans, divided into 5 cm/2 inch lengths
50 g/2 oz unsalted cashew nuts
125 ml/4 fl oz Chicken Stock (see page 141)
2 tablespoons dry sherry
1 tablespoon light soy sauce
1 teaspoon vinegar
1 teaspoon sugar
black pepper

1 Heat the oil in a wok or frying pan. Add the garlic, shallots and ginger, and stir-fry briskly over moderate heat for 1 minute. Stir in the red chilli and salt, and continue stir-frying for 30 seconds.

2 Add the green beans and cashew nuts to the wok and toss well to combine with the garlic, shallots and spices. Stir-fry quickly for 1 minute to brown the cashew nuts.

3 Add the stock, sherry, soy sauce, vinegar and sugar, and bring to the boil. Reduce the heat slightly and continue stir-frying for about 4 minutes, until the beans are cooked and the liquid has thickened. Turn into a warmed serving dish, season with a generous sprinkling of pepper and serve immediately.

Serves 4
Preparation time: 10 minutes
Cooking time: 7–8 minutes

sweet and sour thai vegetables

2 tablespoons groundnut oil
3 garlic cloves, chopped
1 cucumber, halved, deseeded and diagonally chopped into 5 mm/¼ inch slices
4 baby corns, diagonally sliced
1 tomato, cut into 8 pieces
250 g/8 oz can water chestnuts, drained
50 g/2 oz mangetout
1 onion, roughly chopped
4 tablespoons Vegetable Stock (see page 140)
1 tablespoon sugar
1 tablespoon Thai fish sauce or soy sauce
1 tablespoon distilled white vinegar or Chinese rice vinegar
3 spring onions, roughly chopped
salt and pepper

1 Heat the oil in a wok, add the garlic, and fry quickly until it is turning golden, then add the rest of the ingredients except the spring onions. Cook for 2–3 minutes, stirring constantly.

2 Season to taste with salt and pepper, then add the chopped spring onions and cook for 30 seconds. Serve immediately.

Serves 4
Preparation time: 10 minutes
Cooking time: 5 minutes

stir-fried vegetables with cashews

50 g/2 oz cashews
250 g/8 oz Chinese leaves, chopped into 2.5 cm/1 inch pieces
50 g/2 oz cauliflower florets
50 g/2 oz broccoli (preferably Chinese)
50 g/2 oz white cabbage, chopped
2 baby corns, diagonally sliced
1 tomato, cut into 8 pieces
5 garlic cloves, chopped
1½ tablespoons soy sauce

1 teaspoon sugar
100 ml/3½ fl oz water
2½ tablespoons groundnut oil
pepper, to taste

1 Fry the cashew nuts in a dry frying pan over a moderate heat until toasted.

2 Mix all the ingredients, except the oil, in a bowl.

3 Heat a wok or frying pan and add the oil. Throw in the contents of the bowl and cook over a high heat for 2–3 minutes, stirring and turning. Serve immediately.

Serves 4
Preparation time: 20 minutes
Cooking time: 2–3 minutes

thai stuffed omelette

1 tablespoon groundnut oil
3 eggs, beaten
salt and pepper
deep-fried basil leaves, to garnish

Filling:
3 tablespoons groundnut oil
2 garlic cloves, chopped
1 onion, finely chopped
2 tablespoons chopped green beans
2 tablespoons chopped asparagus
3 baby corns, thinly sliced
1 tomato, diced
4 dried shiitake mushrooms, soaked, drained and sliced
1½ teaspoons sugar
2 teaspoons soy sauce
50 ml/2 fl oz water
pinch of salt

1 First make the filling. Heat the oil in a wok or frying pan, add the garlic and onion, and stir-fry for 30 seconds. Add the beans, asparagus, corn, tomato, mushrooms, sugar and soy sauce, and stir-fry for 3–4 minutes, then add the measured water and salt, and continue stir-frying for 2 minutes. Remove the filling and set aside. Wipe the wok clean with kitchen paper.

2 To make the omelette, put the oil in the pan and heat it, making sure it coats not only the base of the wok but as much of the sides as possible. Pour off any excess. Season the eggs, then pour them into the pan, swirling them around to form a large, thin omelette. Loosen the omelette and move it around with a spatula to make sure it is not sticking to the pan, adding more oil if necessary.

3 When the omelette is almost firm, put the filling in the middle and fold both sides and ends over to form an oblong parcel, constantly checking that the omelette is not sticking underneath.

4 Carefully remove the omelette from the wok and place in a serving dish. Garnish with deep-fried basil leaves and serve immediately.

Serves 4
Preparation time: 8–10 minutes, plus soaking
Cooking time: 8–10 minutes

watercress in garlic and oyster sauce

2 tablespoons oil
6 garlic cloves, finely chopped
300 g/10 oz watercress
1 tablespoon oyster sauce
2 tablespoons Vegetable Stock (see page 140)

1 Heat the oil in a wok or frying pan, add the garlic and stir-fry until golden.

2 Add the watercress and stir-fry for 30 seconds, then add the oyster sauce and stock. Continue to stir-fry vigorously for 1 minute, then serve immediately.

Serves 4
Preparation time: 2 minutes
Cooking time: 5 minutes

cauliflower curry

125 g/4 oz ghee or 2 tablespoons vegetable oil
750 g/1½ lb cauliflower, cut into florets
300 ml/½ pint natural yogurt
2 large onions, finely chopped
2 garlic cloves, crushed
4 bay leaves
300 ml/½ pint hot water
salt

Spices:
6 cloves
6 black peppercorns
1 black cardamom
2 green cardamoms
2 x 2.5 cm/1 inch pieces of cinnamon stick
1 teaspoon coriander seeds
1 teaspoon white cumin seeds
1 teaspoon chilli powder

1 Heat 25 g/1 oz of the ghee or ½ tablespoon of the oil in a large saucepan. Add the cauliflower and cook over a medium heat for 5 minutes. Using a slotted spoon, transfer the cauliflower to a bowl and pour the yogurt over the top.

2 Add the remaining ghee or oil to the pan. When it is hot, add the onions, garlic, salt to taste, bay leaves and all the spices except the chilli powder. Fry until the onions are golden and soft, then stir in the chilli powder.

3 Return the cauliflower and yogurt to the pan and stir gently to combine all the ingredients. Cook gently over a low heat for 10 minutes.

4 Pour in the measured hot water and simmer for 25 minutes or until the cauliflower is tender, stirring occasionally. Serve hot.

Serves 4–6
Preparation time: 15 minutes
Cooking time: 45 minutes

spicy stuffed aubergines

4–6 aubergines, halved lengthways
100 ml/3½ fl oz water
1 bay leaf
125 g/4 oz ghee or 2 tablespoons vegetable oil
1 large onion, finely chopped
2 garlic cloves, finely chopped
2 teaspoons coriander seeds, coarsely crushed
1 teaspoon chilli powder
1 teaspoon lovage seeds (optional)
1 teaspoon salt

To garnish:
coriander sprigs
dried red chillies, chopped

1 Place the aubergines in a roasting pan with the cut sides upwards. Pour in the measured water, add the bay leaf and cover the pan tightly with foil. Poach in a preheated oven, 160°C (325°F), Gas Mark 3, for 25 minutes or until soft.

2 Heat the ghee or oil in a heavy-based saucepan, add the onion and garlic, and fry gently for 4–5 minutes until soft. Add the coriander seeds, chilli powder, lovage seeds, if using, and salt. Stir well and fry for about 2–3 minutes.

3 Remove the aubergines from the water and pat dry with kitchen paper. With a teaspoon, scrape out the flesh, reserving the skins. Mash the flesh and add to the spice mixture. Fry for 2–3 minutes, stirring.

4 Grill the aubergine skins for 5 minutes until dried out, and fill with the fried mixture. Arrange on a serving dish, garnish with coriander sprigs and chillies, and serve.

Serves 4–6
Preparation time: 20 minutes
Cooking time: 35 minutes
Oven temperature: 160°C (325°F), Gas Mark 3

thai fried rice with beans and tofu p407

fragrant rice with vegetables and cashew nuts p397

griddled polenta with field mushrooms p396

meat-filled cannelloni p389

prawn vermicelli   p410

spaghetti with sardines, anchovies and fennel   p378

kedgeree p396

tagliatelle with borlotti beans and sage p372

panir mattar

2–3 tablespoons oil
125 g/4 oz panir (curd cheese), cut into
　1 cm/½ inch cubes
2 tablespoons finely chopped onion
75 ml/3 fl oz water
250 g/8 oz shelled peas
½ teaspoon sugar
1 tablespoon grated fresh root ginger
2 fresh green chillies, finely chopped
½ teaspoon garam masala
1 tablespoon finely chopped coriander sprigs
salt

1 Heat the oil in a heavy-based pan, add the panir and fry until golden, turning gently and taking care not to burn it. Remove from the pan and set aside. Add the onions to the pan and fry until coloured, then remove and set aside.

2 Add the measured water, and salt to taste, to the pan and bring to the boil. Add the peas and sugar, cover and simmer until the peas are almost tender. If necessary, uncover and cook for 1 minute to evaporate any liquid.

3 Return the onions to the pan, add the ginger and chillies, and stir well. Cook for 2 minutes, then very gently stir in the panir. Heat through for 2 minutes, then stir in the garam masala and coriander. Serve immediately.

Serves 4
Preparation time: 5 minutes
Cooking time: 25 minutes

aloo sag

This recipe uses frozen spinach, but you could use fresh if you prefer, which would give both a slightly stronger colour and flavour.

6 tablespoons oil
1 onion, chopped
2.5 cm/1 inch piece of fresh root ginger, chopped
2 fresh green chillies, finely chopped
1 teaspoon turmeric
2 garlic cloves, finely chopped
500 g/1 lb potatoes, cut into small pieces
500 g/1 lb frozen leaf spinach, defrosted
salt

1 Heat the oil in a frying pan, add the onion and cook until soft. Add the ginger, chillies, turmeric and garlic, and cook for 5 minutes. Add the potatoes, and salt to taste, stir well, cover, and cook for 10 minutes.

2 Drain the spinach in a colander, pressing down firmly with a wooden spoon to squeeze out excess moisture. Chop the spinach, add to the potatoes and cook for about 5 minutes, until both vegetables are tender. Serve hot.

Serves 4
Preparation time: 5 minutes
Cooking time: 30 minutes

balti mixed vegetables

Use whichever vegetables are in season, finely diced so that they do not take too long to become tender.

2–3 tablespoons vegetable oil
1 small onion, chopped
1 garlic clove, crushed
2.5 cm/1 inch piece of fresh root ginger, grated
1 teaspoon chilli powder
2 teaspoons ground coriander
½ teaspoon turmeric
500 g/1 lb diced mixed vegetables (potatoes, carrots,
　swede, peas, beans, cauliflower)
2–3 tomatoes, skinned and chopped, or 4 tablespoons
　lemon juice
salt

1 Heat the oil in a large wok or heavy-based saucepan, add the onion and fry gently for 5–10 minutes or until lightly browned. Add the garlic, ginger, chilli powder, coriander, turmeric and a pinch of salt, and fry for 2–3 minutes. Add the diced vegetables and stir-fry for a further 2–3 minutes.

2 Add either the chopped tomatoes or the lemon juice. Stir well and add a little water. Cover and cook gently for 10–12 minutes, or until the vegetables are tender, adding a little more water, if necessary, to prevent the vegetables sticking to the bottom of the wok. Serve immediately.

Serves 4
Preparation time: 15 minutes
Cooking time: 20–30 minutes

spiced okra

1 teaspoon cumin seeds
1 teaspoon coriander seeds
2 teaspoons mustard seeds
2 teaspoons sunflower oil
1 large onion, chopped
2 garlic cloves, crushed
2 teaspoons grated fresh root ginger
4 ripe tomatoes, chopped
1 teaspoon turmeric
1 teaspoon chilli powder
500 g/1 lb okra
150 ml/¼ pint Vegetable Stock (see page 140)
2 tablespoons chopped coriander leaves
salt and pepper

1 Dry-fry the cumin, coriander and mustard seeds in a small frying pan until they start to pop and give off a smoky aroma. Remove from the heat and grind to form a rough powder.

2 Heat the oil in a saucepan, add the onion, garlic and ginger, and fry over a moderate heat for 10 minutes until golden. Stir in the tomatoes, cover and continue to cook for a further 10 minutes.

3 Add the roasted spices, turmeric and chilli powder, okra and stock. Bring to the boil, cover and simmer over a very low heat for 20 minutes, until the okra is tender. Stir in the coriander and season to taste with salt and pepper. Serve hot.

Serves 4
Preparation time: 15 minutes
Cooking time: 40 minutes

vegetable curry

3 tablespoons oil
1 teaspoon fennel seeds
2 onions, sliced
1 teaspoon chilli powder
1 tablespoon ground coriander
2.5 cm/1 inch piece of fresh root ginger, finely chopped
2 aubergines, sliced
175 g/6 oz shelled peas
125 g/4 oz potatoes, cubed
250 g/8 oz canned tomatoes
4 green chillies, sliced
salt

1 Heat the oil in a large pan, add the fennel seeds and fry for a few seconds, then add the onions and fry until soft and golden. Add the chilli powder, coriander seeds, ginger and salt to taste. Fry for 2 minutes, stirring.

2 Add the aubergines, peas and potatoes and cook for 5 minutes, stirring occasionally.

3 Add the tomatoes with their juice and the chillies to the pan, cover and simmer for 30 minutes, or until the peas and potatoes are tender and the sauce is thick. Transfer to a warmed serving dish and serve.

Serves 4
Preparation time: 20 minutes
Cooking time: 45 minutes

kidney bean curry

125 ml/4 fl oz vegetable oil
2 teaspoons cumin seeds
1 large onion, chopped
400 g/13 oz can chopped tomatoes
1 tablespoon ground coriander
1 teaspoon chilli powder
1 teaspoon sugar
1 teaspoon salt
2 x 475 g/15 oz cans red kidney beans, drained

1 Heat the oil in a wok or frying pan, add the cumin seeds and onion, and fry until the onion is lightly browned.

2 Stir in the tomatoes and fry for a few seconds, then add the ground coriander, chilli powder, sugar and salt and stir well. Lower the heat and cook for about 5–7 minutes.

3 Add the beans, stir carefully but thoroughly and cook for 10–15 minutes. Serve immediately.

Serves 4–6
Preparation time: 15 minutes
Cooking time: 20–25 minutes

vegetables in malaysian coconut sauce

125 g/4 oz broccoli florets
125 g/4 oz green beans, cut into 2.5 cm/1 inch lengths
1 red pepper, cored, deseeded and sliced
125 g/4 oz courgettes, thinly sliced

Malaysian coconut sauce:
25 g/1 oz dried tamarind
150 ml/¼ pint boiling water
425 g/14 oz can thick coconut milk
2 teaspoons Thai Green Curry Paste (see page 149)
1 teaspoon grated ginger
1 onion, diced
½ teaspoon turmeric
salt

1 First make the sauce. Put the tamarind into a bowl. Pour over the measured boiling water and leave to soak for 30 minutes.

2 Mash the tamarind in the soaking water, then strain through a wire sieve set over a bowl, pressing the tamarind to extract as much pulp as possible.

3 Skim 2 tablespoons of the cream from the coconut milk and place it in a wok or heavy-based saucepan. Add the curry paste, ginger, onion and turmeric, and cook over gentle heat for 2–3 minutes, stirring. Stir in the remaining coconut milk and the tamarind water. Bring to the boil, then lower the heat and season with salt.

4 Add the broccoli and cook for 5 minutes, then add the green beans and red pepper and cook for a further 5 minutes, stirring. Stir in the courgettes and cook for 1–2 minutes, and serve.

Serves 4
Preparation time: 15 minutes, plus soaking
Cooking time: about 20 minutes

masoor dhal

4 tablespoons oil
3 cloves
2 teaspoons ground coriander
1 teaspoon turmeric
6 cardamom pods
2.5 cm/1 inch cinnamon stick
1 onion, chopped
2.5 cm/1 inch piece of fresh root ginger, chopped
1 green chilli, finely chopped
1 garlic clove, chopped
½ teaspoon garam masala
250 g/8 oz masoor dhal (red split lentils)
4 tablespoons lemon juice
salt
marjoram, to garnish

1 Heat the oil in a saucepan, add the cloves, ground coriander, turmeric, cardamom pods and cinnamon, and fry until they start to swell. Add the onion and fry for about 5 minutes until translucent.

2 Add the ginger, chilli, garlic and garam masala, and cook for 5 minutes.

3 Add the lentils, stir thoroughly and fry for 1 minute. Season to taste with salt and add enough water to come about 3 cm/1¼ inches above the level of the lentils. Bring to the boil, cover the pan and simmer for about 20 minutes, until the dhal is really thick and the lentils are tender.

4 Sprinkle with the lemon juice and stir to mix. Garnish with marjoram and serve immediately.

Serves 4
Preparation time: 15 minutes
Cooking time: about 35 minutes

sweet potato and spinach curry

*500 g/1 lb sweet potatoes, peeled and cut
  into large chunks*
3 tablespoons groundnut oil
1 red onion, chopped
2 garlic cloves, crushed
1 teaspoon shrimp paste
1 teaspoon turmeric
1 large red chilli, deseeded and chopped
425 ml/14 fl oz coconut milk
250 g/8 oz young leaf spinach
salt

1 Cook the sweet potato chunks in a saucepan of salted boiling water for 8–10 minutes or until tender. Drain and set aside.

2 Heat the oil in a saucepan, add the onion, garlic, shrimp paste and turmeric, and fry over a gentle heat for 3 minutes, stirring frequently. Stir in the chopped red chilli and fry for a further 2 minutes.

3 Add the coconut milk, stir to mix, and simmer for 3–4 minutes until the coconut milk has thickened slightly. Stir in the sweet potatoes, add salt to taste, and cook for 4 minutes.

4 Stir in the spinach, cover the pan and simmer gently for 2–3 minutes or until the spinach has wilted and the curry has heated through. Taste and adjust the seasoning if necessary and serve immediately.

Serves 4
Preparation time: about 10 minutes
Cooking time: about 25 minutes

balti courgettes

25 g/1 oz ghee or butter
1 small onion, chopped
pinch of asafoetida (optional)
2 small potatoes, quartered
375 g/12 oz courgettes, sliced
½ teaspoon chilli powder
½ teaspoon turmeric
1 teaspoon ground coriander

½ teaspoon salt
150 ml/¼ pint water
½ teaspoon garam masala
chopped coriander leaves, to garnish

1 Heat the ghee or butter in a Balti pan or heavy-based frying pan, add the onion, and fry for 5 minutes, stirring occasionally, until softened.

2 Add the asafoetida, if using, then add the potatoes and fry for about 2–3 minutes.

3 Stir in the courgettes, the chilli powder, turmeric, coriander and salt. Add the measured water, cover the pan and cook gently for 8–10 minutes, until the potatoes are tender. Sprinkle with the garam masala, garnish with chopped coriander and serve immediately.

Serves 4
Preparation time: 10 minutes
Cooking time: about 15 minutes

sri lankan vegetable curry

2 onions, thinly sliced
2 garlic cloves, finely chopped
1 tablespoon grated ginger
4 green chillies, 2 finely chopped and 2 slit
*1 teaspoon powdered lemon grass or finely grated
  lemon rind*
1 teaspoon turmeric
6 curry leaves
600 ml/1 pint thin coconut milk
*250 g/8 oz each courgettes, potatoes, peppers and
  carrots, sliced*
300 ml/½ pint thick coconut milk
salt

1 Put the onions, garlic, ginger, chopped chillies, lemon grass or lemon rind, turmeric, curry leaves, thin coconut milk and salt in a saucepan. Bring to simmering point and cook gently, uncovered, for 20 minutes.

2 Add the vegetables, slit chillies and thick coconut milk, and cook for a further 20 minutes or until the vegetables are tender. Transfer to a warmed serving dish and serve.

Serves 4–6
Preparation time: 15 minutes
Cooking time: 50 minutes

eggs in chilli sauce

½–1 teaspoon small dried red chillies
2 onions, chopped
4 garlic cloves
15 g/½ oz unsalted peanuts
1 teaspoon powdered lemon grass or grated lemon rind
1 teaspoon shrimp paste
1 teaspoon salt
1 teaspoon sugar
2 tablespoons oil
300 ml/½ pint thick coconut milk
6 curry leaves
6 hard-boiled eggs, peeled

1 Put the chillies, onions, garlic, peanuts, lemon grass or lemon rind, shrimp paste, salt and sugar in a food processor or blender, and process until smooth.

2 Heat the oil in a wok or frying pan, add the spice paste and fry for 3–4 minutes; stir well and add a little water if it gets too dry.

3 Stir in the coconut milk and curry leaves, and bring to the boil. Add the eggs and simmer for 15 minutes or until the sauce thickens. Transfer to a warmed serving dish and serve immediately.

Serves 4
Preparation time: 10 minutes
Cooking time: 25–35 minutes

egg and coconut curry

2–3 tablespoons oil
5 cm/2 inch cinnamon stick
6 cardamom pods
6 cloves
2 onions, finely chopped
2 garlic cloves, finely chopped
2.5 cm/1 inch piece of fresh root ginger, grated
4 green chillies, 2 finely chopped and 2 slit
450 ml/¾ pint thick coconut milk
¼ teaspoon freshly grated nutmeg
6 hard-boiled eggs, peeled and halved
salt

1 Heat the oil in a saucepan, add the cinnamon, cardamom pods and cloves, and fry for a few seconds. As the spices change colour, add the onions, garlic, ginger and chopped chillies, and fry gently, stirring, until soft and golden.

2 Pour in the coconut milk and bring to the boil. Add the nutmeg, the slit chillies and salt, and simmer for 10 minutes or until the sauce is thick.

3 Add the eggs and simmer for a further 5 minutes. Transfer to a warmed serving dish and serve.

Serves 4
Preparation time: 10 minutes
Cooking time: 20–25 minutes

huevos rancheros

2 tablespoons oil
2 onions, finely chopped
3 garlic cloves, crushed
2 red peppers, cored, deseeded and chopped
2 fresh red chillies, deseeded and chopped
1 teaspoon dried oregano
½ teaspoon ground cumin
4 large tomatoes, skinned and chopped
125 ml/4 fl oz tomato purée
125 ml/4 fl oz water or Vegetable Stock (see page 140)
4 eggs
salt and pepper

To garnish:
1 tablespoon chopped coriander sprigs
1 large avocado, peeled, stoned and sliced

1 Heat the oil in a deep frying pan, add the onions, garlic, peppers and chillies, and sauté until soft and golden. Stir in the oregano, cumin, and salt and pepper to taste, and cook for 2 minutes.

2 Add the chopped tomatoes, tomato purée and measured water or stock. Bring to the boil, then reduce the heat and simmer gently until the sauce reduces and thickens.

3 Pour the sauce into a large greased ovenproof dish and then make 4 wells, or indentations, in it with the back of a spoon. Carefully break an egg into each well. Bake in a preheated oven, 180°C (350°F), Gas Mark 4, for about 10–12 minutes, until the eggs are set and cooked. Sprinkle with chopped coriander, garnish with avocado slices and serve.

Serves 4
Preparation: 15 minutes
Cooking: 30 minutes
Oven temperature: 180°C (350°F), Gas Mark 4

rösti potatoes

1 kg/2 lb potatoes, halved, or quartered if large
1 large onion, grated
1 egg, beaten
50 g/2 oz butter
salt and pepper

1 Place the potatoes in a large saucepan of salted water, cover, bring to the boil and simmer for 5 minutes. Drain and leave to cool.

2 Grate the potatoes coarsely into a mixing bowl and add the grated onion. Stir in the beaten egg and season to taste with salt and pepper.

3 Heat the butter in a frying pan and add the potato mixture, spreading it over the pan. Cook over a moderate heat for about 15 minutes until lightly browned on both sides. There is no need to turn all the potato at once – just lift one section on to the spatula at a time and turn it over carefully.

4 Use the spatula to press the potato together to form a large pancake, then cook for 2–3 minutes until the underside is browned and crisp.

5 Invert the pancake on to a plate, slide it back into the pan and cook the other side. Cut into wedges and serve immediately.

Serves 4–6
Preparation time: 10 minutes
Cooking time: 30 minutes

roast potatoes with rosemary and garlic

4 tablespoons olive oil
2 tablespoons chopped rosemary
750 g/1½ lb medium potatoes, unpeeled and quartered lengthways
4 garlic cloves, peeled and sliced
salt and pepper

1 Put 2 tablespoons of the oil into a large roasting tin, and place in a preheated oven, 230°C (450°F), Gas Mark 8, to warm through.

2 Make sure the potatoes are dry. Mix together the remaining oil and the rosemary, and toss the potatoes to coat them completely.

3 Add the potatoes to the roasting tin in the oven, shake carefully to give an even layer, then place the tin at the top of the oven and roast for 20 minutes.

4 Remove the tin from the oven and move the potatoes around so that they cook evenly. Scatter the garlic amongst the potatoes, return the tin to the oven and cook for a further 5 minutes. Remove the potatoes from the oven, season to taste with salt and pepper, and serve immediately.

Serves 4
Preparation time: 5 minutes
Cooking time: 25 minutes
Oven temperature: 230°C (450°F), Gas Mark 8

scalloped potatoes with onions

1 kg/2 lb potatoes, thinly sliced
1 large onion, thinly sliced
150 ml/¼ pint Beef Stock (see page 141)
25 g/1 oz butter, melted
salt and pepper
1 tablespoon chopped parsley, to garnish

1 Make layers of the potatoes and onion in a well-buttered ovenproof dish, seasoning them generously with salt and pepper.

2 Bring the stock to the boil and pour over the potatoes, then brush liberally with the melted butter.

3 Cover with foil and cook in a preheated oven, 180°C (350°F), Gas Mark 4, for 1½ hours. Remove the foil and cook for a further 30 minutes or until the potatoes are cooked through and lightly browned.

4 Place under a moderate grill until the potatoes are brown and crispy on top. Serve hot, garnished with parsley.

Serves 4–6
Preparation time: 20 minutes
Cooking time: about 2 hours
Oven temperature: 180°C (350°F), Gas Mark 4

mashed potato with coriander root

Coriander roots can be found still attached to bunches of coriander in some supermarkets or greengrocers. Coriander stalks, chopped very finely, are a suitable alternative.

1 kg/2 lb floury potatoes
6 tablespoons olive oil
5 g/¼ oz coriander roots
2 tablespoons chopped coriander leaves
milk (optional)
salt and pepper

1 Cook the potatoes in a saucepan of salted boiling water for 15–20 minutes until tender. Drain well, then return to the pan and mash until smooth.

2 Meanwhile, heat the oil in a small pan, add the coriander roots, and fry very gently until tender. Remove from the heat and stir in the chopped coriander. Transfer to a liquidizer and process to form a smooth paste.

3 Add the coriander paste to the mashed potatoes with plenty of salt and pepper, and beat gently until evenly combined. Stir in a little milk to form a softer mixture, if liked, and serve at once.

Serves 4
Preparation time: 5 minutes
Cooking time: 15–20 minutes

warm new potato and pancetta salad

500 g/1 lb small new potatoes
2 red onions, cut into wedges with the root ends intact
4 rosemary sprigs
6 tablespoons olive oil
75 g/3 oz smoked pancetta, in thick slices, cut into strips
3 tablespoons red wine vinegar
sea salt and pepper

1 Add the potatoes to a pan of boiling water and parboil for 5 minutes. Drain thoroughly and transfer them to a roasting tin.

2 Add the red onions to the roasting tin with the rosemary. Drizzle over 4 tablespoons of the olive oil. Place the roasting tin in a preheated oven, 200°C (400°F), Gas Mark 6, and roast for 45–60 minutes, until the potatoes are tender and lightly patched with brown.

3 When the potatoes are done, heat the remaining oil in a frying pan. Add the pancetta and fry until crisp and lightly browned. Add the vinegar and bring to the boil, stirring, to deglaze the pan. Pour over the potatoes and toss to coat. Season to taste with sea salt and pepper. Discard the rosemary sprigs just before serving, and serve warm or cold.

Serves 4
Preparation time: 15 minutes
Cooking time: about 1 hour
Oven temperature: 200°C (400°F), Gas Mark 6

potato galette

250–300 g/8–10 oz potatoes
125 g/4 oz butter, melted
salt
parsley or coriander sprigs, to garnish

1 Slice the potatoes very thinly in a food processor or with a mandoline. Place in a bowl of cold water and rinse well. Drain well and dry on kitchen paper.

2 Pour half the butter into a flat-bottomed wok or frying pan. Arrange the potato slices in the pan, overlapping slightly like the scales of a fish. Spoon over some more butter. Continue layering the potato slices in the pan, finishing with butter.

3 Cook for about 2 minutes, shaking the pan with a circular movement to prevent the potatoes from sticking. Press down the galette with the back of a spoon and cook for 10 minutes. Turn over with a spatula and cook the other side for 10 minutes.

4 Drain off the butter, tilting the pan but keeping the galette in position. Slide onto a warmed serving plate, garnish with parsley or coriander, and serve immediately.

Serves 4
Preparation: 10 minutes
Cooking time: 25 minutes

griddled warm new potatoes with fresh mint dressing

750 g/1¾ lb small new potatoes, halved lengthways
finely grated rind and juice of 2 limes
8 tablespoons grapeseed oil
2 tablespoons chopped mint
sea salt and pepper
mint leaves, to garnish

1 Heat a griddle pan or nonstick frying pan. Place a layer of potato halves on the hot griddle and cook for 6 minutes on each side, reducing the heat as required. Remove and keep warm while cooking the remaining potatoes.

2 Combine the lime rind and juice and the oil, beating well with a whisk. Add the chopped mint, salt and pepper, and whisk until evenly combined. Alternatively, place all the ingredients in a screw-top jar and shake well to combine.

3 Toss the potatoes in the dressing, transfer to a warmed serving dish, garnish with mint leaves, and serve.

Serves 4
Preparation time: 10 minutes
Cooking time: about 30 minutes

gratin dauphinois

1 garlic clove, halved
75 g/3 oz butter, softened
1 kg/2 lb waxy potatoes, sliced into thick rounds
freshly grated nutmeg
350 ml/12 fl oz hot milk
250 ml/8 fl oz single cream
salt and pepper

1 Rub the cut garlic clove round the inside of a large earthenware baking dish. Brush the dish thickly with some of the softened butter.

2 Arrange a layer of potatoes in the bottom of the dish and sprinkle with salt, pepper and grated nutmeg. Continue making layers of potatoes, seasoning each layer, until they are all used.

3 Mix together the hot milk and cream, and then pour the mixture over the layered potatoes, making sure that the potatoes are almost totally covered by the liquid. Dot the top with the remaining butter and bake in a preheated oven, 180°C (350°F), Gas Mark 4, for 1–1¼ hours, or until the potatoes are tender when pierced with a skewer. Increase the oven temperature to 200°C (400°F), Gas Mark 6 for the last 10 minutes of cooking time to brown the top layer of potatoes. Serve hot, straight from the baking dish.

Serves 4–6
Preparation time: 15–20 minutes
Cooking time: 1–1¼ hours
Oven temperature: 180°C (350°F) Gas Mark 4

candied sweet potatoes

500 g/1 lb sweet potatoes
250 g/8 oz cooking apples, peeled, cored and thickly sliced
125 g/4 oz soft light brown sugar
4 teaspoons grated orange rind
3 tablespoons fresh orange juice
1 teaspoon ground mixed spice
25 g/1 oz butter
2 tablespoons medium sherry
salt

1 Cook the potatoes in a pan of salted boiling water for 30 minutes. Drain.

2 As soon as the potatoes can be handled, peel off the skins and cut the flesh into 2.5 cm/1 inch cubes. Mix with the apple slices in a 1 litre/1¾ pint ovenproof dish.

3 Put the sugar, orange rind, orange juice, mixed spice, butter, sherry, and salt to taste, in a saucepan, and stir over a low heat until the sugar has dissolved. Pour over the potatoes and apples.

4 Cook, uncovered, in a preheated oven, 180°C (350°F), Gas Mark 4, for 1 hour, stirring occasionally, until the potatoes are tender and lightly browned, and the liquid has been absorbed. Serve immediately.

Serves 4
Preparation time: 15 minutes
Cooking time: 1½ hours
Oven temperature: 180°C (350°F), Gas Mark 4

honey-glazed turnips

750 g/1½ lb baby turnips
50 g/2 oz butter
2 heaped tablespoons clear honey
2 tablespoons flaked almonds
salt and pepper
1½ tablespoons chopped coriander sprigs, to garnish

1 Cook the turnips in salted boiling water for about 10 minutes until tender but still firm to the bite. Drain.

2 Melt the butter with the honey in a frying pan. Add the turnips and cook for 3–5 minutes, stirring, until glossy.

3 Toast the almond flakes in a dry frying pan over moderate heat until golden, then stir into the turnips. Transfer to a warmed serving dish. Season with salt and pepper, pour over the pan juices, sprinkle with the coriander and serve.

Serves 4–6
Preparation time: 5 minutes
Cooking time: 15 minutes

baby glazed carrots

25 g/1 oz butter
500 g/1 lb young carrots, quartered lengthways
pinch of sugar
2 tablespoons orange juice
salt and pepper
chopped parsley, to garnish

1 Melt the butter in a saucepan, add the carrots, sugar, salt and pepper. Pour in just enough water to cover and cook gently, uncovered, for 15–20 minutes until the carrots are tender and the liquid has evaporated. Add the orange juice towards the end of cooking time.

2 Sprinkle with the parsley and serve.

Serves 4
Preparation time: 5 minutes
Cooking time: 15–20 minutes

roasted parsnips dressed with lemon and garlic

750 g/1½ lb parsnips, cut into sticks
6 tablespoons olive oil
1 tablespoon roughly chopped thyme
1 teaspoon finely grated lemon rind
2 tablespoons lemon juice
1 garlic clove, crushed
sea salt and pepper

To serve:
rocket or other salad leaves (optional)
50 g/2 oz Parmesan cheese

1 Add the parsnips to a pan of boiling water and parboil for 4 minutes. Drain well and leave to dry.

2 Transfer the parsnips to a roasting tin large enough to hold them in a single layer. Spoon the olive oil over them and then sprinkle with the thyme. Toss to coat. Place in a preheated oven, 200°C (400°F), Gas Mark 6, and roast for 45–60 minutes, stirring occasionally, until the parsnips are tender and lightly patched with brown. Transfer to a bowl and leave to cool slightly.

3 Add the lemon rind and juice and the garlic to the parsnips and season with sea salt and pepper. Toss well and leave to cool completely.

4 Serve the dressed parsnips as they are, or on a bed of rocket or other salad leaves, and use a mandoline or vegetable peeler to shave Parmesan on top.

Serves 4–6
Preparation time: 15 minutes, plus cooling
Cooking time: 1 hour
Oven temperature: 200°C (400°F), Gas Mark 6

piedmont peppers

4 red peppers
4 tomatoes, skinned and quartered
4–8 anchovy fillets, halved or quartered lengthways
4 tablespoons olive oil
salt and pepper

To garnish:
handful of green or red basil, roughly torn
125 g/4 oz Parmesan cheese

1 Halve the peppers lengthways, leaving the stalks intact, and remove the cores and seeds. Lightly oil a baking sheet and arrange the peppers on it, skin side down.

2 Put 2 tomato quarters into each pepper, make an anchovy cross on top, drizzle with olive oil and sprinkle with salt and pepper. Place in a preheated oven, 200°C (400°F), Gas Mark 6, and cook for 25 minutes.

3 Allow the peppers to cool, then garnish with torn basil leaves. Using a mandoline or vegetable peeler, shave the Parmesan on top.

Serves 4
Preparation time: 5 minutes, plus cooling
Cooking time: 25 minutes
Oven temperature: 200°C (400°F), Gas Mark 6

roast peppers in olive oil

4 red, green and yellow peppers
4 tablespoons olive oil
1 tablespoon chopped parsley
2 garlic cloves, crushed or chopped
sea salt

1 Place the peppers under a hot grill and cook them until they are blackened and blistered on all sides. Place them in a polythene bag until they are cool, and then peel away the skins. Core and deseed, and cut the flesh into thin strips.

2 Arrange the peppers in a serving dish, sprinkle with olive oil and scatter with parsley and garlic. Sprinkle a little sea salt on top and serve.

Serves 4–6
Preparation time: 10 minutes
Cooking time: 15 minutes

leeks à la grecque

150 ml/¼ pint dry white wine
150 ml/¼ pint water
2 tablespoons olive oil
grated rind of 1 lemon
2 tablespoons lemon juice
1 shallot or small onion, thinly sliced
1 small celery stick with leaves
1 parsley sprig
1 thyme sprig or ¼ teaspoon dried thyme
1 bay leaf
¼ teaspoon salt
6 peppercorns
6 coriander seeds or ¼ teaspoon ground coriander
500 g/1 lb leeks

1 Combine the wine and measured water in a large saucepan. Add all the other ingredients except the leeks. Cover the pan, bring to the boil, then lower the heat and simmer for 10 minutes.

2 Meanwhile, trim the leeks so that each measures about 18 cm/7 inches long. Slit each leek along its length, open it out and flush out any grit under cold running water. Place the leeks in the simmering liquid, cover and simmer for 10–15 minutes until tender.

3 Remove the leeks from the pan with a slotted spoon and place on a serving dish. Boil the remaining liquid to reduce to about 150 ml/¼ pint. Pour the liquid over the leeks, removing the herbs and spices if preferred, and leave to cool. Serve at room temperature.

Serves 4
Preparation time: 5 minutes, plus cooling
Cooking time: 25–35 minutes

griddled leeks, asparagus and peppers with balsamic vinegar

2 red peppers, cored, deseeded and quartered
250 g/8 oz baby leeks
250 g/8 oz asparagus
3 tablespoons olive oil
2 tablespoons balsamic vinegar
1 bunch of flat leaf parsley, chopped
sea salt and pepper

1 Heat a griddle pan or nonstick frying pan. Add the red peppers, baby leeks and asparagus and cook for 5 minutes, turning them occasionally.

2 Mix all the vegetables with the olive oil, balsamic vinegar, chopped parsley, salt and pepper. Serve at room temperature.

Serves 4
Preparation time: 10 minutes, plus cooling
Cooking time: 5 minutes

quick italian spinach

The spinach must be dry before you start to cook. Dry it in a salad spinner or press it in a tea towel.

1 tablespoon olive oil
1 red onion, sliced
1 garlic clove, chopped
75 g/3 oz pine nuts
4 tomatoes, skinned, cored and roughly chopped

1 kg/2 lb spinach
50 g/2 oz butter
pinch of nutmeg
salt and pepper

1 Heat the oil in a large saucepan, add the onion and garlic and sauté for 5 minutes.

2 Put the pine nuts into a heavy-based frying pan and dry-fry over moderate heat until browned, stirring constantly. Set aside.

3 Add the tomatoes, spinach, butter and nutmeg to the onions and garlic, and season with salt and pepper. Turn up the heat to high and mix well. Cook for 3 minutes until the spinach has just started to wilt. Remove the pan from the heat, stir in the pine nuts and serve immediately.

Serves 4–6
Preparation time: 10 minutes
Cooking time: 10 minutes

spinach with olive oil and lemon dressing

For this recipe, fresh spinach can be cooked and drained several hours in advance, then tossed with the butter and garlic just before serving. You can also use frozen leaf spinach. Defrost it first and drain it thoroughly, toss with the butter and garlic and continue as for fresh spinach.

625 g/1¼ lb spinach
2 tablespoons butter
2 garlic cloves, finely chopped
4 tablespoons olive oil
2 tablespoons lemon juice
salt and pepper

1 Put the spinach in a large saucepan with just the water left on the leaves, sprinkling the layers with salt to taste. Cover the pan and cook over a medium heat for 5–7 minutes until the spinach has wilted and is tender, shaking the pan vigorously from time to time.

2 Drain the spinach thoroughly in the colander, then return it to the rinsed-out pan and toss over a high heat until any remaining water is driven off. Add the butter and garlic, and continue tossing until combined with the spinach.

3 Transfer to a warmed serving dish. Drizzle over the oil and lemon juice, sprinkle with salt and pepper to taste, and serve.

Serves 4
Preparation time: 5 minutes
Cooking time: about 10 minutes

beetroot with parmesan

4 tablespoons olive oil
2 tablespoons butter
500 g/1 lb cooked beetroot, sliced into rings
75 g/3 oz Parmesan cheese, grated
pepper

1 Heat the oil and butter in a small pan until foaming. Put about one-third of the beetroot in an ovenproof dish and drizzle with some of the oil and butter. Cover with about one-third of the Parmesan and season to taste with salt and pepper.

2 Repeat these layers until all the ingredients are used, then bake in a preheated oven, 200°C (400°F), Gas Mark 6, for 15 minutes. Serve hot, straight from the dish.

Serves 6
Preparation time: 10 minutes
Cooking time: 15 minutes
Oven temperature: 200°C (400°F), Gas Mark 6

baked beetroot with soured cream and onion rings

4 raw beetroot, unpeeled
3 tablespoons light olive oil
1 large onion, sliced
about 50 g/2 oz rocket
few dill sprigs
1 dessert apple
2 teaspoons lemon juice
salt and pepper
150 ml/¼ pint soured cream, to serve

1 Wrap each beetroot in foil and place on a baking sheet. Bake in a preheated oven, 200°C (400°F), Gas Mark 6, for 40–50 minutes, or until tender.

2 Meanwhile, heat the oil in a frying pan. Add the onion slices and cook over a fairly high heat for about 5 minutes, stirring frequently, until browned and beginning to crisp. Transfer to kitchen paper to drain.

3 Just before serving, arrange the rocket and dill on 4 serving plates. Peel and core the apple and finely dice the flesh. Place in a bowl with the lemon juice and toss well to prevent discolouration. Divide the diced apple between the plates.

4 To serve, remove the cooked beetroot from their foil wrappings. Put one on each plate and cut in half or quarters. Scatter the fried onion around the beetroot. Season to taste with salt and pepper and serve with soured cream.

Serves 4
Preparation time: 15 minutes
Cooking time: 40–50 minutes
Oven temperature: 200°C (400°F), Gas Mark 6

fried courgettes with chillies

750 g/1½ lb courgettes, thickly sliced
75 g/3 oz plain flour
oil, for frying
50 g/2 oz butter
½ teaspoon crushed dried chillies
2 garlic cloves, chopped
grated rind and juice of 1 lemon
1 tablespoon green olives, pitted and chopped
salt and pepper

1 Dust the courgette slices with flour.

2 Heat the oil in a frying pan, add the courgettes in batches and fry for 2 minutes on each side, until golden. Remove from the pan and keep warm.

3 When all the courgettes are cooked, pour off the oil from the pan. Add the butter, chillies, garlic, lemon juice and rind and the green olives, and heat until the butter is foaming. Pour over the courgettes, season with salt and pepper, and toss. Serve immediately.

Serves 4
Preparation time: 5 minutes
Cooking time: 10 minutes

braised courgettes

2 tablespoons olive oil
25 g/1 oz butter
1 shallot, finely chopped
6 yellow or green courgettes or a mixture of both, cut into
    5 cm/2 inch sticks
375 g/12 oz tomatoes
2 tablespoons stock
20 black olives, pitted and halved
¼ teaspoon chopped oregano
1 tablespoon chopped parsley
1 mozzarella cheese, cubed
salt and pepper

1 Heat the oil and butter in a large shallow pan, add the shallot and cook over a low heat until softened. Add the courgettes and cook for a few minutes over a high heat, then reduce it to moderate. Add the tomatoes and mash with a fork. Season to taste with salt and pepper and leave to cook until the courgettes are tender, adding a little stock if necessary.

2 Add the olives, oregano and parsley, and scatter the mozzarella cheese over the top. Cover the pan, turn off the heat and leave to rest for a few minutes, then serve.

Serves 4
Preparation time: 10 minutes
Cooking time: 25–30 minutes

crispy courgettes

350 g/12 oz courgettes, halved lengthways and cut
    into 5 cm/2 inch lengths
125 g/4 oz onions, sliced
about 150 ml/¼ pint milk
about 75 g/3 oz plain flour
salt and pepper
oil, for deep-frying

1 Place the courgettes and onions in a large bowl, pour over the milk and toss well, so that the vegetables are coated in the milk.

2 Season the flour with salt and pepper and place in a large plastic bag. Add about a quarter of the vegetables, toss well to coat, then shake off the excess flour.

3 Heat the oil in a large wok – it should come to just over a quarter way up the sides. Drop in the vegetables and fry for about 4–5 minutes, until golden. Remove with a slotted spoon, drain on kitchen paper and keep warm. Repeat with the remaining vegetables.

4 Transfer to a warmed serving dish and serve immediately.

Serves 4–6
Preparation time: 10 minutes
Cooking time: 15–20 minutes

courgettes with orange

750 g/1½ lb courgettes, sliced
grated rind and juice of 2 oranges
25 g/1 oz butter
pepper

1 Place the courgettes and orange rind and juice in a saucepan, cover tightly and simmer for about 6 minutes or until the courgettes are tender.

2 Add the butter and season with pepper. Allow the butter to melt slightly, then toss until the courgettes are well coated. Serve immediately.

Serves 6
Preparation time: 10 minutes
Cooking time: about 6 minutes

courgettes with oregano

4 tablespoons olive oil
50 g/2 oz butter
3 garlic cloves, roughly chopped
750 g/1½ lb green and yellow courgettes, thinly sliced
    diagonally
1 tablespoon chopped oregano, plus extra to garnish
salt and pepper

1 Heat the oil and butter in a large wok or frying pan, add the garlic and cook gently for 1 minute, without browning.

2 Add the courgettes and stir well to coat in the butter and oil. Sauté for 2 minutes, stirring. Season with salt and pepper and stir in the oregano. Cook for 5–6 minutes, stirring constantly, until the courgettes are just tender.

3 Transfer to a warmed serving dish, garnish with sprigs of oregano, if using, and serve immediately.

Serves 4
Preparation time: 5 minutes
Cooking time: 10 minutes

balsamic braised leeks and peppers

2 tablespoons olive oil
2 leeks, cut into 1 cm/½ inch pieces
1 orange pepper, cored, deseeded and cut
  into 1 cm/½ inch chunks
1 red pepper, cored, deseeded and cut
  into 1 cm/½ inch chunks
3 tablespoons balsamic vinegar
handful of flat leaf parsley, chopped
salt and pepper

1 Heat the olive oil in a saucepan, add the leeks and orange and red peppers, stir well, cover the pan and cook very gently for 10 minutes.

2 Add the balsamic vinegar and cook for a further 10 minutes, uncovered. The vegetables should be brown from the vinegar and all the liquid should have evaporated.

3 Season to taste with salt and pepper, and stir in the parsley just before serving.

Serves 4
Preparation time: 5 minutes
Cooking time: 20 minutes

fennel baked with cream and parmesan

750 g/1½ lb fennel heads
small knob of butter
250 ml/8 fl oz double cream
75 g/3 oz Parmesan cheese, freshly grated
salt and pepper

1 Trim the outside leaves from the fennel, remove the hard central core and slice the fennel lengthways. Immerse the leaves in a pan of boiling water and cook for 5 minutes. Drain well.

2 Butter a shallow ovenproof dish, add the fennel and sprinkle with salt and pepper. Pour over the cream and sprinkle with the Parmesan.

3 Place the dish at the top of a preheated oven, 200°C (400°F), Gas Mark 6, and cook for 20 minutes. Allow the top of the fennel to go a deep golden brown. Serve hot.

Serves 4
Preparation time: 5 minutes
Cooking time: 25 minutes
Oven temperature: 200°C (400°F), Gas Mark 6

broccoli with anchovies

75 g/3 oz pine nuts
1 kg/2 lb broccoli, divided into florets
50 g/2 oz butter
4 tablespoons lemon juice
4 anchovy fillets, finely chopped
75 g/3 oz Parmesan cheese, freshly grated
salt and pepper

1 Place the pine nuts in a heavy-based frying pan and dry-fry over a moderate heat, stirring constantly, until golden all over. Set aside.

2 Steam the broccoli or plunge it into boiling water for 2 minutes, then drain well and transfer to a bowl.

3 Melt the butter in a small saucepan, add the lemon juice and anchovies, and heat until the butter foams. Pour the melted butter over the broccoli, sprinkle with salt and pepper and toss. Sprinkle the broccoli with the Parmesan and pine nuts, and serve.

Serves 4
Preparation time: 10 minutes
Cooking time: 10 minutes

stir-fried ginger broccoli

500 g/1 lb broccoli, divided into small florets
2 tablespoons oil
1 garlic clove, thinly sliced (optional)
2.5 cm/1 inch piece fresh root ginger, finely shredded
½–1 teaspoon sesame oil
salt

1 Peel and diagonally slice the broccoli stems. Blanch the florets and stems in salted boiling water for 30 seconds. Drain well, refresh under cold running water, and drain thoroughly.

2 Heat the oil in a large wok or frying pan, add the garlic, if using, and ginger, and stir-fry for 2–3 seconds. Add the blanched broccoli and cook for 2 minutes. Sprinkle over the sesame oil and stir-fry for a further 30 seconds.

3 Spoon into a warmed serving dish and serve immediately.

Serves 4
Preparation time: 3–4 minutes
Cooking time: about 3 minutes

broad beans with bacon

Broad beans have a very short season in early summer, and freshly picked, young broad beans are delicious cooked in this way. For this recipe you will need about 500 g/1 lb broad beans in their shells, and they will need to be boiled for 15–20 minutes. Mature broad beans become woolly and tasteless, and develop a tough skin, so don't bother with them.

250 g/8 oz frozen broad beans
2 tablespoons olive oil
125 g/4 oz pancetta, finely diced
1 onion, finely chopped
1 garlic clove, crushed
400 g/13 oz can chopped tomatoes
1 sage sprig
1 teaspoon sugar
salt and pepper

1 Cook the beans in salted boiling water for 5–6 minutes, or according to the packet instructions.

2 Meanwhile, put the oil and pancetta in a saucepan and heat gently until the fat runs from the pancetta. Add the onion and garlic and cook gently for about 5 minutes until softened but not coloured. Add the tomatoes and their juice, the sage, sugar, and salt and pepper to taste. Bring to the boil, stirring.

3 Drain the beans and add to the tomato sauce, then simmer, uncovered; for 10 minutes, shaking the pan constantly. Taste and adjust the seasoning, if necessary, before serving.

Serves 4–6
Preparation time: 10 minutes
Cooking time: 20 minutes

roast vegetables with olive oil and chillies

4 tablespoons olive oil
250 g/8 oz parsnips, cut into equal-size chunks
250 g/8 oz leeks, cut into 1 cm/½ inch slices
250 g/8 oz red peppers, cored, deseeded and cut into
* squares*
250 g/8 oz aubergines, cut into chunks
½ teaspoon crushed dried chillies
handful of marjoram, chopped
salt and pepper

1 Place the olive oil in a large roasting tin and put it into a preheated oven, 220°C (425°F), Gas Mark 7, for a few minutes to warm.

2 Add the parsnips to the tin, toss well in the oil, then return the tin to the top of the oven and cook the parsnips for 10 minutes.

3 Remove the tin from the oven and add the leeks, red peppers, aubergines and crushed chillies. Toss to coat in the olive oil then return the tin to the oven to cook for a further 15 minutes.

4 Remove the tin from the oven, add the chopped marjoram, salt and pepper, and mix well. Transfer to a warmed serving bowl and serve immediately.

Serves 4
Preparation time: 5 minutes
Cooking time: 25 minutes
Oven temperature: 220°C (425°F), Gas Mark 7

cauliflower with breadcrumbs and hazelnuts

25 g/1 oz butter
50 g/2 oz fresh white breadcrumbs
25 g/1 oz hazelnuts, finely chopped
375 g/12 oz dried fusilli
8 tablespoons hazelnut oil
1 cauliflower, divided into tiny florets
2 garlic cloves, sliced
1 dried red chilli, deseeded and chopped
2 tablespoons chopped parsley
salt and pepper

1 Melt the butter in a frying pan, add the breadcrumbs and hazelnuts and stir-fry over a medium heat for about 3 minutes, until crisp and golden. Drain on kitchen paper and set aside.

2 Cook the pasta until al dente (see page 137).

3 Meanwhile, heat half the oil in a deep frying pan, add the cauliflower, garlic and chilli, and fry for 8–10 minutes until the cauliflower is golden and tender. Add the parsley.

4 Drain the pasta, toss with the remaining oil and pepper and stir into the cauliflower mixture. Serve immediately, topped with the crispy breadcrumb mixture.

Serves 4
Preparation time: 15 minutes
Cooking time: 15–18 minutes

cabbage, beetroot and apple sauté

Buy the vacuum-sealed packets of beetroot cooked without the addition of vinegar for this recipe.

40 g/1½ oz butter
½ red cabbage, thinly shredded
1 tablespoon chopped thyme
2 teaspoons caraway seeds
1 teaspoon ground mixed spice
1 tablespoon sugar
150 ml/¼ pint red wine
2 tablespoons port
2 tablespoons red wine vinegar
2 dessert apples
250 g/8 oz cooked beetroot, cubed
50 g/2 oz pecan nuts, toasted
salt and pepper

1 Melt 25 g/1 oz of the butter in a large frying pan, add the cabbage, thyme, caraway seeds, spice and sugar, and fry for 10 minutes. Add the wine, port and vinegar, and bring to the boil. Cover the pan and cook over a low heat for 20 minutes.

2 Meanwhile, quarter, core and thickly slice the apples. Melt the remaining butter in a clean frying pan and fry the apples for 4–5 minutes until lightly golden. Add to the cabbage with the pan juices and the beetroot. Cover and cook for a further 15–20 minutes until the cabbage is tender.

3 Toast the pecan nuts in a dry frying pan over moderate heat. When the cabbage is cooked, season to taste with salt and pepper, stir in the nuts and serve immediately.

Serves 4
Preparation time: 20 minutes
Cooking time: 55 minutes

cabbage au gratin

750 g/1½ lb white winter cabbage, shredded
25 g/1 oz butter
25 g/1 oz plain flour
1 teaspoon mustard powder
300 ml/½ pint milk
4 tablespoons double cream
50 g/2 oz Cheddar cheese, grated
25 g/1 oz fresh breadcrumbs
salt and pepper

1 Cook the cabbage in a saucepan of salted boiling water for 5 minutes. Drain well and set aside.

2 Melt the butter in a saucepan, stir in the flour and mustard, and cook for 2–3 minutes. Gradually add the milk, stirring constantly until the sauce boils and thickens. Stir in the cabbage and cream, and add salt and pepper to taste.

3 Transfer the mixture to a baking dish. Mix the cheese and breadcrumbs together and sprinkle the mixture over the cabbage cream. Bake in a preheated oven, 180°C (350°F), Gas Mark 4, for 30 minutes. Serve immediately.

Serves 4–6
Preparation time: 10 minutes
Cooking time: 40 minutes
Oven temperature: 180°C (350°F), Gas Mark 4

austrian red cabbage

50 g/2 oz butter
1 large onion, sliced
1 garlic clove, crushed
1 kg/2 lb red cabbage, shredded
2 large cooking apples, peeled, cored and sliced
1 teaspoon caraway seeds
4 tablespoons red wine vinegar
4 tablespoons water
1 tablespoons soft light brown sugar
6 juniper berries, crushed (optional)
salt and pepper

1 Melt the butter in a large saucepan, add the onion and garlic and fry gently for 5 minutes.

2 Stir in the cabbage and apples and simmer for 10 minutes, stirring occasionally.

3 Add the caraway seeds, vinegar, measured water, sugar and juniper berries, if using, and season to taste with salt and pepper. Bring to the boil, lower the heat and simmer for 30–45 minutes, until the cabbage is tender and most of the liquid has been absorbed. Serve immediately.

Serves 6–8
Preparation time: 10 minutes
Cooking time: 45 minutes–1 hour

roasted onions with balsamic vinegar

6 large red onions
3 tablespoons olive oil
1 tablespoon chopped thyme
1 tablespoon chopped rosemary
2 garlic cloves, crushed
1 teaspoon coriander seeds, crushed
4 tablespoons balsamic vinegar
4 tablespoons red wine
1 tablespoon clear honey
salt and pepper

1 Cut the onions into eighths from the stalk to the root without cutting all the way through and press open. Place in a roasting pan.

2 Combine the oil, herbs, garlic, coriander seeds and seasoning. Drizzle over the onions and place in a preheated oven, 220°C (425°F), Gas Mark 7, for 30 minutes.

3 Mix the vinegar, wine and honey together, pour a little over each onion and bake for a further 25–30 minutes until the onions are tender. Serve with the glazed juices.

Serves 6
Preparation time: 10 minutes
Cooking time: 1 hour
Oven temperature: 220°C (425°F), Gas Mark 7

linguine with vegetables

1 red pepper, cored, deseeded and cut into large squares
1 courgette, sliced
1 red onion, sliced
1 small aubergine, sliced into thin rounds
8 asparagus spears, trimmed
5 tablespoons olive oil
300 g/10 oz linguine
3 tablespoons frozen petits pois
125 g/4 oz Parmesan cheese, freshly grated
handful of basil leaves, roughly torn
salt and pepper

1 The vegetables can be either cooked on a griddle or grilled. To griddle, heat a griddle pan, place the pepper squares on it, skin side down, until the skin blisters and blackens, then transfer the peppers to a polythene bag. Griddle the courgette, onion and aubergine slices and the asparagus for 2 minutes on each side. Alternatively, cook all these vegetables under a preheated hot grill.

2 When the pepper is cool, peel off the skin and slice the flesh into ribbons. Place in a dish with the courgettes, onion, aubergine and asparagus, drizzle with olive oil and put into a warm oven to keep warm.

3 Cook the pasta until al dente (see page 137). Add the petits pois for the last minute of the cooking time.

4 Drain the pasta and petits pois in a colander, then return to the saucepan. Add the warm vegetables, season with salt and pepper and add the Parmesan. Toss well, using two spoons, adding a little more olive oil if necessary. Finally, add the torn basil leaves and toss again, then serve immediately.

Serves 4
Preparation time: 10 minutes
Cooking time: 25 minutes

pasta primavera

This recipe uses small, young broad beans. If only the large, mature broad beans are available, shell, skin and cook them first.

2 tablespoons olive oil
1 garlic clove, chopped
2 shallots, chopped
125 g/4 oz shelled peas
125 g/4 oz young broad beans, shelled and skinned
125 g/4 oz asparagus, trimmed and cut into
   5 cm/2 inch lengths
125 g/4 oz spinach, washed and chopped
300 g/10 oz tagliatelle
150 ml/¼ pint whipping cream
75 g/3 oz Parmesan cheese, freshly grated
handful of mint leaves, chopped
salt and pepper

1 Heat the oil in a saucepan then sauté the garlic and shallots for 3 minutes. Add the peas, broad beans, asparagus and spinach to the shallot mixture. Stir well and cook for 2 minutes.

2 Cook the pasta until al dente (see page 137).

3 Stir the cream into the vegetables, mix well and simmer for 3 minutes.

4 Drain the tagliatelle thoroughly, then add the pasta to the vegetable sauce and season to taste with salt and pepper. Add the Parmesan and mint, toss well, and serve immediately.

Serves 4
Preparation time: 15 minutes
Cooking time: 20 minutes

penne with tomato and chilli

3 tablespoons olive oil
1 onion, chopped
2 garlic cloves, chopped
2 pinches of crushed dried chillies, or to taste
300 g/10 oz penne
10 plum tomatoes, skinned, deseeded and cut into strips
1 teaspoon sugar
1 teaspoon vinegar
handful of flat leaf parsley, chopped
salt and pepper
75 g/3 oz Parmesan cheese, freshly grated, to serve

1 Heat the oil in a saucepan, add the onion and garlic, and sauté until soft but not browned. Add the chillies.

2 Cook the pasta until al dente (see page 137).

3 Add the tomatoes to the onion mixture. Over a low heat, add the sugar, vinegar and salt and pepper. Mix gently and simmer slowly until the pasta is cooked.

4 Drain the pasta well. Stir the parsley into the tomato sauce. Add the sauce to the pasta, mix well, adding a dash of olive oil, if liked. Serve with a bowl of grated Parmesan.

Serves 4
Preparation time: 10 minutes
Cooking time: 20 minutes

penne with broad beans, asparagus and mint

500 g/1 lb asparagus, trimmed and cut into 5 cm/2 inch
   lengths
4 tablespoons olive oil
250 g/8 oz broad beans or peas
300 g/10 oz penne
75 ml/3 fl oz double cream
75 g/3 oz Parmesan cheese, freshly grated
4 tablespoons chopped mint
salt and pepper

1 Place the asparagus on a baking sheet, brush generously with olive oil and season with salt and pepper. Place under a preheated grill and cook for 8 minutes, turning as they brown.

2 Meanwhile, cook the broad beans or peas in lightly salted boiling water for 2 minutes.

3 Cook the pasta until al dente (see page 137).

4 Pour the cream into the empty pasta pan over the heat, add the broad beans or peas, asparagus and Parmesan, and season with salt and pepper. Return the pasta to the pan, add the mint, toss well, and serve immediately.

Serves 4
Preparation time: 10 minutes
Cooking time: 18 minutes

spaghetti with rocket and ricotta

You can substitute spinach for the rocket, but be generous with the pepper.

300 g/10 oz spaghetti
1 tablespoon olive oil
25 g/1 oz butter
1 small onion, finely chopped
bunch of rocket, leaves finely chopped
1 garlic clove, finely chopped
125 g/4 oz ricotta cheese
125 ml/4 fl oz dry white wine
salt and pepper
freshly grated Parmesan cheese, to serve

1 Cook the pasta until al dente (see page 137).

2 Meanwhile, heat the oil and butter in a saucepan until foaming. Add the onion and cook gently, stirring for 5 minutes until softened.

3 Add the rocket, garlic, and salt and pepper to taste, and stir for 2–3 minutes until wilted. Add the ricotta and wine, and stir until the ricotta has melted and mixed evenly with the rocket.

4 Drain the spaghetti, return to the pan and add the rocket mixture. Toss well and serve sprinkled with Parmesan.

Serves 4
Preparation time: 10 minutes
Cooking time: 12 minutes

tagliatelle with borlotti beans and sage

3 tablespoons olive oil
75 g/3 oz smoked bacon, rinded and cubed
1 onion, finely chopped
5 sage leaves, plus extra to garnish
250 g/8 oz can borlotti beans
2 tablespoons Chicken Stock (see page 141) or water
¼ teaspoon flour
1 tablespoon tomato purée
2 tablespoons red wine
425 g/14 oz tagliatelle
2 tablespoons freshly grated Parmesan cheese
1 tablespoon grated pecorino cheese

1 Heat the oil in a large, heavy-based saucepan, add the bacon, onion and whole sage leaves, and cook over a moderate heat until golden.

2 Drain the beans, rinse and drain again, then add them to the pan.

3 Heat the stock. Mix the flour and tomato purée in a small bowl; stir in the hot stock and the wine. Pour into the bean mixture, stir with a wooden spoon and simmer over a low heat until the sauce thickens.

4 Cook the pasta until al dente (see page 137).

5 Remove the sage leaves from the sauce, taste and adjust the seasoning. Drain the pasta, mix with the sauce and put in a large heated serving dish. Add the Parmesan and pecorino, and serve hot, garnished with a few sage leaves.

Serves 4
Preparation time: 10 minutes
Cooking time: 20 minutes

spaghetti in pepper and aubergine sauce

4 tablespoons olive oil
1 onion, finely chopped
400 g/13 oz can chopped tomatoes
2 tablespoons tomato purée
150 ml/¼ pint red wine
1 large aubergine, chopped
1 large red pepper, cored, deseeded and finely diced
1 large green pepper, cored, deseeded and finely diced
8 anchovy fillets, drained and chopped
1 garlic clove, crushed
500 g/1 lb spaghetti or linguine
75 g/3 oz black olives, pitted
salt and pepper

1 Heat the oil in a large, heavy-based saucepan, add the onion and fry gently for 3 minutes.

2 Add the tomatoes, tomato purée, red wine, aubergine, red and green peppers, anchovy fillets and garlic. Simmer gently for 20 minutes.

3 Cook the pasta until al dente (see page 137).

4 Drain and toss with the sauce, adding the olives, and salt and pepper to taste. Serve immediately.

Serves 4–6
Preparation time: 10 minutes
Cooking time: about 25 minutes

spaghetti with roasted peppers and coriander and chilli pesto

3 mixed red and yellow peppers
500 g/1 lb spaghetti or fettuccine
50 g/2 oz butter, diced

Coriander and chilli pesto:
50 g/2 oz coriander leaves, roughly chopped
1 chilli, deseeded and roughly chopped
2 garlic cloves, crushed
2 tablespoons pine nuts

finely grated rind of 1 lime
1 teaspoon salt
8 tablespoons olive oil
50 g/2 oz Parmesan cheese, freshly grated

1 Roast the peppers in a preheated oven, 220°C (425°F), Gas Mark 7, until the skins blister and blacken on all sides. Put them in a polythene bag until they are cool, then remove the skins, core and seeds, and chop the flesh into 1 cm/½ inch dice.

2 To make the pesto, put the coriander and chilli in a blender or food processor with the garlic, pine nuts, lime rind and salt. Purée until smooth, gradually adding the olive oil. Transfer to a bowl and mix with the Parmesan.

3 Cook the pasta until al dente (see page 137). Drain and toss with the peppers, sauce and butter. Serve immediately.

Serves 6
Preparation time: 20 minutes
Cooking time: 20–30 minutes
Oven temperature: 220°C (425°F), Gas Mark 7

fettuccine with chanterelles

300 g/10 oz chanterelles, morels or other wild mushrooms
500 ml/17 fl oz Chicken Stock (see page 141)
15 g/½ oz butter
1 tablespoon olive oil
1 bunch of spring onions, finely chopped
4 tablespoons dry white wine
300 g/10 oz fettuccine verde
2 tablespoons pine nuts
350 ml/12 fl oz whipping cream or crème fraîche
salt and pepper

1 Thinly slice the chanterelles, reserving any discarded pieces of stem or peel.

2 Pour the stock into a saucepan and bring to the boil. Add the mushroom trimmings and cook over a medium-high heat until reduced to 125 ml/4 fl oz. Strain through a sieve and discard the mushroom trimmings.

3 Melt the butter with the oil in a large saucepan or deep frying pan, add the mushrooms and spring onions, and cook, stirring, until the mushrooms begin to render liquid. Add the wine and cook over high heat until the liquid has nearly evaporated.

4 Cook the pasta until al dente (see page 137). Set aside and keep warm.

5 Meanwhile, toast the pine nuts under the grill or in a dry pan over a moderate heat. Watch them all the time and move them around to toast evenly.

6 Add the reduced stock and cream to the mushroom mixture. Bring to the boil and reduce the sauce to half its original volume. Season to taste with salt and pepper. Add the drained pasta and pine nuts to the pan and toss to coat with the sauce. Serve immediately.

Serves 4
Preparation time: 15 minutes
Cooking time: 30 minutes

pasta with pesto

1 quantity Pesto (see page 146)
500 g/1 lb tagliatelle
salt and pepper
50 g/2 oz Parmesan cheese, freshly grated, to serve

1 First make the pesto.

2 Cook the pasta until al dente (see page 137). Drain well and return to the pan. Sprinkle with pepper, pour over the pesto sauce, and toss lightly. Transfer to a warmed serving dish, sprinkle with the grated Parmesan and serve hot.

Serves 4
Preparation time: 15–20 minutes
Cooking time: 8–12 minutes

saffron bows

300 g/10 oz farfalle
25 g/1 oz butter
150 ml/¼ pint double cream
½ teaspoon saffron threads
salt and pepper
75 g/3 oz Parmesan cheese, freshly grated, to serve

1 Cook the pasta until al dente (see page 137).

2 Heat the butter and cream in a small saucepan, add the saffron and gently bring to the simmer.

3 Drain the pasta well, place in a warmed serving bowl and pour over the saffron sauce. Season with salt and pepper, and mix well.

4 Serve the Parmesan at the table and sprinkle just a little over each portion.

Serves 4
Preparation time: 5 minutes
Cooking time: 8–12 minutes

fusilli with parmesan and pine nuts

300 g/10 oz fusilli
125 g/4 oz pine nuts
75 g/3 oz butter
2 tablespoons olive oil
75 g/3 oz Parmesan cheese, freshly grated
handful of basil leaves
salt and pepper

1 Cook the pasta until al dente (see page 137).

2 Toast the pine nuts in a dry frying pan over a moderate heat, stirring constantly, until golden.

3 Melt the butter with the oil in a small saucepan. Drain the pasta thoroughly, pour over the butter, season with salt and pepper, and toss well.

4 Turn into a warmed serving dish, sprinkle with the pine nuts, Parmesan and basil leaves, and serve immediately.

Serves 4
Preparation time: 5 minutes
Cooking time: 8–12 minutes

pappardelle with olives and capers

300 g/10 oz pappardelle
125 g/4 oz black or green olives, pitted and roughly
* chopped*
2 pinches crushed dried chillies
2 tablespoons capers, chopped
7 anchovy fillets, drained and chopped
4 large pieces of sun-dried tomatoes in olive oil, roughly
* chopped*
large handful of parsley, chopped
75 g/3 oz Parmesan cheese, freshly grated
salt and pepper

1 Cook the pasta until al dente (see page 137).

2 Meanwhile, put the olives into a saucepan with the chillies, capers and anchovies. Add the sun-dried tomatoes with 4 tablespoons of their oil. Gently heat the mixture for 4 minutes until warm; do not let it fry.

3 Drain the pasta, add the olive mixture, parsley and Parmesan. Season with salt and pepper, mix well and serve. This dish can also be left to stand for a while and served at room temperature.

Serves 4
Preparation time: 10 minutes
Cooking time: 8–12 minutes

lemon and basil orzo

300 g/10 oz orzo
2 garlic cloves, crushed
large handful of basil leaves
5 tablespoons olive oil
rind and juice of 2 lemons
150 g/5 oz Parmesan cheese, freshly grated
salt and pepper

1 Cook the pasta until al dente (see page 137).

2 Using a pestle and mortar or a food processor, blend the garlic, basil, olive oil, lemon rind and juice until smooth.

3 Add the Parmesan to the basil mixture, blend well and season with salt and pepper.

4 Drain the orzo thoroughly. Add the pesto and mix well so that the sauce is distributed evenly throughout the orzo. Serve immediately.

Serves 4
Preparation time: 10 minutes
Cooking time: 8–12 minutes

pappardelle with pesto and potatoes

375 g/12 oz new potatoes, or large red-skinned potatoes
* cut into chunks*
2 tablespoons olive oil
1 tablespoon coarse salt
300 g/10 oz pappardelle
250 g/8 oz Pesto (see page 146)
salt and pepper

To garnish:
2 tablespoons pine nuts
2 tablespoons finely chopped parsley

1 Cook the potatoes in a pan of boiling lightly salted water for 15–20 minutes until just tender.

2 Drain the potatoes, dry them on kitchen paper, then place them in a shallow dish with the olive oil and salt. Toss gently to coat with the oil.

3 Cook the pasta until al dente (see page 137).

4 Meanwhile, toast the pine nuts in a dry frying pan over a moderate heat, stirring constantly, until golden.

5 Drain the pasta well, return to the pan, add the potatoes and pesto, and toss thoroughly. Transfer to a warmed serving bowl, garnish with the pine nuts and parsley, and serve.

Serves 4
Preparation time: 15 minutes
Cooking time: 20–30 minutes

tagliatelle with crab sauce

2 tablespoons olive oil
2 shallots, chopped
200 g/7 oz crab meat
1–2 pinches dried chilli, crumbled
grated rind and juice of 1 lemon
300 g/10 oz tagliatelle
4 tablespoons double cream
handful of chives, snipped
salt and pepper
75 g/3 oz Parmesan cheese, freshly grated, to serve

1 Heat the olive oil in a saucepan, add the shallots and sauté gently until soft, but do not brown.

2 Add the crab meat, chillies, lemon rind and juice, and season with salt and pepper.

3 Cook the pasta until al dente (see page 137).

4 Add the cream to the crab mixture and bring to the boil.

5 Drain the tagliatelle well. Add the chives to the crab mixture. Add the sauce to the tagliatelle, mix well and serve with a bowl of grated Parmesan.

Serves 4
Preparation time: 10 minutes
Cooking time: 15 minutes

linguine with prawn, sun-dried tomato and mushroom sauce

300 g/10 oz linguine verde or spaghetti
8 tablespoons olive oil
375 g/12 oz button mushrooms, sliced
375 g/12 oz large raw prawns, peeled and deveined
  (see page 111)
40 g/1½ oz sun-dried tomatoes in oil, drained and chopped
2 tablespoons lemon juice
1 bunch of spring onions, diagonally sliced
3 tablespoons chopped basil
salt and pepper

1 Cook the pasta until al dente (see page 137).

2 Meanwhile, heat the oil in a large frying pan until almost smoking. Add the button mushrooms and stir-fry for 2 minutes. Add the prawns and sun-dried tomatoes, and stir-fry for 3 minutes.

3 Add the lemon juice and spring onions, and stir-fry for another 2 minutes. Stir in the basil and season to taste with salt and pepper.

4 Drain the pasta, transfer to a warmed serving dish and toss with half of the sauce. Spoon the remaining sauce over the top, and serve immediately.

Serves 4
Preparation time: 10 minutes
Cooking time: 8–12 minutes

tagliarini alla marinara with ginger

1 kg/2 lb mussels, scrubbed and debearded
  (see page 109)
4 slices of fresh root ginger
2 shallots, finely chopped
2 garlic cloves, finely chopped
125 ml/4 fl oz dry white wine
375 g/12 oz tagliarini
1½ tablespoons olive oil
25 g/1 oz unsalted butter

2 tablespoons finely shredded ginger
250 g/8 oz raw prawns, peeled and deveined (see page 111)
250 g/8 oz small scallops
125 ml/4 fl oz double cream
1–2 teaspoons lemon juice
salt and pepper
deep-fried basil leaves, to garnish

1 Place the mussels in a large pan. Scatter with the ginger slices, shallots and half of the garlic and sprinkle with the wine. Cover and steam over a medium-high heat for about 5 minutes until the mussels open.

2 Discard the ginger slices. Remove the mussels and reserve. Pour the cooking juices, shallots and garlic into a small saucepan and cook over a high heat until the liquid is reduced to 125 ml/4 fl oz. Cover and set aside.

3 Cook the pasta until al dente (see page 137). Drain and transfer to a warmed serving dish.

4 Heat a wok or frying pan over a moderate heat. When it is hot, add the oil and the butter, then add the remaining garlic and the shredded ginger, and sauté for about 30 seconds until softened.

5 Add the prawns and sauté for about 1 minute until they just begin to turn pink. Add the scallops and toss to mix. Pour in the reserved cooking juices and the cream, and cook for about 1 minute until the sauce is reduced to a creamy consistency.

6 Add the reserved mussels and lemon juice, and season with salt and pepper. Spoon over the pasta and serve immediately, garnished with the deep-fried basil.

Serves 4–6
Preparation time: 30 minutes
Cooking time: 25 minutes

pasta with smoked salmon

300 g/10 oz penne or other pasta shapes
300 ml/½ pint crème fraîche
125 ml/4 fl oz vodka
2 spring onions, finely chopped (optional)
1 teaspoon finely chopped dill
250 g/8 oz smoked salmon, cut into strips
salt and pepper
dill sprigs, to garnish

1 Cook the pasta until al dente (see page 137).

2 When the pasta is almost ready, pour the crème fraîche and vodka into a separate saucepan and heat gently until it is almost boiling.

3 Add the spring onions, if using, and dill, season with salt and pepper, and cook until heated through. Remove the pan from the heat and stir in the smoked salmon.

4 Drain the pasta and toss with the sauce. Garnish with dill sprigs and serve immediately.

Serves 4
Preparation time: 5 minutes
Cooking time: 8–12 minutes

spaghetti vongole with flat leaf parsley

4 tablespoons olive oil
2 garlic cloves, chopped
1.5 kg/3 lb baby clams, cleaned (see page 109)
125 ml/4 fl oz dry white wine
75 ml/3 fl oz double cream
500 g/1 lb spaghetti
large handful of flat leaf parsley, chopped
salt and pepper
freshly grated Parmesan cheese, to serve

1 Heat the oil in a large saucepan over a low heat, add the garlic and clams, cover, and cook for 3 minutes or until all the clams have opened. Discard any clams that do not open.

2 Lift the clams out of the pan with a slotted spoon. Remove half of them from their shells and return any liquid to the pan. Set the clams aside.

3 Add the wine and cream to the pan and increase the heat to reduce the sauce.

4 Meanwhile, cook the pasta until al dente (see page 137).

5 Return the clams to the sauce, stir well and simmer for 2 minutes. Add the parsley and spaghetti to the clams, season with salt and pepper, and mix well. Serve immediately with freshly grated Parmesan.

Serves 4
Preparation time: 20 minutes
Cooking time: 8–12 minutes

pappardelle with seafood sauce

1 kg/2 lb clams, cleaned (see page 109)
5 tablespoons olive oil
2 onions, finely chopped
250 g/8 oz plum tomatoes, halved and deseeded
250 g/8 oz raw prawns, peeled and deveined
  (see page 111)
250 g/8 oz sole fillets, skinned and cut into
  bite-sized pieces
250 g/8 oz cod fillet, skinned and cut into
  bite-sized pieces
handful of chives, snipped
375 g/12 oz pappardelle or fettuccine
salt and pepper

1 Put the clams in a large shallow frying pan with 1 tablespoon of the oil. Cover and cook over a high heat for 5–8 minutes until the shells open. Discard any that do not open. Remove the clams from their shells and put them in a bowl. Strain the cooking liquid through muslin.

2 Heat the remaining oil in a large saucepan, add the onions, salt and pepper, and cook over a medium heat until golden. Add the strained clam cooking liquid and simmer for 10 minutes, then add the clams and tomatoes. Cook for 10 minutes more. Add the prawns, followed a few minutes later by the fish pieces, and simmer for 15 minutes, until they are cooked through. Sprinkle with chives and keep hot.

3 Meanwhile, cook the pasta until al dente (see page 137). Drain, mix with the sauce and serve immediately.

Serves 4–6
Preparation time: 10 minutes
Cooking time: 50 minutes

linguine with mussels in tomato sauce

1 kg/2 lb mussels, scrubbed and debearded
  (see page 109)
100 ml/3½ fl oz water
3 tablespoons olive oil
1 onion, chopped
3 garlic cloves, crushed
750 g/1½ lb tomatoes, skinned and chopped
500 g/1 lb linguine
3 tablespoons chopped parsley
salt and pepper

1 Place the mussels in a large saucepan with the measured water, cover and cook over a moderate heat until the mussels open, shaking the pan occasionally. Drain the mussels and remove the shells, leaving a few in their shells to garnish.

2 Heat the olive oil in a frying pan, add the onion and garlic, and sauté until golden and tender. Add the chopped tomatoes, season with salt and pepper and cook gently over a low heat until the mixture is thickened and reduced. Gently mix the shelled mussels into the tomato sauce. Simmer over a low heat for 2–3 minutes or until the mussels are heated through.

3 Meanwhile, cook the pasta until al dente (see page 137). Drain well and toss with the sauce.

4 Transfer the pasta and sauce to a warmed serving dish or 4 warmed plates, sprinkle with chopped parsley, garnish with the reserved mussels and serve.

Serves 4
Preparation time: 25 minutes
Cooking time: 20 minutes

spaghetti with sardines, anchovies and fennel

1 fennel head, quartered
8–10 tablespoons olive oil
2 garlic cloves, crushed
500 g/1 lb sardine fillets, cut into 2–3 inch pieces

2 large onions, finely sliced
1 tablespoon sultanas
1 tablespoon pine nuts
6 anchovy fillets, chopped
2 tablespoons chopped parsley
150 ml/5 fl oz dry white wine or Fish Stock (see page 142)
500 g/1 lb spaghetti
lightly browned white breadcrumbs
salt and pepper

1 Cook the fennel in salted boiling water until almost tender. Drain well, reserving the cooking liquid. Chop the fennel coarsely.

2 Heat 3 tablespoons of the oil in a frying pan, add the garlic and cook gently until golden. Add the sardines and cook gently for a further 10 minutes.

3 Meanwhile, heat another 3 tablespoons of oil in a frying pan, add the onions and cook until they are soft and golden brown. Add the fennel, sultanas, pine nuts, anchovies, parsley and wine or fish stock. Season lightly. Cook over a moderate heat for 10 minutes.

4 Cook the spaghetti until al dente (see page 137) in salted boiling water to which the fennel water has been added.

5 Drain the pasta and place half in an ovenproof dish. Cover with half the sardines and a little of the onion and fennel. Repeat the layers and sprinkle breadcrumbs and a little oil over the top. Cook in a preheated oven, 200°C (400°F), Gas Mark 6, for 20 minutes. Serve immediately, sprinkled with pepper.

Serves 4
Preparation time: 10 minutes
Cooking time: 1 hour
Oven temperature: 200°C (400°F), Gas Mark 6

orecchiette with spicy tomato and pancetta sauce

2 tablespoons olive oil
1 onion, chopped
2 garlic cloves, chopped
125 g/4 oz pancetta, chopped
400 g/13 oz can chopped tomatoes
½–1 teaspoon crushed dried chillies

125 ml/4 fl oz red wine
300 g/10 oz orecchiette
handful of flat leaf parsley, chopped
handful of basil, chopped
salt and pepper
75 g/3 oz Parmesan shavings, to garnish

1 Heat the olive oil in a saucepan, add the onion, garlic and pancetta, and sauté for 5 minutes.

2 Add the chopped tomatoes, dried chillies and red wine, and simmer for 15 minutes or until the sauce is rich and thick.

3 Meanwhile, cook the pasta until al dente (see page 137). Drain well.

4 Stir the parsley, basil, and salt and pepper into the sauce. Add to the pasta and toss well. Garnish with some of the Parmesan shavings, place the rest in a separate bowl and serve.

Serves 4
Preparation time: 5 minutes
Cooking time: 20 minutes

penne with chicken livers

1 yellow pepper, halved, cored, and deseeded
300 g/10 oz penne
2 tablespoons olive oil
50 g/2 oz butter
1 red onion, sliced
250 g/8 oz chicken livers, trimmed
1 rosemary sprig, chopped
salt and pepper
75 g/3 oz Parmesan cheese, freshly grated, to serve

1 Roast the yellow pepper in a hot oven or under the grill for 5 minutes until the skin is blistered and blackened all over. Place the pepper in a polythene bag until it is cool, then peel off the skin and cut the flesh into long strips.

2 Cook the pasta until al dente (see page 137).

3 Heat the oil and butter in a large frying pan, add the onion and chicken livers, and cook on a high heat until browned all over. Add the rosemary and pepper strips and season with salt and pepper. Do not overcook the chicken livers, as this dries them out and makes them hard; they are best still pink in the middle.

4 Mix the chicken liver sauce with the pasta and toss well. Serve immediately with a bowl of freshly grated Parmesan.

Serves 4
Preparation time: 10 minutes
Cooking time: 12 minutes

spaghetti carbonara

The traditional Italian way to serve spaghetti carbonara is with an egg yolk in its shell on top of each serving, which is mixed in by the person eating.

1 tablespoon olive oil
175 g/6 oz smoked bacon, rinded and cut into strips
1 garlic clove, crushed and chopped
300 g/10 oz spaghetti
4 tablespoons double cream
3 egg yolks
75 g/3 oz Parmesan cheese, freshly grated
salt and pepper

1 Heat the oil in a saucepan, add the bacon and fry over a low heat for 3 minutes. Add the garlic and cook for 1 minute.

2 Meanwhile, cook the pasta until al dente (see page 137). Drain well and return to the pan.

3 Beat together the cream and egg yolks, add to the bacon and mix well over a low heat.

4 Add the sauce and Parmesan to the spaghetti, season with salt and pepper, toss well and serve immediately.

Serves 4
Preparation time: 10 minutes
Cooking time: 8–12 minutes

penne with sausages and mixed vegetables

3 tablespoons olive oil
25 g/1 oz butter
½ onion, finely chopped
1 small shallot, finely chopped
1 small carrot, finely diced
1 celery stick, sliced
125 g/4 oz Italian sausage, crumbled
1 small yellow pepper, cored, deseeded and diced
4 basil leaves, finely chopped
50 ml/2 fl oz dry red wine
400 g/13 oz can plum tomatoes
425 g/14 oz penne
2 tablespoons freshly grated pecorino cheese
2 tablespoons freshly grated Parmesan cheese
salt and pepper
basil sprigs, to garnish

1 Heat the oil and butter in a flameproof casserole, add the onion, shallot, carrot and celery and cook over a low heat for 4 minutes.

2 Mix well and then add the sausage, pepper and basil. Brown over a medium heat for 3–4 minutes, then add the red wine.

3 When the wine has evaporated, strain the juice from the tomatoes and add the tomatoes to the casserole dish with salt and pepper to taste. Cook the sauce for 30 minutes, stirring from time to time.

4 Meanwhile, cook the pasta until al dente (see page 137). Drain well. Tip the pasta into the casserole and mix well. Sprinkle with the grated cheeses and mix again. Garnish with basil sprigs and serve hot.

Serves 4
Preparation time: 15 minutes
Cooking time: 45 minutes

pappardelle with hare

1 prepared hare, cut into small pieces
500 ml/17 fl oz red wine
1 celery stick, chopped
1 onion, finely sliced
1 bay leaf
a few black peppercorns
75 g/3 oz belly pork
1 carrot, roughly chopped
4 tablespoons olive oil
7 tablespoons Beef Stock (see page 141)
400 g/13 oz pappardelle
75 g/3 oz Parmesan cheese, freshly grated
50 g/2 oz butter, softened
salt and pepper

1 Put the hare, wine, celery, half the onion, the bay leaf and peppercorns in a bowl. Cover and leave to marinate for 3–4 hours, stirring occasionally.

2 Mince the pork with the remaining onion and the carrot. Heat the oil in a frying pan, add the minced mixture and fry for 5 minutes.

3 Drain the hare, reserving the marinade, then add to the pan with salt and pepper to taste. Fry until browned on all sides, then add 2–3 tablespoons of the reserved marinade and the stock. Cover and cook for 1½ hours until the hare is tender, stirring occasionally and adding more marinade and stock as necessary. Transfer the pieces of hare to a warmed serving dish. Strain the cooking juices and keep hot.

4 Meanwhile, cook the pasta until al dente (see page 137), then drain. Pile on a serving dish and moisten with a little liquid from the hare. Add the Parmesan and butter, and mix. Serve with the hare in a separate dish.

Serves 4
Preparation time: 25 minutes, plus marinating
Cooking time: 1½–1¾ hours

spaghetti alla bolognese

500 g/1 lb spaghetti
pepper
50 g/2 oz Parmesan cheese, freshly grated, to serve

Meat sauce:
4 tablespoons olive oil
1 onion, finely chopped
1 garlic clove, crushed
4 streaky bacon rashers, rinded and chopped
1 carrot, diced
1 celery stick, diced
500 g/1 lb minced lean beef
150 ml/¼ pint red wine
125 ml/4 fl oz milk
grated nutmeg
400 g/13 oz can chopped tomatoes
1 tablespoon sugar
1 teaspoon chopped oregano
salt and pepper

1 To make the sauce, heat the oil in a saucepan or deep frying pan, add the onion, garlic, bacon, carrot and celery and sauté until soft and golden. Add the beef and cook until browned, stirring occasionally.

2 Add the red wine and bring to the boil. Reduce the heat slightly and cook over a medium heat until most of the wine has evaporated. Season with salt and pepper.

3 Add the milk and a little nutmeg, and stir well. Continue cooking until the milk has been absorbed by the meat mixture. Add the tomatoes, sugar and oregano. Reduce the heat to a bare simmer and cook uncovered for 2–2½ hours, until the sauce is reduced and richly coloured.

4 Cook the pasta until al dente (see page 137). Drain well and season with freshly ground black pepper. Pour over the meat sauce and serve the Parmesan separately.

Serves 4
Preparation time: 20 minutes
Cooking time: 2½–3 hours

tagliatelle verde with bacon, garlic and fennel

6 unsmoked streaky bacon rashers
2 tablespoons olive oil
2 fennel bulbs, finely chopped
2 garlic cloves, finely chopped
4 tablespoons freshly grated Parmesan cheese
300 ml/½ pint fromage frais
3 tablespoons finely chopped parsley
375 g/12 oz spinach tagliatelle
salt and pepper
fennel fronds, to garnish

1 Grill the bacon until crisp. Drain on kitchen paper and set aside. Heat the oil in a frying pan, add the fennel and garlic, cover and cook gently over a low heat for 5 minutes until the fennel is just tender.

2 Add the Parmesan, fromage frais and parsley, and season to taste with salt and pepper. Simmer over a low heat for 1–2 minutes.

3 Meanwhile, cook the pasta until al dente (see page 137). Drain well, return to the pan, pour over the sauce, and toss. Transfer to a warmed serving dish.

4 Chop the bacon and sprinkle it over the pasta. Garnish with fennel fronds and serve immediately.

Serves 4–6
Preparation time: 15 minutes
Cooking time: 8–12 minutes

conchiglie with pepperoni, onion and balsamic vinegar

5 tablespoons olive oil
3 large onions, thinly sliced
375 g/12 oz conchiglie or other pasta shapes
250 g/8 oz pepperoni, sliced
300 ml/½ pint Vegetable Stock (see page 140)
4 tablespoons chopped flat leaf parsley
1 tablespoon balsamic vinegar
salt and pepper

1 Heat the oil in a large frying pan, add the onions and fry over low heat for 40 minutes, stirring occasionally to prevent them sticking, until very soft and slightly caramelized.

2 Cook the pasta until al dente (see page 137).

3 While the pasta is cooking, add the sliced pepperoni to the onions, increase the heat and stir-fry for a few minutes until the mixture is heated through.

4 Pour in the stock and bring to the boil, scraping up any sediment from the bottom of the pan. Stir in the parsley and vinegar, and season to taste with salt and pepper.

5 Drain the pasta thoroughly, return to the pan, pour over the sauce and. toss. Transfer to a warmed serving dish and serve immediately.

Serves 4
Preparation time: 10–15 minutes
Cooking time: 50 minutes

spinach tortellini with blue cheese dressing

500 g/1 lb spinach tortellini
300 g/10 oz Gorgonzola or dolcelatte cheese
75 g/3 oz butter
150 ml/¼ pint double cream
pepper

1 Cook the pasta until al dente (see page 137).

2 Crumble the cheese into a small saucepan, add the butter and cream and place over a low heat to melt the cheese and warm the mixture. Season with pepper.

3 Drain the pasta well, return to the pan, add the sauce and toss well. Transfer to a warmed serving dish and serve immediately.

Serves 4
Preparation time: 5 minutes
Cooking time: 8–12 minutes

mushroom ravioli

2 tablespoons olive oil
1 onion, finely chopped
1–2 garlic cloves, crushed
500 g/1 lb mushrooms, finely chopped
200 g/7 oz ricotta cheese
1 egg, beaten
2–3 tablespoons white breadcrumbs
1 quantity Basic Egg Pasta (see page 134)
75 g/3 oz butter
salt and pepper
50 g/2 oz Parmesan cheese, freshly grated

1 Heat the oil in a frying pan, add the onion and garlic and fry over a low heat until soft and lightly coloured. Add the mushrooms and continue to cook gently until the mushrooms are soft and any liquid has evaporated.

2 Remove the pan from the heat and beat in the ricotta, egg and sufficient breadcrumbs to give a firm mixture. Season to taste with salt and pepper.

3 Roll out the pasta dough thinly and cut out 6 cm/2½ inch rounds. Place a portion of the mixture on each round, brush around the edge of the dough with cold water, fold over and seal. Alternatively, cut out 2.5 cm/ 1 inch squares or rounds, place the filling in the centre of half of them, brush around the edge with cold water, place another matching pasta shape on top and seal.

4 Bring a large saucepan of salted water to the boil, drop in a few ravioli at a time and cook for 4–5 minutes, until they rise to the surface. Remove with a slotted spoon, drain well and place in a warmed serving dish. Cover and keep hot until all the ravioli are cooked. Just before serving, heat the butter in a saucepan until it is a light golden brown, and pour over the ravioli immediately. Sprinkle a little of the Parmesan over the top, and serve the rest separately. Serve hot.

Serves 4
Preparation time: 30 minutes, plus making the pasta
Cooking time: 30 minutes

cheese ravioli

425 g/14 oz plain flour
4 eggs, beaten
1.5 litres/2½ pints Vegetable Stock (see page 140)
salt

Cheese filling:
250 g/8 oz ricotta cheese
125 g/4 oz Bel Paese cheese, freshly grated
50 g/2 oz Parmesan cheese, freshly grated
2 eggs, beaten
pinch of grated nutmeg

To serve:
125 g/4 oz butter, melted
75 g/3 oz Parmesan cheese, freshly grated

1 To make the pasta, sift the flour and a pinch of salt on to a work surface and make a well in the centre. Add the eggs and mix to a smooth dough. Shape into a ball, wrap in a damp cloth and leave for about 30 minutes.

2 Meanwhile, make the filling. Put the ricotta and Bel Paese into a bowl and beat well. Add the Parmesan, eggs, nutmeg and a pinch of salt and beat thoroughly.

3 Roll out the dough on a lightly floured surface until it is paper-thin. Cut it into 4 cm/1¾ inch squares with a pastry cutter wheel. Put a little filling in the centre of each square, then fold the dough over to make triangles. Turn the corners upwards.

4 Bring the stock to the boil in a large saucepan. Add the ravioli and cook for 5 minutes or until they rise to the surface. Drain and pile into a warmed serving dish. Sprinkle with the melted butter and Parmesan, and serve immediately.

Serves 4
Preparation time: 30–35 minutes, plus standing
Cooking time: about 5 minutes

ravioli with spinach and ricotta

1 quantity Basic Egg Pasta (see page 134)

Filling:
250 g/8 oz spinach, stalks removed
125 g/4 oz ricotta cheese
25 g/1 oz freshly grated Parmesan cheese
grated nutmeg
1 egg, beaten
salt and pepper

To serve:
50 g/2 oz butter, melted
3–4 sage leaves, torn
freshly grated Parmesan cheese

1 First make the filling. Put the spinach into a saucepan with just the water left on the leaves, cover and cook over a very low heat until wilted. Drain in a colander, pressing down firmly with a wooden spoon to squeeze out excess moisture, and then chop roughly.

2 Put the ricotta and Parmesan into a bowl and mix in the spinach. Season with salt, pepper and nutmeg, and add the beaten egg, mixing well to a paste.

3 Roll out the pasta as thinly as possible on a lightly floured surface and cut exactly in half. Place teaspoons of the filling on one piece of pasta, spacing them about 5 cm/2 inches apart.

4 Cover with the second sheet of pasta and press gently around each little mound with your fingers. Using a pastry cutter wheel, cut the pasta into squares.

5 Place the ravioli in a saucepan of gently boiling water and cook for 4–5 minutes, until they rise to the surface. Drain and pile into a warmed serving dish. Sprinkle with the melted butter, sage and grated Parmesan, and serve immediately.

Serves 4–6
Preparation time: 30 minutes, plus making dough
Cooking time: 4–5 minutes

cappelletti with fish stuffing and prawn sauce

250 g/8 oz Basic Egg Pasta (see page 134)
25 g/1 oz butter
salt and pepper
parsley and marjoram, to garnish

Fish stuffing:
1 small onion, halved
1 celery stick, roughly chopped
1 small carrot, roughly chopped
375 g/12 oz sea bass or other white fish, skin removed
175 ml/6 fl oz dry white wine
2 egg yolks
20 g/¾ oz freshly grated Parmesan cheese
1 teaspoon chopped marjoram
pinch of grated nutmeg

Prawn sauce:
4 tablespoons olive oil
2 garlic cloves, crushed
8 tomatoes, skinned, deseeded and chopped
4 tablespoons dry white wine
250 g/8 oz cooked peeled prawns, chopped
300 ml/½ pint double cream
2 tablespoons chopped parsley

1 To make the fish stuffing, put the onion, celery, carrot and fish into a frying pan, pour over the wine and season well with salt and pepper. Bring to the boil and simmer for 10–12 minutes until the fish is tender. Drain and flake the fish into a bowl. Add the egg yolks, Parmesan, marjoram and nutmeg. Mix well and season to taste with salt and pepper.

2 Roll out the pasta very thinly and cut into 3.5 cm/ 1½ inch squares. Place ½ teaspoon of the filling in the centre of each square and dampen the edges of the dough with water. Fold into a triangle and seal the edges. Then take the left and right corners together to form a circle and pinch to seal. Place the cappelletti on a clean dry tea towel and leave to dry for 1 hour.

3 Meanwhile, make the prawn sauce. Put the oil and garlic into a frying pan and cook for 2–3 minutes until the garlic is golden brown. Add the tomatoes and wine, bring to the boil and simmer uncovered for 15–20 minutes, until thickened. Stir in the prawns and season to taste with salt and pepper.

4 Add the cream and gradually bring to the boil, stirring constantly. Stir in the parsley and remove from the heat.

5 Cook the cappelletti in a large saucepan of salted boiling water for 30 seconds–1 minute, until just tender. Drain thoroughly and transfer to a warmed serving dish. Add the butter, toss well, then pour over the sauce. Garnish with parsley and marjoram, and serve hot.

Serves 4
Preparation time: 45 minutes–1 hour, plus making dough and standing
Cooking time: about 45 minutes

mushroom and mozzarella lasagne stacks

2 tablespoons olive oil
50 g/2 oz butter
2 onions, chopped
2 garlic cloves, crushed and chopped
500 g/1 lb mushrooms, sliced
4 tablespoons double cream
4 tablespoons dry white wine
1 teaspoon chopped thyme
8 sheets of lasagne
2 red peppers, cored, deseeded, skinned and thickly sliced
125 g/4 oz baby spinach leaves
125 g/4 oz buffalo mozzarella cheese, sliced
50 g/2 oz fresh Parmesan cheese shavings
salt and pepper

1 Heat the oil and butter in a saucepan, add the onions and sauté for 3 minutes. Add the garlic and cook for 1 minute. Add the mushrooms, turn up the heat and cook for 5 minutes.

2 Add the cream, white wine and thyme, season with salt and pepper and simmer for 4 minutes.

3 If using dried lasagne, cook it until al dente (see page 137). Remove from the pan, pat dry and place 4 pieces on a well-oiled baking sheet.

4 Place a generous spoonful of mushroom mixture on each piece of lasagne, add some red pepper slices and one-eighth of the spinach leaves, and put another piece of lasagne on top. Then add the remaining spinach leaves, a slice of mozzarella, and top with a little more mushroom mixture. Finish with some Parmesan shavings. Place the lasagne stacks under a preheated very hot grill and cook for 5 minutes until the mushroom mixture is bubbling and the Parmesan is golden. Serve immediately.

Serves 4
Preparation time: 10 minutes
Cooking time: 20 minutes

baked lasagne

1 quantity Classic White Sauce (see page 144)
pinch of nutmeg
10–12 sheets of lasagne
50 g/2 oz freshly grated Parmesan cheese
15 g/½ oz butter

Meat sauce:
4 tablespoons olive oil
1 onion, finely chopped
1 garlic clove, crushed
4 streaky bacon rashers, rinded and chopped
1 carrot, diced
1 celery stick, diced
500 g/1 lb minced lean beef
150 ml/¼ pint red wine
400 g/13 oz can chopped tomatoes
1 tablespoon sugar
1 teaspoon chopped oregano
salt and pepper

1 First make the meat sauce. Heat the oil in a saucepan or deep frying pan, add the onion, garlic, bacon, carrot and celery, and sauté until soft and golden. Add the beef and cook until browned, stirring occasionally.

2 Add the red wine and bring to the boil. Reduce the heat slightly and cook over a medium heat until most of the wine has evaporated. Season with salt and pepper.

3 Add the tomatoes, sugar and oregano. Reduce the heat to a bare simmer and cook, uncovered, for 2–2½ hours, until the sauce is reduced and richly coloured.

4 Add a pinch of nutmeg to the white sauce and mix well to combine.

5 If using dried lasagne, cook until al dente (see page 137), drain and pat dry.

6 Put a little of the meat sauce in a buttered ovenproof dish and cover with a layer of lasagne and then another layer of meat sauce, topped with some white sauce. Continue layering up in this way, ending with a layer of lasagne and a topping of white sauce.

7 Sprinkle with grated Parmesan and dot the top with butter. Bake in a preheated oven, 230°C (450°F), Gas Mark 8, for 30 minutes until the lasagne is light golden brown.

Serves 4
Preparation time: 30 minutes
Cooking time: 3½ hours
Oven temperature: 230°C (450°F), Gas Mark 8

spinach lasagne with cheese sauce

500–750 g/1–1½ lb fresh spinach, or 375 g/12 oz frozen
*   leaf spinach*
1½ tablespoons olive oil
2 onions, finely chopped
2 garlic cloves, finely chopped
10 sheets of lasagne
2–3 tablespoons freshly grated Parmesan cheese
salt and pepper

Cheese sauce:
50 g/2 oz butter or margarine
50 g/2 oz flour
750 ml/1¼ pints milk
1–2 eggs (optional)
175 g/6 oz Gruyère or Cheddar cheese, grated
1 teaspoon prepared English mustard

1 Put the fresh spinach into a saucepan with just the water left on the leaves, cover and cook over a very low heat until wilted. Add salt and pepper to taste. Drain in a colander, pressing down firmly with a wooden spoon to squeeze out excess moisture, then chop finely. Cook frozen spinach as instructed on the packet.

2 Heat the oil in a saucepan, add the onions and garlic, and fry until tender. Mix with the spinach.

3 To make the cheese sauce, heat the butter or margarine in a saucepan, stir in the flour, then gradually add the milk. Bring to the boil, then stir or whisk into a smooth sauce.

4 Beat the eggs well, if adding, then whisk into the hot, but not boiling sauce. Do not reheat. Stir most of the Gruyère or Cheddar into the sauce, with the mustard, salt and pepper.

5 If using dried lasagne, cook until al dente (see page 137). Drain well and pat dry.

6 Assemble the lasagne. Place a layer of lasagne in an ovenproof dish, then a layer of spinach and a layer of sauce. Continue layering in this way, ending with lasagne and a coating of sauce. Sprinkle the remaining Gruyère or Cheddar and the Parmesan over the top of the sauce and bake for 25–30 minutes in a preheated oven, 190°C (375°F), Gas Mark 5. Serve hot.

Serves 4
Preparation time: 40 minutes
Cooking time: 45 minutes
Oven temperature: 190°C (375°F), Gas Mark 5

wild mushroom lasagne

15 g/½ oz dried ceps
150 ml/¼ pint boiling water
3 tablespoons olive oil
4 shallots, chopped
2 garlic cloves, chopped
1 tablespoon chopped thyme
750 g/1½ lb mixed cultivated mushrooms
150 ml/¼ pint dry white wine
500 g/1 lb tomatoes, skinned and chopped, or
    400 g/13 oz can chopped tomatoes
50 g/2 oz drained sun-dried tomatoes in oil, chopped
1 tablespoon dark soy sauce
12 sheets of lasagne
1 quantity Cheese Sauce (see page 144)
250 g/8 oz mozzarella cheese
salt and pepper

1 Place the dried ceps in a bowl and pour over the measured boiling water. Leave to soak for 30 minutes, then drain, reserving the liquid. Slice the ceps.

2 Heat the oil in a large frying pan, add the shallots, garlic and thyme, and fry for 5 minutes. Add the ceps and fresh mushrooms and stir-fry for 5–6 minutes until golden. Add the wine and boil rapidly for 5 minutes. Stir in the tomatoes, sun-dried tomatoes, reserved cep liquid and soy sauce, bring to the boil and simmer gently for 15 minutes. Season to taste with salt and pepper.

3 If using dried lasagne, cook until al dente (see page 137), drain and pat dry.

4 Assemble the lasagne. Pour one-third of the mushrooms into a 20 x 25 cm/8 x 10 inch lasagne dish and top with 4 sheets of lasagne, one-third of the cheese sauce and one-third of the mozzarella. Repeat layering with the remaining ingredients, finishing with a layer of cheese sauce and then mozzarella.

5 Place the mushroom lasagne in a preheated oven, 190°C (375°F), Gas Mark 5, for about 45 minutes until bubbling and golden. Serve hot.

Serves 6
Preparation time: 40 minutes, plus soaking
Cooking time: 1¼ hours
Oven temperature: 190°C (375°F), Gas Mark 5

tomato and aubergine soufflé lasagne

2 aubergines, cut into 1 cm/½ inch slices
4 tablespoons sunflower oil
2 large onions, sliced
2 garlic cloves, crushed
8 sheets of no pre-cook lasagne verde
750 g/1½ lb ripe tomatoes, sliced
1 tablespoon chopped basil
150 ml/¼ pint Vegetable Stock (see page 140)
salt and pepper

Soufflé topping:
15 g/½ oz butter
15 g/½ oz plain flour
300 ml/½ pint milk
2 eggs, separated

1 Put the aubergine slices into a colander, sprinkle with salt and set aside for 30 minutes to draw out some of the excess liquid.

2 Heat 1 tablespoon of the oil in a large frying pan, add the onions and garlic, and fry for 5 minutes until soft but not browned. Spoon into a dish and set aside.

3 Rinse the aubergine slices, drain, then dry with kitchen paper. Heat 2 tablespoons of the remaining oil in the pan, add half of the slices and fry on both sides until golden brown. Drain on kitchen paper. Add the rest of the oil to the pan and fry the remaining aubergine slices.

4 Lightly oil a large shallow ovenproof dish. Lay 4 lasagne sheets in the bottom. Cover with a layer of aubergine slices, then a layer of cooked onion, then one of tomato slices. Sprinkle with salt, plenty of pepper and half of the basil. Repeat the layers once more, using all the remaining lasagne, vegetables and herbs. Pour over the stock to rehydrate the pasta.

5 To make the soufflé topping, melt the butter in a small saucepan, stir in the flour and cook for 1 minute. Gradually add the milk, stirring until the sauce boils and thickens. Cool slightly, then stir in the egg yolks and season with salt and pepper.

6 Whisk the egg whites in a grease-free bowl until stiff and fold them carefully into the sauce. Spoon the mixture into the dish, covering the top layer completely. Bake in a preheated oven, 180°C (350°F), Gas Mark 4, for 45 minutes until the soufflé has risen and is browned. Serve hot.

Serves 4–6
Preparation time: 30 minutes, plus standing
Cooking time: 1 hour
Oven temperature: 180°C (350°F), Gas Mark 4

mozzarella and plum tomato lasagne with chilli

6 sheets of lasagne verde
10 large plum tomatoes
125 g/4 oz mozzarella cheese, sliced
125 g/4 oz goats' cheese, sliced
small bunch of oregano, chopped
a few drops of chilli-flavoured oil
salt

1 If using dried lasagne, cook until al dente (see page 137), drain and pat dry.

2 Line a buttered rectangular 1.2 litre/2 pint ovenproof dish with 2 sheets of lasagne, cutting them to fit if necessary. Slice 6 of the tomatoes and arrange half of the slices over the lasagne, packing them in well. Sprinkle with salt and add a few slices of mozzarella and goats' cheese and some oregano. Lay 2 more lasagne sheets on top and cover with the remaining tomato slices, half of the remaining cheese slices and the remaining oregano. Top with the remaining lasagne sheets.

3 Cut the remaining tomatoes into wedges, and scatter over the pasta with the rest of the cheese. Drizzle with the chilli-flavoured oil and cook in a preheated oven, 200°C (400°F), Gas Mark 6, for 20–30 minutes. Remove the lasagne from the oven and leave to rest for 10 minutes before serving.

Serves 4
Preparation time: 20 minutes
Cooking time: 30–40 minutes
Oven temperature: 200°C (400°F), Gas Mark 6

tagliatelle brie bake

15 g/½ oz butter
2 tablespoons olive oil
½ onion, sliced
1 garlic clove, crushed
125 g/4 oz button mushrooms, quartered
50–75 g/2–3 oz basil leaves, torn
500 g/1 lb tagliatelle
2 tablespoons freshly grated Parmesan cheese
2 x 400 g/13 oz cans chopped tomatoes
200 ml/7 fl oz crème fraîche
300 g/10 oz Brie, rinded and chopped
50 g/2 oz dolcelatte cheese, chopped
salt and pepper

1 Melt the butter with 1 tablespoon of the oil in a frying pan, add the onion and garlic, and fry for 5 minutes until softened. Add the mushrooms and cook for 2 minutes. Stir in most of the basil. Season with salt and pepper, then remove from the heat.

2 Cook the pasta until al dente (see page 137). Drain, return to the pan, season and toss in a little oil. Sprinkle a little Parmesan cheese into the pasta, if liked.

3 Drain the juice from the tomatoes into a bowl. Stir the tomatoes into the mushroom mixture and stir the crème fraîche into the tomato juice. Add the mushroom mixture and the crème fraîche mixture to the pasta, toss, sprinkle with some basil and spoon into a buttered 1.8 litre/3 pint deep ovenproof dish. Scatter the Brie and dolcelatte over the top and sprinkle with the remaining Parmesan and a few more basil leaves. Cook in a preheated oven, 180°C (350°F), Gas Mark 4, for about 40 minutes.

Serves 6
Preparation time: 20 minutes
Cooking time: 50–55 minutes
Oven temperature: 180°C (350°F), Gas Mark 4

macaroni with anchovies and garlic

2 anchovy fillets
a little milk
4 tablespoons oil
1 garlic clove
50 g/2 oz smoked bacon, rinded and diced
400 g/13 oz can plum tomatoes, drained and cut into strips
50 g/2 oz pitted black olives, chopped
¼ teaspoon chopped oregano
375 g/12 oz macaroni
25 g/1 oz pecorino cheese, freshly grated
salt and pepper

1 Soak the anchovy fillets in a little milk to remove excess salt, then drain.

2 Heat the oil in a saucepan, add the garlic clove and the anchovies and cook over a moderate heat for a few minutes, then remove the garlic and add the bacon.

3 When the bacon is crisp, add the tomatoes to the pan. Season with salt and pepper, and cook over a low heat for about 10 minutes, then add the olives and oregano. Cook for about another 10 minutes, until a thick sauce has formed.

4 Meanwhile, cook the pasta until al dente (see page 137).

5 Drain the pasta, transfer to a warmed serving bowl, pour on the sauce and sprinkle with the pecorino. Mix well and serve.

Serves 4
Preparation time: 10 minutes
Cooking time: 25 minutes

baked macaroni with prawns

½ quantity Classic White Sauce (see page 144)
90 g/3½ oz butter
175 g/6 oz button mushrooms, sliced
250 g/8 oz cooked peeled prawns
2 tablespoons warmed brandy
50–75 g/2–3 oz Parmesan cheese, freshly grated

pinch of grated nutmeg
250 g/8 oz short macaroni
salt and pepper
basil, to garnish

1 Make the white sauce and keep it warm.

2 Heat half the butter in a frying pan, add the mushrooms and cook until tender. Season to taste with salt and pepper. Add the prawns and heat through, then pour on the warmed brandy and set alight. When the flames have subsided, stir in half the Parmesan and check the seasoning.

3 Meanwhile, cook the pasta until al dente (see page 137). Drain well. Check the seasoning of the white sauce and add a pinch of nutmeg and the remaining cheese.

4 Place one-third of the macaroni in a buttered ovenproof dish and spread with half the mushroom mixture. Repeat the layers, ending with a layer of macaroni.

5 Cover with the white sauce. Heat the remaining butter in a pan and, when it is lightly coloured, pour it over the top. Bake in a preheated oven, 200°C (400°F), Gas Mark 6, for about 20 minutes until golden brown. Garnish with basil and serve hot.

Serves 4
Preparation time: 15–20 minutes
Cooking time: 35–40 minutes
Oven temperature: 200°C (400°F), Gas Mark 6

pasta bake with spinach and ham

2 tablespoons olive oil
1 onion, chopped
1 garlic clove, chopped
750 g/1½ lb spinach, chopped
pinch of grated nutmeg
8 sheets of lasagne
250 g/8 oz ham, chopped into large chunks
125 g/4 oz buffalo mozzarella cheese, thinly sliced
125 g/4 oz fontina cheese, freshly grated
salt and pepper

1 Heat the olive oil in a saucepan, add the onion and garlic, and sauté for 3 minutes.

2 Add the spinach and mix well, cook for 2 minutes over a moderate heat, so that the spinach just starts to wilt. Add nutmeg, salt and pepper to taste.

3 If using dried lasagne, cook until al dente (see page 137), drain well and pat dry.

4 Lightly oil a large shallow baking dish, place a layer of lasagne at the bottom, followed by a layer of spinach, then ham and then a layer of mozzarella. Repeat until all the ingredients are used, finishing with lasagne and the fontina cheese.

5 Place the dish at the top of a preheated oven, 200°C (400°F), Gas Mark 6, and bake for 15 minutes until golden brown and bubbling. Serve hot.

Serves 4
Preparation time: 15 minutes
Cooking time: 25 minutes
Oven temperature: 200°C (400°F), Gas Mark 6

meat-filled cannelloni

The simplest way to fill cannelloni tubes is to put the filling mixture into a piping bag, without the nozzle, and squeeze it gently into the tubes.

1–2 tablespoons olive oil
375 g/12 oz lean stewing veal, finely diced
1 onion, sliced
1 carrot, sliced
150 ml/5 fl oz dry white wine
300 ml/½ pint Chicken Stock (see page 141)
125 g/4 oz chicken, cooked
125 g/4 oz spinach, cooked and chopped
2–3 tablespoons single cream
12 tubes no pre-cook cannelloni
2 quantities Quick Tomato Sauce (see page 147)
40 g/1½ oz Parmesan cheese, freshly grated
salt and pepper

1 Butter an ovenproof dish and set aside. Heat the oil in a frying pan, add the veal and fry until it is golden brown. Remove from the pan, add the onion and carrot, and cook until lightly coloured. Return the veal to the pan with the wine and stock. Season lightly and simmer gently for 40–45 minutes until the meat is tender.

2 Remove the meat and vegetables from the pan and mince or chop finely in a food processor with the chicken. Stir in the chopped spinach. Boil the stock until it has reduced to about 2 tablespoons and stir it into the meat and spinach mixture with sufficient cream to soften the mixture.

3 Pipe or spoon the filling into the cannelloni tubes. Place the filled cannelloni in the ovenproof dish and pour over the tomato sauce. Bake in a preheated oven, 180°C (350°F), Gas Mark 4, for 40–45 minutes.

4 Sprinkle a little Parmesan over the top 5–10 minutes before the end of the cooking time and serve the rest separately.

Serves 4
Preparation time: 20–30 minutes
Cooking time: 1–1½ hours
Oven temperature: 180°C (350°F), Gas Mark 4

vegetable cannelloni

1 tablespoon oil
1 onion, chopped
2 celery sticks, very finely sliced
1 carrot, finely chopped
1 tablespoon oregano
1 tablespoon tarragon
400 g/13 oz can flageolet beans
375 g/12 oz carton fresh mushroom sauce
125 g/4 oz baby curly kale, shredded
10 no pre-cook cannelloni tubes
150 ml/¼ pint single cream (optional)
250 g/8 oz ricotta or mascarpone cheese
2 eggs, beaten
3 tablespoons freshly grated Parmesan cheese
salt and pepper

1 Heat the oil in a large frying pan, add the onion, celery and carrot, and fry for 1 minute. Stir in the oregano and tarragon, then cover the pan and sweat the vegetables for 10 minutes, adding a splash of water if they appear a little dry.

2 Stir in the flageolet beans, mushroom sauce and kale. Season with salt and pepper and simmer for a further 10 minutes.

3 Pipe or spoon the filling into the cannelloni tubes and arrange them in a buttered 1.8 litre/3 pint ovenproof dish. Add the cream, if using, to the remaining vegetable mixture to soften it, and pour over the pasta.

4 Beat together the ricotta or mascarpone, eggs and Parmesan, and season well. Spread over the pasta and cook in a preheated oven, 180°C (350°F), Gas Mark 4, for 45 minutes, covering with foil if over-browning. Serve immediately.

Serves 4–6
Preparation time: 20 minutes
Cooking time: 45 minutes
Oven temperature: 180°C (350°F), Gas Mark 4

gnocchi with pesto

1 quantity Pesto (see page 146)
500 g/1 lb potatoes, freshly boiled
175 g/6 oz plain flour
1 egg, beaten
grated nutmeg
salt and pepper

To serve:
25 g/1 oz butter
freshly grated Parmesan cheese

1 First make the pesto.

2 To make the gnocchi, drain the potatoes well and shake over the heat to dry them thoroughly. Mash them very finely so there are no lumps. Beat in the flour and egg and season with nutmeg and salt and pepper. Mix to a dough and turn out on to a floured board.

3 With floured hands, roll small pieces of dough into croquettes, about the thickness of your thumb. Press them lightly with the prongs of a fork.

4 Bring a large pan of lightly salted water to a rolling boil. Drop the gnocchi into the boiling water, a few at a time, and cook for 3–5 minutes, until they rise to the surface. Remove with a slotted spoon and drain. Arrange the gnocchi in a buttered serving dish, dot with butter and sprinkle with Parmesan cheese. Pour the pesto over the top and serve immediately.

Serves 4
Preparation time: 10 minutes
Cooking time: 40 minutes

roman gnocchi baked with parmesan

600 ml/1 pint milk
125 g/4 oz semolina
pinch of grated nutmeg
125 g/4 oz Gruyère cheese, freshly grated
25–50 g/1–2 oz butter, melted
25–50 g/1–2 oz Parmesan cheese, freshly grated
salt and white pepper

1 Bring the milk to the boil. Remove the pan from the heat and immediately add the semolina all at once. Beat well until smooth, season with a pinch of nutmeg and salt and pepper.

2 Return to the heat, bring to the boil and cook for 5–7 minutes over a moderate heat, beating vigorously all the time until the mixture leave the sides of the pan. Beat in the Gruyère and check the seasoning.

3 Turn out the mixture on to a buttered or oiled baking tray and spread into a sheet approximately 1–1.5 cm/½–¾ inch thick. Leave until cold, then refrigerate until completely firm.

4 Cut the gnocchi into rounds with a 5–6 cm/2–2½ inch pastry cutter. Arrange, overlapping, in a buttered ovenproof dish. (Re-form any leftover mixture and cut out more rounds.) Pour the melted butter over the top and sprinkle with the Parmesan. Bake in a preheated oven, 220°C (425°F), Gas Mark 7, for 20–30 minutes until golden brown. Serve straight from the oven.

Serves 4–6
Preparation time: 20–30 minutes, plus chilling
Cooking time: 30–40 minutes
Oven temperature: 220°C (425°F), Gas Mark 7

gnocchi with fennel sauce

1 kg/2 lb floury potatoes
1 egg, plus 1 egg yolk
175 g/6 oz plain flour
1 teaspoon salt
fennel fronds, to garnish
freshly grated Parmesan cheese, to serve

Fennel sauce:
4 tablespoons olive oil
2 tablespoons boiling water
1 tablespoon lemon juice
2 tablespoons chopped fennel fronds
salt and pepper

1 Bake the potatoes in a preheated oven, 200°C (400°F), Gas Mark 6, for 1 hour or until tender. Leave the oven on.

2 Wearing rubber gloves, peel the potatoes while they are hot. Lightly mash the potato, and beat in the egg, egg yolk, salt to taste, and enough of the flour to form a soft, slightly sticky dough.

3 Bring a large saucepan of lightly salted water to a rolling boil. Roll small pieces of the potato dough in your hands and drop into the boiling water. Cook in batches for 4–5 minutes until they rise to the surface. Remove with a slotted spoon, drain well, and place in an oiled baking dish. Repeat with the remaining mixture.

4 Whisk all the sauce ingredients together, season to taste with salt and pepper and pour over the gnocchi. Heat in the oven for 6–8 minutes until bubbling. Sprinkle with grated Parmesan, garnish with fennel fronds and serve immediately.

Serves 4
Preparation time: 50 minutes
Cooking time: 1¼ hours
Oven temperature: 200°C (400°F), Gas Mark 6

green vegetable risotto

1 litre/1¾ pints Chicken or Vegetable Stock
(see pages 141 and 140)
125 g/4 oz butter
1 tablespoon olive oil
1 garlic clove, chopped
1 onion, finely diced
300 g/10 oz arborio or carnaroli rice
125 g/4 oz cooked green beans, trimmed and
cut into 2.5 cm/1 inch pieces
125 g/4 oz cooked peas
125 g/4 oz broad beans, shelled, skinned and cooked
125 g/4 oz asparagus, trimmed, cut into 2.5 cm/1 inch
pieces, and cooked
125 g/4 oz baby spinach, chopped
75 ml/3 fl oz dry vermouth or white wine
2 tablespoons chopped parsley
125 g/4 oz Parmesan cheese, freshly grated
salt and pepper

1 Place the stock in a saucepan and simmer gently.

2 Melt half of the butter with the olive oil in a heavy-based saucepan, add the garlic and onion, and sauté gently for 5 minutes, but do not brown.

3 Add the rice and stir well to coat each grain with the butter and oil. Add enough stock to just cover the rice, stir again and simmer gently, stirring as frequently as possible.

4 When most of the liquid has been absorbed, add more stock; keep adding stock a little at a time, stirring and simmering gently until all the stock is absorbed. When you add the last of the stock, add the vegetables and dry vermouth or white wine, mix well and cook for 2 minutes.

5 Remove the pan from the heat, season with salt and pepper and add the remaining butter, the chopped parsley and the Parmesan. Mix well and serve immediately.

Serves 4
Preparation time: 10 minutes
Cooking time: 30 minutes

risotto alla milanese

1 litre/1¾ pints Chicken Stock (see page 141)
75 g/3 oz butter
1 tablespoon olive oil
2 onions, finely diced
425 g/14 oz arborio or carnaroli rice
½ teaspoon saffron threads
125 ml/4 fl oz dry vermouth or dry white wine
125 g/4 oz Parmesan cheese, freshly grated
salt and pepper

1 Place the stock in a saucepan and simmer gently.

2 Melt 50 g/2 oz of the butter and the olive oil in a large heavy-based saucepan, add the onions and sauté for 5 minutes.

3 Add the rice to the onions and stir well to coat each grain with the butter. Add enough stock to just cover the rice, stir again and simmer gently, stirring as frequently as possible.

4 When most of the liquid has been absorbed, add more stock; keep adding stock a little at a time, stirring and simmering gently until all the stock is absorbed.

5 Finally, add the vermouth or white wine, Parmesan and the remaining butter in small knobs, and season with salt and pepper. Stir well and serve immediately.

Serves 4
Preparation time: 10 minutes
Cooking time: 30 minutes

red wine risotto

600 ml/1 pint Chicken Stock (see page 141)
450 ml/¾ pint Valpolicella or other red wine
1 tablespoon olive oil
125 g/4 oz butter
2 garlic cloves, chopped
2 red onions, chopped
300 g/10 oz arborio or carnaroli rice
250 g/8 oz field mushrooms, sliced
175 g/6 oz Parmesan cheese, freshly grated
salt and pepper

1 Place the stock and red wine in a large saucepan and simmer gently.

2 Heat the olive oil and half of the butter in a heavy-based saucepan, add the garlic and onions, and gently sauté for 5 minutes, but do not brown.

3 Add the rice and stir well to coat each grain with the butter and oil. Add enough of the stock to just cover the rice, stir again and simmer gently, stirring as frequently as possible. When most of the liquid has been absorbed, add more stock; keep adding stock a little at a time, stirring and simmering gently until all the stock is absorbed.

4 When half of the stock has been incorporated, add the mushrooms and season with salt and pepper. The rice should be stained with the colour of the wine, giving it a rich dark red colour.

5 When all the stock has been added, and the rice is just cooked with a good creamy sauce, add most of the Parmesan and the remaining butter, and mix well. Garnish with a little grated Parmesan and serve.

Serves 4
Preparation time: 10 minutes
Cooking time: 30 minutes

butternut squash risotto

1 butternut squash, weighing 1 kg/2 lb
3 tablespoons olive oil
1 litre/1¾ pints Chicken or Vegetable Stock
  (see pages 141 and 140)
125 g/4 oz butter
1 garlic clove, chopped
1 onion, finely diced
300 g/10 oz arborio or carnaroli rice
150 g/5 oz Parmesan cheese, freshly grated
salt and pepper
pumpkin seed oil, to serve

1 Top and tail the squash, cut in half round the middle, then pare away the skin without losing too much of the flesh. Cut both pieces in half lengthways, remove the seeds and cut the flesh into 5 cm/2 inch dice. Place on a large baking sheet, drizzle with 2 tablespoons of the olive oil and season with salt and pepper. Mix well and cook in the top of a preheated oven, 220°C (425°F), Gas Mark 7, for 15 minutes. The squash should be soft and slightly browned.

2 Meanwhile, place the stock in a saucepan and simmer gently.

3 Melt the remaining olive oil and half of the butter in a heavy-based saucepan, add the garlic and onion, and gently sauté for 5 minutes, but do not brown.

4 Add the rice and stir well to coat each grain with the butter and oil. Add enough of the stock to just cover the rice, stir again and simmer gently, stirring as frequently as possible. When most of the liquid has been absorbed, add more stock; keep adding stock a little at a time, stirring and simmering gently until all the stock is absorbed.

5 Remove the squash from the oven, add to the risotto with the Parmesan and the remaining butter, season with salt and pepper, and stir gently.

6 Serve the risotto on individual warmed plates with a little pumpkin seed oil drizzled on top of each portion.

Serves 4
Preparation time: 10 minutes
Cooking time: 30 minutes
Oven temperature: 220°C (425°F), Gas Mark 7

spinach and lemon risotto

1 litre/1¾ pints Chicken or Vegetable Stock
  (see pages 141 and 140)
125 g/4 oz butter
1 tablespoon olive oil
2 shallots, finely chopped
300 g/10 oz arborio or carnaroli rice
500 g/1 lb spinach, chopped
grated rind and juice of 1 lemon
125 g/4 oz Parmesan cheese, freshly grated
salt and pepper
grated lemon rind, to garnish

1 Place the stock in a saucepan and simmer gently.

2 Melt half of the butter and the olive oil in a saucepan, add the shallots and sauté for 3 minutes.

3 Add the rice and mix well to coat each grain with the butter and oil. Add enough of the stock to just cover the rice, stir again and simmer gently, stirring as frequently as possible. When most of the liquid has been absorbed, add more stock; keep adding stock a little at a time, stirring and simmering gently until all the stock is absorbed.

4 Before you add the last of the stock, stir in the chopped spinach, lemon rind and juice, and season with salt and pepper. Increase the heat, stir well then add the remaining stock and butter. Allow to cook for a few minutes, then add half of the Parmesan and mix in well. Serve garnished with the remaining Parmesan and grated lemon rind, if liked.

Serves 4
Preparation time: 10 minutes
Cooking time: 30 minutes

risotto with tomatoes and beef

2 tablespoons olive oil
65 g/2½ oz butter, softened
1 onion, sliced
250 g/8 oz minced beef
125 g/4 oz kidneys, sliced
1 chicken liver, sliced
400 g/13 oz tomatoes, skinned and mashed
1 litre/1¾ pints Beef Stock (see page 141)
400 g/13 oz arborio rice
75 g/3 oz Parmesan cheese, freshly grated
salt and pepper

1 Heat the oil and half of the butter in a heavy-based saucepan add the onion and fry over a low heat for 5 minutes, until golden. Add the minced beef, kidneys and chicken liver, increase the heat and fry until browned, stirring. Add the tomatoes and season to taste, lower the heat and cook for 30 minutes. Place the stock in a saucepan and simmer gently.

2 Add the rice and mix well to coat each grain with the butter and oil. Add enough of the stock to just cover the rice, stir again and simmer gently, stirring as frequently as possible. When most of the liquid has been absorbed, add more stock; keep adding stock a little at a time, stirring and simmering gently until all the stock is absorbed.

3 When all the liquid has been absorbed and the rice is creamy, remove from the heat. Stir in the remaining butter and the Parmesan, and fold gently to mix. Leave to stand for 2 minutes, then serve.

Serves 4–6
Preparation time: 10 minutes
Cooking time: about 1 hour

country-style risotto

2 tablespoons olive oil
40 g/1½ oz butter
2 shallots, finely chopped
1 small onion, finely chopped
1 rosemary sprig, finely chopped
1 tablespoon finely chopped parsley
¼ teaspoon finely chopped marjoram
4 basil leaves, finely chopped
1 garlic clove, crushed
900 ml/1½ pints Vegetable Stock (see page 140)
375 g/12 oz arborio rice
50 ml/2 fl oz dry white wine
4 plum tomatoes, skinned
2 tablespoons single cream
salt and pepper

1 Heat the oil and butter in a large saucepan over a low heat, add the shallots and onion, the herbs and garlic, and simmer for 5 minutes, stirring occasionally. Place the stock in a saucepan and simmer gently.

2 Sprinkle the rice in the onion pan, allow it to turn golden, moisten with wine, and simmer until the liquid evaporates. Add the tomatoes, mashing with a fork.

3 Mix well and add enough of the stock to just cover the rice, stir again and simmer gently, stirring as frequently as possible. When most of the liquid has been absorbed, add more stock; keep adding stock a little at a time, stirring and simmering gently until all the stock is absorbed.

4 As the rice becomes creamy, add plenty of pepper and stir in the cream just before serving.

Serves 4
Preparation time: 5 minutes
Cooking time: 35–40 minutes

seafood risotto

1 litre/1¾ pints Fish, Chicken or Vegetable Stock
* (see pages 142, 141 and 140)*
good pinch of saffron threads
125 g/4 oz butter
2 tablespoons olive oil
3 shallots, chopped
1 garlic clove, chopped

300 g/10 oz arborio or carnaroli rice
125 g/4 oz small scallops, removed from their shells
125 g/4 oz prepared squid, cut into rings
125 g/4 oz cooked peeled prawns
2 tablespoons roughly chopped flat leaf parsley
75 ml/3 fl oz white wine or dry vermouth
125 g/4 oz Parmesan cheese, freshly grated
salt and pepper

1 Place the stock and saffron in a saucepan and simmer gently.

2 Melt half of the butter and the oil in another saucepan, add the shallots and garlic, and sauté for 5 minutes, but do not brown.

3 Add the rice and mix well to coat each grain with the butter and oil. Add enough of the stock to just cover the rice, stir again and simmer gently, stirring as frequently as possible. When most of the liquid has been absorbed, add more stock; keep adding stock a little at a time, stirring and simmering gently until all the stock is absorbed.

4 When half of the stock has been incorporated, add the scallops, squid and prawns, turn the heat up a little and continue to add the stock by the ladle; stir carefully so as not to break up the seafood.

5 When all the stock has been absorbed, add the parsley, the remaining butter, white wine or vermouth, and half of the Parmesan, and season with salt and pepper. Stir well. Serve garnished with the remaining Parmesan.

Serves 4
Preparation time: 10 minutes
Cooking time: 30 minutes

chicken risotto

1 kg/2 lb oven-ready chicken
2 litres/3½ pints water
2 celery sticks
2 onions
2 carrots
3–4 tablespoons olive oil
7 tablespoons white wine
375 g/12 oz tomatoes, skinned and mashed

500 g/1 lb arborio rice
75 g/3 oz butter, softened
75 g/3 oz Parmesan cheese, freshly grated
salt and pepper

1 Remove the bones from the chicken and place them in a large pan with the measured water. Add 1 celery stick, 1 onion and 1 carrot, and season liberally with salt and pepper. Bring to the boil, lower the heat, cover and simmer for 1½ hours. Strain the stock and keep hot.

2 Meanwhile, dice the chicken meat, removing all the skin, and finely chop the remaining vegetables.

3 Heat the oil in a large, deep frying pan, add the vegetables and fry gently until lightly coloured. Add the chicken and fry for a further 5 minutes, stirring constantly, then add the wine and boil until it evaporates.

4 Add the tomatoes and salt and pepper to taste. Cover and cook gently for 20 minutes, adding a little of the chicken stock if the mixture becomes dry.

5 Stir in the rice, then add 200 ml/7 fl oz chicken stock. Cook for 20–25 minutes until the rice is just tender, adding a little more stock to moisten, as necessary. Remove from the heat, add the butter and Parmesan, and fold in gently to mix. Serve immediately.

Serves 6
Preparation time: 35 minutes
Cooking time: 2¼ hours

grilled polenta with asparagus and parmesan

Parmesan shavings are best made with a mandoline, but you can also use a vegetable peeler. Shave the Parmesan straight on to the prepared dish, as the shavings are very fragile and do not handle well.

600 ml/1 pint water
150 g/5 oz quick-cooking polenta flour
50 g/2 oz butter
500 g/1 lb asparagus, trimmed
3 tablespoons olive oil
1 tablespoon balsamic vinegar
salt and pepper
125 g/4 oz Parmesan cheese, shaved, to garnish

1 Heat the measured water to a gentle simmer, pour in the polenta flour and beat well for 1–2 minutes until it is a smooth paste.

2 Turn the heat down and continue to cook the polenta for 6–8 minutes until it thickens, stirring constantly so that it does not catch on the bottom of the pan or form a skin on the top. When it is thick and cooked add the butter, season with salt and pepper, and mix well.

3 Turn the polenta on to a chopping board, roll out to 1.5 cm/¾ inch thick and leave to set for 5 minutes.

4 Heat a griddle pan until it is hot or preheat a grill to full heat. Cut the polenta into wedges, and cook on each side for 5 minutes. If you are using a griddle it will be easier to get a good colour, but this does not affect the taste.

5 Griddle or grill the asparagus for 4–5 minutes on a high heat, turning it as it colours.

6 Arrange the polenta on a warmed serving dish and place the asparagus on top. Drizzle with the olive oil and balsamic vinegar, shave the Parmesan on top, and serve.

Serves 4
Preparation time: 5 minutes
Cooking time: 25 minutes

griddled polenta with field mushrooms

1 litre/1¾ pints water
250 g/8 oz quick-cooking polenta flour
1 tablespoon olive oil
50 g/2 oz butter
375 g/12 oz field mushrooms, sliced
2 garlic cloves, chopped
1 bunch of thyme, chopped
2 tablespoons white wine
250 g/8 oz Parmesan cheese, shaved, to garnish
sea salt and pepper

1 Bring the measured water to the boil in a large saucepan, add the polenta, season with salt and pepper, and mix until smooth. Turn the heat down and continue to mix for about 5 minutes until the polenta thickens and the water has been absorbed. The mixture will become very thick and hard to work. Using a spatula, spread the polenta out on a chopping board, or in an oiled 23 cm/9 inch springform cake tin. Leave to cool for about 1 hour.

2 Heat the oil and butter in a small saucepan, add the mushrooms, garlic and thyme, and fry for 8 minutes, until soft and dark. Add the white wine and simmer for 2 minutes, then season. Remove from the heat and keep warm.

3 Heat a griddle pan, cut the polenta into slices or wedges, and griddle for about 4 minutes on each side. Arrange the polenta on individual plates with the mushroom mix spooned over one side. Shave the Parmesan on top and serve.

Serves 4
Preparation time: 35 minutes, plus cooling
Cooking time: 25 minutes

kedgeree

125 g/4 oz long-grain rice
500 g/1 lb smoked haddock fillet
2 eggs, hard-boiled
50 g/2 oz butter or margarine
2–3 tablespoons milk or single cream
salt and pepper
chopped parsley, to garnish

1 Cook the rice in boiling salted water for about 12 minutes, or according to the packet instructions, until each grain is dry and fluffy, then set aside.

2 Poach the haddock in a little water for 10 minutes, drain and break the fish into large flakes. Meanwhile, shell the eggs, cut half an egg into wedges for a garnish and chop the rest.

3 Heat the butter or margarine in a large frying pan, add the fish and the cooked rice and just enough milk or cream to moisten. Heat gently, stirring carefully, so the flakes of fish are not broken. Add the chopped eggs to the mixture and season to taste with salt and pepper.

4 Spoon on to a warmed dish, garnish with the egg wedges, sprinkle with the parsley, and serve.

Serves 4
Preparation time: 10 minutes
Cooking time: 20 minutes

paella

2 tablespoons olive oil
1 small oven-ready chicken, cut into 8 portions
125 g/4 oz fat pork or bacon, diced
1 large Spanish onion, chopped
2–3 garlic cloves
500 g/1 lb tomatoes, skinned and chopped
1 red pepper, cored, deseeded and sliced
250–300 g/8–10 oz arborio rice
600 ml/1 pint water
¼ teaspoon saffron threads or powdered saffron
75 g/3 oz chorizo sausage, or any spiced
  sausage, thinly sliced
12 cooked mussels on their half shells (see page 109)
12 large cooked peeled prawns, deveined (see page 111)
salt and pepper

1 Heat the oil in a paella pan or a large, deep frying pan, add the chicken and pork or bacon, and fry until golden and nearly tender. Remove from the pan, add the onion and garlic and cook for 5 minutes or until golden brown.

2 Put in the tomatoes and cook for 2–3 minutes, then add the red pepper and rice.

3 Continue to stir over a gentle heat for 1–2 minutes, mixing the rice with the onion mixture. Boil the measured water, add the saffron and pour over the rice. Season lightly.

4 Cook steadily until the rice is almost tender. Stir from time to time and make sure that you check the amount of liquid regularly. If necessary, add more boiling water.

5 Return the chicken and pork or bacon to the pan and continue cooking until almost ready to serve.

6 Add the sausage to the pan with the mussels and prawns and any extra seasoning required. Cook for 5–7 minutes, then serve straight from the pan.

Serves 4
Preparation time: 50 minutes
Cooking time: 35–40 minutes

fragrant rice with vegetables and cashew nuts

250 g/8 oz long-grain rice
1 cinnamon stick
seeds of 4–6 cardamom pods
3–4 cloves
3 tablespoons vegetable oil
1 green pepper, cored, deseeded and finely chopped
1 onion, finely chopped
1 garlic clove, crushed
125 g/4 oz button mushrooms, thinly sliced
125 g/4 oz frozen peas
175 ml/6 fl oz Vegetable Stock (see page 140), or water
2 carrots, peeled and grated
100 g/3½ oz cashew nuts
salt and pepper

1 Cook the rice in boiling salted water according to packet instructions, with the cinnamon stick, cardamom seeds and cloves until each grain is dry and fluffy. Drain and set aside, removing the spices.

2 Heat a wok or large frying pan until hot, add the oil and cook over a moderate heat until hot. Add the green pepper, onion and garlic, and stir-fry for 2–3 minutes or until slightly softened.

3 Add the mushrooms and peas, increase the heat to high and stir-fry for 3–4 minutes or until tender.

4 Add the cooked rice and stock or measured water and toss to mix with the vegetables, then stir in the carrots and about three-quarters of the nuts. Toss for a further minute. Add salt and pepper to taste, sprinkle with the remaining cashew nuts and serve immediately.

Serves 4
Preparation time: 40 minutes
Cooking time: 15–20 minutes

gingered rice with carrots and tomatoes

250 g/8 oz basmati rice, rinsed
4 tablespoons olive oil
2 garlic cloves, crushed
1 tablespoon grated fresh root ginger
4 carrots, thinly sliced
4 ripe tomatoes, skinned, deseeded and diced
2 cinnamon sticks, bruised
seeds from 3 cardamom pods, bruised
1 dried red chilli
1 tablespoon lemon juice
50 g/2 oz flaked almonds, toasted
salt and pepper

1 Cook the rice in plenty of boiling salted water for 8 minutes. Drain, refresh under cold water and drain again. Spread out on a large baking sheet and set aside to dry.

2 Heat the oil in a wok or large frying pan, add the garlic, ginger and carrots, and fry for 10 minutes. Add the tomatoes and spices, and cook for a further 5 minutes.

3 Stir in the rice, lemon juice and nuts and season to taste with salt and pepper. Stir-fry for 3–4 minutes until the rice is heated through. Serve immediately.

Serves 4
Preparation time: 20 minutes
Cooking time: 25 minutes

caribbean black-eyed beans and rice

2 tablespoons sunflower oil
1 small onion, finely chopped
1 garlic clove, crushed
1 teaspoon grated fresh root ginger
½ teaspoon hot paprika
¼ teaspoon black pepper
2 tomatoes, skinned and chopped
150 ml/¼ pint coconut milk
250 g/8 oz long-grain rice, rinsed

425 g/14 oz can black-eyed beans, drained
600 ml/1 pint Vegetable Stock (see page 140)
1 teaspoon salt
parsley, to garnish

1 Heat the oil in a large saucepan, add the onion, garlic, ginger, paprika and pepper, and fry for 5 minutes, stirring frequently. Add the tomatoes and coconut milk, and simmer gently for 10 minutes.

2 Add the remaining ingredients, bring to the boil, cover and simmer over a low heat for 15 minutes. Remove the saucepan from the heat and leave to stand for 10 minutes. Stir well, taste and adjust the seasoning, garnish with the parsley, and serve.

Serves 4
Preparation time: 10 minutes
Cooking time: 30 minutes, plus standing

trinidad chicken pilau

2 kg/4 lb chicken, cut into pieces
3 tablespoons groundnut oil
15 g/½ oz butter
1 onion, finely chopped
2 garlic cloves, crushed
1 red pepper, deseeded and chopped
1 red chilli pepper, deseeded and finely chopped
375 g/12 oz long-grain rice
2 tomatoes, skinned and chopped
900 ml/1½ pints Chicken Stock (see page 141)
few saffron strands
1 thyme sprig

Seasoning:
1 teaspoon dried mixed herbs
2 allspice berries
1 garlic clove
salt and pepper

To garnish:
50 g/2 oz roasted peanuts
chopped red chilli

1 First prepare the seasoning. Put the mixed herbs, allspice and garlic into a mortar with salt and pepper and pound well with a pestle until all the ingredients are well blended. Rub this mixture all over the chicken pieces and leave in a cool place or the refrigerator for several hours or overnight.

2 Heat the oil and butter in a large, deep frying pan, add the seasoned chicken pieces and fry over a moderate heat, turning several times, until they are golden brown all over. Remove from the pan and keep warm.

3 Add the onion, garlic, red pepper and chilli to the pan, and fry over gentle heat until softened but not browned. Add the rice to the pan and turn in the oil until all the grains are glistening. Stir in the tomatoes, stock, strands of saffron and thyme.

4 Return the chicken to the pan, cover and simmer for about 20 minutes, or until the rice is tender and has absorbed all the liquid, and the chicken is cooked. Keep checking the pan and stirring the rice to prevent it sticking. Add more liquid if necessary. Sprinkle with peanuts and chilli, and serve hot.

Serves 6
Preparation time: 10 minutes, plus marinating
Cooking time: 40 minutes

nut and rice roast

Nut roasts have the unfortunate reputation of being the epitome of a dull vegetarian meal: a poor substitute for meat. This one is moist, nutty and very tasty, and is sure to please even meat-eaters.

15 g/½ oz dried ceps
25 g/1 oz butter
1 onion, very finely chopped
2 celery sticks, very finely chopped
1 garlic clove, crushed
250 g/8 oz button mushrooms, very finely chopped
2 tablespoons chopped parsley
1 tablespoon chopped thyme
175 g/6 oz cooked brown rice
125 g/4 oz each cashew nuts and hazelnuts, toasted and
*   coarsely ground*
50 g/2 oz walnuts, toasted and coarsely ground
125 g/4 oz Gruyère or Cheddar cheese, freshly grated
1 egg, beaten
salt and pepper
oregano, to garnish

1 Pour a little boiling water over the ceps and leave to soak for 30 minutes. Drain and slice the ceps.

2 Melt the butter in a frying pan, add the onion, celery and garlic, and fry for 5 minutes. Stir in the ceps, mushrooms, herbs and rice, and fry, stirring frequently for a further 5 minutes until all the liquid from the mushrooms has evaporated.

3 Transfer the mixture to a large bowl and stir in all the remaining ingredients until evenly combined, and season with salt and pepper. Press into a greased and base lined 1 kg/2 lb loaf tin and smooth the surface. Place in a preheated oven, 190°C (375°F), Gas Mark 5, for 1–1¼ hours until it feels firm and a skewer inserted into the centre comes out clean.

4 Cover the tin with foil and let the loaf rest for 15 minutes. Turn out and slice. Garnish with oregano and serve hot.

Serves 6–8
Preparation time: 30 minutes, plus soaking and resting
Cooking time: 1½ hours
Oven temperature: 190°C (375°F), Gas Mark 5

rice with tomatoes, avocado and black olives

4 tablespoons olive oil
1 small onion, finely chopped
2 plump garlic cloves, crushed
250 g/8 oz basmati rice, rinsed and drained
450 ml/¾ pint Vegetable Stock (see page 140)
1 tomato, deseeded and diced
2 spring onions, including some green, chopped
2 tablespoons chopped parsley
50 g/2 oz black olives, pitted
1 small avocado, diced
salt and pepper

1 Heat 2 tablespoons of the oil in a saucepan, add the onion and garlic, and cook for 1 minute. Add the rice and stir for 2 minutes, then add the stock and bring to the boil. Stir the rice, cover the pan and simmer very gently, without lifting the lid, for about 12 minutes until the rice is just tender.

2 Meanwhile, heat the remaining oil in a frying pan. Add the tomato, spring onions, parsley and salt and pepper, and simmer for 5 minutes. Remove the pan from the heat and stir in the olives and avocado.

3 Fluff up the rice with a fork and carefully stir in the tomato mixture. Serve hot or cold.

Serves 4
Preparation time: 10 minutes
Cooking time: 20–25 minutes

prawn pilau

375 g/12 oz basmati rice
6 tablespoons ghee or vegetable oil
1 tablespoon coriander seeds, crushed
½ teaspoon turmeric
1 small pineapple, cubed, or 250 g/8 oz can pineapple
  cubes, drained
250 g/8 oz cooked peeled prawns
1 teaspoon salt
about 600 ml/1 pint Fish Stock (see page 142)

To garnish:
2 tablespoons ghee or vegetable oil
2 tablespoons sultanas
2 tablespoons cashew nuts
2 hard-boiled eggs, quartered
2 tablespoons chopped fresh coriander

1 Wash the rice under cold running water and drain thoroughly.

2 Heat the ghee or vegetable oil in a large saucepan, add the coriander seeds and fry for 30 seconds. Add the turmeric and stir for a few seconds, then add the pineapple and stir-fry for 30 seconds. Add the prawns, rice and salt. (If using a stock cube, omit the salt.) Stir-fry for 1 minute, then pour in enough stock to cover the rice by 5 mm/¼ inch. Bring to the boil, cover tightly and cook very gently for 25 minutes or until all the liquid has been absorbed and the rice is cooked.

3 Meanwhile, prepare the garnish. Heat the ghee or vegetable oil in a small frying pan and then fry the sultanas and cashews for 1–2 minutes until the sultanas are plump and the nuts lightly coloured.

4 Transfer the rice to a warmed serving dish and gently fork in the sultanas and nuts. Arrange the egg quarters around the edge, sprinkle the coriander on top, and serve hot.

Serves 6
Preparation time: 10 minutes
Cooking time: about 45 minutes

vegetable and panir biriyani

500 g/1 lb basmati rice
3 tablespoons ghee or vegetable oil
1 large onion, finely chopped
2 garlic cloves, chopped
8 cloves
2 x 2.5 cm/1 inch cinnamon sticks
4 green cardamoms
1 teaspoon turmeric
1 teaspoon garam masala
250 g/8 oz mixed diced vegetables (carrots, cauliflower,
  courgettes, okra, peas)
600 ml/1 pint Vegetable Stock (see page 140)
50 g/2 oz panir (curd cheese), diced and lightly fried
50 g/2 oz sultanas
125 g/4 oz chopped mixed nuts (almonds, cashew nuts,
  pistachios)
salt

1 Wash the rice under cold running water and drain thoroughly.

2 Heat the ghee or vegetable oil in a large saucepan, add the onion and fry until golden. Remove half of the fried onion and set aside for the garnish. Add the garlic and spices to the pan and fry for 2–3 minutes.

3 Rinse the rice thoroughly under cold running water, then drain well. Add to the pan and stir well. Cook for a further 5 minutes until all the grains are glistening and translucent.

4 Add the mixed diced vegetables and salt to taste, together with the stock, and bring to the boil. Cover the pan and reduce the heat to a bare simmer. Cook gently for 20–25 minutes until all the liquid has been absorbed and the rice is cooked.

5 Stir in the panir, sultanas and nuts, and mix well. Cover and cook for 5 minutes over a low heat until all the moisture has evaporated. Serve hot, sprinkled with the reserved fried onion.

Serves 4–6
Preparation time: 15 minutes
Cooking time: 40–45 minutes

indian saffron rice

Edible silver leaf is used for decorative purposes. It is very fragile and should therefore be handled with care. It is available from specialist Indian food stores, though you may have to order it.

½ teaspoon saffron threads
750 ml/1¼ pints boiling water
175 g/6 oz ghee or 3 tablespoons vegetable oil
2 large onions, sliced
375 g/12 oz basmati or patna rice
1 teaspoon cloves
4 cardamoms
1 teaspoon salt
1 teaspoon freshly ground black pepper
silver leaf, to garnish (optional)

1 Put the saffron threads in a small bowl with 1 tablespoon of the boiling water and leave to soak for 30 minutes. Heat the ghee or vegetable oil in a large heavy-based saucepan, add the onions and fry gently for 4–5 minutes until soft.

2 Wash the rice thoroughly under cold running water and drain well. Add to the onions in the pan, then stir in the cloves, cardamoms, salt and pepper. Fry for 3 minutes, stirring frequently.

3 Pour the remaining boiling water into the pan, together with the saffron and its soaking liquid, then lower the heat and simmer for 15–20 minutes until the rice is cooked.

4 Drain well, transfer the rice to a serving dish, garnish with silver leaf, if liked, and serve hot.

Serves 4
Preparation time: 15 minutes, plus soaking
Cooking time: 30–35 minutes

pilau rice with sultanas and nuts

2 tablespoons ghee or vegetable oil
6 cardamoms, bruised
5 whole cloves
2 x 3 cm/1½ inch cinnamon sticks
½ teaspoon black peppercorns, lightly crushed
¼ teaspoon saffron threads
375 g/12 oz basmati rice, rinsed and drained
¾ teaspoon salt
½ teaspoon orange flower water (optional)
600 ml/1 pint water
25 g/1 oz sultanas
25 g/1 oz cashew nuts, toasted
25 g/1 oz pistachio nuts

1 Heat the ghee or vegetable oil in a wide heavy-based saucepan, add the cardamoms, cloves, cinnamon sticks and peppercorns, and fry over a gentle heat for 2 minutes, until fragrant, stirring constantly. Add the saffron threads and rice to the pan and fry for a further minute, stirring constantly.

2 Add the salt, orange flower water, if using, and measured water. Stir well to mix. Bring to the boil, then reduce the heat, cover the pan and cook the rice gently for 15 minutes without removing the lid.

3 Remove the pan from the heat and lightly loosen the rice grains with a fork. (All the water should have been absorbed.) Stir the sultanas into the rice, cover the pan with a clean, dry tea towel and allow the rice to cook in its own heat for a further 5 minutes.

4 Stir the cashew nuts and pistachios into the rice just before serving. Serve hot.

Serves 4–6
Preparation time: 10 minutes
Cooking time: 25 minutes

chicken biriyani

2 tablespoons ghee or vegetable oil
1 large onion, finely chopped
1.5 kg/3 lb chicken, jointed
2 garlic cloves, chopped
6 cloves
2 x 2.5 cm/1 inch cinnamon sticks
4 green cardamoms
2 teaspoons turmeric
1 teaspoon garam masala
500 g/1 lb basmati rice, rinsed and drained
600 ml/1 pint Chicken Stock (see page 141)
50 g/2 oz sultanas
50 g/2 oz chopped almonds
salt

1 Heat the ghee or vegetable oil in a large saucepan, add the onion and fry until golden. Remove the fried onion and set aside. Add the chicken pieces to the pan and brown on all sides; cook until almost tender. Add the garlic and spices to the pan and fry for 2–3 minutes. Return half the onion to the pan.

2 Add the rice to the pan and stir well. Cook for a further 5 minutes until all the grains are glistening and translucent.

3 Add salt to taste, together with the stock, and bring to the boil. Cover the pan and reduce the heat to a bare simmer. Cook gently for 20–25 minutes until all the liquid has been absorbed and the rice and chicken are cooked through.

4 Stir in the sultanas and almonds and mix well. Cover and cook for 5 minutes over a low heat until all the moisture has evaporated. Sprinkle with the reserved fried onion and serve hot.

Serves 4–6
Preparation time: 15 minutes
Cooking time: 1 hour

green couscous

300 ml/½ pint olive oil
125 ml/4 fl oz lemon juice
500 g/1 lb cooked couscous
2 bunches of spring onions, chopped
125 g/4 oz rocket, chopped
1 cucumber, halved, deseeded and chopped
salt and pepper

1 Whisk or shake together the oil and lemon juice. Season to taste with salt and pepper.

2 Tip the couscous into a warmed serving dish. Stir in the spring onions, rocket, cucumber, and oil and lemon juice dressing, and serve immediately.

Serves 6
Preparation time: 10 minutes
Cooking time: 10 minutes

couscous and pepper pilaf

3 tablespoons olive oil
1 red onion or small onion, finely chopped
2 plump garlic cloves, crushed
1 red chilli, deseeded and finely chopped
1 red pepper, cored, deseeded and cut lengthways
   into 8 pieces
1 yellow pepper, cored, deseeded and cut lengthways
   into 8 pieces
paprika
250 g/8 oz couscous
300 ml/½ pint boiling Vegetable Stock (see page 140)
small handful of coriander leaves, chopped, to serve
salt

1 Heat the oil in a saucepan, add the onion and cook until it begins to soften. Stir in the garlic, chilli and peppers. Cook for 3–4 minutes, then season to taste with paprika and cook for 1 minute.

2 Add the couscous, give it a good stir, then add the boiling stock. Bring back to the boil, then simmer gently, uncovered, for about 15 minutes until most of the stock has been absorbed and the peppers are tender; if the pilaf becomes too dry add a little more stock or water.

3 Add salt to taste, stir in the coriander, and serve.

Serves 2–4
Preparation time: 10 minutes
Cooking time: 25 minutes

pumpkin and couscous pilaf

150 g/5 oz couscous
200 ml/7 fl oz water
½ teaspoon saffron threads
250 ml/8 fl oz Vegetable Stock (see page 140)
4 tablespoons olive oil
1 onion, finely chopped
400 g/13 oz pumpkin, diced
long strip of lemon rind
1 cinnamon stick
2 bay leaves
125 g/4 oz flaked almonds
salt and pepper
mint or dill, to garnish

1 Put the couscous into a bowl. Pour over the measured water and leave to soak for 15 minutes. Add the saffron to the stock and set aside to soak.

2 Heat 3 tablespoons of the oil in a saucepan, add the onion and fry until translucent. Add the pumpkin and fry until the onion and pumpkin are lightly coloured.

3 Drain the couscous and add to the pan with the saffron stock, lemon rind, cinnamon, bay leaves, and salt and pepper. Bring to the boil, then simmer very gently, uncovered, for about 15 minutes until most of the liquid has been absorbed.

4 Meanwhile, heat the remaining oil in a heavy-based frying pan, add the almonds and cook, stirring frequently, until evenly browned.

5 Remove the cinnamon, bay leaves and lemon rind from the pilaf, if liked, then fork in the almonds. Garnish with mint or dill, and serve.

Serves 2–4
Preparation time: 15 minutes
Cooking time: 25 minutes

couscous with roast vegetables

2 aubergines, cut into 5 cm/2 inch chunks
2 courgettes, cut into 5 cm/2 inch chunks
1 red pepper, cored, deseeded and cut lengthways into 6 pieces
1 yellow pepper, cored, deseeded and cut lengthways into 6 pieces
1 fennel head, root end intact, cut into 6 wedges
3 red onions, root ends intact, each cut into 6 wedges
4 tablespoons olive oil
3 garlic cloves, crushed
2–3 dashes of Tabasco sauce
750 ml/1¼ pints Vegetable Stock (see page 140)
500 g/1 lb couscous
1 onion, finely diced
salt and pepper

1 Put the aubergines, courgettes, red and yellow peppers, fennel and red onions into a roasting tin. Add 3 tablespoons of the olive oil, 2 of the garlic cloves, the Tabasco sauce, and pepper. Stir all the ingredients, then roast for about 35 minutes in a preheated oven, 240°C (475°F), Gas Mark 9, until the vegetables are charred and tender.

2 Meanwhile, bring the stock to the boil in a saucepan, add the couscous, stir, then cover the pan and remove from the heat. Leave to stand until all of the stock has been absorbed.

3 Heat the remaining oil in a frying pan, add the diced onion and fry until tender and golden, adding the remaining garlic towards the end. Stir the onion mixture into the couscous and season to taste with salt and pepper.

4 Pile the roast vegetables on top of the couscous and serve immediately.

Serves 6
Preparation time: 20 minutes
Cooking time: 35 minutes
Oven temperature: 240°C (475°F), Gas Mark 9

saffron millet and lentils with radicchio

pinch of saffron threads
300 ml/1½ pints boiling Vegetable Stock (see page 140)
125 g/4 oz Puy lentils, rinsed
125 g/4 oz millet
50 g/2 oz butter
1 leek, sliced
2 garlic cloves, sliced
1 teaspoon ground cinnamon
50 g/2 oz currants
1 small radicchio head, shredded
salt and pepper

1 Soak the saffron threads in the boiling stock for 10 minutes.

2 Meanwhile, put the lentils in a saucepan and add water to cover the lentils by about 2.5 cm/1 inch. Bring to the boil and boil rapidly for 8–10 minutes, then drain.

3 Place the millet in a small frying pan and heat gently until the grains start to turn golden.

4 Melt the butter in a saucepan, add the leek, garlic and cinnamon, and fry for 3 minutes. Stir in the lentils and millet, then pour in the saffron stock. Bring to the boil, cover and simmer gently for 30 minutes, until the lentils and millet are tender.

5 Stir in the currants and shredded radicchio and heat through for 5 minutes. Season to taste with salt and pepper and serve immediately.

Serves 4–6
Preparation time: 10 minutes, plus soaking
Cooking time: 50 minutes

baked buckwheat and spiced butter

75 g/3 oz unsalted butter, softened
1 small garlic clove, crushed
2 tablespoons chopped coriander leaves
¼ teaspoon ground cumin
¼ teaspoon ground cinnamon
pinch of chilli powder
250 g/8 oz buckwheat, roasted
450 ml/¾ pint boiling Vegetable Stock (see page 140)
sea salt

1 In a small bowl, beat together the butter, garlic, coriander and spices until evenly combined. Cover and leave for at least 30 minutes.

2 Use a little of the spiced butter to grease an ovenproof dish. Put in the roasted buckwheat and pour over the boiling stock. Cover with a tight-fitting lid and place in a preheated oven, 200°C (400°F), Gas Mark 6, for 15 minutes.

3 Remove the dish from the oven and leave to stand for 5 minutes. Stir in the remaining spiced butter and sea salt to taste, and serve immediately.

Serves 4–6
Preparation time: 10 minutes, plus standing
Cooking time: 15 minutes
Oven temperature: 200°C (400°F), Gas Mark 6

barley bake with squash, mushroom and rosemary

175 g/6 oz pearl barley
600 ml/1 pint boiling Vegetable Stock (see page 140)
25 g/1 oz butter, plus extra for greasing
1 onion, sliced
500 g/1 lb peeled squash, cubed
250 g/8 oz shiitake or button mushrooms, halved if large
2 tablespoons chopped rosemary
½ teaspoon cayenne pepper
200 g/7 oz canned chopped tomatoes
150 ml/¼ pint single cream

50 g/2 oz Gruyère or Cheddar cheese, freshly grated
salt and pepper
chopped parsley, to garnish

1 Rinse the barley for several minutes under cold running water, drain well and shake dry. Place in a saucepan, pour over the boiling stock and bring back to the boil. Cover the pan and simmer gently for 40 minutes until the stock is absorbed and the barley is tender.

2 Melt the butter in a frying pan, add the sliced onion and fry over a low heat for 5 minutes, stirring occasionally, until soft but not browned. Add the squash, mushrooms and rosemary to the pan, and fry for a further 5 minutes. Stir into the barley with the remaining ingredients, except the parsley, until evenly combined.

3 Transfer the barley mixture to a greased baking dish and place in a preheated oven, 200°C (400°F), Gas Mark 6, for 20 minutes until golden and bubbling. Garnish with chopped parsley, and serve.

Serves 4–6
Preparation time: 25 minutes
Cooking time: 1 hour
Oven temperature: 200°C (400°F), Gas Mark 6

special egg-fried rice

2–3 eggs
2 spring onions, finely chopped
2 teaspoons salt
3 tablespoons vegetable oil
125 g/4 oz cooked peeled prawns
125 g/4 oz cooked chicken or pork, diced
50 g/2 oz canned bamboo shoots, diced
4 tablespoons fresh or frozen peas, cooked
1 tablespoon light soy sauce
375–500 g/12 oz–1 lb cold, cooked long-grain rice
chopped spring onions, to garnish

1 Break the eggs into a small bowl and add 1 teaspoon of the finely chopped spring onions and a pinch of the salt. Beat lightly together with a fork to combine them.

2 Heat about 1 tablespoon of the oil in a wok or large frying pan, add the beaten egg mixture and cook, stirring constantly, until the eggs are scrambled and set. Remove the scrambled eggs and set aside in a bowl.

3 Heat the remaining oil in the wok or pan, add the prawns, meat, bamboo shoots, peas and the remaining chopped spring onions, and stir-fry briskly for 1 minute, then stir in the soy sauce.

4 Stir-fry for 2–3 minutes, then add the cooked rice, breaking it up, together with the scrambled eggs and the remaining salt. Stir well to break up the scrambled eggs into small pieces and separate the grains of rice. Garnish with spring onions, and serve hot.

Serves 4
Preparation time: 15 minutes
Cooking time: 8–10 minutes

fried rice with ham and bean sprouts

2 tablespoons sunflower oil
2 spring onions, finely chopped
1 garlic clove, crushed
375 g/12 oz cold, cooked long-grain rice
175 g/6 oz cooked ham, diced
2 tablespoons light soy sauce
2 eggs
250 g/8 oz bean sprouts, rinsed and drained
salt and pepper

1 Heat the oil in a wok or large frying pan over a moderate heat, add the spring onions and garlic, and stir-fry for 2 minutes. Add the rice and stir well. Cook gently, stirring as the rice heats through.

2 Stir in the ham and soy sauce.

3 Beat the eggs with salt and pepper to taste. Pour into the rice mixture in a thin stream, stirring all the time. Add the bean sprouts and continue cooking, stirring until all the ingredients are hot and the eggs are set. Serve immediately.

Serves 4
Preparation time: 15 minutes
Cooking time: 8–10 minutes

spicy fried rice with red chillies

375 g/12 oz long-grain rice
2 tablespoons sunflower oil
4 shallots or 1 onion, thinly sliced
2 red chillies, deseeded and thinly sliced
50 g/2 oz chopped pork, beef or bacon
1 tablespoon light soy sauce
1 teaspoon tomato purée
salt

To garnish:
few slices of fried onion
1 plain omelette, made with 1 egg, cut into strips
coriander leaves
cucumber slices

1 Cook the rice according to packet instructions and keep hot.

2 Heat the oil in a wok or large frying pan, add the shallots and chillies, and fry for 1–3 minutes. Add the meat and fry for 3 minutes, stirring constantly. Add the rice, soy sauce and tomato purée and stir-fry for 5–8 minutes, then season to taste with salt.

3 Transfer to a warmed serving dish, garnish with the onion, omelette, coriander and cucumber, and serve immediately.

Serves 4
Preparation time: 15 minutes
Cooking time: about 30 minutes

fried rice with pork

2 tablespoons vegetable oil
1 garlic clove, crushed
150 g/5 oz pork fillet, sliced
3 tablespoons light soy sauce
2 eggs
1 tablespoon tomato purée
1 tablespoon sugar
1 small onion, sliced
750 g/1½ lb cold, cooked long-grain rice

To garnish:
¼ cucumber, thinly sliced
1 lemon, cut into wedges
2 tablespoons chopped coriander
1 red chilli, deseeded and shredded

1 Heat the oil in a wok or large frying pan, add the garlic and stir-fry for 1 minute.

2 Add the pork fillet and 1 teaspoon of the soy sauce and stir-fry for 5 minutes over a moderate heat.

3 Break the eggs into the wok or pan and cook for 2 minutes, stirring vigorously. Add the tomato purée, sugar, the remaining soy sauce and the sliced onion. Stir-fry briskly for 1 minute.

4 Add the rice and continue stir-frying for 5 minutes. Transfer the mixture to a warmed serving dish or 4 warmed plates and garnish with the sliced cucumber, lemon wedges, chopped coriander and shredded red chilli. Serve immediately.

Serves 4
Preparation time: 10–15 minutes
Cooking time: 15 minutes

indonesian spiced coconut rice

375 g/12 oz basmati rice
125 g/4 oz creamed coconut, chopped
750 ml/1¼ pints boiling water
7 cm/3 inch piece of lemon grass, halved lengthways
2 x 2.5 cm/1 inch pieces of cinnamon stick
4 curry leaves
½ teaspoon grated nutmeg
¼ teaspoon ground cloves
1 teaspoon salt
pinch of pepper

1 Wash the rice thoroughly under cold water. Drain and place in a large heavy-based saucepan. Dissolve the creamed coconut in the measured water, and add to the rice with the lemon grass, cinnamon, curry leaves, nutmeg, cloves and salt and pepper.

2 Bring the rice to the boil and then boil, uncovered, over a moderate heat for 8 minutes, stirring frequently, until almost all the liquid is absorbed.

3 Reduce the heat to low, cover the pan with a tight-fitting lid and cook the rice very gently for a further 10 minutes.

4 Remove the pan from the heat and, working quickly, loosen the rice grains with a fork. Cover the pan with a clean, dry tea towel and allow the rice to cook in its own heat for a further 15 minutes. Serve immediately.

Serves 6
Preparation time: 5 minutes
Cooking time: 35 minutes

thai rice with vegetables and chilli

375 g/12 oz rice
1 tablespoon groundnut oil
4 garlic cloves, chopped
4 large red chillies, sliced
50 g/2 oz drained canned straw mushrooms
50 g/2 oz oyster mushrooms, torn
125 g/4 oz drained canned bamboo shoots
1 teaspoon sugar
½ teaspoon salt
1 teaspoon soy sauce
coriander sprigs, to garnish

1 Cook the rice according to the packet instructions.

2 Meanwhile, heat the oil in a wok, add the garlic and chillies, and stir-fry for 30 seconds. Add the mushrooms and bamboo shoots and stir-fry again for 1 minute, then lower the heat and add the sugar, salt and soy sauce. Give the mixture another good stir, then taste and adjust the seasoning.

3 Transfer the rice to a warmed serving bowl, top with the vegetables, garnish with coriander, and serve.

Serves 4
Preparation time: 8 minutes
Cooking time: 15 minutes

thai fried rice with beans and tofu

groundnut oil, for deep-frying
125 g/4 oz block ready-fried tofu, diced
2 eggs
250 g/8 oz cold, cooked long-grain rice
3 teaspoons sugar
1½ tablespoons soy sauce
2 teaspoons crushed dried chillies
1 teaspoon Thai fish sauce or salt
125 g/4 oz green beans, finely chopped
25 g/1 oz deep-fried mint leaves, to garnish

1 Heat the oil for deep-frying in a wok or large frying pan, add the tofu and deep-fry over a moderate heat until golden brown on all sides. Remove from the oil with a slotted spoon, drain on kitchen paper and set aside.

2 Pour the oil out of the wok or pan, leaving behind about 2 tablespoonfuls. Heat this oil until hot, then crack the eggs into it, breaking the yolks and stirring them around.

3 Add the rice, sugar, soy sauce, chillies and fish sauce, increase the heat to high, and stir-fry vigorously for 1 minute.

4 Lower the heat and add the green beans and tofu. Increase the heat again and stir-fry vigorously for 1 minute.

5 Transfer to a warmed serving dish, garnish with deep-fried mint leaves, and serve.

Serves 4
Preparation time: 15 minutes
Cooking time: 6 minutes

crispy rice vermicelli

vegetable oil, for deep-frying
150 g/5 oz rice vermicelli
6 tablespoons vegetable oil
1 egg, beaten
1 tablespoon sliced shallots
1 tablespoon sliced garlic
50 g/2 oz raw prawns, peeled and deveined
  (see page 111) and halved lengthways
50 g/2 oz chicken breast, thinly sliced
2 tablespoons tamarind water
4 tablespoons brown sugar
1 tablespoon salted soya bean flavouring
1 tablespoon Thai fish sauce

To garnish:
1 red chilli, deseeded and sliced
2 tablespoons chopped coriander leaves

1 Heat the oil in a wok or large frying pan to 180–190°C (350–375°F). It will be ready when a piece of vermicelli, dropped into the wok, pops open immediately. Deep-fry the vermicelli in batches until it pops and turns a rich creamy colour. Remove with a slotted spoon, drain on kitchen paper and keep warm without covering, or it will become soft.

2 Heat a little of the vegetable oil in a small pan and add the beaten egg, tilting the pan until it covers the base. Remove the omelette when it is set and cooked, and roll up and cut into thin strips. Keep them warm.

3 Heat the remaining oil in the wok, add the shallots and garlic, and stir-fry until tender and golden. Remove, drain on kitchen paper and keep warm. Add the prawns and sliced chicken to the wok or pan and stir-fry for 5 minutes. Drain off any excess oil.

4 Stir in the tamarind water, sugar, soya bean flavouring and fish sauce. Cook for 5 minutes until sticky. Add the vermicelli, shallots and garlic to the wok, mix well and cook over a very low heat for 2–3 minutes. Transfer to a serving dish, top with the omelette strips, garnish with sliced chilli and coriander, and serve.

Serves 4
Preparation time: 15 minutes
Cooking time: 17–18 minutes

rice vermicelli in coconut milk

250 g/8 oz soaked rice vermicelli
2 teaspoons vegetable oil
2 eggs, beaten
575 ml/18 fl oz coconut milk
½ onion, roughly chopped
250 g/8 oz raw prawns, peeled and deveined
  (see page 111)
4 tablespoons salted soya bean flavouring
2 tablespoons sugar
2 tablespoons tamarind juice or 1 tablespoon lemon juice
300 g/10 oz bean sprouts
125 g/4 oz spring onions, chopped

To garnish:
3 tablespoons chopped coriander leaves
2 red chillies, deseeded and sliced
1 lemon, sliced lengthways

1 Bring a large saucepan of water to the boil, add the soaked rice vermicelli and cook, stirring occasionally, for 15 minutes. Drain well and set aside.

2 Heat a little of the vegetable oil in a small pan and add the beaten egg, tilting the pan until it covers the base. Remove the omelette when it is set and cooked, and roll up and cut into thin strips. Keep them warm.

3 Bring the coconut milk to the boil in a wok or large frying pan. Cook over a high heat for 10 minutes until a film of oil forms on top. Stir in the onion, prawns, soya bean flavouring, sugar and tamarind or lemon juice. Cook for 5 minutes, then transfer half of the mixture to a bowl and keep warm.

4 Add the reserved vermicelli to the mixture in the wok. Mix well and cook for 5 minutes. Stir in half of the bean sprouts and spring onions. Pile the vermicelli mixture on to a serving dish and top with the reserved prawn mixture and shredded omelette. Garnish with coriander, chillies and lemon slices, and serve with the remaining bean sprouts and spring onions.

Serves 4
Preparation time: 15 minutes
Cooking time: 45 minutes

szechuan noodles

350 g/12 oz thin egg noodles
250 g/8 oz minced pork
2 tablespoons dark soy sauce
1 tablespoon dry sherry
½ teaspoon salt
4 tablespoons groundnut or vegetable oil
3 garlic cloves, crushed
2.5 cm/1 inch piece of fresh root ginger, peeled and finely chopped
3 spring onions, chopped
1–2 red chillies, deseeded and finely chopped
1 tablespoon hot soy bean paste
1 tablespoon peanut butter
175 ml/6 fl oz Chicken Stock (see page 141)
pepper
1 red chilli, deseeded and chopped, to garnish

1 Cook the egg noodles according to packet instructions until tender.

2 Meanwhile, put the minced pork into a bowl with the soy sauce, sherry and salt, and mix well to coat the pork thoroughly. Heat the oil in a wok or large frying pan, add the pork and stir-fry until lightly browned. Remove with a slotted spoon and drain on kitchen paper.

3 Add the garlic, ginger, spring onions and chillies to the wok or pan and stir-fry for 1 minute. Add the hot soy bean paste and peanut butter and stir well over a moderate heat for a few seconds.

4 Add the stock, bring to the boil and then simmer for about 5 minutes until thickened. Stir in the pork and continue cooking over a low heat for 1 minute.

5 Drain the noodles well and divide among 4 individual bowls or place in 1 large one. Ladle the sauce over the noodles, sprinkle with plenty of pepper, garnish with chopped chilli, and serve.

Serves 4
Preparation time: 15 minutes
Cooking time: 10 minutes

fried noodles with chicken, seafood and vegetables

4 tablespoons vegetable oil
2 garlic cloves, crushed
125 g/4 oz medium-sized egg noodles, soaked and drained
2 teaspoons dark soy sauce
125 g/4 oz mixed sliced chicken breast, prepared squid (see page 107) and cooked peeled prawns
½ teaspoon pepper
2 tablespoons Thai fish sauce
125 g/4 oz mixed shredded cabbage and broccoli florets
300 ml/½ pint Chicken Stock (see page 141)
1 tablespoon cornflour
2 tablespoons water
1 tablespoon salted soya bean flavouring
2 tablespoons sugar

1 Heat half of the oil in a wok or large frying pan, add half of the garlic and stir-fry for 1 minute until golden. Add the noodles and soy sauce, and cook for 3–5 minutes, stirring. Transfer to a serving dish and keep warm.

2 Heat the remaining oil in the wok or pan and stir-fry the rest of the garlic for 1 minute until golden. Add the chicken breast, squid and prawn mixture, pepper and fish sauce, and stir-fry for 5 minutes.

3 Add the shredded cabbage and broccoli florets and stir-fry for 3 minutes.

4 Stir in the stock. Mix the cornflour with the measured water and stir into the wok or pan. Add the soya bean flavouring and sugar and bring to the boil. Lower the heat and cook for 3 minutes, stirring constantly. Pour the thickened sauce over the noodles and serve immediately.

Serves 4
Preparation time: 10 minutes
Cooking time: 20 minutes

egg noodles in yellow bean sauce

375 g/12 oz egg noodles
3 tablespoons yellow bean paste
2 teaspoons chilli sauce
1 garlic clove, crushed
3 tablespoons oil
2 green peppers, cored, deseeded and thinly sliced
1 onion, thinly sliced
150 g/5 oz bean sprouts
salt

1 Cook the noodles in salted boiling water for 5 minutes, then drain.

2 Mix together the yellow bean paste, chilli sauce and garlic.

3 Heat the oil in a wok or large frying pan on a high heat, add the peppers, onion and bean sprouts, and stir-fry for 2 minutes.

4 Add the noodles and stir in the sauce mixture. Heat through, transfer to a warmed serving dish, and serve.

Serves 4
Preparation time: 10 minutes
Cooking time: 5 minutes

prawn vermicelli

50 g/2 oz pork belly fat
8 tablespoons milk
1 teaspoon dark soy sauce
3 tablespoons oyster sauce
1 teaspoon chopped garlic
5 black peppercorns, crushed
15 g/½ oz coriander leaves, stalk and root
20 g/¾ oz fresh root ginger, peeled and cut into thin strips
125 g/4 oz bean thread vermicelli, soaked
12 large raw prawns, peeled and deveined, tails left intact (see page 111)
2 tablespoons Fish Stock (see page 142) (optional)
coriander sprigs, to garnish

1 Heat the fat in a wok or large frying pan over a high heat until the oil runs, stirring occasionally. Remove from the heat and set aside. Discard the fat but leave the oil in the wok or pan.

2 Meanwhile, combine the milk, soy sauce and oyster sauce in a bowl.

3 When the oil has cooled down a bit – about 5 minutes – add the garlic, peppercorns, coriander and ginger, and stir-fry for 30 seconds. Add the vermicelli and milk mixture, stir together thoroughly over a high heat, then reduce the heat to low, cover the wok or pan and cook for 12 minutes.

4 Turn up the heat, add the prawns, and the stock if the sauce looks too thick, and cook for about 2–3 minutes, stirring, until all the prawns have turned pink.

5 Transfer to a warmed serving bowl, garnish with coriander and serve.

Serves 4
Preparation time: 20 minutes
Cooking time: 20 minutes

mixed seafood rice sticks

4 dried Chinese mushrooms
500 g/1 lb rice stick noodles
2 tablespoons oil
4 spring onions, chopped
2 garlic cloves, sliced
2.5 cm/1 inch piece fresh root ginger, peeled and finely chopped
50 g/2 oz cooked peeled prawns
125 g/4 oz squid, cleaned and sliced (see page 107)
250 g/8 oz can clams, drained
2 tablespoons dry sherry
1 tablespoon soy sauce
salt

1 Soak the mushrooms in warm water for 15 minutes. Squeeze well, discard the stalks, then slice the mushrooms caps.

2 Cook the rice stick noodles in boiling salted water for 7–8 minutes until just tender. Drain and rinse in cold water. Set aside.

3 Heat the oil in a wok or large frying pan, add the spring onions, garlic and ginger, and stir-fry for 30 seconds. Stir in the mushrooms, prawns and squid, if using, and cook for 2 minutes. Stir in the remaining ingredients, then carefully stir in the noodles and heat through.

4 Pile the mixture into a warmed serving dish and serve immediately.

Serves 4–6
Preparation time: 10 minutes, plus soaking
Cooking time: 10–11 minutes

singapore noodles

2 nests of dry noodles
575 ml/18 fl oz water
125 g/4 oz lean pork, cut into 5 cm/2 inch strips
75 g/3 oz raw prawns, peeled and deveined
* (see page 111)*
75 g/3 oz squid, cleaned and sliced (see page 107)
4 tablespoons sunflower oil
2 garlic cloves, crushed
75 g/3 oz bean sprouts
1 tablespoon light soy sauce
1 tablespoon dark soy sauce
½ teaspoon black pepper
1 bunch of chives, snipped
2 eggs

1 Boil the noodles in plenty of water for 2 minutes, then drain. Bring the measured water to the boil in a pan and cook the pork, prawns and squid together for 5 minutes. Drain and reserve the liquid.

2 Heat the oil in a wok or frying pan, add the garlic and fry until golden. Add the bean sprouts and noodles, increase the heat, and stir-fry for 2 minutes. Add the pork, prawns and squid, the soy sauces, pepper and chives and stir-fry for 1 minute more.

3 Push the mixture to one side of the pan and crack in the eggs. Cook for 1 minute and add the reserved liquid. Bring to the boil and cook for 2 minutes, stirring well. Transfer to a warmed serving dish and serve immediately.

Serves 4
Preparation time: 15 minutes
Cooking time: 15 minutes

noodles tossed with meat and vegetables

375 g/12 oz noodles
2 tablespoons oil
2 green chillies, deseeded and thinly sliced
1 garlic clove, thinly sliced
375 g/12 oz minced pork
2 carrots, cut into matchsticks
3 celery sticks, cut into matchsticks
½ cucumber, cut into matchsticks
4 spring onions, sliced
1 small green pepper, cored, deseeded and sliced
1 tablespoon soy sauce
2 tablespoons sweet red bean paste
1 tablespoon dry sherry

1 Cook the noodles according to the packet instructions, then drain well.

2 Meanwhile, heat the oil in a wok or deep frying pan, add the chillies and garlic, and stir-fry for about 30 seconds. Add the pork and cook for 2 minutes.

3 Increase the heat, add the carrots, celery, cucumber, onions and green pepper, and cook for 1 minute. Stir in the soy sauce, bean paste, sherry and noodles. Stir well to mix and heat through.

4 Pile on to a warmed serving dish and serve immediately.

Serves 4–6
Preparation time: 10 minutes
Cooking time: 10 minutes

chow mein

500 g/1 lb egg noodles
4 tablespoons vegetable oil
1 onion, thinly sliced
125 g/4 oz cooked meat (pork, chicken or ham), cut into
* thin shreds*
125 g/4 oz mangetout or green beans

125 g/4 oz bean sprouts
1 teaspoon salt
2–3 spring onions, thinly shredded
2 tablespoons light soy sauce
1 tablespoon sesame seed oil or chilli sauce, to serve

1 Cook the noodles in a large saucepan of boiling salted water according to packet instructions, then drain and rinse under cold running water until cool, and set aside.

2 Heat about 3 tablespoons of the oil in a hot wok or large frying pan, add the onion, meat, mangetout or beans and the bean sprouts, and stir-fry for about 1 minute. Add the salt and stir a few times more, then remove from the wok or pan with a perforated spoon and keep hot.

3 Heat the remaining oil in the wok or pan and add the spring onions and the noodles, with about half of the meat and vegetable mixture. Mix with the soy sauce, then stir-fry for 1–2 minutes, or until heated through.

4 Transfer the mixture to a large warmed serving dish, then pour the remaining meat and vegetable mixture on top. Sprinkle with the sesame seed oil or chilli sauce, or both if preferred, and serve immediately.

Serves 4
Preparation time: 15 minutes
Cooking time: 10 minutes

hot and sour thai noodles

Although this dish can be served when it is still warm, the flavours improve if it is left to cool to room temperature.

2 tablespoons sunflower oil
1 teaspoon sesame oil
2 garlic cloves, crushed
1 teaspoon chilli flakes
2 carrots, cut into matchsticks
50 g/2 oz small broccoli florets
50 g/2 oz small cauliflower florets
125 g/4 oz sugar snap peas
125 g/4 oz shiitake mushrooms, sliced
125 g/4 oz Chinese cabbage, shredded
125 g/4 oz bean sprouts
75 g/3 oz rice vermicelli
50 g/2 oz cashew nuts

Dressing:
2½ tablespoons sunflower oil
1 tablespoon caster sugar
2 tablespoons lime juice
1 tablespoon rice or wine vinegar
1 tablespoon Thai fish sauce or light soy sauce
1 teaspoon Tabasco sauce
1 tablespoon each chopped coriander and mint
salt and pepper

1 Heat the sunflower and sesame oils in a small saucepan with the garlic and chilli flakes until the oil starts to smoke. Carefully strain the oil into a wok or large frying pan.

2 Reheat the oil and, when hot, add the carrots, broccoli, cauliflower, sugar snap peas and mushrooms, and stir-fry for 2 minutes. Add the cabbage and bean sprouts and stir-fry for a further 2 minutes, until the vegetables are just wilted. Remove from the heat.

3 Cook the vermicelli according to the packet instructions. In a small bowl whisk all the dressing ingredients together and season to taste with salt and pepper. Drain the noodles and toss with a little of the dressing.

4 Stir the remaining dressing into the vegetables. Spoon the noodles on to individual plates, top with the vegetables and nuts, and serve immediately. Alternatively, arrange the noodles on a large plate, top with the vegetables and leave to cool for up to 1 hour. Sprinkle over the nuts just before serving.

Serves 4
Preparation time: 15 minutes
Cooking time: 10 minutes

thai noodles in spicy gravy

1 tablespoon groundnut oil
300 g/10 oz dried rice stick noodles, soaked and drained
750 ml/1¼ pints Vegetable Stock (see page 140)
5 tablespoons cornflour
5 tablespoons water
150 g/5 oz broccoli
25 g/1 oz spring onions, cut into 2.5 cm/1 inch lengths
2 red chillies, chopped
1½ teaspoons sugar
¼ teaspoon salt

1 teaspoon soy sauce
1 teaspoon black bean sauce
1 tablespoon deep-fried garlic slices
salt and pepper

1 Heat the oil in a wok or large frying pan, add the noodles and stir-fry for 2–3 minutes until they are softened and cooked. Meanwhile, bring the stock to the boil in a saucepan.

2 Mix the cornflour and measured water thoroughly, then add to the boiling stock, together with the broccoli and spring onions. Boil slowly and add the chillies, sugar, salt, soy sauce and black bean sauce. Stir until the gravy thickens, then add the deep-fried garlic and salt and pepper to taste.

3 Transfer the noodles to a warmed serving bowl, pour the gravy over them and serve immediately.

Serves 4
Preparation time: 15 minutes, plus soaking
Cooking time: 8–9 minutes

egg noodles with oyster mushrooms

200 g/7 oz dried egg noodles
2 tablespoons groundnut oil
3 garlic cloves, chopped
1 teaspoon sugar
1 tablespoon soy sauce
1 tablespoon Thai fish sauce
1/2 teaspoon salt
50 g/2 oz oyster mushrooms, torn
1/2 onion, chopped
125 g/4 oz mangetout, topped and tailed
4 large fresh orange chillies, thinly sliced lengthways
pepper

1 Cook the noodles according to packet instructions and drain well.

2 Heat the oil in a wok or large frying pan, add the garlic and give it a brief stir, then add the noodles, sugar, soy sauce, fish sauce and salt. Stir vigorously over a high heat for 1 minute.

3 Add the vegetables, stir continuously for 2–3 minutes, then lower the heat and check the seasoning.

4 Turn into a warmed dish and serve immediately.

Serves 3–4
Preparation time: 10 minutes
Cooking time: 10 minutes

chilli fried noodles with asparagus

oil, for deep-frying
2 tablespoons chopped shallots
1 tablespoon chopped garlic
1 tablespoon groundnut oil
2 eggs, beaten
325 g/11 oz rice stick noodles, soaked and drained
2 tablespoons sugar
1 1/2 tablespoons soy sauce
50 g/2 oz asparagus, cut into 2.5 cm/1 inch lengths
1 celery stick, finely chopped
1 teaspoon pepper
1 tablespoon crushed dried chillies
salt

1 Heat the oil in a wok or large saucepan to 180–190°C (350–375°F) or until a cube of bread browns in 30 seconds. Throw in the shallots and fry for 1 1/2–2 minutes. Remove with a slotted spoon, then drain on kitchen paper. Repeat with the garlic, cooking for 40 seconds. Reserve the flavoured oil for another recipe.

2 Heat the groundnut oil in a wok or large frying pan. Add the eggs, stir them around, then add the shallots and garlic, and stir-fry for 30 seconds. Add the noodles and fry briefly, then add all the remaining ingredients. Stir-fry vigorously for 2–3 minutes, turn on to a warmed dish and serve.

Serves 3–4
Preparation time: 15 minutes, plus soaking
Cooking time: 10 minutes

salads

rich polenta salad

600 ml/1 pint water
150 g/5 oz quick-cooking polenta flour
25 g/1 oz butter
250 g/8 oz goats' cheese, rinded and thinly sliced or crumbled
1 small radicchio head, separated into leaves
125 g/4 oz rocket
3 tablespoons olive oil
1 tablespoon balsamic vinegar
salt and pepper

1 Heat the measured water to a gentle simmer, pour in the polenta and beat well for 1–2 minutes until it is a smooth paste. Turn the heat down and continue to cook the polenta for 6–8 minutes, until it thickens, stirring constantly so that it does not catch on the bottom of the pan or form a skin on the top.

2 When the polenta is thick and cooked, add the butter, season with salt and pepper, and mix well. Turn it on to a chopping board and spread to 1.5 cm/³/₄ inch thick and allow to set for 5 minutes.

3 Arrange the goats' cheese on the polenta, then cut the polenta into bars or wedges. Place the polenta under a preheated grill and cook until the cheese has melted and starts to bubble.

4 Put the radicchio leaves and the rocket into a bowl. Add the oil and vinegar and season with salt and pepper, then toss the leaves until coated. Arrange the salad leaves on individual plates, place the polenta bars on top, and serve.

Serves 4
Preparation time: 10 minutes
Cooking time: 20 minutes

caesar salad

3 slices of country bread, cubed
1 cos lettuce, torn into pieces
3 tablespoons freshly grated Parmesan cheese
vegetable oil, for frying

Dressing:
1 garlic clove, crushed
4 anchovy fillets, chopped
4 tablespoons lemon juice
2 teaspoons English mustard powder
1 egg yolk
200 ml/7 fl oz olive oil
pepper

1 First make the dressing. Place the garlic, anchovy fillets, lemon juice, mustard and egg yolk in a small bowl and season with pepper. With a hand-held blender or a small whisk, mix well until combined. Slowly drizzle in the olive oil, mixing all the time to form a thick creamy dressing; if it is too thick, add a little water.

2 Heat the vegetable oil in a frying pan until a small piece of bread sizzles immediately when dropped in, then fry the cubes of bread, turning them when they are golden. When they are golden on all sides, drain on kitchen paper.

3 Put the lettuce into a bowl, pour over the dressing and 2 tablespoons of the Parmesan, and mix well.

4 Serve the salad in a large bowl or on individual plates, sprinkled with croûtons and the remaining Parmesan.

Serves 4
Preparation time: 20 minutes
Cooking time: 5 minutes

panzanella

When making this delicious but very simple salad dish, try to cut all the ingredients into pieces of a similar size.

Salad:
4 slices of ciabatta bread, cut or torn into small pieces
4 ripe tomatoes, cored and diced
½ cucumber, peeled, quartered lengthways and diced
1 red onion, chopped
handful of flat leaf parsley, chopped
1 tablespoon chopped black olives

Dressing:
4 tablespoons olive oil
1–2 tablespoons wine vinegar
2 tablespoons lemon juice
salt and pepper

1 Place all the salad ingredients in a large bowl.

2 Whisk all the dressing ingredients together in a small bowl or place them in a screw-top jar and shake well to combine.

3 Pour the dressing over the salad and mix well. Cover and leave to stand at room temperature for at least 1 hour before serving, to allow all the flavours to develop and mingle.

Serves 4
Preparation time: 15 minutes, plus standing

caponata

6 tablespoons olive oil
2 aubergines, cubed
1 red onion, chopped
3 celery sticks, chopped
5 tomatoes, skinned and roughly chopped
3 tablespoons red wine vinegar
1 tablespoon sugar
1 tablespoon capers
50 g/2 oz black olives, pitted
handful of flat leaf parsley, chopped
salt and pepper

1 Heat the oil in a saucepan, add the aubergines and fry until golden and soft. Remove from the pan and drain on kitchen paper.

2 Add the onion and celery to the pan and sauté for 6 minutes until soft but not brown.

3 Add the tomatoes and cook for 3 minutes, then add the vinegar, sugar, capers, olives and parsley, and season to taste with salt and pepper. Simmer for 5 minutes. Remove the pan from the heat, add the aubergines and mix well. Allow to cool, then serve.

Serves 4
Preparation time: 10 minutes, plus cooling
Cooking time: 20 minutes

roast vegetable salad

2 Spanish onions, unpeeled
500 g/1 lb small aubergines
2 red peppers
3 large, firm but ripe tomatoes
8 garlic cloves
1 teaspoon cumin seeds
3 tablespoons lemon juice
4 tablespoons virgin olive oil
3 tablespoons white wine vinegar
salt
2 tablespoons finely chopped parsley or torn
*   basil leaves, to garnish*

1 Place the onions on a baking sheet and bake in a preheated oven, 180°C (350°F), Gas Mark 4, for 10 minutes. Add the aubergines and bake for a further 10 minutes. Add the peppers and bake for 10 minutes, then add the tomatoes and 6 of the garlic cloves.

2 Cook for a further 15 minutes, until all the vegetables are tender. If necessary, remove any vegetables that have cooked more quickly than the others. When the vegetables are cool enough to handle, peel them carefully with your fingers.

3 Core and deseed the peppers and cut the flesh into strips. Halve the tomatoes, deseed, and slice the flesh. Slice the aubergines into strips and the onions into rings. Arrange the peppers, tomatoes, aubergines and onions in a serving dish.

4 Pound the roasted and raw garlic and the cumin seeds to a paste. Use a pestle and mortar or the end of a rolling pin in a small bowl. Gradually beat in the lemon juice, oil and vinegar, then add salt to taste. Pour over the vegetables and sprinkle with parsley or basil. Serve warm or cold.

Serves 4
Preparation time: 5–10 minutes
Cooking time: 45 minutes, plus cooling
Oven temperature: 180°C (350°F), Gas Mark 4

greek country salad

4 tablespoons olive oil
1 tablespoon red wine vinegar
1 garlic clove, crushed
½ cucumber, halved lengthways, deseeded
*   and thinly sliced*
1 small round lettuce, torn
1 small cos lettuce, shredded
3 firm but ripe tomatoes, cut into wedges
1 Spanish onion, thinly sliced into rings
1 green pepper, cored, deseeded and thinly sliced into
*   rings*
125 g/4 oz feta cheese, crumbled
12 or more black olives (Kalamata if possible)
salt and pepper

To garnish:
1–2 tablespoons roughly chopped parsley
2 teaspoons chopped oregano

1 Whisk together the oil, vinegar, garlic and salt and pepper to taste. Cover and set aside for 1 hour.

2 Sprinkle the cucumber slices with salt and leave to drain. Rinse the cucumber and dry with kitchen paper.

3 Place the lettuce in a bowl. Whisk the oil and vinegar again, then toss a little of it with the lettuce.

4 Layer the tomatoes, cucumber, onion, green pepper, cheese and olives on the lettuce. Pour over the remaining dressing, then scatter over the chopped parsley and the oregano, and serve.

Serves 4
Preparation time: 25–30 minutes, plus standing

salade niçoise

1 garlic clove, bruised
1 lettuce
125 g/4 oz celery hearts, thinly sliced
125 g/4 oz cucumber, peeled and thinly sliced
250 g/8 oz small green beans
250 g/8 oz canned artichoke hearts, thinly sliced
500 g/1 lb tomatoes, skinned, deseeded and quartered
1 green pepper, cored, deseeded and sliced
1 onion, sliced

griddled asparagus salad   p434

bulgar wheat salad   p435

mesclun with croûtons and cheese dressing   p428

roast vegetable salad   p416

tomato salad with anchovies p426

tabbouleh and fennel salad p436

salade niçoise p416

tomato and coriander salad p431

4 eggs, hard-boiled and halved
50 g/2 oz black olives, pitted
8 anchovy fillets
250 g/8 oz can tuna in oil, drained

Dressing:
7 tablespoons olive oil
4 basil leaves, finely chopped
salt and pepper

1 Rub around the inside of a large salad bowl with the bruised garlic clove. Line the bowl with lettuce leaves. Chop the remaining lettuce leaves roughly and arrange them in the bottom of the bowl.

2 Mix the celery and cucumber with the green beans and artichoke hearts. Arrange on top of the lettuce in the salad bowl.

3 Arrange the tomatoes, sliced pepper, onion, eggs, olives and anchovies on top of the mixed vegetables in the bowl.

4 Cut the tuna into chunks and place in the bowl.

5 To make the dressing, mix together the olive oil and chopped basil with salt and pepper to taste.

6 Pour the dressing over the salad, toss to mix well, transfer to individual plates and serve.

Serves 4
Preparation time: 20 minutes

aubergine salad

4 tablespoons olive oil
1 onion, chopped
2 garlic cloves, chopped
2 aubergines, cubed
75 g/3 oz pine nuts
4 tomatoes, skinned and roughly chopped
4 anchovy fillets, chopped
2 tablespoons black olives, pitted
2 tablespoons chopped capers
handful of flat leaf parsley, chopped
salt and pepper

Dressing:
1 tablespoon white wine vinegar
3 tablespoons olive oil
2 tablespoons lemon juice
1 teaspoon Dijon mustard

1 Heat the olive oil in a saucepan, add the onion, garlic and aubergines, and sauté for 15 minutes.

2 Meanwhile, make the dressing. Whisk all the ingredients together in a small bowl or place them in a screw-top jar and shake well to combine. Season to taste with salt and pepper and set aside.

3 Toast the pine nuts in a dry frying pan over moderate heat until golden, stirring constantly.

4 Add the tomatoes, anchovies, olives, pine nuts, capers and parsley to the aubergine mixture and season to taste with salt and pepper. Pour in the salad dressing, mix well, then allow the salad to cool before serving.

Serves 4
Preparation time: 10 minutes, plus cooling
Cooking time: 15 minutes

marinated mushroom salad with straw potatoes

500 g/1 lb flat mushrooms, very thinly sliced
250 g/8 oz potatoes, peeled and cut into matchsticks
125 g/4 oz salad leaves
6 spring onions, thinly sliced
salt and pepper
vegetable oil, for frying

Dressing:
4 teaspoons balsamic vinegar
4 teaspoons coarse grain mustard
150 ml/5 fl oz olive oil
salt and pepper

1 First make the dressing. Whisk together the vinegar and mustard, then gradually whisk in the oil. Season to taste with salt and pepper.

2 Place the mushrooms on a large plate. Pour half the dressing over the mushrooms. Set aside for 1 hour, turning occasionally until softened.

3 Heat 1 cm/½ inch of oil in a frying pan, add the potato straws and fry for 2–3 minutes until crisp and golden. Drain on kitchen paper.

4 Place the salad leaves in a large bowl and toss with the remaining dressing, then place on serving plates. Arrange the marinated mushrooms on the leaves and top with the spring onions and straw potatoes. Serve immediately.

Serves 4
Preparation time: 15 minutes, plus marinating
Cooking time: 2–3 minutes

red leaf salad with pecan cheese balls

175 g/6 oz mixed red salad leaves (red chicory, lollo rosso, red oakleaf, radicchio)
small handful of nasturtiums, pansies or other edible flowers
½ red onion, thinly sliced

Cheese balls:
250 g/8 oz medium-soft goats' cheese, rinded, or cream cheese
40 g/1½ oz pecan nuts, very finely chopped
2 tablespoons paprika

Yogurt dressing:
150 ml/¼ pint natural yogurt
1 tablespoon lemon juice
1 teaspoon clear honey
½ teaspoon Dijon mustard
salt and pepper

1 Make the cheese balls first. Mix the cheese and pecan nuts in a small bowl. Shape into about 16 small balls. Spread out the paprika on a sheet of foil and lightly roll the cheese balls in it to coat. Place on a baking sheet and chill for at least 20 minutes or until required.

2 To make the yogurt dressing, beat all the ingredients together in a small bowl with a wooden spoon. Season to taste with salt and pepper.

3 Arrange all the salad leaves and flowers in a shallow serving bowl. Add the onion and spoon the dressing over. Add the cheese balls and serve immediately.

Serves 4
Preparation time: 20 minutes, plus chilling

mozzarella salad with pesto dressing

Bocconcini are miniature balls of mozzarella cheese. They are available from some supermarkets and Italian delicatessens, but if you cannot obtain them you can use regular mozzarella cut into cubes.

1 cos or other crisp green lettuce, separated into leaves
1 small head of frisé
250 g/8 oz bocconcini or diced mozzarella cheese
1 red onion, chopped
salt and pepper
1 quantity Pesto (see page 146), to serve

To garnish:
basil leaves, roughly chopped
oregano sprigs

1 Tear the salad leaves into bite-sized pieces and arrange on a platter or shallow serving dish. Scatter the bocconcini or diced mozzarella over the leaves and sprinkle with the red onion. Add salt and pepper to taste.

2 Spoon the pesto over the mozzarella, sprinkle the salad with the basil leaves and sprigs of oregano, to garnish, and serve.

Serves 4
Preparation time: 10 minutes

fresh apricot and rice salad with grilled goats' cheese

175 g/6 oz cooked white or brown rice
2 tablespoons finely chopped parsley
1 tablespoon finely chopped mint
1 quantity French Dressing (see page 146)
6 large ripe apricots, halved and stoned

2 tablespoons chopped toasted almonds
4 thick slices of goats' cheese log, with rind
salt and pepper
herb sprigs (sage or salad burnet) or salad leaves,
    to garnish

1 Combine the rice and herbs in a bowl. Add 4 tablespoons of the dressing, with salt and pepper to taste, and mix well. Reserve the remaining dressing in a jug.

2 Fill the apricot cavities with the rice salad, piling it up in the centre. Arrange on 4 individual serving plates. Scatter the toasted almonds over the top.

3 Place the goats' cheese slices on a baking sheet. Cook under a preheated hot grill for 3–4 minutes until bubbling and patched with brown. Lift on to the serving plates, garnish with herbs or salad leaves, and serve immediately. Hand the remaining dressing round separately at the table.

Serves 4
Preparation time: 15 minutes
Cooking time: 3–4 minutes

herb salad with grilled haloumi

Haloumi is a traditional Cypriot cheese with a firm texture and a deliciously salty flavour. It is superb for grilling or frying as it develops a golden crust and does not melt. It is available in large supermarkets or Greek or Cypriot stores.

1 cos lettuce, torn into bite-sized pieces
about 50 g/2 oz rocket or young leaf spinach
handful of mixed herbs (dill, chervil, coriander, basil,
    parsley), roughly torn
250 g/8 oz haloumi cheese, cut into cubes less than
    2.5 cm/1 inch
1–2 tablespoons olive oil
½ quantity French Dressing (see page 146)
pepper

1 Place the lettuce in a large, shallow salad bowl with the rocket or leaf spinach and mixed herbs.

2 Place the cubes of haloumi in a baking tin large enough to hold them in one layer. Add the olive oil, season with pepper and toss gently to coat the cheese. Cook under a preheated hot grill for about 8 minutes, stirring occasionally, until golden brown on all sides. Scatter the haloumi over the salad leaves.

3 Pour the dressing over the salad and toss well. Serve immediately.

Serves 4–6
Preparation time: 20 minutes
Cooking time: about 8 minutes

spinach and goats' cheese salad

175 g/6 oz young spinach leaves
2 oranges, peeled and segmented
175 g/6 oz goats' cheese, diced
5 tablespoons olive oil
50 g/2 oz hazelnuts, roughly chopped
1 garlic clove, crushed
6 tablespoons orange juice
1 bunch of watercress, leaves stripped from the stalks,
    very finely chopped
2 tablespoons chopped mixed herbs (parsley, tarragon,
    mint, dill, basil)
salt and pepper

1 Combine the spinach leaves, orange segments and goats' cheese in a large salad bowl.

2 Heat the olive oil in a small frying pan, add the hazelnuts and garlic, and cook for 1–2 minutes. Stir in the orange juice, watercress and herbs. Heat through, then quickly pour the hot dressing on to the spinach, orange and goats' cheese. Add salt and pepper to taste, toss well and serve immediately.

Serves 4
Preparation time: 15 minutes
Cooking time: about 2 minutes

thai egg salad with crispy basil

4 hard-boiled eggs, halved lengthways
3 shallots, finely sliced
5 small green chillies, finely chopped
1 large garlic clove, finely sliced
4 tablespoons lime juice
2 tablespoons Thai fish sauce or soy sauce
½ teaspoon sugar
groundnut oil, for frying
25–50 g/1–2 oz basil leaves

1 Put the eggs, yolk side up, on a serving dish or in a bowl and sprinkle the shallots over them. Put the chillies, garlic, lime juice, fish sauce and sugar in a small bowl and mix well together. Spoon the mixture over the eggs.

2 Heat some oil in a wok, add the basil leaves and fry until crispy, then quickly remove them from the oil with a slotted spoon and drain on kitchen paper.

3 Scatter the crispy basil over the salad and serve.

Serves 4
Preparation time: 4–5 minutes
Cooking time: 1½ minutes

rocket, tuna and haricot bean salad

4 tomatoes, skinned, cored and roughly chopped
125 g/4 oz rocket
425 g/14 oz can haricot beans, drained
200 g/7 oz can tuna in olive oil
1 red onion, chopped
125 g/4 oz artichoke hearts in olive oil
2 young celery sticks with leaves, chopped
1 tablespoon black olives, pitted
4 tablespoons lemon juice
1 tablespoon red wine vinegar
¼ teaspoon crushed dried chilli
handful of flat leaf parsley, roughly chopped
salt and pepper

1 Put the tomatoes into a large salad bowl with the rocket and stir in the haricot beans and the tuna with its oil, roughly breaking the tuna into large flakes. Stir in the chopped red onion.

2 Add the artichoke hearts and their oil, celery, olives, lemon juice, vinegar, chilli and parsley, and season to taste with salt and pepper.

3 Mix all the ingredients together well and allow to stand for 30 minutes for the flavours to mingle. Serve at room temperature.

Serves 4
Preparation time: 15 minutes

tuna and olive salad

6 whole carrots, cooked and finely sliced
2 potatoes, boiled and diced
500 g/1 lb tuna in oil, drained and chopped, oil reserved
4 tablespoons black olives, pitted and halved
2 tablespoons wine vinegar
salt and pepper
4 basil leaves, to garnish

1 Put the carrots, potatoes, tuna and olives in a bowl.

2 Put the tuna oil and vinegar into a screw-top jar, season to taste with salt and pepper and shake well to combine.

3 Pour the dressing over the salad, mix, garnish with basil leaves and serve.

Serves 4
Preparation time: 25 minutes

coronation prawn and pasta salad

300 g/10 oz fusilli or other pasta shapes
1 tablespoon olive oil
15 g/½ oz butter
500 g/1 lb large raw prawns, peeled, deveined and halved lengthways (see page 111)

2 celery sticks, finely chopped
3 tablespoons crème fraîche
125 ml/4 fl oz Mayonnaise (see page 145)
1 teaspoon lemon juice
2 teaspoons medium-hot curry paste
salt and pepper

To serve:
salad leaves
lemon wedges

1 Cook the pasta until al dente (see page 137).

2 Meanwhile, heat the oil and butter in a frying pan, add the prawns and cook over a medium-high heat for about 2 minutes, until they turn pink and start to brown in places. Remove the prawns and drain on kitchen paper.

3 Drain the pasta, rinse under cold running water, drain again and set aside.

4 Place the pasta in a large bowl with the prawns, celery, crème fraîche, mayonnaise, lemon juice, curry paste and pepper, and mix thoroughly. Adjust the seasoning to taste. Cover and chill for 20 minutes.

5 Arrange the lettuce leaves on individual plates, divide the salad among them and serve with the lemon wedges.

Serves 4
Preparation time: 10 minutes, plus chilling
Cooking time: 8–12 minutes

mussel salad with bacon and tomato vinaigrette

1 kg/2 lb mussels, scrubbed and debearded (see page 109)
2 shallots, finely chopped
6 tablespoons dry white wine or water
6 smoked streaky bacon rashers, rinded
50 g/2 oz Parmesan cheese
basil or parsley, to garnish (optional)

Dressing:
6 tablespoons tomato juice
4 tablespoons olive oil
2 tablespoons red wine vinegar
½ garlic clove, crushed
¼ teaspoon caster sugar
1 tablespoon finely shredded basil
salt and pepper

1 First make the dressing. Whisk all the ingredients together in a small bowl or place them in a screw-top jar and shake well to combine. Set aside.

2 Place the mussels in a large saucepan with the shallots and white wine or water, cover and cook over a high heat for 3–4 minutes, or until the shells have opened. Drain, discarding the cooking liquid and any unopened mussels. Transfer the mussels and shallots to a bowl and leave to cool. Remove some of the shells, if you like, for ease of eating.

3 Meanwhile, cook the bacon under a preheated hot grill until crisp. Drain on kitchen paper. Crumble or snip into small pieces.

4 Pour the dressing over the mussel mixture, toss together lightly, then scatter the bacon over the top. Adjust the seasoning to taste. Shave the Parmesan over the top of the salad with a mandoline or vegetable peeler, garnish with basil or parsley, if liked, and serve.

Serves 4
Preparation time: 25 minutes
Cooking time: 8–9 minutes

thai squid salad

½ red onion, sliced
1 tomato, cut into 8 pieces
5 g/¼ oz coriander leaves, roughly chopped
5 small green or red chillies, finely sliced
125 g/4 oz squid, cleaned and sliced
3 tablespoons lime juice
2 teaspoons palm sugar or light muscovado sugar
3 tablespoons Thai fish sauce
15 g/½ oz carrot, shredded
15 g/½ oz white cabbage, shredded

1 Place the onion, tomato, coriander and chillies in a salad bowl.

2 Put the squid briefly in a saucepan of boiling water and cook for about 1½ minutes. Remove from the pan and combine with the onion and tomato mixture.

3 Add the lime juice, sugar and fish sauce and mix together for 1–2 minutes.

4 Finally add the carrot and cabbage, give the salad a quick stir, and serve.

Serves 4
Preparation time: 8 minutes
Cooking time: 1–2 minutes

crab salad

1 large cooked crab, about 1 kg/2 lb
1–2 tablespoons lemon juice
300 ml/½ pint Mayonnaise (see page 145)
about 250 g/8 oz mixed salad leaves (frisé, red oakleaf,
* lollo rosso, batavia, lamb's lettuce, rocket, chicory)*
handful of herb sprigs (chervil, dill, parsley, coriander)
3 spring onions, finely shredded
½ cucumber, peeled and finely diced
salt and pepper
lemon wedges, to garnish

1 Remove the white and brown meat from the crab and flake into a bowl.

2 Add the lemon juice and mayonnaise to the crab, adjusting the quantities according to taste, and season to taste with salt and pepper. Mix thoroughly.

3 Just before serving, arrange the salad leaves on a serving platter or on individual plates. Scatter over the herb sprigs, the spring onion shreds and the cucumber. Place the crab meat on to the platter or plates. Serve at once, garnished with lemon wedges.

Serves 4
Preparation time: 30 minutes

chicken and parmesan salad

2 boneless, skinless chicken breasts
1 garlic clove, chopped
150 ml/¼ pint olive oil
3 anchovy fillets, roughly chopped
2 tablespoons lemon juice
1 teaspoon English mustard powder
1 egg yolk
1 cos lettuce, torn into pieces
handful of basil, roughly torn
3 slices of ciabatta or white country bread, cubed and
* fried in oil*
75 g/3 oz Parmesan cheese
pepper

1 Place the chicken breasts on a hot griddle pan or under a preheated hot grill and cook on each side for 5 minutes.

2 Put the garlic, olive oil, anchovies, lemon juice, mustard and egg yolk into a blender, season with pepper and mix until blended.

3 Put the lettuce into a large bowl, pour over the dressing and toss.

4 Arrange the lettuce on serving plates and sprinkle with torn basil leaves and the croûtons.

5 Slice the chicken into long lengths and place on top of the lettuce. Shave the Parmesan on to the chicken with a mandoline or vegetable peeler, and serve.

Serves 4
Preparation time: 10 minutes
Cooking time: 15 minutes

warm chorizo salad

about 250 g/8 oz salad leaves (radicchio, chicory, frisé)
small handful of sage leaves
5 tablespoons olive oil
300 g/10 oz chorizo sausage, skinned and thinly sliced
1 small red onion, thinly sliced
1 garlic clove, chopped
2 tablespoons red wine vinegar
salt and pepper

1 Arrange the salad leaves on individual plates, or tear the leaves into bite-sized pieces and place in a large salad bowl. Scatter over the sage leaves.

2 Heat the olive oil in a frying pan until fairly hot, add the chorizo and fry over a high heat for 1 minute. Add the onion and garlic and fry for 1–2 minutes more, or until the chorizo is browned. Remove the pan from the heat.

3 Stir the vinegar into the pan, with salt and pepper to taste. Quickly spoon the mixture over the salad leaves and toss lightly. Serve at once.

Serves 4
Preparation time: 15 minutes
Cooking time: 2–3 minutes

warm duck and orange salad

4 boneless duck breasts
1 tablespoon olive oil
2 teaspoons sesame oil
2 courgettes, sliced
1 garlic clove, chopped (optional)
2 small oranges, peeled and segmented
about 375 g/12 oz salad leaves (chicory, rocket, spinach,
*   lollo rosso)*
salt and pepper

Dressing:
4 tablespoons olive oil
1 teaspoon sesame oil
1 tablespoon red wine vinegar
1 teaspoon grated orange rind
1 teaspoon finely chopped parsley
pinch of dried sage

To garnish:
toasted sesame seeds
long strips of orange rind

1 Using a sharp knife, make 4 diagonal slashes in the skin of each duck breast. Season with salt and pepper, rubbing the mixture into the skin and flesh.

2 Heat both the oils in a large frying pan, add the duck breasts and fry over a fairly high heat for 5–7 minutes, turning once, until well browned on the outside but still rosy pink on the inside. Transfer the duck breasts to a plate and keep warm.

3 Add the courgettes to the oil remaining in the pan, and stir in the garlic, if using. Cook for 1–2 minutes, stirring, until the courgettes have started to soften. Using a slotted spoon, transfer to a bowl. Add the orange segments to the bowl.

4 To make the dressing, whisk all the ingredients together in a small bowl or place them in a screw-top jar and shake well to combine.

5 Arrange the salad leaves on 4 individual plates. Slice the duck breasts and arrange the slices next to the leaves, with portions of the courgette and orange salad next to the duck. Spoon the dressing over the salad, garnish with the sesame seeds and orange rind, and serve warm.

Serves 4
Preparation time: 20 minutes
Cooking time: 6–9 minutes

lamb salad with minted yogurt

3 small carrots
1 small cauliflower, divided into florets
425 g/14 oz can pimientos, drained
½ cucumber, peeled, deseeded and diced
4 spring onions, shredded
375 g/12 oz cold roast lamb, sliced
salt and pepper
mint leaves, to garnish (optional)

Dressing:
150 ml/¼ pint natural yogurt
2 tablespoons mint jelly

1 Using a vegetable peeler, pare the carrots into long thin strips or 'ribbons'. Place in a bowl of iced water and leave to curl and crisp.

2 Cook the cauliflower florets in boiling water for 3–4 minutes until barely tender. Drain and refresh under cold running water.

3 To make the dressing, mix the yogurt and mint jelly together until smooth. Season to taste with salt and pepper.

4 Rinse the pimientos, drain on kitchen paper and then slice thinly.

5 Put all the prepared ingredients together in a large bowl. Season and toss lightly. Drizzle over the dressing, garnish with a few mint leaves, if liked, and serve.

Serves 4
Preparation time: 20 minutes
Cooking time: 3–4 minutes

hot chicken liver salad

25 g/1 oz butter
5 tablespoons light olive oil
500 g/1 lb chicken livers, halved
2 tablespoons red wine vinegar
1 teaspoon coarse grain mustard
about 250 g/8 oz mixed salad leaves (red oakleaf, frisé, radicchio, chicory)
2 spring onions, thinly sliced
salt and pepper
flat leaf parsley sprigs, to garnish

1 Heat the butter and the oil in a large frying pan, add the chicken livers and fry over a high heat for 3–4 minutes, stirring, until sealed and browned on the outside but still lightly pink within. Remove from the heat and stir in the vinegar and mustard, and season to taste with salt and pepper.

2 Arrange the salad leaves on 4 serving plates.

3 Spoon the hot chicken liver mixture on top of the salad leaves and sprinkle with the spring onions. Garnish with sprigs of flat leaf parsley and serve at once.

Serves 4
Preparation time: 20 minutes
Cooking time: 3–4 minutes

curried chicken mayonnaise

1 tablespoon olive oil
1 onion, finely chopped
2 teaspoons ground coriander
1 teaspoon ground cumin
1 teaspoon grated fresh root ginger
2 teaspoons lemon juice
1 teaspoon apricot jam
2 tablespoons red wine
300 ml/½ pint thick Mayonnaise (see page 145)
750 g/1½ lb cold cooked chicken, cut into pieces
salt and pepper

To garnish:
coriander leaves, finely chopped
½ avocado, peeled, sliced and dipped in lemon juice

1 Heat the oil in a frying pan, add the onion and fry gently for 5 minutes, until soft and lightly coloured. Stir in the coriander, cumin and ginger. Cook for 2 minutes more.

2 Add the lemon juice, jam and wine, and simmer for 2 minutes. Remove from the heat and leave to cool for 5 minutes.

3 Put the mayonnaise in a large bowl and add the curry mixture, stirring very thoroughly. Add the chicken and turn in the curried mayonnaise until thoroughly coated. Garnish with chopped coriander and avocado slices, and serve.

Serves 4–6
Preparation time: 8 minutes
Cooking time: 11 minutes

gado gado with chicken

250 g/8 oz carrots, cut into matchsticks
175 g/6 oz celery, cut into matchsticks
175 g/6 oz leek, cut into matchsticks
125 g/4 oz mangetout, halved diagonally
½ cucumber, peeled, halved lengthways, deseeded and sliced
175 g/6 oz bean sprouts
about 175 g/6 oz pak choi
2 cooked chicken breasts, skinned and shredded
salt and pepper
chopped coriander leaves, to garnish (optional)

Spicy peanut dressing:
25 g/1 oz creamed coconut, chopped
4 tablespoons milk
½ small onion, chopped
1 garlic clove, crushed
4 tablespoons smooth peanut butter
1 teaspoon soft light brown sugar
2 teaspoons soy sauce
½ teaspoon ground cumin
½ teaspoon chilli powder
salt and pepper

1 First make the dressing. Place the creamed coconut in a small saucepan with the milk. Heat gently for about 2 minutes, stirring, until the coconut melts and forms a paste with the milk.

2 Transfer to a liquidizer or food processor, add all the remaining ingredients and purée until smooth. Scrape into a small bowl, cover and set aside until required.

3 Blanch the carrot, celery and leek matchsticks in boiling water for 1–2 minutes. Drain in a colander, refresh under cold running water, and then drain again thoroughly. Tip into a large bowl.

4 Add the mangetout, cucumber and bean sprouts to the bowl. Season to taste with salt and pepper. Gently toss to mix thoroughly.

5 Arrange the pak choi leaves on a serving platter or individual plates, with the shredded chicken and the vegetable mixture. Spoon the dressing over, garnish with a sprinkling of chopped coriander, if liked, and serve.

Serves 4
Preparation time: 40 minutes
Cooking time: 3–4 minutes

pear and stilton salad

4 pears, cut into eighths and cored
4 tablespoons lemon juice
250 g/8 oz baby spinach or lettuce
4 walnuts, chopped
250 g/8 oz blue Stilton cheese, crumbled
4 tablespoons walnut oil

1 Heat a griddle pan or nonstick frying pan and cook the slices of pear on each side for 1 minute. Remove and sprinkle them with the lemon juice.

2 Pile the spinach on a large platter and arrange the pears on top. Sprinkle with walnuts and crumbled Stilton and spoon over the walnut oil. Serve immediately.

Serves 4
Preparation time: 10 minutes
Cooking time: 2 minutes

waldorf salad

4 dessert apples, unpeeled, cored and diced
1 celery head, finely diced, some leaves reserved for
  garnish
small bunch of grapes, halved and deseeded
50 g/2 oz walnuts or pecan nuts, coarsely chopped
1 quantity Mayonnaise (see page 145)

1 Mix the apples, celery, grapes and walnuts or pecan nuts with the mayonnaise, reserving some of the nuts to garnish.

2 Spoon into a bowl, arrange a few celery leaves around the edge and top with the remaining nuts.

Serves 4–6
Preparation time: 15–20 minutes

chicory salad

Pancetta is a type of cured pork that looks and tastes similar to bacon, and you can use unsmoked streaky bacon instead. Both pancetta and pecorino cheese tend to be salty, which is why there is no salt in this recipe.

2 chicory heads
4 tablespoons olive oil
125 g/4 oz pancetta, finely diced
125 g/4 oz hard pecorino cheese, grated
1 tablespoon lemon juice
pepper

1 Separate the chicory leaves and wash and dry them carefully. Arrange them, rounded-side down, on a large serving platter.

2 Heat 1 tablespoon of the oil in a nonstick frying pan, add the pancetta and cook over a low heat until the fat runs. Increase the heat to moderate and cook, stirring constantly, until the pancetta begins to colour and crisp. Remove the pan from the heat and, using a slotted spoon, transfer the pancetta to kitchen paper to drain.

3 Sprinkle the pancetta inside the chicory leaves, then sprinkle over the pecorino and pepper to taste.

4 Add the remaining oil and the lemon juice to the pan juices and return the pan to a medium heat. Stir until sizzling, then drizzle over the chicory and serve immediately.

Serves 4
Preparation time: 10 minutes
Cooking time: about 5 minutes

classic potato salad

Choose potato varieties with a waxy texture, such as Charlotte or Pink Fir Apple. They will retain their shape better than floury baking potatoes.

750 g/1½ lb waxy salad potatoes
4 spring onions, finely chopped
2 tablespoons snipped chives, to garnish
salt and pepper

Dressing:
6 tablespoons Mayonnaise (see page 145)
3 tablespoons single cream
1 teaspoon Dijon mustard

1 Cook the potatoes, whole in their skins, in a large pan of boiling water for about 15 minutes, or until tender. Drain and refresh under cold running water, then drain thoroughly and allow to cool.

2 Thickly slice the potatoes and place in a serving bowl with the spring onions. Season with salt and pepper to taste.

3 To make the dressing, stir together the mayonnaise, cream and mustard. Spoon over the salad and toss lightly to mix. Serve the salad sprinkled with the snipped fresh chives.

Serves 6
Preparation time: 15 minutes, plus cooling
Cooking time: about 15 minutes

tomato salad with anchovies

1 heaped tablespoon French mustard
2 tablespoons white or red vinegar
75 ml/3 fl oz olive oil
4–5 firm tomatoes, sliced
1 stick celery, cut into thin finger-length strips
1 red onion, diced
1 teaspoon cumin seeds
2 anchovy fillets, chopped
salt and pepper
2 hard-boiled eggs to garnish (optional)

1 Place the mustard in a small bowl and stir in the vinegar. Season lightly with salt and plenty of pepper.

2 Whisk in the olive oil until the mixture is well blended.

3 Place the tomatoes in a salad bowl with the celery, onion, cumin seeds and anchovy fillets. Pour over the dressing, mix well, garnish with the hard-boiled eggs if using, and serve.

Serves 4
Preparation time: 20 minutes

mushroom and butter bean salad

250 g/8 oz dried butter beans, soaked overnight
250 g/8 oz button mushrooms, thinly sliced
1–2 tablespoons snipped chives
large handful of flat leaf parsley, roughly torn
50 g/2 oz Parmesan cheese (optional)

Dressing:
5 tablespoons olive oil
½ garlic clove, crushed
1 teaspoon finely grated lemon rind
2 tablespoons lemon juice
½ teaspoon mustard
pinch of sugar
salt and pepper

1 Drain the butter beans, then put them in a large saucepan of cold water. Bring to the boil and boil briskly for 10 minutes, then lower the heat, cover and simmer for 30–40 minutes, until the beans are tender. Drain and rinse under cold running water, then drain thoroughly and leave to cool.

2 To make the dressing, whisk all the ingredients together in a small bowl, or place them in a screw-top jar and shake well to combine.

3 Place the mushrooms in a large bowl, add the cooled butter beans and pour over the dressing. Toss well to mix and leave to stand for at least 20 minutes before serving, to allow the flavours to develop.

4 Sprinkle the chives and parsley over the salad and toss lightly. Use a mandoline or vegetable peeler to shave Parmesan over the top, if liked.

Serves 4–6
Preparation time: 15 minutes, plus soaking and standing
Cooking time: 40–50 minutes

white bean and sun-dried tomato salad

2 tablespoons olive oil
1 onion, sliced
1 garlic clove, chopped
425 g/14 oz can white beans, drained
125 g/4 oz sun-dried tomatoes in oil, drained and roughly chopped
1 tablespoon chopped black olives
2 teaspoons chopped capers
2 teaspoons chopped thyme
1 tablespoon olive oil
2 tablespoons lemon juice
salt and pepper

1 Heat the oil in a frying pan, add the onion and garlic, fry over a high heat until golden, then remove from the pan.

2 Put the beans into a mixing bowl and stir in the onion and garlic. Add the sun-dried tomatoes, olives, capers, thyme, olive oil, lemon juice, and salt and pepper to taste, and mix well. Check the seasoning and serve.

Serves 4
Preparation time: 10 minutes
Cooking time: 5 minutes

fennel, orange and olive salad

4 fennel heads, halved and thinly sliced lengthways
2 oranges, peeled and thinly sliced crossways
125 g/4 oz black olives, pitted and chopped
5 tablespoons olive oil
2 tablespoons lemon juice
¼ teaspoon cumin seeds
salt and pepper

1 Put the fennel in a large salad bowl.

2 Remove the pith and seeds from the orange slices and cut each slice into 4. Add to the bowl, with the olives.

3 Mix the oil with the lemon juice in a small bowl, and season with a little salt and plenty of pepper. Pour this dressing over the salad and sprinkle on the cumin seeds. Mix together and leave to rest in a cool place (not the refrigerator) for about 1 hour before serving.

Serves 4
Preparation time: 20 minutes, plus standing

chicory and pear salad with roquefort

2 large ripe pears
1 tablespoon lemon juice
1 orange, peeled and segmented
2 chicory heads, trimmed and separated into leaves
175 g/6 oz Roquefort cheese
2 tablespoons snipped chives

Dressing:
3 tablespoons walnut oil
2 tablespoons white wine vinegar
½ teaspoon finely grated orange rind
pinch of sugar
salt and pepper

1 Frist make the dressing. Whisk all the ingredients together in a small bowl or place them in a screw-top jar and shake well to combine.

2 Peel, core and thinly slice the pears and place in a small bowl with the lemon juice. Toss well to prevent them from discolouring. Arrange the pear slices, orange segments and chicory leaves on individual plates or in a large shallow bowl. Pour the dressing over.

3 Crumble the Roquefort over the salad, sprinkle with the chives, and serve immediately.

Serves 4–6
Preparation time: 15 minutes

green salad with a mixed herb sauce

Batavia, also called escarole, is a type of endive. Though it is slightly less curly-leaved than endive, it has a similar, slightly bitter taste.

1 round lettuce
1 batavia lettuce
125 g/4 oz lamb's lettuce

Herb sauce:
2 hard-boiled eggs, peeled
2 tablespoons double cream
2 tablespoons olive oil
2 teaspoons white wine vinegar
1 tablespoon chopped chives
1 tablespoon chopped dill
1 tablespoon chopped tarragon
salt and pepper

1 Break the round lettuce leaves in pieces and pile in a salad bowl. Using only the pale green inner leaves of the batavia lettuce, scatter them over the lettuce and put the lamb's lettuce on top.

2 To make the herb sauce, separate the whites and yolks of the hard-boiled eggs. Chop the egg whites and scatter over the green salad. Mash the egg yolks to a paste with the cream, and stir in the oil very gradually. Add the vinegar slowly and stir until blended. Add salt and pepper to taste, and stir in the herbs.

3 Pour the herb sauce over the salad, mix well and serve.

Serves 4
Preparation time: 10 minutes

mesclun with croûtons and cheese dressing

250 g/8 oz mixed salad leaves
25 g/1 oz flat leaf parsley
4 thick slices of day-old white bread
1 large garlic clove, halved

Dressing:
25 g/1 oz dolcelatte cheese, softened
25 g/1 oz ricotta cheese, softened
6 tablespoons olive oil
1 tablespoon white wine vinegar
1 tablespoon boiling water
salt and pepper

1 Wash all the salad leaves and the parsley, shake off the excess water and transfer to a plastic bag. Tie the bag and chill for 30 minutes.

2 To make the dressing, place both the cheeses in a bowl and gradually beat in the oil, vinegar, boiling water, salt and pepper to form a smooth, thick sauce.

3 Place the salad leaves in a large bowl. Toast the bread lightly on both sides and, while still warm, rub all over with the garlic. Cut the bread into cubes and add to the bowl with the salad leaves.

4 Pour the dressing over the salad leaves, toss well and serve immediately.

Serves 4
Preparation time: 10 minutes, plus chilling
Cooking time: 2–3 minutes

country salad with horseradish dressing

250 g/8 oz shelled fresh broad beans
125 g/4 oz thin green beans, halved
500 g/1 lb firm ripe plum tomatoes, cut into wedges
½ small cucumber, thickly sliced
2 celery sticks, sliced
175 g/6 oz cooked beetroot, sliced
1 small red onion, thinly sliced
2 tablespoons capers
2 soft-boiled eggs, peeled and halved
salt

Dressing:
2 tablespoons grated horseradish or 1 tablespoon creamed horseradish
4 tablespoons olive oil
2 teaspoons red wine vinegar
pinch of sugar
2 tablespoons chopped herbs

1 Blanch the broad beans in boiling salted water for 1 minute, drain, refresh under cold water and pat dry on kitchen paper. Peel and discard the tough outer skin.

2 Boil the green beans for 4–5 minutes, drain, refresh under cold water and pat dry on kitchen paper.

3 Place the beans in a large bowl and add the tomatoes, cucumber, celery, beetroot, onion and capers.

4 Whisk all the dressing ingredients together and season with salt and pepper to taste. Pour over the salad and toss gently until all the ingredients are evenly coated. Transfer the salad to a serving dish and top with the egg halves. Serve at once.

Serves 4
Preparation time: 20 minutes
Cooking time: 6 minutes

green salad with walnuts and parmesan

large bowl of mixed salad leaves, (rocket, lamb's lettuce, spring spinach, red oakleaf, frisé, chicory)
½ mild onion, chopped
50 g/2 oz walnut pieces
about 40 g/1½ oz Parmesan cheese

Dressing:
5 tablespoons walnut oil
2 tablespoons red wine vinegar
½–1 teaspoon coarse grain mustard
pinch of sugar
salt and pepper

1 If the salad leaves are large, tear them roughly, and place them in a serving bowl with the onion.

2 Lightly toast the walnuts in a dry frying pan over moderate heat, then roughly chop them and leave to cool.

3 To make the dressing, whisk all the ingredients together in a small bowl or place them in a screw-top jar and shake well to combine.

4 Add the walnuts to the salad and pour over the dressing. Toss lightly to mix. Using a mandoline or vegetable peeler, shave the Parmesan over the salad and serve immediately.

Serves 4–6
Preparation time: 10 minutes
Cooking time: 2 minutes

mixed leaf salad with spiced toasted nuts

175–250 g/6–8 oz mixed salad leaves (lollo rosso, lamb's
lettuce, young spinach, frisé, rocket, red oakleaf)
small handful of chervil or dill sprigs
6 tablespoons French Dressing (see page 146)

Spiced nuts:
25 g/1 oz butter
50 g/2 oz blanched almonds
50 g/2 oz pecan nuts
2 tablespoons pine nuts
1 teaspoon Worcestershire sauce
1 teaspoon mild chilli powder
pinch of ground cumin
salt

1 To make the spiced nuts, melt the butter in a pan, add all the remaining ingredients, and cook over a moderate heat for 1 minute. Tip into a baking tin and place under a preheated moderate grill. Cook, turning frequently, for 5–10 minutes, until the nuts are toasted. Allow to cool.

2 Mix the salad leaves and herbs in a large salad bowl. Spoon over the dressing, toss to coat the leaves, scatter the spiced nuts over the top, and serve.

Serves 4–6
Preparation time: 10 minutes
Cooking time: 6–12 minutes

spiced coleslaw

Make the dressing before shredding the cabbage, so that the cabbage does not become dry. Similarly, avoid making the coleslaw too far ahead, as the ingredients should remain as crisp as possible.

1 dessert apple, unpeeled, cored and diced
2 carrots, grated
2 tablespoons diced gherkins
2 teaspoons capers
2 tablespoons chopped parsley
¼–½ white cabbage or cabbage heart, shredded

Spiced dressing:
3 tablespoons Mayonnaise (see page 145)
½ teaspoon curry powder
½ teaspoon ground nutmeg
½ teaspoon paprika
1 teaspoon prepared English mustard
1 tablespoon olive oil
1 tablespoon lemon juice
salt and pepper

1 To make the dressing, whisk all the ingredients together until blended.

2 Add the apple and carrots to the dressing with the gherkins, capers and parsley. Mix together thoroughly.

3 Pour the dressing over the cabbage, toss to mix, and serve.

Serves 4
Preparation time: 25–30 minutes

chickpea salad with garlic and olives

250 g/8 oz dried chickpeas, soaked overnight
1 bay leaf
1 parsley sprig
1 thyme sprig
3 tablespoons olive oil
1 onion, finely chopped
2 garlic cloves, crushed
125 g/4 oz black olives, pitted
½ red onion, finely sliced
salt and pepper
thyme sprigs, to garnish

Dressing:
6 tablespoons olive oil
1 tablespoon red wine vinegar
2 tablespoons lemon juice
2 tablespoons chopped herbs, such as parsley and thyme

1 Drain the chickpeas, rinse thoroughly under cold running water, and place in a saucepan of cold water. Add the bay leaf, parsley and thyme, bring to the boil, boil for 10 minutes, then cook at a bare simmer for about 2 hours, or until the chickpeas are tender. Drain and discard the herbs.

2 Meanwhile, heat the olive oil in a frying pan, add the onion and garlic, and gently fry until the onion is softened but not brown.

3 To make the dressing, whisk all the ingredients together in a small bowl or place them in a screw-top jar and shake well to combine. Place the drained chickpeas and sautéed onion in a bowl and pour over the dressing.

4 While the chickpeas are still hot, season to taste with salt and pepper, and toss gently. Add the olives and red onion and leave to cool. Garnish with thyme and serve at room temperature.

Serves 6–8
Preparation time: 15 minutes, plus soaking and cooling
Cooking time: 2¼ hours

tomato and coriander salad

1 kg/2 lb mixed tomatoes, sliced or quartered (include
  yellow cherry tomatoes if available)
2 teaspoons grated lime rind
½ small red onion, thinly sliced
1 tablespoon sesame seeds, toasted (optional)

Dressing:
2 tablespoons chopped coriander leaves
1 tablespoon lime juice
1 garlic clove, crushed
½ teaspoon clear honey
pinch of cayenne pepper
4 tablespoons olive oil
salt and pepper

1 First make the dressing. Whisk together the coriander, lime juice, garlic, honey, cayenne and salt and pepper, and then whisk in the oil.

2 Arrange the tomatoes in a large serving bowl and scatter over the lime rind, onion and toasted sesame seeds, if using.

3 Whisk the dressing ingredients again and pour over the salad. Cover the salad and set aside for 30 minutes for the flavours to develop, then serve.

Serves 4
Preparation time: 10 minutes, plus standing

grilled pepper and onion salad

3 onions, cut into wedges with root ends intact
3 red peppers, halved lengthways, cored and deseeded
3 yellow peppers, halved lengthways, cored and
  deseeded
15 garlic cloves
1½ tablespoons fennel seeds
6 tablespoons olive oil
2 tablespoons balsamic vinegar
3 tablespoons roughly chopped parsley
salt and pepper

1 Bring a saucepan of water to the boil, and cook the onions for 1 minute, then drain well.

2 Place the peppers, skin side up, in a grill pan. Add the onions and garlic cloves. Cook under a preheated hot grill for 10–15 minutes, turning occasionally, until the pepper skins are blistered and blackened all over. Turn the onions and garlic as necessary but let them char too.

3 Place the peppers in a polythene bag until they are cool, then peel off the skin. Arrange the peppers, onions and 12 of the garlic cloves on individual plates.

4 Toast the fennel seeds in a dry frying pan over moderate heat for a few minutes until they begin to pop and smell aromatic. Using a mortar and pestle, or a small strong bowl and the end of a rolling pin, roughly crush the fennel seeds with the 3 remaining grilled garlic cloves.

5 Whisk in the oil and vinegar, and season to taste with salt and pepper.

6 Sprinkle the parsley over the salad, then spoon over the dressing and serve at room temperature.

Serves 6
Preparation time: 20 minutes, plus cooling
Cooking time: 11–16 minutes

baby corn and alfalfa salad

To make this salad more substantial, add cooked chicken, or if you are vegetarian, add other types of nuts and a variety of sprouting beans.

500 g/1 lb baby corn cobs
125 g/4 oz alfalfa sprouts
5 tablespoons light olive oil or groundnut oil
½ onion, chopped
25 g/1 oz flaked almonds
2 tablespoons white wine vinegar
½ teaspoon finely grated lemon rind
½ teaspoon soft brown sugar
1 tablespoon chopped parsley
salt and pepper

1 Unless they are very small, halve the baby corn cobs lengthways. Cook in a saucepan of boiling water for about 3–4 minutes or until barely tender. Drain in a colander and refresh under cold running water. Drain again thoroughly and place in a large shallow bowl with the alfalfa sprouts.

2 Heat 2 tablespoons of the oil in a small frying pan, add the onion and fry for about 3 minutes or until softened. Transfer to a small bowl.

3 Add the almonds to the pan and cook, stirring, for 1–2 minutes, until lightly browned. Add the almonds, including the oil, to the onion with the remaining ingredients. Stir well and season to taste with salt and pepper.

4 Spoon the onion dressing over the corn and alfalfa, toss lightly and serve.

Serves 4–6
Preparation time: 15 minutes
Cooking time: 8–10 minutes

cucumber and pineapple salad with guacamole

Make the guacamole just before serving, as it tends to discolour if left to stand. If you have to make the guacamole in advance, put the avocado stones back into the middle of the guacamole to lessen the discolouration, and cover with clingfilm.

½ cucumber, peeled and very thinly sliced
1 teaspoon salt
½ ripe pineapple, peeled, cored and cut into bite-sized pieces
1 bunch of coriander, to garnish
salt and pepper

Guacamole:
2 ripe avocados, roughly chopped
1 garlic clove, crushed
2 tablespoons lime juice
1 red chilli, finely chopped
1 tomato, skinned and finely chopped
2 spring onions, finely chopped

1 Put the cucumber slices in a colander and sprinkle with the salt. Leave to drain over a large plate or in the sink for 20–30 minutes.

2 Place the pineapple in a bowl. Roughly tear about half of the coriander leaves into the bowl.

3 Rinse the cucumber slices under cold running water. Drain thoroughly, tip on to kitchen paper to dry slightly, then add to the pineapple mixture, with salt and pepper to taste. Toss lightly to mix.

4 To make the guacamole, place all the ingredients in a bowl. Using a fork, mash together thoroughly. Season to taste with salt and pepper. Garnish with coriander, and serve at once with the salad.

Serves 4–6
Preparation time: 20 minutes, plus draining

cucumber and dill salad

1 cucumber, peeled and very thinly sliced
2 teaspoons salt
dill sprigs, to garnish

Dressing:
4 tablespoons thick natural yogurt or Greek yogurt
1 teaspoon white wine vinegar
2 tablespoons chopped dill
pepper

1 Put the cucumber slices in a colander set over a large plate or in the sink. Sprinkle the salt over the cucumber and leave to stand for 20–30 minutes, to allow the excess moisture to drain away. Rinse the cucumber under cold running water, then drain thoroughly and place in a shallow serving dish.

2 To make the dressing, stir all the ingredients together in a small bowl.

3 Spoon the dressing over the cucumber and toss lightly to mix. Garnish with sprigs of dill and serve.

Serves 4–6
Preparation time: 10 minutes, plus standing

carrot and caraway salad

500 g/1 lb carrots, cut into sticks
2 teaspoons caraway seeds
2 teaspoons soft light brown sugar
150 ml/¼ pint water
chopped herbs, to garnish

Dressing:
3 tablespoons orange juice
½ teaspoon finely grated orange rind
4 tablespoons grapeseed oil, or 2 tablespoons sunflower
   oil plus 2 tablespoons olive oil
salt and pepper

1 Place the carrots in a saucepan with the caraway seeds, sugar and the measured water. Bring to the boil and cook, uncovered, on a fairly high heat for about 5 minutes, stirring once or twice, until all the water has evaporated and the carrots are still just firm. Transfer to a shallow serving dish.

2 Meanwhile, prepare the dressing. Put the orange juice and rind into a small bowl and gradually whisk in the oil, or place all the ingredients together in a screw-top jar and shake well to combine. Season well to taste with salt and pepper.

3 Pour the orange dressing over the carrots while they are still hot. Allow to cool. Sprinkled with chopped herbs, and serve.

Serves 4
Preparation time: 15 minutes, plus cooling
Cooking time: 5 minutes

beetroot and orange salad

3 oranges, peeled and pith removed
375 g/12 oz cooked beetroot, cut into matchstick lengths
1 tablespoon wine or cider vinegar
1 teaspoon lemon juice
pinch of sugar
1 small garlic clove, crushed
¼ teaspoon mustard powder
1 tablespoon chopped mixed herbs
3 tablespoons oil
salt and pepper
watercress, to garnish

1 Holding the oranges over a bowl to catch the juice, divide them into segments, remove the flesh from the membranes and cut them in half. Arrange the orange pieces in a serving dish, with the beetroot.

2 Add the vinegar, lemon juice, sugar, garlic, mustard and herbs to the bowl containing the orange juice. Whisk to mix, then gradually whisk in the oil. Taste the dressing and add salt and pepper if necessary. Pour the dressing over the salad, garnish with the watercress and serve.

Serves 4
Preparation time: 15 minutes

celeriac salad

1 large celeriac, cut into matchstick lengths
2–3 tablespoons thick Mayonnaise (see page 145)
¼ teaspoon Dijon mustard
salt

To garnish:
chopped parsley
paprika

1 Blanch the celeriac in a saucepan of salted boiling water for 2–3 minutes, or until just tender. Drain thoroughly and allow to cool.

2 Blend the mayonnaise with the mustard in a salad bowl. Add the celeriac and toss well. Sprinkle with the parsley and a little paprika and serve immediately.

Serves 4
Preparation time: 15 minutes, plus cooling
Cooking time: 2–3 minutes

leeks vinaigrette

If you cannot get very young leeks – ones that are not much fatter than a pencil – use 4 medium-sized leeks and halve them lengthways.

24 very young leeks

Dressing:
4 tablespoons olive oil
1 tablespoon white wine vinegar
½ teaspoon Dijon mustard
salt and pepper

To garnish:
1 hard-boiled egg, peeled and finely chopped
1 tablespoon chopped parsley
2 tablespoons chopped walnuts

1 Rinse the leeks thoroughly to remove any dirt. Boil them in shallow water in a frying pan or steam until just tender. Drain thoroughly.

2 Meanwhile, make the dressing. Whisk together all the ingredients in a small bowl or place them in a screw-top jar and shake well to combine. Season to taste with salt and pepper.

3 Transfer the drained leeks, while still hot, to a shallow serving dish. Pour over the dressing and leave to cool. Just before serving, sprinkle with the chopped egg, parsley and walnuts.

Serves 4
Preparation time: 10 minutes, plus cooling
Cooking time: 3–5 minutes

moroccan radish salad

2–3 bunches of radishes, trimmed and thinly sliced
2 oranges, peeled and segmented
2–3 tablespoons lemon juice
1 teaspoon caster sugar
orange flower water (optional)
salt
ground cinnamon or chopped coriander, to garnish

1 Toss together the radishes and oranges.

2 Mix the lemon juice with the sugar, a few drops of orange flower water, if using, and salt to taste, stirring until the sugar and salt have dissolved. Pour over the salad and toss lightly.

3 Sprinkle with a fine dusting of cinnamon or chopped coriander, and serve immediately.

Serves 4–6
Preparation time: 15 minutes

griddled asparagus salad

This salad can be made in the morning and left to marinate all day.

3 tablespoons olive oil (optional)
500 g/1 lb asparagus, trimmed
125 g/4 oz rocket or other green leaves
2 spring onions, finely sliced
4 radishes, thinly sliced
sea salt and pepper

Tarragon and lemon dressing:
2 tablespoons tarragon vinegar
finely grated rind of 1 lemon
¼ teaspoon Dijon mustard
pinch of sugar
1 tablespoon chopped tarragon
5 tablespoons olive oil or grapeseed oil
salt and pepper

To garnish:
herbs (tarragon, parsley, chervil and dill), roughly
    chopped
thin strips of lemon rind

1 First make the dressing. Whisk together the vinegar, lemon rind, mustard, sugar and tarragon in a small bowl, then gradually whisk in the oil, or place all the ingredients in a screw-top jar and shake well to combine. Season to taste with salt and pepper.

2 Heat the oil (if using) in a griddle pan or nonstick frying pan and place the asparagus on in a single layer. Cook for about 5 minutes, turning occasionally. The asparagus should be tender when pierced with the tip of a sharp knife, and lightly patched with brown. Remove from the pan to a shallow dish and sprinkle with sea salt and pepper. Pour on the dressing and toss gently, then leave to cool for 5 minutes.

3 Arrange the rocket on a platter, sprinkle the spring onions and radishes over the top and arrange the asparagus in a pile in the middle of the leaves. Garnish with chopped herbs and strips of lemon rind, and serve.

Serves 4
Preparation time: 20 minutes, plus cooling
Cooking time: about 5 minutes

bulgar wheat salad

125–150 g/4–5 oz bulgar wheat
2 tablespoons French Dressing (see page 146)
2 tablespoons diced cucumber
1 tablespoon sliced spring onions
3 tomatoes, sliced
2 tablespoons cooked peas
2 tablespoons sweetcorn kernels
1 tablespoon chopped chives
1 tablespoon chopped mint

To garnish:
black olives, pitted
lemon wedges
coriander sprigs

1 Place the wheat in a bowl. Cover it completely with boiling water and leave for 25 minutes. Drain well and place on kitchen paper to dry.

2 Put the wheat into a bowl with the dressing. Add the other ingredients, mix together thoroughly, garnish with black olives, lemon wedges, and coriander sprigs, and serve.

Serves 4
Preparation time: 15 minutes, plus standing

bulgar wheat with tomatoes, broad beans, feta and mint

250 g/8 oz bulgar wheat
475 ml/16 fl oz boiling water
250 g/8 oz frozen broad beans
½ cucumber, peeled, halved lengthways and deseeded
1 small red onion, chopped
4 tomatoes, chopped
2 tablespoons finely chopped mint
250 g/8 oz feta cheese, crumbled or diced

Dressing:
6 tablespoons olive oil
2 tablespoons wine vinegar
1 garlic clove, crushed
½ teaspoon sugar
salt and pepper

1 Put the wheat in large bowl and pour over the measured boiling water. Stir well and leave to stand for about 30 minutes until all the water is absorbed. Transfer to a serving dish and allow to cool.

2 Meanwhile, add the frozen broad beans to a pan of boiling water for 1 minute to blanch. Drain and cool under cold running water and then drain well. By hand, remove the waxy outer skins from the broad beans, reserving the bright green beans inside. Add these to the wheat in the serving dish.

3 Slice or dice the cucumber flesh and add to the salad with the red onion, tomatoes and mint. Season well with salt and pepper, and toss lightly to mix.

4 Sprinkle the feta cheese over the salad.

5 Whisk all the dressing ingredients together in a small bowl or place them in a screw-top jar and shake well to combine. Just before serving, pour the dressing over the salad and toss together lightly.

Serves 4–6
Preparation time: 15 minutes, plus standing and cooling
Cooking time: 1 minute

tabbouleh and fennel salad

250 g/8 oz bulgar wheat
1 fennel head, very finely sliced
1 red onion, finely sliced
5 tablespoons chopped mint
5 tablespoons chopped parsley
2 tablespoons fennel seeds
2 tablespoons olive oil
finely grated rind and juice of 2 lemons
salt and pepper

1 Place the wheat in a bowl, add enough cold water to cover, then leave to stand for 30 minutes, until all the water has been absorbed. Line a colander with muslin or a clean tea towel. Drain the wheat into the colander, then gather up the sides of the cloth or towel and squeeze to extract as much of the liquid as possible. Tip the wheat into a salad bowl.

2 Stir in the fennel, onion, mint, parsley, fennel seeds, oil, lemon rind and half the lemon juice. Add salt and pepper to taste. Cover and set aside for 30 minutes, then taste the salad and add more lemon juice, if required.

Serves 6
Preparation time: 20 minutes, plus soaking and standing

warm lentil salad

375 g/12 oz green lentils
2 carrots
1 onion, studded with 1 clove
1 bay leaf
pinch of dried thyme
1 garlic clove
1 leek, thinly sliced
125 g/4 oz celery, chopped
1 tablespoon oil
200 g/7 oz smoked streaky bacon, rinded and diced
1 tablespoon snipped chives

Dressing:
200 ml/7 fl oz walnut oil
6 tablespoons sherry or wine vinegar
1 tablespoon Dijon mustard
salt and pepper

1 Put the lentils in a bowl, cover them with water and leave to soak for 3–4 hours. Drain well and put them in a large saucepan.

2 Add 1 of the carrots, the onion studded with the clove, bay leaf, thyme and garlic. Cover with cold water, bring to the boil and simmer gently for 30–35 minutes. Discard the vegetables, bay leaf and garlic, and drain the lentils.

3 Slice the remaining carrot thinly and blanch with the leek and celery in a saucepan of lightly salted boiling water. Drain well.

4 Meanwhile, make the dressing. Whisk together all the ingredients in a small bowl or place them in a screw-top jar and shake well to combine.

5 Heat the oil in a frying pan, add the bacon and fry until crisp.

6 Stir the blanched vegetables and fried bacon gently into the lentils, pour over the dressing and toss. Sprinkle with snipped chives and serve warm.

Serves 4
Preparation: 10 minutes, plus soaking
Cooking: 45 minutes

couscous, chickpea and prawn salad

175 g/6 oz cooked couscous
400 g/13 oz can chickpeas, drained and rinsed
500 g/1 lb cooked peeled prawns
2 spring onions, thinly sliced
3 tomatoes, deseeded and chopped
1 bunch of mint, chopped
lemon wedges, to garnish

Dressing:
6 tablespoons olive oil
3 tablespoons lemon juice
pinch of caster sugar
paprika, to taste
salt and pepper

1 To make the dressing, whisk all the ingredients together in a small bowl or place them in a screw-top jar and shake well to combine. Add salt and pepper to taste.

2 Mix the couscous with the chickpeas, prawns, spring onions, tomatoes and mint.

3 Pour over the dressing and toss to coat all the ingredients. Garnish with lemon wedges and serve.

Serves 4
Preparation time: 10 minutes

lemon rice and wild rice salad with nuts, seeds and papaya

50 g/2 oz wild rice, rinsed
250 g/8 oz long-grain rice, rinsed
2 tablespoons lemon juice
1 teaspoon sugar
1 teaspoon salt
1 small papaya
1 bunch of spring onions, sliced
25 g/1 oz pecan nuts, toasted and chopped
25 g/1 oz sunflower seeds, toasted
1 tablespoon poppy seeds

Dressing:
6 tablespoons olive oil
1 tablespoon lemon juice or lime juice
2 tablespoons chopped parsley
salt and pepper

1 Cook the wild rice according to the packet instructions.

2 Meanwhile, put the long-grain rice in a pan with plenty of cold water, add the lemon juice, sugar and salt, bring to the boil and simmer gently for 10–12 minutes until cooked.

3 Drain both the wild and long-grain rice and place in a large bowl.

4 To make the dressing, whisk all the ingredients together in a small bowl or place them in a screw-top jar and shake well to combine. Season to taste with salt and pepper.

5 Pour the dressing over the rice, toss to mix thoroughly and set aside until cold.

6 Just before serving, cut the papaya in half, discard the seeds, peel, and dice the flesh. Add to the rice with the spring onions, nuts and seeds. Taste and adjust the seasoning, if necessary, and serve immediately.

Serves 6
Preparation time: 15 minutes, plus cooling
Cooking time: 35 minutes

herbed pasta salad with courgettes and tomatoes

250 g/8 oz dried pasta shapes
250 g/8 oz baby courgettes, sliced very thinly
175 g/6 oz cherry tomatoes, halved
2 tablespoons pine nuts, toasted

Dressing:
4 tablespoons olive oil
1 tablespoon capers
1 tablespoon chopped parsley
1 tablespoon chopped basil
1 teaspoon grated lime rind
1 tablespoon white wine vinegar
salt and pepper

To garnish:
coriander sprigs
basil sprigs

1 Cook the pasta until al dente (see page 137).

2 Meanwhile, prepare the dressing. Place the ingredients in a liquidizer and process until fairly smooth. Season to taste with salt and pepper.

3 Drain the pasta and immediately toss with the dressing. Stir in the courgettes and tomatoes and leave to cool to room temperature. Scatter over the pine nuts, garnish with coriander and basil sprigs, and serve.

Serves 4
Preparation time: 15 minutes
Cooking time: 8–12 minutes

pasta and broad bean salad

500 g/1 lb shelled fresh broad beans
500 g/1 lb dried pasta shells or twists
175 g/6 oz salami, diced
salt
lemon thyme sprigs, to garnish

Lime and thyme dressing:
6 tablespoons Mayonnaise (see page 145)
2 hard-boiled eggs, peeled and diced
2 tablespoons lime juice
2 teaspoons finely grated lime rind
4 tablespoons snipped chives
2 tablespoons chopped lemon thyme

1 Cook the broad beans in a pan of salted boiling water for 5 minutes. Drain and set aside.

2 Cook the pasta until al dente (see page 137). Drain the pasta in a colander, rinse under cold running water and drain again.

3 Transfer the pasta to a large bowl, and stir in the beans and salami.

4 To make the dressing, mix together all the ingredients in a small bowl. Fold into the pasta and bean mixture. Spoon the salad into a serving bowl, garnish with a sprig of lemon thyme and serve.

Serves 4–6
Preparation time: 10 minutes
Cooking time: 8–12 minutes

chicory, orange and pasta salad

500 g/1 lb tagliatelle, cut into shorter lengths
4 chicory heads, sliced
6 large oranges, divided into segments
2 tablespoons chopped tarragon
4 tablespoons snipped chives
salt

Orange dressing:
6 tablespoons olive oil
2 tablespoons orange juice
2 tablespoons lemon juice
½ teaspoon coarse grain mustard
1 teaspoon clear honey
1 teaspoon chopped mixed herbs
1 teaspoon finely grated orange rind

1 Cook the pasta until al dente (see page 137). Drain the pasta in a colander, rinse under cold running water and drain again.

2 To make the dressing, whisk together all the ingredients.

3 Pour the dressing over the pasta. Stir in the chicory, orange segments and herbs. Transfer to a serving dish and serve immediately.

Serves 4–6
Preparation time: 5–10 minutes
Cooking time: 8–12 minutes

chicken and mushroom penne salad

300 g/10 oz penne or other pasta shapes
250 g/8 oz cold cooked chicken, cut into strips
125 g/4 oz button mushrooms, sliced
1 red pepper, cored, deseeded and finely sliced
2 tablespoons sesame oil
1 teaspoon sesame seeds
1 tablespoon lemon juice
4 spring onions, diagonally sliced
salt and pepper
2 tablespoons chopped parsley, to garnish

1 Cook the pasta until al dente (see page 137), drain in a colander under cold running water and drain again. Put the drained pasta in a large salad bowl.

2 Add the chicken, sliced mushrooms and red pepper strips. Pour in the oil, sesame seeds, lemon juice and spring onions. Add salt and pepper to taste and toss well to combine all the ingredients. Garnish with the chopped parsley and serve at room temperature.

Serves 4
Preparation time: 15 minutes
Cooking time: 8–12 minutes

goats' cheese and watercress conchiglie

300 g/10 oz conchiglie or other pasta shapes
3 spring onions, diagonally sliced
3 tablespoons raspberry vinegar
6 tablespoons olive oil
125 g/4 oz soft goats' cheese, diced
1 orange or grapefruit, peeled and sliced into rings
1 bunch of watercress, trimmed
salt and pepper

1 Cook the pasta until al dente (see page 137), drain in a colander under cold running water and drain again. Put the drained pasta in a large salad bowl.

2 Mix the spring onions, raspberry vinegar and oil in a small bowl. Add salt and pepper to taste, whisk well to combine, then pour over the pasta.

3 Fold in the goats' cheese, the orange or grapefruit slices and the watercress. Toss the salad and chill until required. Do not make this salad too far in advance as the dressing will cause the watercress to wilt.

Serves 4
Preparation time: 10 minutes
Cooking time: 8–12 minutes

crunchy pasta salad

300 g/10 oz conchiglie or other pasta shapes
¼ red cabbage, shredded
2 celery sticks, chopped
1 Granny Smith apple, cored
1 tablespoon lemon juice
25 g/1 oz sultanas
4 tablespoons Mayonnaise (see page 145)
4 tablespoons milk
salt and pepper

To garnish:
pinch of cayenne pepper
celery leaves

1 Cook the pasta until al dente (see page 137), drain in a colander under cold running water and drain again. Put the drained pasta in a large salad bowl.

2 Add the cabbage and celery to the pasta in the bowl and mix well.

3 Quarter the apple, slice it into a small bowl and sprinkle with lemon juice to prevent it browning. Fold the apple slices into the pasta with the sultanas.

4 Mix together the mayonnaise and milk, add salt and pepper to taste, then fold it into the salad. Garnish with cayenne pepper and celery leaves and serve.

Serves 4
Preparation time: 20 minutes
Cooking time: 8–12 minutes

bruschetta

Bruschetta is a very useful snack, as the bread does not have to be fresh.

8 slices of ciabatta bread
2 garlic cloves, peeled
small handful of flat leaf parsley, chopped
5 tablespoons olive oil
salt

1 Toast the ciabatta bread under a preheated grill until golden brown.

2 Rub the garlic over one side of the bread; the bread acts as a grater and the garlic is evenly spread over it.

3 Sprinkle the bruschetta with the parsley and salt and drizzle with olive oil. Serve immediately or keep warm until required, but not for too long or the bruschetta will lose its crunchiness.

Serves 4
Preparation time: 5 minutes
Cooking time: 5 minutes

crostini

1–2 red peppers
8 slices of ciabatta bread
2 garlic cloves, peeled
small handful of flat leaf parsley, chopped
5 tablespoons olive oil
75 g/3 oz black olives, pitted
125 g/4 oz goats' cheese, crumbled
salt and pepper

1 Roast the red peppers in a hot oven or under the grill until the skin is blistered and black all over. Place them in a polythene bag until they are cool, then remove the skin, core and seeds, and cut the flesh into strips.

2 Toast the ciabatta bread under a preheated grill until golden brown.

3 Rub the garlic over one side of the bread; the bread acts as a grater and the garlic is evenly spread over it. Sprinkle with parsley and salt, and drizzle with olive oil.

4 Mix together the red peppers, olives and crumbled goats' cheese and season to taste with pepper.

5 Spread the mixture evenly over the toasted bruschetta and place under a preheated low grill for 2 minutes to just melt the cheese, and serve immediately.

Serves 4
Preparation time: 10 minutes
Cooking time: 5 minutes

artichoke and goats' cheese pizzas

2 quantities Basic Pizza Dough (see page 133), divided
    into 4 pieces
2 onions, finely sliced
1 kg/2 lb artichoke hearts in oil
2 tablespoons black olives, pitted
175 g/6 oz mild goats' cheese, thinly sliced or crumbled
handful of oregano, chopped
salt and pepper

1 Roll out each piece of dough to a 23 cm/9 inch round. Place the pizza bases on oiled baking sheets.

2 Mix together the onions and artichokes and season well with salt and pepper.

3 Divide the mixture between the bases and spread over evenly. Sprinkle with the olives and top with the goats' cheese, oregano and salt and pepper. Put the pizzas in a preheated oven, 230°C (450°F), Gas Mark 8, bake for 10–15 minutes and serve immediately.

Serves 4
Preparation time: 8–10 minutes, plus making the dough and rising
Cooking time: 10–15 minutes
Oven temperature: 230°C (450°F), Gas Mark 8

fresh vegetable pizzas

2 quantities Basic Pizza Dough (see page 133), divided
    into 4 pieces
5 tablespoons olive oil
2 garlic cloves, chopped
1 red onion, finely sliced
2 courgettes, thinly sliced lengthways
1 red pepper, cored, deseeded and cut into thin strips
1 yellow pepper, cored, deseeded and cut into thin strips
4 plum tomatoes, skinned, cored and cut into small
    wedges
500 g/1 lb asparagus, trimmed
4 thyme sprigs, separated into leaves
handful of basil leaves, roughly torn
salt and pepper
75 g/3 oz fresh Parmesan shavings (optional), to garnish

1 Roll out each piece of dough to a 23 cm/9 inch round. Place the pizza bases on oiled baking sheets and brush them with a little olive oil. Arrange the vegetables on the bases, sprinkling them with the thyme leaves and roughly torn basil.

2 Season the pizzas generously with salt and pepper, drizzle with olive oil, and bake at the top of a preheated oven, 230°C (450°F), Gas Mark 8, for 10 minutes. The vegetables should be slightly charred around the edges as this adds to the flavour. Garnish with fresh Parmesan shavings, if liked, and serve.

Serves 4
Preparation time: 20 minutes, plus making the dough and rising
Cooking time: 10 minutes
Oven temperature: 230°C (450°F), Gas Mark 8

anchovy and red pepper pizzas

4 tablespoons olive oil
2 red onions, sliced
4 red peppers, cored, deseeded and cut into strips
2 garlic cloves, chopped
2 quantities Basic Pizza Dough (see page 133), divided
    into 4 pieces
50 g/2 oz can anchovies
handful of marjoram, chopped
1 tablespoon black olives, pitted and chopped
250 g/8 oz buffalo mozzarella, sliced
salt and pepper

1 Heat the olive oil in a saucepan, add the onions and red peppers, and fry for about 5 minutes until soft. Add the garlic and mix well.

2 Roll out each piece of dough to a 23 cm/9 inch round. Place the pizza bases on oiled baking sheets. Spoon and spread the cooked peppers over them. Arrange the anchovies on top of the pizzas and sprinkle with salt and pepper, chopped marjoram and olives, and add the slices of mozzarella.

3 Put the pizzas into a preheated oven, 230°C (450°F), Gas Mark 8, and bake for 10 minutes. Serve the pizzas immediately.

Serves 4
Preparation time: 10 minutes, plus making the dough and rising
Cooking time: 15 minutes
Oven temperature: 230°C (450°F), Gas Mark 8

many tomato pizzas

1 quantity Basic Pizza Dough (see page 133), divided in half
2 large ripe plum tomatoes, sliced
125 g/4 oz red cherry tomatoes, halved
125 g/4 oz yellow pear tomatoes, halved
4 sun-dried tomatoes in oil, drained and roughly chopped
handful of basil leaves, torn into pieces
2 teaspoons grated lemon rind
12 black olives, pitted
4 tablespoons olive oil
sea salt and pepper

1 Roll out each piece of dough to a 23 cm/9 inch round. Place the pizza bases on an oiled baking sheet.

2 Dry the tomato slices on kitchen paper. Arrange all the tomatoes over the pizzas, scattering over the basil, lemon rind and olives. Season well and drizzle over a little olive oil.

3 Place at the top of a preheated oven, 230°C (450°F), Gas Mark 8, for 20 minutes until the bases are crisp and the tops golden. Serve immediately.

Serves 2
Preparation time: 10 minutes, plus making dough and rising
Cooking time: 20 minutes
Oven temperature: 230°C (450°F), Gas Mark 8

vegetable calzone

A calzone is a stuffed pizza or one that is simply folded in half and sealed.

1 tablespoon olive oil
1 large onion, thinly sliced
1 red pepper, cored, deseeded and sliced
1 garlic clove, crushed
500 g/1 lb frozen leaf spinach, defrosted
175 g/6 oz mozzarella cheese, diced
50 g/2 oz pine nuts, toasted
40 g/1½ oz sultanas
¼ teaspoon grated nutmeg
2 quantities Basic Pizza Dough (see page 133), divided into 6 pieces
salt and pepper

1 Heat the oil in a frying pan, add the onion, pepper and garlic, and fry until golden. Remove from the heat.

2 Drain the spinach in a colander, pressing down firmly to squeeze out any moisture, then chop finely. Stir into the onion mixture, then stir in the remaining ingredients, except the pizza dough, and set aside to cool.

3 Roll out each piece of dough to an 18 cm/7 inch round. Divide the filling between the rounds, brush the edges with water and fold the dough over, pressing together firmly to seal the edges and enclose the filling.

4 Transfer the parcels to a large oiled baking sheet and lightly brush each one with water. Place at the top of a preheated oven, 200°C (400°F), Gas Mark 6, for 20 minutes until the calzone are golden. Remove from the oven and leave to rest for 10 minutes before serving.

Serves 6
Preparation time: 20 minutes, plus making the dough, rising and resting
Cooking time: 25–30 minutes
Oven temperature: 200°C (400°F), Gas Mark 6

vegetable frittata

2 tablespoons olive oil
2 onions, finely sliced
2 garlic cloves, chopped
2 potatoes, boiled and sliced

2 red peppers, cored, deseeded and cut into strips
6 courgettes, sliced
1 thyme sprig, chopped
5 eggs, beaten
50 g/2 oz Parmesan cheese, freshly grated
salt and pepper

1 Heat the olive oil in a frying pan with a heatproof handle, add the onions, garlic, potatoes, red peppers and courgettes, and sauté for 5 minutes.

2 Add the thyme, season with salt and pepper and mix well. Pour in the beaten eggs and cook over a moderate heat for 3 minutes.

3 Sprinkle with the Parmesan and put the pan in a preheated oven, 200°C (400°F), Gas Mark 6, and cook for 15 minutes. The frittata should be set and golden.

4 Remove the pan from the oven, ease a palette knife all the way round the edge and under the frittata, slide it on to a large plate and serve immediately.

Serves 4–6
Preparation time: 10 minutes
Cooking time: 25 minutes
Oven temperature: 200°C (400°F), Gas Mark 6

asparagus omelette

500 g/1 lb young asparagus, trimmed
5 eggs
2 tablespoons milk
4 tablespoons finely chopped flat leaf parsley
2 tablespoons olive oil
15 g/½ oz butter
2 tablespoons grated Parmesan cheese
salt and pepper

1 Cook the asparagus in plenty of salted boiling water for 10 minutes. Drain and refresh under cold running water, then cut into 1 cm/½ inch lengths.

2 Beat the eggs, milk and parsley in a bowl and season with salt and pepper to taste. Add the pieces of asparagus and stir to mix.

3 Heat the oil and butter in a 30 cm/12 inch nonstick frying pan until foaming. Pour in the egg mixture and let it settle, then cover the pan and cook over a low heat for 10 minutes or until the omelette is almost set.

4 Sprinkle the Parmesan evenly over the omelette, then put it under a preheated grill for 2–3 minutes until golden brown and set. Serve warm or cold.

Serves 4
Preparation time: 15 minutes
Cooking time: about 25 minutes

spanish tortilla

150 ml/¼ pint olive oil
750 g/1½ lb potatoes, thinly sliced
1 large onion, sliced
5 large eggs, beaten
salt and pepper

1 Heat all but 2 tablespoons of the oil in a 20 cm/8 inch nonstick frying pan, add the potato slices and onions, and cook for 15 minutes, stirring frequently, until they are golden and tender.

2 Stir the potato mixture into the beaten eggs and season generously with salt and pepper. Set aside for 15 minutes.

3 Clean out the frying pan. Heat the remaining oil in the clean pan and tip in the tortilla mixture. Cook over a low heat for 10 minutes until almost cooked through. Carefully slide the tortilla on to a large plate, invert the pan over the tortilla and flip the tortilla back into the pan.

4 Return the pan to the heat and cook for a further 5 minutes or until the tortilla is cooked on both sides. Allow to cool, cut into wedges and serve.

Serves 4–6
Preparation time: 10 minutes
Cooking time: 30 minutes, plus standing

onion tortilla

40 g/1½ oz butter
1 large onion, halved and thinly sliced
125 g/4 oz cabbage, finely shredded
3 eggs, beaten

1 tablespoon cold water
125 g/4 oz Cheddar or Edam cheese, finely grated
salt and pepper
tomato wedges, to garnish

1 Melt 25 g/1 oz of the butter in a saucepan, add the onion and cabbage, and fry over low heat for 3 minutes, stirring frequently.

2 Beat the eggs with the measured water in a bowl. Add salt and pepper to taste. Stir in half the cheese.

3 Melt the remaining butter in a 23 cm/9 inch frying pan. Add the softened onion and cabbage, pour over the egg and cheese mixture, and cook over moderately high heat for 3 minutes or until lightly golden on the underside.

4 Sprinkle the surface of the tortilla with the remaining cheese. Place under a preheated moderately hot grill for 2–3 minutes until the cheese is melted and the tortilla is set. Cut into wedges, garnish with tomatoes and serve immediately.

Serves 4
Preparation time: 10 minutes
Cooking time: 15 minutes

chicken liver and bacon kebabs

375 g/12 oz chicken livers
375 g/12 oz streaky bacon rashers, rinded
4 teaspoons Worcestershire sauce
4 teaspoons mushroom ketchup
2 tablespoons mustard powder
1 teaspoon lemon juice
1 tablespoon tomato purée
50 g/2 oz butter, melted
lemon wedges, to garnish
radicchio and rocket leaves, to serve

1 Trim the chicken livers and cut into 2.5 cm/1 inch pieces. Stretch the bacon rashers with the back of a knife. Cut each rasher in half and roll up the pieces with the point of a knife.

2 Thread the liver pieces and bacon rolls alternately on to small skewers. Blend together the Worcestershire sauce, mushroom ketchup, mustard, lemon juice, tomato purée and butter. Place the kebabs close together in a deep dish and pour the sauce over them. Cover closely and marinate in the refrigerator overnight.

3 Place the kebabs on a grill rack and cook under a preheated hot grill for 5–10 minutes, turning and basting with the sauce as they cook. Garnish with lemon wedges and serve hot with the radicchio and rocket leaves.

Serves 8
Preparation time: 10 minutes, plus marinating
Cooking time: 5–10 minutes

potato pancakes

500 g/1 lb potatoes
4 tablespoons boiling milk
4 tablespoons plain flour
3 eggs, plus 4 egg whites
1/2 teaspoon dried mixed herbs (optional)
4 tablespoons double cream
oil, for frying
salt and pepper
parsley sprigs, to garnish

1 Boil the potatoes in their skins until tender. When cool enough to handle, remove the skins, then mash the potatoes until very smooth. Beat in the boiling milk and leave to cool completely.

2 Using a wooden spoon, beat in the flour, whole eggs and egg whites. Stir in the herbs, if using, and cream, and season with salt and pepper. Beat until very smooth – it should resemble a thick batter.

3 Pour a little oil into a frying pan, swirl it around to just cover the base of the pan, pouring off any excess, and heat the pan. When the oil begins to give off a slight haze, drop in tablespoons of the batter, a little apart, and cook for 2 minutes on each side, until golden brown.

4 Place the pancakes in layers in a clean dry tea towel and put into a cool oven to keep warm. Repeat with the remaining batter.

5 Garnish with parsley and serve very hot.

Serves 4
Preparation time: 10 minutes, plus cooling
Cooking time: about 25 minutes

breakfast gratin

4 tablespoons olive oil
175 g/6 oz button mushrooms, quartered if large
1 onion, roughly chopped
4 small cooked potatoes, cubed
4 small tomatoes, halved
4 small eggs
125 g/4 oz Cheddar cheese, grated
salt and pepper
2 tablespoons chopped chives or parsley, to garnish

1 Heat half the oil in a large frying pan, add the mushrooms and onion, and fry for 5 minutes until golden. Remove with a slotted spoon and set aside. Add the remaining oil and fry the potatoes for 5–6 minutes until golden.

2 Increase the heat, stir in the tomatoes, and fry over a high heat for 2–3 minutes until lightly golden. Return the mushrooms and onions to the pan and season to taste.

3 Make 4 holes in the mixture and carefully break an egg into each hole. Scatter over the cheese and place under a preheated hot grill for 4–5 minutes until the eggs are set and the cheese bubbling and golden.

4 Sprinkle over the chopped chives or parsley and serve immediately.

Serves 4
Preparation time: 15 minutes
Cooking time: 18–20 minutes

eggs benedict

1 quantity Hollandaise Sauce (see page 144)
6 large mushrooms, stalks trimmed
6 tablespoons olive oil
500 g/1 lb spinach, trimmed
6 small eggs
cayenne pepper, to garnish

1 Make the hollandaise sauce first. Place a piece of clingfilm over the surface of the sauce and sit the bowl over a pan of hot water to keep warm.

2 Arrange the mushrooms, cap side down, in an ovenproof dish. Drizzle over the olive oil, cover with foil and place in a preheated oven, 200°C (400°F), Gas Mark 6, for 20 minutes.

3 Meanwhile, wash the spinach and place in a large saucepan with just the water left on the leaves. Heat gently until just wilted. Drain in a colander, pressing down firmly with a wooden spoon to squeeze out excess moisture, and chop roughly.

4 Poach the eggs for 3–4 minutes until just cooked. Remove the mushrooms from the oven, spoon the chopped spinach around them and carefully place a poached egg on top of each one.

5 Pour over the hollandaise sauce and place the dish under a preheated hot grill for 3–4 minutes until browned. Sprinkle with a little cayenne pepper and serve immediately.

Serves 6
Preparation time: 20 minutes
Cooking time: 25–30 minutes
Oven temperature: 200°C (400°F), Gas Mark 6

smoked salmon with scrambled eggs

25 g/1 oz butter
6 large eggs
2 tablespoons milk
2 tablespoons cream (optional)
75 g/3 oz smoked salmon, cut into narrow strips
2 teaspoons finely snipped chives
2–4 slices wheaten bread, toasted and buttered
salt and pepper

1 Melt the butter in a saucepan until foaming. Place the eggs in a bowl and mix well with a fork. Add the milk and season with salt and pepper. Pour the eggs into the foaming butter. Stir with a wooden spoon, over a gentle heat, scraping the bottom of the pan and bringing the outside edges to the middle.

2 When the eggs form soft creamy curds and are barely set, remove the pan from the heat, stir in the cream, if using, salmon and chives. Place the hot brown toast on warmed serving plates, pile the eggs on top, and serve immediately.

Serves 2
Preparation time: 5 minutes
Cooking time: 3–4 minutes

smoked salmon and poached egg salad on muffins

4 eggs
2 plain muffins, halved
125 g/4 oz frisé lettuce
250 g/8 oz smoked salmon
1 tablespoon poppy seeds
snipped chives, to garnish

Anchovy butter:
25 g/1 oz butter, softened
1¹/₂ teaspoons mashed anchovy fillets
¹/₂ teaspoon lemon juice

Dressing:
2 teaspoons champagne or white wine vinegar
1 teaspoon Dijon mustard
1 tablespoon snipped chives
6 tablespoons olive oil
2 ripe tomatoes, skinned, deseeded and diced
salt and pepper

1 First make the anchovy butter. Cream together all the ingredients, season with pepper and set aside.

2 Poach the eggs until just set.

3 Meanwhile, grill both sides of the muffins under a preheated grill until golden; split, spread the insides with anchovy butter and return to the grill for a further 1–2 minutes.

4 Blend together all the dressing ingredients except the tomatoes, taste and adjust the seasoning, if necessary, and toss half with the frisé lettuce. Stir the diced tomato into the remaining dressing.

5 Arrange the muffins on serving plates, top each with smoked salmon and dressed frisé, and sprinkle over the poppy seeds. Carefully remove the poached eggs from the water with a slotted spoon, drain on kitchen paper and place 1 egg on top of each muffin. Pour the tomato dressing around each muffin, garnish with the snipped chives, and serve.

Serves 4
Preparation time: 25 minutes
Cooking time: 10 minutes

spicy toasts

2 eggs
2¹/₂ teaspoons mixed spice
50 g/2 oz caster sugar
4 thick slices of white bread
oil, for shallow frying

1 Beat the eggs with 2 teaspoons of the mixed spice. Mix the remaining mixed spice with the sugar.

2 Dip the slices of bread into the egg mixture.

3 Heat the oil in a frying pan, add the bread and fry, turning to brown both sides.

4 Drain well on kitchen paper, then sprinkle with the spiced sugar, cut into quarters and serve warm.

Serves 2–4
Preparation time: 10 minutes
Cooking time: 10 minutes

hot cheesy garlic bread

1 French bread stick
125 g/4 oz butter or margarine, softened
1 garlic clove, crushed
1¹/₂ tablespoons snipped chives or chopped parsley
125 g/4 oz Red Leicester or Cheddar cheese, finely grated

1 Carefully cut the loaf into 2.5 cm/1 inch thick slices, cutting almost through to the bottom crust but keeping the slices together at the base.

2 Using a wooden spoon, cream the butter or margarine with the garlic, chives or parsley and cheese in a bowl.

3 Spread the savoury butter on either side of each slice of bread and over the top of the loaf. Wrap the loaf tightly in foil.

4 Place the loaf on a baking sheet and bake in a preheated oven, 190°C (375°F), Gas Mark 5, for 15 minutes. Then carefully open up the foil and fold it back to expose the top of the loaf. Bake for 5 minutes more. Cut into slices and serve hot.

Serves 4–6
Preparation time: 10 minutes
Cooking time: 20 minutes
Oven temperature: 190°C (375°F), Gas Mark 5

mini pissaladière

4 tablespoons olive oil
1 kg/2 lb onions, thinly sliced
2 garlic cloves, crushed
2 teaspoons chopped thyme
1 teaspoon salt
1 teaspoon sugar
6 anchovy fillets, halved lengthways
6 black olives, pitted
3 tablespoons freshly grated Parmesan cheese

Pastry:
125 g/4 oz plain flour
¹/₄ teaspoon salt
50 g/2 oz butter, diced
1–2 tablespoons iced water

1 To make the pastry, sift the flour and salt into a bowl and rub in the butter until the mixture resembles fine breadcrumbs. Work in enough of the measured water to form a soft dough. Knead lightly and chill for 30 minutes.

2 Heat the oil in a heavy-based frying pan, add the onions, garlic, thyme, salt and sugar, and fry for about 25 minutes, until golden and caramelized. Set aside to cool.

3 Divide the pastry into 6 pieces, roll each piece out on a lightly floured surface and use to line six 7 cm/3 inch tartlet tins. Prick the bases with a fork and chill for a further 20 minutes.

4 Line the pastry cases with greaseproof paper and fill with baking beans or dried beans. Bake in a preheated oven, 200°C (400°F), Gas Mark 6, for 10 minutes. Lift out the paper and beans and bake for a further 10 minutes or until light golden brown.

5 Divide the onion mixture between the pastry cases, place a cross of anchovies and an olive on top of each one, sprinkle over the Parmesan, and bake for 10 minutes. Serve warm or cool on a wire rack.

Serves 6
Preparation time: 20 minutes, plus chilling
Cooking time: 50 minutes
Oven temperature: 200°C (400°F), Gas Mark 6

cornish pasties

Pastry:
500 g/1 lb plain flour
¹/₄ teaspoon salt
125 g/4 oz butter
125 g/4 oz hard white fat
150 ml/¹/₄ pint cold water
beaten egg, to glaze

Filling:
500 g/1 lb braising steak, trimmed and cut into thin strips
250 g/8 oz potatoes, peeled and cut into thin flakes
175 g/6 oz swede, peeled and cut into thin flakes
2 onions, finely chopped
25 g/1 oz butter, cut into 8 equal pieces
salt and pepper

To garnish:
lettuce leaves
tomato wedges

1 To make the pastry, sift the flour with the salt into a mixing bowl, add the butter and fat and rub in until the mixture resembles coarse breadcrumbs. Add the measured water and mix to form a soft dough. Knead gently until free from cracks. Wrap and chill while preparing the filling.

2 Put the meat, potatoes, swede and onions into a bowl and season well with salt and pepper. Stir to mix.

3 Roll out the pastry on a lightly floured surface and cut out eight 18 cm/7 inch rounds, using a plate as a guide, and re-rolling the trimmings as required.

4 Spoon equal portions of the filling on to the centre of each pastry round. Place a piece of butter on each portion of filling, dampen the pastry edges and draw up both sides to meet on top of the filling, taking care not to stretch the pastry. Seal the edges firmly and form a 1 cm/½ inch high edge on top of each pasty. Crimp the edge decoratively with the fingertips, folding and tucking the edge under to give a 'rope' effect down the length of each pasty. Place the pasties on a lightly greased baking sheet.

5 Make a small hole at the side of each join and brush each pastry with beaten egg. Place in a preheated oven, 190°C (375°F), Gas Mark 5, and bake for 1 hour or until golden brown and cooked through. (Cover with foil if necessary to prevent over-browning.) To test if the vegetables are tender, insert a fine metal skewer or wooden cocktail stick into the hole in each pasty. Serve hot or cold, garnished with lettuce and tomato.

Serves 8
Preparation time: 30 minutes
Cooking time: 1 hour
Oven temperature: 190°C (375°F), Gas Mark 5

smoked mozzarella and tomato puff tartlets

Smoked mozzarella is available from good cheese shops or supermarkets. Use another smoked cheese or plain mozzarella as an alternative.

250 g/8 oz frozen puff pastry, defrosted, and divided into 8 pieces
2 tablespoons Pesto (see page 146)
2 large ripe tomatoes, each cut into 4 slices
125 g/4 oz smoked mozzarella, cut into 8 slices
salt and pepper

1 Roll out each piece of the pastry thinly on a lightly floured surface. Using a 10 cm/4 inch pastry cutter, stamp out 8 circles. Prick the pastry circles with a fork and place on baking sheets.

2 Spread each circle of pastry with pesto, leaving a thin border around the edges. Top with a slice of tomato and then a slice of mozzarella. Season with salt and pepper.

3 Bake the tartlets at the top of a preheated oven, 220°C (425°F), Gas Mark 7, for 10–15 minutes until puffed up and golden. Serve warm.

Serves 8
Preparation time: 10 minutes
Cooking time: 10–15 minutes
Oven temperature: 220°C (425°F), Gas Mark 7

quiche lorraine

250 g/8 oz plain flour
pinch of salt
125 g/4 oz butter
1 egg yolk
2–3 tablespoons iced water

Filling:
50 g/2 oz butter
150 g/5 oz smoked bacon, cut into small pieces
350 ml/12 fl oz double cream
3 eggs
¼ teaspoon freshly grated nutmeg
salt and pepper

1 To make the pastry, sift the flour and salt into a large mixing bowl and rub in the butter until the mixture resembles breadcrumbs. Mix in the egg yolk and enough of the measured water to bind the ingredients. Knead the dough lightly and then chill in the refrigerator for 30 minutes.

2 Roll out the pastry on a lightly floured surface and use to line a buttered 23 cm/9 inch loose-bottomed flan tin. Prick the base of the flan with a fork.

3 Melt half of the butter in a frying pan, add the bacon pieces and cook gently until lightly coloured. Put the cream and eggs in a bowl and whisk together. Add the grated nutmeg and season with salt and pepper.

4 Sprinkle the cooked bacon pieces over the base of the pastry case and dot with the remaining butter. Pour in the cream and egg mixture. Bake in a preheated oven, at 200°C (400°F), Gas Mark 6, for 30 minutes, or until set and golden brown. Serve warm.

Serves 6
Preparation time: 20 minutes, plus chilling
Cooking time: 30 minutes
Oven temperature: 200°C (400°F), Gas Mark 6

focaccia sandwich with mediterranean vegetables and mozzarella p463

hamburgers with mustard mayonnaise and radicchio p456

many tomato pizzas   p442

grilled mushrooms with garlic oil   p452

marinated goats' cheese   p452

baked garlic with brie   p452

crostini p440

fresh vegetable pizzas p441

cheese and onion flan

Oat pastry:
125 g/4 oz wholemeal flour
125 g/4 oz medium oatmeal
pinch of salt
125 g/4 oz butter or margarine
2–3 tablespoons water

Filling:
2 tablespoons oil
2 onions, chopped
2 eggs
150 ml/¼ pint milk
250 g/8 oz Cheddar cheese, grated
salt and pepper

1 To make the pastry, place the flour, oatmeal and salt in a mixing bowl and rub in the butter or margarine until the mixture resembles breadcrumbs. Add enough of the water to mix to a firm dough. Turn on to a floured surface and knead lightly until smooth. Roll out and use to line a 20 cm/8 inch flan dish. Chill for 15 minutes.

2 Meanwhile, make the filling. Heat the oil in a frying pan, add the onions and fry gently until translucent. Mix the eggs and milk together, then stir in the cheese, onions, and salt and pepper to taste.

3 Pour into the flan case and bake in a preheated oven, 190°C (375°F), Gas Mark 5, for 35–40 minutes. Serve hot or cold.

Serves 4–6
Preparation time: 25 minutes, plus chilling
Cooking time: 40–45 minutes
Oven temperature: 190°C (375°F), Gas Mark 5

french onion flan

Pastry:
250 g/8 oz plain flour
50 g/2 oz butter
50 g/2 oz hard white fat
3 tablespoons iced water

Filling:
40 g/1½ oz butter
500 g/1 lb onions, thinly sliced
2 teaspoons tomato purée
3 eggs
150 ml/¼ pint milk
salt and pepper

1 Melt the butter in a frying pan. Add the onions with the tomato purée, sprinkle lightly with salt and pepper, stir well and cook over gentle heat for 15 minutes, stirring occasionally. Remove from the heat and leave to cool.

2 Meanwhile, make the pastry. Sift the flour with the salt into a mixing bowl and rub in the butter and fat until the mixture resembles fine breadcrumbs. Stir in the measured water and mix to form a fairly firm dough. Knead lightly until free from cracks.

3 Roll out the pastry on a lightly floured surface and line a 25 cm/10 inch loose-bottomed fluted flan tin set on a baking sheet. Line the pastry case with greaseproof paper and fill with baking beans or dried beans. Bake in a preheated oven, 200°C (400°F), Gas Mark 6, for 15 minutes. Lift out the paper and beans and bake for a further 5–10 minutes until the pastry is dry and cooked through. Remove from the oven.

4 Arrange the onions in the flan case. Beat the eggs with the milk in a bowl and add salt and pepper to taste. Strain into the flan case. Lower the oven temperature to 180°C (350°F), Gas Mark 4, and bake for 30–35 minutes until the filling is set and lightly golden. Serve hot or cold.

Serves 6–8
Preparation time: 30 minutes
Cooking time: about 1 hour
Oven temperatute: 200°C (400°F), Gas Mark 6

little pizza pies

175 g/6 oz frozen puff pastry, defrosted
15 g/½ oz butter
1 onion, thinly sliced
1 garlic clove, finely chopped
2 teaspoons tomato purée
400 g/13 oz can chopped tomatoes
5 basil leaves, shredded
salt and pepper

Topping:
75 g/3 oz mature Cheddar cheese, finely grated
6 black olives, pitted and halved
6 anchovy fillets, halved

1 Roll out the pastry thinly on a lightly floured work surface and use to line twelve 6 cm/2½ inch tartlet tins. Chill.

2 To make the filling, melt the butter in a frying pan, add the onion and garlic and fry gently for about 5 minutes. Add the tomato purée and canned tomatoes and simmer for 30 minutes. Stir in the basil and salt and pepper. Leave to cool.

3 Divide the tomato mixture among the pies and sprinkle with cheese. Put half an olive in the centre of each pie and arrange a piece of anchovy around it.

4 Bake the pies in a preheated oven, 200°C (400°F), Gas Mark 6, for 12–15 minutes or until the pastry is browned and cheese melted. Serve warm.

Makes 12
Preparation time: 20 minutes, plus chilling
Cooking time: 50 minutes
Oven temperature: 200°C (400°F), Gas Mark 6

sausage slice

1 tablespoon oil
1 small onion, chopped
500 g/1 lb sausagemeat
1 teaspoon dried mixed herbs
1 egg, beaten
400 g/13 oz frozen puff pastry, defrosted
1 small cooking apple, peeled, cored and sliced
salt and pepper

1 Heat the oil in a small frying pan, add the onion and fry gently until soft. Tip into a bowl, cool slightly, then add the sausagemeat with the herbs. Season to taste and stir in half the egg.

2 Roll out three-quarters of the pastry to a 25 cm/10 inch square. Place on a greased baking sheet. Spread the mixture over the pastry to within 1 cm/½ inch of the edge. Arrange the apple slices on top. Dampen the edges of the pastry with water.

3 Roll out the remaining pastry. Cut into 1 cm/½ inch wide strips and make a woven trellis over the top of the apples. Brush with the remaining egg and chill for 30 minutes.

4 Place in a preheated oven, 220°C (425°F), Gas Mark 7, for 15 minutes. Reduce the oven temperature to 180°C (350°F), Gas Mark 4, and cook for a further 15–30 minutes. Serve hot.

Serves 6
Preparation time: 15 minutes, plus chilling
Cooking time: 30–45 minutes
Oven temperature: 220°C (425°F), Gas Mark 7

piperade

4 large red peppers
7 tablespoons olive oil
4 large onions, thinly sliced
1 hot pimento, thinly sliced
2 garlic cloves, crushed
pinch of sugar
1 kg/2 lb tomatoes, skinned, deseeded and chopped
1 bouquet garni
6 thick slices of ham, preferably Bayonne
6 eggs
salt and pepper

1 Place the red peppers under a preheated hot grill until the skins become blistered and blackened, turning them frequently. Place them in a polythene bag until they are cool, then remove the skin, core and seeds, and slice the flesh thinly.

2 Heat 6 tablespoons of oil in a frying pan, add the pepper strips and cook over a moderate heat until soft, stirring frequently. Add the onions, pimento and garlic and fry gently for 10 minutes, stirring. Add the sugar, tomatoes, bouquet garni, and season to taste with salt and pepper. Cook gently for a further 10 minutes, stirring occasionally, then remove the bouquet garni.

3 Heat the remaining oil in a separate pan and gently warm the ham.

4 Beat the eggs together lightly in a bowl. Pour the beaten eggs into a lightly oiled or greased frying pan and cook for 2–3 minutes over very low heat without stirring. Stir in the vegetable mixture, and keep stirring until the eggs start to scramble and cook through. Adjust the seasoning to taste. Serve the pipérade straight from the pan accompanied by the slices of ham.

Serves 6
Preparation time: 15–20 minutes
Cooking time: 25–30 minutes

aubergine and pepper layer

1 aubergine, cut into 5 mm/¼ inch thick slices
4 tablespoons olive oil
2 large red peppers, quartered
4 slices of day old rustic bread
1 garlic clove, peeled
1 ripe tomato, halved
175 g/6 oz goats' cheese, cut into 8 slices
pepper

1 Brush the aubergine with oil and cook under a preheated grill for 2–3 minutes on each side until charred and tender. Let cool.

2 Grill the peppers for 4–5 minutes each side. Place them in a polythene bag until they are cool, then peel off the skins, deseed and cut the flesh into wide strips.

3 Meanwhile, toast the bread on both sides and rub all over the surface firstly with the garlic clove and then with the tomato.

4 Brush over any remaining oil and layer the aubergine and peppers on the toast. Arrange 2 slices of goats' cheese on top of each toast. Season with pepper. Return to the grill for 1–2 minutes until the cheese is bubbling and melted, serve immediately.

Serves 4
Preparation time: 25 minutes, plus cooling
Cooking time: 20 minutes

spinach and ricotta stuffed pancakes

Pancake batter:
scant 125 g/4 oz plain flour
¼ teaspoon salt
2 small eggs
1 teaspoon oil
150 ml/¼ pint milk
6 tablespoons water

Stuffing:
250 g/8 oz frozen chopped spinach, cooked and squeezed dry
250 g/8 oz ricotta or curd cheese
25 g/1 oz Parmesan cheese, freshly grated
1 egg, beaten
grated nutmeg
salt and pepper

Topping:
25 g/1 oz butter
3 tablespoons freshly grated Parmesan cheese
5 tablespoons Vegetable Stock (see page 140)

1 To make the batter, sift the flour and salt into a bowl. Make a well in the centre and add the eggs, oil and milk. Beat until smooth, then stir in the measured water. Cover and chill for 1–2 hours.

2 Lightly oil an 18 cm/7 inch frying pan and place it over a moderate heat. When it is hot, pour in just enough batter to cover the base. When the pancake is set and the underside browned, turn and briefly cook the other side. Repeat with the remaining batter, making 8 pancakes.

3 To make the stuffing, combine the spinach, ricotta or curd cheese, Parmesan and the egg in a mixing bowl and season liberally with nutmeg, salt and pepper. Divide the mixture among the pancakes, roll up loosely and arrange in a greased ovenproof dish. Dot with the butter, sprinkle with the Parmesan and pour in the stock.

4 Bake the pancakes in a preheated oven, 200°C (400°F), Gas Mark 6, for about 20 minutes until golden. Serve immediately.

Serves 4
Preparation time: 15 minutes, plus chilling
Cooking time: 45 minutes
Oven temperature: 200°C (400°F), Gas Mark 6

marinated goats' cheese

1 teaspoon fennel seeds
1 teaspoon pink peppercorns
250 g/8 oz goats' cheese, such as Sainte-Maure
2 garlic cloves
2 small green chillies, bruised
2 rosemary sprigs, bruised
2 bay leaves, bruised
olive oil, to cover
crusty bread, to serve

1 Put the fennel seeds and peppercorns in a small, heavy-based frying pan and heat gently until they start to pop and release an aroma. Leave to cool completely.

2 Roll the cheese into small balls and place in a bowl or jar. Add the cooled fennel seeds and peppercorns, then add the remaining ingredients with sufficient olive oil to cover.

3 Store in a cool place for at least 3 days but no longer than 1 week. Serve the cheese balls with a little of the oil and chunks of French bread.

Serves 8
Preparation time: 15 minutes, plus cooling and marinating

baked garlic with brie

2 garlic heads
150 ml/¼ pint olive oil
2 rosemary sprigs, bruised
salt and pepper

To serve:
wedge of ripe Brie
crusty bread

1 Cut a small slice from the top of each head of garlic and sit them in a small baking tin. Pour over half the oil and top with the rosemary sprigs. Season well with salt and pepper, cover with foil and bake in a preheated oven, 200°C (400°F), Gas Mark 6, for 1 hour.

2 Remove the foil, baste and bake for a further 15–20 minutes until caramelized.

3 Split each garlic head in two and then transfer each half to a small plate, drizzle over the remaining oil and serve with a wedge of Brie and plenty of crusty bread.

Serves 4
Preparation time: 5 minutes
Cooking time: 1¼ hours
Oven temperature: 200°C (400°F), Gas Mark 6

grilled mushrooms with garlic oil

75 ml/3 fl oz olive oil
2 garlic cloves, crushed
grated rind and juice of ½ lime
1 small red chilli, deseeded and finely chopped
2 tablespoons chopped parsley
12 large flat mushrooms
salt and pepper

1 In a small bowl combine all the ingredients except the mushrooms, and season to taste with salt and pepper.

2 Arrange the mushrooms, stalk side down, on a foil-lined grill pan and cook under a preheated grill, as close to the heat as possible, for 3–4 minutes until beginning to moisten.

3 Flip the mushrooms over and cook for a further 4–5 minutes until cooked through. Transfer to a serving plate and pour over the dressing. Leave to cool to room temperature, then serve.

Serves 4
Preparation time: 5 minutes, plus cooling
Cooking time: 8–10 minutes

chicken satay

Soak the bamboo skewers in cold water for 30 minutes before use to prevent them from burning under the grill.

500 g/1 lb boneless, skinless chicken breasts
1 small onion, finely chopped
2 teaspoons grated fresh root ginger
2 garlic cloves, crushed

2 tablespoons lime juice
1 tablespoon dark soy sauce
1 tablespoon garam masala
½ teaspoon salt

Satay sauce:
1 tablespoon groundnut oil
1 garlic clove, crushed
4 tablespoons crunchy peanut butter
¼ teaspoon dried chilli flakes
1 tablespoon dark soy sauce
1 tablespoon lime juice
1 teaspoon clear honey
2 tablespoons coconut cream

1 Cut the chicken breasts diagonally into very thin strips and place in a shallow dish. Combine the remaining ingredients for the marinade and pour over the chicken. Stir once, cover and leave to marinate overnight.

2 To make the satay sauce, heat the groundnut oil in a small pan and then gently fry the garlic for 2–3 minutes until softened. Stir in the remaining ingredients and heat gently until boiling.

3 Drain the chicken and pat dry. Thread the chicken strips on to 8 pre-soaked bamboo skewers, zig-zagging back and forwards as you go. Cook under a preheated grill for 2–3 minutes on each side until charred and cooked through. Serve with the satay sauce, to dip.

Serves 4–8
Preparation time: 20 minutes, plus marinating
Cooking time: 4–6 minutes

souvlakia

500 g/1 lb neck of lamb, cut into 2.5 cm/1 inch cubes
1 tablespoon chopped rosemary
2 teaspoons dried oregano
2 teaspoons dried mint
2 bay leaves
1 small onion, chopped
2 garlic cloves, chopped
150 ml/¼ pint red wine
4 tablespoons olive oil
2 pitta breads
50 g/2 oz feta cheese, crumbled
salt and pepper

1 Place the lamb in a shallow dish. Combine the herbs, onion, garlic, wine and oil. Season with salt and pepper and pour over the lamb. Stir well, cover and leave to marinate overnight.

2 Thread the lamb on to metal skewers and cook over a barbecue or under a preheated grill for 10 minutes, turning and basting frequently. Leave to rest for 5 minutes.

3 Grill or toast the pitta bread and cut into quarters. Serve the souvlakia on the pitta pieces, scattered with the feta cheese.

Serves 8
Preparation time: 10 minutes, plus marinating
Cooking time: 10 minutes

prawn and rocket piadina

Piadina, the precursor of the pizza, is a small disc of unleavened dough that is dry-fried on a very hot griddle.

Dough:
125 g/4 oz plain flour
½ teaspoon salt
5 g/¼ oz butter, softened
65 ml/2½ fl oz tepid water

Topping:
4 tablespoons olive oil, plus extra to serve
2 large garlic cloves, crushed
pinch of crushed chilli flakes
½ teaspoon dried oregano
500 g/1 lb raw tiger prawns, peeled and deveined
  (see page 111)
175 g/6 oz rocket
175 g/6 oz feta cheese, crumbled
pepper

1 To make the dough, sift the flour and salt into a bowl and rub in the butter until the mixture resembles breadcrumbs. Add the measured water and mix to form a soft dough. Knead on a lightly floured surface for 10 minutes. Wrap in cling film and leave to rest for 30 minutes.

2 Divide the dough into 4 pieces and roll each one out to a 12.5 cm/5 inch round. Cover with a clean tea towel while preparing the topping.

3 Heat the oil in a large frying pan. As soon as it stops foaming, add the garlic, chilli flakes and dried oregano, stir well and immediately add the prawns. Cook for 3–4 minutes until the prawns are cooked. Stir in the rocket and cook until wilted. Keep warm.

4 Heat a griddle or heavy-based frying pan until hot. Cook 1 dough base at a time for about 1 minute, flip over and cook the other side for a further 30 seconds until dotted brown.

5 Transfer the piadina to warmed plates and top with the prawn and rocket mixture, scatter over the feta, drizzle with extra olive oil and serve immediately.

Serves 4
Preparation time: 15–20 minutes, plus resting
Cooking time: 15 minutes

piquant potatoes

4 baking potatoes
25 g/1 oz butter
125 g/4 oz Cheddar cheese, grated
125 g/4 oz sliced cooked ham, chopped
2 tablespoons sweetcorn or tomato relish
salt and pepper

1 Prick the potatoes all over and wrap in foil. Bake in a preheated oven, 200°C (400°F), Gas Mark 6, for 1–1½ hours, until soft when squeezed gently.

2 Cut a large cross in each potato, cutting through the foil. Very carefully squeeze each potato and scoop out the flesh into a bowl, taking care not to pierce the potato skins or foil.

3 Add the butter to the potato and mash well until smooth. Stir in the cheese, ham and relish. Add salt and pepper to taste, and mix well.

4 Spoon the mixture back into the skins, return to the oven and cook for a further 15 minutes. Serve immediately.

Serves 4
Preparation time: 15 minutes
Cooking time: 1¼–1¾ hours
Oven temperature: 200°C (400°F), Gas Mark 6

spring rolls

Wrappers:
250 g/8 oz plain flour
pinch of salt
1 egg
about 300 ml/½ pint cold water
1 tablespoon flour blended with 1 tablespoon water
sunflower oil, for deep-frying

Filling:
1 tablespoon sunflower oil
250 g/8 oz lean pork, shredded
1 garlic clove, crushed
2 celery sticks, sliced
125 g/4 oz mushrooms, sliced
2 spring onions, chopped
125 g/4 oz bean sprouts
125 g/4 oz cooked peeled prawns
2 tablespoons light soy sauce

1 Sift the flour and salt into a bowl and beat in the egg and measured water to make a smooth batter.

2 Lightly oil a 20 cm/8 inch frying pan and set it over moderate heat. Pour in sufficient batter to cover the base of the pan. Cook until the underside is pale golden and then turn the pancake over and cook the other side. Repeat until all the batter is used.

3 To make the filling, heat the oil in a wok or frying pan, add the pork and stir-fry for 2–3 minutes until it is evenly browned. Add the garlic and vegetables and stir-fry for 2 minutes. Mix in the prawns and soy sauce, then remove from the heat and allow to cool.

4 Place 2–3 tablespoons of the filling in the centre of each pancake. Fold in the sides and roll them up tightly, sealing the edges with a little of the flour and water paste.

5 Heat the oil in a wok or deep frying pan to 180–190°C (350–375°F) or until a cube of bread browns in 30 seconds, and deep-fry the spring rolls, 2 at a time, until golden. Drain on kitchen paper and serve hot.

Serves 4–6
Preparation time: 15 minutes
Cooking time: 30 minutes

vegetarian spring rolls

12 spring roll wrappers (see page 454)
oil, for deep-frying
coriander sprigs, to garnish

Filling:
1 tablespoon groundnut oil
2 garlic cloves, finely chopped
50 g/2 oz bean sprouts
50 g/2 oz white cabbage, shredded
2 fresh shiitake mushrooms, shredded
25 g/1 oz celery stick and leaves, finely chopped
1 teaspoon sugar
2 teaspoons soy sauce
50 g/2 oz dried bean thread noodles, soaked, drained and
   cut into short lengths with scissors

1 Make the wrappers, following the instructions on page 454. To make the filling, heat a wok or large frying pan, add the oil, garlic, bean sprouts, cabbage, mushrooms and celery, and stir-fry for 30 seconds. Add the sugar, soy sauce and noodles, stir-fry for 1 minute, then remove from the heat and place the ingredients on a plate. Wipe the wok or pan clean with kitchen paper.

2 Place 2–3 tablespoons of the filling in the centre of each pancake. Fold in the sides and roll them up tightly, sealing the edges with a little of the flour and water paste.

3 Heat the oil in a wok or deep frying pan to 180–190°C (350–375°F) or until a cube of bread browns in 30 seconds, and deep-fry the spring rolls, 2 at a time, until golden. Drain on kitchen paper and serve hot, garnished with coriander sprigs.

Serves 4–6
Preparation time: 15–20 minutes, plus soaking
Cooking time: 30 minutes

crab rolls

Wrappers:
4 tablespoons plain flour
½ teaspoon salt
4 tablespoons water
4 eggs, beaten
1 tablespoon plain flour blended with 1 tablespoon water
vegetable oil, for deep-frying

Filling:
2 tablespoons vegetable oil
1 egg, beaten
1 spring onion, shredded
300 g/10 oz crab meat, flaked
1 tablespoon dry sherry
salt and pepper
1 tablespoon cornflour blended with 3 tablespoons water

1 To make the wrappers, sift the flour and salt into a bowl, then gradually beat in the measured water and eggs to form a smooth batter. Place a small lightly oiled frying pan over moderate heat and pour in 4 tablespoons of batter, rotating it until the base is covered. Cook until the edges curl then flip over and cook the other side. Cook all the pancakes in this way.

2 To make the filling, heat the oil in a frying pan, add the egg, spring onion and crab meat, and stir-fry for a few seconds. Add the sherry and salt and pepper. Blend the cornflour with the measured water and add to the pan, stirring until thickened. Remove from the heat and cool.

3 Place 2 tablespoons of the filling on half of each pancake. Fold over the other half, fold in the sides, roll up and seal with the flour and water paste.

4 Heat the oil in a wok or deep frying pan to 180–190°C (350–375°F) or until a cube of bread browns in 30 seconds, and deep-fry the crab rolls, a few at a time, until golden brown all over. Drain on kitchen paper and cut into pieces diagonally. Serve immediately.

Serves 6–8
Preparation time: 30 minutes
Cooking time: 30 minutes

deep-fried drumsticks

2 tablespoons dry sherry
2 tablespoons soy sauce
pinch of sugar
4 garlic cloves, crushed
2 teaspoons finely chopped fresh root ginger
4 spring onions, chopped
8 chicken drumsticks
50 g/2 oz plain flour
1–2 eggs, beaten
oil, for deep-frying
lemon slices and parsley sprigs, to garnish

1 Mix the sherry, soy sauce, sugar, garlic, ginger and spring onions in a bowl, add the chicken and turn to coat. Leave for 30 minutes. Remove the chicken; reserving the marinade.

2 Sift the flour into a bowl and beat in the egg. Gradually beat in the marinade, to form a smooth paste. Dip the chicken into the batter and turn to coat evenly.

3 Heat the oil in a deep frying pan to 180–190°C (350–375°F) or until a cube of bread browns in 30 seconds, and deep-fry the chicken drumsticks for 12–15 minutes, until golden brown and cooked through. Drain on kitchen paper. Garnish with lemon and parsley, and serve immediately.

Serves 4
Preparation time: 10 minutes, plus marinating
Cooking time: 12–15 minutes

spicy beefburgers

1 kg/2 lb minced beef
2 tablespoons green peppercorns
1 tablespoon chopped thyme
2 teaspoons Worcestershire sauce
2 teaspoons French mustard
salt

To serve:
8 burger buns
8 lettuce leaves
selection of relishes
1 onion, sliced
4 tomatoes, sliced

1 Put the beef in a bowl and season well with salt. Stir in the peppercorns, thyme, Worcestershire sauce and mustard; mix well. Divide into 8 portions and form into flat patties.

2 Cook under a preheated moderate grill, or on a barbecue grid 10 cm/4 inches above the coals, for 3–5 minutes each side, according to taste.

3 Cut the buns in half and toast the cut sides. Arrange a lettuce leaf on each bun base, top with a burger and relish. Arrange onion and tomato slices on top and replace the bun lid. Serve immediately.

Serves 4–8
Preparation time: 10–15 minutes
Cooking time: 5–10 minutes

hamburgers with mustard mayonnaise and radicchio

750 g/1½ lb lean beef, finely minced
1 small onion, finely chopped
2 tablespoons Worcestershire sauce
4 brown baps or ciabatta rolls
1 large radicchio head, cut into 8 wedges
2 beef tomatoes, skinned and sliced
sea salt and pepper

Mustard mayonnaise:
2 egg yolks
1 tablespoon white wine vinegar
1 tablespoon Dijon mustard
1 tablespoon coarse grain mustard
300 ml/½ pint grapeseed oil

1 Place the meat, onion, Worcestershire sauce and seasoning in a bowl and mix with a fork. With wet hands, shape the meat into 4 patties to fit into the baps or rolls.

2 To make the mustard mayonnaise, place the egg yolks, vinegar and both mustards in a bowl. Using a hand-held blender, blend. Slowly pour in the oil, continuing to blend, until the mixture is smooth and creamy. Season to taste with salt and pepper. Alternatively, make the mayonnaise in a food processor.

3 Heat a griddle pan or nonstick frying pan and cook the prepared burgers for 3 minutes on each side for rare, or 5 minutes for well done. Remove from the griddle and keep warm. Cut the baps in half and place cut-side down on the griddle to toast and absorb any meat juices. Cook the radicchio wedges for 1 minute on each side.

4 To assemble, spread the bottom half of each bap with mustard mayonnaise, then place on a wedge of radicchio, a burger, more mustard mayonnaise, half a slice of tomato, another radicchio wedge and more mustard mayonnaise. Cover with the top half of the bap and serve immediately.

Serves 4
Preparation time: 30 minutes
Cooking time: 15 minutes

de luxe cheeseburgers

500 g/1 lb lean minced beef
1 small onion, finely chopped
2 tablespoons corn oil
4 slices of processed Cheddar cheese
8 crisp lettuce leaves
1 small onion, thinly sliced and separated into rings
4 sesame seed baps, split and warmed
1 large tomato, sliced
2 tablespoons relish
salt and pepper

1 Put the minced beef into a bowl. Add the chopped onion, season to taste and mix well.

2 Divide the mixture into 4 and shape each portion into a 10 cm/4 inch round burger, about 1 cm/½ inch thick.

3 Heat the oil in a frying pan, add the burgers and fry over moderate heat for 5–6 minutes on each side. Top each with a slice of cheese and remove from heat.

4 Place 2 lettuce leaves and some onion rings on each warmed bap base, then place a burger on each. Top with tomato slices and relish. Cover with the remaining bap halves and serve.

Serves 4
Preparation time: 10 minutes
Cooking time: 10–12 minutes

winchester sausages

Sausage casings are available from some butchers. They should be soaked overnight in cold water and drained before use.

250 g/8 oz belly pork, minced
250 g/8 oz lean pork, minced
25 g/1 oz pork fat, minced
6 tablespoons milk
75 g/3 oz wholemeal breadcrumbs
1 garlic clove, crushed
¼ teaspoon each ground mace and allspice
1 tablespoon each chopped parsley and sage
1 teaspoon chopped thyme
salt and pepper
about 1 metre/3 ft sausage casing

1 Mix the pork and fat together in a bowl. Pour the milk over the breadcrumbs and leave for 10 minutes. Squeeze the breadcrumbs dry and add to the meat. Add the garlic, spices, herbs, and salt and pepper and mix together thoroughly.

2 Using a piping bag fitted with a large plain nozzle, carefully force the sausage mixture into the casings. Push the mixture evenly along the casing then twist to form sausages.

3 Separate the sausages, prick the skins and cook under a preheated moderate grill, or on a barbecue grid 10 cm/4 inches above the coals, for 15–20 minutes, until golden brown and thoroughly cooked.

Makes 10–12
Preparation time: 20 minutes, plus soaking
Cooking time: 15–20 minutes

chicken-stuffed tortillas

6 boneless, skinless chicken breasts, cut into thin strips
2 tablespoons olive oil
2 large onions, sliced
2 red peppers, cored, deseeded and cut into strips
2 tablespoons sesame seeds, toasted
12 soft tortillas, warmed
300 ml/½ pint soured cream
1 tablespoon chopped coriander
1 quantity Guacamole (see page 459)

Marinade:
8 tablespoons lime juice
3 tablespoons olive oil
1 teaspoon dried oregano
1 teaspoon dried coriander

1 To make the marinade, combine the ingredients in a bowl. Add the chicken strips and stir well. Cover and leave in the refrigerator for 4 hours.

2 Put the chicken strips and marinade in a roasting tin. Cover with foil and bake in a preheated oven, 200°C (400°F), Gas Mark 6, for 30 minutes. Remove the foil for the last 10 minutes of the cooking time.

3 Meanwhile, heat the oil in a frying pan, add the onions and peppers, and sauté until they are soft and melting. It does not matter if they become a little brown and caramelized.

4 Toast the sesame seeds in a dry frying pan over moderate heat.

5 Make the guacamole, following the instructions on page 459.

6 Place a little of the onions and peppers on each warmed tortilla and top with some chicken. Add a little guacamole, some soured cream and sesame seeds. Sprinkle with coriander, roll up, and serve.

Serves 4
Preparation time: 30 minutes, plus marinating
Cooking time: 45 minutes
Oven temperature: 200°C (400°F), Gas Mark 6

empanadas

250 g/8 oz flour
¼ teaspoon salt
75 g/3 oz hard white fat, diced
50 g/2 oz butter, diced
6–8 tablespoons iced water
beaten egg, to glaze
sesame seeds

Filling:
1½ tablespoons oil
75 g/3 oz chopped onion
1 garlic clove, crushed
250 g/8 oz pork fillet, diced
175 g/6 oz sweet potato, shredded
4 juicy prunes, stoned
125 ml/4 fl oz unsweetened pineapple juice
1 tablespoon tomato purée
2 teaspoons chilli powder
salt

1 First make the filling. Heat the oil in a frying pan, add the onion and garlic, and sauté until soft. Add the pork and cook, stirring, until lightly browned. Stir in the remaining ingredients and continue cooking until the excess liquid has evaporated. Remove from the heat and cool.

2 Put the flour, salt and fats in a food processor, and process until the mixture resembles breadcrumbs. Add enough iced water to make a soft dough. Shape into a ball and chill for 20–30 minutes.

3 Divide the dough into 8 equal portions and roll them out on a lightly floured surface to make 15 cm/6 inch rounds.

4 Put one-eighth of the filling on each round. Dampen the edges and fold over to make half-moon shapes. Press the edges together and crimp with a fork. Place on a greased baking sheet, brush with beaten egg and sprinkle with sesame seeds. Bake in a preheated oven, 190°C (375°F), Gas Mark 5, for 35–40 minutes. Serve hot.

Serves 4–6
Preparation time: 30 minutes, plus cooling and chilling
Cooking time: 45–50 minutes
Oven temperature: 190°C (375°F), Gas Mark 5

vegetable fajitas

2 tablespoons olive oil
2 large onions, thinly sliced
2 garlic cloves, crushed
2 red peppers, cored, deseeded and thinly sliced
2 green peppers, cored, deseeded and thinly sliced
4 green chillies, deseeded and thinly sliced
2 teaspoons chopped oregano
250 g/8 oz button mushrooms, sliced
salt and pepper

To serve:
12 soft tortillas, warmed
salsa
soured cream

1 Heat the olive oil in a large frying pan, add the onions and garlic, and gently sauté for about 5 minutes until they are soft and golden brown. They should be melting and almost caramelized.

2 Add the peppers, chillies and oregano, and stir well. Sauté gently for 10 minutes more, until cooked and tender.

3 Add the mushrooms and cook quickly for 1 more minute, stirring to mix thoroughly with the other vegetables. Season to taste with salt and pepper.

4 Spoon the sizzling hot vegetable mixture into the warmed tortillas and fold over or roll up. Serve very hot with salsa and plenty of soured cream.

Serves 4
Preparation time: 15 minutes
Cooking time: 16 minutes

chimichangas

2 tablespoons olive oil
1 small onion, chopped
1 red pepper, cored, deseeded and diced
125 g/4 oz button mushrooms, thinly sliced
250 g/8 oz small broccoli florets
2 tomatoes, skinned and chopped
2 red chillies, finely chopped
175 g/6 oz Cheddar cheese, grated

8 soft tortillas
oil, for deep-frying
salt and pepper
150 ml/¼ pint soured cream, to serve

Guacamole:
2 ripe avocados, roughly chopped
1 garlic clove, crushed
2 tablespoons lime juice
1 red chilli, finely chopped
1 tomato, finely chopped
2 spring onions, finely chopped
salt and pepper

1 Heat the olive oil in a large heavy-based frying pan, add the onion and red pepper and gently sauté until just tender but still slightly crisp. Add the mushrooms and broccoli florets, tomatoes and chillies and stir-fry over a medium heat for 3–4 minutes. Season to taste with salt and pepper.

2 Remove the pan from the heat, and mix the cheese into the vegetables. Stir gently until the cheese melts.

3 Divide the vegetable and cheese mixture into 8 portions and put one in the centre of each tortilla. Roll up carefully, tucking in the edges at the sides so that the filling is completely sealed and cannot escape.

4 To make the guacamole, place all the ingredients in a bowl. Using a fork, mash together thoroughly. Season to taste with salt and pepper.

5 Heat the oil in a deep frying pan to 180–190°C (350–375°F) or until a cube of bread browns in 30 seconds, and deep-fry the tortillas, a few at a time, until crisp and golden, turning once. Drain on kitchen paper and serve with soured cream and guacamole.

Serves 4
Preparation time: 20 minutes
Cooking time: 15–20 minutes

greek-style peppers

3 tablespoons sunflower oil
1 small onion, finely chopped
1 garlic clove, crushed (optional)
1 celery stick, finely chopped
125 g/4 oz brown long-grain rice
250 g/8 oz canned tomatoes

125–175 g/4–6 oz cooked minced lamb
200 ml/7 fl oz Chicken Stock (see page 141)
¼ teaspoon dried oregano
1 bay leaf
4 green or red peppers
50 g/2 oz Cheddar cheese, finely grated
salt and pepper

1 Heat 2 tablespoons of the oil in a saucepan, add the onion, garlic and celery, and fry gently for 2 minutes. Add the rice and fry, stirring, for a further 3 minutes.

2 Add the tomatoes and their juice, breaking up with a spoon. Stir in the lamb, stock, oregano and bay leaf, and season to taste. Stir to mix. Bring to the boil, cover, lower the heat and simmer for 40–50 minutes until the liquid is absorbed and the rice tender. Discard the bay leaf.

3 Cut a 1 cm/¼ inch slice off the stalk end of each pepper and reserve. Core and deseed the peppers, then blanch with the 'lids' in a pan of boiling water for 2 minutes. Drain, plunge into cold water for 5 minutes, then drain again.

4 Stuff each pepper with the tomato mixture, arrange in a greased ovenproof dish and sprinkle with the cheese. Place the lids in position and brush each pepper lightly with the remaining oil.

5 Cover loosely with foil and cook in a preheated oven, 180°C (350°F), Gas Mark 4, for 20 minutes. Remove the foil, cook for a further 25 minutes, and serve.

Serves 4
Preparation time: 15 minutes
Cooking time: 1½ hours
Oven temperature: 180°C (350°F), Gas Mark 4

swiss cheese fondue

1 garlic clove, halved
150 ml/¼ pint dry white wine
1 teaspoon lemon juice
175 g/6 oz Gruyère cheese, grated
175 g/6 oz Emmental cheese, grated
1 teaspoon cornflour
2 tablespoons kirsch
pepper
grated nutmeg
day-old French bread, cut into bite-sized cubes, to serve

1 Rub the inside of a fondue dish with the cut garlic. Pour in the wine and lemon juice, and heat gently until bubbling. Gradually stir in the cheeses and heat slowly, stirring, until the cheeses melt and begin to cook.

2 Blend the cornflour with the kirsch. Add to the cheese and cook for 2–3 minutes, stirring, until the mixture is thick and creamy. Add pepper and nutmeg to taste.

3 Place over a spirit burner and keep at a simmer. Use long fondue forks to dip the bread cubes into the hot fondue.

Serves 4–6
Preparation time: 10 minutes
Cooking time: 15 minutes

anchovy and prawn fondue

1 garlic clove, halved
150 ml/¼ pint dry white wine
125 g/4 oz Gruyère cheese, grated
250 g/8 oz Cheddar cheese, grated
1 teaspoon cornflour
2 tablespoons sherry
2 teaspoons anchovy essence
Tabasco sauce
cayenne pepper

To serve:
125 g/4 oz cooked peeled prawns
day-old French bread, cut into bite-sized cubes

1 Rub the inside of a fondue dish with the cut garlic. Pour in the wine and heat gently until bubbling. Gradually stir in the cheeses and heat gently, stirring, until the cheeses melt and begin to cook.

2 Blend the cornflour with the sherry and add the anchovy essence, Tabasco and cayenne to taste. Stir into the cheese and heat gently, stirring, for 2–3 minutes, until the mixture is thick and creamy.

3 Place over a spirit burner and keep at a simmer. Use long fondue forks to dip the prawns and bread cubes into the hot fondue.

Serves 4–6
Preparation time: 10 minutes
Cooking time: 15 minutes

pan bagnat slices

Pan bagnat is a Niçoise stuffed bread. It makes a great picnic dish as well as a snack.

2 red peppers
1 short French stick
1–2 garlic cloves
8 tablespoons olive oil
1 tablespoon balsamic or sherry vinegar
4 ripe tomatoes, sliced
150 g/5 oz buffalo mozzarella, sliced
12 large basil leaves
salt and pepper

1 Place the red peppers on a foil-lined grill pan and grill under a preheated grill for 15–20 minutes, turning frequently until the skin is blistered and blackened on all sides. Place them in a polythene bag until they are cool.

2 Meanwhile, cut the bread in half horizontally and scoop out and discard most of the middle, leaving a good 1 cm/½ inch thick edge. Leave to one side to dry out slightly.

3 Peel, core and deseed the peppers over a bowl to catch the juices, and cut the flesh into quarters. Rub the insides of the bread with garlic and drizzle generously with the oil and vinegar.

4 Arrange the peppers, tomato slices, mozzarella slices and basil in layers in one half of the bread, season with salt and pepper, and pour over the reserved pepper juices and any remaining olive oil.

5 Replace the remaining half of the bread, wrap tightly in cling film and leave to chill overnight. Return to room temperature and cut the bread into 2.5 cm/1 inch thick slices to serve.

Serves 2
Preparation time: 30 minutes, plus chilling
Cooking time: 15–20 minutes

cucumber sandwiches

1 small bunch of watercress, trimmed and finely chopped
50 g/2 oz butter, softened
4 thin slices of white bread
4 thin slices of wholemeal bread
5 cm/2 inch piece of cucumber, very thinly sliced
watercress sprigs and cucumber slices, to garnish
**   (optional)**

1 Beat the watercress with the butter until smooth.

2 Spread the white and wholemeal bread with the butter and arrange the cucumber on the white slices of bread. Top with the wholemeal bread. Wrap and chill until ready to serve.

3 Trim the crusts from the sandwiches and cut them into triangles. Serve garnished with watercress sprigs and cucumber slices, if liked.

Serves 4
Preparation time: 15 minutes

granary roll fillers

4 granary rolls
125 g/4 oz full-fat soft cheese
1 tablespoon snipped chives
7.5 cm/3 inch piece of cucumber, halved lengthways and
**   thinly sliced**
25 g/1 oz butter, softened
2 hard-boiled eggs, peeled
1½ tablespoons Mayonnaise (see page 145)
a little mustard and cress
salt and pepper

1 Using a sharp knife, carefully make 2 vertical cuts in each roll, taking care not to cut through the bottom crust, to give 2 'pockets' for filling.

2 Mix the cheese with the chives in a bowl, and spread inside one pocket in each roll. Arrange halved cucumber slices in each cheese-filled pocket, protruding slightly above the top crust.

3 Spread the remaining pocket in each roll with the butter. Mash the hard-boiled eggs, stir in the mayonnaise, add salt and pepper to taste and use to fill the buttered pockets. Arrange a little mustard and cress along each egg-filled pocket. Serve immediately.

Serves 4
Preparation time: 15 minutes

salami stacks

50 g/2 oz butter, softened
50 g/2 oz full-fat soft cheese
6 slices of crusty white or brown bread
6 thin slices of salami, rinded
50 g/2 oz coleslaw
a little mustard and cress
crisp lettuce leaves
1 large tomato, thinly sliced
salt and pepper

1 In a bowl, combine the butter and soft cheese, and mix well using a wooden spoon.

2 Place 2 slices of bread on a board and spread with the cheese mixture. Add 3 slices of salami to each and top both with coleslaw and a little mustard and cress.

3 Spread 2 more slices of bread with the cheese mixture and place, spread side down, on each sandwich. Spread the exposed surfaces of the bread with more of the cheese mixture.

4 Add a layer of lettuce and tomato to each stacked sandwich and season with salt and pepper. Spread the remaining slices of bread with cheese mixture and invert on each sandwich. Press down firmly, then cut each sandwich into quarters. Keep the layers together with a cocktail stick, if necessary. Serve immediately.

Serves 2
Preparation time: 15 minutes

chunky pan-fried sandwiches

8 medium-thick slices of white or wholemeal bread, crusts removed if liked
4 slices of cooked ham
1 onion, thinly sliced and separated into rings
125 g/4 oz Cheddar cheese, thinly sliced
50 g/2 oz butter, softened
watercress sprigs, to garnish

1 Place 4 slices of the bread on a board and cover each one with a slice of ham. Top with onion rings to taste and then cover with slices of cheese. Top with the remaining bread slices and press down lightly.

2 Spread a little butter on the top of each sandwich. Heat a large frying pan over moderate heat, without added fat. Fry two of the sandwiches, buttered sides down, over a low heat for 2–3 minutes, until golden brown on the undersides.

3 Butter the exposed tops of the sandwiches, then carefully turn them over, and fry for a further 3–4 minutes, pressing the sandwiches down with a spatula or fish slice until golden brown on both sides.

4 Keep warm while frying the remaining sandwiches in the same way. Cut each sandwich into 4 triangles, garnish with watercress sprigs and serve immediately.

Serves 4
Preparation time: 8 minutes
Cooking time: 5–7 minutes each

souffléd ham rarebits

4 slices of bread, crusts removed if liked
125 g/4 oz Red Leicester cheese, thinly sliced
4 thin slices of cooked ham
4 eggs, separated
2 teaspoons milk
salt and pepper
parsley sprigs, to garnish

1 Toast the bread slices on one side only. Arrange, toasted sides down, on a baking sheet. Top each with a slice of cheese and a slice of ham.

2 Beat the egg yolks with the milk in a bowl. Add salt and pepper to taste.

3 In a separate, grease-free bowl, whisk the egg whites until stiff peaks form, then gently fold into the egg yolk mixture, using a large metal spoon.

4 Spoon a portion of the egg mixture over each rarebit. Bake in a preheated oven, 180°C (350°F), Gas Mark 4, for 15–20 minutes until the soufflé topping is set and golden brown. Garnished with parsley sprigs and serve immediately.

Serves 4
Preparation time: 10 minutes
Cooking time: 15–20 minutes each
Oven temperature: 180°C (350°F), Gas Mark 4

piperade baps

50 g/2 oz butter
1 tablespoon sunflower oil
1 large onion, chopped
1 garlic clove, crushed
1 green pepper, cored, deseeded and cut into thin strips
4 streaky bacon rashers, rinded and diced
4 eggs, beaten
1½ tablespoons cold water
salt and pepper
4 floury baps, warmed

1 Melt 15 g/½ oz of the butter with the oil in a 23 cm/9 inch frying pan with a flameproof handle, add the onion, garlic, green pepper and bacon and fry gently for about 5 minutes, stirring from time to time.

2 Meanwhile, whisk the eggs with the measured water in a bowl. Add salt and pepper to taste. Pour into the onion mixture in the pan and stir lightly with a fork. Cook over a gentle heat for about 3 minutes, until the omelette is golden brown underneath.

3 Place the pan under a preheated hot grill for 2–3 minutes until the open omelette is set on top. Turn on to a board and cut into quarters. Split the baps and spread with the remaining butter. Place an omelette quarter in each bap and serve immediately.

Serves 4
Preparation time: 15 minutes
Cooking time: 12 minutes

focaccia sandwich with mediterranean vegetables and mozzarella

1 small aubergine, sliced
2 courgettes, sliced lengthways
1 red onion, sliced into rings
2 red peppers, cored, deseeded and halved
1 loaf of focaccia bread
1 garlic clove, halved (optional)
1 mozzarella cheese, sliced
75 g/3 oz rocket
olive oil, for drizzling
sea salt and pepper

1 Heat a griddle pan or nonstick frying pan and griddle the aubergine, courgettes and red onion for about 5 minutes, turning occasionally. Leave to cool.

2 Griddle or grill the peppers on the skin side until the skin is blistered and blackened. Place them in a polythene bag until cool, then peel off the skin and cut the flesh into wide strips.

3 Split the focaccia in half and place on the griddle or under a grill to toast lightly. Rub the cut garlic edges all over the toasted bread. Place the sliced mozzarella on the base of the toasted focaccia.

4 Evenly layer the griddled vegetables on top of the mozzarella. Start with the aubergine and then add the courgettes, peppers, onion and rocket. Season each layer with salt and pepper as you arrange it.

5 Finally, drizzle with a little olive oil, season and place the top of the focaccia bread on top of the vegetables. Push together gently but firmly. Cut into 4 even-sized pieces and serve.

Serves 4
Preparation time: 10 minutes, plus cooling
Cooking time: 20 minutes

special occasions

figs with parma ham

This recipe is very simple and relies heavily on the quality of ingredients used, so it is best made when figs are in season and then only if they look ripe and delicious. It is also important to buy your Parma ham from a delicatessen where the ham is carved to order. If you like, the figs can be replaced with a fragrant, ripe melon, peeled, deseeded and cut into wedges.

4 figs
2 tablespoons lemon juice
4 tablespoons extra virgin olive oil
handful of basil, roughly torn
12 paper-thin slices of Parma ham
salt and pepper

1 Cut the figs into quarters and remove the stems. Place them in a dish with the lemon juice, olive oil, roughly torn basil leaves and season with salt and pepper. Mix well and allow to stand for 5 minutes.

2 Arrange the Parma ham on a serving plate then spoon the figs over the ham. Serve at room temperature.

Serves 4
Preparation time: 5 minutes, plus standing

baked scallops with butter and breadcrumbs

This is the simplest method of cooking scallops, and relies completely on the freshness of the fish. Use only the finest scallops for this recipe.

8–10 scallops with their shells, washed and prepared
125 g/4 oz butter
4 tablespoons fresh breadcrumbs
salt and pepper
2 tablespoons chopped parsley, to garnish

1 Remove the scallops from their shells, reserving 4 of the rounded shell halves. Chop the white flesh of the scallops coarsely, leaving the orange coral whole.

2 Divide the chopped scallops and coral evenly between the 4 shells and season to taste with salt and pepper. Dot the scallops with half the butter.

3 Sprinkle the breadcrumbs equally between the shells and use the remaining butter to dot over the tops.

4 Cook in the middle of a preheated oven, 180°C (350°F), Gas Mark 4, for about 30 minutes, or until the top is crisp and bubbly. Serve immediately, sprinkled with the parsley.

Serves 4
Preparation time: 10 minutes
Cooking time: 30 minutes
Oven temperature: 180°C (350°F), Gas Mark 4

smoked salmon blinis

250–300 ml/8–10 fl oz milk
50 g/2 oz plain flour
100 g/3½ oz buckwheat flour
½ teaspoon salt
15 g/½ oz fast-action dried yeast
50 g/2 oz butter
2 eggs, separated
2 tablespoons soured cream

To serve:
125 g/4 oz smoked salmon
175 g/6 oz crème fraîche

To garnish:
salmon eggs
dill sprigs

1 Pour 175 ml/6 fl oz of the milk into a pan. Heat until the milk rises, remove from the heat and leave to stand until it is luke warm.

2 Sift the flours and salt into a bowl. Mix thoroughly, then make a well in the centre. Add the yeast and the scalded milk, and gradually incorporate the flour. Beat for 2 minutes until smooth. Cover with a damp tea towel and put in a warm place for 2–3 hours to rise.

3 Melt half of the butter in a pan and allow to cool a little. Add a further 50 ml/2 fl oz of the milk to the risen batter and stir it in thoroughly. Stir in the egg yolks, soured cream and melted butter until the mixture has the consistency of double cream. (If it is too thick to pour, add more milk.)

4 Whisk the egg whites until stiff peaks form. Fold into the batter, a little at a time, until thoroughly mixed.

5 Heat half of the remaining butter in a frying pan. Pour enough batter into the pan to make a small pancake. Cook for 1–2 minutes, turning when browned. Keep warm while making the remaining blinis. Add more butter to the pan as necessary until all the batter is used. Serve hot with smoked salmon and crème fraîche, and garnished with salmon eggs and dill sprigs.

Makes 8
Preparation time: 10 minutes, plus standing
Cooking time: about 20 minutes

luxurious liver pâté

250 g/8 oz chicken livers, trimmed
2 shallots, coarsely chopped
2 garlic cloves, halved
2 duck breasts, cooked, skinned and chopped
2 eggs, beaten
2 tablespoons sherry
150 ml/¼ pint double cream
fresh bay leaves
juniper berries
10 streaky bacon rashers
salt and pepper

1 Using a food processor or blender, process the chicken livers, shallots, garlic and duck breasts until smooth. Gradually add the eggs, sherry and cream, and season well with salt and pepper.

2 Arrange the bay leaves and juniper berries in the base of a 500 g/1 lb loaf tin. Stretch the bacon rashers to line the base and sides of tin. Spoon in the chicken mixture and fold the excess bacon over the top.

3 Put the loaf tin in a roasting tin half-filled with boiling water. Bake in a preheated oven, 180°C (350°F), Gas Mark 4, for 1 hour or until a skewer inserted in the centre comes out quite dry and the mixture is shrinking around the sides.

4 Leave to cool with a weight placed on the top and chill.

Serves 10
Preparation time: 15 minutes, plus cooling and chilling
Cooking time: 1 hour
Oven temperature: 180°C (350°C) Gas Mark 4

aubergine, haloumi and cumin bruschetta

Haloumi is a cheese from Cyprus, which griddles particularly well.

1 tablespoon cumin seeds
4 tablespoons extra virgin olive oil, plus extra for drizzling
grated rind of 1 lemon
2 small aubergines, each cut lengthways into 4 slices
4 thick slices of day-old country bread
250 g/8 oz haloumi, cut into 4 slices
2 garlic cloves, cut in half
125 g/4 oz rocket leaves

1 Dry roast the cumin seeds in a small frying pan until they start to pop and give off a smoky aroma. Add the oil and lemon rind, remove from the heat and leave to infuse for several hours.

2 Heat a griddle pan or nonstick frying pan and cook the aubergine slices for 4–5 minutes on each side. Remove from the pan and dip each slice into the cumin-scented oil, reserving the remaining oil. Spread out the aubergine slices on a plate to cool to room temperature.

3 Just before serving, prepare the bruschetta. Heat the griddle pan again, add the slices of bread and toast each side well. Add the haloumi and cook on each side for 1–2 minutes, turning it carefully with a palette knife or spatula. Rub the toast all over with the cut garlic halves and drizzle with olive oil. Toss the rocket in the remaining cumin oil and heap on top of the bruschetta. Arrange slices of aubergine and haloumi on top and serve immediately.

Serves 4
Preparation time: 5 minutes, plus infusing and cooling
Cooking time: 30 minutes

fennel soup

25 g/1 oz butter
1 onion, chopped
4 fennel heads, chopped
1 bouquet garni
900 ml/1½ pints Chicken or Vegetable Stock (see pages 141 and 140)
3 egg yolks
4 tablespoons lemon juice
salt and pepper

To garnish:
fennel leaves
croûtons

1 Melt the butter in a large pan, add the onion and fry for 5 minutes, without browning. Stir in the fennel, then add the bouquet garni, stock and salt and pepper to taste. Bring to the boil, cover and simmer for 30 minutes, until the vegetables are very tender.

2 Remove the bouquet garni and cool slightly. Sieve or work in a electric blender until smooth, then reheat. Mix the egg yolk and lemon juice together with a few tablespoons of the soup.

3 Stir the egg mixture into the soup and serve immediately, garnished with fennel leaves and croûtons.

Serves 6
Preparation time: 20 minutes
Cooking time: 40 minutes

iced cucumber soup

25 g/1 oz butter
1 cucumber, chopped
2 shallots, chopped
300 ml/½ pint milk
2 garlic cloves, crushed
1 bay leaf
1 tablespoon chopped mint
1 tablespoon chopped chives
250 g/8 oz cooked peeled prawns
300 ml/½ pint single cream
salt and pepper

To garnish:
mint sprigs
cucumber slices
cooked peeled prawns

1 Melt the butter in a saucepan, add the cucumber and shallots, cover and cook gently for 5 minutes, until softened but not browned.

2 Add the milk, garlic, bay leaf, and salt and pepper to taste, and simmer for 10 minutes. Remove the bay leaf. Pour the soup into a food processor or blender and work until smooth. Pour into a soup tureen and stir in the herbs, prawns and cream. Chill for 2 hours.

3 To serve, garnish the soup with mint, cucumber slices and prawns.

Serves 4
Preparation time: 20 minutes, plus chilling
Cooking time: 20 minutes

gravad lax

750 g–1 kg/1½–2 lb salmon tailpiece, scaled and filleted
mustard, to serve

Pickle:
1 heaped tablespoon sea salt
1 tablespoon sugar
1 teaspoon black peppercorns, crushed
1 tablespoon brandy
1 tablespoon chopped dill

To garnish:
dill leaves
lime slices

1 Mix together the pickle ingredients in a small bowl and transfer approximately a quarter of the mixture to a flat dish.

2 Place one salmon fillet, skin side down, in the pickle mixture. Spread half of the remaining pickle over the cut side of the salmon. Place the other piece of salmon, skin side up, on top.

3 Cover with the remaining pickle mixture, rubbing it into the skin. Cover with foil, lay a board on top and weight it down.

4 Chill for between 12 hours and 5 days before serving. Drain well and slice the salmon. Garnish with dill and lime slices and serve with mustard.

Serves 4–6
Preparation time: 10 minutes, plus chilling

oysters in cream sauce

12 fresh oysters in shells, opened, rinsed and liquor
  strained and reserved
about 50 ml/2 fl oz dry white vermouth or wine
2 tablespoons unsalted butter
2 spring onions, chopped
1 garlic clove, crushed
1 tablespoon flour
Tabasco sauce, to taste
1 egg yolk
50 ml/2 fl oz double cream
25 g/1 oz button mushrooms, finely chopped
75 g/3 oz cooked peeled prawns, finely chopped
15 g/½ oz Parmesan cheese, grated
2 tablespoons fine dry breadcrumbs
salt and white pepper

1 Measure the oyster liquor and make up to 250 ml/8 fl oz with dry white vermouth or wine. Scrub the deeper shell halves and place an oyster in each. Arrange on crumpled foil in a pan. Keep cool.

2 Melt the butter in a saucepan, then add the spring onions and garlic. Cook, stirring, until softened but not browned. Stir in the flour and continue cooking for 1 minute, then gradually stir in the oyster liquor and vermouth or wine. Bring to the boil, lower the heat and simmer for 5 minutes, stirring constantly. Season to taste with salt and pepper, adding a little Tabasco sauce.

3 Blend the egg yolk and cream. Add 2 tablespoons of the hot sauce, then stir into the remaining sauce in the pan. Gently stir until thickened, without boiling. Remove from heat and stir in the mushrooms and prawns. Spoon over the oysters in the shells.

4 Mix together the Parmesan and breadcrumbs and sprinkle over the tops of the oysters. Bake in a preheated oven, 200°C (400°F), Gas Mark 6, for 15–20 minutes or until golden brown and the edges of the oysters begin to curl. Serve hot.

Serves 2–4
Preparation time: 15 minutes
Cooking time: 30–40 minutes
Oven temperature: 200°C (400°F), Gas Mark 6

timbales of smoked salmon

175 g/6 oz smoked salmon, thinly sliced
50 ml/2 fl oz crème fraîche, chilled
1 tablespoon red caviar or salmon roe, plus extra to garnish
pinch of cayenne pepper or dash of Tabasco sauce
2 ripe tomatoes, skinned, deseeded and chopped
salt and pepper
whole chives or dill, to garnish

1 Rinse 2 small soufflé dishes and line with clingfilm. Line with 150 g/5 oz of the smoked salmon slices, allowing them to overlap the sides. Chop the remaining salmon finely. Beat the crème fraîche until soft peaks form, and fold in the chopped salmon, caviar and cayenne pepper or Tabasco.

2 Fill the moulds with the mixture, fold over the sides of overlapping salmon, cover and chill overnight. To make a tomato purée, rub the tomato flesh through a fine sieve. Season with salt and pepper and chill.

3 Unmould the timbales on to individual serving plates and spoon a circle of tomato purée around each one. Garnish the top of the timbales with chives or dill.

Serves 2
Preparation time: 30 minutes, plus chilling

ceviche of salmon

175 g/6 oz piece of salmon fillet
lemon juice, for sprinkling
olive oil, for sprinkling
salt and pepper
chopped dill or fennel, to garnish
brown bread and butter, to serve

1 Using a sharp knife, cut down through the fillet of salmon into very thin slices – about the same thickness as sliced smoked salmon. Arrange the raw salmon on two plates in a single layer.

2 Sprinkle the salmon with lemon juice and olive oil, and season to taste with salt and pepper. Garnish with dill or fennel. Serve immediately with brown bread and butter.

Serves 2
Preparation time: 20 minutes

grilled seafood shells with garlic and mushrooms

600 ml/1 pint mussels, scrubbed and debearded (see page 109)
175 g/6 oz queen scallops
50 g/2 oz butter
1 tablespoon finely chopped onion
1 garlic clove, crushed
50 g/2 oz button mushrooms, sliced
50 g/2 oz fresh white breadcrumbs
150 ml/¼ pint dry white wine
1 tablespoon lemon juice
1 tablespoon chopped parsley
salt and pepper

1 Place the mussels in an ovenproof dish with a little water. Put in a preheated oven, 180°C (350°F), Gas Mark 4, until they open. Remove the mussels from the shells. Separate the white and coral parts of the scallops.

2 Melt half of the butter in a frying pan and sauté the onion, garlic and mushrooms until they are lightly coloured. Mix in the mussels and scallops and heat through gently.

3 Butter 4 deep scallop shells or ramekin dishes and sprinkle in half of the breadcrumbs. Divide the seafood mixture between the shells. Boil 4 tablespoons of water with the wine and lemon juice until well reduced and spoon over the shells.

4 Combine the remaining breadcrumbs with the chopped parsley and seasoning and scatter over the shells. Melt the remaining butter and pour over the top. Place the shells on a baking tray and bake in a preheated oven, 180°C (350°F), Gas Mark 4, for 15 minutes until golden brown.

Serves 4
Preparation time: 30 minutes
Cooking time: 15 minutes
Oven temperature: 180°C (350°F), Gas Mark 4

roasted asparagus with coriander and lime

750 g/1½ lb asparagus
8 tablespoons olive oil
3 tablespoons lime juice
sea salt and pepper
torn coriander leaves, to garnish

1 Trim the asparagus and use a potato peeler to peel the skin from about 5 cm/2 inches of the base of each stalk. Arrange the asparagus in a single layer in a shallow roasting tin.

2 Spoon 4 tablespoons of the olive oil over the asparagus and shake lightly to mix. Roast in a preheated oven, 200°C (400°F), Gas Mark 6, for about 20 minutes, until just tender, turning the asparagus once during cooking. Leave to cool.

3 Transfer the roasted asparagus spears to a shallow dish and spoon the remaining olive oil and the lime juice over the top. Sprinkle with the salt and pepper and toss lightly. Garnish with torn coriander leaves.

Serves 4–6
Preparation time: 10 minutes
Cooking time: 20 minutes
Oven temperature: 200°C (400°F), Gas Mark 6

risotto with wild mushrooms and sage

1 litre/1¾ pints Vegetable Stock (see page 140)
125 g/4 oz butter
1 tablespoon olive oil
1 garlic clove, chopped
1 onion, finely diced
250 g/8 oz wild mushrooms (morel, porcini, chanterelle or field mushrooms), halved or quartered
300 g/10 oz arborio or carnaroli rice
75 ml/3 fl oz dry white wine
1 tablespoon chopped sage
salt and pepper
125 g/4 oz Parmesan cheese, grated, to serve

1 Pour the stock into a saucepan and simmer gently. Heat half the butter with the oil in a heavy-based saucepan, add the garlic and onion and sauté gently for 3 minutes without browning

2 Add the mushrooms to the onions and continue to cook for 2 minutes. Add the rice and mix well so that the grains are coated in the oil and butter. Add just enough stock to cover the rice, stir well and simmer gently, stirring as frequently as possible throughout cooking. As the liquid evaporates, continue adding stock and stirring well. Repeat until all the stock has been absorbed.

3 Finally add the white wine, the remaining butter, the sage and salt and pepper to the rice and stir well. Serve with the Parmesan in a separate bowl.

Serves 4
Preparation time: 10 minutes
Cooking time: 30 minutes

beetroot ravioli with dill cream

1 quantity Basic Egg Pasta dough (see page 134)
1 tablespoon extra virgin olive oil
1 small onion, finely chopped
½ teaspoon caraway seeds
175 g/6 oz cooked beetroot, chopped
175 g/6 oz ricotta or curd cheese
25 g/1 oz dried breadcrumbs

1 egg yolk
2 tablespoons grated Parmesan cheese
grated nutmeg
salt and pepper

Dill cream:
4 tablespoons walnut oil
4 tablespoons chopped dill
1 tablespoon green peppercorns in brine, drained and
 crushed
6 tablespoons crème fraîche

1 Make the pasta dough, wrap in clingfilm and leave
to rest.

2 Heat the oil in a frying pan, add the onion and caraway
seeds and fry over a medium heat for 5 minutes until
light golden. Add the beetroot and cook for a further
5 minutes.

3 Process the beetroot mixture in a liquidizer until
smooth then leave to cool. Beat in the ricotta or curd
cheese, breadcrumbs, egg yolk, Parmesan and nutmeg.
Season to taste with salt and pepper.

4 Roll out the pasta dough to form 8 sheets; cut each in
half widthways. Lay one sheet on a floured surface and
place 5 heaped teaspoons of the filling at 2.5 cm/1 inch
intervals over the dough.

5 Dampen around the mounds of filling with a wet
pastry brush and lay a second sheet of pasta over the
top; press around the mounds to seal well. Cut into
round ravioli using a cutter or into squares using a sharp
knife and place on a floured tea towel. Repeat to make
40 ravioli.

6 Bring a large saucepan of lightly salted water to a
rolling boil and add 2 teaspoons of salt. Drop the ravioli
into the boiling water, return to the boil and cook for
3–4 minutes until al dente.

7 Meanwhile, make the dill cream. Heat the oil in a small
saucepan, add the chopped dill and green peppercorns
and remove from the heat. Stir in the crème fraîche.

8 Drain the ravioli well, transfer to a warmed serving dish
and toss with the dill cream. Serve at once.

Serves 4–6
Preparation time: 1 hour, including making pasta
Cooking time: 25 minutes

morels with wild rice

*Wild rice is actually not a rice at all but a grass native to
the Great Lakes region of the USA and Canada. It has a
deliciously nutty flavour which complements mushrooms
very well.*

150 g/5 oz fresh morels, trimmed and halved lengthways,
 or 25 g/1 oz dried morels plus 125 g/4 oz field
 mushrooms, trimmed
150 g/5 oz wild rice, rinsed
50 g/2 oz butter
75 ml/3 fl oz double cream
1 tablespoon brandy
salt and pepper

1 If using dried mushrooms, soak them in a bowl of
warm water for 15 minutes, then drain.

2 Place the wild rice in a saucepan of salted boiling
water and cook for 18–20 minutes until the grains begin
to split. Drain well.

3 Meanwhile, melt half of the butter in a heavy-based
frying pan, add all the mushrooms and sauté over a
moderately high heat for 2–3 minutes. Season to taste
with salt and pepper, add the cream and brandy, then
reduce the heat and continue cooking until the liquid
has almost all evaporated. Transfer the mushrooms to a
bowl, cover and keep warm.

4 Melt the remaining butter in the pan, add the wild rice
and reheat, stirring to coat it well with the buttery juices.
Season to taste and serve topped with the mushrooms.

Serves 2
Preparation time: 10 minutes, plus soaking
Cooking time: about 20 minutes

tagliatelle with fresh truffles

*Truffles are in season in the autumn and early winter
months, and you can find them in specialist
delicatessens. They are very expensive but a great treat.
It really isn't worth using truffles from a can or jar as they
bear no resemblance to the flavour of fresh truffles.*

300 g/10 oz dried tagliatelle
125 g/4 oz truffles
125 g/4 oz butter
½ tablespoon truffle oil
handful of flat leaf parsley, chopped
75 g/3 oz Parmesan cheese, grated
salt and pepper

1 Cook the pasta in a saucepan of lightly salted boiling water until al dente (see page 137).

2 While the pasta is cooking, clean the truffles with a clean, dry soft brush, dusting away any dirt. Finely slice the truffles using a mandoline.

3 Drain the pasta, add the butter, truffle oil, parsley and Parmesan and season to taste with salt and pepper. Toss well.

4 Add half of the sliced truffles to the pasta and toss again. Serve garnished with the remaining truffles.

Serves 4
Preparation time: 5 minutes
Cooking time: 8–12 minutes

mixed mushroom fricassee

Any mixture of cultivated or wild mushrooms can be used for this dish, or use one type only, depending on taste and availability. The fricassee is also delicious with finger strips of fried bacon stirred in just before serving. Smaller portions make an excellent starter.

75 g/3 oz butter
1 onion, finely chopped
1 garlic clove, crushed
875 g/1¾ lb mixed mushrooms, sliced if large
1 teaspoon finely chopped marjoram
1 tablespoon finely chopped parsley
150 ml/¼ pint red wine
1 egg yolk
1 teaspoon cornflour
2 tablespoons cream
salt and pepper

To serve:
8 slices of bread
2 tablespoons finely chopped parsley

1 Melt two-thirds of the butter in a large frying pan and fry the onion and garlic until soft but not coloured. Add the prepared mushrooms and continue to cook over a gentle heat for about 10 minutes to draw out their juices. The mushrooms should stew rather than fry. Add the marjoram, parsley and red wine and season with salt and pepper. Bring to the boil.

2 Blend the egg yolk with the cornflour and cream, pour into the pan and stir to combine. Cook over a low heat until the sauce thickens. Keep warm.

3 Toast the bread and cut a circle from each slice using an 8 cm/3½ inch cutter. Lay the circles of hot toast overlapping on 4 individual plates and divide the frigasse between them, piling it on the bread. Sprinkle with parsley and serve immediately.

Serves 4
Preparation time: 15–20 minutes
Cooking time: 20–25 minutes

griddled vegetables with creamed polenta

Polenta is a cornmeal porridge traditionally eaten in northern Italy. It is very versatile and can be used for many different dishes.

1 red pepper, cored, deseeded and quartered
4 baby aubergines, quartered
4 baby courgettes, quartered
8 baby sweetcorn
8 baby leeks
1 red onion, cut into wedges, root end left intact
8 baby tomatoes
600 ml/1 pint water
150 g/5 oz instant polenta flour
50 g/2 oz butter, plus extra for greasing
2 tablespoons olive oil, plus extra for drizzling
1 bunch of oregano, chopped
175 g/6 oz rindless soft goats' cheese
sea salt and pepper
salad, to serve (optional)

1 Heat a griddle pan or nonstick frying pan and griddle all the vegetables for 2–4 minutes on each side. Alternatively, grill them under a medium hot grill. Keep warm in a large dish.

2 Heat the water to a gentle boil, pour in the polenta and beat well for 1–2 minutes until it becomes a smooth paste. Reduce the heat and cook the polenta for 6–8 minutes until it thickens, stirring constantly so that it does not catch on the bottom of the pan.

3 Add the butter, olive oil and oregano, and season to taste with salt and pepper. Mix well. The polenta should be the consistency of soft mashed potatoes.

4 Grease a large serving dish with butter, spread the polenta over the bottom of it and arrange the griddled vegetables on top. Crumble the goats' cheese over the top, drizzle with olive oil and place under a hot grill until the cheese has melted. Serve with a leafy salad, if liked.

Serves 4
Preparation time: 15 minutes
Cooking time: 20 minutes

sesame prawns

Splitting and pressing the prawns before cooking is not absolutely essential, but it does help prevent them shrivelling up during deep-frying and adds to the appearance of the finished dish.

12 raw king or tiger prawns, peeled and deveined, with tails left on
2 tablespoons plain flour
1 large egg
2 tablespoons sesame seeds
vegetable oil, for deep-frying
salt and pepper
flat leaf parsley, to garnish
soy sauce, to serve

1 Rinse the prawns under cold running water, then pat dry with kitchen paper. With a sharp pointed knife, slit the prawns along their undersides. Open them out carefully, place cut side down on a board and press firmly to flatten them slightly.

2 Sprinkle the flour on a work surface or plate, add the prawns and turn to coat in the flour. Beat the egg in a bowl with the sesame seeds and salt and pepper to taste.

3 Heat the oil in a deep pan to 180–190°C (350–375°F) or until a cube of bread browns in 30 seconds.

4 Holding the prawns by their tails, dip them one at a time into the egg mixture, then immediately drop them into the hot oil. Deep-fry for 1–2 minutes or until crisp and light golden, then lift out with a slotted spoon and place on kitchen paper to drain. Keep hot while deep-frying the remaining prawns in the same way. Serve at once, garnished with flat leaf parsley, with a bowl of soy sauce for dipping.

Makes 12
Preparation time: 30 minutes
Cooking time: about 10 minutes

seafood brochettes with chilli butter

4 tablespoons lime juice
2 tablespoons olive oil
2 garlic cloves, crushed
500 g/1 lb mixed seafood (raw prawns, fresh tuna, scallops)
50 g/2 oz butter, softened
2 hot chillies, chopped (preferably jalapeño)
salt and pepper
torn coriander leaves, to garnish
plain boiled rice, to serve

1 To make the marinade, put the lime juice, olive oil and garlic in a large bowl. Mix thoroughly to blend and add some salt and pepper. Put the prepared seafood in the marinade (cut the scallops in half if they are very large) and stir gently until completely coated. Cover and refrigerate for at least 1 hour.

2 Remove the seafood from the marinade and thread on to wooden or metal skewers. Place them on the rack of a grill pan and brush with the remaining marinade. Grill, turning occasionally, until cooked and tender, about 5 minutes. Baste with more marinade if necessary.

3 To make the chilli butter, blend the softened butter with the chopped chillies until they are thoroughly mixed. Arrange the seafood brochettes on 4 serving plates on a bed of rice and put a pat of chilli butter on top of each one. Scatter with torn coriander leaves.

Serves 4
Preparation time: 20 minutes, plus marinating
Cooking time: 5 minutes

tagliatelle with smoked salmon and asparagus

250 g/8 oz asparagus tips
375 g/12 oz tagliatelle or fettuccine (fresh or dried)
125 g/4 oz smoked salmon, cut into thin strips
300 ml/½ pint double cream
1 tablespoon chopped tarragon
salt and pepper
fresh Parmesan cheese shavings, to garnish

1 Blanch the asparagus tips in boiling salted water for 5 minutes. Drain under cold running water and pat dry.

2 Meanwhile, cook the pasta in a saucepan of salted boiling water until al dente (see page 137). Drain and return to the pan. Toss over a low heat with the asparagus, smoked salmon, cream, tarragon and salt and pepper, until it is completely heated through.

3 Transfer to a warmed serving dish and garnish with wafer-thin shavings of Parmesan.

Serves 4
Preparation time: 10 minutes
Cooking time: 15 minutes

creamy crab pasta with artichoke hearts

The unusual combination of crab and artichoke hearts, served in a rich creamy sauce, makes a lovely dish for special occasions.

300 g/10 oz fresh linguine verde
750 ml/1¼ pints whipping cream
50 g/2 oz unsalted butter, at room temperature
125 g/4 oz canned artichoke hearts, drained and halved
3 spring onions, cut into 2.5 cm/1 inch lengths
50 g/2 oz Parmesan cheese, freshly grated
250 g/8 oz cooked crab meat
salt and pepper
flat leaf parsley, to garnish

1 Cook the linguine in a saucepan of salted boiling water until al dente (see page 137). Drain and keep warm.

2 Meanwhile, pour the cream into a saucepan and boil until reduced to 350 ml/12 fl oz. Add a little of the butter, then add the artichoke hearts and spring onions and sauté for 2–3 minutes. Add half of the Parmesan and the crab meat and cook until just heated through.

3 Toss the pasta with the remaining butter, then pour the sauce over the pasta and toss again. Season to taste with salt and pepper and sprinkle with the remaining Parmesan. Garnish with parsley and serve immediately.

Serves 4
Preparation time: 10 minutes
Cooking time: 8–12 minutes

spicy crab salad

large lettuce leaves
Chinese leaves, shredded
250 g/8 oz cooked crab meat
2 tomatoes, cut into wedges
2 hard-boiled eggs, peeled and cut into wedges

Dressing:
125 ml/4 fl oz Mayonnaise (see page 145)
50 ml/2 fl oz chilli sauce
2 spring onions, chopped
1 tablespoon chopped parsley
1 teaspoon tomato purée
dash of Worcestershire sauce
50 ml/2 fl oz double cream, whipped
salt and pepper

1 First make the dressing. Combine the mayonnaise, chilli sauce, spring onions, parsley, tomato purée and Worcestershire sauce in a bowl, and season to taste with salt and pepper. Stir well to mix, then fold in the whipped cream. Cover and refrigerate for at least 1 hour.

2 Line a serving platter with the lettuce leaves and make an even layer of shredded Chinese leaves in the centre. Pile the crab meat on top. Arrange the tomato and egg wedges around the crabmeat. Spoon some of the dressing over the crab and serve the rest separately.

Serves 2
Preparation time: 15 minutes, plus chilling

sesame-crusted salmon fillet salad

The crust on this salmon makes it really special. The dressing is a must as it complements the slightly oriental salmon so well. This is a great dinner party dish, because it is not only easy to prepare, but also sensational both to look at and to eat.

500 g/1 lb thick salmon fillet
2 egg whites, lightly beaten
1 tablespoon white sesame seeds
1 tablespoon black sesame seeds
2 bunches of watercress
1 frisé lettuce, divided into leaves
4 spring onions, cut into thin strips and placed in water
sea salt and pepper

Dressing:
3 tablespoons white wine vinegar
5 tablespoons vegetable oil
1 tablespoon soy sauce
1 tablespoon sesame oil
1 teaspoon caster sugar
1 bunch of chives, chopped

1 Dry the salmon with kitchen paper, then dip in the egg white. Mix the sesame seeds and seasoning together on a large plate. Roll the salmon in the sesame seeds and pat on the seeds all over to give a good even coating. Heat a griddle pan or nonstick frying pan, put on the salmon and cook for 2 minutes on each side for rare, or 5 minutes for well done.

2 Process the dressing ingredients in a blender or place in a screw-top jar and shake well to combine. Toss the watercress and frisé in the dressing and arrange on a large serving dish.

3 Slice the salmon fillet with a sharp, thin-bladed knife and arrange on top of the salad. Drain the spring onions, dry on kitchen paper and sprinkle over the salmon.

Serves 4
Preparation time: 15 minutes
Cooking time: 10 minutes

quick griddled scottish scallops with sage

Fresh sage leaves add a lovely subtle flavour. This is a quick and simple dish, perfect for the busy host to serve as an impressive starter.

16 Scottish scallops
1 bunch of sage leaves
3 tablespoons olive oil
1 tablespoon balsamic vinegar
sea salt and pepper
4 lemon wedges, to garnish

1 Dry the scallops thoroughly with kitchen paper. Heat a griddle pan or nonstick frying pan, add the scallops and cook on each side for 2–3 minutes. Add the sage leaves and cook until just wilting.

2 Mix together the olive oil and the balsamic vinegar in a shallow dish. Remove the scallops and sage from the heat and toss well in the dressing. Season and serve immediately with wedges of lemon.

Serves 4
Preparation time: 10 minutes
Cooking time: 6 minutes

griddled mahi mahi with lime and wasabi butter

Mahi mahi is similar in texture to tuna and swordfish, which can be substituted for it. The wasabi butter also goes well with other fish and chicken.

125 g/4 oz butter, at room temperature
grated rind and juice of 1 lime
2 teaspoons wasabi paste
4 x 175 g/6 oz mahi mahi steaks
sea salt and pepper

1 Place the butter, lime rind and juice and wasabi paste in a food processor and blend well. Spoon the butter on to greaseproof paper, wrap the paper round and roll into a sausage shape. Refrigerate for 30 minutes until firm.

2 Heat a griddle pan or nonstick frying pan and cook the fish for 4 minutes on each side. To get a criss-cross effect if using a ridged griddle pan, cook the fish on one side for 2 minutes on a high heat, then give the fish a quarter turn and cook for another 2 minutes. Repeat for the other side. The fish is cooked when firm to the touch and charred.

3 Cut the butter into 8 equal slices. Top each piece of fish with 2 slices of butter and serve immediately.

Serves 4
Preparation time: 10 minutes, plus chilling
Cooking time: 8 minutes

dublin lawyer

1 live lobster, approximately 1 kg/2 lb
50 g/2 oz butter
1 small onion, finely chopped
4 tablespoons Irish whiskey
150 ml/¼ pint double cream
1 teaspoon prepared English mustard
1 teaspoon lemon juice
salt and pepper

To garnish:
watercress sprigs
lemon wedges

1 Plunge the lobster, head first, into fast boiling salted water for 2 minutes. Remove and hold under cold running water to stop the cooking. Set the lobster on a chopping board, upside down, and cut in half lengthways. Discard the stomach sac in the head, the feathery gills and the dark intestinal vein running down the centre of the tail. Remove the meat from the shells and cut into chunks. Crack the claws and remove the meat. Place the body shells into a very low oven to keep warm.

2 Heat the butter in a large frying pan and fry the onion until soft. Add the lobster meat and fry until just cooked, then add the coral and green liver from the head. Warm the whiskey, pour over and carefully ignite with a lighted taper. When the flames have died down add the rest of the ingredients and mix well.

3 Put the lobster meat in the warmed shells. Boil the liquid to reduce and thicken, pour over the lobster and serve immediately garnished with watercress and lemon wedges.

Serves 2
Preparation time: 20–30 minutes
Cooking time: 20 minutes

griddled lobster tails with oregano butter

125 g/4 oz butter, at room temperature
1 large bunch of oregano, chopped
4 raw lobster tails, halved lengthways
sea salt and pepper

To serve:
2 lemons, cut into wedges
new potatoes
salad

1 Place the butter and oregano in a bowl, mix together and season to taste with salt and pepper. Place the butter in a rough sausage shape on some greaseproof paper, roll and twist the ends tightly and place in the freezer to chill and harden for 10 minutes.

2 Heat a griddle pan or nonstick frying pan, place the lobster tails on the griddle and cook for 5 minutes on each side. The shell will turn pink and the flesh white.

3 Place the lemons on the griddle for 3 minutes to colour up and warm the lemon juice.

4 Serve the lobsters with the lemon wedges, accompanied by a salad and new potatoes. Remove the oregano butter from the freezer. Slice and arrange on top of the cooked lobsters to serve.

Serves 4
Preparation time: 15 minutes
Cooking time: 10 minutes

lobster and asparagus salad with herb dressing

500 g/1 lb asparagus
2 x 750 g/1½ lb lobsters, cooked
mixed salad leaves, to serve

Herb dressing:
1 small garlic clove, crushed
2 anchovy fillets
1 tablespoon snipped chives
1 tablespoon chopped parsley
1 teaspoon chopped tarragon
125 ml/4 fl oz Mayonnaise (see page 145)
1 teaspoon tarragon vinegar
a few tablespoons soured cream (optional)
salt and pepper

1 First make the dressing. Put the garlic, anchovy fillets and herbs in a food processor and process until well blended. Add the mayonnaise and process to mix. Add the vinegar and season to taste with salt and pepper. Pour into a bowl, cover and refrigerate for at least 1 hour. Before serving, stir in a few tablespoons of soured cream, if liked.

2 Trim the woody ends from the asparagus spears, making them all the same length. Cook the asparagus in a pan of boiling salted water for 4–8 minutes, until tender but still crisp. Drain and refresh under cold running water, then drain again. Leave to cool.

3 Crack the claws and tails of the lobsters and remove the meat. Keep the claw meat whole, and slice the tail meat across into neat rounds.

4 Arrange the asparagus spears and lobster meat on a bed of salad leaves. Spoon over a little of the dressing and serve the rest separately.

Serves 2
Preparation time: 20 minutes, plus chilling
Cooking time: 8 minutes

spaghetti with lobster

This dish makes an excellent quick supper to serve to friends – the addition of lobster makes it really special.

8 plum tomatoes
1 kg/2 lb lobster, cooked and cut in half lengthways
300 g/10 oz spaghetti
4 tablespoons olive oil
2 shallots, chopped
4 tablespoons lemon juice
handful of chives, chopped
salt and pepper

1 First skin the tomatoes. Place them in a bowl and cover with boiling water. Leave for 1 minute, then remove from the water and slip off the skins. Cut into quarters, remove and discard the seeds, then chop the flesh.

2 Remove all the meat from the lobster and cut it into bite-sized chunks. Cook the pasta in a saucepan of salted boiling water until al dente (see page 137). Drain well.

3 Meanwhile, heat the oil in a saucepan, add the shallots and sauté for 3 minutes. Add the tomatoes and lemon juice, season with salt and pepper and cook for a further 3 minutes. Add the lobster to the tomato sauce, stir, reduce the heat and cook for 4 minutes.

4 Add the sauce to the pasta with the chopped chives, toss with two wooden spoons and serve immediately.

Serves 4
Preparation time: 15 minutes
Cooking time: 8–12 minutes

chicken salad with warm lemon hollandaise

If you find it difficult to bone a chicken yourself, ask your butcher to do it for you.

1.75 kg/3½ lb chicken, boned
1 frisé lettuce, divided into leaves
375 g/12 oz new potatoes, cooked
8 plum tomatoes, skinned and sliced
1 onion, cut into wedges and griddled until tender
175 g/6 oz asparagus, steamed until tender
125 g/4 oz green beans, cooked
1 bunch of radishes, sliced
1 bunch of flat leaf parsley, chopped
sea salt and pepper

Lemon hollandaise:
175g /6 oz unsalted butter
2 large egg yolks
1 teaspoon Dijon mustard
4 tablespoons lemon juice

1 Heat a griddle pan or nonstick frying pan, put on the chicken, skin side down first, and cook for 20 minutes on each side. The outside of the chicken should be beautifully charred when cooked. To test that it is cooked through, insert a sharp knife into the thickest part of the thigh – the juices should run clear.

2 Meanwhile, line a large serving platter with lettuce leaves, then arrange the potatoes, tomatoes, onion, asparagus, beans and radishes on top.

3 To make the hollandaise, melt the butter slowly in a small saucepan. Using a food processor or hand-held blender, process the egg yolks, mustard and lemon juice until smooth. With the machine still running, slowly pour in the butter. Season with salt and pepper, then pour the sauce into a small bowl and place it in a bain marie, or over a saucepan of warm water, so that it keeps warm.

4 Remove the chicken from the heat, place on a carving board and slice thinly. Arrange the chicken over the salad and season. Sprinkle with the chopped parsley and spoon over the hollandaise sauce.

Serves 4
Preparation time: 40 minutes
Cooking time: about 40 minutes

breast of pheasant with savoy cabbage and mustard sauce

4–6 tablespoons clarified butter
4 boneless, skinless pheasant breasts
salt and pepper
herb sprigs, to garnish

Sauce:
300 ml/½ pint Chicken Stock (see page 141)
   or game stock
300 ml/½ pint red wine
2 tablespoons port
2–4 tablespoons coarse grain mustard
300 ml/½ pint single cream

To serve:
425 g/14 oz Savoy cabbage, shredded
50 g/2 oz butter

1 Heat the butter in a large frying pan and cook the pheasant breasts, skin side down, over a gentle heat for 3–4 minutes. Turn and cook on the other side for a further 3–4 minutes. Remove from the heat, season with salt and pepper to taste and leave to rest for 3 minutes before serving. Cooking times will vary with the thickness of the pheasant breasts. When cooked, the flesh should feel firm but springy to the touch and when sliced should only just be cooked through.

2 Make the sauce by combining the stock, wine and port in a saucepan and reducing by half. Stir in the mustard and cream and reduce until the sauce thickens and coats the back of a spoon. Season to taste with salt and pepper.

3 Meanwhile, cook the cabbage, drain, toss in the butter and season to taste with salt and pepper. Divide between 4 plates, piling it in the centre. Carve each pheasant breast into 3 flat slices and arrange in a fan on top of the cabbage. Spoon a little sauce over each breast and serve immmediately, garnished with herb sprigs.

Serves 4
Preparation time: 15 minutes
Cooking time: 6–8 minutes

celebration roast goose

4.5–5 kg/9–10 lb oven-ready goose with giblets
300 ml/½ pint water

Stuffing:
500 g/1 lb canned unsweetened chestnut purée
350 g/12 oz potatoes, boiled and mashed
8 back bacon rashers, rinded and chopped
1 tablespoon chopped lemon thyme
1 tablespoon chopped sage
finely grated rind of 1 lemon

Sauce:
25 g/1 oz butter
1 large onion, chopped
250 g/8 oz sharp-flavoured dessert apples, peeled, cored
   and chopped
1 tablespoon clear honey
4 tablespoons lemon juice
½ teaspoon powdered cardamom
salt and pepper

1 Remove the giblets from the goose, chop the liver and set aside. Remove all visible fat from the cavity of the goose and prick the skin of the lower breast and legs.

2 Mix the stuffing ingredients together thoroughly, adding the chopped goose liver and pepper. Use to fill the cavity. Truss the goose firmly, securing the vent with string.

3 Put the remaining giblets in a roasting pan. Place a rack in the pan and put the goose on top. Pour the water into the pan. Cover loosely with foil and cook in a preheated oven, 190°C (375°F), Gas Mark 5, for 30 minutes, then lower the temperature to 180°C (350°F), Gas Mark 4. Cook for 3½–3¾ hours, until the juices run clear. Baste occasionally with the liquid and add more water if necessary. Remove the foil after 3 hours to allow the skin to become golden and crisp.

4 To make the sauce, melt the butter in a pan and add the onion, apple, honey and lemon juice. Cover and cook for 12–15 minutes until the onion is soft, then add the cardamom and salt and pepper to taste. Using a food processor or electric blender, work to a smooth sauce, or rub through a sieve.

5 Transfer the goose to a warmed serving dish and serve with the sauce separately, and gravy made from the pan juices (see page 101).

Serves 6–8
Preparation time: 25 minutes
Cooking time: about 4 hours
Oven temperature: 190°C (375°F), Gas Mark 5

thanksgiving turkey

6–8 kg/12–16 lb oven-ready turkey with giblets
12–16 button onions
12–16 cloves
125 g/4 oz unsalted butter, softened and diced
150 ml/¼ pint water
300 ml/½ pint white wine or cider
1 bay leaf
salt and pepper
herb sprigs, to garnish

Pomegranate sauce:
1 pomegranate
50 g/2 oz walnuts, chopped
finely grated rind and juice of 1 orange
finely grated rind and juice of 1 lemon
4 egg yolks

1 Set aside the turkey giblets. Season the cavity of the turkey with salt and pepper. Stud each onion with a clove and use these and half the butter to fill the cavity. Spread the remaining butter over the skin of the bird.

2 Chop the giblets and place in a large roasting pan with the water, wine or cider, and bay leaf. Place the turkey in the pan and cover loosely with foil. Cook in a preheated oven, 190°C (375°F), Gas Mark 5, for 15 minutes per 500 g/1 lb or until the juices run clear; remove the foil for the last 30 minutes. Transfer to a warmed serving dish and keep warm. Strain the juices and reserve.

3 To make the pomegranate sauce, cut the pomegranate in half crossways and extract the juice with a lemon squeezer. Add the walnuts, orange and lemon rind and juice, and reserved turkey juices to make up to 600 ml/1 pint. Pour into a saucepan and simmer gently.

4 Lightly whisk the egg yolks in a bowl; gradually add 5 to 6 tablespoons of the pomegranate sauce. Remove the pan from the heat, add the egg yolk mixture and whisk well; do not reheat.

5 To serve, garnish the turkey with herb sprigs. Serve a clove-studded onion with each portion and hand the sauce separately.

Serves 12–16
Preparation time: 30 minutes
Cooking time: 3–4 hours
Oven temperature: 190°C (375°F), Gas Mark 5

griddled duck with oranges and cranberries

4 Barbary duck breasts
2 oranges
125 g/4 oz cranberries
50 g/2 oz light brown sugar
1 tablespoon honey
sea salt and pepper

1 Heat a griddle pan or nonstick frying pan. Score the skin of the duck breast through to the flesh – this allows the fat to be released and the skin to go crispy. Place the duck breasts on the griddle pan or nonstick frying pan and cook them on the skin side for 6–10 minutes and then on the other side for 4–6 minutes.

2 Remove the rind and pith from the oranges, then segment the flesh. Place the oranges, cranberries, sugar and seasoning in a saucepan and simmer to soften the cranberries. Finally, add the honey to the sauce.

3 Remove the duck from the griddle, slice and serve with the orange and cranberry sauce.

Serves 4
Preparation time: 10 minutes
Cooking time: 20 minutes

roast pheasant flambéed with calvados

2 oven-ready pheasants
2 small onions, halved
50 g/2 oz butter
4 sharp-flavoured dessert apples, peeled,
  cored and thickly sliced

Sauce:
25 g/1 oz plain flour
300 ml/½ pint dry white wine
4 tablespoons Calvados
125 ml/4 fl oz double cream
2 tablespoons chopped parsley
salt and pepper

1 Place the pheasants in a roasting tin. Tuck the onion halves under the birds and sprinkle with a little salt and pepper. Dot with the butter and place in a preheated oven, 190°C (375°F), Gas Mark 5. Roast for about 45 minutes, or until the pheasants are cooked through and tender.

2 Add the apples to the tin 15–20 minutes before the end of the cooking time. Remove the pheasants from the roasting tin and transfer to a warmed serving dish. Place the apple slices in a separate dish and keep them hot while making the Calvados sauce.

3 Stir the flour into the pan juices and cook over a moderate heat for 1 minute. Stir in the wine and bring to the boil, stirring all the time. Remove from the heat.

4 Heat the Calvados in a small saucepan until it is just warm, set it alight and then, when the flames die down, add it to the sauce. Stir in the double cream and chopped parsley and adjust the seasoning to taste, then reheat the sauce without boiling.

5 Pour a little of the sauce around the pheasants and arrange the apples in the dish. Serve the pheasants immediately with the remaining sauce served separately.

Preparation time: 20 minutes
Cooking time: 50 minutes
Oven temperature: 190°C (375°F), Gas Mark 5

duck with blackcurrant sauce

1.5 kg/3 lb oven-ready duck, halved
1 tablespoon chopped rosemary
4 tablespoons brandy
olive oil, for sprinkling
salt and pepper
rosemary sprigs, to garnish

Sauce:
25 g/1 oz butter
1 small onion, finely chopped
300 g/10 oz blackcurrants in syrup
2 tablespoons red wine vinegar

1 Put the duck halves into a large shallow dish. Pierce in a few places with a fine skewer. Add salt and pepper to taste, the chopped rosemary, brandy and a sprinkling of olive oil. Cover and marinate in the refrigerator for at least 6 hours or overnight.

2 Remove the duck, reserving any marinade. Place the duck halves on a rack in a roasting tin, skin side uppermost. Rub a little olive oil into the duck skin. Roast in a preheated oven, 200°C (400°F), Gas Mark 6, for 1 hour or until the duck is tender.

3 Meanwhile, prepare the sauce. Melt the butter in a saucepan, add the onion and fry gently for 3 minutes. Add the blackcurrants in their syrup, the wine vinegar and reserved duck marinade. Bring to the boil and simmer gently for 5 minutes.

4 Purée the sauce in a food processor or blender until smooth. Return to the saucepan and heat through. Taste and adjust the seasoning if necessary.

5 Place the duck halves on a warmed serving dish, spoon the sauce over the top and garnish with rosemary.

Serves 2
Preparation time: 20 minutes, plus marinating
Cooking time: 1 hour
Oven temperature: 200°C (400°F), Gas Mark 6

venison with port and fresh figs

2 slices of venison fillet or chump steaks,
   approximately 150 g/5 oz each
75 ml/3 fl oz port
25 ml/1 fl oz red wine vinegar
1 teaspoon olive oil
40 g/1½ oz shallots, finely sliced
1 teaspoon wholemeal flour
50 ml/2 fl oz Beef Stock (see page 141)

2 ripe figs
½ teaspoon mild mustard
salt and pepper
freshly cooked pasta, to serve

1 Trim any fat from the steaks. Place them in a shallow dish. Add the port and vinegar. Cover and refrigerate overnight.

2 Heat the oil in a large, flameproof casserole and sauté the shallots until they have softened.

3 Lift the meat out of the marinade, reserving the liquid. Add the steaks to the casserole and sauté them for about 2 minutes to seal each side. Remove the steaks.

4 Add the flour to the casserole and cook for 1 minute. Stir in the stock and the marinade. Bring to the boil, stirring. Scoop the flesh from one of the figs and add to the casserole with the mustard, salt and pepper.

5 Return the steaks to the casserole. Lower the heat, cover and simmer gently for 45 minutes, stirring occasionally, until tender. Garnish with the remaining fig, sliced. Serve with pasta.

Serves 2
Preparation time: 20 minutes, plus marinating
Cooking time: 50 minutes

venison steak with redcurrant and cranberry sauce

Venison steak from the loin or fillet is not always available, so ask your butcher if you can use another cut. This makes a lovely winter dinner, rich in colour and flavour.

1 teaspoon crushed juniper berries
4 venison steaks, from the fillet or loin
sea salt and pepper

Sauce:
125 g/4 oz redcurrant jelly
125 g/4 oz cranberries
grated rind and juice of 1 orange
2 tablespoons red wine

timbales of smoked salmon p468

sesame-crusted salmon fillet salad p474

griddled duck with oranges and cranberries   p479

griddled lobster tails with oregano butter   p475

griddled vegetables with creamed polenta p471

mixed pepper-crusted venison fillet p481

tagliatelle with smoked salmon and asparagus p473

chocolate truffles p494

1 Mix the juniper berries with salt and pepper and spread over both sides of the venison steaks. Set aside for at least 1 hour or preferably overnight to absorb the flavours.

2 To make the sauce, place the ingredients in a small saucepan and then simmer gently for 10 minutes, stirring constantly.

3 Meanwhile, heat a griddle pan or nonstick frying pan. Put on the venison steaks and cook for 3 minutes on each side for rare, 5 minutes for well done. Serve immediately with the redcurrant and cranberry sauce.

Serves 4
Preparation time: 10 minutes, plus marinating
Cooking time: 15 minutes

mixed pepper-crusted venison fillet

75 g/3 oz mixed peppercorns, crushed
25 g/1 oz juniper berries, crushed
750 g/1½ lb venison fillet, cut from the haunch
1 egg white
sea salt

To serve:
redcurrant jelly
pink sweet potato chips

1 Mix the peppercorns, juniper berries and salt together and place on a large shallow dish. Dip the venison into the egg white, then roll the venison in the peppercorn mix, covering all over with an even layer of the crust ingredients.

2 Heat a griddle pan or preheat a hot grill. Cook the venison for 4 minutes on each side, turning carefully so that the crust stays intact. Cook evenly on all sides, then transfer the fillet to a lightly oiled roasting tin and cook in a preheated oven, 200°C (400°F), Gas Mark 6, for a further 15 minutes for rare, and up to 30 minutes for well done. The time will depend on the thickness of the venison fillet.

3 Slice the venison and serve with redcurrant jelly and pink sweet potato chips.

Serves 4
Preparation time: 10 minutes
Cooking time: up to 45 minutes
Oven temperature: 200°C (400°F), Gas Mark 6

pork chops with gingered apple and rosemary sauce and grilled parsnips

This combination of griddled pork, parsnips and apple sauce makes a memorable meal. The sauce can be made a few hours in advance and warmed up before serving.

4 apples, peeled, cored and cut into 8 wedges
1 teaspoon rosemary leaves
2 tablespoons clear honey
½ tablespoon finely chopped fresh root ginger
2 tablespoons water
1 garlic clove, chopped
3 tablespoons olive oil
1 tablespoon sherry vinegar
2 teaspoons Dijon mustard
4 boneless pork loin chops
500 g/1 lb young parsnips, peeled and cut into thin
   lengths
25 g /1 oz melted butter
sea salt and pepper

1 Place the apples in a saucepan with the rosemary, honey, ginger and water. Cover and bring to the boil, then lower the heat and simmer for 10 minutes, until the apples are tender. Remove from the heat.

2 Mix the garlic, olive oil, vinegar and Dijon mustard in a bowl.

3 Heat a griddle pan or nonstick frying pan, add the chops and cook for 10 minutes on each side.

4 Meanwhile, brush the parsnips with melted butter, sprinkle with salt and pepper, and cook under a preheated hot grill for 10 minutes on each side.

5 To serve, pour the mustard dressing over the chops and serve with the gingered apple sauce and grilled parsnips.

Serves 4
Preparation time: 15 minutes
Cooking time: 25–30 minutes

rare roast beef and tomatoes with mustard sauce

This is a lavish but delicious meal, perfect for serving at a supper party.

1.25 kg/2½ lb beef fillet
1 tablespoon olive oil
1 garlic clove, sliced
2 red onions, sliced
16 small tomatoes
2 tablespoons chopped coriander leaves
2 tablespoons Dijon mustard
2 tablespoons coarse grain mustard
2 tablespoons clear honey
sea salt and pepper

1 Heat a griddle pan or nonstick frying pan. Season the beef fillet, rubbing in the seasoning. Place the fillet on the griddle or pan and cook for 20–25 minutes, turning frequently, until charred on all sides.

2 Transfer to a lightly oiled roasting tin and cook in a preheated oven, 220°C (425°F), Gas Mark 7, for 10–15 minutes for rare and 20–25 minutes for medium. Remove from the oven and allow to rest for 10 minutes.

3 Heat the oil in a pan. Add the garlic and onions and cook for 5 minutes. Add the tomatoes, season to taste with salt and pepper and warm through for 3 minutes. Stir in the coriander.

4 Warm the two mustards in a small saucepan with the honey. Stir until blended. Slice the beef and serve on a bed of the tomato mixture, with the mustard sauce drizzled over the top.

Serves 8
Preparation time: 20 minutes
Cooking time: 30–50 minutes
Oven temperature: 220°C (425°F), Gas Mark 7

griddled italian lamb with rosemary oil

2 lamb fillets, trimmed of fat
4 garlic cloves, cut into slivers
a few small rosemary sprigs
2 red onions, quartered
1 tablespoon chopped rosemary
4 tablespoons olive oil
sea salt and pepper
freshly cooked pasta, to serve

To garnish:
fresh Parmesan cheese shavings
flat leaf parsley

1 Make small incisions with a sharp knife all over the fillets and insert the garlic slivers and rosemary sprigs. Heat a griddle pan or nonstick frying pan, put on the fillets, and cook, turning occasionally, until charred all over (about 20 minutes for rare, and 30–40 minutes for well done). Add the onions for the last 10 minutes and char on the outside.

2 Place the chopped rosemary and oil in a pestle and mortar and work to release the flavours. Season.

3 Allow the lamb to rest for 5 minutes before carving into slices. Spoon the rosemary oil over the top and serve at once with the griddled onions. Serve with fresh pasta, garnished with flat leaf parsley and Parmesan shavings.

Serves 4
Preparation time: 15 minutes
Cooking time: 20–40 minutes

fillet steak with cashel blue cheese and croûtons

Cashel Blue is one of Ireland's most famous cheeses and, in addition to being an important element on the cheese board, has many uses in the kitchen. It is perfect in soup, as a topping for toasted bread, scones and pies and it can also be used in stuffings for fillet of beef and breast of chicken.

1 fillet steak, 4 cm/1½ inches thick
25 g/1 oz butter
50 g/2 oz Cashel Blue cheese, rinded and sliced
salt and pepper

To garnish:
thyme sprigs
croûtons
watercress sprigs

1 Season the fillet with salt and pepper and seal on both sides in a little butter in a very hot pan. Transfer to a buttered baking sheet and set the cheese slices on top.

2 Put into a very hot oven, 220°C (425°F), Gas Mark 7, for 5 minutes for rare; 8 minutes for medium rare and 15 minutes for well done, allowing the cheese to melt and lightly colour. Transfer the steak from the baking sheet to a hot plate, scatter round the croûtons and a few sprigs of thyme and pour around the cooking juices. Garnish with sprigs of watercress. Serve immediately.

Serves 1
Preparation time: 5 minutes
Cooking time: 6–16 minutes
Oven temperature: 220°C (425°F), Gas Mark 7

gaelic steak

25 g/1 oz butter
2 tablespoons oil
1 onion, finely chopped
2 fillet or sirloin steaks, trimmed of fat
50 ml/2 fl oz Irish whiskey
150 ml/¼ pint double cream
2 tablespoons finely chopped parsley
salt and pepper
watercress sprigs, to garnish

1 Heat the butter and oil in a frying pan and fry the onion until soft but not coloured. Scrape to the side of the pan, increase the heat and fry the steaks on both sides, until cooked as required. Remove the meat from the pan and keep warm.

2 Add the whiskey to the pan and set alight; when the flames have subsided, pour on the cream and mix with the onion and meat juices. Bring to the boil, add salt and pepper to taste, add the parsley and pour the sauce over the meat. Serve immediately, garnished with watercress.

Serves 2
Preparation time: 10 minutes
Cooking time: 5–15 minutes

fillet steak with smoked oysters

300 g/10 oz beef fillet, cut into 2 steaks
1 tablespoon soya or sunflower oil
50 g/2 oz onion, finely sliced
75 g/3 oz button mushrooms, finely sliced
25 ml/1 fl oz red wine
25 ml/1 fl oz Beef Stock (see page 141)
1 tablespoon tomato purée
50 g/2 oz canned smoked oysters, drained
salt and pepper
watercress sprigs, to garnish

1 Carefully cut three-quarters of the way through each steak and open out butterfly fashion. Place between 2 sheets of greaseproof paper and beat with a rolling pin to an even thickness. Season and brush lightly with a little oil. Place under a preheated hot grill and cook for 6–10 minutes, turning once.

2 Meanwhile, heat the remaining oil in a pan and sauté the onions and mushrooms for a few minutes until they have softened. Add the wine, stock and tomato purée and simmer for 3–4 minutes, until the liquid is slightly reduced and the sauce thickened. Stir in the oysters.

3 Spoon the sauce over the steaks and garnish with sprigs of watercress.

Serves 2
Preparation time: 10 minutes
Cooking time: 6–10 minutes

sirloin steaks with tomato garlic sauce

4 sirloin steaks, trimmed
15 g/½ oz butter
basil sprigs, to garnish

Sauce:
750 g/1½ lb tomatoes
3 garlic cloves, crushed
1 tablespoon chopped basil or 1 teaspoon dried basil
salt and pepper

1 First skin the tomatoes. Place them in a bowl and cover with boiling water. Leave for 1 minute, then remove from the water and slip off the skins. Cut into quarters, remove and discard the seeds, then chop the flesh.

2 Beat the steaks with a meat mallet or rolling pin until fairly thin, then dot with the butter. Cook under a preheated hot grill for 8–10 minutes, or as preferred, turning once.

3 Meanwhile, make the sauce. Combine the tomatoes, garlic and basil in a saucepan. Add salt and pepper to taste. Simmer for about 10 minutes until the tomatoes are soft.

4 Transfer the steaks to a warmed serving dish and pour over the sauce. Serve immediately, garnished with the basil sprigs.

Serves 4
Preparation time: 15 minutes
Cooking time: about 10 minutes

noisettes of lamb with pomegranates

4 lamb noisettes, trimmed of fat
½ pomegranate
1 spring onion, finely chopped
a few black peppercorns, lightly crushed
50 ml/2 fl oz lamb or Beef Stock (see page 141)
50 ml/2 fl oz red wine
parsley sprigs, to garnish

1 Place the noisettes in a shallow dish in one layer. Using a lemon squeezer, squeeze the juice from the pomegranate and pour it over the lamb. Add the spring onion and peppercorns. Cover and leave to marinate for at least 2 hours.

2 Drain the noisettes, reserving the marinade, and dry them on kitchen paper. Fry the lamb noisettes in a nonstick frying pan, without added fat, to seal them on both sides. Pour over the stock and red wine. Simmer, uncovered, until the liquid has reduced by about half. Add the reserved marinade and bring to the boil.

3 Remove the noisettes from the pan with a slotted spoon and arrange on a warmed serving plate. Garnish with parsley sprigs. Pour the sauce over and serve.

Serves 2
Preparation time: 15 minutes, plus marinating
Cooking time: 20 minutes

steak en croûte

Homemade flaky pastry is delicious, but frozen puff pastry will do just as well if you do not have time to make it.

40 g/1½ oz butter
1 tablespoon oil
2 small onions, finely chopped
1 garlic clove, crushed
125 g/4 oz mushrooms, finely chopped
pinch of ground nutmeg
4 fillet steaks, trimmed
250 g/8 oz Flaky Pastry (see page 125)
*   or frozen puff pastry, defrosted*
1 egg, beaten
4 slices of ham
salt and pepper
chervil or parsley sprigs, to garnish

1 Heat two-thirds of the butter and the oil in a frying pan and gently cook the onions and garlic until soft. Add the mushrooms, nutmeg and salt and pepper to taste and stir over a gentle heat until the mushrooms are cooked and the moisture has evaporated. Remove from the pan, divide into 8 portions and leave to cool.

2 Heat the remaining butter in a clean frying pan, add the steaks and sear quickly on both sides. Remove from the pan, cool quickly and keep chilled until required.

3 Roll out the pastry on a lightly floured surface and cut into 8 rounds slightly larger than the steaks. Brush a 2.5 cm/1 inch border around the edge of each pastry round with beaten egg. Cut the ham into 8 rounds the same size as the steaks.

4 Place one piece of ham on each of 4 pastry rounds. Cover the ham with a portion of the mushroom mixture, a fillet steak, another portion of mushrooms and another round of ham. Top with a pastry circle. Press the edges of the two pastry rounds between your fingers to make neat parcels and then seal with a fork. Cut any pastry trimmings into leaves and use to decorate the croûtes. Brush with beaten egg and cook in a preheated oven, 220°C (425°F), Gas Mark 7, for 20 minutes until golden brown. Serve with chervil or parsley sprigs.

Serves 4
Preparation time: 30 minutes
Cooking time: 30–35 minutes
Oven temperature: 220°C (425°F), Gas Mark 7

beef stroganoff

25 g/1 oz butter
2 onions, sliced
1–2 garlic cloves, crushed
750 g/1½ lb rump or sirloin steak
2 tablespoons dry red wine
125 g/4 oz button mushrooms, sliced
1 teaspoon French mustard
150 g/5 oz natural yogurt
1 tablespoon each chopped thyme and parsley
salt and pepper
fried bread croûtons, to serve

1 Melt the butter in a large frying pan, add the onions and garlic and fry until lightly browned. Cut the steak into thin strips, add to the pan and brown on all sides. Add the wine and boil for 5 minutes, until the liquid has reduced.

2 Add the mushrooms, mustard, yogurt, and salt and pepper to taste and simmer for 5 minutes. Just before serving, stir in the herbs. Garnish with croûtons and serve immediately.

Serves 4
Preparation time: 10 minutes
Cooking time: 20 minutes

lamb cutlets with sherry sauce

8 lamb cutlets
1 garlic clove, sliced
1 egg, beaten
50 g/2 oz white breadcrumbs
1–2 tablespoons oil
25 g/1 oz unsalted butter
1 tablespoon each chopped thyme, parsley, sage and chives
150 ml/¼ pint dry sherry
150 ml/¼ pint double cream
salt and pepper

To garnish:
125 g/4 oz green olives
sage leaves

1 Cut small slits in the cutlets and push in the garlic slices. Coat each cutlet with egg and breadcrumbs, then chill for 20 minutes.

2 Heat the oil and butter in a frying pan, add the cutlets and brown on both sides. Lower the heat and cook for 6 minutes on each side. Drain on kitchen paper and arrange on a warmed serving dish; keep warm.

3 Add the herbs and sherry to the pan and boil rapidly for 2 minutes, until thickened. Stir in the cream, and salt and pepper to taste.

4 Spoon the sauce over the cutlets and serve immediately, garnished with the olives and sage.

Serves 4
Preparation time: 15 minutes, plus chilling
Cooking time: 15–20 minutes

gammon with cumberland sauce

1 gammon, on the bone, weighing about 5 kg/10 lb
4 bay leaves
1 tablespoon black peppercorns
1 onion
8 cloves
175 g/6 oz dried breadcrumbs

Sauce:
2 oranges
2 lemons
500 g/1 lb redcurrant jelly
150 ml/¼ pint port

To garnish:
1 orange, sliced and twisted
watercress sprigs

1 Place the gammon in a large pan with the bay leaves, peppercorns and onion studded with the cloves. Cover with cold water, bring to the boil and skim the surface. Simmer for 3–3½ hours, allowing 20 minutes per 500 g/1 lb plus 20 minutes over. Leave to cool in the cooking liquid.

2 Meanwhile prepare the sauce. Peel the rind thinly from the oranges and lemons and cut into fine shreds. Cover with cold water, bring to the boil and boil for 2 minutes, then drain.

3 Squeeze the juice from the fruit, place in a pan with the redcurrant jelly and heat gently, stirring, until the jelly melts. Simmer for 5 minutes, then add the port and shredded rind. Leave to cool.

4 Remove the skin from the gammon and press the breadcrumbs into the fat. Carve and arrange on a serving platter. Garnish with orange twists and watercress. Serve with the sauce.

Serves 20
Preparation time: 20 minutes, plus cooling
Cooking time: 3–3½ hours

pappardelle with prosciutto and porcini

Fresh or dried porcini may be used for this recipe. If you use dried porcini, use 125 g/4 oz and soak them in hot water for 15 minutes to rehydrate before use.

2 tablespoons olive oil
1 garlic clove, chopped
250 g/8 oz porcini, sliced
250 g/8 oz prosciutto
300 g/10 oz pappardelle
150 ml/¼ pint whipping cream
handful of flat leaf parsley, chopped
75 g/3 oz Parmesan cheese, grated
salt and pepper

1 Heat the olive oil in a saucepan, add the garlic and porcini and sauté for 4 minutes over a moderate heat. Cut the prosciutto into strips; try and keep them separate.

2 Cook the pasta in a saucepan of salted boiling water until al dente (see page 137). Drain well.

3 Add the prosciutto, cream and parsley to the porcini and season with salt and pepper to taste. Bring to the boil and simmer for 1 minute.

4 Add the pappardelle to the sauce and toss well using two spoons to mix evenly. Sprinkle with the Parmesan, toss well and serve immediately.

Serves 4
Preparation time: 10 minutes
Cooking time: 15 minutes

cucumber and strawberry salad

This refreshing salad epitomizes a perfect summer's day. Serve it with cold salmon or on its own as a light starter.

1 small cucumber, peeled and very thinly sliced
1 tablespoon grapeseed oil or light olive oil
1 teaspoon white wine vinegar
250 g/8 oz strawberries, hulled and thinly sliced
salt and pepper
mint leaves and edible flowers, to garnish

1 Place the cucumber slices in a bowl. Add the oil and vinegar, with salt and pepper to taste. Toss lightly.

2 Arrange the cucumber and strawberry slices on a serving platter or individual plates. Scatter a few mint leaves and edible flowers on top. Chill for at least 30 minutes before serving.

Serves 4
Preparation time: 15 minutes, plus chilling

green bean and apricot salad

A pretty salad to make the most of the all-too-brief season for fresh apricots, with toasted almonds to bring out the apricots' flavour.

500 g/1 lb green beans, topped and tailed
6 ripe apricots, halved, stoned and sliced
a few parsley sprigs, roughly torn
1 tablespoon chopped tarragon
1 quantity French Dressing (see page 146)
salt and pepper
25 g/1 oz flaked almonds, to garnish

1 Bring a saucepan of water to the boil, add the beans and cook for 2–3 minutes, or until just tender. Drain in a colander, refresh under cold running water and drain again. Blot the excess water with kitchen paper and place the beans in a serving bowl.

2 Add the sliced apricots to the bowl with the green beans, then add the herbs. Season to taste with salt and pepper.

3 Add the dressing to the salad and toss lightly. Toast the flaked almonds in a dry frying pan until golden. Garnish the salad with a sprinkling of toasted almond flakes.

Serves 4–6
Preparation time: 10 minutes
Cooking time: 5 minutes

champagne sorbet

300 g/10 oz sugar
250 ml/8 fl oz water
600 ml/1 pint Champagne or sparkling white wine
3 tablespoons lemon juice
2 egg whites
4 tablespoons icing sugar

1 Dissolve the sugar in the water in a saucepan over low heat, then bring to the boil. Boil for about 5 minutes or until thick but not beginning to brown. Cool, then stir in 350 ml/12 fl oz of the Champagne or sparking wine and the lemon juice. Pour into freezer trays and freeze for about 1 hour or until mushy.

2 Pour the mixture into a bowl and beat well for 2 minutes. Return to the freezer trays and freeze for a further 30 minutes. Beat again. Repeat the freezing and beating every 30 minutes for the next 2 hours.

3 Beat the egg whites until stiff. Gradually beat in the icing sugar. Beat the frozen mixture well to break down the ice crystals, then fold in the meringue. Return to the freezer and freeze until firm.

4 About 30 minutes before required, put the sorbet in the refrigerator to soften slightly. Before serving, pour a little of the remaining Champagne or sparkling wine over each portion.

Serves 8
Preparation time: 30 minutes, plus freezing
Cooking time: 10 minutes

passion fruit sorbet

10 passion fruit
1 tablespoon lime juice
100 ml/3½ fl oz water
1 egg white
1 teaspoon caster sugar

Sorbet syrup:
300 g/10 oz sugar
300 ml/½ pint water

1 First prepare the sorbet syrup. Place the sugar and water in a pan. Heat to boiling point, stirring continuously to dissolve the sugar. Allow to cool.

2 Scoop the flesh out of the passion fruit. Liquidize with the lime juice and water for about 10 seconds. Strain the juice into a freezer container and combine with the sorbet syrup. Place the freezer container in the freezer and freeze for 2–3 hours or until almost solid.

3 Whisk the egg white and caster sugar until stiff. Remove the sorbet from the freezer and beat in the egg white. Return the sorbet to the freezer for 1–2 hours or until set. If the sorbet has been in the freezer for 24 hours or longer, transfer to the refrigerator 15 minutes before serving to soften slightly.

Serves 4
Preparation time: 25 minutes, plus cooling and freezing
Cooking time: 5 minutes

blackcurrant sorbet

500 g/1 lb blackcurrants
150 ml/¼ pint water
125 g/4 oz caster sugar
2 tablespoons lemon juice
1 egg white, lightly whisked
mint leaves, to garnish

1 Place the blackcurrants in a saucepan with 2 tablespoons of the water and simmer until tender. Rub through a sieve: there should be 300 ml/½ pint blackcurrant purée.

2 Place the sugar and the remaining water in a saucepan and heat gently, stirring constantly, until the sugar has dissolved. Bring to the boil and simmer for 5 minutes. Leave to cool.

3 Add the sugar syrup to the blackcurrant purée with the lemon juice. Turn the purée into a rigid freezerproof container. Cover and freeze until partially set.

4 When the sorbet is half frozen, fold in the egg white. Freeze until firm. Transfer the sorbet to the refrigerator 10 minutes before serving to soften a little. Serve on chilled plates.

Serves 4
Preparation time: 15 minutes, plus freezing
Cooking time: 15 minutes

chestnut roulade

3 eggs, separated
125 g/4 oz caster sugar
250 g/8 oz unsweetened chestnut purée
grated rind and juice of 1 orange
icing sugar, for sprinkling
300 ml/½ pint double cream
2 tablespoons Grand Marnier
finely shredded orange rind, to decorate

1 Whisk the egg yolks with the sugar until thick and creamy. Put the chestnut purée in a bowl with the orange juice and beat until blended, then whisk into the egg mixture. Whisk the egg whites until fairly stiff and fold in carefully.

2 Turn into a lined and greased 20 x 30 cm/8 x 12 inch Swiss roll tin. Bake in a preheated oven, 180°C (350°F), Gas Mark 4, for 25–30 minutes, until firm. Cool for 5 minutes, then cover with a clean damp cloth and leave until cold. Carefully turn the roulade onto a sheet of greaseproof paper, sprinkled thickly with icing sugar. Peel off the lining paper.

3 Place the cream, grated rind and liqueur in a bowl and whip until stiff. Spread three-quarters over the roulade and roll up like a Swiss roll. Transfer to a serving dish, pipe the remaining cream along the top and decorate with orange rind.

Serves 8
Preparation time: 30 minutes, plus cooling
Cooking time: 25–30 minutes
Oven temperature: 180°C (350°F), Gas Mark 4

hot chocolate liqueur soufflé

50 g/2 oz butter, plus extra for greasing
50 g/2 oz plain flour
300 ml/½ pint milk
75 g/3 oz plain or white chocolate, broken into pieces
2 tablespoons crème de menthe
3 eggs, separated, plus 1 egg white
50 g/2 oz caster sugar, plus extra for dusting
icing sugar, for dusting

Sauce:
150 ml/¼ pint double cream
50 g/2 oz plain or white chocolate, broken into pieces
2 tablespoons crème de menthe
1 egg yolk

1 Butter an 18 cm/7 inch soufflé dish and dust with caster sugar.

2 Combine the butter, flour and milk in a medium saucepan. Stirring continuously, heat gently until boiling. Stir vigorously until a thick paste is formed. Cook for 2–3 minutes, still stirring.

3 Away from the heat, add the chocolate and stir until smooth and completely blended into the mixture. Beat in the liqueur and egg yolks.

4 Whisk the 4 egg whites until very stiff, then add the sugar. Whisk again until very stiff and, using a metal spoon, fold the chocolate mixture into the egg whites, taking care not to knock the air out of the whites.

5 Pour the mixture into the prepared soufflé dish and bake in a preheated oven, 180°C (350°F), Gas Mark 4, for 45–50 minutes, until well risen. Do not open the oven door until ready to serve.

6 Make the sauce while the soufflé is cooking. Pour the cream into a small saucepan and add the chocolate. Heat gently, stirring constantly until the chocolate has melted and is thoroughly smooth. Do not boil. Stir in the liqueur and egg yolk. Pour into a jug.

7 To serve, dust the soufflé with icing sugar and take it directly from the oven to a heatproof mat on the table. Serve the soufflé with the sauce.

Serves 6
Preparation time: 30 minutes
Cooking time: 50–55 minutes
Oven temperature: 180°C (350°F), Gas Mark 4

strawberry meringue heart

4 egg whites
250 g/8 oz caster sugar
a few drops vanilla essence
½ teaspoon lemon juice
125 g/4 oz ground almonds
450 ml/¾ pint double cream, whipped
250 g/8 oz fresh strawberries

1 Line 2 baking sheets with lightly greased greaseproof paper and draw a 23 cm/9 inch wide heart on each.

2 To make the nut meringue, whisk the egg whites until stiff. Add the sugar, 1 tablespoon at a time, whisking constantly until the mixture holds its shape. Fold in the vanilla essence, lemon juice and ground almonds.

3 Spoon the nut meringue into a piping bag fitted with a large star nozzle. Pipe star shapes on to the paper, following the outline of the hearts. Then fill in the middles of the hearts with smaller stars to make a solid base. Bake in a preheated oven, 180°C (350°F), Gas Mark 4, for about 40–45 minutes, until crisp and lightly coloured, then cool.

4 Lift the meringues off the greaseproof paper with a palette knife. Sandwich the 2 hearts together with two-thirds of the cream and half the strawberries. Use the remaining cream to pipe rosettes around the edge of the heart and decorate with the remaining strawberries.

Serves 2–4
Preparation time: 45 minutes, plus cooling
Cooking time: 40–45 minutes
Oven temperature: 180°C (350°F), Gas Mark 4

crème caramel

500 ml/17 fl oz milk
1 vanilla pod, split in half lengthways
4 eggs
50 g/2 oz sugar

Caramel:
50 g/2 oz sugar
1 tablespoon water
1 teaspoon lemon juice

1 Put the milk and vanilla pod in a heavy-based saucepan and bring to the boil. Remove from the heat and leave for 5 minutes to infuse.

2 While the milk is infusing, make the caramel. Put the sugar, water and lemon juice in a small saucepan and cook over moderate heat, stirring well until the sugar dissolves. When it turns a rich golden caramel colour, remove from the heat immediately. Pour the caramel into 6 small moulds or 1 large 1 litre/1¾ pint charlotte mould. Rotate the moulds quickly so that the caramel coats the base and sides evenly.

3 Whisk the eggs and sugar together in a bowl until thoroughly combined. Discard the vanilla and whisk the milk into the egg and sugar mixture. Strain the custard through a fine sieve. Pour into the moulds and stand in a roasting tin half-filled with water (a bain marie). Cook in a preheated oven, 150°C (300°F), Gas Mark 2, for about 45 minutes, or until set.

4 Leave to cool and then chill in the refrigerator before unmoulding. To unmould, dip the base of the moulds into a bowl of hot water for 30 seconds and then turn out on to a serving plate.

Serves 6
Preparation time: 15 minutes, plus chilling
Cooking time: 1 hour
Oven temperature: 150°C (300°F), Gas Mark 2

crêpes suzette

125 g/4 oz plain flour
¼ teaspoon salt
3 eggs
2 tablespoons oil
50 g/2 oz butter, melted
1 tablespoon caster sugar
2 teaspoons vanilla sugar
350 ml/12 fl oz milk
25 g/1 oz butter, for frying

Syrup:
125 g/4 oz softened butter, diced
125 g/4 oz caster sugar
grated rind and juice of 1 orange
6 tablespoons Cointreau or Grand Marnier
3 tablespoons brandy

1 To make the batter, sift the flour and salt into a bowl and make a well in the centre. Tip in the eggs, oil, melted butter, sugars and milk, and beat until smooth. Use a hand-held electric whisk, if wished.

2 Melt a little of the butter in a small frying pan and when it is really hot, ladle some of the batter into the pan. Tilt the pan so that the batter covers the base evenly and fry until golden brown on the underside. Flip the crêpe over and cook the other side. Slide it on to a warmed plate and keep warm while you cook the other crêpes.

3 To make the syrup, put the butter and sugar in a bowl and beat together until smooth and creamy. Beat the orange rind and juice into the creamed mixture, and then beat in 3 tablespoons of the orange liqueur and 1 tablespoon of the brandy.

4 Transfer the orange mixture to a large frying pan and heat gently. Boil rapidly for 1–2 minutes, then reduce the heal. Add the crêpes, one at a time, folding each one in half and then in half again in the syrup. Simmer gently until hot. Warm the remaining liqueur and brandy in a small pan, set alight and pour flaming over the crêpes just before serving.

Serves 6–8
Preparation time: 25 minutes
Cooking time: 20 minutes

lemon soufflé pancakes with raspberry sauce

50 g/2 oz plain flour, sifted
1 egg, beaten
200 ml/7 fl oz milk
butter, for greasing
25 g/1 oz icing sugar

Lemon soufflé filling:
25 g/1 oz butter
25 g/1 oz plain flour
300 ml/½ pint milk
25 g/1 oz caster sugar
grated rind and juice of 1 lemon
2 eggs, separated, plus 1 egg white

Sauce:
250 g/8 oz raspberries
50 g/2 oz icing sugar
4 tablespoons lemon juice

1 To make the pancake batter, sift the flour into a mixing bowl. Make a well in the centre and drop in the egg. Mix well. Gradually add half the milk, beating well and drawing in the surrounding flour to make a thick smooth batter. Stir in the remaining milk. Grease a 15 cm/6 inch frying pan and make 8 small pancakes, then set aside.

2 To make the filling, melt the butter in a pan, stir in the flour and cook for 2–3 minutes. Stir in the milk, sugar, lemon rind and juice. Bring to the boil, stirring until the filling thickens. Cool slightly, then beat in the egg yolks. Whisk the egg whites in a grease-free bowl until stiff, then lightly fold into the mixture.

3 Put 1 tablespoon of the lemon mixture into each pancake, then fold it over. Arrange the pancakes carefully in a single layer in a baking dish and sift a little icing sugar over each. Bake in a preheated oven, 200°C (400°F), Gas Mark 6, for 10–15 minutes.

4 To make the sauce, sieve the raspberries into a bowl, then add the icing sugar and lemon juice and mix well. Serve the pancakes hot, with the raspberry sauce in a jug.

Serves 4
Preparation time: 30 minutes
Cooking time: 30 minutes
Oven temperature: 200°C (400°F), Gas Mark 6

tarte tatin

1.5 kg/3 lb crisp dessert apples
75 g/3 oz caster sugar
75 g/3 oz butter
250 g/8 oz Flaky Pastry (see page 125) or frozen puff pastry, defrosted
cream or crème fraîche, to serve

Caramel:
75 g/3 oz caster sugar
3 tablespoons water
25 g/1 oz butter

1 First make the caramel. Put the sugar and water in a flameproof oval or round baking dish and place over a low heat. Stir well to dissolve the sugar completely, then turn up the heat and cook until the sugar starts to caramelize and go golden brown. Remove quickly from the heat and stir in the butter. Add a little hot water if necessary to thin the caramel, standing well back.

2 Peel and core the apples. Cut each one in half and pack tightly into the dish, arranging them in concentric circles so that each round side fits neatly into a hollowed-out side. Sprinkle the apples with the caster sugar. Cut the butter into small dice and scatter across the top of the apples. Cook in a preheated oven, 190°C (375°F), Gas Mark 5, for 20 minutes.

3 Roll out the pastry on a lightly floured board and place on top of the apples. Tuck in the pastry edges around the sides of the dish. Increase the oven temperature to 220°C (425°F), Gas Mark 7, and bake for a further 15–20 minutes until the pastry is well-risen and golden brown. Cool a little and then invert the tart on to a serving platter. Serve warm with cream or crème fraîche.

Serves 6
Preparation time: 20 minutes
Cooking time: 40–45 minutes
Oven temperature: 190°C (375°F), Gas Mark 5

tarte citron

250 g/8 oz plain flour
pinch of salt
125 g/4 oz butter
1 egg yolk
2–3 tablespoons iced water

Filling:
grated rind and juice of 3 lemons
75 g/3 oz caster sugar
2 eggs, plus 1 egg white
75 ml/3 fl oz double cream
125 g/4 oz ground almonds
pinch of ground cinnamon

Topping:
2 lemons, thinly sliced
125 g/4 oz caster sugar

1 To make the pastry, sift the flour and salt into a bowl and rub in the butter until the mixture resembles breadcrumbs. Stir in the egg yolk and sufficient iced water to make a soft and pliable dough. Chill in the refrigerator for 30 minutes.

2 Next make the filling. Put the lemon rind, juice and sugar in a mixing bowl. Break in the eggs and add the egg white. Beat well together and then beat in the cream, ground almonds and cinnamon. The mixture should be thick and smooth.

3 Roll out the pastry on a lightly floured surface, and use to line a 25 cm/10 inch loose-bottomed flan tin. Prick the base with a fork and pour in the filling mixture. Bake in a preheated oven, 190°C (375°F), Gas Mark 5, for 30 minutes, or until it is set and golden. Set aside to cool.

4 Heat the lemon slices in a little water over low heat for 10 minutes, or until tender. Remove and drain the slices, keeping about 75 ml/3 fl oz of the liquid. Add the sugar and stir over gentle heat until dissolved. Bring to the boil, add the lemon slices and cook rapidly until they are well coated with thick syrup. Remove and use to decorate the tart. Leave to cool and serve.

Serves 6–8
Preparation time: 30 minutes, plus chilling and cooling
Cooking time: 30 minutes
Oven temperature: 190°C (375°F), Gas Mark 5

crème brûlée

300 ml/10 fl oz double cream
12 drops of vanilla essence
2 egg yolks
125 g/4 oz caster sugar

1 Place the cream and vanilla essence in a small pan and heat very gently. Whisk the egg yolks with 2 tablespoons of the sugar in a heatproof basin. Stir in the cream and stand the basin over a pan of simmering water. Stir constantly until the mixture thickens slightly.

2 Pour into 4 ramekin dishes and bake in a preheated oven, 160°C (325°F), Gas Mark 3, for 8 minutes. Cool slightly, then place in the refrigerator until thoroughly chilled, preferably overnight.

3 Sprinkle evenly with the remaining sugar and place under a preheated hot grill until the sugar has caramelized. Cool, then chill for 2 hours before serving.

Serves 4
Preparation time: 15 minutes, plus chilling
Cooking time: 20 minutes
Oven temperature: 160°C (325°F), Gas Mark 3

white chocolate profiteroles

25 g/1 oz chopped hazelnuts
1 quantity Choux Pastry dough (see page 123)
175 ml/6 fl oz double cream
1 tablespoon icing sugar, sifted
2–3 drops of vanilla essence

Chocolate sauce:
175 g/6 oz white chocolate
150 ml/¼ pint water
125 g/4 oz sugar

1 Toast the chopped nuts in a dry frying pan, stirring continuously, until they turn a light golden brown. Stir into the choux pastry. Put the pastry mixture into a piping bag fitted with a plain 1 cm/½ inch nozzle, and pipe small mounds on a damp baking sheet. Bake in a preheated oven, 220°C (425°F), Gas Mark 7, for 10 minutes, then lower the heat to 190°C (375°F), Gas Mark 5 and bake for a further 20–25 minutes until golden. Make a slit in each bun and cool on a wire rack.

2 Meanwhile, make the sauce, gently melt together the chocolate and 2 tablespoons of the water in a small saucepan. Add the remaining water and the sugar and heat gently, stirring, until dissolved, then simmer uncovered for 10 minutes. Leave to cool.

3 Next make the filling. Whip the cream in a bowl, then fold in the sugar and vanilla essence. Pipe or spoon a little into each profiterole. Pile the profiteroles on a serving dish. Pour over the chocolate sauce and serve.

Serves 4–6
Preparation time: 25 minutes, plus cooling
Cooking time: 30–35 minutes
Oven temperature: 220°C (425°F), Gas Mark 7

panettone pudding

This is an elegant version of the well-loved bread and butter pudding, perfect for serving at a supper party.

50 g/2 oz butter
5 slices of panettone (Italian fruit bread)
apricot jam, for spreading
250 ml/8 fl oz milk
250 ml/8 fl oz double cream
2 eggs, plus 1 egg yolk
50 g/2 oz brown sugar, plus extra for sprinkling

1 Butter a 1.2 litre/2 pint ovenproof dish. Spread the panettone slices with the remaining butter, and then with the jam. Cut them into triangles and place in the buttered dish, arranged in overlapping layers.

2 Place the milk and cream in a saucepan and bring gently to the boil.

3 Whisk together the eggs, egg yolk and sugar in a bowl until creamy and fluffy. Continue whisking and slowly add the hot milk and cream. When it is all combined, carefully pour it over the panettone, making sure it is all covered by the custard mixture. Sprinkle with a little extra sugar to make a crunchy crust. Chill for at least an hour, or overnight, to allow the custard to soak into the panettone.

4 Half-fill a roasting tin with boiling water. Place the pudding in its dish in the tin and bake in a preheated oven, 180°C (350°F), Gas Mark 4, for 25 minutes or until set.

Serves 4
Preparation time: 10 minutes, plus chilling
Cooking time: 30 minutes
Oven temperature: 180°C (350°F), Gas Mark 4

orange syllabub

grated rind and juice of 2 oranges
grated rind and juice of 1 lemon
75 g/3 oz caster sugar
2 tablespoons Cointreau
300 ml/½ pint double cream

1 Place the orange and lemon rinds in a bowl with the juices and sugar. Add the Cointreau, cover and refrigerate for 1 hour.

2 Add the orange mixture to the cream and whisk on medium speed until it holds its shape. Pour into glasses and chill until required. Serve with crisp biscuits.

Serves 6
Preparation time: 15 minutes, plus chilling

spiced burgundy peaches

1 orange
3 tablespoons clear honey
125 ml/4 fl oz water
½ cinnamon stick
1 clove
pared rind of ½ lemon
300 ml/½ pint red Burgundy
4 large peaches, peeled, halved and stoned
1 tablespoon arrowroot or cornflour

1 Cut the rind from the orange and reserve. Squeeze the juice into a large frying pan. Add the honey, water, cinnamon stick and clove. Add the lemon rind and a thin strip of the orange rind. Cover and bring to the boil over a high heat. Add the wine and peaches. Bring back to the boil, reduce the heat and simmer for 20 minutes.

2 Meanwhile, remove any pith from the remaining orange rind, then cut the rind into very thin strips and reserve for decoration.

3 When the peaches are tender, lift them out of the cooking liquid with a slotted spoon and allow to cool slightly. Slice each peach half and fan out the segments.

4 In a cup, blend the arrowroot or cornflour to a paste with a little water until smooth. Stir it into the cooking liquid and bring to the boil, stirring constantly until thickened. Strain the sauce into a jug.

5 Pour a little of the sauce on to 4 individual dessert plates. Divide the peaches between the plates and decorate with the reserved orange rind. Serve hot or well chilled.

Serves 4
Preparation time: 25 minutes
Cooking time: 30 minutes

avocado ice cream

2 ripe avocados, peeled and stoned
150 ml/¼ pint single cream
300 ml/½ pint double cream
75 g/3 oz caster sugar
2 tablespoons lemon juice
50 g/2 oz split almonds, finely chopped and toasted

1 Place the avocados and single cream in a food processor or blender and work until smooth. Whip the double cream until it forms soft peaks. Fold in the sugar, the avocado mixture, lemon juice and almonds. Place in a rigid freezerproof container. Cover, seal and freeze until firm.

2 Transfer the ice cream to the refrigerator 30 minutes before serving to soften. Scoop into 4 chilled glasses.

Serves 4
Preparation time: 15 minutes, plus freezing

chocolate truffles

3 tablespoons double cream
325 g/11 oz plain chocolate, broken into small pieces
½–1 tablespoon whisky or cognac (optional)
2 tablespoons cocoa powder

1 Heat the cream gently until tepid. Put 125 g/4 oz of the chocolate pieces into a small basin and melt gently over hot, but not boiling, water, stirring occasionally. Do not rest the basin in the hot water. Remove the bowl from the heat and slowly pour in the cream, stirring thoroughly.

2 Cool the mixture and add the whisky or cognac, if using. Whisk for 3–4 minutes until the mixture becomes lighter and stands in peaks. Cool in the refrigerator for about 20 minutes.

3 Sieve the cocoa powder on to a tray or board. Form spoonfuls of the chocolate paste into balls about 2.5 cm/1 inch in diameter. Roll each one into the cocoa powder to cover. Leave to cool until firm.

4 To cover the truffle balls in chocolate, melt the remaining chocolate over hot water. Spear each truffle on a skewer and dip them one by one into the melted chocolate. Place them on a marble slab or a sheet of foil to set.

Makes about 10
Preparation time: 40 minutes, plus cooling
Cooking time: 5 minutes

moroccan almond pastry

A moist, aromatic pastry with all the scents of North Africa – this is delicious served cut into small wedges with coffee after a special meal, or as part of an elegant tea party.

250 g/8 oz ground almonds
175 g/6 oz icing sugar, plus extra
    for sprinkling
1 egg, separated
a few drops of almond extract
1¹/₂ tablespoons rosewater
6 sheets of filo pastry
4 tablespoons olive oil
pinch of ground cinnamon, plus extra
    for sprinkling

1 Stir the ground almonds and icing sugar together and mix to a paste with the egg white, almond extract and rosewater. Divide into 3 equal pieces. Sift icing sugar over a work surface, then roll out each piece of almond paste with your hands to form a sausage about 50 cm/20 inches long and about 1 cm/¹/₂ inch thick.

2 Brush a sheet of filo pastry with oil, cover with a second sheet of pastry and brush that with oil. Cover the remaining pastry with a damp tea towel. Place an almond sausage along one edge of the oiled pastry, about 2.5 cm/1 inch in from the side. Roll up the pastry enclosing the almond filling.

3 Form the pastry-covered sausage into a loose coil, starting in the centre of an oiled 20 cm/8 inch round loose-bottomed tin. Repeat with the remaining almond sausages and pastry. Join one to the end of the coil in the tin, continue to coil outwards, then repeat with the last sausage to form a large coil, filling the tin.

4 Beat the egg yolk with the cinnamon and brush over the top of the coil. Bake in a preheated oven, 180°C (350°F), Gas Mark 4, for 30 minutes until golden and crisp on top.

5 Remove the sides of the tin, carefully turn the coil over, return to the base of the tin and place in the oven for a further 10 minutes until the other side is golden.

6 Invert on to a wire rack and leave to cool slightly. Sift with icing sugar and cinnamon and serve warm, cut into small wedges.

Serves 12–16
Preparation time: 30 minutes
Cooking time: 40 minutes
Oven temperature: 180°C (350°F), Gas Mark 4

almond brittle

Serve this tasty almond brittle with ice cream or with good strong coffee after a meal. Store it in an airtight container to keep it crisp.

250 g/8 oz blanched almonds
250 g/8 oz sugar

1 Line a baking sheet with baking parchment.

2 Put the almonds on a grill pan and place under a preheated hot grill until lightly browned. Allow to cool a little, then chop roughly.

3 Heat a nonstick frying pan over a moderate heat, add the sugar and allow to melt into caramel. Take care that the heat is not too high or the caramel will burn and have a very bitter flavour.

4 Add the almonds and mix in, then pour the almond brittle into the prepared baking tray. Leave the brittle to cool and set, then break into small serving pieces.

Serves 8
Preparation time: 5 minutes, plus cooling
Cooking time: 10 minutes

desserts

treacle pudding with hot treacle sauce

Treacle pudding is one of the great British traditions, and tastes absolutely wonderful. Steamed to a light, fluffy texture, it readily absorbs the delicious, aromatic sauce.

125 g/4 oz butter or margarine, plus extra for greasing
125 g/4 oz caster sugar
2 large eggs
125 g/4 oz self-raising flour, sifted
4 tablespoons golden syrup

Treacle sauce:
4 tablespoons golden syrup
1 tablespoon water

1 Grease a 900 ml/1½ pint pudding basin.

2 Cream together the butter or margarine and sugar in a bowl until light and fluffy. Beat in the eggs, one at a time, adding a little of the flour with the second egg. Fold in the remaining flour.

3 Spoon the golden syrup into the buttered pudding basin, then put the sponge mixture on top. Cover with buttered foil, making a pleat across the centre to allow the pudding to rise. Steam for 1½–2 hours.

4 To make the sauce, heat the syrup and water in a small pan. Turn out the pudding on to a warmed serving dish and pour over the hot sauce just before serving.

Serves 4
Preparation time: 20–30 minutes
Cooking time: 1½–2 hours

apple pie with almond pastry

750 g/1½ lb apples, peeled, cored and sliced
2 teaspoons lemon juice
125 g/4 oz caster sugar
a little milk, for glazing
clotted cream, to serve

Pastry:
175 g/6 oz plain flour
2 rounded tablespoons ground almonds
125 g/4 oz butter, at room temperature
25 g/1 oz icing sugar, sifted
1 egg yolk
2 tablespoons cold water

1 First make the pastry. Put the flour and almonds into a basin, then add the butter. Cut into small pieces and rub into the flour with your fingertips until the mixture resembles breadcrumbs. Add the sifted icing sugar, mix thoroughly and make a well in the centre. Mix together the egg yolk and water and pour into the well. Mix to a rough dough in the basin with a fork.

2 Turn on to a lightly floured surface and knead gently until the dough is quite smooth. Roll into a ball and chill for at least 30 minutes before using.

3 Divide the pastry in half. Roll out the first half and use to line a greased 20 cm/8 inch shallow pie plate. Fill the pie with the apples, lemon juice and the sugar. Moisten the edges, roll out the second piece of pastry and lay on top, pressing down the edges with finger and thumb.

4 Make a small slit in the middle to let the air out, or prick lightly all over the top, and brush with a little milk. Bake in the centre of a preheated oven, 200°C (400°F), Gas Mark 6, for 20 minutes, then reduce the oven temperature to 160°C (325°F), Gas Mark 3 and bake for a further 15–20 minutes. Serve warm with clotted cream.

Serves 4–6
Preparation time: 30 minutes, plus chilling
Cooking time: 40 minutes
Oven temperature: 200°C (400°F), Gas Mark 6

rhubarb, apple and double ginger crumble

125 g/4 oz plain flour
50 g/2 oz ginger biscuits, crushed or ground in a food processor
25 g/1 oz porridge oats
100 g/3½ oz unsalted butter, plus extra for greasing
3 tablespoons light muscovado sugar
500 g/1 lb rhubarb, chopped

2 tablespoons chopped preserved stem ginger, plus 2 tablespoons syrup from jar
50 g/2 oz caster sugar
4 tablespoons water
375 g/12 oz dessert apples, peeled, cored and sliced

1 Sift the flour into a bowl and stir in the ground ginger biscuits and oats. Rub in the butter until the mixture resembles breadcrumbs, then stir in the muscovado sugar.

2 Place the rhubarb in a saucepan with the chopped ginger, ginger syrup, caster sugar and water. Heat gently, cover and simmer for 10 minutes.

3 Place the sliced apples in a greased pie dish. Add the rhubarb mixture and sprinkle over the crumble topping. Place in a preheated oven, 190°C (375°F), Gas Mark 5, for 40 minutes until the filling is bubbling and the topping is golden. Serve hot.

Serves 8
Preparation time: 20 minutes
Cooking time: 50 minutes
Oven temperature: 190°C (375°F), Gas Mark 5

autumn fruit crumble

250 g/8 oz blackberries
2 cooking apples, peeled, cored and sliced
2 teaspoons cornflour
125–150 g/4–5 oz sugar
125 g/4 oz plain flour
50 g/2 oz butter, diced
50 g/2 oz demerara sugar
25 g/1 oz bran flakes, coarsely crushed
50 g/2 oz chopped mixed nuts

1 Place the blackberries and apple slices in a bowl. Mix together the cornflour and sugar and sprinkle over the fruit. Toss well until thoroughly coated. Turn the mixture into a 1.2 litre/2 pint pie dish.

2 Sift the flour into a mixing bowl, add the butter and rub in with the fingertips until the mixture resembles coarse breadcrumbs. Stir in the demerara sugar, bran flakes and chopped nuts. Spoon the mixture over the fruit and flatten slightly with the back of a spoon.

3 Cook in a preheated oven, 190°C (375°F), Gas Mark 5, for 40–45 minutes until the fruit is tender and the topping light golden. Serve hot or cold.

Serves 4–5
Preparation time: 20 minutes
Cooking time: 40–45 minutes
Oven temperature: 190°C (375°F), Gas Mark 5

chocolate puddle pudding

This delicious oven-baked pudding separates while baking to produce a gooey chocolate sauce under a light, spongy crust. Serve it hot, well dusted with cocoa powder and with plenty of whipped cream.

250 g/8 oz plain chocolate, broken into pieces
300 ml/½ pint milk
2 tablespoons brandy (optional)
50 g/2 oz unsalted butter, softened
150 g/5 oz caster sugar
2 eggs, separated
25 g/1 oz self-raising flour
25 g/1 oz cocoa powder, plus extra for dusting
whipped cream, to serve

1 Put the chocolate in a small saucepan with the milk and heat gently until the chocolate has melted. Stir in the brandy, if using.

2 Beat together the butter and sugar until pale and creamy. Gradually beat in the egg yolks, flour, cocoa and melted chocolate mixture.

3 Whisk the egg whites in a separate bowl until they hold their shape. Using a large metal spoon, fold a quarter of the egg whites into the chocolate mixture, then fold in the rest of the egg whites.

4 Turn into a 1.5 litre/2½ pint pie dish and place the dish in a roasting tin. Pour boiling water into the tin to a depth of 2.5 cm/1 inch. Bake in a preheated oven, 180°C (350°F), Gas Mark 4, for about 35 minutes until a crust has formed.

5 Dust generously with cocoa powder and serve hot with whipped cream.

Serves 5–6
Preparation time: 20 minutes
Cooking time: about 35 minutes
Oven temperature: 180°C (350°F), Gas Mark 4

hot chocolate pecan pie

A rich pudding, grand enough for a dinner party, combining the texture and flavour of pecan nuts with chocolate and maple syrup, served in a chocolate pastry case.

Pastry:
175 g/6 oz plain flour
25 g/1 oz cocoa powder
125 g/4 oz unsalted butter
50 g/2 oz caster sugar
2 egg yolks
1–2 tablespoons cold water

Filling:
175 g/6 oz caster sugar
150 ml/¼ pint maple syrup
50 g/2 oz unsalted butter
1 teaspoon vanilla extract
3 tablespoons cocoa powder
3 eggs
200 g/7 oz pecan halves, very lightly chopped

To serve:
crème fraîche
ground cinnamon or icing sugar

1 To make the pastry, sift the flour and cocoa powder into a bowl. Add the butter, cut into small pieces, and rub in gently with the fingertips until the mixture resembles fine breadcrumbs. Add the sugar, egg yolks and enough cold water to make a firm dough. Knead lightly, then wrap closely and chill for 30 minutes.

2 Roll out the pastry on a lightly floured surface and use to line a greased 23 cm/9 inch x 2.5 cm/1 inch deep loose-bottomed flan tin. Trim off the excess pastry around the rim.

3 Line the pastry case with greaseproof paper and fill with baking beans or dried beans. Bake in a preheated oven, 200°C (400°F), Gas Mark 6, for 10 minutes. Lift out the paper and beans and bake for a further 5 minutes. Reduce the oven temperature to 160°C (325°F), Gas Mark 3.

4 To make the filling, put the sugar and syrup in a small saucepan and heat until the sugar dissolves. Remove from the heat and stir in the butter until melted. Leave to cool slightly, then stir in the vanilla extract, cocoa powder and eggs.

5 Scatter the chopped pecans in the pastry case and pour over the syrup mixture. Bake for about 50 minutes until just set. Serve sprinkled with cinnamon or icing sugar, with crème fraîche to accompany it.

Serves 10
Preparation time: 25 minutes, plus chilling
Cooking time: about 1 hour
Oven temperature: 200°C (400°F), Gas Mark 6

marbled chocolate pudding with hazelnut butter sauce

125 g/4 oz plain chocolate, broken into pieces
125 g/4 oz white chocolate, broken into pieces
175 g/6 oz unsalted butter, softened
175 g/6 oz caster sugar
3 eggs, beaten
175 g/6 oz self-raising flour, sifted

Sauce:
60 g/2½ oz hazelnuts
75 g/3 oz caster sugar
75 ml/3 fl oz water
2 tablespoons lemon juice
40 g/1½ oz unsalted butter

1 Grease and line the base of a 1.2 litre/2 pint pudding basin. Melt the plain and white chocolate in separate bowls over simmering water.

2 Beat together the butter and sugar until light and creamy. Gradually beat in the eggs, adding a little flour to prevent the mixture curdling. Fold in the remaining flour, then turn half the mixture into a separate bowl. Stir the plain chocolate into one half and the white into the other.

3 Place alternate spoonfuls of the white and dark chocolate mixtures into the pudding basin. Level the surface, then swirl a skewer through the mixtures to marble them together. Cover the basin with a double thickness of greaseproof paper, securing under the rim with string. Cover with foil, crumpling this under the rim to seal.

4 Cook the pudding in a steamer for 2–2½ hours, topping up with boiling water if necessary. (Alternatively, position the basin on an upturned saucer in a large saucepan. Pour water into the pan to a depth of about 5 cm/2 inches, and cover tightly. Simmer gently.)

5 Meanwhile, make the sauce. Toast the hazelnuts in a dry frying pan until they turn a golden brown. Allow to cool a little and then roughly chop them. Heat the sugar and water in a small, heavy-based saucepan, stirring until the sugar dissolves. Bring to the boil and boil rapidly until caramel-coloured. Immerse the base of the pan in cold water to prevent further cooking. Add the lemon juice, hazelnuts and butter and heat, stirring until smooth.

6 Invert the pudding on to a serving plate and pour over a little sauce. Serve the remaining sauce separately.

Serves 8
Preparation time: 25 minutes
Cooking time: 2–2½ hours

creamy kumquat baskets

25 g/1 oz butter
25 g/1 oz caster sugar
1½ tablespoons golden syrup
½ teaspoon lemon juice
25 g/1 oz plain flour, sifted
½ teaspoon ground ginger

Filling:
15 kumquats, thinly sliced
50 g/2 oz caster sugar dissolved in 125 ml/4 fl oz orange juice
250 g/8 oz cream cheese
150 ml/5 fl oz double cream

1 Heat the butter, sugar, syrup and lemon juice together, stirring, until well blended. Remove from the heat and beat in the flour and ginger. Leave until cold.

2 Divide the mixture into 8 and roll into balls. Place 3 balls well apart on a baking sheet lined with nonstick paper and bake in a preheated oven, 180°C (350°F), Gas Mark 4, for 8–10 minutes, until golden. Cool for 1 minute, then mould each over the base of an inverted glass to form a basket shape. Leave to set for 1 minute, then remove carefully and cool on a wire rack. Repeat with the remaining mixture.

3 Reserve one-third of the kumquats; cook the remainder in the orange juice syrup for 2–3 minutes, until transparent. Remove and set aside. Boil the syrup for 1 minute, then allow to cool. Whisk the cheese and cream together until smooth, then gradually whisk in the cooled orange syrup until thick. Fold in the cooked kumquats. Spoon into the baskets and decorate with the reserved kumquats to serve.

Serves 8
Preparation time: 25 minutes, plus cooling
Cooking time: 30 minutes
Oven temperature: 180°C (350°F), Gas Mark 4

summer pudding

This favourite English pudding may be made with other fruits in season, including gooseberries and strawberries. For a luxury pudding, replace the bread with thinly sliced plain cake.

500 g/1 lb mixed redcurrants, blackcurrants and
  blackberries
125 g/4 oz caster sugar
250 g/8 oz raspberries
8 slices of white bread, crusts removed
whipped cream, to serve

1 Place the currants and blackberries in a heavy-based pan with the sugar. Cook gently, stirring occasionally, for 10–15 minutes until tender. Add the raspberries and leave to cool. Strain the fruit, reserving the juice.

2 Cut 3 circles of bread the same diameter as a 900 ml/1½ pint pudding basin. Shape the remaining bread to fit round the sides of the basin. Soak all the bread in the reserved fruit juice.

3 Line the bottom of the basin with one of the circles, then arrange the shaped bread around the sides. Pour in half the fruit and place another circle of bread on top. Cover with the remaining fruit, then top with the remaining bread circle.

4 Cover with a saucer small enough to fit inside the basin and put a 500 g/1 lb weight on top. Chill in the refrigerator overnight.

5 Turn on to a serving plate and pour over any remaining fruit juice. Serve with whipped cream.

Serves 8
Preparation time: 20 minutes, plus chilling
Cooking time: 10–15 minutes

hazelnut and strawberry roulade

50 g/2 oz ground hazelnuts
3 eggs
125 g/4 oz caster sugar
50 g/2 oz plain flour, sifted
1 tablespoon light vegetable oil
caster sugar, for dredging

Filling:
250 g/8 oz double cream
250 g/8 oz strawberries, chopped

Sauce:
175 g/6 oz strawberries
1 tablespoon icing sugar
2 tablespoons double cream

1 Grease and line a 20 x 30 cm/8 x 12 inch Swiss roll tin. Toast the ground hazelnuts in a dry frying pan and stir continuously until they turn a golden brown. Whisk the eggs and sugar together until very thick and mousse-like. Carefully fold in the flour and hazelnuts, adding the oil at the last moment.

2 Turn the mixture into the Swiss roll tin. Bake in a preheated oven, 200°C (400°F), Gas Mark 6, for 8–10 minutes until the cake springs back when lightly pressed in the centre.

3 Wring out a clean tea towel in hot water and lay it on a work surface. Place a sheet of greaseproof paper on top and sprinkle it with caster sugar. Turn the sponge upside down on to the greaseproof paper then remove the lining paper. Trim off the crisp sides of the cake and roll up with the greaseproof inside the sponge. Place on a wire rack, with the join underneath, and leave to cool.

4 To make the filling, whisk the cream until it stands in soft peaks and fold in the chopped strawberries. Unroll the cooled sponge and remove the greaseproof paper. Spread the filling evenly over the sponge and roll up again.

5 To make the sauce, put the strawberries and sugar into a food processor or blender and process to a purée. Rub through a nylon sieve to remove the pips. Cover each serving plate with some strawberry sauce, then put a slice of roulade in the centre. Place a few drops of cream on the sauce and drag a skewer through the sauce to make an attractive design.

Serves 8
Preparation time: 30 minutes, plus cooling
Cooking time: 8–10 minutes
Oven temperature: 200°C (400°F), Gas Mark 6

raspberry cheese roulade

5 eggs, separated
175 g/6 oz caster sugar
2 tablespoons clear honey
75 g/3 oz hazelnuts, finely ground

Filling:
175 g/6 oz cream cheese, softened
150 ml/5 fl oz single cream
2 tablespoons icing sugar, sifted, plus extra for dredging
250 g/8 oz raspberries

1 Place the egg yolks and sugar in a bowl and whisk until thick and pale. Whisk the egg whites until stiff, then whisk in the honey until thick and glossy. Fold into the egg yolk mixture with the hazelnuts until evenly mixed. Pour into a lined and greased 30 x 20 cm/12 x 8 inch Swiss roll tin. Bake in a preheated oven, 160°C (325°F), Gas Mark 3, for 20–25 minutes, until firm. Cover with a damp tea towel and leave until cold.

2 Beat together the cheese, cream and the icing sugar and place 2 rounded tablespoons of the mixture in a piping bag fitted with a small star nozzle.

3 Turn the roulade out on to a piece of greaseproof paper dredged with icing sugar. Cover with the remaining cheese mixture and the raspberries, reserving 8 raspberries for decoration. Carefully roll up from a short edge. Place on a serving dish and decorate with the reserved cheese mixture and raspberries.

Serves 6
Preparation time: 20 minutes, plus cooling
Cooking time: 20–25 minutes
Oven temperature: 160°C (325°F), Gas Mark 3

bread and butter pudding

40 g/1½ oz butter
4 slices of white bread, crusts removed
4 tablespoons apricot jam
25 g/1 oz chopped mixed peel
25 g/1 oz sultanas
450 ml/¾ pint milk
2 tablespoons sugar
2 eggs, beaten

1 Grease a 1.2 litre/2 pint ovenproof serving dish with one-third of the butter.

2 Butter the bread and spread with the apricot jam. Cut the slices into small triangles. Layer the bread in the dish, sprinkling the mixed peel and sultanas between the layers.

3 Place the milk and sugar in a saucepan and heat to just below boiling point. Remove from the heat and whisk in the eggs. Strain the mixture over the bread and leave to soak for 30 minutes.

4 Place the dish in a roasting tin and fill with water to halfway up the sides; bake in a preheated oven, 180°C (350°F), Gas Mark 4, for 45 minutes. Increase the heat to 190°C (375°F), Gas Mark 5, and cook for a further 10–15 minutes until crisp and golden on top and just set. Serve at once.

Serves 4
Preparation time: 10 minutes, plus soaking
Cooking time: 1 hour
Oven temperature: 180°C (350°F), Gas Mark 4

steamed chocolate sponge

*The chocolate sauce must be served as soon as it is
ready or kept warm over a very low heat.*

125 g/4 oz butter
125 g/4 oz caster sugar
2 eggs, beaten
150 g/5 oz self-raising flour
15 g/½ oz cocoa powder, mixed with 2 tablespoons milk

Chocolate sauce:
25 g/1 oz unsalted butter
125 g/4 oz plain dark chocolate, broken into squares
25 ml/1 fl oz double cream

1 Grease a 900 ml/1½ pint pudding basin. Place the
butter and sugar in a bowl and cream together until light
and fluffy. Gradually add the eggs, beating well between
each addition. Sift the flour and fold it in until thoroughly
blended using a figure of eight motion. Add the cocoa
and milk mixture.

2 Spoon the sponge mixture into the pudding basin.
Cover with a pleated piece of greased greaseproof paper
and a sheet of foil large enough to allow for expansion
and tie with string.

3 Place the basin in a large heavy-based saucepan, two-
thirds full of hot water, cover and steam over a low heat
for about 1½ hours, topping up with more hot water as
and when necessary.

4 While the pudding is steaming, prepare the chocolate
sauce. Put the butter and chocolate into a flameproof
bowl set over a pan of simmering water. When the
chocolate has melted, beat in the double cream.

5 To serve, remove the string, paper and foil and turn
out the pudding on to a warmed serving dish. Pour a
little hot chocolate sauce over the pudding and serve the
rest separately.

Serves 4–6
Preparation time: 30 minutes
Cooking time: about 1½ hours

sussex pond pudding

250 g/8 oz self-raising flour
125 g/4 oz shredded suet
pinch of salt
25 g/1 oz sugar
50–75 ml/2–3 fl oz water
1 large lemon
125 g/4 oz light soft brown sugar
125 g/4 oz butter or margarine, diced
lemon slices, to decorate

1 Combine the flour, suet, salt and sugar in a mixing
bowl. Gradually add enough water to make a soft dough.

2 Turn on to a lightly floured surface. Roll out the
dough to a large circle and cut out a wedge about one-
third of its size. Use the cut circle to line a greased
1.2 litre/2 pint pudding basin. Seal the edges together.

3 Prick the lemon all over with a fork and place it, with
the brown sugar and margarine or butter, in the pastry-
lined basin. Re-roll the remaining dough to make a lid
and use to cover the pudding, pressing the edges
together firmly.

4 Cover with a circle of greased greaseproof paper with a
pleat in the centre to allow for expansion. Tie securely
round the rim. Cover loosely with foil.

5 Place the basin on an upturned saucer or trivet in a
roasting tin, pour in boiling water to come halfway up
the sides of the basin and bake in a preheated oven,
160°C (325°F), Gas Mark 3, for about 1¾ hours until
cooked through.

6 Remove the coverings and turn the pudding out
on to a serving plate. Serve hot, decorated with the
lemon slices.

Serves 4
Preparation time: 20 minutes
Cooking time: 1¾ hours
Oven temperature: 160°C (325°F), Gas Mark 3

traditional christmas puddings

In the past, Christmas puddings were made during the last week of November – everyone in the family taking a turn at stirring on 'Stir-up Sunday' – and the puddings were eaten the following year. Nowadays it is more usual to make the puddings 3–6 months in advance, although you can make them at the last minute if you have to. If you follow the tradition of putting a silver coin in your pudding, be sure to tell your guests to look out for it.

125 g/4 oz self-raising flour
175 g/6 oz fresh white breadcrumbs
175 g/6 oz currants
175 g/6 oz sultanas
125 g/4 oz stoned dates
250 g/8 oz seedless raisins
175 g/6 oz shredded suet
50 g/2 oz chopped mixed peel
50 g/2 oz blanched almonds, chopped
1 small apple, peeled, cored and grated
grated rind and juice of 1 small orange
½ teaspoon mixed spice
¼ teaspoon ground or grated nutmeg
½ teaspoon salt
3 eggs
4 tablespoons brown ale or cider
250 g/8 oz dark soft brown sugar
butter, for greasing
3–4 tablespoons brandy, to serve

1 Place all the ingredients except the butter and brandy in a large bowl, and stir well to mix.

2 Grease a 1.2 litre/2 pint pudding basin and a 600 ml/ 1 pint pudding basin with butter. Fill each basin just over three-quarters full with the mixture and, if you like, bury one silver coin, wrapped in foil, in each one. Cover the basin with greased greaseproof paper and foil or a pudding cloth. Tie securely with string.

3 Place each pudding in a saucepan and pour in boiling water to come halfway up the sides. Boil for 6–8 hours depending on size, topping up with more boiling water as necessary. Remove the puddings from the pans and leave overnight to cool completely.

4 Remove the coverings and cover again with fresh greased greaseproof paper and foil or a pudding cloth. Store the puddings in a cool, dry place.

5 To serve, boil the puddings again for 3–4 hours, depending on size, then turn out on to a warm dish. To ignite the pudding, warm the brandy, pour all over the pudding and set alight carefully. Serve immediately.

Makes 1 large and 1 small pudding
Preparation time: 30 minutes, plus cooling
Cooking time: 6–8 hours, plus 3–4 hours to reheat before serving

moroccan rice pudding

about 1 litre/1¾ pints milk
50 g/2 oz short-grain pudding rice,
*   rinsed and drained*
50 g/2 oz sugar
1–1½ tablespoons orange flower water

To decorate:
chopped pistachio nuts
chopped almonds
crystallized violets or rose petals

1 Heat the milk in a heavy, nonstick saucepan. Sprinkle over the rice and bring to the boil, stirring. Lower the heat and cook very gently, stirring occasionally, until the pudding is thick, velvety and falls easily from the spoon. This may take anything up to about 2 hours. Use a heat-diffusing mat, if necessary, to prevent the rice cooking too quickly and sticking to the pan.

2 When the rice pudding is cooked, stir in the sugar and the orange flower water, to taste.

3 Pour into a serving dish or into individual dishes. Serve warm or cold with pistachio nuts, almonds and crystallized violets or rose petals scattered over the top.

Serves 4
Preparation time: 10 minutes
Cooking time: about 2 hours

traditional rice pudding scented with rosewater

A good rice pudding is a true delicacy, so it is worthwhile knowing how to make it. This recipe has an exquisite balance of flavour and texture.

75 g/3 oz pudding rice
125 g/4 oz sugar
½ teaspoon ground nutmeg
¼ teaspoon ground coriander
½ teaspoon salt
2 tablespoons grated suet
600 ml/1 pint milk
4 egg yolks, plus 1 egg white
4 tablespoons fresh white breadcrumbs
2 tablespoons rosewater
lemon peel slivers, to decorate (optional)
brown sugar, to serve

1 Combine the rice, sugar, spices, salt, suet and milk in a saucepan. Cook over low heat, stirring occasionally, for about 30 minutes, or until the mixture is thick and creamy.

2 Beat in the egg yolks and the egg white, the breadcrumbs and rosewater until thoroughly blended. Serve warm, sprinkled with brown sugar and decorated with slivers of lemon peel, if using.

Serves 4
Preparation time: 10 minutes
Cooking time: 30–35 minutes

chocolate risotto

50 g/2 oz hazelnuts
600 ml/1 pint milk
25 g/1 oz sugar
50 g/2 oz butter
125 g/4 oz arborio or carnaroli rice

50 g/2 oz sultanas
125 g/4 oz plain dark chocolate, grated
splash of brandy (optional)
grated chocolate, to decorate

1 Toast the hazelnuts in a dry frying pan until they turn a golden brown. Allow to cool a little and then roughly chop them.

2 Put the milk and sugar into a small saucepan and heat to simmering point.

3 Melt the butter in a heavy-based saucepan, add the rice and stir well to coat the grains. Add a ladleful of hot milk and stir well. When the rice has absorbed the milk, add another ladleful. Continue to stir and add the milk until it is all absorbed. The rice should be slightly al dente, with a creamy sauce.

4 Finally add the hazelnuts, sultanas and grated chocolate and mix quickly. Try not to over-mix the chocolate as the marbled effect looks good. For a special treat add a splash of brandy just before serving. Decorate with grated chocolate.

Serves 4
Preparation time: 10 minutes
Cooking time: 30 minutes

chocolate profiteroles

1 quantity Choux Pastry (see page 123)
300 ml/½ pint double cream
175 g/6 oz plain dark chocolate
50 g/2 oz butter
50 g/2 oz white chocolate, melted

1 Make the choux pastry, then put teaspoonfuls of the mixture on to wetted baking sheets. Bake in a preheated oven, 200°C (400°F), Gas Mark 6, for 15 minutes or until puffy and golden. Using a small knife, make a slit in the side of each bun and return to the oven for 2 minutes. Transfer to a wire rack to cool.

2 Lightly whip the cream until thick, but not too stiff. Spoon into a piping bag fitted with a small plain nozzle and use to fill the buns. Melt the plain chocolate and butter in a heatproof bowl set over gently simmering water. Dip the tops of the buns in the chocolate mixture. Spoon the white chocolate into a paper piping bag and pipe fine lines across the buns. Allow the chocolate to set before serving.

Serves 6
Preparation time: 30 minutes, plus making pastry
Cooking time: 20 minutes
Oven temperature: 200°C (400°F), Gas Mark 6

apple and walnut whirls

75 g/3 oz butter
50 g/2 oz soft brown sugar
125 g/4 oz plain flour, sifted
75 g/3 oz ground walnuts
chopped walnuts, to decorate

Filling:
1 tablespoon apricot jam
500 g/1 lb dessert apples, peeled, cored and sliced
½ teaspoon ground cinnamon
250 ml/8 fl oz double cream, whipped

1 Cream the butter and sugar together until light and fluffy. Stir in the sifted flour and ground walnuts and mix to a firm dough using your hand. Turn on to a floured surface and knead lightly until smooth. Roll the dough out thinly; cut out ten 7.5 cm/3 inch and ten 5 cm/2 inch circles.

2 Place on a greased baking sheet and bake in a preheated oven, 180°C (350°F), Gas Mark 4, for 12–15 minutes, until golden. Transfer to a wire rack to cool.

3 To make the filling, put the apricot jam and apples into a saucepan, cover and cook gently for 15–20 minutes, until softened. Add the cinnamon and leave to cool.

4 Spread the cooled apple mixture over the larger rounds, pipe two-thirds of the cream over the apple and top with the small rounds. Decorate with the remaining cream and the chopped walnuts.

Serves 10
Preparation time: 20 minutes, plus cooling
Cooking time: 25 minutes
Oven temperature: 180°C (350°F), Gas Mark 4

hazelnut shortcake

75 g/3 oz hazelnuts, ground
75 g/3 oz butter or margarine
50 g/2 oz light muscovado sugar
125 g/4 oz wholemeal flour
1 egg white
1 tablespoon chopped hazelnuts
whipped cream, to serve

Filling:
500 g/1 lb dessert apples, peeled, cored and sliced
2 tablespoons apple juice
50 g/2 oz raisins
50 g/2 oz sultanas
1 teaspoon ground mixed spice

1 Toast the ground hazelnuts in a dry frying pan until they turn a golden brown. Allow to cool. Beat the margarine or butter and sugar together until soft. Stir in the flour and ground hazelnuts and mix to a firm dough. Turn on to a floured surface and knead lightly until smooth. Divide in half, roll each piece into a 20 cm/8 inch round and place on a greased baking sheet. Brush one round with egg white and sprinkle with the chopped nuts.

2 Bake both rounds in a preheated oven, 190°C (375°F), Gas Mark 5, for 10–15 minutes. Cut the nut-covered round into 8 sections while still warm. Transfer both rounds to a wire rack to cool.

3 Meanwhile, place the apples and juice in a pan, cover and cook gently for 15 minutes, stirring occasionally. Add the remaining filling ingredients and leave to cool.

4 Spread the filling over the hazelnut round and arrange the cut triangles on top. Serve with whipped cream.

Serves 6–8
Preparation time: 20 minutes, plus cooling
Cooking time: 20 minutes
Oven temperature: 190°C (375°F), Gas Mark 5

fruit shortcake with fresh nectarines

375 g/12 oz plain flour, sifted
250 g/8 oz soft margarine or butter
125 g/4 oz soft brown sugar
½ teaspoon vanilla extract
175 g/6 oz curd cheese
1 tablespoon clear honey
2 nectarines

1 Lightly grease 2 baking sheets. Place the sifted flour in a large mixing bowl and rub in the margarine or butter. Stir in the sugar, then add the vanilla extract. Bring the mixture together with your hand to make a ball and knead lightly. Divide the dough in half. Roll out each half on a lightly floured surface to a 20 cm/8 inch round. Flute the edges with a fork.

2 Place both rounds on the prepared baking sheets and mark one into 8 sections. Bake in a preheated oven, 160°C (325°F), Gas Mark 3, for 50 minutes–1 hour until lightly browned. Remove from the oven. Cut through the sections on the marked round. Leave to cool slightly. Transfer to a wire rack and leave to cool completely before filling.

3 Cream the curd cheese and honey in a bowl. Peel, stone and chop one nectarine and add it to the curd cheese. Spread this mixture carefully on to the uncut round of shortbread.

4 Arrange the shortbread wedges neatly on the cheese mixture, each at a slight angle and overlapping a little. Thinly slice the remaining nectarine, without peeling it, and use the nectarine slices to decorate the top of the shortcake.

Serves 8
Preparation time: 20 minutes, plus cooling
Cooking time: 50 minutes–1 hour
Oven temperature: 160°C (325°F), Gas Mark 3

chocolate peach puffs

These quick and easy little pies can be made using white chocolate or, for those with a less sweet tooth, luxury plain dark chocolate.

75 g/3 oz white or plain dark chocolate, broken into pieces
4 small ripe peaches or nectarines
375 g/12 oz Flaky Pastry (see page 125)
    or frozen puff pastry
beaten egg, to glaze
icing sugar, for dusting
grated chocolate, to decorate (optional)
single cream, to serve

1 Grease and lightly dampen a baking sheet. Put the chocolate in a heatproof bowl over a pan of simmering water and leave until melted.

2 Halve and stone the peaches, then slice them very thinly. Roll out the pastry thinly on a lightly floured surface and cut out four 12 cm/5 inch rounds using a small bowl or saucer as a guide.

3 Place the pastry rounds on the baking sheet. Spoon the melted chocolate on to the pastry, spreading to within 2.5 cm/1 inch of the edges.

4 Arrange the peach slices in an overlapping circle over the chocolate. Make small flutes around the edges of the pastry with the back of a knife. Brush the pastry with a little beaten egg. Bake in a preheated oven, 200°C (400°F), Gas Mark 6, for 15 minutes until the pastry is golden.

5 Dust the pastries with icing sugar and place under a preheated hot grill for 1–2 minutes, watching closely, until lightly caramelized. Leave to cool slightly, then decorate with grated chocolate, if liked. Serve with single cream.

Serves 4
Preparation time: 20 minutes
Cooking time: 15–20 minutes
Oven temperature: 200°C (400°F), Gas Mark 6

plum and almond crisp

50 g/2 oz butter
125 g/4 oz fresh white breadcrumbs
50 g/2 oz light soft brown sugar
50 g/2 oz flaked almonds
½ teaspoon ground cinnamon
500 g/1 lb plums, stoned and lightly poached in
    150 ml/¼ pint water and 2 tablespoons sugar
whipped cream, to serve

1 Melt the butter in a saucepan. Stir in the breadcrumbs, sugar, almonds and cinnamon.

2 Put the plums in a pie dish, then sprinkle the breadcrumb mixture over the top. Bake in a preheated oven, 180°C (350°F), Gas Mark 4, for 30–35 minutes. Serve cold with cream.

Serves 4
Preparation time: 15 minutes
Cooking time: 30–35 minutes
Oven temperature: 180°C (350°F), Gas Mark 4

pear and cardamom flan

175 g/6 oz plain flour
¼ teaspoon salt
100 g/3½ oz unsalted butter, diced,
    plus extra for greasing
2 tablespoons caster sugar
1 egg yolk
1–2 tablespoons cold water

Filling:
125 g/4 oz unsalted butter, softened
75 g/3 oz caster sugar
2 small eggs, lightly beaten
75 g/3 oz ground hazelnuts
25 g/1 oz ground rice
seeds from 2 cardamom pods, crushed
1 teaspoon grated lemon rind
4 tablespoons soured cream
3 small firm pears

To serve:
1 teaspoon caster sugar
whipped cream (optional)

1 Sift the flour and salt into a bowl and rub in the butter until the mixture resembles fine breadcrumbs. Stir in the sugar and gradually work in the egg yolk and enough cold water to form a soft dough. Knead lightly, wrap in cling film and chill for 30 minutes.

2 Roll out the pastry on a lightly floured surface and use to line a greased 23 cm/9 inch fluted flan tin. Prick the base and chill for a further 30 minutes.

3 Line the pastry case with nonstick baking paper and baking beans and bake 'blind' (see page 122) in a preheated oven, 220°C (425°F), Gas Mark 7, for 10 minutes. Remove the paper and beans and bake for a further 10–12 minutes until the pastry is crisp. Reduce the oven temperature to 180°C (350°F), Gas Mark 4.

4 In a bowl, beat together the butter and sugar for the filling until pale and light and then gradually beat in the eggs, a little at a time until incorporated. Lightly beat in all the remaining ingredients, except the pears. Pour the mixture into the prepared pastry case.

5 Peel and halve the pears and scoop out the cores. Thinly slice each pear lengthways. Be careful to keep the slices together. Then, using a palette knife, carefully transfer the sliced pear halves to the pastry case, arranging them neatly on the filling. Bake the flan for 55 minutes–1 hour until golden and firm in the middle. Serve the flan warm, sprinkled all over with a little caster sugar and some whipped cream, if liked.

Serves 6
Preparation time: 25 minutes, plus chilling
Cooking time: about 1¼ hours
Oven temperature: 220°C (425°F), Gas Mark 7

butterscotch flan

175 g/6 oz plain flour
75 g/3 oz butter, cut into small pieces
25 g/1 oz caster sugar
1–2 tablespoons water
whipped cream, to decorate

Filling:
125 g/4 oz dark soft brown sugar
40 g/1½ oz butter
40 g/1½ oz plain flour, sifted
300 ml/½ pint milk
150 ml/¼ pint single cream

1 Sift the flour into a bowl, add the butter and rub in until the mixture resembles breadcrumbs. Stir in the sugar with enough water to mix to a firm dough; knead lightly. Roll out the pastry on a floured surface and use to line a 23 cm/9 inch fluted flan dish. Prick the base and chill for 30 minutes.

2 Line the pastry case with nonstick baking paper and baking beans and bake 'blind' (see page 122) in a preheated oven, 190°C (375°F), Gas Mark 5, for 15 minutes. Remove the paper and beans and cook for 5–10 minutes, until firm. Leave to cool.

3 Next prepare the filling. Place the sugar, butter, flour, milk and cream in a saucepan, bring to the boil, whisking, then cook gently for 1 minute. Pour into the pastry case and chill until set. Decorate with cream.

Serves 6
Preparation time: 20 minutes, plus chilling
Cooking time: 30 minutes
Oven temperature: 190°C (375°F), Gas Mark 5

spicy pumpkin flan

Pastry:
175 g/6 oz wholemeal flour
1 teaspoon ground mixed spice
75 g/3 oz butter or margarine, cut into small pieces
25 g/1 oz soft brown sugar
2 tablespoons water

Filling:
4 tablespoons mincemeat
2 eggs, beaten
500 g/1 lb cooked pumpkin, puréed
75 g/3 oz caster sugar
1 teaspoon ground mixed spice
150 ml/¼ pint double cream

1 Place the flour and spice in a bowl and rub in the butter or margarine until the mixture resembles breadcrumbs. Stir in the sugar and water, mix to a firm dough and knead lightly. Roll out and use to line a 23 cm/9 inch fluted flan tin. Chill for 30 minutes.

2 Line the pastry case with nonstick baking paper and baking beans and bake 'blind' (see page 122) in a preheated oven, 190°C (375°F), Gas Mark 5, for 15 minutes. Remove the paper and beans and cook for a further 10 minutes.

3 Cover the flan base with the mincemeat. Beat the eggs, pumpkin purée, sugar, spice and 3 tablespoons of the cream together. Pour into the pastry case and return to the oven for 20–25 minutes, until set. Leave in the tin until cool, then carefully place on a serving plate. Whip the remaining cream and pipe swirls around the edge.

Serves 6
Preparation time: 20 minutes, plus chilling
Cooking time: 50 minutes
Oven temperature: 190°C (375°F), Gas Mark 5

peach, apricot and blueberry gratin

This quick and simple dessert is best made when fresh apricots and peaches are in season. American blueberries are available most of the year, or raspberries make a good substitute.

4 firm ripe peaches, halved, stoned and thinly sliced
6 firm ripe apricots, halved, stoned and thinly sliced
175 g/6 oz blueberries
250 g/8 oz mascarpone cheese
250 g/8 oz Greek yogurt
3 tablespoons light muscovado sugar
1 teaspoon ground cinnamon

1 Spoon the peaches, apricots and blueberries into a gratin dish. Beat the mascarpone and yogurt together and spread over the fruit.

2 Combine the sugar and cinnamon, sprinkle over the gratin to cover the surface and cook under a preheated hot grill for 5–6 minutes until the sugar is caramelized. Leave to cool for a few minutes before serving.

Serves 6
Preparation time: 20 minutes
Cooking time: 5–6 minutes

white chocolate cherry tart

2 eggs
40 g/1½ oz caster sugar
150 g/5 oz white chocolate, finely chopped
300 ml/½ pint double cream
500 g/1 lb fresh black or red cherries or 1 kg/2 lb canned cherries, drained
ground cinnamon, for dusting

Pastry:
175 g/6 oz plain flour
½ teaspoon ground cinnamon
125 g/4 oz unsalted butter
25 g/1 oz caster sugar
2–3 teaspoons cold water

1 First make the pastry. Sift the flour and cinnamon into a bowl. Add the butter, cut into small pieces, and rub in with the fingertips until the mixture resembles fine breadcrumbs. Add the sugar and enough water to mix to a firm dough. Wrap and chill for 30 minutes.

2 Roll out the dough on a floured surface and use to line a 23 cm/9 inch x 2.5 cm/1 inch deep loose-based flan tin. Trim off the excess pastry around the rim.

3 Line the pastry case with greaseproof paper and fill with baking beans. Bake 'blind' (see page 122) in a preheated oven, 200°C (400°F), Gas Mark 6, for 10 minutes. Lift out the greaseproof paper and baking beans and bake for a further 5 minutes. Reduce the oven temperature to 180°C (350°F), Gas Mark 4.

4 Meanwhile, make the filling. Beat together the eggs and sugar. Heat the chocolate and cream gently in a small heavy-based saucepan until the chocolate has melted. Pour over the egg mixture, stirring constantly.

5 Stone the cherries, if using fresh, or thoroughly drain the canned cherries. Arrange in the flan case. Pour the chocolate mixture over the cherries. Bake in the oven for about 45 minutes until the chocolate cream is set. Dust with cinnamon and serve warm.

Serves 6–8
Preparation time: 30 minutes, plus chilling
Cooking time: about 1 hour
Oven temperature: 200°C (400°F), Gas Mark 6

apricot lattice tart

Drained canned apricots may be used instead of fresh ones in this tart. Alternatively, dried apricots – presoaked in cold water – can be used.

250 g/8 oz plain flour
2 teaspoons ground mixed spice
175 g/6 oz butter
25 g/1 oz caster sugar
1 egg, separated
about 1 tablespoon iced water
cream, to serve (optional)

Filling:
750 g/1½ lb apricots, stoned
2 tablespoons lemon juice
1 tablespoon clear honey
3 tablespoons cornflour
2 tablespoons water
1 egg yolk mixed with 1 teaspoon water, to glaze

1 Sift the flour and spice into a bowl. Rub in the butter until the mixture resembles fine breadcrumbs. Stir in the caster sugar, the egg yolk and enough water to mix to a fairly stiff dough.

2 Turn the dough on to a floured surface, knead lightly until smooth, then roll out and use to line a 20 cm/8 inch flan ring. Reserve the pastry trimmings. Chill the flan case and pastry trimmings in the refrigerator for 30 minutes.

3 Prick the base and sides of the dough and line with greaseproof paper and baking beans. Bake 'blind' (see page 122) in a preheated oven, 200°C (400°F), Gas Mark 6, for 15 minutes, then remove the paper and beans. Brush the base with egg white and return to the oven for a further 3 minutes.

4 To make the filling, place the apricots in a pan with the lemon juice and honey. Cover and simmer gently for 5–10 minutes or until softened. Cool slightly, then process in a food processor or blender until smooth. Return the purée to the pan.

5 Blend the cornflour to a smooth paste with the water and add to the apricot purée. Cook over a low heat for 2–3 minutes until thickened, stirring constantly. Allow to cool, then turn into the pastry case and level the surface.

6 Roll out the reserved pastry trimmings and cut into strips. Make a lattice pattern over the fruit, attaching the pastry with a little water.

7 Brush the pastry lattice with the egg glaze, then bake in a preheated oven, 200°C (400°F), Gas Mark 6, for 25–30 minutes until golden brown. Cover the rim of the pastry with foil if it appears to brown too quickly.

8 Serve the tart hot or cold, with cream if liked.

Serves 6
Preparation time: 25–30 minutes, plus cooling and chilling
Cooking time: 45–50 minutes
Oven temperature: 200°C (400°F), Gas Mark 6

apple and nectarine flan

Pastry:
250 g/8 oz plain flour
pinch of salt
125 g/4 oz butter
1 egg yolk
2–3 tablespoons iced water

Filling:
1 kg/2 lb cooking apples, peeled, cored and chopped
2 tablespoons water
6 cloves
1 cinnamon stick
125 g/4 oz light soft brown sugar
25 g/1 oz butter
finely grated rind and juice of 1 lemon
3 nectarines, halved, stoned and thinly sliced

Glaze:
2 tablespoons apricot jam
1 tablespoon boiling water
1 tablespoon lemon juice

1 First make the pastry. Sift the flour and salt into a bowl and rub in the butter until the mixture resembles breadcrumbs. Stir in the egg yolk and sufficient iced water to make a soft and pliable dough. Chill in the refrigerator for 30 minutes.

2 Place the apples in a saucepan with the water, cloves and cinnamon. Bring gently to the boil over a moderate heat, then simmer until the apples have broken down to form a thick purée. Stir in the sugar, butter and lemon rind and juice. Allow to cool.

3 Roll out the pastry on a lightly floured surface and use to line a 25 cm/10 inch loose-bottomed flan tin. Prick the base with a fork. Remove the cloves and cinnamon from the apple mixture, then pour the purée into the flan case. Arrange the nectarine slices on top, overlapping in neat circles. Bake in a preheated oven, 190°C (375°F), Gas Mark 5, for 25 minutes or until golden.

4 Meanwhile make the glaze. Mix the jam with the boiling water and lemon juice and beat welll to combine. When the tart comes out of the oven, brush the glaze generously all over the surface and leave the tart to cool on a wire rack.

Serves 6
Preparation time: 30 minutes, plus chilling and cooling
Cooking time: 35 minutes
Oven temperature: 190°C (375°F), Gas Mark 5

key lime pie

200 g/7 oz digestive biscuits, crushed
25 g/1 oz sugar
75 g/3 oz butter, melted
lime slices, to decorate (optional)

Filling:
3 eggs, separated
400 g/13 oz condensed milk
125 ml/4 fl oz lime juice
1 tablespoon lemon juice
2 teaspoons grated lime rind
a few drops of green food colouring (optional)
25 g/1 oz sugar

Topping:
250 ml/8 fl oz double or whipping cream
1 tablespoon icing sugar, sifted
a few drops of vanilla extract

1 Mix together the crushed digestive biscuits, sugar and melted butter and press over the bottom and up the sides of a 23 cm/9 inch springform cake tin. Chill while making the filling.

2 Lightly beat the egg yolks until creamy. Add the condensed milk, lime and lemon juices and lime rind and beat until well mixed and slightly thickened. Tint a pale green with food colouring, if liked.

3 In another bowl, beat the egg whites until frothy. Add the sugar and continue beating until the meringue forms soft peaks. Fold gently but thoroughly into the lime mixture using a large metal spoon.

4 Spoon the filling into the pie shell and smooth the top. Bake in a preheated oven, 160°C (325°F), Gas Mark 3, for 15–20 minutes or until the filling is just firm and lightly browned on top. When cool, chill the pie for at least 3 hours.

5 To make the topping, whip the cream until it begins to thicken. Add the sugar and vanilla and continue whipping until quite thick but not stiff. Spread the cream over the top of the chilled pie. If desired, decorate with twisted lime slices.

6 Remove the pie from the cake tin just before serving, and serve well chilled.

Serves 8–10
Preparation time: 25–30 minutes, plus chilling
Cooking time: 15–20 minutes
Oven temperature: 160°C (325°F), Gas Mark 3

apricot and almond filo pie

1 kg/2 lb apricots, halved and stoned
2 tablespoons lemon juice
50 g/2 oz blanched almonds, chopped
50 g/2 oz caster sugar
250 g/8 oz filo pastry
50 g/2 oz butter, melted
icing sugar, for dusting

1 Mix the apricots, lemon juice, almonds and caster sugar in a bowl.

2 Place 1 sheet of filo pastry over a greased 20 cm/8 inch flan tin. Brush with butter and place a second sheet on top of the first, at an angle. Continue layering the filo in this manner, with each successive sheet at a different angle, until only 2 sheets remain. Gently compress the filo sheets so that they take the shape of the tin, with the edges of the pastry sheets overlapping the tin.

3 Fill the pastry case with the apricot mixture, then layer the remaining 2 sheets of filo on top, brushing each with butter. Scrunch the overlapping edges of the pastry all round the top edge of the pie.

4 Brush the pie with any remaining butter and bake in a preheated oven, 190°C (375°F), Gas Mark 5, for 35–40 minutes, until the pastry is crisp and golden brown. Dust with icing sugar and serve warm or cold.

Serves 6
Preparation time: 20 minutes
Cooking time: 35–40 minutes
Oven temperature: 190°C (375°F), Gas Mark 5

nectarine baked alaska

A spectacular dessert that normally needs to be prepared at the last minute, but this one can be frozen fully prepared and baked just a few minutes before serving. It is best not to keep it in the freezer for more than 1–2 days.

2 eggs
75 g/3 oz caster sugar
50 g/2 oz plain flour, sifted
4 tablespoons sweet sherry
2–3 nectarines
1 tablespoon lemon juice
600 ml/1 pint vanilla ice cream

Meringue:
4 egg whites
250 g/8 oz caster sugar

1 Grease a 20 cm/8 inch sandwich tin, line the base with greased greaseproof paper. Dust the inside of the tin lightly with flour.

2 Put the eggs and sugar into a bowl and whisk with an electric beater until thick and mousse-like. Carefully fold in the flour. Turn the mixture into the prepared tin and level the surface. Bake in a preheated oven, 190°C (375°F), Gas Mark 5, for 15–20 minutes until the cake springs back when lightly pressed in the centre. Turn out on to a wire rack, peel off the lining paper, turn the cake the right way up and leave to cool.

3 Place the sponge on a heatproof serving dish and sprinkle over the sherry. Stone and finely slice the nectarines and sprinkle with the lemon juice. Arrange the nectarines over the sponge.

4 To make the meringue, whisk the egg whites until stiff, then gradually whisk in the sugar. Set aside.

5 Soften the ice cream slightly, then shape it into a dome over the nectarines, leaving a 2.5 cm/1 inch margin all round. Quickly spoon the meringue over the ice cream and sponge to cover them completely.

6 Open-freeze the alaska until solid, then pack into a rigid freezerproof container. Return to the freezer for up to 2 days.

7 Bake from frozen in a preheated oven, 220°C (425°F), Gas Mark 7, for 8–10 minutes until the meringue has browned lightly. Serve the baked alaska immediately.

Serves 6–8
Preparation time: 35 minutes, plus cooling and freezing
Cooking time: 25–30 minutes
Oven temperature: 190°C (375°F), Gas Mark 5

chocolate and spiced apple strudel

6 sheets of filo pastry
50 g/2 oz unsalted butter, melted
icing sugar, for dusting
clotted or whipped cream, to serve

Filling:
1 kg/2 lb cooking apples
2 tablespoons lemon juice
50 g/2 oz unsalted butter
50 g/2 oz breadcrumbs
1 teaspoon ground mixed spice
50 g/2 oz demerara sugar
50 g/2 oz sultanas
50 g/2 oz walnut pieces
125 g/4 oz plain dark chocolate, chopped

1 Lightly grease a large baking sheet with slightly raised sides. To make the filling, peel, core and slice the apples and put them into a bowl of water with the lemon juice to prevent discoloration.

2 Melt the butter in a frying pan and fry the breadcrumbs for about 3 minutes until golden. Drain the apples and add to the pan with the remaining filling ingredients.

3 Lay one sheet of filo pastry on a work surface and brush with a little of the melted butter. Cover with another sheet and brush with more butter. Add a third sheet and spoon half the filling over the pastry to within 2.5 cm/1 inch of the edges. Fold the two short ends over the filling, then roll up the pastry like a Swiss roll, starting from a long side. Transfer to the baking sheet with the join underneath.

4 Use the remaining pastry, filling and butter to make a second strudel in the same way. Bake in a preheated oven, 190°C (375°F), Gas Mark 5, for about 30 minutes until golden. Cool slightly, dust with icing sugar and serve sliced with clotted or whipped cream.

Serves 8
Preparation time: 35 minutes
Cooking time: about 30 minutes
Oven temperature: 190°C (375°F), Gas Mark 5

cherry japonaise

125 g/4 oz ground almonds
50 g/2 oz cornflour
150 g/5 oz caster sugar
3 egg whites
125 g/4 oz cream cheese
2 tablespoons black cherry jam
150 ml/¼ pint double cream, whipped
250 g/8 oz cherries, pitted

1 Line 2 baking sheets with nonstick paper and draw a 20 cm/8 inch circle on each piece.

2 Mix together the ground almonds, cornflour and half the sugar. In a large bowl, whisk the egg whites until stiff, then whisk in the remaining sugar. Carefully fold in the almond mixture.

3 Place half the mixture in a piping bag fitted with a small star nozzle and pipe a lattice design inside one circle of paper, then pipe a border around the edge. Spread the remaining mixture evenly over the second circle. Bake in a preheated oven, 160°C (325°F), Gas Mark 3, for 25–30 minutes, until firm. Cool, then remove the paper carefully.

gâteau ganache with chocolate cream filling   p517

iced chocolate mousse with whipped cream   p533

mango with thai sticky rice   p537

poached figs in cassis with cinnamon sauce   p525

traditional rice pudding scented with rosewater p504

treacle pudding with hot treacle sauce p496

raspberry sorbet p532

ricotta and rum bombe p534

4 Beat the cheese and jam together until soft, then fold in the cream and two-thirds of the cherries. Place the japonaise base on a serving plate and spread with the cherry mixture. Very carefully lay the lattice design on top and decorate with the reserved cherries.

Serves 6
Preparation time: 20 minutes, plus cooling
Cooking time: 25–30 minutes
Oven temperature: 160°C (325°F), Gas Mark 3

oeufs à la neige au citron

5 eggs, separated
175 g/6 oz caster sugar
finely grated rind of ½ lemon
600 ml/1 pint milk
strip of lemon rind
extra lemon rind, to decorate

1 Put the egg whites into a large clean bowl and whisk well until they form firm peaks. Gradually whisk in two-thirds of the sugar. Fold in the grated lemon rind.

2 Beat the egg yolks together and add 2 tablespoons of the milk. Bring the rest of the milk to the boil in a large saucepan, add the strip of lemon rind and stir in the remaining sugar. Reduce the heat.

3 Drop teaspoons of the beaten egg white into the hot milk and poach gently for 2 minutes. Remove with a slotted spoon, drain on kitchen paper and set aside while you make the lemon custard.

4 Cool the milk and stir in the beaten egg yolks. Heat the mixture gently in a double boiler, or basin, over simmering water, stirring continuously until the custard thickens. Do not allow the mixture to boil. Remove the lemon rind and let the custard cool. Pour into a shallow serving dish and float the meringues on top. Cover and chill well before serving, sprinkled with extra lemon rind.

Serves 4
Preparation time: 15–20 minutes, plus cooling and chilling
Cooking time: 20–30 minutes

panettone with peaches and clotted cream

Griddled panettone is delicious and makes an interesting base for a dessert. Other fruits, such as apples, apricots and pears, can be griddled and used instead of the peaches.

4 peaches, halved and stoned
4 slices of panettone
ground cinnamon, for dusting
4 tablespoons clotted cream
icing sugar, for dusting

1 Heat a griddle pan or nonstick frying pan and cook the peaches on each side until slightly charred, about 5 minutes.

2 Toast the panettone slices for 1–2 minutes on each side until golden.

3 Place the peaches on the panettone and dust with cinnamon. Spoon on the clotted cream, dust with icing sugar and serve immediately.

Serves 4
Preparation time: 5 minutes
Cooking time: 10–15 minutes

banana rum fritters

4 large, ripe bananas
25 g/1 oz sugar
5 tablespoons dark rum
oil, for deep-frying

Batter:
75 g/3 oz plain flour
pinch of salt
1 tablespoon olive oil
150 ml/¼ pint water
2 egg whites

To serve:
vanilla sugar
ground cinnamon

1 Peel the bananas and cut them diagonally into slices about 1 cm/½ inch thick. Place them in a shallow dish and sprinkle with the sugar. Pour the rum over the top and set aside for 1½ hours, turning from time to time.

2 Meanwhile, make the batter. Sift the flour and salt into a bowl. Make a well in the centre and gradually mix in the oil and water. Mix to a smooth batter and leave to stand for 1 hour.

3 Just before the batter is needed, beat the egg whites stiffly and then lightly fold them into the batter. Drain the banana slices and dip them into the batter so that they are completely coated.

4 Heat the oil for deep-frying to 180–190°C (350–375°F) or until a cube of bread browns in 30 seconds. Fry the banana pieces, a few at a time, until golden brown on both sides. Drain on absorbent kitchen paper. Serve the fritters really hot, sprinkled with vanilla sugar and cinnamon.

Serves 4
Preparation time: 15 minutes, plus standing
Cooking time: 10 minutes

filo horns with mixed berries and raspberry sauce

6 large sheets of filo pastry
75 g/3 oz unsalted butter, melted, plus extra for greasing
25 g/1 oz ground almonds
175 g/6 oz ricotta or curd cheese
1 tablespoon clear honey
625 g/1¼ lb mixed summer berries
flaked almonds, to decorate

Sauce:
250 g/8 oz raspberries
2 tablespoons Grand Marnier (optional)
3 tablespoons icing sugar, plus extra for dusting

1 Cut each sheet of pastry into two 15 cm/6 inch squares, brush each square with butter and fold in half diagonally to form a triangle. Wrap each triangle around a greased cream horn mould, brush with the remaining butter and place on a large greased baking sheet, seam-side down. Bake the filo horns in a preheated oven, 190°C (375°F), Gas Mark 5, for 15 minutes until crisp and golden. Leave to cool, then carefully remove the pastry from the moulds.

2 Toast the ground almonds in a dry frying pan and stir continuously until they turn a golden brown. Allow to cool a little, then beat together with the ricotta or curd cheese and the honey. Hull and slice the fruits as necessary and stir into the cheese mixture.

3 To make the sauce, put the raspberries into a food processor or blender and process until smooth. Pass through a fine sieve and whisk in the Grand Marnier, if using, and the icing sugar. Toast the flaked almonds in the same way as the ground almonds and leave to cool a little.

4 Fill the filo horns with the cheese and fruit mixture and arrange on a plate. Pour a little sauce on the side and sprinkle lightly with icing sugar and scatter over the toasted, flaked almonds.

Serves 6
Preparation time: 40 minutes, plus cooling
Cooking time: 15 minutes
Oven temperature: 190°C (375°F), Gas Mark 5

coffee meringues

2 egg whites
125 g/4 oz caster sugar
1 tablespoon instant coffee powder
300 ml/½ pint double cream
2 tablespoons Tia Maria or other coffee-flavoured liqueur
pistachios or almonds, to decorate

1 Line 2 baking sheets with nonstick paper or baking parchment. Draw six 7.5 cm/3 inch circles and six 5 cm/2 inch circles on the paper with a pencil.

2 Whisk the egg whites until stiff, then whisk in the sugar, 1 tablespoon at a time. Add the coffee powder and continue whisking until the meringue is very stiff and holds its shape. Spoon into a piping bag fitted with a 1 cm/½ inch plain nozzle and pipe within the circles to form meringue disks.

3 Bake in a preheated oven, 110°C (225°F), Gas Mark ¼, for 1½ hours until crisp. Peel the paper carefully off the meringues, then cool on a wire rack.

4 Whip the cream and liqueur together in a bowl until stiff. Spoon into a piping bag fitted with a large fluted nozzle and pipe three-quarters of the cream on to the larger meringue circles. Top with the small circles, then pipe a whirl of cream on each one. Toast the pistachios or almonds in a dry frying pan, stirring continuously until they turn a golden brown. Allow to cool slightly, then use to decorate the meringues. Serve the meringues with the remaining cream.

Serves 6
Preparation time: 35–40 minutes
Cooking time: 1½ hours
Oven temperature: 110°C (225°F), Gas Mark ¼

pavlova

Vary the filling of the pavlova as you like. Raspberries, strawberries, grapes, figs and redcurrants are all delicious.

4 egg whites
250 g/8 oz caster sugar
1 tablespoon cornflour
2 teaspoons vinegar
¼ teaspoon vanilla extract

Filling:
300 ml/½ pint double cream
2 bananas, sliced
1 small pineapple, cut into cubes
flesh of 2 passion fruits
2 peaches, skinned and sliced

1 Whisk the egg whites until stiff. Add the sugar, a tablespoon at a time, whisking until the meringue is very stiff. Whisk in the cornflour, vinegar and vanilla.

2 Pile the meringue on to a baking sheet lined with silicone paper and spread into a 23 cm/9 inch round. Hollow out the centre slightly and bake in a preheated oven, 150°C (300°F), Gas Mark 2, for 1½ hours.

3 Let the pavlova cool, then remove the paper and place the pavlova on a serving dish. Whip the cream until stiff and fold in some of the fruit. Pile into the pavlova and decorate with the remaining fruit.

Serves 6–8
Preparation time: about 20 minutes, plus cooling
Cooking time: 1½ hours
Oven temperature: 150°C (300°F), Gas Mark 2

mini meringues

3 egg whites
175 g/6 oz golden caster sugar
1 tablespoon instant coffee powder
150 ml/¼ pint double cream
1 teaspoon vanilla extract

1 Whisk the egg whites until they are stiff, but not dry. Gradually whisk in the sugar and coffee powder, until stiff and glossy.

2 Spoon or pipe small mounds of meringue on to baking sheets lined with baking parchment. Bake in a preheated oven, 110°C (225°F), Gas Mark ¼, for 2–2½ hours, or until the meringues are crisp and dry. Leave to cool.

3 Whisk the cream with the vanilla extract until it just holds its shape. Stick pairs of meringues together with a little flavoured cream and serve.

Makes 20
Preparation time: 20 minutes
Cooking time: 2–2½ hours
Oven temperature: 110°C (225°F), Gas Mark ¼

white chocolate creams with orange and cranberry sauce

2 teaspoons powdered gelatine
2 tablespoons cold water
4 egg yolks
25 g/1 oz caster sugar
1 teaspoon cornflour
1 teaspoon vanilla extract
300 ml/½ pint milk
200 g/7 oz white chocolate, chopped
300 ml/½ pint double cream
grated chocolate, to decorate

Sauce:
3 clementines or 2 small oranges
125 g/4 oz fresh or frozen cranberries
75 g/3 oz caster sugar
150 ml/¼ pint cold water

1 Lightly oil 6 individual 150 ml/¼ pint ramekin dishes, pudding basins or metal moulds. Sprinkle the gelatine over the water in a small bowl.

2 Whisk the egg yolks in a bowl with the sugar, cornflour, vanilla extract and a little of the milk. Bring the remaining milk to the boil in a heavy-based saucepan. Pour over the egg mixture, stirring to combine. Return to the saucepan and heat gently, stirring until the mixture is slightly thickened. (Do not allow to boil or the mixture might curdle.) Remove from the heat and stir in the gelatine until dissolved. Add the chocolate and stir until melted. Leave to cool.

3 Whip the cream until just peaking. Using a large metal spoon, fold the cream into the custard. Spoon the mixture into the prepared containers. Place on a tray and chill for 4–5 hours or overnight.

4 To make the sauce, pare thin strips of rind from one of the clementines and cut into fine shreds. Remove the peel from all the fruit and slice the fruit thinly.

5 Put the cranberries into a small, heavy-based saucepan with the sugar and water. Heat gently until the sugar dissolves and then simmer until the cranberries have softened. Remove the cranberries from the pan and reserve.

6 Boil the cranberry liquid until very syrupy, then return the cranberries to the pan with the sliced clementines and shredded rind. Mix together and turn into a small bowl. Leave to cool.

7 Dip the chocolate moulds very briefly into warm water to loosen, then invert on to serving plates. Spoon a little sauce over and around the creams and serve decorated with grated chocolate.

Serves 6
Preparation time: 30 minutes, plus chilling
Cooking time: about 10 minutes

moroccan rosewater pudding

The texture of this delightful pudding is very reminiscent of nursery food – light, silky, soothing and not quite set. The sophisticated flavouring of rosewater makes it into an adult dessert.

5 tablespoons cornflour
3–5 tablespoons sugar, to taste
750 ml/1¼ pints creamy milk
2 tablespoons rosewater
½ teaspoon grated lemon rind

Topping:
25 g/1 oz blanched almonds, chopped
25 g/1 oz pistachio nuts, chopped

1 Blend the cornflour, a little sugar and a few spoonfuls of the milk to a paste. Bring the remaining milk to the boil in a nonstick saucepan, then stir some into the paste. Return the paste and milk to the saucepan and cook, stirring, until thick enough to coat the back of a spoon.

2 Remove the pan from the heat and stir in the rosewater and lemon rind. Add more sugar, to taste, and stir to dissolve.

3 Pour into a large serving dish, or individual dishes, and leave until a skin forms on the surface.

4 Scatter the chopped almonds and pistachios over the top of the pudding, then leave until cold. Cover and chill before serving.

Serves 4–6
Preparation time: 15 minutes, plus chilling
Cooking time: 10 minutes

gâteau ganache with chocolate cream filling

Meringue:
125 g/4 oz ground hazelnuts
4 egg whites
275 g/9 oz caster sugar
a few drops of vanilla extract
1 teaspoon white wine vinegar
125 g/4 oz ground hazelnuts

Filling:
75 g/3 oz plain dark chocolate, broken into small pieces
3 tablespoons water
300 ml/½ pint double cream

To decorate:
25 g/1 oz plain dark chocolate
2–3 physalis (optional)

1 Grease two 20 cm/8 inch sandwich tins, line the bases with greaseproof paper, then grease the paper. Toast the ground hazelnuts in a dry frying pan, stirring continuously, until they turn a golden brown.

2 Whisk the egg whites until stiff, then whisk in the sugar, 1 tablespoon at a time. Continue whisking until the meringue is very stiff and holds its shape. Carefully fold in the vanilla extract, vinegar and hazelnuts.

3 Turn the mixture into the prepared tins and level the surface. Bake in a preheated oven, 180°C (350°F), Gas Mark 4, for 45–50 minutes. Loosen the meringues from the tins with a sharp knife, turn out and carefully peel off the paper. Place on a wire rack and leave to cool.

4 To make the filling, melt the chocolate with the water in a heatproof bowl over a pan of gently simmering water. Remove from the heat and leave to cool.

5 Whip the cream until it begins to thicken, then whisk in the cooled chocolate and continue whisking until stiff. Sandwich the meringue rounds together with the chocolate cream.

6 To decorate the meringue, melt the chocolate in a heatproof bowl over a pan of gently simmering water, remove from the heat and leave to cool.

7 Put the cooled chocolate in a greaseproof piping bag, snip off the tip, then drizzle the chocolate across the top of the meringue. Leave to set. Decorate with physalis, if liked, and serve as soon as possible.

Serves 6–8
Preparation time: 45–50 minutes
Cooking time: 45–50 minutes
Oven temperature: 180°C (350°F), Gas Mark 4

lemon polenta syrup cake

175 g/6 oz butter
175 g/6 oz caster sugar
125 g/4 oz ground almonds
50 g/2 oz flaked almonds
½ teaspoon vanilla extract
2 large eggs
finely grated rind and juice of 1 lemon
75 g/3 oz polenta flour
½ teaspoon baking powder
single cream, to serve

Syrup:
grated rind and juice of 2 lemons
50 g/2 oz caster sugar
2 tablespoons of water

1 Line a 15 cm/6 inch cake tin with baking parchment.

2 Beat together the butter and sugar until light and creamy. Add the ground and flaked almonds, vanilla extract and eggs and mix well. Add the lemon rind and juice, polenta and baking powder and mix well. Spoon into the prepared tin and bake in a preheated oven, 180°C (350°F), Gas Mark 4, for 25 minutes.

3 While the cake is cooking, make the syrup. Put the lemon rind and juice, caster sugar and water in a saucepan and heat through. Spoon over the cake as soon as it comes out of the oven, allowing the syrup to drizzle through. Serve the cake hot or cold with cream.

Serves 4–6
Preparation time: 10 minutes
Cooking time: 25 minutes
Oven temperature: 180°C (350°F), Gas Mark 4

baked ricotta cheesecake

50 g/2 oz butter or margarine
175 g/6 oz digestive biscuits, crushed
250 g/8 oz ricotta cheese
2 eggs, separated
50 g/2 oz ground almonds
finely grated rind of 1 lemon
150 ml/¼ pint single cream
50 g/2 oz caster sugar

To decorate:
icing sugar, for dusting
lemon rind slivers

1 Oil a 20 cm/8 inch springform cake tin.

2 Melt the butter in a small pan, then mix in the biscuit crumbs. Press the mixture over the base of the cake tin, then chill in the refrigerator for about 15 minutes until firm.

3 Beat the ricotta cheese with the egg yolks, almonds and lemon rind until smooth, then gradually stir in the cream.

4 Whisk the egg whites until stiff, then whisk in the sugar a little at a time. Carefully fold into the cheese mixture, then spoon over the biscuit base and level the surface.

5 Bake in a preheated oven, 160°C (325°F), Gas Mark 3, for 1–1¼ hours until firm. Turn off the heat and leave the cheesecake in the oven until cold. Put in the refrigerator and chill. To serve, dust with a sifted icing sugar and sprinkle with lemon rind.

Serves 8
Preparation time: 40 minutes, plus cooling and chilling
Cooking time: 1–1¼ hours
Oven temperature: 160°C (325°F), Gas Mark 3

blackcurrant cheesecake

50 g/2 oz butter, melted
125 g/4 oz digestive biscuits, finely crushed
25 g/1 oz demerara sugar
300 g/10 oz curd cheese
50 g/2 oz caster sugar
2 eggs, separated

grated rind and juice of ½ orange
15 g/½ oz gelatine
300 ml/½ pint whipping cream, whipped

Topping:
200 g/7 oz can blackcurrants in syrup
2 teaspoons arrowroot
finely grated rind and juice of 1 orange

1 Combine the butter, biscuit crumbs and demerara sugar. Spread the mixture over the base of an oiled 20 cm/8 inch loose-bottomed cake tin and chill until firm.

2 Place the curd cheese in a bowl and beat in the sugar, egg yolks and orange rind. Soak the gelatine in the orange juice, then heat gently until dissolved. Stir into the curd cheese mixture with the cream.

3 Whisk the egg whites until stiff. Fold 2 tablespoons into the mixture to soften it. Fold in the remaining egg white and spread evenly over the biscuit base. Chill until set.

4 Drain the blackcurrants. Heat the syrup in a small pan. Blend the arrowroot with the orange rind and juice, then pour into the pan, stirring. Bring to the boil, stirring, until thickened. Add the blackcurrants and allow to cool.

5 Remove the cheesecake from the tin and pour the blackcurrant mixture over the top. Cool, then chill until ready to serve.

Serves 8
Preparation time: 25 minutes, plus cooling and chilling
Cooking time: about 10 minutes

chocolate and orange cheesecake

50 g/2 oz butter or margarine
125 g/4 oz digestive biscuits, finely crushed
25 g/1 oz demerara sugar
175 g/6 oz plain dark chocolate, broken into small pieces
250 g/8 oz full-fat soft cheese
finely grated rind of 2 oranges
75 g/3 oz caster sugar
2 eggs, separated
150 ml/¼ pint whipping cream
1 teaspoon powdered gelatine dissolved in
    1 tablespoon water

To decorate:
150 ml/¼ pint double cream, whipped
2 oranges, peeled and thinly sliced

1 Melt the butter or margarine in a small pan, then mix in the biscuit crumbs and demerara sugar. Press the mixture over the base of a lightly oiled 20 cm/8 inch loose-bottomed cake tin, then chill in the refrigerator for about 15 minutes until firm.

2 Melt the chocolate in a heatproof bowl over a pan of gently simmering water. Beat together the soft cheese, orange rind, caster sugar and egg yolks until thoroughly blended. Whip the cream until it stands in soft peaks. Fold the warm chocolate into the cheese mixture with the dissolved gelatine, then fold in the whipped cream.

3 Whisk the egg whites until fairly stiff and quickly fold into the chocolate mixture. Spoon over the biscuit base, level the surface and chill in the refrigerator for 1–1½ hours or until set. Remove from the tin.

4 Pipe a decorative border of whipped cream around the edge of the cheesecake and decorate with the orange slices. Serve chilled.

Serves 6
Preparation time: 25 minutes, plus chilling
Cooking time: about 5 minutes

creamy plum cheesecake

125 g/4 oz butter
2 tablespoons golden syrup
300 g/10 oz digestive biscuits, finely crushed
350 g/12 oz yellow plums, stoned and sliced
50 g/2 oz ratafia biscuits, crushed
65 g/2½ oz caster sugar
250 g/8 oz cottage cheese, sieved
250 g/8 oz cream cheese
150 ml/¼ pint soured cream

To decorate:
ratafia biscuits
whipped cream

1 Place the butter and syrup in a pan and heat gently until melted. Stir in the biscuit crumbs and spread over the base and up the side of a 23 cm/9 inch loose-bottomed cake tin.

2 Arrange the plums on the biscuit base and sprinkle with the ratafia crumbs and 15 g/½ oz of the sugar.

3 Beat together the cheeses, soured cream and the remaining sugar until well blended, then pour the mixture over the plums.

4 Bake the cheesecake in a preheated oven, 150°C (300°F), Gas Mark 2, for 1 hour. Turn off the heat and leave it in the oven until cool. Chill overnight or for several hours.

5 Carefully transfer the cheesecake to a serving plate and decorate with ratafia biscuits and piped cream.

Serves 6
Preparation time: 20 minutes, plus cooling and chilling
Cooking time: about 1 hour
Oven temperature: 150°C (300°F), Gas Mark 2

coeurs à la crème

Try serving other fresh soft fruit with these cheese and yogurt creams, such as raspberries, blackberries, cooked blackcurrants or redcurrants.

250 g/8 oz cream cheese
150 ml/¼ pint natural yogurt
2 tablespoons clear honey, plus extra for serving
1 egg white
250 g/8 oz strawberries
redcurrant sprigs, to decorate

1 Place the cream cheese, yogurt and honey in a bowl and mix well. Whisk the egg white until fairly stiff then fold into the cream cheese mixture.

2 Line 6 heart-shaped perforated moulds with muslin, spoon in the cream cheese mixture and smooth the tops. Place on a plate and leave to drain in the refrigerator for 3–4 hours. Turn out on to individual dishes and surround with strawberries.

3 Alternatively, spoon the cheese mixture into ramekin dishes, arrange the strawberries on top and chill.

4 To serve, drizzle honey round each little cream and decorate with sprigs of redcurrants.

Serves 6
Preparation time: 15 minutes, plus draining or chilling

baked lemon and bay custards

This recipe is a variation of the old classic lemon tart. Here, the lemon custard is infused with bay leaves, giving it a heady scent. The custard is baked in a very low oven; if the oven is too hot the custard will curdle. Check after 40 minutes – the centres should be almost set but still move a little – they will firm up as they cool.

2 bay leaves, bruised
2 tablespoons pared lemon rind
150 ml/¼ pint double cream
4 eggs, plus 1 egg yolk
150 g/5 oz caster sugar
100 ml/3½ fl oz lemon juice

1 Put the bay leaves, lemon rind and cream in a small saucepan and heat gently until it reaches boiling point. Remove from the heat and set aside for 2 hours to infuse.

2 Whisk together the eggs, egg yolk and sugar until the mixture is pale and creamy and then whisk in the lemon juice. Strain the cream mixture through a fine sieve into the egg mixture and stir until combined.

3 Pour the custard into 8 individual ramekin dishes and place on a baking sheet. Bake in a preheated oven, 120°C (250°F), Gas Mark ½, for 50 minutes or until the custards are almost set in the middle. Leave until cold and chill until required. Return to room temperature before serving.

Serves 8
Preparation time: 15 minutes, plus infusing and chilling
Cooking time: about 1 hour
Oven temperature: 120°C (250°F), Gas Mark ½

tiramisu with raspberry surprise

This dish is best made the night before so that it can set completely.

4 tablespoons very strong espresso coffee
2 tablespoons grappa or brandy
10 sponge fingers
125 g/4 oz raspberries
175 g/6 oz mascarpone cheese
2 eggs, separated
50 g/2 oz icing sugar
25 g/1 oz plain dark chocolate

1 Combine the coffee and grappa or brandy. Dip the sponge fingers into the liquid to coat them evenly, then arrange them on a small shallow dish or a serving platter, pouring over any excess liquid. Sprinkle the raspberries evenly over the soaked sponge fingers.

2 In a bowl, whisk together the mascarpone, egg yolks and icing sugar until smooth and well blended.

3 In another bowl, whisk the egg whites until stiff and glossy, then fold together the egg whites and the mascarpone mixture until well blended. Spoon the mixture over the sponge fingers and smooth the surface. Finely grate the chocolate straight on to the mixture. Cover and chill until set.

Serves 4
Preparation time: 15 minutes, plus chilling

zabaglione

4 egg yolks
75 g/3 oz caster sugar, plus extra for frosting the glasses
grated rind of ½ lemon
½ teaspoon ground cinnamon, plus extra to serve
1 drop of vanilla extract
150 ml/¼ pint Marsala
125 g/4 oz fruit (peaches, apricots, berries), sliced

1 Place the egg yolks, caster sugar, lemon rind, cinnamon and vanilla extract in a heatproof bowl and beat with an electric whisk until thick, pale and creamy.

2 Place the bowl over a saucepan of simmering water and continue whisking. Slowly add the Marsala and whisk until the mixture is warm, frothy and thick.

3 To serve, dip the rims of 4 tall stemmed glasses in water, then in sugar to frost them. Divide the fruit among the glasses, then spoon in the zabaglione. To serve, dust with a little extra cinnamon.

Serves 4
Preparation time: 5 minutes
Cooking time: 10 minutes

italian trifle

This dessert is very good if made the night before to allow all the flavours to blend together.

8 sponge fingers
2 tablespoons blueberry jam
50 ml/2 fl oz Marsala or sweet sherry
250 g/8 oz blueberries
300 ml/¹/₂ pint milk
1 tablespoon cornflour
2 egg yolks
2 tablespoons sugar
300 ml/¹/₂ pint whipping cream
50 g/2 oz chocolate, grated

1 Spread the sponge fingers with the jam and arrange in a glass serving bowl. Sprinkle over the Marsala or sherry and add half of the blueberries.

2 Mix a little milk with the cornflour to make a smooth paste. Stir the paste into the rest of the milk. Pour into a saucepan and bring to the boil, stirring all the time as the milk thickens; when it is boiling and smooth, remove it from the heat.

3 Whisk the egg yolks and sugar in a large bowl until they are light and creamy. Add the thickened milk to the beaten egg mixture, whisking all the time. Blend well and pour over the blueberries, then top with the remaining blueberries. Allow to cool.

4 Softly whip the cream and spread over the trifle, then top with the grated chocolate.

Serves 4
Preparation time: 10 minutes
Cooking time: 10 minutes

amaretti and chocolate trifle

50 g/2 oz blanched almonds
50 g/2 oz caster sugar
50 ml/2 fl oz cold water
1 teaspoon vanilla extract
750 g/1¹/₂ lb apricots, halved and stoned
175 g/6 oz amaretti biscuits
4 tablespoons Amaretto di Saronno liqueur
300 ml/¹/₂ pint double cream
cocoa powder, for dusting

Custard:
2 egg yolks
2 tablespoons cocoa powder
1 teaspoon cornflour
50 g/2 oz caster sugar
150 ml/¼ pint milk
300 ml/½ pint double cream
200 g/7 oz plain dark chocolate, broken into pieces

To decorate:
chocolate shavings
sugared almonds, coarsely chopped

1 First make the custard. Lightly whisk the egg yolks with the cocoa powder, cornflour, sugar and half the milk. Put the remaining milk into a saucepan with the cream and chocolate. Heat gently, stirring, until the chocolate has melted. Bring almost to the boil, then pour it over the egg mixture, whisking well.

2 Return the custard to the saucepan and whisk well over a moderate heat until the custard has thickened slightly. Transfer to a bowl and cover the surface with greaseproof paper to prevent a skin forming. Leave to cool.

3 Toast the almonds in a dry frying pan, stirring continuously, until they turn a golden brown. Allow to cool. Heat the sugar and water in a saucepan until the sugar dissolves. Add the vanilla and apricots, and cover with a lid. Simmer gently for 2–5 minutes (depending on the ripeness of the fruit) until just softened.

4 Drain the apricots, reserving 3 tablespoons of the syrup. Place the apricots in a glass serving dish. Scatter the biscuits over the apricots.

5 Mix the reserved syrup with the liqueur and spoon over the biscuits. Scatter with the almonds. Spoon the cooled custard into the dish and leave to stand for several hours to set.

6 Whip the cream until just peaking. Spoon over the custard and dust with cocoa powder. Decorate the trifle with chocolate shavings and sugared almonds.

Serves 8–10
Preparation time: 30 minutes, plus cooling and standing
Cooking time: about 7 minutes

almond soufflés

15 g/½ oz butter, plus extra for greasing
25 g/1 oz plain flour, plus extra for dusting
200 ml/7 fl oz milk
75 g/3 oz ground almonds
3 eggs, separated
25 g/1 oz caster sugar
75 ml/3 fl oz Amaretto di Saronno liqueur
4 amaretti biscuits, crushed
icing sugar, to serve

1 Butter 4 small soufflé dishes and dust with flour.

2 Melt the butter in a small saucepan, add the flour and stir to a smooth paste. Slowly pour in the milk, stirring constantly, to make a smooth sauce. Add the ground almonds and egg yolks; mix well and rapidly. Do not leave the pan on the heat. Add the sugar and Amaretto and mix well.

3 Quickly whisk the egg whites until stiff. Fold in the almond sauce, then quickly fold in the crushed biscuits.

4 Divide the mixture between the prepared soufflé dishes and cook in a preheated oven, 220°C (425°F), Gas Mark 7, for about 12 minutes until risen and golden. Dust with icing sugar and serve immediately.

Serves 4
Preparation time: 20 minutes
Cooking time: 12 minutes
Oven temperature: 220°C (425°F), Gas Mark 7

white chocolate soufflés

5 g/¼ oz unsalted butter, melted
250 g/8 oz white chocolate, broken into pieces
50 ml/2 fl oz double cream
25 ml/1 fl oz milk
40 g/1½ oz caster sugar
6 eggs, separated
1 teaspoon vanilla extract
cocoa powder or icing sugar, for dusting

Raspberry sauce:
375 g/12 oz raspberries
1 tablespoon lemon juice
2 tablespoons icing sugar

1 Use the melted butter to brush the bases and sides of six 150 ml/¼ pint ovenproof soufflé dishes. Place the dishes on a baking sheet.

2 Put the white chocolate in a heatproof bowl together with the double cream and the milk, and then heat over a pan of gently simmering water until the chocolate has melted completely. Stir the mixture lightly to blend together.

3 Stir the sugar, egg yolks and vanilla extract into the chocolate and cream mixture. Whisk the egg whites in a large bowl until stiff and with soft but formed peaks. Using a large metal spoon, fold a quarter of the egg whites into the chocolate sauce, then fold in the remainder.

4 Spoon the mixture into the dishes, filling them almost to the rims, and bake in a preheated oven, 200°C (400°F), Gas Mark 6, for 15–20 minutes until well risen and golden.

5 To make the sauce, lightly blend the raspberries in a blender or food processor, or mash thoroughly. Press through a sieve into a saucepan and discard the pips. Add the lemon juce and icing sugar and heat through thoroughly. When the soufflés are cooked, dust with cocoa powder or icing sugar and serve immediately with the sauce.

Serves 6
Preparation time: 20 minutes
Cooking time: 20 minutes
Oven temperature: 200°C (400°F), Gas Mark 6

creamy coffee chocolate pots

Use a good quality dark chocolate with a high percentage of cocoa butter – at least 75 per cent.

175 g/6 oz plain dark chocolate, chopped
250 ml/8 fl oz strong espresso coffee
2 tablespoons whisky
50 g/2 oz sugar
6 egg yolks
50 ml/2 fl oz double cream
grated nutmeg

1 Place the chocolate in a small pan with the coffee and whisky, and heat gently until the chocolate has melted. Add the sugar and stir until dissolved. Remove the pan from the heat.

2 Immediately beat in the egg yolks until thickened. Pour through a fine sieve into 8 small espresso cups or ramekins. Cool and chill for 4 hours or overnight, until set.

3 Whip the cream until it just holds its shape and spoon a little on to each chocolate pot. Sprinkle with nutmeg. Pour a small amount of boiling water into a roasting dish to a depth of about 1 cm/½ inch. Sit the chocolate pots in the boiling water for 1 minute, then remove and serve immediately.

Serves 8
Preparation time: 10 minutes, plus chilling
Cooking time: 5 minutes

lemon syllabub

grated rind and juice of 1 lemon
125 ml/4 fl oz white wine
75 g/3 oz caster sugar
300 ml/½ pint double cream
1 egg white
biscuits, to serve

1 Place the lemon rind and juice in a bowl with the white wine and half of the sugar. Cover and leave to soak for about 1 hour.

2 Whip the cream until it stands in peaks, then gradually add the wine mixture and continue whipping until it holds its shape.

3 Whisk the egg white until stiff then whisk in the remaining sugar. Carefully fold into the cream mixture. Spoon into 4 glasses and serve with biscuits.

Serves 4
Preparation time: 15 minutes, plus soaking

irish whiskey syllabub

grated rind and juice of 1 large lemon
6 tablespoons clear honey
8 tablespoons Irish whiskey
300 ml/½ pint double cream, chilled
grated nutmeg, to decorate

1 Put the lemon rind and juice, honey and whiskey into a large bowl and leave to stand for as long as possible to develop the flavours. Gradually whisk in the cream until the mixture begins to thicken. Spoon into wine glasses and chill until required.

2 If the syllabub is left for several hours, it will separate into a thick cream on top and a clear liquid at the bottom. Whether served immediately as a thick creamy concoction or after a few hours as a two-layered dessert, the syllabub should be decorated with grated nutmeg.

Serves 4–6
Preparation time: 15 minutes, plus standing and chilling

chocolate mousse

75 g/3 oz bitter dark chocolate, broken into pieces
25 g/1 oz plain dark chocolate, broken into pieces
25 g/1 oz butter
2 eggs, separated
1 tablespoon ginger wine
150 ml/¼ pint double cream
50 g/2 oz caster sugar
chopped crystallized ginger, to decorate

1 Place the chocolate in a heatproof bowl with the butter. Stand the bowl over a pan of hot water and stir until the chocolate has melted. Allow to cool slightly.

2 Whisk the egg yolks with the ginger wine until creamy. Whip the cream until thick.

3 Stir the whisked egg yolk mixture into the melted chocolate, then fold in the whipped cream. Whisk the egg whites until thick and foamy. Add half the sugar and whisk until stiff. Finally, whisk in the remaining sugar. Fold into the chocolate mixture lightly but thoroughly. Spoon into stemmed sundae dishes and chill.

4 Serve decorated with a little chopped crystallized ginger.

Serves 4–6
Preparation time: 20–25 minutes, plus chilling

mango mousse

2 mangoes
75 g/3 oz icing sugar, sifted
2 tablespoons lime or lemon juice
2 teaspoons gelatine, soaked in 2 tablespoons cold water
300 ml/½ pint double cream, whipped
lime or lemon twists, to decorate

1 Cut the mangoes in half lengthways, scrape out the flesh and place in a food processor or blender. Add the icing sugar and lime or lemon juice and purée until smooth. Alternatively, work the mangoes through a sieve, then stir in the juice and sugar.

2 Heat the gelatine gently until dissolved. Cool slightly, then mix into the mango purée with the whipped cream. Pour into individual glass bowls and leave to set.

3 To serve, decorate with lime or lemon twists.

Serves 6
Preparation time: 15 minutes, plus setting

gooseberry fool

The flavours of gooseberries and elderflowers combine beautifully in desserts. If you do not have any elderflowers, try using a little elderflower cordial instead: add 1–2 teaspoons to the gooseberries and sugar as they cook.

500 g/1 lb gooseberries, topped and tailed
150 g/5 oz caster sugar
2 elderflower heads, tied in muslin (optional)
250 ml/8 fl oz whipping cream, whipped
a few drops of green food colouring (optional)
biscuits, to serve

1 Place the gooseberries in a pan with the sugar and elderflowers, if using. Cover and cook for 10–15 minutes until tender. Remove the elderflowers and leave to cool. Rub through a sieve or work in a blender until smooth.

2 Fold the cream and colouring, if using, into the fruit mixture. Spoon into individual dishes and chill before serving with biscuits.

Serves 6
Preparation time: 15 minutes, plus cooling and chilling
Cooking time: 10–15 minutes

chilled raspberry fool

Try adding 1 tablespoon of Grand Marnier or orange Curaçao when you whip the cream, to give a specially interesting flavour to this fruit fool.

250 g/8 oz fresh raspberries
50 g/2 oz caster sugar
grated rind and juice of ½ orange
250 ml/8 fl oz double cream

1 Reserve 4 of the raspberries and put the rest into a food processor or blender with the sugar, orange rind and juice and purée until smooth. Rub the raspberry purée through a sieve to remove the pips.

2 Place the cream in a large bowl and whip until thick. Fold the raspberry purée lightly but thoroughly into the cream.

3 Spoon the fool into 4 stemmed glasses and chill for 3–4 hours. Decorate with the reserved raspberries just before serving.

Serves 4
Preparation time: 20 minutes, plus chilling

peaches brûlée

6 peaches, skinned
2 tablespoons Cointreau
300 ml/¹/² pint double cream, whipped
125 g/4 oz soft brown sugar

1 Halve the peaches, discard the stones and place the peach halves cut sides up in a shallow ovenproof dish. Pour over the Cointreau.

2 Spread the cream over the peaches to cover them completely and sprinkle with the sugar. Place under a preheated hot grill for 3 minutes or until the sugar has caramelized. Cool, then chill before serving.

Serves 6
Preparation time: 10 minutes, plus chilling
Cooking time: 3 minutes

griddled figs with greek yogurt and honey

Warm figs with Greek yogurt and honey drizzled over them make a delicious and quick dessert. Buy figs when they are in season, when they are full of taste and juice.

8 ripe figs
4 tablespoons Greek yogurt
2 tablespoons clear honey

1 Heat a griddle pan or hot grill and add the figs. Cook for 8 minutes, turning occasionally, until they are charred on the outside. Remove and cut in half. Arrange the figs on 4 plates and serve with a spoonful of Greek yogurt and some honey spooned over the top.

Serves 4
Preparation time: 5 minutes
Cooking time: 10 minutes

baked bananas with chocolate fudge sauce

4 firm bananas, skins left on
1 tablespoon lemon juice
lightly whipped cream or vanilla ice cream, to serve

Sauce:
100 ml/3¹/² fl oz double cream
125 g/4 oz plain dark chocolate, broken into pieces
25 g/1 oz unsalted butter
125 g/4 oz golden syrup

1 Place the bananas in a shallow ovenproof dish. Brush the skins with the lemon juice and bake in a preheated oven, 180°C (350°F), Gas Mark 4, for 20 minutes or until the bananas have darkened in colour and feel soft.

2 Meanwhile, make the sauce. Put the cream, chocolate, butter and golden syrup into a small, heavy-based saucepan. Heat gently, stirring frequently, until the chocolate has melted. Bring to the boil and boil for 2 minutes until thickened slightly.

3 Transfer the bananas to warmed serving plates. Split lengthways to reveal the flesh. Top with cream or ice cream and serve with the hot sauce.

Serves 4
Preparation time: 10 minutes
Cooking time: 20 minutes
Oven temperature: 180°C (350°F), Gas Mark 4

poached figs in cassis with cinnamon sauce

Fresh figs can be disappointingly lacking in flavour. The best figs are those enjoyed straight from the tree. However, this method of poaching them in a blackcurrant liqueur and red wine will add flavour to the fruit.

300 ml/½ pint red wine
150 ml/¼ pint cassis
2 cinnamon sticks
2 strips of lemon rind
2 strips of orange rind
300 ml/½ pint water
12 large firm ripe figs, washed

Sauce:
150 g/5 oz Greek yogurt
2 tablespoons Greek honey
1 teaspoon ground cinnamon

1 Place the wine, cassis, cinnamon sticks, citrus peel and water in a large saucepan and bring to the boil.

2 Add the figs, cover the pan and simmer gently for 10 minutes until the figs are just tender. Do not overcook or the figs will fall apart.

3 Remove the figs with a slotted spoon and place in a serving dish. Bring the poaching liquid to a rolling boil and simmer until it is reduced by half and is thick and syrupy. Pour over the figs and leave to cool.

4 Meanwhile, combine all the sauce ingredients and set aside to allow the flavours to develop. Serve the figs at room temperature with the cinnamon sauce.

Serves 4
Preparation time: 10 minutes, plus chilling
Cooking time: 15 minutes

baked peaches with almonds and honey

50 g/2 oz butter, plus extra for greasing
4 large ripe peaches, halved and stoned
50 g/2 oz flaked almonds
4 tablespoons clear honey
a little ground cinnamon
crème fraîche, to serve

1 Butter a shallow baking dish, large enough to take 8 peach halves.

2 Place the peaches in the baking dish, skin side down. Dot with butter, sprinkle with the almonds, drizzle with the honey and dust with cinnamon.

3 Bake the peaches at the top of a preheated oven, 200°C (400°F), Gas Mark 6, for 10–15 minutes. You want to get a little colour into the peaches and get the almonds lightly browned.

4 Serve the peaches with the juices drizzled over and topped with a spoonful of crème fraîche.

Serves 4
Preparation time: 5 minutes
Cooking time: 15 minutes
Oven temperature: 200°C (400°F), Gas Mark 6

caramelized oranges and pineapple

4 oranges
175 g/6 oz sugar
125 ml/4 fl oz water
1 small pineapple

1 With a very sharp knife, remove the rind from 2 of the oranges and slice it into very fine strips. Place the rind in a pan of boiling water and simmer for 2 minutes. Remove and drain well.

2 Put the sugar and water into a saucepan and heat gently, swishing the pan constantly until the sugar is dissolved. Increase the heat and boil the syrup until it turns a golden brown. Take care not to overcook the caramel as it will continue to cook in the pan once it is golden as it has reached such a high temperature. If it does get too dark, carefully add 2 tablespoons of water. Stand back when adding the water as the caramel spits. When it is golden, place it to one side.

3 To peel the oranges, cut a slice off the top and bottom of each one, then place the orange on one of these cut sides and take a knife around the side of the orange, cutting away the skin and pith. Cut each orange into 6 or 7 slices.

4 To prepare the pineapple, top and tail it and slice away the skin from top to bottom. Make sure that you remove the 'eyes' close to the skin. Cut the pineapple into quarters and remove the core. Cut the remaining flesh into slices.

5 Make alternate layers of orange and pineapple in a heatproof dish, sprinkle with the orange rind, pour over the hot caramel and leave to stand until required.

Serves 4
Preparation time: 15 minutes
Cooking time: 10 minutes

poached pears with honey and cinnamon

grated rind and juice of 1 lemon
450 ml/³/₄ pint red wine
150 ml/¹/₄ pint water
5 tablespoons clear honey
1 mace blade
1 cinnamon stick
6 cloves
4 ripe pears, peeled
Greek yogurt, to serve

1 Put the lemon rind and juice, red wine, water, honey, mace, cinnamon and cloves into a saucepan and bring to a gentle boil.

2 Add the pears and simmer for 10 minutes, or until they are soft, turning them occasionally.

3 Remove the pears with a slotted spoon and set aside. Transfer the liquid to a saucepan with a larger surface area. Place the pan on a high heat and boil rapidly to make a rich, thick, sticky syrup. Spoon the liquid over the pears and serve with Greek yogurt.

Serves 4
Preparation time: 5 minutes
Cooking time: 20 minutes

papaya and pineapple flambé

2 papayas
1 small pineapple
50 g/2 oz butter
50 g/2 oz soft brown sugar

grated rind and juice of 1 lime
¹/₂ teaspoon ground cinnamon
4 tablespoons tequila
slivers of lime rind, to decorate

1 Peel the papayas and scoop out the seeds. Cut the flesh into slices. Peel the pineapple and cut into thin slices. Remove the central core so that you are left with pineapple rings.

2 Melt the butter in a large heavy-based frying pan, then stir in the sugar over a low heat, stirring until it is thoroughly dissolved. Add the lime juice and grated rind.

3 Increase the heat slightly and let the sugary mixture bubble for a few minutes until thickened. Take care that it does not burn or turn to caramel. Add the papaya and pineapple and cook gently for 2 minutes. Sprinkle with ground cinnamon.

4 Add the tequila to the pan, then stand well back and set it alight, using a long taper. When the flames die down, divide the flambéed papaya and pineapple among 4 individual serving dishes. Decorate each one with slivers of lime rind.

Serves 4
Preparation time: 10 minutes
Cooking time: 10 minutes

almond fruit salad

4 dessert apples, cored
4 peaches, skinned and stoned
125 g/4 oz strawberries
4 slices of pineapple
125 g/4 oz lychees, skinned and stoned

Almond syrup:
2 tablespoons ground almonds
450 ml/³/₄ pint water
1 tablespoon cornflour, blended with 2 tablespoons water
3 tablespoons sugar

1 First make the syrup. Put the almonds, water, blended cornflour and sugar in a pan and mix well. Gradually bring to the boil, stirring, then simmer for 10 minutes, stirring constantly. Remove from the heat and leave to cool, stirring occasionally to prevent a skin forming.

2 Slice the apples, peaches and strawberries; cut the pineapple into cubes. Put all the fruit in a bowl and mix well. Spoon over the almond syrup and chill before serving.

Serves 4–6
Preparation time: 15 minutes, plus cooling and chilling
Cooking time: 10 minutes

melon, grape and kiwi salad

1 large Galia melon
125 g/4 oz seedless green grapes
3 kiwi fruits, peeled and thinly sliced
300 g/10 oz canned lychees, drained
2 apples, peeled, cored and thinly sliced
3 tablespoons kirsch
mint sprigs, to decorate

1 Cut a thin slice from the base of the melon so that it stands firmly. Slice the top off the melon, remove the seeds and discard. Scoop out the flesh in small balls, using a melon baller or teaspoon. Reserve the shell.

2 Place the melon balls in a bowl with the grapes, kiwi fruit, lychees and apples and sprinkle with the kirsch. Cover and chill until ready to serve.

3 Place the melon shell on a serving plate. Pile the fruit into the shell and decorate with mint sprigs.

Serves 4–6
Preparation time: 15 minutes, plus chilling

fruit baskets

Use whatever fresh seasonal fruit you wish to fill these little biscuit baskets. Blueberries and sliced fresh figs are a good choice, but any combination of small or sliced fruits, such as strawberries, raspberries or green grapes, can be used. Arrange the fruit in the baskets just before serving them.

125 g/4 oz plain flour
125 g/4 oz icing sugar
3 egg whites
a few drops of orange extract
25 g/1 oz flaked almonds
4 oranges, for moulds

Pineapple sauce:
2 slices of pineapple, peeled, cored and chopped
125 ml/4 fl oz pineapple juice
1–2 drops yellow food colouring
125 ml/4 fl oz natural yogurt

Filling and decoration:
375 g/12 oz seasonal fruit
1 tablespoon icing sugar, sifted

1 Sift the flour and icing sugar into a bowl, then beat in the egg whites until smooth. Cover and leave to stand for 1–2 hours. Stir in the orange extract and almonds.

2 Mark four 18 cm/7 inch circles on silicone paper and spread out on 2 baking sheets. Spread the batter in the marked circles, then bake in a preheated oven, 180°C (350°F) Gas Mark 4, for 8 minutes or until pale golden.

3 While the biscuits are cooking, prepare 4 oranges for moulds. Cut a fine slice off each, so that they stand up well, and grease lightly with oil.

4 Allow the cooked biscuits to cool for about 1 minute, then ease them off the baking sheets and mould over the prepared oranges.

5 To make the pineapple sauce, place the pineapple, juice and yellow food colouring in a small saucepan and simmer for 2 minutes. Transfer to a food processor or blender and work to a purée. Chill, then mix in the yogurt.

6 To serve, place each biscuit basket on a pool of pineapple sauce on a dessert plate. Fill the baskets with seasonal fruit and dust with icing sugar.

Serves 4
Preparation time: 30 minutes, plus standing and chilling
Cooking time: 10 minutes
Oven temperature: 180°C (350°F) Gas Mark 4

melon and raspberries in sauternes

1 small ripe Galia melon
175 g/6 oz raspberries
½ bottle Sauternes, chilled

1 Halve the melon and either scoop out small balls using a melon baller or a teaspoon or cut the flesh into small cubes.

2 Divide the melon and raspberries equally among 4 glass dishes. Pour over any melon juice, cover and chill in the refrigerator for at least 2 hours.

3 Just before serving, pour some of the chilled Sauternes into each dish to almost cover the fruit. Serve at once.

Serves 4
Preparation time: 15 minutes, plus chilling

summer fruit compôte

500 g/1 lb mixed redcurrants, blackcurrants and blackberries, washed
125 g/4 oz caster sugar
250 g/8 oz raspberries
whipped cream, to serve

1 Place the currants and blackberries in a heavy-based saucepan with the sugar. Cook gently over a low heat, stirring occasionally, for 10 minutes until tender.

2 Remove the pan from the heat, add the raspberries, and set aside to cool.

3 Spoon the fruit into individual serving bowls and serve with whipped cream.

Serves 6
Preparation time: 10 minutes, plus cooling
Cooking time: 10 minutes

pineapple with rumbled mascarpone

1 pineapple, peeled and sliced
6 tablespoons mascarpone cheese
2 tablespoons rum
2 tablespoons fine brown sugar

1 Heat a griddle pan or hot grill, add the pineapple and cook for 2 minutes on each side.

2 Mix together the mascarpone, rum and brown sugar. Serve the griddled pineapple with the mascarpone mixture spooned on top.

Serves 4
Preparation time: 5 minutes
Cooking time: 10 minutes

sticky glazed apples

4 cooking apples, cored
50 g/2 oz sultanas
50 g/2 oz light soft brown sugar
25 g/1 oz butter, cut into 4 pieces
6 tablespoons orange juice
125 g/4 oz golden syrup

1 Using a sharp knife, make a circular cut around the waist of each apple, to prevent the skin from bursting. Arrange the apples in a buttered shallow ovenproof dish.

2 Mix the sultanas and sugar in a bowl; spoon into the cavities in the apples. Top each with a piece of butter.

3 Heat the orange juice and golden syrup in a small saucepan until the syrup has melted, then spoon over the apples in the dish.

4 Cook in a preheated oven, 190°C (375°F) Gas Mark 5, basting with the orange mixture occasionally, for 50 minutes or until the apples are tender. Serve hot with custard, cream or ice cream.

Serves 4
Preparation time: 10 minutes
Cooking time: 50 minutes
Oven temperature: 190°C (375°F) Gas Mark 5

caribbean fruit kebabs

1 pineapple
1 ripe mango
125 g/4 oz strawberries
50 g/2 oz raspberries

Sauce:
175 g/6 oz plain dark chocolate, chopped
175 g/6 oz milk chocolate, chopped
150 ml/¼ pint double cream
2 tablespoons dark rum

1 First make the sauce. Put the dark and milk chocolate into a heatproof bowl set over a pan of gently simmering water. Heat until melted, stirring occasionally. Stir the cream into the chocolate mixture, then add the rum.

2 Meanwhile, prepare the fruits. Peel, core and chop the pineapple. Skin, stone and chop the mango. Hull and quarter the strawberries. Thread the fruits on to wooden skewers and serve with the chocolate sauce.

Serves 4–6
Preparation time: 20 minutes
Cooking time: 5 minutes

lemon honey granita

4 large or 6 medium lemons
about 4 tablespoons water
2 tablespoons clear honey
50 g/2 oz caster sugar
1 fresh bay leaf or 1 lemon balm sprig
450 ml/¾ pint natural yogurt or fromage frais
lemon balm sprigs, to decorate

1 Cut a slice from the base of each lemon so that it stands upright.

2 Slice off the top of each lemon and reserve. Carefully scoop out all the pulp and juice with a teaspoon: do this over a bowl, so that no juice is wasted. Discard any white pith, skin and pips from the fruit you have removed. Sieve or liquidize the pulp and juice. You need 150 ml/¼ pint. If there is less than this, dilute it with water. Cut out excess pith from the lemon shells and from the tops. Cover and set aside.

3 Put the 4 tablespoons of water into a pan with the honey, sugar and bay leaf or lemon balm. Stir over a low heat until the sugar has dissolved, then leave to cool. Blend with the lemon purée and the yogurt or fromage frais. Do not remove the herb at this stage.

4 Pour into a freezing tray or shallow dish and leave until lightly frozen, then gently fork the mixture and remove the herb. Re-freeze the granita for a short time, until it is sufficiently firm to spoon into the lemon shells. Replace the tops of the lemons and place the fruit in the freezer.

5 Transfer the granitas to the refrigerator about 20 minutes before serving. Serve decorated with sprigs of lemon balm.

Serves 4–6
Preparation time: 20 minutes, plus cooling and freezing
Cooking time: 5 minutes

blood orange granita

1 kg/2 lb blood oranges
250 g/8 oz sugar

1 Using a sharp knife, cut off the top and bottom of the oranges, then cut away the pith and peel. Working over a bowl to catch the juice, cut the segments out of the oranges and squeeze any excess juice from each one.

2 Strain the juice into a saucepan, add the sugar and heat until it has dissolved.

3 Place the orange flesh in a food processor or blender and whizz until smooth. Mix in the juice and pour into ice cube trays to freeze.

4 When you serve the granita, first chill the serving dishes for a short while in the freezer. To serve, remove the granita ice cubes from the freezer, put them in the food processor or blender and whizz for 30 seconds, then transfer them to the serving dishes and serve immediately.

Serves 4
Preparation time: 20 minutes, plus freezing
Cooking time: 5 minutes

redcurrant sherbet

Frosted currant leaves, which add a pretty finishing touch here, are simple to make. Paint egg white all over the leaves with a fine paintbrush, brush off any excess and dip in caster sugar until completely coated. Place on greaseproof paper to dry for 1–2 hours.

500 g/1 lb redcurrants
125 g/4 oz icing sugar, sifted
4 tablespoons orange juice
1 egg white

To decorate:
frosted currant leaves (see above)
a few redcurrant sprigs

1 Place the redcurrants, icing sugar and orange juice in a food processor or blender and work to a purée. Rub through a sieve to remove the pips. Place in a freezerproof container, cover and freeze for 2–3 hours. Whisk to break up the crystals.

2 Whisk the egg white until stiff, then whisk into the half-frozen purée. Return to the freezer until firm. Transfer the sherbet to the refrigerator 15 minutes before serving to soften.

3 To serve, scoop into chilled glasses and decorate with frosted currant leaves and redcurrant sprigs.

Serves 4
Preparation time: 15 minutes, plus freezing

lychee sorbet

500 g/1 lb canned lychees
125 g/4 oz granulated sugar
2 tablespoons lemon or lime juice
2 egg whites
thinly pared rind of 1 lime, to decorate

1 Drain the juice from the lychees into a measuring jug and make up to 300 ml/½ pint with cold water. Pour into a saucepan and stir in the sugar. Heat gently, stirring, until the sugar has dissolved. Bring to the boil, then simmer gently for 10 minutes. Remove from the heat and allow to cool slightly.

2 Purée the lychees in a food processor or blender or work through a sieve. Mix the purée with the sugar syrup and lemon or lime juice. Pour the mixture into a shallow freezerproof container and freeze for 1–2 hours, until nearly frozen.

3 Whisk the egg whites in a clean, dry bowl until fairly stiff. Cut the frozen lychee mixture into small pieces and then work in a food processor or blender to break down the crystals. Transfer to a bowl and quickly fold in the whisked egg white. Pour into a freezerproof container and freeze for 2–3 hours until firm.

4 Transfer the sorbet to the refrigerator 15 minutes before serving to soften. Plunge the pared lime rind into a saucepan of boiling water and blanch for 2 minutes. Drain, refresh and pat dry. Cut into thin strips and serve sprinkled over the sorbet.

Serves 6
Preparation time: 35 minutes, plus freezing
Cooking time: 15 minutes

mango and passion fruit sorbet

The combination of mango and passion fruit makes for a different but highly delicious flavour in this unusual sorbet.

2 ripe mangoes
4 passion fruits
1 tablespoon lemon juice
75 g/3 oz caster sugar
150 ml/¼ pint water
1–2 egg whites (optional)

1 Cut the skin from the mangoes and cut the pulp from the stones. Halve the passion fruit and scoop out all the pulp. Put the mango and passion fruit pulp into a food processor or blender and work to a purée or rub through a sieve.

2 Put the lemon juice, sugar and water into a saucepan and heat just until the sugar has dissolved. Stir into the fruit purée and allow to cool.

3 Turn the fruit purée into a freezerproof container, cover, seal and freeze until firm, stirring once or twice during freezing.

4 If liked, whisk 1–2 egg whites until stiff, then fold them into the fruit purée when it is slightly frozen. This extends the purée and gives a greater volume, but the egg whites do take away some of the natural fruit flavour.

5 Transfer the sorbet to the refrigerator 15 minutes before serving, to soften.

Serves 4
Preparation time: 10–15 minutes, plus cooling and freezing
Cooking time: about 4 minutes

watermelon sorbet

500 g/1 lb watermelon, skinned, deseeded and chopped
200 g/7 oz caster sugar
250 ml/8 fl oz water
2 cinnamon sticks
40 ml/1½ fl oz lime juice
1 egg white

1 Put the watermelon into a heavy-based saucepan over a low heat. Cook gently until it softens.

2 In a separate saucepan, dissolve the sugar in the water and add the cinnamon sticks. Bring to the boil and cook for 5 minutes, then remove from the heat. Cover the pan and leave the syrup to cool and infuse.

3 Strain the syrup into the watermelon purée and stir in the lime juice. Pour the mixture into a freezer container, cover and freeze for 2 hours, removing it at 30 minute intervals and beating it with a fork to ensure no ice crystals form.

4 Beat the egg white until stiff and add it to the mixture, blending it in thoroughly.

5 Freeze for a further 1 hour, beating once with a fork after 30 minutes. Transfer the mixture to the refrigerator 30 minutes before serving.

Serves 4
Preparation time: 10 minutes, plus cooling and freezing
Cooking time: 12–15 minutes

raspberry sorbet

500 g/1 lb raspberries
125 g/4 oz sugar
300 ml/½ pint water
2 egg whites

1 Pass the raspberries through a sieve and discard the pips. Put the sugar and water into a saucepan and stir over a gentle heat until the sugar has dissolved.

2 Increase the heat and boil briskly, without stirring, for 8 minutes or until a syrup has formed. Allow to cool.

3 Stir the syrup into the raspberry purée and pour into an ice tray or shallow rigid container.

4 Place in the freezer for 1 hour or until just smooth. Whisk the egg whites until stiff and fold into the raspberry mixture.

5 Return to the container. Cover and seal, then return to the freezer.

6 Transfer the sorbet to the refrigerator 10–15 minutes before serving, to soften slightly.

Serves 4–6
Preparation time: 10 minutes, plus cooling and freezing
Cooking time: 10 minutes

strawberry and yogurt ice

125 g/4 oz caster sugar
300 ml/½ pint water
375 g/12 oz strawberries
300 ml/½ pint strawberry yogurt
1 egg white
150 ml/¼ pint double or whipping cream

1 Put the sugar and water into a small saucepan and heat gently to dissolve the sugar, then boil rapidly until the thread stage is reached. The thread stage temperature is 107°C (225°F) on a sugar thermometer: to test without a thermometer, remove a little of the syrup with a small spoon and allow it fall from the spoon on to a dish. The syrup should form a fine thread.

2 Reserving 4 strawberries for decoration, slice the remainder and put them into a food processor or blender with the syrup. Blend for a few seconds, then pour the purée into a bowl.

3 Stir the yogurt into the strawberries and pour into a 1.2 litre/2 pint freezerproof container. Freeze for about 2 hours, stirring once or twice, until mushy.

4 Spoon the strawberry mixture into a large mixing bowl and put the egg white and cream into two slightly small bowls.

5 Using an electric whisk, beat the egg white until it is stiff but not too dry. Whisk the cream until it forms soft peaks, and whisk the strawberry mixture until smooth. There is no need to wash the whisk in between if you keep to this order.

6 With a large metal spoon, turn the egg white and cream into the strawberry mixture and gently fold all three together until smoothly blended.

7 Return to the container and freeze for about 3 hours until the ice cream is setting round the edges. Spoon into a bowl and whisk again until smooth and light.

8 Pour the ice cream back into the container, cover and freeze for at least 6 hours. Transfer the ice cream to the refrigerator about 40 minutes before serving to soften slightly. Scoop or spoon the ice cream into glasses and serve decorated with the reserved strawberries.

Serves 4
Preparation time: 30 minutes, plus freezing
Cooking time: 10 minutes

coffee parfait

1 tablespoon instant coffee powder
1 teaspoon drinking chocolate powder
2 teaspoons boiling water
¼ teaspoon vanilla extract
300 ml/½ pint whipping cream
2 egg whites
50 g/2 oz caster sugar
40 g/1½ oz plain dark chocolate, grated
fan wafers, to serve

1 Dissolve the coffee and drinking chocolate in the boiling water in a cup or mug then leave to cool. Add the vanilla extract.

2 Whisk the cream in a bowl until stiff, then fold in the coffee and chocolate mixture, using a metal spoon.

3 Whisk the egg whites in a grease-free bowl until stiff peaks form, then gradually add the sugar, whisking well after each addition until very stiff and glossy.

4 Lightly fold the egg whites and two-thirds of the grated chocolate into the cream mixture, using a metal spoon.

5 Spoon the mixture into 6 individual serving dishes, sprinkle with the remaining grated chocolate and serve chilled, with fan wafers.

Serves 6
Preparation time: 15 minutes, plus chilling

iced chocolate mousse with whipped cream

4 eggs, separated
125 g/4 oz caster sugar
125 g/4 oz plain dark chocolate, broken into pieces
3 tablespoons water
300 ml/½ pint double cream

To decorate:
8 tablespoons double cream, whipped
grated chocolate

1 Put the egg yolks and sugar into a bowl and whisk with a hand-held beater until the mixture is thick and fluffy.

2 Melt the chocolate with the water in a heatproof bowl over a pan of gently simmering water. Remove from the heat and cool slightly.

3 Whisk the chocolate into the egg yolk mixture. Whip the cream until it will stand in soft peaks, then carefully fold it into the chocolate mixture.

4 Whisk the egg whites in a bowl until stiff, carefully fold 1 tablespoon into the mousse, then fold in the remainder.

5 Pour the chocolate mousse mixture into 8 individual dishes and chill. Decorate with whipped cream and grated chocolate.

Serves 8
Preparation time: 15 minutes, plus chilling

ricotta and rum bombe

5 egg yolks
125 g/4 oz caster sugar
5 tablespoons rum
500 g/1 lb fresh ricotta cheese, sieved
Amaretti biscuits or brandy snaps, to serve

1 Line a 1.2 litre/2 pint freezerproof mould with foil.

2 Put the egg yolks and sugar into a bowl, and whisk with an electric blender or whisk until light and fluffy.

3 Fold in the rum until well amalgamated, then fold in the ricotta a little at a time. Spoon the mixture into the prepared mould, smooth the surface and cover with foil.

4 Freeze until solid. Unmould on to a serving plate and serve immediately with Amaretti or brandy snaps.

Serves 4–6
Preparation time: 20 minutes, plus freezing

cassata siciliana

600 ml/1 pint vanilla ice cream
450 ml/¾ pint chocolate ice cream
150 ml/¼ pint double or whipping cream
50 g/2 oz icing sugar
125 g/4 oz candied fruits, finely chopped

1 Soften three-quarters of the vanilla ice cream slightly, then use it to line a 1.2 litre/2 pint bombe mould, pudding basin or foil container. Transfer the vanilla ice cream to the freezer and freeze until solid.

2 Soften the chocolate ice cream slightly, then use to make a layer inside the vanilla ice cream, leaving a well in the centre. Freeze until solid.

3 Whip the cream until it just holds its shape, then add the icing sugar and continue whipping until thick. Fold in the fruits, then spoon the mixture into the well in the centre of the cassata. Freeze until solid.

4 Soften the remaining vanilla ice cream slightly, then spread over the top of the cream to cover it completely. Cover the mould with a lid or foil, then freeze until required.

5 To serve, dip the mould in hot water for 1–2 seconds, then unmould the cassata on to a chilled serving platter. Serve immediately.

Serves 6–8
Preparation time: 20 minutes, plus freezing

mango and papaya ice cream

Choose fully ripe fruits for this luscious tropical ice cream, and use a plastic sieve or a food processor or blender to purée the fruit.

250 ml/8 fl oz milk
4 egg yolks
125 g/4 oz sugar
pinch of salt
250 ml/8 fl oz fresh mango purée
1–2 teaspoons lime juice
250 ml/8 fl oz double cream
150 ml/¼ pint fresh papaya purée
2 tablespoons white rum
icing sugar, to taste

1 Scald the milk in a heavy saucepan. Place the egg yolks in a bowl with the sugar and salt and beat lightly until pale. Gradually stir in the hot milk, then return the mixture to the pan and cook over low heat, stirring until the custard thickens. Do not allow to boil or the custard will curdle.

2 Pour the custard into a bowl and let cool. Stir in the mango purée and lime juice. Whip the cream until thick and beat lightly into the mango mixture. Pour into a freezerproof container, cover and freeze until just firm.

3 Mix together the papaya purée and rum, then sweeten to taste with some icing sugar.

4 Put alternate spoonfuls of mango ice cream and the papaya mixture into a freezerproof container, and stir gently with a spoon to make a swirled effect. Cover and return to the freezer until firm. The whole freezing process should take 4–5 hours. Soften at room temperature for about 10 minutes before serving.

Serves 6–8
Preparation time: 20 minutes, plus cooling and freezing
Cooking time: 5–10 minutes

vanilla ice cream

Here is the perfect vanilla ice cream: rich and creamy, it is delicious in its own right, and can be used as the base for other ice creams, too.

2 eggs, plus 2 egg yolks
75 g/3 oz caster sugar
450 ml/¾ pint single cream
2–3 drops of vanilla extract
300 ml/½ pint double cream, whipped
biscuits, to serve

1 Mix together the eggs, egg yolks and sugar in a bowl. Bring the single cream gently to the boil and pour on to the egg mixture, stirring vigorously. Strain, then stir in the vanilla extract. Leave to cool, then fold in the whipped cream.

2 Pour into a rigid freezerproof container. Cover, seal and freeze for 1 hour. Remove and stir well, then re-freeze until firm.

3 Transfer the ice cream to the refrigerator 20 minutes before serving to soften. Scoop into chilled glasses and serve with biscuits.

Serves 8
Preparation time: 15 minutes, plus cooling and freezing
Cooking time: 3 minutes

strawberry ice cream

Raspberries could replace the strawberries in this ice cream: omit the food colouring if you wish.

375 g/12 oz strawberries, plus extra to decorate
15 g/½ oz gelatine, soaked in 3 tablespoons cold water
450 ml/¾ pint evaporated milk, chilled
175 g/6 oz caster sugar
a few drops of red food colouring
2 tablespoons lemon juice

1 Rub the strawberries through a sieve or purée in a food processor or blender, then sieve to remove the pips: there should be 300 ml/½ pint purée.

2 Place the soaked gelatine in a bowl over a pan of simmering water and stir until dissolved. Add the dissolved gelatine to the strawberry purée.

3 Whisk the evaporated milk until thick, then add the sugar, strawberry purée, red food colouring and lemon juice. Turn into a freezerproof container. Cover and freeze for 1 hour.

4 Remove the ice cream from the freezer and stir well, then re-freeze until solid.

5 Transfer to the refrigerator 1 hour before serving, to soften. To serve, scoop into chilled glasses and decorate each one with a strawberry.

Serves 8
Preparation time: 20 minutes, plus freezing
Cooking time: 2 minutes

pineapple ice cream

The pineapple halves, when the flesh and juice have been removed, can make attractive containers for serving this ice cream.

1 large pineapple
3 egg whites
175 g/6 oz caster sugar
300 ml/½ pint double cream, whipped

1 Cut the pineapple in half lengthways. Scrape out the flesh and juice into a bowl, discarding the hard core. Chop the flesh finely or purée in a food processor or blender.

2 Whisk the egg whites until stiff, then gradually add the sugar, whisking continuously. Fold in the cream and chopped pineapple.

3 Place the ice cream in a freezerproof container. Cover and freeze for 1 hour. Remove from the freezer, stir well, then re-freeze until solid.

4 Transfer the ice cream to the refrigerator 20 minutes before serving, to soften. Scoop into the chilled pineapple shells and arrange on a serving dish. Scoop into chilled glass dishes to serve.

Serves 6–8
Preparation time: 15 minutes, plus freezing

coffee and brandy ice cream

3 eggs
75 g/3 oz caster sugar
300 ml/½ pint single cream
3 tablespoons instant coffee powder
300 ml/½ pint double cream
3 tablespoons brandy

1 Beat the eggs and sugar together until smooth. Bring the single cream and coffee just to the boil in a small pan, then stir into the egg mixture.

2 Transfer to the top of a double boiler, or to a heatproof bowl over a pan of gently simmering water. Cook gently, stirring continuously, until the custard is thick enough to coat the back of a spoon.

3 Strain into a bowl and leave to cool, stirring occasionally to prevent a skin forming.

4 Whip the double cream until it will stand in soft peaks, then fold it into the cold custard with the brandy.

5 Pour into a rigid container, cover and freeze for 2–3 hours until half-frozen. Remove from the freezer and stir well, then return to the container and freeze until solid.

6 Transfer the ice cream to the refrigerator about 20 minutes before serving to allow it to soften. Scoop into chilled glasses or dishes and serve immediately.

Serves 6–8
Preparation time: 20 minutes, plus freezing
Cooking time: 10 minutes

peking toffee apples

125 g/4 oz plain flour
1 egg
100 ml/3½ fl oz water
4 crisp apples, peeled, cored and cut into fat slices
600 ml/1 pint sunflower oil

Syrup:
6 tablespoons sugar
2 tablespoons water
1 tablespoon sunflower oil
3 tablespoons golden syrup

1 Mix together the flour, egg and 100 ml/3½ fl oz of the water in a bowl to make a batter. Dip each piece of apple into the batter.

2 Heat 600 ml/1 pint of the oil in a wok or deep frying pan to 180–190°C (350–375°F) or until a cube of bread browns in 30 seconds. Deep-fry the apple pieces for 2 minutes, then remove and drain on kitchen paper.

3 To make the syrup, heat together the sugar, water and oil in another pan. Dissolve the sugar over a gentle heat, then simmer for 5 minutes, stirring constantly. Add the golden syrup and boil until the hard crack stage is reached, at 151°C/304°F, or until it forms brittle threads when dropped into iced water. Put in the fried apples and turn to coat each piece.

4 Remove the apple pieces with a slotted spoon and drop into iced water. Remove immediately and serve.

Serves 4
Preparation time: 15 minutes
Cooking time: 15–20 minutes

rice fritters

175 g/6 oz cooked medium-grain rice
2 eggs, beaten
3 tablespoons sugar
½ teaspoon vanilla extract
50 g/2 oz plain flour
1 tablespoon baking powder
pinch of salt
25 g/1 oz desiccated coconut
vegetable oil, for deep-frying
sifted icing sugar, for sprinkling

1 Put the rice, eggs, sugar and vanilla in a bowl and mix well. Sift together the flour, baking powder and salt, then stir into the rice mixture. Stir in the coconut.

2 Heat the oil in a deep fat fryer to 180–190°C (350–375°F) or until a cube of bread browns in 30 seconds. Drop tablespoonfuls of the mixture into the hot oil, one at a time, and deep-fry until golden on all sides. Drain on absorbent kitchen paper.

3 Transfer the fritters to a warmed serving dish and sprinkle generously with icing sugar. Serve hot.

Makes about 20
Preparation time: 10 minutes
Cooking time: about 5–10 minutes

bananas in coconut milk

1 large or 2 small bananas
200 ml/7 fl oz coconut milk
100 ml/3½ fl oz water
3 tablespoons palm sugar or light muscovado sugar

1 Peel the banana(s) and halve lengthways. Cut each half into 4 pieces.

2 Put the coconut milk, water and sugar into a saucepan and simmer, stirring occasionally, for about 6 minutes. Add the bananas and cook for 4 minutes until heated through. Serve hot.

Serves 2
Preparation time: 2 minutes
Cooking time: 10 minutes

mango with thai sticky rice

500 g/1 lb glutinous rice, soaked for at least 6 hours
  or overnight
150 g/5 oz sugar
300 ml/½ pint coconut milk
2 ripe mangoes

1 Drain and rinse the rice well. Cook in a steamer for about 30 minutes. Give the rice a good shake halfway through steaming to ensure it is evenly cooked.

2 While the rice is steaming, combine the sugar and coconut milk in a large bowl and stir well.

3 When the rice is cooked, transfer it to the coconut mixture and stir thoroughly for 2–3 minutes to achieve a rather creamy consistency. Cover with a lid and allow to stand at room temperature for 30 minutes.

4 Before serving, slice the mangoes and arrange them attractively on a dish around the rice.

Serves 4
Preparation time: 15 minutes, plus standing
Cooking time: 30 minutes

baking

basic white bread

750 g/1½ lb strong white or unbleached flour
2 teaspoons salt
15 g/½ oz lard or vegetable fat
450 ml/¾ pint water
15 g/½ oz fresh yeast or 1½ teaspoons fast-action dried
yeast with 1 teaspoon caster sugar

1 To make the dough with fresh yeast, sift the flour and salt into a mixing bowl and warm gently for 5–6 minutes. Rub in the lard or vegetable fat lightly. Warm the measured water until tepid and blend in the yeast. Add all the water at once to the dry ingredients. Mix into a soft dough and beat well with a wooden spoon or by hand, until the dough leaves the sides of the bowl clean, adding a little extra flour if sticky.

2 To make the dough with dried yeast, heat a cupful of the measured water until hand-hot and add the sugar. Sprinkle the dried yeast on top, swirl it around and leave for about 10 minutes or until frothy. Add with the remaining water to the warm dry ingredients and mix to a dough as for fresh yeast.

3 Gather the dough into a ball (add more flour if sticky), turn it on to a floured board, and knead for about 10 minutes until firm, elastic and smooth. Round the dough into a ball and place in an oiled container. Leave to rise until doubled in bulk, then turn on to a board and knock back with your knuckles before shaping.

4 Mould the dough according to the type of loaf required (see page 132), taking care not to work in extra flour as this will affect the colour and finish of the crust. Place the shaped dough in tins or hand mould on a baking sheet, cover with an oiled plastic bag and leave to rise until doubled in bulk – it will be springy to the touch when sufficiently proved. Remove the bag and bake the loaves in the centre of a preheated oven, 230°C (450°F), Gas Mark 8, for 30–40 minutes according to size. The bread is ready when the loaf begins to shrink from the sides of the tin.

5 Remove from the oven, turn out of the tin or turn upside down if hand-moulded and tap the bottom. The loaf will sound hollow when cooked. Cool on a wire rack.

Makes 1 large or 2 small loaves
Preparation time: 25 minutes, plus proving
Cooking time: 30–40 minutes
Oven temperature: 230°C (450°F), Gas Mark 8

quick brown bread

*500 g/1 lb wholemeal flour or 250 g/8 oz wholemeal and
    250 g/8 oz strong white flour*
2 teaspoons salt
1 teaspoon caster sugar (optional)
25 g/1 oz butter or lard, plus extra for greasing
*15 g/½ oz fresh yeast or 1½ teaspoons fast-action dried
    yeast with 1 teaspoon caster sugar*
about 350 ml/12 fl oz warm water

1 Sift the flour and salt into a mixing bowl with the sugar,
if using, and rub in the fat. Prepare the yeast liquid. If
using fresh yeast, blend it with a cupful of the warm
water, then add it to the flour, salt and fat all at once with
the remaining warm water. If using dried yeast, dissolve
it in a cup of hand-hot water and add the sugar. Leave in
a warm place for 15 minutes until frothy, then add to the
dry ingredients with the remaining warm water. Beat with
a wooden spoon into a fairly soft dough, adding more
water if necessary.

2 Turn on to a floured board and knead well for
10 minutes. Stretch the dough to fit 1 large loaf tin or
divide in half to fit 2 small tins. Fold or roll up and put
into the warmed and greased tins. Put into an oiled
polythene bag and leave to rise in a warm place until
the dough reaches the top edge of the tin.

3 Brush with lightly salted water and bake in the centre
of a preheated oven, 230°C (450°F), Gas Mark 8, for
15 minutes. Reduce the temperature to 200°C (400°F),
Gas Mark 6, and cook for a further 30–40 minutes,
according to size. When cooked, the loaves will shrink
slightly from the tin.

4 Turn out and tap the base to see if it sounds hollow.
Remove from the oven and cool on a wire rack.

Makes 1 large or 2 small loaves
Preparation time: 25 minutes, plus proving
Cooking time: 45–55 minutes
Oven temperature: 230°C (450°F), Gas Mark 8

soft wholemeal rolls

*Soft rolls are made with milk, or at least half milk and
half water, in order to produce a soft texture. To get a soft
crust, dust with flour just before baking, instead of
glazing with salted water.*

250 g/8 oz wholemeal flour
1 teaspoon salt
25 g/1 oz butter or lard
*15 g/½ oz fresh yeast or 1½ teaspoons fast-action dried
    yeast with 1 teaspoon sugar*
about 150 ml/¼ pint warm milk

1 Sift the flour and salt into a warmed mixing bowl. Rub
in the fat. Blend the fresh yeast with the warm milk and
leave for 10 minutes to froth. If using dried yeast,
dissolve the sugar in the warm milk, sprinkle in the dried
yeast and leave for 15–20 minutes until frothy.

2 Pour the yeast liquid into the flour and mix, adding a
little more milk if necessary. Beat until the dough leaves
the sides of the bowl clean, turn on to a floured board
and knead for 10 minutes.

3 Put the dough into an oiled polythene bag and leave to
rise until doubled in bulk. Knock back the dough, make
a fat sausage shape and cut across into 8 equal-sized
pieces. Shape into rounds or ovals. Press down firmly
with the heel of your hand and release.

4 Place the pieces of dough on a floured baking sheet,
leaving space between them for expansion. Cover and
prove for 15 minutes or until doubled in size.

5 Dust with flour and bake in the centre of a preheated
oven, 230°C (450°F), Gas Mark 8, for 15–20 minutes.
When cooked, remove to a wire rack, cover with a tea
towel and leave to cool.

Makes 8 rolls
Preparation time: 25 minutes, plus proving
Cooking time: 15–20 minutes
Oven temperature: 230°C (450°F), Gas Mark 8

olive foccacia with herb oil

500 g/1 lb strong plain flour
2 teaspoons fast-action dried yeast
2 teaspoons sea salt, plus extra for scattering
½ teaspoon caster sugar
300 ml/½ pint warm water
4 tablespoons herb oil, such as rosemary or thyme
50 g/2 oz pitted black olives, roughly chopped
extra virgin olive oil, to serve

1 Sift the flour into a bowl and stir in the yeast, salt and sugar. Make a well in the centre and gradually work in the warm water and half of the infused oil to form a soft dough. Turn out and knead on a lightly floured surface for 10 minutes. Cover the bowl with an oiled plastic bag and leave to rise in a warm place for about 1 hour until doubled in size.

2 Knock back the dough, divide in half and roll each half out to a 1 cm/½ inch thick oval. Transfer to 2 greased baking sheets, cover with an oiled plastic bag and leave to rise for a further 30 minutes.

3 Remove the bag and press indentations all over the surface of each oval with your fingers. Scatter over a little extra sea salt, the olives and drizzle over the remaining herb oil.

4 Bake in a preheated oven, 220°C (425°F), Gas Mark 7, for 25–30 minutes until risen and golden. Cool slightly and serve warm cut into fingers with a bowl of extra virgin olive oil, for dipping.

Makes 2 loaves
Preparation time: 15 minutes, plus proving
Cooking time: 25–30 minutes
Oven temperature: 220°C (425°F), Gas Mark 7

soda bread with oatmeal

375 g/12 oz plain wholemeal flour, plus extra for dusting
50 g/2 oz pinhead oatmeal
1 teaspoon bicarbonate of soda
½ teaspoon salt
300 ml/½ pint buttermilk or natural yogurt

1 In a bowl, mix together the flour, oatmeal, bicarbonate of soda and salt. Make a well in the centre and gradually work in the buttermilk or yogurt to form a soft dough.

2 Turn out on to a lightly floured surface and knead gently for 5 minutes until the dough is smooth.

3 Shape the dough into a flattish round and place on a greased baking sheet. Using a sharp knife, slash a cross on the top of the bread and place in a preheated oven, 230°C (450°F), Gas Mark 8, for 15 minutes. Reduce the temperature to 200°C (400°F), Gas Mark 6 and continue to bake for a further 30 minutes until the bread is risen and golden and sounds hollow when tapped on the base.

4 Wrap the bread in a clean tea towel and leave to cool completely on a wire rack. Slice and serve with butter and jam or marmalade.

Makes 1 small loaf
Preparation time: 5 minutes
Cooking time: 45 minutes
Oven temperature: 230°C (450°F), Gas Mark 8

herb bread

375 g/12 oz strong plain flour
2 teaspoons dried tarragon
2 teaspoons caster sugar
2 teaspoons salt
2 teaspoons fast-action dried yeast
250 ml/8 fl oz milk
1 egg, beaten
1 tablespoon fennel seeds

1 Grease a 23 x 12 cm/9 x 5 inch loaf tin. Stir the flour, tarragon, sugar, salt and yeast in a bowl. Mix together the milk and egg and work into the dry mixture. Knead well for 10 minutes.

2 Shape the dough to fit the loaf tin and roll it in the fennel seeds to coat before turning into the tin. Cover with an oiled plastic bag and leave in a warm place to prove for 30 minutes.

3 Bake in a preheated oven, 200°C (400°F), Gas Mark 6, for 25–30 minutes. Transfer the loaf to a wire rack to cool before serving.

Makes 1 large loaf
Preparation time: 20 minutes, plus proving
Cooking time: 25–30 minutes
Oven temperature: 200°C (400°F), Gas Mark 6

granary bread

1.5 kg/3 lb malted granary flour
2 teaspoons salt
4 teaspoons fast-action dried yeast
1 teaspoon brown sugar or black treacle
900 ml/1½ pints warm water
beaten egg, to glaze
a little buckwheat, for sprinkling (optional)

1 Mix the flour, salt and yeast in a large warmed bowl. Add the sugar or treacle to the measured water and stir into the flour to make a soft pliable dough.

2 Knead the dough on a lightly floured surface for about 10 minutes until smooth and elastic. Return to the cleaned bowl and place in an oiled plastic bag. Leave in a warm place for 1 hour, or until the dough has doubled in bulk.

3 Turn the dough on to a lightly floured surface and cut in half. Knead each piece until smooth, then place in two 1 kg/2 lb loaf tins. Place the tins in the oiled plastic bag and tie loosely. Leave in a warm place to prove until the dough rises above the sides of the tin.

4 Brush the loaves with beaten egg and sprinkle with buckwheat, if using. Bake in a preheated oven, 220°C (425°F), Gas Mark 7, for 30–45 minutes. Leave to cool on a wire rack.

Makes 2 large loaves
Preparation time: 20 minutes, plus proving
Cooking time: 30–45 minutes
Oven temperature: 220°C (425°F), Gas Mark 7

poppy seed plaits

500 g/1 lb strong white flour
1 teaspoon salt
40 g/1½ oz butter
300 ml/½ pint milk
15 g/½ oz fresh yeast
2 tablespoons caster sugar
1 egg, beaten

Topping:
1 egg, beaten
2 tablespoons poppy seeds

1 Grease a baking sheet. Sift the flour and salt into a warmed mixing bowl. Melt the butter in a small pan over a gentle heat then add the milk and heat the mixture until tepid. Remove from the heat.

2 Place the yeast and sugar in a small bowl, pour on a little of the milk mixture and cream until the yeast has dissolved. Pour the yeast mixture back into the remaining milk, then add the beaten egg and stir well.

3 Make a well in the centre of the flour and pour in the liquid. Beat the flour and liquid together with your hands until a dough is formed. Turn out the dough on a lightly floured surface and knead it for 8–10 minutes until smooth and no longer sticky.

4 Return the dough to the bowl, place the bowl in an oiled plastic bag and set aside in a warm place until the dough has doubled in bulk.

5 Turn the risen dough on to a floured board, punch to deflate the air bubbles and knead gently for 1–2 minutes. Divide the dough into 6 equal pieces and roll each one into a sausage shape. Cut in 3 lengthways, leaving one end joined together. Plait the 3 pieces over each other, and turn the ends under. Make 5 more plaits in the same way.

6 Place the plaits on the prepared baking sheet and leave to prove in a warm place for 20–30 minutes. Brush with the beaten egg, sprinkle with poppy seeds and bake in a preheated oven, 200°C (400°F), Gas Mark 6, for 15–25 minutes, or until golden brown. Remove from the oven and cool on a wire rack.

Makes 6
Preparation time: 25 minutes, plus proving
Cooking time: 20–30 minutes
Oven temperature: 200°C (400°F), Gas Mark 6

rye bread

375 g/12 oz rye flour
500 g/1 lb wholemeal flour
2 teaspoons salt
25 g/1 oz fresh yeast
450–600 ml/¾–1 pint warm water
2 tablespoons black treacle
2 tablespoons oil
milk, for brushing
1 teaspoon caraway seeds

1 Mix the flours and salt together in a bowl. Cream the yeast with a little of the water and leave until frothy. Add to the flour mixture with the remaining water, the treacle and oil and mix thoroughly to form a firm dough.

2 Turn on to a floured surface and knead for 5 minutes until smooth and elastic. Place in a clean bowl, cover with a damp cloth and leave to rise in a warm place for 2 hours, until doubled in bulk.

3 Turn on to a floured surface and knead for a few minutes. Shape into 2 oval loaves and place on greased baking sheets. Prick with a fork in 8 or 9 places. Leave to rise in a warm place for 1½ hours, until doubled in size again.

4 Brush with milk and sprinkle with caraway seeds. Bake in a preheated oven, 220°C (425°F), Gas Mark 7, for 15 minutes. Lower the heat to 190°C (375°F), Gas Mark 5, and bake for a further 30–40 minutes. Transfer to a wire rack to cool.

Makes 2 loaves
Preparation time: 20 minutes, plus proving
Cooking time: 45–55 minutes
Oven temperature: 220°C (425°F), Gas Mark 7

cheese and bacon loaf

75 g/3 oz streaky bacon, rinded and chopped
1 small onion, finely chopped
250 g/8 oz self-raising flour
1 teaspoon salt
pinch of pepper
50 g/2 oz butter or margarine
125 g/4 oz matured Cheddar cheese, grated
2 eggs
150 ml/¼ pint milk
1 teaspoon prepared mustard
1 tablespoon chopped parsley

1 Place the bacon in a nonstick pan and heat gently until the fat runs. Add the onion and cook for 5–7 minutes until soft. Drain on kitchen paper and leave to cool.

2 Sift the flour, salt and pepper into a bowl. Rub in the fat until the mixture resembles breadcrumbs. Stir in the cheese, bacon and onion.

3 Beat the eggs with the milk, mustard and parsley. Add to the dry ingredients and beat thoroughly. Turn into a greased 500 g/1 lb loaf tin and bake in a preheated oven, 190°C (375°F), Gas Mark 5, for 45–55 minutes, or until firm and golden. Leave in the tin for 5 minutes, then cool on a wire rack. Serve with butter.

Makes 1 loaf
Preparation time: 15 minutes
Cooking time: about 1 hour
Oven temperature: 190°C (375°F), Gas Mark 5

french brioche

500 g/1 lb strong plain flour
1 teaspoon salt
25 g/1 oz caster sugar
4 teaspoons fast-action dried yeast
4 eggs, lightly beaten
125 g/4 oz butter, melted, plus extra for greasing
beaten egg, to glaze

1 Butter 12 brioche moulds. Sift the flour, salt and sugar into a bowl. Stir in the yeast, eggs and melted butter. Beat with your fingers for 10 minutes.

2 Transfer the mixture to an oiled bowl, cover and leave in a warm place for about 1¼ hours to double in bulk.

3 Knead the dough on a lightly floured surface and divide into 12 pieces. To make each brioche, cut off one quarter of the dough. Shape the larger piece into a ball and set in the mould, then make the smaller piece into a pear shape.

4 Using a floured finger, make a hole in the centre of the dough in the tin. Gently press the pointed end of the small ball into the hole. Cover and leave for about 45 minutes.

5 Glaze the brioche with beaten egg, then bake in a preheated oven, 230°C (450°F), Gas Mark 8, for 10 minutes. Cool on a wire rack.

Makes 12
Preparation time: 25 minutes, plus proving
Cooking time: 10 minutes
Oven temperature: 230°C (450°F), Gas Mark 8

milk rolls

300 ml/½ pint milk
50 g/2 oz butter
15 g/½ oz fresh yeast
1 teaspoon caster sugar
500 g/1 lb strong white flour
1 teaspoon salt
1 small egg, beaten

To finish:
beaten egg
poppy seeds

1 Place the milk and butter in a saucepan and heat until lukewarm. Cream the yeast and sugar, add a little of the warm milk and leave until frothy.

2 Sift the flour and salt into a bowl. Make a well in the centre and pour in the yeast, the milk mixture and the egg. Mix to a soft dough, then knead well until the dough is smooth and elastic.

3 Place the dough in a clean, warmed bowl. Cover with a damp cloth and leave to rise in a warm place for about 30 minutes, or until doubled in bulk. Turn out on to a floured surface and knead for 2 minutes. Cut into 14 pieces and shape into rolls.

4 Place on a greased baking sheet, cover and leave in a warm place until doubled in size, about 15 minutes. Glaze with the beaten egg, sprinkle with poppy seeds and bake in a preheated oven, 220°C (425°F), Gas Mark 7, for 20 minutes. Cool on a wire rack.

Makes 14
Preparation time: 20 minutes, plus proving
Cooking time: 20 minutes
Oven temperature: 220°C (425°F), Gas Mark 7

cheese-topped scones

250 g/8 oz self-raising flour
1 teaspoon mustard powder
pinch of cayenne
pinch of salt
50 g/2 oz butter
125 g/4 oz Cheddar cheese, grated
1 egg, beaten
about 4 tablespoons milk, plus extra to glaze

1 Sift the flour, mustard, cayenne and salt into a bowl and rub in the fat until the mixture resembles breadcrumbs. Stir in three-quarters of the cheese, the egg and enough milk to mix to a soft dough.

2 Turn on to a floured surface, knead lightly and roll out to 2 cm/¾ inch thick. Cut into 5 cm/2 inch rounds and place on a floured baking sheet. Brush with milk and sprinkle with the remaining cheese.

3 Bake in a preheated oven, 200°C (400°F), Gas Mark 6, for 15 minutes. Transfer to a wire rack to cool. Serve with butter.

Makes about 12
Preparation time: 15 minutes
Cooking time: 15 minutes
Oven temperature: 200°C (400°F), Gas Mark 6

sesame thins

175 g/6 oz wholemeal flour
50 g/2 oz medium oatmeal
pinch of salt
1 teaspoon baking powder

75 g/3 oz butter or margarine
1 tablespoon malt extract
2 tablespoons milk
25 g/1 oz sesame seeds

1 Place the flour, oatmeal and salt in a mixing bowl, sift in the baking powder and mix well. Rub in the butter or margarine until the mixture resembles breadcrumbs.

2 Whisk together the malt extract and milk until blended, then add to the dry ingredients with the sesame seeds. Mix to a firm dough.

3 Turn the dough on to a floured surface and roll out thinly. Cut into 6 cm/2½ inch rounds with a plain cutter. Place on a baking sheet and bake in a preheated oven, 190°C (375°F), Gas Mark 5, for 12–15 minutes, until golden. Transfer to a wire rack to cool.

Makes 20–24
Preparation time: 10 minutes
Cooking time: 12–15 minutes
Oven temperature: 190°C (375°F), Gas Mark 5

crumpets

125 g/4 oz strong white flour
125 g/4 oz plain flour
2 teaspoons salt
5 g/¼ oz fresh yeast
1 teaspoon sugar
300 ml/½ pint mixed milk and water, warmed
1 tablespoon vegetable oil
½ teaspoon bicarbonate of soda
150 ml/¼ pint warm water

1 Sift the flours and salt into a warmed bowl. Cream the yeast with the sugar. Add the warmed milk and water, then the oil. Stir into the flour to make a batter and beat vigorously until smooth and elastic. Cover the bowl, put it in a warm place and leave until the mixture rises and the surface is full of bubbles (about 1½ hours). Break down the batter by beating with a wooden spoon.

2 Dissolve the bicarbonate of soda in the warm water and stir into the batter. Cover and leave in a warm place to prove for about 30 minutes.

3 To cook the crumpets, heat and lightly grease a flat-based griddle pan. Grease five or six 8–9 cm/3–3½ inch crumpet rings or scone cutters and put them on the griddle to heat.

4 Put 1 cm/½ inch of batter into each ring. Cook gently for 7–10 minutes, or until the surface sets and is full of tiny bubbles. Using an oven glove for protection, lift off the ring and if the base of the crumpet is pale gold, flip it over and cook for another 3 minutes until the other side is just coloured.

5 If the crumpet batter is set but sticks slightly in the ring, push it out gently with the back of a wooden spoon. Wipe, grease and reheat the rings for each batch of crumpets. Try to cook as many as possible in each batch as the batter will not remain bubbly for long.

Makes 12–14
Preparation time: 20 minutes, plus proving
Cooking time: 10–13 minutes per batch

muffins

These are cooked on the griddle like crumpets, but are made with a yeast dough instead of a batter. They should be served very hot and generously buttered.

500 g/1 lb strong white flour
1 tablespoon salt
15 g/½ oz fresh yeast or 1½ teaspoons fast-action dried yeast
1 teaspoon sugar
250 ml/8 fl oz mixed milk and water, warmed
50 g/2 oz butter, melted, plus extra for greasing

1 Sift the flour and salt into a bowl and leave in a warm place. Dissolve the yeast and sugar in half of the warm milk and water. Leave to froth, then mix in the butter. Stir all the liquid into the warm flour and beat well until smooth and elastic. Cover and prove in a warm place for 50 minutes or until doubled in bulk.

2 Turn on to a well floured surface and knead, working in a little more flour if necessary to make the dough easy to shape. Round up the dough, roll into a thick sausage shape and divide into 8–10 portions, each about 2 cm/¾ inch thick.

crumpets p544

madeira cake p556

cherry cake p556

cream horns p553

baked scones with whipped cream p549

banana cake p559

custard tarts p552

fresh lemon slices p551

3 Shape each one into a round with straight sides. Put on to a greased baking sheet. Cover and put in a warm place to prove for 30–40 minutes, or until springy to the touch. Leave room for expansion and be careful not to over-prove as the muffins will lose their shape.

4 Warm a griddle or nonstick frying pan and grease lightly. Lift the muffins carefully on to the griddle and cook over a very moderate heat for 8–10 minutes until they are pale gold underneath. Turn them over and cook the other side. Wrap the muffins in a cloth and keep them warm in a low oven if you are cooking in batches.

5 To serve, insert a knife in the side, then with fingers, pull the top and bottom apart and insert thin slices of butter. If reheating from cold, toast the top and bottom, then pull apart and add the butter.

Makes 8–10
Preparation time: 20–25 minutes, plus proving
Cooking time: 12–14 minutes per batch

drop scones

These are sometimes called Scotch pancakes as they are made with a batter, not a dough. There are a variety of recipes but the following one is excellent for tea-time, being quick and easy to make.

125 g/4 oz self-raising flour
2 tablespoons caster sugar
1 egg, beaten
about 150 ml/¼ pint milk

1 Sift the flour into a mixing bowl and mix in the sugar. Make a well in the centre and drop in the egg. Stir in the milk gradually and mix to a creamy batter. The thicker the batter, the thicker the pancakes will be.

2 Heat a griddle or nonstick frying pan and grease it lightly. Using a large spoon, drop the batter off the point in round 'puddles' on to the griddle, leaving space for spreading. Cook over a moderate heat until the top surface is covered with bubbles, and when the underneath is golden, turn over with a palette knife and cook the other side.

3 When the scones are golden, lift them off the griddle and wrap in a cloth to keep warm while cooking the others. Serve as soon as possible with butter, honey or preserves.

4 If any scones are left until the next day, they can be crisped under the grill before serving.

Makes 18
Preparation time: 10 minutes
Cooking time: 15–20 minutes

croissants

500 g/1 lb strong flour
1 teaspoon salt
1 teaspoon sugar
15 g/½ oz fresh yeast or 1½ teaspoons fast-action dried yeast
125 ml/4 fl oz warm water mixed with 125 ml/4 fl oz warm milk
125 g/4 oz butter
1 egg, beaten with a little milk

1 Sift the flour and salt into a warmed bowl. Add the sugar. Blend the yeast and a little of the warm liquid in a small bowl then stir into the flour with the remaining liquid. Mix to a fairly stiff dough and knead lightly on a floured surface for 8 minutes or until smooth. Place in a greased bowl, cover with a damp cloth and leave to rise in a warm place until it has doubled in bulk. Turn out and knead the dough on a floured surface until smooth.

2 Roll out the dough into a rectangle measuring about 50 x 20 cm/20 x 8 inches. Divide the butter into 3 and dot one portion of butter over two-thirds of the dough. Fold the dough into 3, bringing the bottom, unbuttered third up and folding the top third over the top of it. Give the dough a quarter turn and seal the folded edges with the rolling pin. Repeat the process twice more, rolling out, folding over and turning the dough, using up the remainder of the butter. Place the dough in an oiled plastic bag and chill in the refrigerator for 30 minutes.

3 Roll out the dough and repeat the rolling, folding and turning process, without butter, 3 more times. Replace the dough in the plastic bag and chill in the refrigerator for a further 1 hour.

4 Roll out the dough on a lightly floured surface to a 50 x 20 cm/20 x 8 inch rectangle, divide in half lengthways and cut each strip into 10 cm/4 inch squares. Divide the squares into 2 triangles. Roll up each one, starting at the longest edge, and rolling towards the point. Tuck the end under and bend into a crescent shape. Arrange on greased and floured baking sheets, place inside a large oiled plastic bag and leave for 15–20 minutes.

5 Brush the croissants with beaten egg and milk and bake in a preheated oven, 220°C (425°F), Gas Mark 7, for 15–20 minutes. Serve warm.

Makes 20
Preparation time: 30 minutes, plus proving
Cooking time: 15–20 minutes
Oven temperature: 220°C (425°F), Gas Mark 7

tea cakes

500 g/1 lb plain flour
1 teaspoon salt
2 teaspoons sugar
125 g/4 oz currants
25 g/1 oz fresh yeast
300 ml/½ pint warm milk
melted butter, for brushing

1 Sift the flour and salt into a mixing bowl and add the sugar and currants.

2 Cream the yeast with a little extra sugar and some of the warm milk. Pour the yeast mixture into a well in the centre of the flour and leave in a warm place for 10 minutes.

3 Add the remaining milk to the yeast mixture, mix to a light dough and knead well. Cover the bowl with a clean tea towel and put in a warm place to rise for about 1–1½ hours until doubled in bulk.

4 Knead the dough again, then divide it into 8 pieces and roll and shape them into round tea cakes. Prick each one with a fork. Put the tea cakes on a greased baking sheet, cover with a cloth and leave in a warm place to prove for 30 minutes.

5 Transfer the tea cakes to a preheated oven, 220°C (425°F), Gas Mark 7, and bake for 10–12 minutes. Remove the tea cakes from the oven, brush them with melted butter, then return to the oven for a further 10 minutes. Cool on a wire rack.

6 To serve, split each tea cake in half, toast lightly and spread with butter.

Makes 8
Preparation time: 25 minutes, plus proving
Cooking time: 20–22 minutes
Oven temperature: 220°C (425°F), Gas Mark 7

walnut and sultana bread

15 g/½ oz fresh yeast
500 g/1 lb granary flour, plus extra for dusting
1 teaspoon sugar
300 ml/½ pint warm water
1 teaspoon salt
25 g/1 oz butter
50 g/2 oz organic oats, plus extra for sprinkling
50 g/2 oz walnuts, roughly chopped
50 g/2 oz sultanas
2 tablespoons malt extract
vegetable oil, for greasing

1 Blend the yeast with 4 tablespoons of the flour, the sugar and half the water until well combined then leave in a warm place for 10 minutes until frothy.

2 In a large bowl, mix together the remaining flour and the salt, rub in the butter and stir in the oats, nuts and sultanas. Make a well in the centre and gradually work in the frothed yeast, malt extract and remaining water to form a stiff dough.

3 Turn out on to a lightly floured surface and knead for 8–10 minutes until the dough is smooth and elastic. Place in an oiled bowl, turn once to coat the dough with oil, cover and leave to rise in a warm, draught-free place for about 45 minutes or until doubled in bulk.

4 Knock back the dough by gently kneading it once more, then shape into an oval loaf. Place the loaf on an oiled baking sheet, cover with an oiled plastic bag and leave to rise for a further 20 minutes. Brush the surface of the loaf with water and scatter over extra oats.

5 Slash the top of the loaf several times and place in a preheated oven, 220°C (425°F), Gas Mark 7, for 35–40 minutes until the bread has risen and sounds hollow when tapped on the bottom. Leave to cool completely on a wire rack before slicing.

Makes 1 large loaf
Preparation time: 20 minutes, plus proving
Cooking time: 35–40 minutes
Oven temperature: 220°C (425°F), Gas Mark 7

apple teabread

50 g/2 oz butter or margarine, softened
50 g/2 oz soft light brown sugar
1 egg, beaten
125 g/4 oz plain wholemeal flour
125 g/4 oz fresh wholemeal breadcrumbs
1½ teaspoons baking powder
¼ teaspoon ground cinnamon
½ teaspoon ground mixed spice
½ teaspoon grated nutmeg
125 g/4 oz sultanas
500 g/1 lb dessert apples, peeled, cored and sliced
2 tablespoons apple juice

1 Line and grease a 500 g/1 lb loaf tin. In a bowl, cream the butter or margarine and sugar until fluffy. Gradually beat in the egg. Fold in the flour, breadcrumbs, baking powder and spices. Stir in the sultanas, apple slices and apple juice.

2 Press the mixture into the prepared tin. Bake in a preheated oven, 180°C (350°F), Gas Mark 4, for 1 hour, or until firm and slightly risen. Cool on a wire rack.

Makes 1 loaf
Preparation time: 20 minutes
Cooking time: 1 hour
Oven temperature: 180°C (350°F), Gas Mark 4

malt loaf

375 g/12 oz wholemeal or strong white flour
½ teaspoon salt
25 g/1 oz butter, diced
25 g/1 oz currants
25 g/1 oz sultanas

25 g/1 oz chopped mixed peel
15 g/½ oz fresh yeast
150 ml/¼ pint warm milk
1 tablespoon golden syrup
1 tablespoon malt extract

1 Sift the flour and salt into a bowl and rub in the butter until the mixture resembles breadcrumbs. Add the fruit and mixed peel. Blend the yeast with the milk; add to the dry ingredients with the syrup and malt extract and mix to a soft dough.

2 Turn out on to a floured surface and knead until smooth and elastic. Place in a clean, greased bowl, cover with a damp cloth and leave to rise in a warm place until doubled in bulk.

3 Turn out the dough on to a floured surface and knead once more, then shape into a loaf and place in a 500 g/1 lb greased loaf tin. Cover and prove until the dough rises to the top of the tin.

4 Bake in a preheated oven, 230°C (450°F), Gas Mark 8, for 10 minutes, reduce the heat to 190°C (375°F), Gas Mark 5, and bake for 25 minutes more, or until it sounds hollow when tapped on the bottom. Turn out and cool on a wire rack.

Makes 1 loaf
Preparation time: 15 minutes, plus proving
Cooking time: 35 minutes
Oven temperature: 230°C (450°F), Gas Mark 8

stollen

25 g/1 oz fresh yeast or 15 g/½ oz fast-action dried yeast
2 tablespoons warm water
75 g/3 oz caster sugar
pinch of salt
6 tablespoons warm milk
2 tablespoons rum
a few drops of almond extract
425 g/14 oz plain flour
1 egg, beaten
150 g/5 oz unsalted butter, softened
50 g/2 oz raisins
50 g/2 oz glacé cherries, washed, dried and chopped
50 g/2 oz currants

25 g/1 oz angelica, chopped
50 g/2 oz chopped mixed peel
40 g/1½ oz flaked almonds
sifted icing sugar, to serve

1 Blend the yeast in the warm water. Dissolve two-thirds of the sugar and the salt in the milk. Add the rum, almond extract and yeast liquid.

2 Sift the flour into a bowl, making a well in the centre. Add the yeast mixture, egg, half of the softened butter cut into small pieces, and the fruit and nuts. Mix to a soft dough and knead for 10 minutes by hand, or 4–5 minutes in a large electric mixer fitted with a dough hook.

3 Return the dough to the bowl, cover with a damp cloth and leave to rise in a warm place until doubled in size – about 2 hours.

4 Knock back the dough and knead it until smooth, then roll it out on a lightly floured surface to a rectangle about 30 x 20 cm/12 x 8 inches.

5 Melt the remaining butter and brush it liberally over the dough, then sprinkle with the remaining caster sugar. Fold one long side over just beyond the centre, and then fold over the other long side to overlap the first piece well. Press lightly together and slightly taper the ends.

6 Place the loaf on a greased baking sheet, brush with melted butter and leave in a warm place until almost doubled in size.

7 Bake in a preheated oven, 190°C (375°F), Gas Mark 5, for about 45 minutes until well risen and browned. Cool on a wire rack. To serve, dredge heavily with sifted icing sugar and cut into fairly thin slices.

Serves 6
Preparation time: 30 minutes, plus proving
Cooking time: about 45 minutes
Oven temperature: 190°C (375°F), Gas Mark 5

panettone

50 g/2 oz caster sugar
25 g/1 oz fresh yeast
150 ml/¼ pint lukewarm water
3 egg yolks
salt
475 g/15 oz strong plain flour
125 g/4 oz butter, softened
50 g/2 oz sultanas
50 g/2 oz raisins
50 g/2 oz chopped mixed peel
25 g/1 oz butter, melted

1 Stir 1 teaspoon of the sugar and all of the yeast into the lukewarm water. Leave to stand for about 10 minutes until frothy. Beat the egg yolks in a large bowl and stir in the yeast mixture, salt and the remaining sugar. Beat in half the flour and then gradually beat in the softened butter, a little at a time. Knead in the remaining flour to make a dough.

2 Turn out the dough on to a lightly floured surface and knead well until it is firm and elastic. Place in a lightly oiled plastic bag and leave in a warm place until well risen and doubled in size.

3 Turn out the dough on to a lightly floured surface and knead in the sultanas, raisins and mixed peel. Continue kneading until the fruit is evenly distributed. Place the dough in a greased 18 cm/7 inch round cake tin and cover with an oiled plastic bag. Leave in a warm place until the dough rises to the top of the tin.

4 Remove the plastic bag and brush the top of the dough with some of the melted butter. Bake in a preheated oven, 200°C (400°F), Gas Mark 6, for 20 minutes. Reduce the oven temperature to 180°C (350°F), Gas Mark 4 and cook for a further 20–30 minutes. Remove from the tin and brush the top and sides with the remaining melted butter. Serve warm or cold, cut into thin slices.

Serves 10
Preparation time: 30 minutes, plus proving
Cooking time: 40–50 minutes
Oven temperature: 200°C (400°F), Gas Mark 6

bath buns

These light, sugary buns are thought to be the invention of the famous Dr Oliver of Bath. He was also responsible for creating the Bath Oliver biscuit.

15 g/½ oz fresh yeast or 1½ teaspoons fast-action dried yeast
1 teaspoon sugar
300 ml/½ pint lukewarm milk
375 g/12 oz plain flour
125 g/4 oz butter
75 g/3 oz caster sugar
2 eggs, beaten
50 g/2 oz chopped mixed peel
50 g/2 oz lump sugar, coarsely crushed

1 Cream the yeast with the sugar and add to the warm milk. (If using dried yeast, mix with the sugar and half the milk. Leave in a warm place until frothy, then add the rest of the milk.)

2 Put the flour in a bowl and pour the yeast mixture into a well in the centre. Leave until frothy, then mix to a dough. Cream the butter and sugar, add the eggs, reserving a little to glaze, and work into the dough. Reserve a little peel for decoration, then add the rest to the dough. Cover the dough with a cloth and leave in a warm place to rise for about 40 minutes.

3 Turn out the dough on to a lightly floured surface and knead until smooth, then shape into buns measuring 7.5 cm/3 inches across and place well spaced out on a greased baking sheet.

4 Leave to rise for a further 15–20 minutes, then brush with the rest of the egg, sprinkle with the crushed sugar and a little chopped peel.

5 Bake the buns in a preheated oven, 180°C (350°F), Gas Mark 4, for about 30 minutes. Transfer to a wire rack to cool.

Makes 10
Preparation time: 25 minutes, plus proving
Cooking time: 30 minutes
Oven temperature: 180°C (350°F), Gas Mark 4

baked scones with whipped cream

250 g/8 oz plain flour
1 teaspoon cream of tartar
½ teaspoon bicarbonate of soda
pinch of salt
50 g/2 oz butter or margarine
25 g/1 oz caster sugar
about 125 ml/4 fl oz milk, plus extra to glaze

To serve:
whipped cream
jam

1 Sift the flour, cream of tartar, soda and salt into a mixing bowl and rub in the fat with your fingertips until the mixture resembles breadcrumbs. Stir in the sugar and add enough milk to mix to a soft dough.

2 Turn out the dough on to a floured surface, knead lightly and roll out to 2 cm/¾ inch thick. Cut into 5 cm/2 inch rounds. Place the rounds on a floured baking sheet and brush with milk.

3 Bake in a preheated oven, 220°C (425°F), Gas Mark 7, for 10 minutes. Transfer to a wire rack to cool. Serve with whipped cream and jam.

Makes 10
Preparation time: 10 minutes
Cooking time: 10 minutes
Oven temperature: 220°C (425°F), Gas Mark 7

almond scones

175 g/6 oz plain flour
¼ teaspoon salt
2 teaspoons baking powder
2 tablespoons ground almonds
50 g/2 oz butter, diced
50 g/2 oz sultanas
125 ml/4 fl oz milk, plus extra to glaze
a few drops of almond extract

1 Sift the flour, salt and baking powder into a bowl, then stir in the ground almonds. Add the butter, rubbing it in until the mixture resembles fine breadcrumbs. Stir in the sultanas. Make a well in the centre of the mixture and pour in the milk and almond extract. Mix lightly with a wooden spoon or fork until a soft dough is formed.

2 Turn the dough on to a floured surface and knead gently until smooth. Roll out to a thickness of 1 cm/½ inch and cut into rounds with a 5 cm/2 inch cutter. Place the scones on a lightly greased baking sheet and brush the tops gently with milk.

3 Bake the scones in a preheated oven, 200°C (400°F), Gas Mark 6, for 7–10 minutes, or until they are well risen and golden brown. Remove from the oven and cool on a wire rack.

Makes 10
Preparation time: 10 minutes
Cooking time: 7–10 minutes
Oven temperature: 200°C (400°F), Gas Mark 6

chocolate chip muffins

175 g/6 oz plain dark chocolate, broken into pieces
60 g/2½ oz unsalted butter
350 ml/12 fl oz milk
375 g/12 oz self-raising flour
1 tablespoon baking powder
60 g/2½ oz cocoa powder
100 g/3½ oz caster sugar
100 g/3½ oz milk chocolate polka dots
100 g/3½ oz white chocolate polka dots
2 teaspoons vanilla extract
1 egg, plus 1 egg yolk
icing sugar, for dusting

1 Line the sections of a muffin tin with paper muffin cases. Put the dark chocolate in a small heavy-based saucepan with the butter and half the milk. Heat gently until the chocolate has melted. Leave to cool.

2 Sift the flour, baking powder and cocoa powder into a bowl. Stir in the sugar and polka dots.

3 Beat the remaining milk with the vanilla extract, egg and egg yolk, and add to the bowl with the chocolate mixture. Using a large metal spoon, fold the ingredients together until only just combined.

4 Spoon the mixture into the paper cases until almost filled. Bake in a preheated oven, 220°C (425°F), Gas Mark 7, for 25 minutes or until well risen and just firm. Transfer to a wire rack to cool. Serve the muffins dusted with icing sugar.

Makes 12
Preparation time: 15 minutes
Cooking time: about 25 minutes
Oven temperature: 220°C (425°F), Gas Mark 7

hot apple muffins

These American muffins are quite delicious split and buttered for breakfast and are very quick and easy to make. They are served hot and can be reheated on a baking sheet covered loosely with foil in a hot oven at 220°C (425°F), Gas Mark 7, for 5–6 minutes.

250 g/8 oz plain flour
1 teaspoon salt
1 tablespoon baking powder
50 g/2 oz caster sugar
2 eggs, beaten
150 ml/¼ pint milk
50 g/2 oz butter, melted
*250 g/8 oz cooking or dessert apples, peeled, cored and
    finely chopped*

1 Grease twenty-four 5 cm/2 inch bun or muffin tins.

2 Sift the flour, salt, baking powder and sugar into a mixing bowl. In a small bowl beat the eggs with the milk and mix in the melted butter. Stir the liquid quickly into the flour mixture. Speed is essential once the liquid is added to the baking powder, so do not beat the mixture or bother about any lumps. Fold in the chopped apples.

3 Spoon the mixture into the greased bun or muffin tins so they are one-third full. Bake in a preheated oven, 220°C (425°F), Gas Mark 7, for 15–20 minutes or until the muffins are well risen and golden brown. Turn out of the tins and serve hot.

Makes 24
Preparation time: 10 minutes
Baking time: 15–20 minutes
Oven temperature: 220°C (425°F), Gas Mark 7

fresh lemon slices

250 g/8 oz butter or margarine, softened
75 g/3 oz icing sugar
1 teaspoon vanilla extract
250 g/8 oz plain flour
4 eggs
175 g/6 oz granulated sugar
grated rind of 1 lemon
6 tablespoons lemon juice

1 Generously grease a 30 x 23 cm/12 x 9 inch shallow baking tin.

2 Put the butter, two-thirds of the icing sugar and the vanilla extract into a bowl and cream until light and fluffy. Sift the flour and fold into the creamed mixture, a little at a time, until completely incorporated. Spread the mixture evenly in the prepared tin and bake in a preheated oven, 190°C (375°F), Gas Mark 5, for 20 minutes.

3 Meanwhile, put the eggs, granulated sugar, lemon rind and lemon juice into a bowl. Stir to blend the ingredients but do not beat together. Pour the mixture over the baked pastry layer.

4 Return the tin to the oven and bake for about 20 minutes until the topping is set and lightly browned.

5 Remove the tin from the oven and sift the remaining icing sugar over the warm cake to cover it generously. Cut the cake into slices. Remove from the tin when cool.

Makes 36
Preparation time: 15 minutes
Baking time: about 40 minutes
Oven temperature: 190°C (375°F), Gas Mark 5

sticky gingerbread

250 g/8 oz plain flour
3 teaspoons ground ginger
1 teaspoon ground mixed spice
1 teaspoon bicarbonate of soda
125 g/4 oz butter or margarine
75 g/3 oz black treacle
125 g/4 oz golden syrup
50 g/2 oz soft brown sugar
150 ml/¼ pint milk
2 eggs, beaten
25 g/1 oz shredded almonds

1 Line and grease an 18 cm/7 inch square cake tin.

2 Sift the flour, spices and soda into a mixing bowl. Put the fat, treacle, syrup and sugar into a saucepan and heat gently. Cool slightly then add to the dry ingredients with the milk and eggs and mix thoroughly.

3 Pour the mixture into the prepared tin and sprinkle with the almonds. Bake in a preheated oven, 160°C (325°F), Gas Mark 3, for 1½–2 hours, or until a skewer inserted into the centre comes out clean.

4 Leave in the tin for 15 minutes, then turn on to a wire rack to cool. Store in an airtight tin for some days before eating to improve the texture.

Makes 1 cake
Preparation time: 15 minutes
Cooking time: 1½–2 hours
Oven temperature: 160°C (325°F), Gas Mark 3

chocolate eclairs

1 quantity Choux Pastry (see page 123)
300 ml/½ pint double cream
1 tablespoon icing sugar
125 g/4 oz plain dark chocolate, broken into pieces
40 g/1½ oz white chocolate, broken into pieces

1 Lightly grease, then dampen a large baking sheet. Put the choux pastry into a large piping bag fitted with a 1 cm/½ inch plain nozzle. Pipe 7.5 cm/3 inch fingers on to the baking sheet. Alternatively, use a teaspoon to place similar-sized lengths of dough on the baking sheet.

2 Bake in a preheated oven, 200°C (400°F), Gas Mark 6, for about 35 minutes until well risen, crisp and golden. Make a slit down the side of each bun to release the steam, then transfer to a wire rack to cool.

3 Whip the cream with the icing sugar until just peaking. Spoon or pipe into the éclairs.

4 Melt the dark and white chocolates in separate bowls over saucepans of simmering water. Spread a little dark chocolate over each bun, then spoon a little white chocolate over the centre of each one, swirling the two together with a spoon or cocktail stick. Leave the chocolate to set lightly before serving.

Makes about 14
Preparation time: 15 minutes, plus cooling and setting
Cooking time: about 35 minutes
Oven temperature: 200°C (400°F), Gas Mark 6

strawberry tartlets

4 tablespoons redcurrant jelly
1 tablespoon water
250 g/8 oz strawberries

Pastry:
125 g/4 oz plain flour
50 g/2 oz butter, softened
50 g/ 2 oz caster sugar
2 egg yolks
a few drops of vanilla extract

1 First make the pastry. Sift the flour on to the work surface, make a well in the centre and place the butter, sugar, egg yolks and vanilla extract in the well. Using the fingertips of one hand, work these ingredients together until well blended, then draw in the flour. Knead lightly until smooth, then chill for 1 hour.

2 Roll out the pastry very thinly and use to line 14 patty tins, then press a piece of foil into each one. Bake in a preheated oven, 190°C, (375°F), Gas Mark 5, for 10 minutes or until golden. Cool, then remove the foil and turn out.

3 To make the glaze, heat the redcurrant jelly with the water. Bring to the boil, sieve and reheat. Brush the cases with some of the glaze. Arrange the strawberries in the cases and brush with the remaining glaze.

Makes 14
Preparation time: about 25 minutes, plus chilling
Cooking time: about 10 minutes
Oven temperature: 190°C (375°F), Gas Mark 5

custard tarts

Pastry:
250 g/8 oz plain flour
pinch of salt
50 g/2 oz butter
50 g/2 oz lard or vegetable fat
25 g/1 oz caster sugar
1 egg yolk
about 2 tablespoons water

Custard:
450 ml/¾ pint milk
2 eggs
2–3 teaspoons sugar
¼ teaspoon vanilla extract
grated nutmeg, to finish

1 To make the pastry, sift the flour and salt into a bowl. Rub the fat into the flour until the mixture resembles breadcrumbs, then mix in the sugar. Beat the egg yolk with the water and stir in to bind to a fairly firm dough, adding a little more water if necessary. Knead lightly until smooth but do not overwork. Cover and chill in the refrigerator for at least 30 minutes before rolling out.

2 Grease eight deep 5 cm/2 inch muffin tins.

3 Roll out the pastry thinly. Cut out 7 cm/3 inch rounds and use to line the muffin tins. Line the pastry cases with foil and fill with baking beans. Bake 'blind' (see page 122) in a preheated oven, 200°C (400°F), Gas Mark 6, for 12–15 minutes until set but not brown. Remove from the oven and lift out the foil and beans. Lower the heat to 160°C (325°F), Gas Mark 3.

4 To make the custard, warm the milk over a low heat and while it is heating beat together the eggs and sugar. Stir the warm milk into the beaten eggs and flavour with vanilla extract. Strain the custard into the partially baked tart cases. Sprinkle the tops with grated nutmeg and return the tarts to the centre of the oven for 15–20 minutes until the custard is set. Serve cold.

Makes 8
Preparation time: 30 minutes, plus chilling
Cooking time: 30–35 minutes
Oven temperature: 200°C (400°F), Gas Mark 6

cream horns

250 g/8 oz frozen puff pastry, defrosted
beaten egg, to glaze
strawberry jam
175 ml/6 fl oz double cream, whipped

To decorate:
glacé cherries, halved
angelica
icing sugar

1 Roll out the pastry into a rectangle about 25 x 33 cm/ 10 x 13 inches and trim the edges. Cut into 10 strips 2.5 cm/1 inch wide.

2 Dampen one long edge of each strip with water and wind round a cornet mould, starting at the point and overlapping the dampened edge. Gently press the edges together. Repeat with the 9 remaining strips and cornet moulds. Place on a dampened baking sheet, cover and chill for 15 minutes.

3 Brush with egg and bake in a preheated oven, 220°C (425°F), Gas Mark 7, for 15–20 minutes until golden brown. Leave for 5 minutes before carefully removing the moulds. Cool on a wire rack.

4 Spoon a little jam into each horn then pipe in the cream. Decorate with pieces of cherry and angelica and sprinkle with icing sugar.

Makes 10
Preparation time: 20 minutes, plus chilling
Cooking time: 15–20 minutes
Oven temperature: 220°C (425°F), Gas Mark 7

frangipane tartlets

1 quantity Shortcrust Pastry (see page 124)
50 g/2 oz butter
50 g/2 oz caster sugar
1 egg, beaten
1 tablespoon flour
50 g/2 oz ground almonds
2 drops of almond extract
25 g/1 oz flaked almonds

Glaze:
2 tablespoons apricot jam
2 tablespoon hot water

1 Roll out the pastry thinly, cut into ten 7 cm/3 inch circles and use to line 10 deep patty tins. Chill for 15 minutes.

2 To make the glaze, beat together the jam and hot water. Sieve the mixture to make a smooth glaze.

3 To make the filling, cream together the butter and sugar until light and fluffy, add the egg, then beat in the flour. Mix in the ground almonds and almond extract.

4 Spoon the filling mixture into a piping bag fitted with a 1 cm/½ inch plain nozzle and two-thirds fill the pastry cases. Sprinkle the tartlets with flaked almonds. Bake in a preheated oven, 200°C (400°F), Gas Mark 6, for 20 minutes. Transfer to a wire rack then brush with the apricot glaze and leave to set.

Makes 10
Preparation time: 20 minutes, plus chilling and setting
Cooking time: 20 minutes
Oven temperature: 200°C (400°F), Gas Mark 6

rich mince pies

250 g/8 oz plain flour
75 g/3 oz chilled butter, diced
50 g/2 oz ground almonds
25 g/1 oz caster sugar
grated rind of 1 orange
1 egg, beaten
2–3 tablespoons orange juice
250 g/8 oz mincemeat

To decorate:
egg white, to glaze
caster sugar, for sprinkling

1 To make the pastry, place the flour in a bowl, add the diced butter and rub in with the fingertips until the mixture resembles fine breadcrumbs. Stir in the ground almonds, sugar and orange rind, then add the egg and orange juice and mix to a firm dough.

2 Knead the dough briefly on a lightly floured surface, then roll out thinly and stamp out twelve 7.5 cm/3 inch rounds with a pastry cutter. Line 12 greased bun tins with the pastry, adding 1 teaspoon mincemeat to each pastry case.

3 Re-roll the remaining pastry and cut into 5 cm/2 inch rounds to cover the mince pies. Dampen the edges and press down lightly to seal. Brush the tops of the mince pies with egg white and sprinkle lightly with the sugar.

4 Bake in a preheated oven, 200°C (400°F), Gas Mark 6, for 20 minutes until golden. Leave to cool slightly in the tins, then transfer to a wire rack.

Makes 12
Preparation time: 20 minutes, plus cooling
Cooking time: 20 minutes
Oven temperature: 200°C (400°F), Gas Mark 6

butterfly cakes

125 g/4 oz butter
125 g/4 oz caster sugar
2 eggs, beaten
½ teaspoon vanilla extract
125 g/4 oz self-raising flour

Butter icing:
50 g/2 oz butter, softened
¼ teaspoon vanilla extract
125 g/4 oz icing sugar, sifted

1 Put paper cases into 16 bun tins. Beat together the butter and sugar until pale and creamy. Gradually beat in the eggs and vanilla extract. Sift the flour and fold into the creamed mixture.

2 Divide the cake mixture among the paper cases and bake in a preheated oven, 190°C (375°F), Gas Mark 5, for 15–20 minutes. Turn on to a wire rack to cool.

3 Beat the ingredients for the butter icing until smooth.

4 Cut a small circular slice from the top of each cake, then cut this in half to form wings. Spoon or pipe the butter icing on to the top of the cakes, then set the wings on top and pipe a little more icing around them.

Makes 16
Preparation time: 25 minutes
Cooking time: 15–20 minutes
Oven temperature: 190°C (375°F), Gas Mark 5

chocolate cup cakes

125 g/4 oz butter
125 g/4 oz caster sugar
2 eggs, beaten
2 tablespoons cocoa powder
2 tablespoons boiling water
125 g/4 oz self-raising flour

Icing:
125 g/4 oz plain dark chocolate, chopped
50 g/2 oz butter

1 Put paper cases into 20 bun tins. In a large bowl, beat the butter and sugar until pale and creamy. Gradually beat in the eggs.

2 Mix the cocoa powder with the boiling water and fold into the creamed mixture with the flour. Divide the mixture among the paper cases and bake in a preheated oven, 190°C (375°F), Gas Mark 5, for 12–15 minutes. Transfer to a wire rack to cool.

3 Melt the chocolate with the butter in a heatproof bowl set over a pan of gently simmering water. Stir, then spoon over the chocolate cakes and leave to set.

Makes 20
Preparation time: 15 minutes
Cooking time: 12–15 minutes
Oven temperature: 190°C (375°F), Gas Mark 5

american banana loaf

250 g/8 oz plain flour
1 teaspoon bicarbonate of soda
½ teaspoon cream of tartar
pinch of salt
125 g/4 oz butter
175 g/6 oz caster sugar
1 teaspoon lemon juice

1 teaspoon grated lemon rind
3 tablespoons milk
2 bananas, mashed
2 eggs, beaten
25 g/1 oz granulated sugar

1 Grease and line the base of a 23 x 12 cm/9 x 5 inch loaf tin. Sift the flour, soda, cream of tartar and salt into a bowl. Rub in the fat until the mixture resembles fine breadcrumbs. Stir in the sugar. In another bowl, mix the lemon juice and rind, milk, bananas and eggs.

2 Stir the banana mixture into the rubbed-in mixture. Turn into the prepared tin and sprinkle with the granulated sugar. Bake in a preheated oven, 180°C (350°F), Gas Mark 4, for 1¼ hours or until a skewer inserted in the centre comes out clean. Serve the loaf sliced and buttered.

Makes 1 loaf
Preparation time: 15 minutes
Cooking time: 1¼ hours
Oven temperature: 180°C (350°F), Gas Mark 4

victoria sandwich cake

125 g/4 oz butter or margarine
125 g/4 oz caster sugar
2 eggs
125 g/4 oz self-raising flour, sifted
1 tablespoon hot water

To finish:
150 ml/¼ pint double cream, lightly whipped
3 tablespoons jam
caster sugar

1 Line and grease two 18 cm/7 inch sandwich tins.

2 Cream together the fat and sugar until light and fluffy. Beat in the eggs, one at a time, adding a tablespoon of the flour with the second egg. Fold in the rest of the flour, then the water.

3 Divide the mixture between the prepared tins and bake in a preheated oven, 180°C (350°F), Gas Mark 4, for 20–25 minutes, until the cakes are golden and spring back when lightly pressed. Turn on to a wire rack to cool.

4 Sandwich the cakes together with the cream and jam and sprinkle the top with caster sugar.

Makes 1 cake
Preparation time: 15 minutes
Cooking time: 20–25 minutes
Oven temperature: 180°C (350°F), Gas Mark 4

swiss roll

3 eggs
75 g/3 oz caster sugar
75 g/3 oz plain flour, sifted
1 tablespoon hot water
3 tablespoons warmed jam
caster sugar, for dredging

1 Line and grease an 18 x 28 cm/7 x 11 inch Swiss roll tin.

2 Whisk the eggs and sugar in a mixing bowl over a saucepan of hot water until thick enough to leave a trail. (Hot water is unnecessary if you are using an electric whisk.) Fold in the flour and water, then turn into the prepared Swiss roll tin.

3 Bake in a preheated oven, 200°C (400°F), Gas Mark 6, for 8–10 minutes, until the cake springs back when lightly pressed.

4 Turn out the roll on to a sheet of greaseproof paper dredged with sugar. Peel off the lining paper and trim the edges. Spread lightly with the jam and roll up quickly. Hold in position for a few minutes, then transfer to a wire rack to cool. Dredge with caster sugar before serving.

Makes 1 Swiss roll
Preparation time: 15 minutes
Cooking time: 8–10 minutes
Oven temperature: 200°C (400°F), Gas Mark 6

lemon cream swiss roll

75 g/3 oz butter or margarine, softened
200 g/7 oz caster sugar
3 eggs
175 g/6 oz self-raising flour, sifted
½ teaspoon finely grated lemon rind
150 ml/¼ pint whipping cream
2 tablespoons lemon curd
sifted icing sugar, for dredging

1 Grease a 33 x 23 cm/13 x 9 inch Swiss roll tin and line the base and sides with nonstick baking paper or greaseproof paper.

2 Put the butter or margarine, 175 g/6 oz of the sugar, the eggs, flour and lemon rind in a mixing bowl and beat well with a wooden spoon for 2–3 minutes, or with a hand-held electric mixer for 1 minute.

3 Turn the mixture into the prepared Swiss roll tin and spread out evenly. Bake in a preheated oven, 190°C (375°F), Gas Mark 5, for 12–15 minutes or until well risen, light golden and cooked through.

4 Meanwhile, have ready on a work surface a large sheet of nonstick baking paper or greaseproof paper, placed over a dampened tea towel. Dredge the paper evenly with the remaining caster sugar.

5 Turn out the sponge on to the sugared paper. Quickly but carefully remove the lining paper and trim the edges of the sponge neatly. Still working quickly, roll up the Swiss roll, starting with a short end and using the paper to help you form a neat roll. Wrap closely in the paper to hold in shape and leave to cool completely.

6 Whip the cream in a bowl until soft peaks form, then add the lemon curd and whisk again until thick and evenly mixed.

7 Unroll the Swiss roll and spread evenly with the lemon cream mixture. Re-roll neatly. Sprinkle with icing sugar and cut into chunky slices to serve.

Makes 1 Swiss roll
Preparation time: 20 minutes
Cooking time: 12–15 minutes
Oven temperature: 190°C (375°F), Gas Mark 5

cherry cake

175 g/6 oz butter or margarine
175 g/6 oz caster sugar
3 eggs
300 g/10 oz self-raising flour, sifted
250 g/8 oz glacé cherries, halved
50 g/2 oz ground almonds
about 5 tablespoons milk

1 Line and grease a deep 18 cm/7 inch cake tin.

2 Cream the fat and sugar until light and fluffy. Beat in the eggs, one at a time, adding a tablespoon of flour with the last two.

3 Carefully fold in the remaining flour, then fold in the cherries, ground almonds and enough milk to give a dropping consistency.

4 Put the mixture into the prepared tin and bake in a preheated oven, 160°C (325°F), Gas Mark 3, for 1½–2 hours.

5 Leave the cherry cake in the tin for 5 minutes, then turn on to a wire rack to cool.

Makes 1 cake
Preparation time: 20 minutes
Cooking time: 1½–2 hours
Oven temperature: 160°C (325°F), Gas Mark 3

madeira cake

175 g/6 oz butter
175 g/6 oz caster sugar
175 g/6 oz self-raising flour
75 g/3 oz plain flour
3 eggs
grated rind and juice of 1 lemon

1 Grease and line an 18 cm/7 inch round cake tin.

2 Cream the butter with the sugar until light, fluffy and very pale.

3 Sift together the self-raising and plain flours. Beat the eggs into the creamed mixture, one at a time, adding a tablespoon of sifted flour after each one.

4 Fold in the remaining flour, followed by the grated lemon rind and juice. Transfer to the prepared tin and bake in a preheated oven, 160°C (325°F), Gas Mark 3, for 1¼ hours, or until well-risen, firm to the touch and golden brown.

5 Cool in the tin for 5–10 minutes, then turn on to a wire rack and leave until cold. Do not peel off the lining paper but wrap the cake in foil or store in an airtight container until required.

Makes 1 cake
Preparation time: 20 minutes
Cooking time: 1¼ hours
Oven temperature: 160°C (325°F), Gas Mark 3

carrot cake

Quark, a slightly acidic German soft cheese, makes an excellent filling and topping for this carrot cake. Quark is generally available at large supermarkets.

175 g/6 oz butter or margarine
175 g/6 oz soft brown sugar
3 large eggs
175 g/6 oz wholemeal self-raising flour
50 g/2 oz ground almonds
175 g/6 oz young carrots, finely grated
75 g/3 oz walnuts, coarsely chopped
1 tablespoon milk

To decorate:
375 g/12 oz Quark or curd cheese (optional)
2 tablespoons halved or chopped walnuts (optional)

1 Grease and flour or line a 20 cm/8 inch cake tin.

2 Cream the butter or margarine and sugar until soft and light. Beat the eggs and gradually blend into the creamed mixture.

3 Fold in the flour with the ground almonds. Add the carrots, walnuts and milk. Mix thoroughly, then spoon into the prepared tin.

4 Bake in a preheated oven, 180°C (350°F), Gas Mark 4, for 1 hour or until firm to the touch. Cool for 5 minutes in the tin, then transfer to a wire rack.

5 When cool, decorate the cake, if you like. Split the cake through the centre and spread with a thick layer of cheese. Spread the rest of the cheese on the top of the cake and scatter with chopped or halved walnuts.

Makes 1 cake
Preparation time: 25 minutes
Cooking time: 1 hour
Oven temperature: 180°C (350°F), Gas Mark 4

chocolate gâteau with rum and walnuts

Sponge:
175 g/6 oz butter
175 g/6 oz caster sugar
3 large eggs
1 tablespoon rum
125 g/4 oz self-raising flour, sifted with ½ teaspoon baking powder
40 g/1½ oz walnuts, finely chopped
40 g/1½ oz digestive biscuits, crushed

Filling:
75 g/3 oz sultanas
3 tablespoons rum
175 g/6 oz plain dark chocolate
150 g/5 oz icing sugar
150 g/5 oz butter
50 g/2 oz walnuts, coarsely chopped

1 Line a 1 kg/2 lb loaf tin with greaseproof paper or baking parchment.

2 Cream the butter and sugar until soft and light. Beat the eggs with the rum. Gradually beat the eggs and rum into the creamed mixture, adding a little flour and baking powder if the mixture shows signs of curdling. When all the egg mixture has been incorporated, add the rest of the flour, the nuts and biscuit crumbs.

3 Spoon into the tin and bake in a preheated oven, 180°C (350°F), Gas Mark 4, for about 45 minutes, or until firm to the touch. Cool for about 10 minutes in the tin, then turn out the cake and allow to cool on a wire rack. Split into three layers.

4 Soak the sultanas in the rum while the sponge is cooking.

5 Melt 150 g/5 oz of the chocolate and coarsely grate the remainder. Sift the icing sugar and cream it with the butter. Add the melted chocolate and beat until light in texture. Add the sultanas, rum and half the walnuts.

6 Sandwich the cake layers together with some of the chocolate and rum mixture. Spread the remainder over the top but not the sides of the gâteau. Sprinkle the remaining walnuts and the grated chocolate over the top of the cake. Chill well before serving.

Serves 6–8
Preparation time: 45 minutes, plus chilling
Cooking time: 45 minutes
Oven temperature: 180°C (350°F), Gas Mark 4

rich christmas cake

125 g/4 oz self-raising flour
200 g/7 oz plain flour
¼ teaspoon salt
1 teaspoon ground mixed spice
½ teaspoon ground cinnamon
½ teaspoon ground nutmeg
250 g/8 oz butter or margarine
250 g/8 oz dark soft brown or dark muscovado sugar
2 teaspoons black treacle
5 eggs
50 ml/2 fl oz medium dry sherry or strained cold tea
1½ teaspoons vanilla extract
250 g/8 oz currants
250 g/8 oz sultanas
250 g/8 oz seedless raisins
75 g/3 oz chopped mixed peel
50 g/2 oz ground almonds
75 g/3 oz glacé cherries
finely grated rind of 1 lemon
3–4 tablespoons brandy

1 Grease and line a 23 cm/9 inch round or 20 cm/8 inch square cake tin, using a double thickness of greased greaseproof paper. Line the outside with several thicknesses of brown paper, standing at least 5 cm/2 inches above the top of the tin.

2 Sift the flours into a bowl with the salt, mixed spice, cinnamon and nutmeg.

3 In a large bowl, cream the butter or margarine with the sugar until light. Beat in the treacle. Lightly beat together the eggs, sherry or tea and vanilla extract.

4 Gradually beat half of the egg mixture into the creamed mixture. Fold in a third of the mixed flours. Continue to add the egg and flour mixtures alternately. Mix in all the remaining ingredients except the brandy. Turn the cake into the prepared tin and smooth the top.

5 Bake in a preheated oven, 140°C (275°F), Gas Mark 1, for 4–4½ hours until a skewer inserted into the centre of the cake comes out clean. Cover the cake with a double layer of greaseproof paper if it starts to brown too much during cooking.

6 Leave the cake to cool in the tin, then turn out on to a wire rack to cool completely. Prick all over with a fine skewer and spoon the brandy on top.

7 Store the cake in an airtight tin and leave to mature for about 3 months.

Makes 1 cake
Preparation time: 45 minutes
Cooking time: 4–4½ hours
Oven temperature: 140°C (275°F), Gas Mark 1

chocolate yule log

3 eggs
75 g/3 oz caster sugar
75 g/3 oz plain flour, sifted twice
1 tablespoon hot water
1 teaspoon vanilla extract
icing sugar, for dusting

Filling and topping:
175 g/6 oz sugar
125 ml/4 fl oz water
6 egg yolks
375 g/12 oz unsalted butter, softened
250 g/8 oz plain dark chocolate, melted and cooled

1 Place the eggs and caster sugar in a large bowl and whisk together until very thick and fluffy. Fold in the flour, water and vanilla extract gently but thoroughly. Pour the mixture into a lined and greased 33 x 23 cm/ 13 x 9 inch Swiss roll tin, and bake in a preheated oven, 220°C (425°F), Gas Mark 7, for 8–10 minutes until golden.

2 Turn out the cake on to a sheet of sugared greaseproof paper set on a damp tea towel. Trim the crusty edges, then roll up with the paper inside and leave to cool.

3 To make the filling and topping, place the sugar and water in a small saucepan and stir over a low heat until the sugar is dissolved. Bring to the boil, then boil without stirring until the temperature reaches 110°C (225°F) on a sugar thermometer.

4 Whisk the eggs yolks in a large bowl and continue to whisk while pouring on the syrup in a thin stream. Whisk until thick and cool. Gradually whisk in the butter and finally fold in the melted chocolate.

5 Unroll the cake and spread with half of the chocolate butter cream. Roll up neatly and place on a silver cakeboard. Cut off the end of the roll at an angle and attach to one side of the roll to resemble a branch.

6 Cover the cake evenly with the remaining chocolate butter cream and score the surface with the tines of a fork to resemble bark. Chill in the refrigerator until firm. To serve, dust the cake with icing sugar.

Makes 1 log
Preparation time: 1 hour, plus cooling and chilling
Cooking time: 8–10 minutes
Oven temperature: 220°C (425°F), Gas Mark 7

ginger cake

175 g/6 oz butter or margarine
175 g/6 oz caster sugar
3 eggs
250 g/8 oz self-raising flour
½ teaspoon ground ginger
75 g/3 oz preserved stem ginger, chopped, plus
  2 tablespoons syrup from the jar

Ginger icing:
175 g/6 oz icing sugar, sifted
2 tablespoons ginger syrup
preserved stem ginger strips, to decorate

1 Line and grease an 18 cm/7 inch cake tin.

2 Cream the fat and sugar until light and fluffy. Add the eggs one at a time, adding a tablespoon of flour with the last two. Sift and fold in the remaining flour and the ground ginger, then fold in the preserved ginger and syrup. Turn into the prepared tin.

3 Bake in a preheated oven, 180°C (350°F), Gas Mark 4, for 1–1¼ hours. Turn out on to a wire rack to cool.

4 To make the ginger icing, beat the icing sugar and syrup together until smooth. Pour over the cake and leave until set. Decorate with ginger strips.

Makes 1 cake
Preparation time: 20 minutes
Cooking time: 1–1¼ hours
Oven temperature: 180°C (350°F), Gas Mark 4

banana cake

125 g/4 oz butter or margarine
125 g/4 oz caster sugar
2 eggs
125 g/4 oz self-raising flour, sifted
2 bananas, mashed
icing sugar, to dust

Filling:
50 g/2 oz ground almonds
50 g/2 oz icing sugar, sifted
1 small banana, mashed
1/2 teaspoon lemon juice

1 Line and grease two 18 cm/7 inch sandwich tins.

2 Cream the fat and sugar until light and fluffy. Add the eggs, one at a time, adding a tablespoon of flour with the second egg. Fold in the remaining flour with the mashed bananas.

3 Divide the mixture between the prepared sandwich tins. Bake in a preheated oven, 180°C (350°F), Gas Mark 4, for 20–25 minutes until the cakes spring back when lightly pressed. Turn out the cakes on to a wire rack to cool.

4 To make the filling, mix the ground almonds with the icing sugar, then add the banana and lemon juice and mix to a smooth paste. Sandwich the cakes together with the filling and dust with icing sugar.

Makes 1 cake
Preparation time: 15 minutes
Cooking time: 20–25 minutes
Oven temperature: 180°C (350°F), Gas Mark 4

white chocolate gâteau

4 eggs
125 g/4 oz caster sugar
125 g/4 oz plain flour
50 g/2 oz white chocolate, finely grated

To finish:
3 tablespoons rosewater
150 ml/¼ pint crème fraîche
200 g/7 oz white chocolate, broken into pieces
75 g/3 oz unsalted butter
3 tablespoons single cream
125 g/4 oz icing sugar
grated white chocolate
icing sugar, for dusting

1 Grease and line the bases of two 20 cm/8 inch round sandwich tins. Put the eggs and sugar in a large heatproof bowl over a pan of simmering water and whisk until the mixture is thick enough to leave a trail when the whisk is lifted from the bowl. Remove from the heat and whisk until cool.

2 Sift the flour into the bowl. Add the grated chocolate and fold in using a large metal spoon.

3 Turn into the prepared tins and bake in a preheated oven, 180°C (350°F), Gas Mark 4, for 20–25 minutes until just firm. Transfer to a wire rack to cool.

4 Stir the rosewater into the crème fraîche and use to sandwich the two cakes together on a serving plate.

5 Put the white chocolate and butter in a heatproof bowl over a pan of gently simmering water and leave until melted. Stir in the cream and icing sugar, and beat until smooth.

6 Leave the mixture to cool until it forms soft peaks, then spread it over the top and sides of the cake using a palette knife.

7 Decorate the top of the cake with grated white chocolate and a light dusting of icing sugar.

Serves 12
Preparation time: 45 minutes, plus cooling
Cooking time: 20–25 minutes
Oven temperature: 180°C (350°F), Gas Mark 4

peach gâteau

This gâteau is best made with fresh peaches, but canned peaches may be used when they are out of season.

3 eggs, separated
125 g/4 oz caster sugar
finely grated rind and juice of ½ lemon
50 g/2 oz semolina
25 g/1 oz ground almonds

To serve:
4 ripe peaches, stoned and thinly sliced
300 ml/½ pint double cream, whipped
4 tablespoons apricot jam
2 teaspoons lemon juice
50 g/2 oz ground hazelnuts

1 Grease a deep 20 cm/8 inch cake tin, line the base with greaseproof paper, then grease the paper. Dust the inside of the tin lightly with flour.

2 Put the egg yolks, sugar, lemon rind and juice into a bowl and whisk with an electric beater until thick and mousse-like. Stir in the semolina and ground almonds. Whisk the egg whites until stiff, then fold in.

3 Turn the mixture into the prepared tin and level the surface. Transfer to a preheated oven, 180°C, (350°F), Gas Mark 4, and bake for 35–40 minutes until the cake springs back when lightly pressed in the centre. Turn out on to a wire rack, peel off the lining paper, turn the cake the right way up and leave to cool.

4 Cut the cooled cake into two layers. Fold half of the peach slices into three-quarters of the cream and use to sandwich the layers together.

5 Toast the ground hazelnuts in a dry frying pan, stirring continuously, until they turn a golden brown. Allow to cool.

6 Put the apricot jam and lemon juice into a small saucepan and heat gently, stirring until the jam has melted. Sieve and reheat. Arrange the remaining peach slices overlapping in a circle on top of the cake. Brush the peaches and the sides of the cake with the warm jam glaze. Press the hazelnuts around the sides, then pipe the remaining cream around the top. Serve chilled.

Serves 8
Preparation time: 40 minutes, plus chilling
Cooking time: 40–45 minutes
Oven temperature: 180°C (350°F), Gas Mark 4

sachertorte

175 g/6 oz butter, softened
175 g/6 oz caster sugar
175 g/6 oz plain dark chocolate, melted
8 eggs, separated
150 g/5 oz plain flour, sifted

Filling and icing:
5 tablespoons apricot jam, warmed and sieved
250 g/8 oz plain dark chocolate
2 tablespoons milk
25 g/1 oz milk chocolate
sugar flowers, to decorate

1 Grease and flour a 23 cm/9 inch round cake tin.

2 Place the butter and sugar in a mixing bowl and beat with a wooden spoon for about 10 minutes until pale and fluffy. Gradually beat in the melted chocolate until evenly mixed, then beat in the egg yolks.

3 Whisk the egg whites in a grease-free bowl until stiff peaks form, then fold carefully into the mixture, using a metal spoon. Carefully fold in the sifted flour.

4 Pour the mixture into the prepared tin. Bake in a preheated oven, 160°C (325°F), Gas Mark 3, for 1 hour until firm to the touch. Cool in the tin for 10 minutes, then turn the cake out on to a wire rack and leave to cool completely before filling and icing.

5 Split the cake in half and sandwich together with half the jam. Brush the top and sides with the remaining jam. Melt the plain chocolate in a bowl set over a saucepan of hot water, and then remove from the heat and stir in the milk. Pour the chocolate evenly over the cake, using a palette knife to coat the sides. Leave to set completely.

6 Melt the milk chocolate in a heatproof bowl set over a pan of gently simmering water. Place in a greaseproof paper piping bag fitted with a thin writing nozzle. Pipe the word 'sacher' in flowing writing over the cake. Decorate with a few sugar flowers, attaching them to the cake with dabs of melted chocolate so that they adhere firmly to the chocolate icing.

Makes 1 cake
Preparation time: 40 minutes, plus cooling and setting
Cooking time: 1 hour
Oven temperature: 160°C (325°F), Gas Mark 3

langues de chat

These delicate biscuits are ideal for serving with desserts such as mousses, creams and ice creams.

50 g/2 oz butter
50 g/2 oz caster sugar
2 egg whites
50 g/2 oz plain flour, sifted
a few drops of vanilla extract

1 Cream the butter and sugar together until light and fluffy. Whisk the egg whites lightly and gradually beat into the creamed mixture. Carefully fold in the flour and vanilla extract.

2 Place the mixture in a piping bag fitted with a 2 cm/¾ inch plain nozzle. Pipe 7 cm/3 inch lengths on to a greased and floured baking sheet.

3 Bake in a preheated oven, 200°C (400°F), Gas Mark 6, for 10 minutes; the biscuits should be pale golden but darker around the edges. Transfer to a wire rack to cool.

Makes 20–24
Preparation time: 15 minutes
Cooking time: 10 minutes
Oven temperature: 200°C (400°F), Gas Mark 6

chocolate chip cookies

125 g/4 oz butter or margarine
50 g/2 oz soft brown sugar
1 egg, beaten
150 g/5 oz self-raising flour
125 g/4 oz plain dark chocolate, finely chopped

1 Lightly grease a baking sheet. Cream the butter or margarine and sugar together until light and fluffy. Beat in the egg, then sift in the flour. Add the chocolate pieces and mix thoroughly.

2 Put 25 teaspoonfuls of the mixture, slightly apart, on the baking sheet and bake in a preheated oven, 180°C (350°F), Gas Mark 4, for 15–20 minutes until golden brown.

3 Leave the cookies on the baking sheet for 1 minute, then transfer to a wire rack and leave to cool.

Makes 25
Preparation time: 10 minutes
Cooking time: 15–20 minutes
Oven temperature: 180°C (350°F), Gas Mark 4

almond butter cookies

175 g/6 oz plain flour
½ teaspoon baking powder
125 g/4 oz butter or margarine, softened
75 g/3 oz sugar
½ teaspoon vanilla extract
2 tablespoons water

Praline:
125 g/4 oz sugar
25 g/1 oz almonds

1 First make the praline. Put the sugar and almonds in a small, heavy-based pan over medium-high heat and stir occasionally until the sugar dissolves and turns a pale amber colour.

2 Pour out the caramel mixture on to a greased and lined baking sheet, to make a layer 5 mm/¼ inch thick and spread with an oiled palette knife. Set aside until cold.

3 Break the praline into pieces and put them into a plastic bag. Crush the pieces coarsely with a rolling pin.

4 To make the cookies, sift the flour and baking powder into a bowl, then set aside.

5 Put the butter and sugar into a large bowl and cream until light and fluffy. Add the vanilla extract and mix well.

6 Add the flour mixture alternately with the water, mixing until smooth after each addition. Stir the crushed praline into the mixture.

7 Drop rounded teaspoonfuls, 5 cm/2 inches apart, on to well-greased baking sheets. Bake in a preheated oven, 160°C (325°F), Gas Mark 3, for about 15 minutes or until the edges are lightly browned. Leave the cookies on the baking sheets for 2 minutes, then carefully transfer to wire racks to cool completely.

Makes about 36
Preparation time: 15 minutes
Cooking time: 20–25 minutes
Oven temperature: 160°C (325°F), Gas Mark 3

shortbread fingers

250 g/8 oz butter
125 g/4 oz caster sugar
50 g/2 oz cornflour
300 g/10 oz plain flour
caster sugar, for sprinkling

1 Cream the butter and sugar until light and fluffy. Sift in the 2 flours and mix well to combine. Press the mixture into an oblong tin about 30 x 20 cm/12 x 8 inches and mark with the tines of a fork.

2 Bake in a preheated oven, 140°C (275°F), Gas Mark 1, for 30 minutes, then reduce the temperature to 120°C (250°F), Gas Mark ½ and cook for a further 1–1½ hours.

3 Remove the shortbread from the oven and cut into 32 fingers. Sprinkle with caster sugar and leave to cool slightly in the tin before transferring to a wire rack to cool completely. Store in an airtight tin.

Makes 32
Preparation time: 15 minutes
Cooking time: 1½–2 hours
Oven temperature: 140°C (275°F), Gas Mark 1

cinnamon shortbread

150 g/5 oz plain flour
1 teaspoon ground cinnamon
25 g/1 oz ground rice
50 g/2 oz caster sugar
125 g/4 oz butter
caster sugar and a little ground cinnamon, for sprinkling

1 Sift the flour, cinnamon, ground rice and caster sugar into a bowl. Rub in the butter. Gradually work the mixture to a smooth dough. Wrap and chill for 15 minutes.

2 Roll out the dough on a lightly floured surface and cut into shapes using biscuit cutters or shortbread moulds. Alternatively, roll out the dough into a circle on a baking sheet and gently mark into 8 portions. Chill for 30 minutes.

3 Bake the shortbread in a preheated oven, 160°C (325°F), Gas Mark 3, for 30–40 minutes until pale golden. Leave on the baking sheet or in the moulds for 5 minutes then transfer to a wire rack to cool. Sprinkle with a little caster sugar and cinnamon before serving.

Makes 8
Preparation time: 20 minutes, plus chilling
Cooking time: 30–40 minutes
Oven temperature: 160°C (325°F), Gas Mark 3

brandy snaps

The biscuits are rolled into their distinctive tube shapes when they come out of the oven. If the biscuits cool too much and are too brittle to roll, return them to the oven for 1 minute to soften.

125 g/4 oz butter
125 g/4 oz demerara sugar
125 g/4 oz golden syrup
125 g/4 oz plain flour
1 teaspoon ground ginger

1 Put the butter, sugar and syrup into a saucepan and heat gently until the butter has melted and the sugar dissolved. Cool slightly, then sift in the flour and ginger and beat well.

2 Place teaspoonfuls of the mixture on a greased baking sheet at least 10 cm/4 inches apart. Bake in a preheated oven, 180°C (350°F), Gas Mark 4, for 10–12 minutes.

3 Leave to cool slightly then remove with a palette knife and roll round the greased handle of a wooden spoon. Leave for 1–2 minutes to set, then slip them off on to a wire rack to cool. Serve plain or filled with whipped cream.

Makes 35
Preparation time: 15 minutes
Cooking time: 10–12 minutes
Oven temperature: 180°C (350°F), Gas Mark 4

moroccan almond biscuits

These rich biscuits are delicious served with coffee, or creamy or fruity desserts. You may find that the mixture becomes too sticky to handle, depending on the warmth of your hands and the kitchen; if this does happen, pop the mixture into the refrigerator to firm up.

2 small eggs
200 g/7 oz icing sugar, plus extra for coating
2 teaspoons baking powder
400 g/13 oz ground almonds
grated rind of ½ lemon
orange flower water or rosewater, to taste
oil, for greasing

1 Break 1 whole egg and 1 egg yolk into a bowl then beat in the sugar and baking powder until thoroughly combined. Work in the ground almonds, lemon rind and orange flower water or rosewater to taste. Knead well so the warmth of your hands releases the oil in the almonds to make a soft, workable paste; if necessary, add the extra egg white.

2 With oiled hands, roll walnut-size pieces of the mixture into egg-shaped balls. Cover a plate with icing sugar. Flatten the balls on the plate, covering them in the sugar.

3 Place the almond balls, spaced well apart, on an oiled baking sheet and bake in a preheated oven, 180°C (350°F), Gas Mark 4, for about 15 minutes until golden. Transfer to a wire rack to cool. Store in an airtight tin.

Makes about 30
Preparation time: 15 minutes
Cooking time: 15 minutes
Oven temperature: 180°C (350°F), Gas Mark 4

drinks & finger food

white wine punch

3 bottles dry white wine, well chilled
½–¾ bottle dry sherry
4–6 tablespoons Curaçao or Grand Marnier
900 ml/1½ pints tonic water, well chilled, or a mixture of
  tonic water and lemonade
crushed ice

To decorate:
cucumber slices
1 orange, thinly sliced
1 lemon, thinly sliced
1 apple, cored and sliced

1 Pour the white wine, sherry and Curaçao or Grand Marnier into a large bowl. Cover and chill in the refrigerator until required.

2 Just before serving, add the tonic water or tonic water and lemonade mixture.

3 To serve, put handfuls of crushed ice into serving jugs and pour in the punch. Decorate the jugs of punch with the cucumber, orange, lemon and apple slices.

Serves 20
Preparation time: 15 minutes, plus chilling

claret cup

75 ml/3 fl oz light rum
1 miniature bottle of orange-flavoured liqueur
thinly pared rind of 1 lemon
2 bottles claret or other red wine
3 bottles ginger ale
ice cubes

1 Put the rum and orange-flavoured liqueur into a small jug. Add the lemon rind, cover and leave to marinate for about 2 hours.

2 Pour the claret and ginger ale into a large bowl, add the rum and orange-flavoured liqueur mixture with the lemon rind and stir to mix. Add a handful of ice cubes and serve immediately.

Serves 12
Preparation time: 10 minutes, plus marinating

loving cup

An ideal drink to welcome guests on Christmas day.

8 sugar cubes
2 lemons
½ bottle medium sweet or sweet sherry
¼ bottle brandy
1 bottle sparkling dry white wine

1 Rub the sugar cubes over the lemons to absorb the zest. Thinly peel the lemons and remove as much of the pith as possible. Thinly slice the lemons and set aside.

2 Put the lemon rind, sherry, brandy and sugar cubes into a jug and stir until the sugar has dissolved. Cover and chill in the refrigerator for about 30 minutes.

3 To serve, add the wine to the cup and float the lemon slices on top.

Serves 12
Preparation time: 10 minutes, plus chilling

peach cup

2 ripe peaches, skinned, halved and stoned
2 bottles still Moselle, chilled
3 tablespoons caster sugar
1 bottle sparkling Moselle, chilled

1 Chop the peaches into a large bowl. Pour one bottle of still Moselle over the fruit. Add the sugar, stir gently, cover and chill for 30 minutes.

2 Add the second bottle of still Moselle. Just before serving, pour in the sparkling Moselle.

Serves 8–10
Preparation time: 10 minutes, plus chilling

champagne strawberry cup

175 ml/6 fl oz Fraises des Bois or other strawberry liqueur, chilled
1 bottle dry champagne or sparkling dry white wine, chilled
125 g/4 oz strawberries, sliced

1 Pour the Fraises des Bois into a large jug. Gradually add the champagne or sparkling wine, stirring very gently so as not to lose the bubbles.

2 Divide the strawberry slices among individual glasses and top up with strawberry-flavoured champagne. Serve immediately.

Serves 6
Preparation time: 10 minutes

brandy and lemon sparkler

juice of 15 lemons
juice of 4 oranges
625 g/1¼ lb caster sugar
ice cubes (optional)
300 ml/½ pint Curaçao
2 measures grenadine
2.5 litres/4 pints brandy
2.5 litres/4 pints sparkling mineral water

To decorate:
lemon slices
orange slices

1 Pour the lemon and orange juices into a jug. Add the caster sugar and stir until dissolved.

2 To serve, put the ice cubes, if using, into a punch bowl. Add the lemon and orange juice mixture and the remaining ingredients. Stir well. Decorate with lemon and orange slices.

Serves 30
Preparation time: 10–15 minutes

claret punch

250 g/8 oz caster sugar
5 bottles claret
2.4 litres/4 pints sparkling mineral water
300 ml/½ pint lemon juice
2 measures Curaçao
ice
seasonal fruits, to decorate

1 Place all the ingredients in a large punch bowl containing plenty of ice. Stir gently until the sugar has dissolved.

2 Decorate with slices of fresh fruits in season. Keep the punch bowl packed with ice.

Serves 20–25
Preparation time: 15 minutes

fruit punch

A delicious non-alcoholic punch, ideal for children.

600 ml/1 pint orange juice
600 ml/1 pint apple juice
150 ml/¼ pint water
½ teaspoon ground ginger
½ teaspoon mixed spice
brown or white sugar (optional)
1 apple, thinly sliced, to decorate

1 Place the orange and apple juices, water and spices in a saucepan and bring gently to the boil, adding sugar to taste if required. Simmer the mixture for 5 minutes.

2 Pour the punch into a warmed bowl and float the apple slices on top.

Serves 6
Preparation time: 5 minutes
Cooking time: 10 minutes

grape punch

An unusual non-alcoholic punch.

600 ml/1 pint sparkling apple juice
600 ml/1 pint grape juice
600 ml/1 pint ginger ale
4 tablespoons lime juice cordial
4 tablespoons clear honey

Tea liquor:
25 g/1 oz Indian tea leaves
600 ml/1 pint cold water

To decorate:
ice cubes (optional)
12 lemon slices
seedless grapes

1 First make the tea liquor. Put the tea leaves into a jug and pour over the cold water. Cover and leave to stand overnight.

2 Strain 450 ml/¾ pint of the tea liquor into a large bowl, add the remaining ingredients and stir well.

3 To serve, pour the punch into individual glasses, add the ice cubes, if liked, and decorate with lemon slices and seedless grapes.

Serves 12
Preparation time: 10 minutes, plus standing

sauternes punch

Any other medium sweet white wine can be used in place of Sauternes.

250 g/8 oz caster sugar
3 bottles Sauternes
ice
1 measure maraschino
1 measure Curaçao
1 measure Grand Marnier
seasonal fruits, to decorate

1 Dissolve the sugar in the wine in a large jug, then pour over a large quantity of ice in a punch bowl and stir in the remaining ingredients. Add slices of fruits in season.

Serves 10–15
Preparation time: 15 minutes

champagne punch

250 g/8 oz caster sugar
3 bottles Champagne
1.2 litres/2 pints sparkling mineral water
2 measures brandy
2 measures maraschino
2 measures Curaçao
ice cubes
seasonal fruits, to decorate

1 Put all the ingredients into a large punch bowl with plenty of ice cubes and stir until the sugar has dissolved. Add slices of fruits in season.

Serves 15–20
Preparation time: 15 minutes

cranberry crush

crushed ice
1.8 litres/3 pints sweetened cranberry juice
600 ml/1 pint fresh orange juice
600 ml/1 pint ginger ale
orange and lemon wedges, to decorate

1 Half fill a large punch bowl with crushed ice. Pour in the cranberry juice and orange juice and stir to mix.

2 Top up with the ginger ale and decorate with orange and lemon wedges. Serve at once.

Serves 15
Preparation time: 10 minutes

tropical cooler

125 g/4 oz caster sugar
125 ml/4 fl oz lemon juice
1 bottle dry white wine
½ bottle golden or light rum
1 can crushed pineapple
ice
seasonal fruits, to decorate

1 Stir the caster sugar with the lemon juice until dissolved. Add the wine, rum and crushed pineapple and stir to mix.

2 Cover and chill for several hours. When ready to serve, add ice cubes and garnish with fruit.

Serves 12
Preparation time: 10 minutes

cardinal punch

juice of 6 lemons
250 g/8 oz icing sugar
300 ml/½ pint brandy
300 ml/½ pint light rum
2 bottles claret
150 ml/¼ pint sweet vermouth
300 ml/½ pint strong black tea
ice block
125 ml/4 fl oz sparkling wine
450 ml/¾ pint soda water
seasonal fruits, to decorate

1 Stir together the lemon juice and sugar until the sugar has dissolved. Add the brandy, rum, claret, vermouth and tea and stir to mix.

2 Pour over a large block of ice in a punch bowl and add the sparkling wine and soda water. Decorate with fruit and serve.

Serves 18–20
Preparation time: 10 minutes

sparkling sorbet punch

500 ml/17 fl oz lemon sorbet
½ bottle sweet or medium sweet white wine, chilled
1 bottle sparkling white wine, chilled
lemon slices, to decorate

1 Scoop the sorbet into a punch bowl. Add the wine and garnish with lemon slices. Serve immediately.

Serves 8
Preparation time: 10 minutes

kir punch

250 g/8 oz ripe strawberries
1–2 measures Crème de Cassis
3 bottles dry white wine, chilled
soda water, chilled, to taste

1 Place the strawberries in a bowl, add the Crème de Cassis and chill for 1–2 hours.

2 Add the wine and stir. If liked, add with soda water to taste.

Serves 18–20
Preparation time: 5 minutes, plus chilling

summer fruit cup

4 measures Grand Marnier
4 measures Kirsch or cherry brandy
375 g/12 oz ripe summer fruits, such as peaches, apricots, nectarines and strawberries, prepared and sliced
orange and lime slices
1 bottle medium dry white wine, chilled

1 Combine the Grand Marnier, Kirsch or cherry brandy, summer fruits and orange and lime slices in a bowl.

2 Stir, then cover and chill for about 1 hour. Add the wine and stir to mix.

Serves 8
Preparation time: 10 minutes, plus chilling

sangria

4 tablespoons Curaçao
125 g/4 oz caster sugar
1 orange, thinly sliced
1 bottle rosé wine, chilled
1½ bottles light or medium-bodied red wine, such as Rioja
300 ml/½ pint orange juice
ice cubes

1 Combine the Curaçao, half the sugar and the sliced orange in a mixing bowl. Stir to dissolve the sugar, then cover and chill for 30 minutes.

2 Tip the orange mixture into a punch bowl or large jug and add wine, orange juice and the remaining sugar. Stir well to mix and dissolve the sugar. Taste and add more sugar if you would like a sweeter punch. Add ice cubes and serve immediately.

Serves 18
Preparation time: 15 minutes, plus chilling

sherry cobbler

1 teaspoon icing sugar
2 measures soda water or water
ice
2 measures sherry
fresh fruit slices, to decorate

1 Combine the sugar and water in a wine glass and stir to dissolve the sugar. Add ice and sherry and decorate with fruit.

Serves 1
Preparation time: 5 minutes

bishop

½ tablespoon lemon juice
1 tablespoon orange juice
1 teaspoon icing sugar
2–3 ice cubes
125 ml/4 fl oz medium red wine
3 dashes white rum or brandy (optional)
orange and lemon slices, to decorate

1 Combine the lemon and orange juices and sugar in a highball glass or squat tumbler and stir to dissolve the sugar. Add the ice cubes and fill the glass with wine. Float rum or brandy on top, if liked, and decorate with orange and lemon slices.

Serves 1
Preparation time: 5 minutes

kir

6 measures dry white wine
½ measure Crème de Cassis
ice (optional)

1 Combine the wine and Crème de Cassis in a large wine glass and stir. Add ice cubes, if liked.

Serves 1
Preparation time: 2 minutes

brandy punch

juice of 5 oranges
juice of 5 lemons
250 g/8 oz caster sugar
ice
150 ml/¼ pint Curaçao
1.2 litres/2 pints brandy
1.2 litres/2 pints sparkling mineral water
orange wedges, to decorate

1 Pour the fruit juices into a jug. Add the sugar and stir well until dissolved.

2 Place some ice in a punch bowl, add all the remaining ingredients and stir well to combine. Decorate with orange wedges and serve.

Serves 10
Preparation time: 10 minutes

cider cup

1 measure maraschino
1 measure Curaçao
1 measure brandy
1.2 litres/2 pints medium dry cider
ice
seasonal fruits, to decorate

1 Pour the maraschino, Curaçao, brandy and cider into a large glass jug or bowl. Add ice and stir gently. Decorate with fruits in season.

Serves 4–6
Preparation time: 5 minutes

between the sheets

dash of lemon juice
1 measure brandy
1 measure Cointreau
1 measure dark rum
ice

1 Shake all the ingredients together in a cocktail shaker and strain into a cocktail glass.

Serves 1
Preparation time: 3 minutes

piña colada

2 measures light rum
2 measures cream of coconut
3–4 measures pineapple juice
6–8 ice cubes, crushed
fresh fruit, to decorate

1 Combine the rum, cream of coconut, pineapple juice and crushed ice in a blender.

2 Blend at high speed for about 10 seconds. Pour into a chilled glass and decorate with slices of fresh fruit.

Serves 1
Preparation time: 5 minutes

tequila sunrise

2 measures tequila
4 measures orange juice
ice cubes
¾ measure grenadine

1 Combine the tequila and orange juice in a glass and stir to combine. Add several ice cubes.

2 Slowly pour in the grenadine which will sink to the bottom, creating the 'sunrise'. Stir gently before drinking.

Serves 1
Preparation time: 4 minutes

tom collins

2 tablespoons lemon juice
1½ teaspoons caster sugar
2 measures gin
ice cubes
soda water, to taste

To decorate:
lemon slices
cocktail cherries

1 Put the lemon juice, sugar and gin into a cocktail shaker and shake well with some ice cubes then strain into a tall tumbler. Add fresh ice and a good dash of soda water, to taste. Serve decorated with lemon slices and cocktail cherries.

Serves 1
Preparation time: 2 minutes

silver streak

1 measure kummel
1 measure gin
ice cubes

1 Put the kummel and gin into a cocktail shaker with several ice cubes. Shake together thoroughly and strain into a cocktail glass.

Serves 1
Preparation time: 2 minutes

bloody mary

This popular drink was probably created in the United States in the 1930s, and may have been named for Mary Pickford, the famous Hollywood star of the thirties. The seasonings may be altered to individual taste.

1½ measures vodka
3 measures tomato juice
dash of lemon juice
1–2 dashes of Worcestershire sauce
2–3 drops Tabasco sauce
salt, or celery salt, and pepper
ice cubes (optional)
celery stick, to decorate

1 Combine the vodka, tomato juice, lemon juice, Worcestershire sauce, Tabasco sauce and salt, or celery salt, and pepper to taste in a cocktail shaker and shake well. Strain into a tumbler. Add ice cubes, if liked, and decorate with the celery stick.

Serves 1
Preparation time: 5 minutes

harvey wallbanger

1–2 measures vodka
4 measures orange juice
ice cubes
½ measure Galliano

1 Pour the vodka and orange juice into a glass. Add several ice cubes and stir. Float the Galliano on top.

Serves 1
Preparation time: 2 minutes

planter's punch

4 tablespoons lime juice
2 teaspoons icing sugar
2 measures golden or light rum
ice cubes
1–2 measures soda water

To decorate:
1 lime slice
1 fresh pineapple wedge
1 maraschino cherry

1 Combine the lime juice and sugar in a tall glass and stir until the sugar has dissolved. Stir in the rum. Add several ice cubes and fill the glass with soda water. Stir again. Decorate with the fruit.

Serves 1
Preparation time: 2 minutes

scorpion

1 measure light rum
1 measure brandy
2 measures orange juice
1 measure lemon juice
½ measure orgeat, or 2 teaspoons almond extract
ice cubes

To decorate:
1 orange slice
1 mint sprig

1 Combine the rum, brandy, orange and lemon juices, orgeat or almond extract and some ice in a blender and blend at low speed for 15 seconds.

2 Pour into a chilled glass over ice cubes and decorate with an orange slice and a sprig of mint.

Serves 1
Preparation time: 5 minutes

highball

2 measures whisky
ice
ginger ale or soda water, to taste
lemon and lime slices, to decorate

1 Pour the whisky over ice cubes in a glass. Fill with ginger ale or soda water and stir gently. Decorate with lemon and lime slices.

Serves 1
Preparation time: 2 minutes

brandy flip

The Flip, which originated in the United States, is a combination of spirit, whole egg and sugar shaken vigorously with ice and then strained. It can be made with many spirits instead of the brandy given here – port, sherry and Marsala are also popular.

1½–2 measures brandy
1 egg
1 teaspoon icing sugar
2 teaspoons double cream (optional)
ice
chocolate curls, to decorate

1 Shake the brandy, egg, sugar and cream, if using, vigorously with ice, then strain into a chilled glass. Sprinkle the top with a few chocolate curls.

Serves 1
Preparation time: 5 minutes

americano

2 measures sweet vermouth
1 measure Campari
ice cubes
soda water, to taste
strip of lemon rind, to decorate

1 Combine the vermouth and Campari in a glass. Add several ice cubes and top up with soda water. Twist the lemon rind over the glass to decorate.

Serves 1
Preparation time: 2 minutes

moscow mule

1½ measures vodka
1 tablespoon lime juice
ice cubes
ginger beer, to taste
lime wedge, to decorate

1 Combine the vodka and lime juice in a tall glass. Add several ice cubes and ginger beer to taste and decorate with a lime wedge.

Serves 1
Preparation time: 2 minutes

white lady

½ measure lemon juice
½ measure Cointreau
1 measure gin
ice cubes
orange slice, to decorate

1 Put the lemon juice, Cointreau and gin in a cocktail shaker with several ice cubes and shake well. Strain into a cocktail glass. Add more ice cubes, if liked, and decorate with an orange slice.

Serves 1
Preparation time: 2 minutes

gin fix

crushed ice
1 tablespoon sugar
1 tablespoon lemon juice
1 measure water
2 measures gin
seasonal fruits, to decorate

1 Two-thirds fill a tall tumbler with crushed ice. Add all the remaining ingredients and stir well.

2 Decorate the rim of the glass with slices of any fruits in season.

Serves 1
Preparation time: 2 minutes

gin sling

1 teaspoon sugar
2 measures gin
ice cubes
mineral or soda water, to taste

1 Dissolve the sugar in a little water in a tall tumbler. Add the gin and several ice cubes.

2 Top up with mineral water or soda water to taste and serve with straws.

Serves 1
Preparation time: 2 minutes

silver fizz

2 measures gin
2 tablespoons lemon juice
1 teaspoon icing sugar
1 egg white
ice cubes
soda water, to taste
orange or lemon slices, to decorate

1 Put the gin, lemon juice, sugar and egg white into a cocktail shaker with ice and shake well, then strain into a glass. Add fresh ice cubes, top up with soda water and stir. Decorate with orange or lemon slices.

Serves 1
Preparation time: 3 minutes

new orleans fizz

2 measures gin
1½ measures double cream
1 tablespoon egg white
1 tablespoon lemon juice
1 tablespoon caster sugar
3 dashes of orange flower water
crushed ice
2 measures soda water
fresh fruit, to decorate

1 Combine the gin, cream, egg white, lemon juice, sugar and orange flower water in a blender with some crushed ice. Blend for about 10 seconds.

2 Add the soda water and blend again, then strain into a tall glass. Decorate with fresh fruit.

Serves 1
Preparation time: 5 minutes

singapore sling

1 teaspoon icing sugar or grenadine
2 tablespoons lemon juice
1½–2 measures gin
ice cubes
soda water, to taste
½ measure cherry brandy
fruits in season, to decorate

1 If using icing sugar, combine it with the lemon juice in a glass and stir until the sugar has dissolved. Stir in the gin and grenadine, if using.

2 Add small ice cubes or crushed ice and fill the glass with soda water. Float the cherry brandy on top and decorate with fresh fruits.

Serves 1
Preparation time: 5 minutes

cuba libre

½ lime
2 measures light rum
ice cubes
Coca-Cola, to taste

To decorate:
1 lime wedge
cocktail cherries

1 Squeeze the juice from the lime into a glass, then drop in a piece of the lime. Add the rum and ice cubes and top up with Coca-Cola. Stir gently to mix. Decorate with a lime wedge and cherries.

Serves 1
Preparation time: 3 minutes

manhattan

The Manhattan is thought to have been created around the turn of the century in New York City. Originally the sweet cocktail did not contain bitters.

2 measures Canadian whisky
1 measure sweet red vermouth
dash of bitters
ice
2 cocktail cherries, to decorate

1 Combine the whisky, vermouth and bitters in a mixing glass with ice and stir to mix. Strain into a cocktail glass and decorate with 2 cherries over the edge of the glass.

Serves 1
Preparation time: 3 minutes

old fashioned

1 small sugar lump
dash of bitters
1 teaspoon water
2 measures Canadian whisky or bourbon whiskey
ice cubes

To decorate:
strip of lemon rind
1 cocktail cherry
1 orange, lemon or lime slice

1 Combine the sugar, bitters and water in a glass and crush to mix.

2 Pour in the whisky and stir, then add several ice cubes. Decorate with lemon rind, a cocktail cherry and a citrus fruit slice.

Serves 1
Preparation time: 3 minutes

pink lady

1½–2 measures gin
1 egg white
1 teaspoon grenadine
1 teaspoon double cream
ice cubes
1 halved strawberry, to decorate

1 Put the gin, egg white, grenadine and cream in a cocktail shaker with ice cubes and shake vigorously.

2 Strain into a glass and decorate with a halved strawberry on a cocktail stick.

Serves 1
Preparation time: 3 minutes

martini

1 measure gin
1 measure dry vermouth
ice cubes
stuffed olive or lemon rind, to decorate

1 Put the gin and vermouth into a mixing glass with ice and stir well then strain into a cocktail glass. Decorate with a stuffed olive or a twist of lemon rind.

Serves 1
Preparation time: 2 minutes

dry martini

2 measures gin
½ measure dry vermouth
ice cubes
green olive or lemon rind, to decorate

1 Put the gin and vermouth into a mixing glass with ice and stir well then strain into a chilled cocktail glass. Decorate with a green olive or a twist of lemon rind.

Serves 1
Preparation time: 3 minutes

sweet martini

2 measures gin
1 measure sweet vermouth
ice cubes

1 Put the gin and vermouth into a cocktail shaker with several ice cubes and shake well. Strain into a cocktail glass.

Serves 1
Preparation time: 2 minutes

gimlet

2 measures gin
1 measure unsweetened lime cordial
ice cubes
1 lime slice, to decorate

1 Put the gin and lime cordial into a cocktail shaker with ice and shake to mix. Strain into a glass and decorate with a lime slice.

Serves 1
Preparation time: 2 minutes

brave bull

1½ measures tequila
1½ measures Kahlua or Tia Maria
ice
strip of lemon rind, to decorate

1 Put the tequila and Kahlua or Tia Maria into a mixing glass with ice and stir to mix. Strain into a glass, add fresh ice and decorate with a twist of lemon rind.

Serves 1
Preparation time: 3 minutes

rusty nail

2 measures Drambuie
1 measure Scotch whisky
ice cubes

1 Pour the Drambuie and whisky into a glass over ice cubes and stir gently to mix.

Serves 1
Preparation time: 2 minutes

whisky sour

The classic Sour cocktail was originally made with brandy when it was first introduced in the 1860s. The substitution of whisky for brandy was made some 30 years later, and the Whisky Sour quickly became a great hit so much so that a special-shaped glass was named for the cocktail.

2 measures Canadian or Scotch whisky
2 tablespoons lemon juice
½–1 teaspoon icing sugar
ice

To decorate:
1 cocktail cherry
1 orange or lemon slice

1 Combine the whisky, lemon juice and sugar in a cocktail shaker with ice and shake to mix. Strain into a chilled glass and decorate with a cherry and an orange or lemon slice.

Serves 1
Preparation time: 3 minutes

stinger

1½ measures brandy
½ measure white crème de menthe
ice cubes
mint sprig, to decorate

1 Put the brandy and crème de menthe into a cocktail shaker with ice and shake to mix. Strain into a glass and decorate with mint.

Serves 1
Preparation time: 2 minutes

sidecar

The Sidecar is thought to have made its first appearance in Paris during World War I, and was once very popular.

2 measures brandy
1 measure Curaçao
½ measure lemon juice
ice
lemon and lime twists, to decorate

1 Put the brandy, Curaçao and lemon juice into a cocktail shaker with ice and shake to mix. Strain into a glass and decorate with lemon and lime twists.

Serves 1
Preparation time: 2 minutes

depth bomb

This cocktail is also sometimes called a Depth Charge.

1½ measures brandy
1½ measures Calvados
2 dashes of lemon juice
dash of grenadine
ice cubes
fresh apple, to decorate

1 Put the brandy, Calvados, lemon juice and grenadine into a cocktail shaker with ice and shake well. Strain into a glass over ice cubes. Cut a piece of apple into 'chevron' shape and fix it on to the rim of the glass.

Serves 1
Preparation time: 5 minutes

crusta

½ lemon
caster sugar
2 measures brandy
½ measure Curaçao

1 teaspoon maraschino liqueur or grenadine
1 teaspoon lemon juice
1–2 dashes of bitters
ice cubes

1 Rub the rim of a glass with the cut side of the lemon half to moisten it, then dip in sugar to coat the rim evenly.

2 Thinly pare the rind from the lemon half in a spiral and place in the glass. Put the brandy, Curaçao, maraschino, lemon juice and bitters into a cocktail shaker with ice and shake to mix. Strain into the glass.

Serves 1
Preparation time: 5 minutes

adonis

2 measures dry sherry
1 measure sweet red vermouth
1–2 dashes of bitters
ice cubes
orange and nectarine slices, to decorate

1 Put the sherry, vermouth and bitters into a mixing glass with ice and stir to mix. Strain into a glass and decorate with slices of orange and nectarine.

Serves 1
Preparation time: 2 minutes

daiquiri

1 tablespoon lemon or lime juice
2 measures light rum
1 teaspoon caster sugar
ice cubes
cocktail cherry, to decorate

1 Put the lemon or lime juice, rum and caster sugar into a cocktail shaker with some ice cubes and shake well.

2 Strain into a chilled cocktail glass and decorate with a cocktail cherry.

Serves 1
Preparation time: 2 minutes

salted almonds   p584

fruity iced tea   p583

briks   p592

grape punch   p566

raw vegetables with yellow bean sauce   p588

russian iced tea   p581

marinated olives   p585

thai egg strips   p589

little devil

½ measure lemon juice
½ measure Cointreau
1 measure dark rum
1 measure gin
ice cubes

1 Put the lemon juice, Cointreau, rum and gin into a cocktail shaker with some ice cubes and shake well. Strain into a cocktail glass.

Serves 1
Preparation time: 2 minutes

parisian blonde

1 measure double cream
pinch of caster sugar
1 measure Curaçao
1 measure dark rum
ice
orange slices, to decorate

1 Put the cream, caster sugar, Curaçao and rum into a cocktail shaker with some ice and shake well. Strain into a cocktail glass and decorate with orange slices.

Serves 1
Preparation time: 2 minutes

screwdriver

2 measures vodka
ice cubes
orange juice
orange slices, to decorate

1 Pour the vodka over ice cubes in a tumbler and top up with orange juice, to taste.

2 Stir well and decorate with orange slices.

Serves 1
Preparation time: 2 minutes

black russian

2 measures vodka
1 measure Kahlua or Tia Maria
ice cubes

1 Pour the vodka and Kahlua or Tia Maria into a glass over ice cubes and stir gently to mix.

Serves 1
Preparation time: 2 minutes

margarita

lime or lemon rind
1 tablespoon salt
1½ measures tequila
½ measure Curaçao
1 measure lime or lemon juice
ice

1 Rub the rim of a glass with lime or lemon rind, then dip into salt to coat the rim. Put the tequila, Curaçao and lime or lemon juice in a cocktail shaker with ice and shake to mix. Strain into the salt-rimmed glass.

Serves 1
Preparation time: 5 minutes

zombie

The Zombie is very strong, as it contains the highest percentage of alcohol of all cocktails.

2 measures light rum
½ measure dark rum
½ measure apricot brandy
1 measure unsweetened pineapple juice
1 measure passion fruit juice
2 tablespoons lime juice
3 tablespoons orange juice
1 teaspoon icing sugar
crushed ice
151-proof rum (optional)

To decorate:
1 fresh pineapple wedge
½ orange slice
1 cocktail cherry

1 Combine the light and dark rums, apricot brandy, fruit juices and sugar in a blender with 4–5 crushed ice cubes.

2 Blend at low speed for 1 minute, then strain into a glass. Carefully float a little 151-proof rum on top, if using. Decorate with the pineapple, orange and cherry.

Serves 1
Preparation time: 5 minutes

mai tai

2 measures dark rum
½ measure Curaçao
½ measure apricot brandy
1 tablespoon lime juice
1 teaspoon grenadine
crushed ice

To decorate:
1 fresh pineapple wedge
1 cocktail cherry

1 Put the rum, Curaçao, brandy, lime juice and grenadine in a cocktail shaker with some ice and shake to mix. Strain into a glass over fresh crushed ice and decorate with the pineapple and cherry.

Serves 1
Preparation time: 5 minutes

mint julep

This is a traditional drink from the southern states of the USA, where it was originally a non-alcoholic minted fruit drink.

1 teaspoon icing sugar
a few drops of cold water
6–8 fresh mint sprigs
shaved or crushed ice
2½–3 measures bourbon whiskey

1 Combine the sugar, water and 4–5 mint sprigs in a glass and crush gently to release the flavour from the mint and dissolve the sugar.

2 Fill the glass with shaved or crushed ice and add the bourbon. Stir gently to mix, then garnish with the remaining mint sprigs.

Serves 1
Preparation time: 5 minutes

sloe 'n' comfortable

¾ measure sloe gin
¾ measure Southern Comfort
3 measures orange juice
ice cubes
1 cocktail cherry, to decorate

1 Combine the sloe gin, Southern Comfort and orange juice in a glass.

2 Add some ice and stir to mix. Decorate with a cherry.

Serves 1
Preparation time: 2 minutes

bullshot

This is supposed to be a good hangover cure. As a variation, you can serve it hot.

1½ measures vodka
4 measures beef consommé
dash of Worcestershire sauce
ice
salt and pepper

1 Put the vodka and beef consommé into a cocktail shaker with a dash of Worcestershire sauce. Add some ice, season with salt and pepper and shake to mix. Strain into a glass and serve.

Serves 1
Preparation time: 4 minutes

angel face

1 measure gin
1 measure apricot brandy
1 measure Calvados
ice

1 Put the gin, apricot brandy and Calvados into a cocktail shaker with ice and shake well. Strain into a cocktail glass.

Serves 1
Preparation time: 2 minutes

corpse reviver

½ measure sweet vermouth
½ measure Calvados
1 measure brandy
ice

1 Put the sweet vermouth, Calvados and brandy into a cocktail shaker with some ice and shake well. Strain into a cocktail glass.

Serves 1
Preparation time: 2 minutes

sicilian kiss

2 measures Southern Comfort
1 measure Amaretto de Saronno
crushed ice
lemon slice, to decorate

1 Combine the Southern Comfort and Amaretto de Saronno in a tumbler with plenty of crushed ice and stir to mix. Decorate with a slice of lemon.

Serves 1
Preparation time: 2 minutes

blue hawaiian

2 measures light rum
½ measure blue Curaçao
½ measure Curaçao
¾ measure double cream
1 teaspoon cream of coconut
ice

1 Put the rum, blue Curaçao, Curaçao, double cream and cream of coconut into a cocktail shaker with some ice and shake thoroughly to mix. Strain into a glass.

Serves 1
Preparation time: 3 minutes

golden cadillac

1 measure Galliano
1–2 measures white crème de cacao
1 measure double cream

1 Combine the Galliano, crème de cacao and double cream in a blender and blend at low speed for 10 seconds. Pour into a chilled glass.

Serves 1
Preparation time: 2 minutes

grasshopper

1 measure white crème de menthe
1 measure green crème de menthe
1 measure double cream
ice

1 Put the two crème de menthes into a cocktail shaker, add the double cream and some ice and shake to mix thoroughly. Strain into a glass.

Serves 1
Preparation time: 2 minutes

brandy alexander

1 measure brandy
1 measure white crème de cacao
1 measure double cream
ice cubes
grated nutmeg

1 Put the brandy, crème de cacao and cream in a cocktail shaker with some ice cubes and shake vigorously. Strain into a chilled cocktail glass and sprinkle with a pinch of nutmeg.

Serves 1
Preparation time: 2 minutes

heartwarmer

200 ml/7 fl oz red grape juice
250 g/8 oz brown sugar
350 ml/12 fl oz dark rum
1.5 litres/2½ pints dry white wine
450 ml/¾ pint red wine

1 Put the grape juice into a saucepan, add the sugar and stir over a gentle heat until the sugar has completely dissolved. Stir in the dark rum and set aside.

2 Pour the white wine and red wine into a large saucepan and heat until hot but not boiling. Add the rum and grape juice mixture and stir together. Serve hot.

Serves 12
Preparation time: 5 minutes
Cooking time: 10 minutes

spiced mulled wine

1 bottle red wine
¼ bottle port
600 ml/1 pint boiling water
brown or white sugar, to taste
pinch of ground nutmeg
1 cinnamon stick
pared orange rind

1 Heat the red wine and port in a saucepan until almost boiling. Add the boiling water.

2 Stir in the sugar and nutmeg, pour into a large bowl and add a cinnamon stick and some pared orange rind. Serve warm.

Serves 10
Preparation time: 5 minutes
Cooking time: 5 minutes

mulled ale

Mulls were traditionally mixed at the fireside and heated by plunging a red-hot poker into the pan.

1.2 litres/2 pints brown ale
150 ml/¼ pint rum or brandy
3 tablespoons brown sugar
6 cloves
1 teaspoon ground ginger
pinch of ground nutmeg
pinch of ground cinnamon
thinly pared rind and juice of 1 lemon
thinly pared rind and juice of 1 orange
600 ml/1 pint water
orange slices, to decorate

1 Put all the ingredients into a large saucepan. Bring the mixture slowly to the boil, stirring all the time to dissolve the sugar. Turn off the heat and leave to stand for a few minutes.

2 To serve, strain into a warmed jug and float orange slices on top.

Serves 12
Preparation time: 10 minutes, plus standing
Cooking time: 10 minutes

irish coffee

Many other liqueurs and spirits can be substituted for Irish whiskey in this popular after-dinner drink. Cointreau or Grand Marnier, brandy and Tia Maria are excellent.

1–2 teaspoons caster sugar
5 measures strong hot black coffee
1½ measures Irish whiskey
whipped or double cream

1 Combine the sugar and coffee in a heatproof glass and stir to dissolve the sugar.

2 Add the whisky, and top with whipped or double cream. If using double cream, pour it slowly on to the coffee over the back of a spoon so that it will float on the surface.

Serves 1
Preparation time: 5 minutes

hot toddy

1 sugar cube
4–6 measures boiling water
2 measures whisky

To decorate:
1 lemon slice
1 cinnamon stick

1 Place the sugar cube and boiling water in a mug or heatproof glass and stir to dissolve the sugar. Add the whisky and stir to mix. Decorate with a lemon slice and a stick of cinnamon, for stirring.

Serves 1
Preparation time: 2 minutes

brandy blazer

1 sugar cube
strip of orange rind
strip of lemon rind
2–3 measures brandy

1 Combine the sugar with orange and lemon rinds in a heatproof glass and crush to mix. Add the brandy and stir. Set alight and serve flaming.

Serves 1
Preparation time: 2 minutes

temperance mocktail

2 measures lemon juice
2 dashes grenadine
1 egg yolk
ice
1 cocktail cherry, to decorate

1 Shake the ingredients well with ice and strain into a cocktail glass. Decorate with a cocktail cherry.

Serves 1
Preparation time: 2 minutes

cool passion

500 ml/17 fl oz orange and passionfruit juice
1 litre/1¾ pints pineapple juice
1.5 litres/2½ pints lemonade
crushed ice

1 Pour the fruit juices into a large jug and stir well to mix. Just before serving, stir in the lemonade. Pour into glasses containing a little crushed ice.

Serves 20
Preparation time: 2 minutes

russian iced tea

375 g/12 oz granulated sugar
250 ml/8 fl oz water
1 bunch of mint leaves
250 ml/8 fl oz lemon juice
900 ml/1½ pints prepared Indian tea, cooled
crushed ice

To decorate:
lemon slices
mint sprigs

1 Dissolve the sugar in the water, then bring to the boil and boil for 10 minutes to make a syrup. Add the mint and leave to steep for about 2 hours. Strain through a sieve into a jug, then stir in the lemon juice and tea.

2 To serve, divide the tea among 10 glasses and top with crushed ice. Decorate with lemon slices and mint sprigs.

Serves 10
Preparation time: 10 minutes, plus steeping
Cooking time: 15 minutes

appleade

2 large dessert apples
600 ml/1 pint boiling water
½ teaspoon sugar
ice cubes
apple slices, to decorate

1 Chop the apples and place in a bowl. Pour the boiling water over the apples and add the sugar. Leave to stand for 10 minutes, then strain into a jug and allow to cool. Pour over ice cubes in tall tumblers and decorate with apple slices. Serve with straws.

Serves 3
Preparation time: 5 minutes, plus standing

san francisco

1 measure orange juice
1 measure lemon juice
1 measure pineapple juice
1 measure grapefruit juice
2 dashes grenadine
1 egg white
ice cubes
soda water, to taste
fruit slices, to decorate

1 Shake the fruit juices, grenadine and egg white together well with ice and strain into a wine glass. Top up with soda water and decorate with fruit slices speared on to a cocktail stick. Serve with a straw.

Serves 1
Preparation time: 4 minutes

carib cream

1 small banana, chopped
1 measure lemon juice
1 measure milk
crushed ice
1 teaspoon finely chopped walnuts

1 Place the banana, lemon juice and milk in a blender with some crushed ice and blend on maximum speed until smooth. Pour into a cocktail glass and sprinkle the chopped walnuts on top just before serving.

Serves 1
Preparation time: 2 minutes

tenderberry

6–8 strawberries, plus extra to decorate
1 measure grenadine
1 measure double cream
1 measure dry ginger ale
pinch of ground ginger

1 Place the strawberries, grenadine and cream in a blender with some crushed ice and blend on maximum speed for 30 seconds. Pour into a tumbler. Add the dry ginger ale and stir. Sprinkle a little ground ginger on top and decorate with a strawberry.

Serves 1
Preparation time: 2 minutes

café astoria

1½ measures coffee extract
2 measures milk
¼ measure pineapple juice
¼ measure lemon juice
chocolate sugar strands, to decorate

1 Place the ingredients in a blender with some crushed ice and blend on maximum speed for about 30 seconds. Pour into a cocktail glass and sprinkle sugar strands on top just before serving.

Serves 1
Preparation time: 2 minutes

fruity iced tea

600 ml/1 pint strong prepared Indian tea
175 g/6 oz caster sugar
4 tablespoons lemon juice
300 ml/½ pint orange juice
ice cubes
75 g/3 oz strawberries, hulled and sliced
½ a lemon, sliced
½ an orange, sliced
mint sprigs, to decorate

1 Stir the tea and sugar together in a jug until the sugar has dissolved. Add the lemon and orange juices. Cover and chill for 1 hour.

2 Pour into a punch bowl and add the ice cubes and sliced fruit. Decorate with mint sprigs and serve.

Serves 4
Preparation time: 10 minutes, plus chilling

middle eastern cinnamon tea

1 tablespoon aniseed
1 teaspoon ground cinnamon
900 ml/1½ pints water
sugar, to taste
chopped almonds and walnuts, to decorate

1 Put the aniseed and cinnamon into a saucepan with the water. Bring to the boil and boil for 3 minutes.

2 Pour into teacups and add sugar to taste. Sprinkle with chopped nuts and serve immediately.

Serves 4
Preparation time: 10 minutes
Cooking time: 5 minutes

quick curried nuts

These deliciously spicy nuts are wonderful served almost straight from the oven, whilst still warm.

40 g/1½ oz butter or sunflower oil
1 tablespoon curry powder
500 g/1 lb mixed skinned nuts, such as almonds, brazils, walnuts, pecans and hazelnuts
1 teaspoon salt

1 Melt the butter in a roasting tin and stir in the curry powder. Cook, stirring, for 30 seconds. Add the nuts and stir until well coated.

2 Roast in a preheated oven, 150°C (300°F), Gas Mark 2 for 30 minutes, stirring from time to time.

3 Remove the nuts from the oven and toss with the salt. Allow to cool completely. These nuts can be stored in an airtight container for up to 2 weeks.

Serves 15
Preparation time: 5 minutes, plus cooling
Cooking time: about 30 minutes
Oven temperature: 150°C (300°F), Gas Mark 2

spicy glazed cashews

25 g/1 oz unsalted butter
3 tablespoons clear honey
1 teaspoon salt
¼ teaspoon cayenne pepper
1 tablespoon water
250 g/8 oz cashew nuts

1 Melt the butter in a small, heavy-based frying pan and then stir in the honey, salt, cayenne and water. Bring to the boil.

2 Add the cashew nuts and stir over a medium heat for 5 minutes until the nuts are toasted and well coated with the glaze. Tip out on to a greased baking sheet and leave to cool. These nuts are best eaten the same day.

Serves 8
Preparation time: 3 minutes
Cooking time: 6–7 minutes

salted almonds

6 tablespoons olive oil
250 g/8 oz blanched almonds
sea salt

1 Heat the oil in a small, heavy-based frying pan, add the nuts in several batches and stir-fry over a medium heat until evenly browned.

2 Using a slotted spoon, transfer the nuts to a bowl. Add plenty of sea salt and stir to coat the nuts. These nuts can be kept in an airtight container for up to 3 days.

Serves 8
Preparation time: 3 minutes
Cooking time: 6–7 minutes

spiced chickpeas

400 g/13 oz can chickpeas, drained and rinsed
2 tablespoons olive oil
2 plump garlic cloves, crushed
paprika and ground cumin, for sprinkling
salt and pepper

1 Spread the chickpeas on a baking sheet. Mix the oil with the garlic and pour over the chickpeas, stirring everything together.

2 Transfer the baking sheet to a preheated oven, 200°C (400°F), Gas Mark 6, and cook the chickpeas for about 15 minutes, stirring them occasionally so that they cook evenly.

3 Tip the chickpeas on to kitchen paper to dry them, then toss while still warm with paprika, cumin and salt and pepper. Eat while warm or store in an airtight jar in a cool place for up to 2 weeks.

Serves 2–4
Preparation time: 5 minutes
Cooking time: 15 minutes
Oven temperature: 200°C (400°F), Gas Mark 6

spicy palmiers

250 g/8 oz puff pastry
2 tablespoons olive oil
½ teaspoon paprika
pinch of cayenne pepper
3 tablespoons grated Parmesan cheese

1 Roll out the puff pastry thinly on a lightly floured surface and trim to make a rectangle roughly 20 x 25 cm/8 x 10 inches.

2 Combine the oil, paprika, cayenne and Parmesan and brush three-quarters of the paste all over the pastry to give an even coating.

3 Fold over both long sides of pastry in to meet in the middle, spread over a layer of the remaining paste and fold the pastry in half lengthways. Press down firmly.

4 Using a sharp knife, cut the pastry into 24 thin slices and transfer, cut side down, to 2 greased baking sheets.

5 Bake the pastries in a preheated oven, 200°C (400°F), Gas Mark 6, for 10 minutes, then turn them over and bake for a further 4–5 minutes until they are crisp and golden. Cool on a wire rack. These pastries are best eaten the same day.

Makes 24
Preparation time: 10 minutes
Cooking time: 15 minutes
Oven temperature: 200°C (400°F), Gas Mark 6

parmesan curls

500 g/1 lb puff pastry
2 tablespoons coarse grain mustard
50 g/2 oz Parmesan, grated
1 tablespoon poppy seeds
1 tablespoon sesame seeds

1 Roll out the pastry on a lightly floured work surface and trim to make a rectangle 30 x 35 cm/12 x 14 inches. Spread with the mustard and sprinkle with the cheese. Fold in half and roll lightly.

2 Cut the pastry into about 20 long, thin strips. Sprinkle half with poppy seeds and the other half with sesame seeds. Twist the strips into loose spirals and arrange them on baking sheets. Bake in a preheated oven, 230°C (450°F), Gas Mark 8, for 15 minutes or until puffy and golden.

Makes about 20
Preparation time: 15 minutes
Cooking time: 15 minutes
Oven temperature: 230°C (450°F), Gas Mark 8

marinated olives

250 g/8 oz large green olives
2 garlic cloves, sliced
grated rind of ½ lemon
1 tablespoon balsamic vinegar
½ teaspoon chilli flakes
4 tablespoons extra virgin olive oil

1 Place the olives in a bowl, add all the remaining ingredients and stir well. If you are not serving the olives immediately, they may be kept, covered, in the refrigerator for up to 3 days.

Serves: 8
Preparation time: 5 minutes

olives marinated with asian flavours

250 g/8 oz mixed green and black olives
1 garlic clove, crushed
1 teaspoon grated ginger
2 lime leaves, shredded, or grated rind of 1 lime
2 red chillies, bruised
2 tablespoons dark soy sauce
extra virgin olive oil, to cover

1 Place all the ingredients in a bowl and stir well. If you are not serving the olives immediately, they may be kept, covered, in the refrigerator for up to 3 days.

Serves: 8
Preparation time: 5 minutes

root vegetable crisps

2 beetroots
1 large potato
1 small sweet potato
2 carrots
2 parsnips
vegetable oil, for deep-frying
cayenne pepper, for sprinkling
sea salt

1 Slice the vegetables into fine wafers using a potato peeler or mandoline, keeping them in separate batches. It is best to cut the carrots and parsnips lengthways.

2 Heat 5 cm/2 inches of vegetable oil in a deep saucepan until it reaches 180–190°C (350–375°F), or until a cube of bread browns in 30 seconds. Pat the vegetables dry with kitchen paper.

3 Again, keeping the vegetables separate, deep-fry them in batches for 30 seconds–1½ minutes, until crisp and golden. Drain on kitchen paper and leave to cool on a wire rack.

4 Transfer the crisps to a large bowl and sprinkle with sea salt and a little cayenne. Pass the crisps around in small bowls.

Serves 4
Preparation time: 15 minutes, plus cooling
Cooking time: 8–10 minutes

chive biscuits

125 g/4 oz butter
125 g/4 oz creamy soft cheese
125 g/4 oz plain flour, sifted
1 tablespoon chopped chives

1 Cream the butter and cheese together until well blended. Stir in the flour and chives and mix with a fork until well combined. Roll the dough into a ball and wrap in foil. Chill in the refrigerator for at least 1 hour.

2 Roll out the dough to 5 mm/¼ inch thick and cut into 4 cm/1½ inch rounds with a plain cutter.

3 Place well apart on greased baking sheets and bake in a preheated hot oven, 220°C (425°F), Gas Mark 7, for 10 minutes. Cool on a wire rack.

4 Serve the biscuits on their own or with dips, or use as a base for savoury spreads and canapés.

Makes about 60
Preparation time: 20 minutes, plus chilling
Cooking time: 10 minutes
Oven temperature: 220°C (425°F), Gas Mark 7

caraway crackers

Serve these savoury crackers as a nibble with an aperitif, or with cheese. Fennel seeds can be substituted for the caraway seeds, if liked.

125 g/4 oz plain flour
¼ teaspoon salt
½ teaspoon ground cumin
50 g/2 oz butter, diced
1–2 teaspoons caraway seeds
2–3 tablespoons water

1 Sift the plain flour, salt and cumin into a bowl. Rub in the butter until the mixture resembles fine breadcrumbs. Stir in the caraway seeds, to taste, and then gradually work in 2–3 tablespoons water to form a soft dough.

2 Knead lightly until smooth, cover with clingfilm and leave to rest for 30 minutes. Roll the dough out thinly on a lightly floured surface and, using a 7 cm/3 inch pastry cutter, stamp out rounds.

3 Re-roll the trimmings and repeat to make 16–18 rounds. Transfer the crackers to a large baking sheet, prick the surfaces with a fork and bake in a preheated oven, 190°C (375°F), Gas Mark 5, for 10 minutes. Turn the crackers over and bake for a further 5 minutes until crisp and lightly golden. Cool on a wire rack. These crackers will keep in an airtight container for up to 2 days.

Makes 16–18
Preparation time: 15–20 minutes, plus resting
Cooking time: 15 minutes
Oven temperature: 190°C (375°F), Gas Mark 5

taramasalata

75 g/3 oz fresh white bread
2 tablespoons milk
125 g/4 oz smoked cod's roe, skinned
1 large garlic clove, crushed
125 ml/4 fl oz olive oil
2 tablespoons lemon juice
Kalamata olives, to garnish
pitta bread, to serve

1 Trim the crusts from the bread and soak the bread slices in the milk for about 15 minutes. Remove the bread slices and squeeze them as dry as possible. Mash the bread with the smoked cod's roe and crushed garlic.

2 Put the mixture into a food processor or blender and gradually add the olive oil, a little at a time, blending well after each addition. Add the lemon juice and blend until smooth. Turn the taramasalata into a bowl, cover and chill in the refrigerator for at least 1 hour.

3 Garnish with olives and serve with warm pitta bread.

Serves 4
Preparation time: 25 minutes, plus chilling

hummus

This dip will keep for up to 1 week, covered, in the refrigerator.

250 g/8 oz chickpeas, soaked overnight
150 ml/¼ pint tahini
3 garlic cloves
6 tablespoons lemon juice
salt and pepper

To finish:
1 tablespoon olive oil blended with 1 teaspoon paprika
1 teaspoon chopped parsley

1 Drain the chickpeas, place in a pan and cover with cold water. Bring to the boil, cover and boil rapidly for 10 minutes, then simmer gently for 1½–2 hours, until soft; the time will vary with the age and quality of the chickpeas. Drain, reserving 300 ml/½ pint of the liquid.

2 Place the chickpeas in a food processor or blender and add the tahini, garlic, lemon juice and enough of the reserved liquid to blend to a soft creamy paste. Season to taste with salt and pepper,

3 Turn the hummus into a shallow serving dish, dribble over the blended oil and sprinkle with the parsley.

Serves 8–10
Preparation time: 20 minutes, plus soaking
Cooking time: 1¾ –2¼ hours

tzatsiki

500 g/1 lb Greek yogurt
1 cucumber, peeled and grated
3 garlic cloves, crushed
salt and pepper
1 tablespoon chopped mint, to garnish
pitta bread, to serve

1 Beat the yogurt with a fork until smooth. Drain the cucumber and place in a bowl. Add the yogurt with the garlic, and season to taste with salt and pepper.

2 Chill for 2 hours, then turn into a serving bowl and sprinkle with the mint. Serve with pitta bread.

Serves 6
Preparation time: 10 minutes, plus chilling

guacamole

2 large ripe avocados
3 tablespoons lemon or lime juice
2 garlic cloves, crushed
40 g/1½ oz spring onions, chopped
1–2 tablespoons chopped mild green chillies
2 tablespoons chopped coriander leaves
125 g/4 oz tomatoes, skinned, deseeded and chopped
salt and pepper
tortilla chips, to serve

1 Cut the avocados in half and remove the stones. Scoop the flesh into a mixing bowl, add the lemon or lime juice and mash coarsely.

2 Add the garlic, spring onions, chillies and coriander and season to taste with salt and pepper. Mix in the chopped tomatoes. Cover the bowl and place in the refrigerator for at least 1 hour. Serve the guacamole with tortilla chips, to dip.

Serves 6
Preparation time: 10 minutes, plus chilling

broad bean & mint dip

This very simple, fresh-tasting dip will undoubtedly be at its best if you use fresh young broad beans, but frozen ones will be quite acceptable.

500 g/1 lb shelled broad beans
leaves from 6–8 mint sprigs
3–4 tablespoons olive oil
2 tablespoons lemon juice
salt and pepper
crudités or bread, to serve
small mint sprigs, to garnish

1 Cook the broad beans in boiling salted water until tender. Drain, reserving the cooking liquid. Rinse the beans under running cold water.

2 Put the beans into a food processor or blender. Add the mint, olive oil and lemon juice and mix to a purée, adding enough of the reserved cooking liquid to give a soft consistency. Season to taste with salt and pepper and adjust the levels of lemon juice and oil, if necessary.

3 Transfer the dip to a small serving dish. Serve at room temperature with crudités or bread, garnished with small mint sprigs.

Serves 4
Preparation time: 10 minutes
Cooking time: 5–10 minutes

aubergine purée

2 aubergines
2 garlic cloves, sliced
½ teaspoon ground cumin
1 teaspoon paprika
about 50 ml/2 fl oz extra virgin olive oil,
*   plus extra to serve*
4 tablespoons lemon juice
salt and pepper
mint or coriander sprigs, to garnish

1 Cut slits in the aubergines and insert the garlic slices. Bake in a preheated oven, 220°C (425°F), Gas Mark 7, for 30–40 minutes until the skins are charred and blistered. Remove from the oven and leave to cool.

2 Cut the aubergines in half and scoop out the flesh and the garlic slices. Squeeze out and discard the juices. Put the aubergine flesh, garlic, cumin and paprika into a food processor and mix to a purée. With the motor running, slowly pour in the olive oil to give the consistency of a soft dip. Add the lemon juice and salt and pepper to taste.

3 Transfer the purée to a bowl. Just before serving, dribble over some olive oil and garnish with mint or coriander sprigs.

Serves 4
Preparation time: 15 minutes
Cooking time: 30–40 minutes
Oven temperature: 220°C (425°F), Gas Mark 7

walnut dip

125 g/4 oz walnut pieces
1 garlic clove
1 tablespoon olive oil
1 teaspoon lemon juice
250 g/8 oz natural yogurt
¼ cucumber, peeled
salt and pepper
crisp fresh vegetables, or biscuits, to serve

1 Put the walnut pieces, garlic, oil and lemon juice in a food processor or blender and purée until smooth.

2 Add the yogurt and blend in quickly. Season to taste with salt and pepper.

3 Transfer the dip to a serving bowl. Chop the cucumber finely and stir it in. Serve chilled, with crisp fresh vegetables or biscuits.

Serves 10
Preparation time: 15 minutes

avocado and cheese dip

2 avocados, peeled and stoned
1 tablespoon lemon juice
2 tomatoes, skinned, deseeded and chopped
2 garlic cloves, crushed
½ onion, grated
625 g/1¼ lb creamy soft cheese
salt and pepper
crisps or biscuits, to serve

1 Mash the avocado flesh with the lemon juice. Beat in the remaining ingredients, with salt and pepper to taste.

Serves 6
Preparation time: 10 minutes

raw vegetables with yellow bean sauce

Good vegetables to choose for this dish are peeled broccoli stalks, carrot, cucumber and courgette sticks, green beans, Chinese leaves, cauliflower florets and strips of red and yellow pepper.

500 g/1 lb vegetables of your choice
1 large red chilli, sliced lengthways, to decorate

Yellow bean sauce:
125 ml/4 fl oz yellow bean sauce
½ onion, chopped
1 tablespoon tamarind water
200 ml/7 fl oz coconut milk
200 ml/7 fl oz water
2 eggs
3 tablespoons sugar
1 tablespoon soy sauce

1 Chop the raw vegetables into bite-sized pieces.

2 To make the sauce, blend the yellow bean sauce and the onion in a food processor or blender and transfer to a saucepan. Add the remaining sauce ingredients and bring gradually to the boil, stirring. Remove from the heat and pour into a bowl.

3 Decorate the sauce with the sliced chilli and serve warm, with the vegetables.

Preparation time: 15 minutes
Cooking time: 5–6 minutes

thai egg strips

3 eggs, beaten
1 shallot, finely sliced
green shoots of 1 spring onion, sliced
1–2 small red chillies, finely chopped
1 tablespoon chopped coriander leaves
1 tablespoon groundnut oil
salt and pepper
spring onion strips, to garnish (optional)

1 Mix all the ingredients, except the oil and garnish, in a bowl.

2 Heat the oil in a frying pan or wok, pour in the egg mixture and swirl it around the pan to produce a large thin omelette. Cook for 1–2 minutes until firm.

3 Slide the omelette out on to a plate and roll it up as though it were a pancake. Allow to cool.

4 When the omelette is cool, cut the roll crossways into 5 mm–1 cm/¼–½ inch sections. Serve the egg strips still rolled up or straightened out, in a mound. Decorate with strips of spring onion, if liked.

Serves 4
Preparation time: 5 minutes
Cooking time: 2–3 minutes

falafel

These savoury patties are a traditional Middle Eastern snack. The mixture is quite wet and crumbly when you come to shape them, but this ensures a perfect, light texture once fried.

125 g/4 oz dried broad beans, soaked overnight in
*   cold water*
2 tablespoons Greek yogurt, plus extra to serve
1 tablespoon tahini
1 tablespoon lemon juice
1 garlic clove, crushed
1 teaspoon ground coriander
½ teaspoon ground cumin
½ teaspoon cayenne pepper
1 tablespoon chopped coriander leaves
1 tablespoon chopped mint
salt and pepper
vegetable oil, for shallow-frying

1 Drain the broad beans and dry thoroughly. Place in a food processor and blend to form a fairly smooth paste. Transfer the puréed beans to a bowl. Stir in all the remaining ingredients, season with salt and pepper then cover and chill for 1 hour.

2 Form the mixture into small patties. Heat a shallow layer of oil in a nonstick frying pan and fry the patties, a few at a time, for 1–2 minutes on each side until golden. Serve with Greek yogurt.

Makes about 12
Preparation time: 10 minutes, plus soaking and chilling
Cooking time: 6–12 minutes

griddled sweet potato chips

750 g/1½ lb sweet potatoes, peeled
sea salt and pepper

Dip:
150 g/5 oz Greek yogurt
1 shallot, finely diced
1 cool red chilli, deseeded and finely diced
1 handful of coriander sprigs, chopped
a few drops of Tabasco sauce

1 Cut the sweet potato into slices 2.5 cm/1 inch wide, then cut the slices into 2.5 cm/1 inch chips. Heat a griddle pan or nonstick frying pan and add a single layer of chips, leaving a little space between each one. Cook for about 3 minutes on each side, 12 minutes in total. Remove from the griddle and keep warm. Repeat until all the sweet potato is cooked. Sprinkle the chips with sea salt and pepper and arrange on a large platter

2 To make the dip, mix the yogurt, shallot, chilli, coriander and Tabasco. Season to taste with salt and pepper and pour into a small bowl. Serve with the griddled sweet potato chips.

Serves 4
Preparation time: 15 minutes
Cooking time: about 25 minutes

fried wontons

30 square wonton wrappers
egg yolk, to seal
groundnut oil, for deep-frying
plum sauce, to serve

Filling:
3 tablespoons groundnut oil
2 garlic cloves, chopped
3 baby corns, very finely sliced
5 fresh shiitake mushrooms, finely chopped
25 g/1 oz green beans, very finely sliced
½ onion, finely chopped
1 egg
½ teaspoon sugar
1 tablespoon soy sauce
salt and pepper

1 First make the filling. Heat two-thirds of the oil in a wok, add the garlic and give it a stir, then add the corn, mushrooms, beans and onion and stir-fry for 1–2 minutes. Push the vegetables to one side of the wok, pour in the remaining oil and break the egg into it.

2 Break the yolk and stir it around for about 1 minute, gradually mixing in the vegetables, Add the sugar and soy sauce, season to taste with salt and pepper and mix well. Remove the pan from the heat and set the mixture aside in a bowl.

3 Put a spoonful of the filling in the centre of a wonton wrapper. Fold the wrapper over to make a triangle, then seal the edges with a little egg yolk. Repeat with the remaining wrappers and filling.

4 Heat the oil for deep-frying in a wok, pop in a batch of wontons and cook over a moderate heat for 3–4 minutes until golden brown on all sides. Remove from the oil with a slotted spoon and drain on kitchen paper. Repeat the frying process with the remaining wontons. Serve hot, with plum sauce for dipping.

Makes 30
Preparation time: 20 minutes
Cooking time: 25–30 minutes

crispy ricotta parcels

250 g/8 oz ricotta cheese
125 g/4 oz frozen spinach, thawed, chopped and
*   squeezed dry*
125 g/4 oz smoked ham, finely chopped
¼ teaspoon ground nutmeg
8 sheets of filo pastry
75 g/3 oz butter, melted
pepper

1 Place the ricotta in a bowl with the spinach, ham and nutmeg and add pepper to taste. Mix well.

2 Put the sheets of filo pastry on a plate and cover with a damp tea towel. Working with 1 sheet of pastry at a time, cut it into 3 equal strips and brush well with butter. Place a teaspoon of the cheese mixture at one end of each strip. Fold one corner of the pastry diagonally over to enclose the filling in a triangle of pastry and continue folding to make a neat triangular parcel.

3 Brush the parcel with more butter and place on a baking sheet. Repeat with the remaining filling, pastry and butter, to make 24 small parcels.

4 Bake the parcels in a preheated oven, 220°C (425°F), Gas Mark 7, for 8–10 minutes until golden brown. Serve hot.

Makes 24
Preparation time: 30 minutes
Cooking time: 8–10 minutes
Oven temperature: 220°C (425°F), Gas Mark 7

pakoras

These spicy nibbles, from northern India, can be served as a starter or with drinks. Discard the seeds from the chillies for a less spicy version.

125 g/4 oz gram or chickpea flour
1 teaspoon salt
½ teaspoon chilli powder
about 150 ml/¼ pint water or yogurt
2 green chillies, finely chopped
1 tablespoon finely chopped coriander leaves
1 teaspoon melted butter or ghee
2 onions, cut into rings
8 small fresh spinach leaves
2–3 potatoes, parboiled and sliced
oil, for deep-frying
chilli sauce, to serve (optional)

1 Sift the flour, salt and chilli powder into a bowl. Stir in sufficient water or yogurt to make a thick batter and beat well until smooth. Cover the bowl and leave to stand for 30 minutes.

2 Stir the chillies and coriander into the batter, then add the melted butter or ghee. Drop in the onion rings to coat thickly with batter.

3 Heat the oil in a deep pan to 180–190°C (350–375°F) or until a cube of bread browns in 30 seconds. Add the onion rings and deep-fry until crisp and golden. Remove from the pan with a slotted spoon, drain on kitchen paper and keep warm.

4 Dip the spinach leaves into the batter and deep-fry in the same way, adding more oil to the pan if necessary.

5 Finally, repeat the process with the potato slices. Serve hot, with chilli sauce, if liked.

Serves 4
Preparation time: 15–20 minutes, plus standing
Cooking time: about 25 minutes

walnut and gorgonzola chicory

2 chicory heads
125 g/4 oz Gorgonzola cheese, cubed
50 g/2 oz walnuts, roughly chopped
4 tablespoons crème fraîche
flat leaf parsley, to garnish

1 Remove the leaves from the chicory stalks, discarding any blemished leaves. Stir together the cheese, walnuts and crème fraîche.

2 Spoon the cheese mixture on to the chicory leaves, dividing it between them. Arrange on a serving platter and garnish with flat leaf parsley.

Serves 8–10
Preparation time: 15 minutes

polenta triangle sandwiches

These are triangles of set polenta, sandwiched together with mozzarella cheese. They are then coated in breadcrumbs and deep-fried. The mozzarella melts and starts to ooze as it cooks, making a rich and delicious morsel.

900 ml/1½ pints water
15 g/½ oz butter
½ teaspoon sea salt
75 g/3 oz quick-cooking polenta
15 g/½ oz freshly grated Parmesan cheese
175 g/6 oz mozzarella cheese
18 large basil leaves
4 tablespoons seasoned flour
2 eggs, beaten
50 g/2 oz dried white breadcrumbs
vegetable oil, for deep-frying
black pepper

1 Grease a 20 x 30 cm/8 x 12 inch shallow tin. Bring the water to a rolling boil, add the butter and salt and then gradually whisk in the polenta in a steady stream.

2 Simmer over a low heat for 5–6 minutes, stirring constantly until the mixture comes away from the sides of the pan. Stir in the Parmesan, season with black pepper and pour into the prepared tin. Smooth the surface and set aside to cool.

3 Turn out the set polenta and trim into two 15 cm/6 inch squares. Cut each into nine 5 cm/2 inch squares and then cut each square in half diagonally, to make 36 triangles. Cut the mozzarella into thin slices and then into triangles, roughly the same size as the polenta.

4 Place a slice of mozzarella on half the polenta triangles, top with a basil leaf and another piece of polenta. Dip the polenta sandwiches in the seasoned flour, then into the beaten egg and finally in the breadcrumbs to coat well. Chill for 1 hour.

5 Heat 5 cm/2 inches of vegetable oil in a deep saucepan until it reaches 180–190°C (350–375°F), or until a cube of bread browns in 30 seconds. Deep-fry the triangles in batches for 1–2 minutes until crisp and golden. Drain on kitchen paper and keep warm in a hot oven while frying the rest. Serve hot.

Makes 36
Preparation time: 20 minutes, plus setting and chilling
Cooking time: 5–10 minutes

briks

These little turnovers originate in Tunisia. Traditionally briks are deep fried and must be served as soon as they are cooked otherwise they become heavy and greasy, but they can be baked, as in this recipe.

250 g/8 oz filo pastry
olive oil, for brushing
sesame seeds, for sprinkling

Filling:
50 g/2 oz olives, pitted
3 anchovy fillets
3 sun-dried tomatoes in oil, drained and chopped
2 tablespoons chopped almonds
2 tablespoons chopped mixed coriander and parsley
3 soft-boiled eggs, chopped
lemon juice, to taste
pepper

1 To make the filling, finely chop the olives and anchovy fillets together then mix them with the tomatoes, almonds, herbs, eggs and lemon juice and season with pepper.

2 Cut the pastry into 10 x 25 cm/4 x 10 inch strips. Work with 3 or 4 strips at a time, keeping the remaining pastry covered with clingfilm.

3 Brush the strips lightly with oil and put a heaped teaspoon of the filling at the top right-hand corner of each one. Fold the corner down to make a triangle. Continue folding the triangle along the length of the strip. Place on a baking sheet and brush with oil. Repeat until all the filling has been used.

4 Sprinkle the briks with sesame seeds and bake in a preheated oven, 190°C (375°F), Gas Mark 5, for about 20 minutes until crisp and golden. Serve hot or warm.

Makes 24
Preparation time: 30 minutes
Cooking time: 20 minutes
Oven temperature: 190°C (375°F), Gas Mark 5

potatoes wrapped in parma ham

12 small new potatoes, boiled
12 very thin slices of Parma ham
2 tablespoons olive oil
sea salt

1 Roll each potato in a slice of Parma ham, patting with your hands to mould the ham to the shape of the potato.

2 Lightly oil a roasting tin, add the potatoes and cook in a preheated oven, 200°C (400°F), Gas Mark 6, for 20 minutes. Keep an eye on the potatoes while they are cooking as they may need turning, or moving around; often the ones on the edge get more colour than the ones in the middle.

3 Serve the potatoes sprinkled with sea salt.

Serves 4
Preparation time: 5 minutes
Cooking time: 20 minutes
Oven temperature: 200°C (400°F), Gas Mark 6

sesame chicken wings

8 chicken wings
grated rind and juice of ½ lemon
4 tablespoons clear honey
2 tablespoons sesame seeds
salt and pepper

1 Put the chicken wings in a single layer in an ovenproof dish. Stir the lemon rind and juice with the honey and sesame seeds. Season with salt and pepper and pour over the chicken. Cover and leave in a cool place for at least 30 minutes, turning the wings at least once.

2 Cook the wings, uncovered, in a preheated oven, 200°C (400°F), Gas Mark 6, for 15 minutes. Pour off the marinade and return the wings to the oven for a further 10 minutes or until golden and cooked through.

Serves 8
Preparation time: 10 minutes, plus standing
Cooking time: 25 minutes
Oven temperature: 200°C (400°F), Gas Mark 6

chicken skewers with thai sweet dip

2 teaspoons sesame seeds
3 boneless, skinless chicken breasts
4 tablespoons sesame oil

Dip:
2.5 cm/1 inch piece of galangal, peeled and finely
*   chopped*
1 garlic clove, crushed
1 small red chilli, deseeded and finely chopped
125 ml/4 fl oz dark soy sauce
1 tablespoon Thai basil, finely chopped, plus extra to
*   garnish*

1 Toast the sesame seeds in a dry frying pan, stirring continuously, until golden. Cut the chicken into fine strips and thread on to 8 wooden skewers which have been soaked in water for 20 minutes. Drizzle with sesame oil and sprinkle with sesame seeds. Cook under a preheated hot grill for 15 minutes, turning the skewers frequently and brushing with more oil.

2 While the chicken is cooking, stir together all the ingredients for the dip. Spoon the dip into a small bowl.

3 Serve the hot chicken kebabs with the dip. Garnish with Thai basil.

Makes 8
Preparation time: 10 minutes, plus soaking
Cooking time: 15 minutes

spicy sausage rolls

750 g/1½ lb good quality sausagemeat
1½ tablespoons hot pepper sauce
3 tablespoons snipped chives
500 g/1 lb puff pastry
1 egg yolk, beaten
caraway seeds, for sprinkling

1 Put the sausagemeat, hot pepper sauce and snipped chives in a bowl and mix together well. Divide the pastry in half and roll out each piece to form a rectangle measuring 50 x 12 cm/20 x 5 inches.

2 Divide the sausagemeat mixture in half and form a long sausage on each pastry strip, arranging it to one side. Dampen the long edge of pastry with a little egg yolk and fold the pastry over to enclose the sausagemeat.

3 Brush the rolls with the beaten egg yolk and sprinkle with caraway seeds. Cut each roll into 25 equal pieces and arrange on baking sheets. Bake in a preheated oven, 220°C (425°F), Gas Mark 7, for 20 minutes.

Makes 50
Preparation time: 20 minutes
Cooking time: 20 minutes
Oven temperature: 220°C (425°F), Gas Mark 7

lamb and courgette koftas

2 courgettes, finely grated
2 tablespoons sesame seeds
250 g/8 oz minced lamb
2 spring onions, finely chopped
1 garlic clove, crushed
1 tablespoon chopped mint

½ teaspoon ground mixed spice
2 tablespoons dried breadcrumbs
1 egg, lightly beaten
salt and pepper
vegetable oil, for shallow-frying
lemon wedges, to garnish

1 Place the courgettes in a sieve and press down to extract as much liquid as possible. Place in a bowl. Dry-fry the sesame seeds in a frying pan for 1–2 minutes until they are golden and release their aroma. Add to the courgettes together with the lamb and all the remaining ingredients except the oil and lemon. Season liberally with salt and pepper.

2 Form the mixture into 20 small balls and shallow-fry in batches for 5 minutes, turning frequently until evenly browned. Keep the koftas warm in a hot oven while cooking the rest. Serve hot, garnished with the lemon wedges.

Serves 6
Preparation time: 20 minutes
Cooking time: 10 minutes

1 Place all the ingredients except the filo pastry and oil in a bowl and stir well until combined. Cover and chill for 1 hour to allow the flavours to develop.

2 Meanwhile, prepare the dipping sauce. Place all the ingredients in a small saucepan and heat gently, stirring until the sugar is dissolved. Bring to the boil and remove from the heat. Leave until cold and transfer to a small serving bowl.

3 Cut the filo pastry into 12 cm/5 inch squares. Brush each one with oil and place a spoonful of the chicken mixture in the centre. Draw the edges up to a point and pinch together. Place the parcels on a large greased baking sheet, brush them with oil and bake in a preheated oven, 190°C (375°F), Gas Mark 5, for 20–25 minutes until golden and crisp.

4 Serve the parcels hot with the dipping sauce.

Makes 24
Preparation time: 10 minutes, plus chilling
Cooking time: 20–25 minutes
Oven temperature: 190°C (375°F), Gas Mark 5

chicken parcels with sweet and sour dipping sauce

250 g/8 oz cooked chicken, minced
50 g/2 oz cooked pork, minced
1 garlic clove, crushed
2 spring onions, chopped
1 tablespoon basil, chopped
¼ teaspoon chilli powder
1 tablespoon light soy sauce
grated rind and juice of ½ lemon
4 filo pastry sheets
4 tablespoons olive oil, plus extra for greasing
*   and brushing*

Dipping sauce:
50 g/2 oz sugar
3 tablespoons rice or wine vinegar
½ teaspoon salt
1 teaspoon dried chilli flakes
2 tablespoons water

mackerel pâté

250 g/8 oz peppered mackerel fillets
200 ml/7 fl oz crème fraîche
50 g/2 oz butter, melted
grated rind of 1 lemon
4 slices of medium sliced white bread
mustard and cress, to serve

1 Remove the skin and bones from the mackerel. Put the fish in a food processor or blender with the crème fraîche and process until smooth. With the motor running, gradually add the melted butter and lemon rind. Spoon the pâté into a serving bowl and chill.

2 Trim the crusts from the slices of bread and toast on both sides. Carefully cut in half horizontally to form 2 thin squares. Cut into triangles and grill on the untoasted side until golden and curled. Serve the pâté with the crisp toast triangles, with mustard and cress.

Serves 10
Preparation time: 15 minutes
Cooking time: 5 minutes

deep-fried calamari

500 g/1 lb small squid, cleaned
vegetable oil, for deep-frying
2–4 tablespoons flour
pinch of cayenne pepper
2 eggs, lightly beaten
salt and pepper

To serve:
sea salt
lemon juice
Mayonnaise (see page 145)

1 Cut the squid into rings and halve the tentacles, if large. Wash well and dry thoroughly on kitchen paper.

2 In a deep saucepan, heat 5 cm/2 inches of vegetable oil until it reaches 180–190°C (350–375°F), or until a cube of bread browns in 30 seconds.

3 Meanwhile, mix the flour with the cayenne pepper and add salt and pepper to taste. Dip the squid into the beaten egg and coat with the seasoned flour. Deep-fry in batches for 1–2 minutes until crisp and golden. Drain each batch on kitchen paper.

4 Keep the cooked squid warm in a hot oven while cooking the remainder. Serve hot sprinkled with sea salt, drizzled with lemon juice and accompanied by a bowl of mayonnaise, to dip.

Serves 4
Preparation time: 15 minutes
Cooking time: 4–8 minutes each batch

moroccan mussel and tomato pastries

24 live mussels, scrubbed and debearded (see page 109)
2 tablespoons olive oil, plus extra for brushing
3 tomatoes, skinned, deseeded and cut into
    8 pieces each
1 small garlic clove, crushed
1½ tablespoons lemon juice
1½ tablespoons finely chopped parsley
2 sheets of filo pastry
melted butter or beaten egg, to glaze
salt and pepper

1 Bring about 2.5 cm/1 inch of salted water to the boil in a large saucepan. Add the mussels, cover the pan and allow the mussels to steam for 2–3 minutes, tossing the pan frequently, until the shells open. Tip the mussels into a colander and discard any that remain closed. Remove the mussels from their shells.

2 Heat the oil in a saucepan over a low heat, add the tomatoes and simmer until soft. Drain through a sieve, retaining the juices and the tomatoes. Pour the juices back into the saucepan, add the garlic and lemon juice and boil until syrupy. Leave to cool, then add the tomatoes, mussels and parsley and season with salt and pepper.

3 Place one sheet of filo pastry on top of the other, brushing each one with oil. Cut into twelve 10 cm/4 inch squares. Wet the edges. Spoon 2 mussels with some of the sauce on to each square, then fold the pastry over and press the edges together to seal.

4 Oil a baking sheet and place the pastries on it. Glaze the tops with melted butter or beaten egg and bake in a preheated oven, 200°C (400°F), Gas Mark 6, for 10–12 minutes until golden. Carefully transfer the pastries to a wire rack. Serve warm or at room temperature.

Makes 12
Preparation time: 30 minutes
Cooking time: 25–30 minutes
Oven temperature: 200°C (400°F), Gas Mark 6

index